MGMT 36100 OPERATION MANAGEMENT

PURDUE UNIVERSITY
KRANNERT SCHOOL OF MANAGEMENT

CONTAINS SELECT MATERIAL FROM

OPERATIONS MANAGEMENT
TENTH EDITION

WILLIAM J. STEVENSON
ROCHESTER INSTITUTE OF TECHNOLOGY

and

OPERATIONS AND SUPPLY CHAIN MANAGEMENT
THIRTEENTH EDITION

F. ROBERT JACOBS
INDIANA UNIVERSITY

RICHARD B. CHASE
UNIVERSITY OF SOUTHERN CALIFORNIA

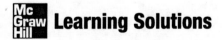

Boston   Burr Ridge, IL   Dubuque, IA   New York   San Francisco   St. Louis
Bangkok   Bogotá   Caracas   Lisbon   London   Madrid
Mexico City   Milan   New Delhi   Seoul   Singapore   Sydney   Taipei   Toronto

The McGraw·Hill Companies

MGMT 36100
Operation Management
Purdue University
Krannert School of Management

This book is a McGraw-Hill Learning Solutions textbook and contains select material from the following sources:
Operations Management, Tenth Edition by William J. Stevenson. Copyright © 2009, 2007, 2005, 2002, 1999, 1996, 1993, 1990, 1986, 1982 by The McGraw-Hill Companies, Inc.
Operations and Supply Chain Management, Thirteenth Edition by F. Robert Jacobs and Richard B. Chase. Copyright © 2011, 2009, 2006, 2004, 2001, 1998, 1995, 1992, 1989, 1985, 1981, 1977, 1973 by The McGraw-Hill Companies, Inc.
Both are reprinted with permission of the publisher. Many custom published texts are modified versions or adaptations of our best-selling textbooks. Some adaptations are printed in black and white to keep prices at a minimum, while others are in color.

2 3 4 5 6 7 8 9 0 QDB QDB 12 11 10

ISBN-13: 978-0-07-746377-9
ISBN-10: 0-07-746377-3

Learning Solutions Specialist: Liz Recker
Production Editor: Jennifer Beecher
Printer/Binder: Quad/Graphics

CONTENTS IN BRIEF

CONTENTS

part 1

INTRODUCTION

Chapter 1 introduces you to the field of operations management. It describes the nature and scope of operations management, and how operations management relates to other parts of the organization. Among the important topics it covers are a comparison of manufacturing and service operations, a brief history of operations management, supply chain management, and a list of trends in business that relate to operations. After you have read this chapter, you will have a good understanding of what the operations function of a business organization encompasses.

Introduction to operations management include this chapter:

1   Introduction to Operations Management, Chapter 1

chapter 1

INTRODUCTION TO OPERATIONS MANAGEMENT

This book is about operations management. The subject matter is fascinating and timely: Productivity, quality, e-business, global competition, and customer service are very much in the news, and all are part of operations management. This first chapter presents an introduction and overview of operations management. Among the issues it addresses are: What is operations management? Why is it important? What do operations management professionals do?

The chapter also provides a brief description of the historical evolution of operations management and a discussion of the trends and issues that impact operations management.

Learning Objectives

After completing this chapter, you should be able to:

1. Define the term *operations management*.
2. Identify the three major functional areas of organizations and describe how they interrelate.
3. Compare and contrast service and manufacturing operations.
4. Describe the operations function and the nature of the operations manager's job.
5. Identify the two major aspects of process management.
6. Describe the key aspects of operations management decision making.
7. Briefly describe the historical evolution of operations management.
8. Identify current trends in business that impact operations management.

In the late 1970s, Wal-Mart was a niche marketer, with about 200 stores, mostly in the South. At the time, Sears, JC Penney, and Kmart dominated the retail market. Over the years, Wal-Mart gained market share at the expense of the previous market leaders, and it has now become the largest and most profitable retailer in the world!

In the 1990s, the Boeing Company ran into trouble when it could not meet production deadlines. As a result, Boeing lost some orders, which had a negative impact on earnings and its stock price.

Why do some companies thrive while others struggle or fail? There are a variety of reasons, to be sure. However, an important key in a company's success or failure is how well it manages its operations.

INTRODUCTION

Goods

Services

Operations is that part of a business organization that is responsible for producing goods and/ or services. Goods are physical items that include raw materials, parts, subassemblies such as motherboards that go into computers, and final products such as cell phones and automobiles. Services are activities that provide some combination of time, location, form, or psychological value. Examples of goods and services are found all around you. Every book you read, every video you watch, every e-mail you send, every telephone conversation you have, and every medical treatment you receive involves the operations function of one or more organizations. So does everything you wear, eat, travel in, sit on, and access the Internet with. The operations function in business can also be viewed from a more far-reaching perspective: The collective success or failure of companies' operations functions has an impact on the ability of a nation to compete with other nations, and on the nation's economy.

The ideal situation for a business organization is to achieve a match of supply and demand. Having excess supply or excess capacity is wasteful and costly; having too little means lost opportunity and possible customer dissatisfaction. The key functions on the supply side are operations and supply chains, and sales and marketing on the demand side.

While the operations function is responsible for producing products and/or delivering services, it needs the support and input from other areas of the organization. Business organizations have three basic functional areas, as depicted in Figure 1.1: finance, marketing, and operations. It doesn't matter whether the business is a retail store, a hospital, a manufacturing firm, a car wash, or some other type of business; all business organizations have these three basic functions.

Finance is responsible for securing financial resources at favorable prices and allocating those resources throughout the organization, as well as budgeting, analyzing investment proposals, and providing funds for operations. Marketing and operations are the primary, or "line," functions. Marketing is responsible for assessing consumer wants and needs, and selling and promoting the organization's goods or services. Operations is responsible for producing the goods or providing the services offered by the organization. To put this into perspective, if a business organization were a car, operations would be its engine. And just as the engine is the core of what a car does, in a business organization, operations is the core of what the organization does. Operations management is responsible for managing that core.

Operations management

Hence, operations management is the management of systems or processes that create goods and/or provide services.

Supply chain

Operations and supply chains—one couldn't exist without the other, and no business organization could exist without both. A supply chain is the sequence of organizations—their facilities, functions, and activities—that are involved in producing and delivering a product or service. The sequence begins with basic suppliers of raw materials and extends all the way to the final customer, as seen in Figure 1.2. Facilities might include warehouses, factories, processing centers, offices, distribution centers, and retail outlets. Functions and activities

figure 1.1   The Three Basic Functions of Business Organizations

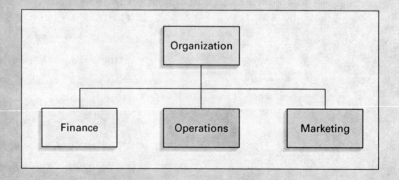

include forecasting, purchasing, inventory management, information management, quality assurance, scheduling, production, distribution, delivery, and customer service. Figure 1.3 provides another illustration of a supply chain: a chain that begins with wheat growing on a farm and ends with a customer buying a loaf of bread in a supermarket. Notice that the value of the product increases as it moves through the supply chain.

Supply chains are both external and internal to the organization. The external parts of a supply chain provide raw materials, parts, equipment, supplies, and/or other inputs to the organization, and they deliver outputs that are goods to the organization's customers. The internal parts of a supply chain are part of the operations function itself, supplying operations with parts and materials, performing work on products and/or services, and passing the work on to the next step in the process.

A Simple Product Supply Chain

figure 1.2

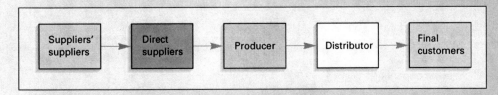

A Supply Chain for Bread

figure 1.3

The creation of goods or services involves transforming or converting inputs into outputs. Various inputs such as capital, labor, and information are used to create goods or services using one or more *transformation processes* (e.g., storing, transporting, repairing). To ensure that the desired outputs are obtained, an organization takes measurements at various points in the transformation process (*feedback*) and then compares them with previously established standards to determine whether corrective action is needed (*control*). Figure 1.4 depicts the conversion system.

Table 1.1 provides some examples of inputs, transformation processes, and outputs. Although goods and services are listed separately in Table 1.1, it is important to note that

figure 1.4

The Operations Function Involves the Conversion of Inputs into Outputs

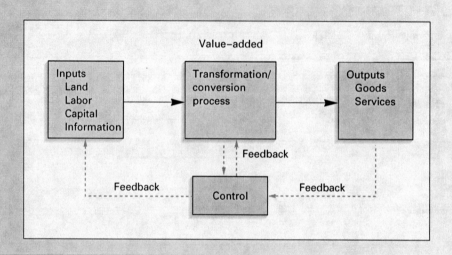

table 1.1

Examples of Inputs, Transformation, and Outputs

INPUTS	TRANSFORMATION	OUTPUTS
Land	Processes	High goods percentage
Human	Cutting, drilling	Houses
Physical labor	Transporting	Automobiles
Intellectual labor	Teaching	Clothing
Capital	Farming	Computers
Raw materials	Mixing	Machines
Water	Packing	Televisions
Metals	Copying, faxing	Food products
Wood	Analyzing	Textbooks
Equipment	Developing	CD players
Machines	Searching	High service percentage
Computers	Researching	Health care
Trucks	Repairing	Entertainment
Tools	Innovating	Car repair
Facilities	Debugging	Legal
Hospitals	Selling	Banking
Factories		Communication
Retail stores		
Energy		
Other		
Information		
Time		
Legal constraints		
Government regulations		

goods and services often occur jointly. For example, having the oil changed in your car is a service, but the oil that is delivered is a good. Similarly, house painting is a service, but the paint is a good. The goods–service combination is a continuum. It can range from primarily goods, with little service, to primarily service, with few goods. Figure 1.5 illustrates this continuum. Because there are relatively few pure goods or pure services, companies usually sell *product packages,* which are a combination of goods and services. There are elements of both goods production and service delivery in these product packages. This makes managing operations more interesting, and also more challenging.

Table 1.2 provides some specific illustrations of the transformation process.

The essence of the operations function is to *add value* during the transformation process: Value-added is the term used to describe the difference between the cost of inputs and the   Value-added

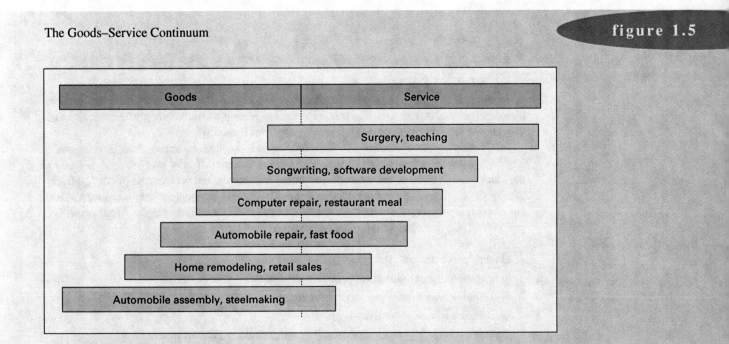

The Goods–Service Continuum   figure 1.5

Goods	Service

- Surgery, teaching
- Songwriting, software development
- Computer repair, restaurant meal
- Automobile repair, fast food
- Home remodeling, retail sales
- Automobile assembly, steelmaking

Illustrations of the Transformation Process   table 1.2

FOOD PROCESSOR	INPUTS	PROCESSING	OUTPUT
	Raw vegetables	Cleaning	Canned vegetables
	Metal sheets	Making cans	
	Water	Cutting	
	Energy	Cooking	
	Labor	Packing	
	Building	Labeling	
	Equipment		

HOSPITAL	INPUTS	PROCESSING	OUTPUT
	Doctors, nurses	Examination	Treated patients
	Hospital	Surgery	
	Medical supplies	Monitoring	
	Equipment	Medication	
	Laboratories	Therapy	

value or price of outputs. In nonprofit organizations, the value of outputs (e.g., highway construction, police and fire protection) is their value to society; the greater the value-added, the greater the effectiveness of these operations. In for-profit organizations, the value of outputs is measured by the prices that customers are willing to pay for those goods or services. Firms use the money generated by value-added for research and development, investment in new facilities and equipment, worker salaries, and *profits.* Consequently, the greater the value-added, the greater the amount of funds available for these purposes. Value can also be psychological, as in *branding.*

Many factors affect the design and management of operations systems. Among them are the degree of involvement of customers in the process and the degree to which technology is used to produce and/or deliver a product or service. The greater the degree of customer involvement, the more challenging it can be to design and manage the operation. Technology choices can have a major impact on productivity, costs, flexibility, and quality and customer satisfaction.

PRODUCTION OF GOODS VERSUS DELIVERY OF SERVICES

Although goods and services often go hand in hand, there are some very basic differences between the two, differences that impact the management of the goods portion versus management of the service portion. This section explores those differences.

Production of goods results in a *tangible output,* such as an automobile, eyeglasses, a golf ball, a refrigerator—anything that we can see or touch. It may take place in a factory, but can occur elsewhere. For example, farming produces *nonmanufactured* goods. Delivery of service, on the other hand, generally implies an *act.* A physician's examination, TV and auto repair, lawn care, and the projection of a film in a theater are examples of services. The majority of service jobs fall into these categories:

Govern'ment (federal, state, local).

Wholesale/retail (clothing, food, appliances, stationery, toys, etc.).

Financial services (banking, stock brokerages, insurance, etc.).

Health care (doctors, dentists, hospitals, etc.).

Personal services (laundry, dry cleaning, hair/beauty, gardening, etc.).

Business services (data processing, e-business, delivery, employment agencies, etc.).

Education (schools, colleges, etc.).

Manufacturing and service are often different in terms of *what* is done but quite similar in terms of *how* it is done. For example, both involve design and operating decisions. Manufacturers must decide what size factory is needed. Service organizations (e.g., hospitals) must decide what size building is needed. Both must make decisions on location, work schedules, capacity, and allocation of scarce resources.

Manufacturing and service organizations differ chiefly because manufacturing is goods-oriented and service is act-oriented. The differences involve the following:

1. Degree of customer contact.
2. Uniformity of input.
3. Labor content of jobs.
4. Uniformity of output.
5. Measurement of productivity.
6. Production and delivery.
7. Quality assurance.
8. Amount of inventory.
9. Evaluation of work.
10. Ability to patent design.

Let us consider each of these differences.

1. Often, by its nature, service involves a much higher degree of customer contact than manufacturing. The performance of a service often occurs at the point of consumption. For example, repairing a leaky roof must take place where the roof is, and surgery requires the presence of the surgeon and the patient. On the other hand, manufacturing allows a separation between production and consumption, so that manufacturing can occur away from the consumer. This permits a fair degree of latitude in selecting work methods, assigning jobs, scheduling work, and exercising control over operations. Service operations, because of their contact with customers, can be much more limited in their range of options. Moreover, customers are sometimes a part of the system (e.g., self-service operations such as gas stations, shopping), so tight control is impossible. In addition, product-oriented operations can build up inventories of finished goods (e.g., cars, refrigerators), enabling them to absorb some of the shocks caused by varying demand. Service operations, however, cannot build up inventories of *time* and are much more sensitive to demand variability—banks and supermarkets alternate between lines of customers waiting for service and idle tellers or cashiers waiting for customers. Note: If a service system has little or no customer contact, it functions in much the same manner as a goods-producing operation.

2. Service operations are subject to greater variability of inputs than typical manufacturing operations. Each patient, each client, each customer, and each auto repair presents a specific problem that often must be diagnosed before it can be remedied. Manufacturing operations often have greater ability to control the amount of variability of inputs and thus achieve low variability in outputs. Consequently, job requirements for manufacturing are generally more uniform than those for services.

3. Many services involve a higher labor content than manufacturing operations.

4. Because high mechanization generates products with low variability, manufacturing tends to be smooth and efficient; service activities sometimes appear to be slow and awkward, and output is more variable. Automated services are an exception to this.

5. Measurement of productivity is more straightforward in manufacturing due to the high degree of uniformity of most manufactured items. In service operations, variations in demand intensity and in requirements from job to job make productivity measurement considerably more difficult. For example, compare the productivity of two doctors. One may have a large number of routine cases while the other does not, so their productivity appears to differ unless a very careful analysis is made.

6. In many instances customers receive the service as it is performed (e.g., haircut, dental care).

7. Quality assurance is more challenging in services when production and consumption occur at the same time. Moreover, the higher variability of input creates additional opportunity for the quality of output to suffer unless quality assurance is actively managed. Quality at the point of creation is typically more evident for services than for manufacturing, where errors can be corrected before the customer receives the output.

8. Due to the nature of manufacturing, manufacturing systems usually have more inventory on hand (e.g., raw materials, partially completed items, finished goods inventories) than service firms. Nonetheless, all business organizations carry at least some items in inventory that are necessary for the operation of their businesses (e.g., office supplies, spare parts for equipment). And some service organizations have substantial amounts of inventory (e.g., firms that supply replacement parts for automobiles, construction equipment, or farm equipment). Hence, in spite of differing inventory requirements, managers in both manufacturing and service organizations must make decisions concerning inventory (e.g., which items to stock, how much to stock, when to reorder).

9. Because goods are tangible and there is often a time interval between production and delivery, evaluation of output is less demanding than it is for services.

10. Product designs are often easier to patent than service designs, and some service designs cannot be patented, making it easier for competitors to copy them.

Service jobs are sometimes categorized as professional or nonprofessional. Wholesale/retail and personal services generally fall into the nonprofessional category. Often these jobs tend to be on the low end of the pay scale, whereas professional services (e.g., surgery, consulting) tend to be on the high end of the pay scale. Manufacturing jobs, on the other hand, don't show this bimodal tendency, and few salaries fall in either the high or low range.

Note that many service activities are essential in goods-producing companies. These include training, human resource management, customer service, equipment repair, procurement, and administrative services.

Table 1.3 provides an overview of the differences between production of goods and service operations. Remember, though, that most systems involve a blend of goods and services.

table 1.3   Typical Differences Between Production of Goods and Provision of Services

CHARACTERISTIC	GOODS	SERVICES
Customer contact	Low	High
Uniformity of input	High	Low
Labor content	Low	High
Uniformity of output	High	Low
Output	Tangible	Intangible
Measurement of productivity	Easy	Difficult
Opportunity to correct quality problems before delivery to customer	High	Low
Inventory	Much	Little
Evaluation	Easier	More difficult
Patentable	Usually	Not usually

READING: THE CHALLENGES OF MANAGING SERVICES

Services can pose a variety of managerial challenges for managers—challenges that in manufacturing are either much less or nonexistent. And because services represent an increasing share of the economy, this places added importance to understanding and dealing with the challenges of managing services. Here are some of the main factors:

1. Jobs in service environments are often less structured than in manufacturing environments.

2. Customer contact is usually much higher in services.

3. In many services, worker skill levels are low compared to those of manufacturing workers.

4. Services are adding many new workers in low-skill, entry-level positions.

5. Employee turnover is often higher, especially in the low-skill jobs.

6. Input variability tends to be higher in many service environments than in manufacturing.

7. Service performance can be adversely affected by workers' emotions, distractions, customers' attitudes, and other factors, many of which are beyond managers' control.

Because of these factors, quality and costs are more difficult to control, productivity tends to be lower, the risk of customer dissatisfaction is greater, and employee motivation is more difficult.

Questions

1. What managerial challenges do services present that manufacturing does not?

2. Why does service management present more challenges than manufacturing?

PROCESS MANAGEMENT

A key aspect of operations management is process management. A process consists of one or more actions that transform inputs into outputs. In essence, the central role of all management is process management.

Businesses are composed of many interrelated processes. Generally speaking, there are three categories of business processes:

Process

1. *Upper-management processes.* These govern the operation of the entire organization. Examples include organizational governance and organizational strategy.
2. *Operational processes.* These are the core processes that make up the value stream. Examples include purchasing, production and/or service, marketing, and sales.
3. *Supporting processes.* These support the core processes. Examples include accounting, human resources, and IT (information technology).

Business processes, large and small, are composed of a series of supplier–customer relationships, where every business organization, every department, and every individual operation is both a customer of the previous step in the process and a supplier to the next step in the process. Figure 1.6 illustrates this concept.

A major process can consist of many subprocesses, each having its own goals that contribute to the goals of the overall process. Business organizations and supply chains have many such processes and subprocesses and they benefit greatly when management is using a process perspective. Business process management (BPM) activities include process design, process execution, and process monitoring. Two basic aspects of this for operations and supply chain management are managing processes to meet demand and dealing with process variability.

MANAGING A PROCESS TO MEET DEMAND

Ideally, the capacity of a process will be such that its output just matches demand. Excess capacity is wasteful and costly; too little capacity means dissatisfied customers and lost revenue. Having the right capacity requires having accurate forecasts of demand, the ability to translate forecasts into capacity requirements, and a process in place capable of meeting expected demand. Even so, process variation and demand variability can make the achievement of a match between process output and demand difficult. Therefore, to be effective, it is also necessary for managers to be able to deal with variation.

PROCESS VARIATION

Variation occurs in all business processes. It can be due to variety or variability. For example, random variability is inherent in every process; it is always present. In addition, variation can occur as the result of deliberate management choices to offer customers variety.

Business Processes Form a Sequence of Suppliers and Customers

figure 1.6

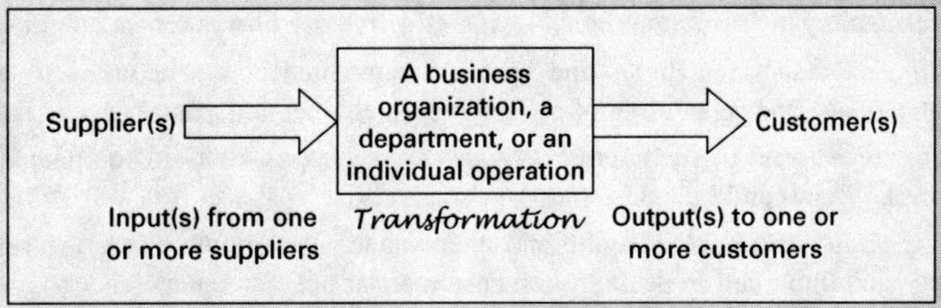

There are four basic sources of variation:

1. *The variety of goods or services being offered.* The greater the variety of goods and services, the greater the variation in production or service requirements.
2. *Structural variation in demand.* These variations, which include trends and seasonal variations, are generally predictable. They are particularly important for capacity planning.
3. *Random variation.* This natural variability is present to some extent in all processes, as well as in demand for services and products, and it cannot generally be influenced by managers.
4. *Assignable variation.* These variations are caused by defective inputs, incorrect work methods, out-of-adjustment equipment, and so on. This type of variation can be reduced or eliminated by analysis and corrective action.

Variations can be disruptive to operations and supply chain processes, interfering with optimal functioning. Variations result in additional cost, delays and shortages, poor quality, and inefficient work systems. Poor quality and product shortages or service delays can lead to dissatisfied customers and damage an organization's reputation and image. It is not surprising, then, that the ability to deal with variability is absolutely necessary for managers.

Throughout this book, you will learn about some of the tools managers use to deal with variation. An important aspect of being able to deal with variation is to use metrics to describe it. Two widely used metrics are the *mean* (average) and the *standard deviation.* The standard deviation quantifies variation around the mean. The mean and standard deviation are used throughout this book in conjunction with variation.

THE SCOPE OF OPERATIONS MANAGEMENT

The scope of operations management ranges across the organization. Operations management people are involved in product and service design, process selection, selection and management of technology, design of work systems, location planning, facilities planning, and quality improvement of the organization's products or services.

The operations function includes many interrelated activities, such as forecasting, capacity planning, scheduling, managing inventories, assuring quality, motivating employees, deciding where to locate facilities, and more.

We can use an airline company to illustrate a service organization's operations system. The system consists of the airplanes, airport facilities, and maintenance facilities, sometimes spread out over a wide territory. The activities include:

Forecasting such things as weather and landing conditions, seat demand for flights, and the growth in air travel.

Capacity planning, essential for the airline to maintain cash flow and make a reasonable profit. (Too few or too many planes, or even the right number of planes but in the wrong places, will hurt profits.)

Facilities and layout, important in achieving effective use of workers and equipment.

Scheduling of planes for flights and for routine maintenance; scheduling of pilots and flight attendants; and scheduling of ground crews, counter staff, and baggage handlers.

Managing inventories of such items as foods and beverages, first-aid equipment, in-flight magazines, pillows and blankets, and life preservers.

Assuring quality, essential in flying and maintenance operations, where the emphasis is on safety, and important in dealing with customers at ticket counters, check-in, telephone

SCHEDULING PLANES, CARGO, AND FLIGHT AND GROUND CREWS IS AN OPERATIONS FUNCTION FOR AN AIRLINE.

and electronic reservations, and curb service, where the emphasis is on efficiency and courtesy.

Motivating and training employees in all phases of operations.

Locating facilities according to managers' decisions on which cities to provide service for, where to locate maintenance facilities, and where to locate major and minor hubs.

Now consider a bicycle factory. This might be primarily an *assembly* operation: buying components such as frames, tires, wheels, gears, and other items from suppliers, and then assembling bicycles. The factory also might do some of the *fabrication* work itself, forming frames, making the gears and chains, and it might buy mainly raw materials and a few parts and materials such as paint, nuts and bolts, and tires. Among the key management tasks in either case are scheduling production, deciding which components to make and which to buy, ordering parts and materials, deciding on the style of bicycle to produce and how many, purchasing new equipment to replace old or worn out equipment, maintaining equipment, motivating workers, and ensuring that quality standards are met.

Obviously, an airline company and a bicycle factory are completely different types of operations. One is primarily a service operation, the other a producer of goods. Nonetheless, these two operations have much in common. Both involve scheduling activities, motivating employees, ordering and managing supplies, selecting and maintaining equipment, satisfying quality standards, and—above all—satisfying customers. And in both businesses, the success of the business depends on short- and long-term planning.

The operations function consists of all activities *directly* related to producing goods or providing services. Hence, it exists both in manufacturing and assembly operations, which are *goods-oriented,* and in areas such as health care, transportation, food handling, and retailing, which are primarily *service-oriented.*

A primary function of an operations manager is to guide the system by decision making. Certain decisions affect the *design* of the system, and others affect the *operation* of the system.

System design involves decisions that relate to system capacity, the geographic location of facilities, arrangement of departments and placement of equipment within physical structures, product and service planning, and acquisition of equipment. These decisions usually, but

A WORKER IS MAKING THE BOTTOM BRACKET LUG FOR A TREK OCLV CARBON ROAD BIKE AT TREK BICYCLE COMPANY IN WATERLOO, WISCONSIN, WORLD HEADQUARTERS FOR TREK. TREK IS A WORLD LEADER IN BICYCLE PRODUCTS AND ACCESSORIES, WITH 1,500 EMPLOYEES WORLDWIDE. DESIGNERS AND ENGINEERS INCORPORATE THE MOST ADVANCED TECHNOLOGY INTO TREK PRODUCTS, RESULTING IN AWARD-WINNING BIKES AND COMPONENTS.

www.trekbikes.com

not always, require long-term commitments. Moreover, they are typically *strategic* decisions. *System operation* involves management of personnel, inventory planning and control, scheduling, project management, and quality assurance. These are generally *tactical* and *operational* decisions. Feedback on these decisions involves *measurement* and *control*. In many instances, the operations manager is more involved in day-to-day operating decisions than with decisions relating to system design. However, the operations manager has a vital stake in system design because *system design essentially determines many of the parameters of system operation.* For example, costs, space, capacities, and quality are directly affected by design decisions. Even though the operations manager is not responsible for making all design decisions, he or she can provide those decision makers with a wide range of information that will have a bearing on their decisions.

A number of other areas are part of the operations function. They include purchasing, industrial engineering, distribution, and maintenance.

Purchasing has responsibility for procurement of materials, supplies, and equipment. Close contact with operations is necessary to ensure correct quantities and timing of purchases. The purchasing department is often called on to evaluate vendors for quality, reliability, service, price, and ability to adjust to changing demand. Purchasing is also involved in receiving and inspecting the purchased goods.

Industrial engineering is often concerned with scheduling, performance standards, work methods, quality control, and material handling.

Distribution involves the shipping of goods to warehouses, retail outlets, or final customers.

Maintenance is responsible for general upkeep and repair of equipment, buildings and grounds, heating and air-conditioning; removing toxic wastes; parking; and perhaps security.

The operations manager is the key figure in the system: He or she has the ultimate responsibility for the creation of goods or provision of services.

The kinds of jobs that operations managers oversee vary tremendously from organization to organization largely because of the different products or services involved. Thus, managing a banking operation obviously requires a different kind of expertise than managing a steelmaking operation. However, in a very important respect, the jobs are the same: They are both essentially *managerial*. The same thing can be said for the job of any operations manager regardless of the kinds of goods or services being created.

The service sector and the manufacturing sector are both important to the economy. The service sector now accounts for more than 70 percent of jobs in the United States, and it is growing in other countries as well. Moreover, the number of people working in services is increasing, while the number of people working in manufacturing is not. (See Figure 1.7.) The reason for the decline in manufacturing jobs is twofold: As the operations function in

U.S. Manufacturing Versus Service Employment, 1940–2005

figure 1.7

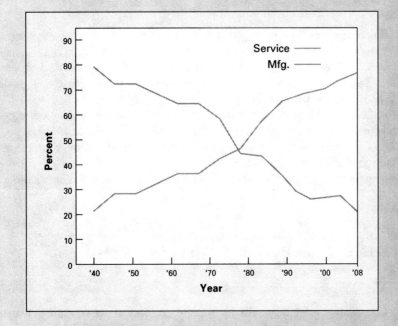

SOURCE: U.S. BUREAU OF LABOR STATISTICS.

READING: WHY MANUFACTURING MATTERS

The U.S. economy is becoming more and more service based. The percentage of employment in manufacturing continues to decrease while the percentage employed in services continues to increase. However, it would be unwise to assume that manufacturing isn't important to the economy, or that service is more important. Let's see why.

In a press release issued by the office of the White House press secretary, a number of key points were made:

1 Over 18 million workers are employed in manufacturing jobs.

2 Manufacturing accounts for over 70 percent of the value of U.S. exports.

3 The average full-time manufacturing worker's total compensation package is about 20 percent greater than the average of all workers in the United States. Compared to service workers, manufacturing workers are more likely to have access to benefits such as health and life insurance, disability, retirement plans, and vacation and sick leave.

4 Productivity growth in manufacturing in the last five years has been more than double that of the U.S. economy at large due to the investments made in technology development and diffusion.

(continued)

(concluded)

5   Manufacturing industries are the economy's most prolific creators and disseminators of technology, accounting for more than half the total R&D performed.

Additional insight comes from testimony before a California Senate committee:

6   While service jobs range from highly paid to minimum wage, California manufacturing workers earn an average of about $25,000 a year more than workers in service jobs.

7   When a California manufacturing job is lost, an average of 2.5 service jobs also disappear.

Questions

1   Why do you suppose the percentage of workers employed in manufacturing in the United States is decreasing?

2   Should business leaders and government officials be concerned when manufacturing jobs are lost?

SOURCE: "WHY MANUFACTURING MATTERS TO THE U.S. ECONOMY," PRESS RELEASE, OFFICE OF THE WHITE HOUSE PRESS SECRETARY, FEBRUARY 5, 2000; FROM TESTIMONY GIVEN BY DOROTHY ROTHROCK, VICE PRESIDENT OF THE CALIFORNIA MANUFACTURERS & TECHNOLOGY ASSOCIATION, BEFORE A CALIFORNIA SENATE COMMITTEE, OCTOBER 10, 2002.

manufacturing companies finds more productive ways of producing goods, the companies are able to maintain or even increase their output using fewer workers. Furthermore, some manufacturing work has been *outsourced* to more productive companies, many in other countries, that are able to produce goods at lower costs. Outsourcing and productivity will be discussed in more detail in this and other chapters.

Many of the concepts presented in this book apply equally to manufacturing and service. Consequently, whether your interest at this time is on manufacturing or on service, these concepts will be important, regardless of whether a manufacturing example or service example is used to illustrate the concept.

The reading on page 15 gives another reason for the importance of manufacturing jobs.

WHY LEARN ABOUT OPERATIONS MANAGEMENT?

There are many career-related reasons for wanting to learn about operations management, whether you plan to work in the field of operations or not. This is because every aspect of business affects or is affected by operations. Operations and sales are the two line functions in a business organization. All other functions—accounting, finance, marketing, IT, and so on—support the two line functions. Among the service jobs that are closely related to operations are financial services (e.g., stock market analyst, broker, investment banker, and loan officer), marketing services (e.g., market analyst, marketing researcher, advertising manager, and product manager), accounting services (e.g., corporate accountant, public accountant, and budget analyst), and information services (e.g., corporate intelligence, library services, management information systems design services).

Apart from the career-related reasons is a not so obvious one: Through learning about operations and supply chains, you will have a much better understanding of the world you live in, the global dependencies of companies and nations, some of the reasons that companies succeed or fail, and the importance of working with others.

Working together successfully means that all members of the organization understand not only their own role, they also understand the roles of others. This is precisely why all business students, regardless of their particular major, are required to take a common core of courses that will enable them to learn about all aspects of business. Because operations management is central to the functioning of every business organization, it is included in the core of courses business students are required to take. And even though individual courses have a narrow focus (e.g., accounting, marketing), in practice, there is significant interfacing and *collaboration* among the various functional areas, involving *exchange of information* and *cooperative decision making*. For example, although the three primary functions in business

The Three Major Functions of Business Organizations Overlap

figure 1.8

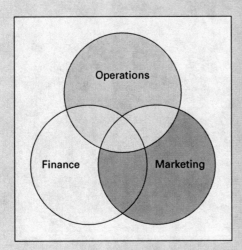

organizations perform different activities, many of their decisions impact the other areas of the organization. Consequently, these functions have numerous interactions, as depicted by the overlapping circles shown in Figure 1.8.

Finance and operations management personnel cooperate by exchanging information and expertise in such activities as the following:

1. *Budgeting.* Budgets must be periodically prepared to plan financial requirements. Budgets must sometimes be adjusted, and performance relative to a budget must be evaluated.
2. *Economic analysis of investment proposals.* Evaluation of alternative investments in plant and equipment requires inputs from both operations and finance people.
3. *Provision of funds.* The necessary funding of operations and the amount and timing of funding can be important and even critical when funds are tight. Careful planning can help avoid cash-flow problems.

Marketing's focus is on selling and/or promoting the goods or services of an organization. Marketing is also responsible for assessing customer wants and needs, and for communicating those to operations people (short term) and to design people (long term). That is, operations needs information about demand over the short to intermediate term so that it can plan accordingly (e.g., purchase materials or schedule work), while design people need information that relates to improving current products and services and designing new ones. Marketing, design, and production must work closely together to successfully implement design changes and to develop and produce new products. Marketing can provide valuable insight on what competitors are doing. Marketing also can supply information on consumer preferences so that design will know the kinds of products and features needed; operations can supply information about capacities and judge the *manufacturability* of designs. Operations will also have advance warning if new equipment or skills will be needed for new products or services. Finance people should be included in these exchanges in order to provide information on what funds might be available (short term) and to learn what funds might be needed for new products or services (intermediate to long term). One important piece of information marketing needs from operations is the manufacturing or service lead time in order to give customers realistic estimates of how long it will take to fill their orders.

Lead time

Thus, marketing, operations, and finance must interface on product and process design, forecasting, setting realistic schedules, quality and quantity decisions, and keeping each other informed on the other's strengths and weaknesses.

figure 1.9   Operations Interfaces with a Number of Supporting Functions

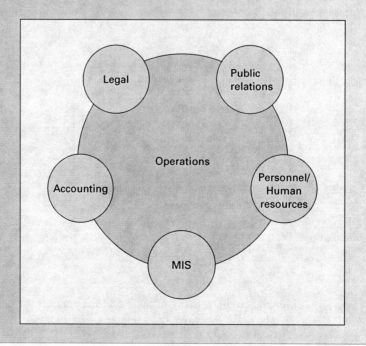

People in every area of business need to appreciate the importance of managing and coordinating operations decisions that affect the supply chain and the matching of supply and demand, and how those decisions impact other functions in an organization.

Operations also interacts with other functional areas of the organization, including legal, management information systems (MIS), accounting, personnel/human resources, and public relations, as depicted in Figure 1.9.

The *legal* department must be consulted on contracts with employees, customers, suppliers, and transporters, as well as on liability and environmental issues.

Accounting supplies information to management on costs of labor, materials, and overhead, and may provide reports on items such as scrap, downtime, and inventories.

Management information systems (MIS) is concerned with providing management with the information it needs to effectively manage. This occurs mainly through designing systems to capture relevant information and designing reports. MIS is also important for managing the control and decision-making tools used in operations management.

The *personnel* or *human resources* department is concerned with recruitment and training of personnel, labor relations, contract negotiations, wage and salary administration, assisting in manpower projections, and ensuring the health and safety of employees.

Public relations has responsibility for building and maintaining a positive public image of the organization. Good public relations provides many potential benefits. An obvious one is in the marketplace. Other potential benefits include public awareness of the organization as a good place to work (labor supply), improved chances of approval of zoning change requests, community acceptance of expansion plans, and instilling a positive attitude among employees.

CAREER OPPORTUNITIES

There are many career opportunities in the operations management and supply chain fields. Among the numerous job titles are operations manager, production analyst, production manager, industrial engineer, time study analyst, inventory manager, purchasing manager, schedule coordinator, distribution manager, supply chain manager, quality analyst, and quality manager.

People who work in the operations field should have a skill set that includes both people skills and knowledge skills. People skills include political awareness; mentoring ability; and collaboration, negotiation, and communication skills. Knowledge skills, necessary for credibility and good decision making, include product and/or service knowledge, process knowledge, industry and global knowledge, and financial and accounting skills.

If you are thinking of a career in operations management, you can benefit by joining one or more of the professional societies.

APICS, the Association for Operations Management 8430 West Bryn Mawr Avenue, Suite 1000, Chicago, Illinois 60631   www.apics.org

American Society for Quality (ASQ) 230 West Wells Street, Milwaukee, Wisconsin 53203   www.asq.org

Institute for Supply Management (ISM) 2055 East Centennial Circle, Tempe, Arizona 85284   www.ism.ws

Institute for Operations Research and the Management Sciences (INFORMS) 901 Elkridge Landing Road, Linthicum, Maryland 21090-2909   www.informs.org

The Production and Operations Management Society (POMS) College of Engineering, Florida International University, EAS 2460, 10555 West Flagler Street, Miami, Florida 33174   www.poms.org

The Project Management Institute (PMI) 4 Campus Boulevard, Newtown Square, Pennsylvania 19073-3299   www.pmi.org

Council of Supply Chain Management Professionals (CSCMP) 333 East Butterfield Road, Suite 140, Lombard, Illinois 60148   http//esemp.org

APICS, ASQ, ISM, and other professional societies offer a practitioner certification examination that can enhance your qualifications. Information about job opportunities can be obtained from all of these societies as well as from other sources, such as the Decision Sciences Institute (University Plaza, Atlanta, Georgia, 30303) and the Institute of Industrial Engineers (25 Technology Park, Norcross, Georgia, 30092).

OPERATIONS MANAGEMENT AND DECISION MAKING

The chief role of an operations manager is that of planner and decision maker. In this capacity, the operations manager exerts considerable influence over the degree to which the goals and objectives of the organization are realized. Most decisions involve many possible alternatives that can have quite different impacts on costs or profits. Consequently, it is important to make *informed* decisions.

Operations management professionals make a number of key decisions that affect the entire organization. These include the following:

What: What resources will be needed, and in what amounts?

When: When will each resource be needed? When should the work be scheduled? When should materials and other supplies be ordered? When is corrective action needed?

Where: Where will the work be done?

How: How will the product or service be designed? How will the work be done (organization, methods, equipment)? How will resources be allocated?

Who: Who will do the work?

Throughout this book, you will encounter the broad range of decisions that operations managers must make, and you will be introduced to the tools necessary to handle those decisions. This section describes general approaches to decision making, including the use of models, quantitative methods, analysis of trade-offs, establishing priorities, ethics, and the systems approach. Models are often a key tool used by all decision makers.

MODELS

Model

A model is an abstraction of reality, a simplified representation of something. For example, a child's toy car is a model of a real automobile. It has many of the same visual features (shape, relative proportions, wheels) that make it suitable for the child's learning and playing. But the toy does not have a real engine, it cannot transport people, and it does not weigh 2,000 pounds.

Other examples of models include automobile test tracks and crash tests; formulas, graphs and charts; balance sheets and income statements; and financial ratios. Common statistical models include descriptive statistics such as the mean, median, mode, range, and standard deviation, as well as random sampling, the normal distribution, and regression equations. Models are sometimes classified as physical, schematic, or mathematical:

Physical models look like their real-life counterparts. Examples include miniature cars, trucks, airplanes, toy animals and trains, and scale-model buildings. The advantage of these models is their visual correspondence with reality.

Schematic models are more abstract than their physical counterparts; that is, they have less resemblance to the physical reality. Examples include graphs and charts, blueprints, pictures, and drawings. The advantage of schematic models is that they are often relatively simple to construct and change. Moreover, they have some degree of visual correspondence.

Mathematical models are the most abstract: They do not look at all like their real-life counterparts. Examples include numbers, formulas, and symbols. These models are usually the easiest to manipulate, and they are important forms of inputs for computers and calculators.

The variety of models in use is enormous. Nonetheless, all have certain common features: They are all decision-making aids and simplifications of more complex real-life phenomena. Real life involves an overwhelming amount of detail, much of which is irrelevant for any particular problem. Models omit unimportant details so that attention can be concentrated on the most important aspects of a situation.

Because models play a significant role in operations management decision making, they are heavily integrated into the material of this text. For each model, try to learn (1) its purpose, (2) how it is used to generate results, (3) how these results are interpreted and used, and (4) what assumptions and limitations apply.

The last point is particularly important because virtually every model has an associated set of assumptions or conditions under which the model is valid. Failure to satisfy all of the assumptions will make the results suspect. Attempts to apply the results to a problem under such circumstances can lead to disastrous consequences.

Managers use models in a variety of ways and for a variety of reasons. Models are beneficial because they

1. Are generally easy to use and less expensive than dealing directly with the actual situation.
2. Require users to organize and sometimes quantify information and, in the process, often indicate areas where additional information is needed.
3. Increase understanding of the problem.
4. Enable managers to analyze "What if ?" questions.
5. Serve as a consistent tool for evaluation and provide a standardized format for analyzing a problem.
6. Enable users to bring the power of mathematics to bear on a problem.

This impressive list of benefits notwithstanding, models have certain limitations of which you should be aware. The following are three of the more important limitations:

1. Quantitative information may be emphasized at the expense of qualitative information.
2. Models may be incorrectly applied and the results misinterpreted. The widespread use of computerized models adds to this risk because highly sophisticated models may be placed in the hands of users who are not sufficiently knowledgeable to appreciate the subtleties of a particular model; thus, they are unable to fully comprehend the circumstances under which the model can be successfully employed.
3. The use of models does not guarantee good decisions.

QUANTITATIVE APPROACHES

Quantitative approaches to problem solving often embody an attempt to obtain mathematically optimal solutions to managerial problems. *Linear programming* and related mathematical techniques are widely used for optimum allocation of scarce resources. *Queuing techniques* are useful for analyzing situations in which waiting lines form. *Inventory models* are widely used to control inventories. *Project models* such as PERT (program evaluation and review technique) and CPM (critical path method) are useful for planning, coordinating, and controlling large-scale projects. *Forecasting techniques* are widely used in planning and scheduling. *Statistical models* are currently used in many areas of decision making.

In large measure, *quantitative approaches* to decision making in operations management (and in other functional business areas) have been accepted because of calculators and computers capable of handling the required calculations. Computers have had a major impact on operations management. Moreover, the growing availability of software packages for quantitative techniques has greatly increased management's use of those techniques.

Although quantitative approaches are widely used in operations management decision making, it is important to note that managers typically use a combination of qualitative and quantitative approaches, and many important decisions are based on qualitative approaches.

PERFORMANCE METRICS

All managers use metrics to manage and control operations. There are many metrics in use, including those related to profits, costs, quality, productivity, flexibility, assets, inventories, schedules, and forecast accuracy. As you read each chapter, note the metrics being used and how they are applied to manage operations.

ANALYSIS OF TRADE-OFFS

Operations personnel frequently encounter decisions that can be described as *trade-off* decisions. For example, in deciding on the amount of inventory to stock, the decision maker must take into account the trade-off between the increased level of customer service that the additional inventory would yield and the increased costs required to stock that inventory.

Throughout this book you will be presented with decision models that reflect these kinds of trade-offs. Decision makers sometimes deal with these decisions by listing the advantages and disadvantages—the pros and cons—of a course of action to better understand the consequences of the decisions they must make. In some instances, decision makers add weights to the items on their list that reflect the relative importance of various factors. This can help them "net out" the potential impacts of the trade-offs on their decision.

DEGREE OF CUSTOMIZATION

A major influence on the entire organization is the degree of customization of products or services being offered to its customers. Providing highly customized products or services such as home remodeling, plastic surgery, and legal counseling tends to be more labor intensive than providing standardized products such as those you would buy "off the shelf" at a mall store or a supermarket or standardized services such as public utilities and Internet services. Furthermore, production of customized products or provision of customized services is generally more time consuming, requires more highly skilled people, and involves more flexible equipment than what is needed for standardized products or services. Customized processes tend to have a much lower volume of output than standardized processes, and customized output carries a higher price tag. The degree of customization has important implications for process selection and job requirements. The impact goes beyond operations and supply chains. It affects marketing, sales, accounting, finance, and information systems.

A SYSTEMS APPROACH

System

A systems viewpoint is almost always beneficial in decision making. A system can be defined as a set of interrelated parts that must work together. In a business organization, the organization can be thought of as a system composed of subsystems (e.g., marketing subsystem, operations subsystem, finance subsystem), which in turn are composed of lower subsystems. The systems approach emphasizes interrelationships among subsystems, but its main theme is that *the whole is greater than the sum of its individual parts.* Hence, from a systems viewpoint, the output and objectives of the organization as a whole take precedence over those of any one subsystem. An alternative approach is to concentrate on efficiency within subsystems and thereby achieve overall efficiency. But that approach overlooks the fact that organizations must operate in an environment of scarce resources and that subsystems are often in direct competition for those scarce resources, so that an orderly approach to the allocation of resources is called for.

A systems approach is essential whenever something is being designed, redesigned, implemented, improved, or otherwise changed. It is important to take into account the impact on all parts of the system. For example, if the upcoming model of an automobile will add antilock brakes, a designer must take into account how customers will view the change, instructions for using the brakes, chances for misuse, the cost of producing the new brakes, installation procedures, recycling worn-out brakes, and repair procedures. In addition, workers will need training to make and/or assemble the brakes, production scheduling may change, inventory procedures may have to change, quality standards will have to be established, advertising must be informed of the new features, and parts suppliers must be selected.

Global competition and outsourcing are increasing the length of companies' supply chains, making it more important than ever for companies to use a systems approach to take the "big picture" into account in their decision making.

ESTABLISHING PRIORITIES

In virtually every situation, managers discover that certain issues or items are more important than others. Recognizing this enables the managers to direct their efforts to where they will do the most good.

Pareto phenomenon

Typically, a relatively few issues or item are very important, so that dealing with those factors will generally have a disproportionately large impact on the results achieved. This well-known effect is referred to as the Pareto phenomenon. The implication is that a manager should examine each situation, searching for the few factors that will have the greatest impact, and give them the highest priority. This is one of the most important and pervasive concepts in operations management. In fact, this concept can be applied at all levels of management and to every aspect of decision making, both professional and personal.

READING: NEED A SYSTEMS APPROACH?

Healthcare today is experiencing both the best and worst of times. Countless lives are saved daily by medical breakthroughs, dedicated practitioners and state-of-the-art technologies. Yet, within this trillion-dollar industry amazing medical feats are juxtaposed against systemic failures and disgruntled stakeholders. Workforce shortages further constrain a system facing a rising demand for services. Advanced technology is often overlaid on archaic processes. As some emergency departments are forced to close, others find themselves overcrowded and understaffed.

SOURCE: HTTP://HEALTHCARE.ISIXSIGMA.COM/LIBRARY/CONTENT/C031028A.ASP.

ETHICS

The financial difficulties of companies such as Enron, WorldCom, Global Crossings, Adelphia, Arthur Andersen, and ImClone Systems brought into question ethical standards and behavior of high-ranking company officials.

In making decisions, managers must consider how their decisions will affect shareholders, management, employees, customers, the community at large, and the environment. Finding solutions that will be in the best interests of all of these stakeholders is not always easy, but it is a goal that all managers should strive to achieve. Furthermore, even managers with the best intentions will sometimes make mistakes. If mistakes do occur, managers should act responsibly to correct those mistakes as quickly as possible, and to address any negative consequences.

Operations managers, like all managers, have the responsibility to make ethical decisions. Ethical issues arise in many aspects of operations management, including

- Financial statements: accurately representing the organization's financial condition.
- Worker safety: providing adequate training, maintaining equipment in good working condition, maintaining a safe working environment.
- Product safety: providing products that minimize the risk of injury to users or damage to property or the environment.
- Quality: honoring warranties, avoiding hidden defects.
- The environment: not doing things that will harm the environment.
- The community: being a good neighbor.
- Hiring and firing workers: avoiding false pretenses (e.g., promising a long-term job when that is not what is intended).
- Closing facilities: taking into account the impact on a community, and honoring commitments that have been made.
- Workers' rights: respecting workers' rights, dealing with workers' problems quickly and fairly.

Many organizations have developed *codes of ethics* to guide employees' or members' conduct.

THE HISTORICAL EVOLUTION OF OPERATIONS MANAGEMENT

Systems for production have existed since ancient times. The production of goods for sale, at least in the modern sense, and the modern factory system had their roots in the Industrial Revolution.

THE INDUSTRIAL REVOLUTION

The Industrial Revolution began in the 1770s in England and spread to the rest of Europe and to the United States during the 19th century. Prior to that time, goods were produced in small shops by craftsmen and their apprentices. Under that system, it was common for one person to be responsible for making a product, such as a horse-drawn wagon or a piece of furniture, from start to finish. Only simple tools were available; the machines in use today had not been invented.

Then, a number of innovations in the 18th century changed the face of production forever by substituting machine power for human power. Perhaps the most significant of these was the steam engine, because it provided a source of power to operate machines in factories. Ample supplies of coal and iron ore provided materials for generating power and making machinery. The new machines, made of iron, were much stronger and more durable than the simple wooden machines they replaced.

Craft production

In the earliest days of manufacturing, goods were produced using craft production: highly skilled workers using simple, flexible tools produced goods according to customer specifications.

Craft production had major shortcomings. Because products were made by skilled craftsmen who custom fitted parts, production was slow and costly. And when parts failed, the replacements also had to be custom made, which was also slow and costly. Another shortcoming was that production costs did not decrease as volume increased; there were no *economies of scale,* which would have provided a major incentive for companies to expand. Instead, many small companies emerged, each with its own set of standards.

A major change occurred that gave the Industrial Revolution a boost: the development of standard gauging systems. This greatly reduced the need for custom-made goods. Factories began to spring up and grow rapidly, providing jobs for countless people who were attracted in large numbers from rural areas.

Despite the major changes that were taking place, management theory and practice had not progressed much from early days. What was needed was an enlightened and more systematic approach to management.

SCIENTIFIC MANAGEMENT

The scientific management era brought widespread changes to the management of factories. The movement was spearheaded by the efficiency engineer and inventor Frederick Winslow Taylor, who is often referred to as the father of scientific management. Taylor believed in a "science of management" based on observation, measurement, analysis and improvement of work methods, and economic incentives. He studied work methods in great detail to identify the best method for doing each job. Taylor also believed that management should be responsible for planning, carefully selecting and training workers, finding the best way to perform each job, achieving cooperation between management and workers, and separating management activities from work activities.

Taylor's methods emphasized maximizing output. They were not always popular with workers, who sometimes thought the methods were used to unfairly increase output without a corresponding increase in compensation. Certainly some companies did abuse workers in their quest for efficiency. Eventually, the public outcry reached the halls of Congress, and hearings were held on the matter. Taylor himself was called to testify in 1911, the same year in which his classic book, *The Principles of Scientific Management,* was published. The publicity from those hearings actually helped scientific management principles to achieve wide acceptance in industry.

A number of other pioneers also contributed heavily to this movement, including the following:

Frank Gilbreth was an industrial engineer who is often referred to as the father of motion study. He developed principles of motion economy that could be applied to incredibly small portions of a task.

Henry Gantt recognized the value of nonmonetary rewards to motivate workers, and developed a widely used system for scheduling, called Gantt charts.

Harrington Emerson applied Taylor's ideas to organization structure and encouraged the use of experts to improve organizational efficiency. He testified in a congressional hearing that railroads could save a million dollars a day by applying principles of scientific management.

Henry Ford, the great industrialist, employed scientific management techniques in his factories.

During the early part of the 20th century, automobiles were just coming into vogue in the United States. Ford's Model T was such a success that the company had trouble keeping up with orders for the cars. In an effort to improve the efficiency of operations, Ford adopted the scientific management principles espoused by Frederick Winslow Taylor. He also introduced

ROW OF COMPLETED "TIN LIZZIES," OR MODEL T'S, COME OFF THE FORD ASSEMBLY LINE.

the *moving assembly line,* which had a tremendous impact on production methods in many industries.

Among Ford's many contributions was the introduction of mass production to the automotive industry, a system of production in which large volumes of standardized goods are produced by low-skilled or semiskilled workers using highly specialized, and often costly, equipment. Ford was able to do this by taking advantage of a number of important concepts. Perhaps the key concept that launched mass production was interchangeable parts, sometimes attributed to Eli Whitney, an American inventor who applied the concept to assembling muskets in the late 1700s. The basis for interchangeable parts was to standardize parts so that any part in a batch of parts would fit any automobile coming down the assembly line. This meant that parts did not have to be custom fitted, as they were in craft production. The standardized parts could also be used for replacement parts. The result was a tremendous decrease in assembly time and cost. Ford accomplished this by standardizing the gauges used to measure parts during production and by using newly developed processes to produce uniform parts.

A second concept used by Ford was the division of labor, which Adam Smith wrote about in *The Wealth of Nations* (1776). Division of labor means that an operation, such as assembling an automobile, is divided up into a series of many small tasks, and individual workers are assigned to one of those tasks. Unlike craft production, where each worker was responsible for doing many tasks, and thus required skill, with division of labor the tasks were so narrow that virtually no skill was required.

Together, these concepts enabled Ford to tremendously increase the production rate at his factories using readily available inexpensive labor. Both Taylor and Ford were despised by many workers, because they held workers in such low regard, expecting them to perform like robots. This paved the way for the human relations movement.

Mass production

Interchangeable parts

Division of labor

ASSEMBLY LINES

Assembly lines are one of several approaches to the production of goods and delivering services. But the importance of assembly lines to business and society is hard to overstate. Often associated with Henry Ford's automobile production, they were the hallmark of mass production, achieving high volumes of standardized products. As such, they played a pivotal role in the development of what we now refer to as industrialized nations. By shifting from craft production methods to assembly lines, producers were able to successfully employ large numbers of unskilled workers. By using assembly lines, they achieved tremendous gains in industrial productivity, produced affordable products, and in the process greatly increased the standard of living of people in industrial nations. As you will learn later in the book, assembly lines also play an important role in a newer approach to operations called lean production or, more generally, lean operations.

THE HUMAN RELATIONS MOVEMENT

Whereas the scientific management movement heavily emphasized the technical aspects of work design, the human relations movement emphasized the importance of the human element in job design. Lillian Gilbreth, a psychologist and the wife of Frank Gilbreth, worked with her husband, focusing on the human factor in work. (The Gilbreths were the subject of a classic 1950s film, *Cheaper by the Dozen.*) Many of her studies in the 1920s dealt with worker fatigue. In the following decades, there was much emphasis on motivation. During the 1930s, Elton Mayo conducted studies at the Hawthorne division of Western Electric. His studies revealed that in addition to the physical and technical aspects of work, worker motivation is critical for improving productivity. During the 1940s, Abraham Maslow developed motivational theories, which Frederick Hertzberg refined in the 1950s. Douglas McGregor added Theory X and Theory Y in the 1960s. These theories represented the two ends of the spectrum of how employees view work. Theory X, on the negative end, assumed that workers do not like to work, and have to be controlled—rewarded and punished—to get them to do good work. This attitude was quite common in the automobile industry and in some other industries, until the threat of global competition forced them to rethink that approach. Theory Y, on the other end of the spectrum, assumed that workers enjoy the physical and mental aspects of work and become committed to work. The Theory X approach resulted in an adversarial environment, whereas the Theory Y approach resulted in empowered workers and a more cooperative spirit. In the 1970s, William Ouchi added Theory Z, which combined the Japanese approach with such features as lifetime employment, employee problem solving, and consensus building, and the traditional Western approach that features short-term employment, specialists, and individual decision making and responsibility.

DECISION MODELS AND MANAGEMENT SCIENCE

The factory movement was accompanied by the development of several quantitative techniques. F. W. Harris developed one of the first models in 1915: a mathematical model for inventory management. In the 1930s, three coworkers at Bell Telephone Labs, H. F. Dodge, H. G. Romig, and W. Shewhart, developed statistical procedures for sampling and quality control. In 1935, L. H. C. Tippett conducted studies that provided the groundwork for statistical-sampling theory.

At first, these quantitative models were not widely used in industry. However, the onset of World War II changed that. The war generated tremendous pressures on manufacturing output, and specialists from many disciplines combined efforts to achieve advancements in the military and in manufacturing. After the war, efforts to develop and refine quantitative tools for decision making continued, resulting in decision models for forecasting, inventory management, project management, and other areas of operations management.

During the 1960s and 1970s, management science techniques were highly regarded; in the 1980s, they lost some favor. However, the widespread use of personal computers and user-friendly software in the workplace contributed to a resurgence in the popularity of these techniques.

Historical Summary of Operations Management

table 1.4

APPROXIMATE DATE	CONTRIBUTION/CONCEPT	ORIGINATOR
1776	Division of labor	Adam Smith
1790	Interchangeable parts	Eli Whitney
1911	Principles of scientific management	Frederick W. Taylor
1911	Motion study, use of industrial psychology	Frank and Lillian Gilbreth
1912	Chart for scheduling activities	Henry Gantt
1913	Moving assembly line	Henry Ford
1915	Mathematical model for inventory management	F. W. Harris
1930	Hawthorne studies on worker motivation	Elton Mayo
1935	Statistical procedures for sampling and quality control	H. F. Dodge, H. G. Romig, W. Shewhart, L. H. C. Tippett
1940	Operations research applications in warfare	Operations research groups
1947	Linear programming	George Dantzig
1951	Commercial digital computers	Sperry Univac, IBM
1950s	Automation	Numerous
1960s	Extensive development of quantitative tools	Numerous
1960s	Industrial dynamics	Jay Forrester
1975	Emphasis an manufacturing strategy	W. Skinner
1980s	Emphasis on flexibility, time-based competition, lean production	T. Ohno, S. Shingo, Toyota
1980s	Emphasis on quality	W. Edwards Deming, J. Juran, K. Ishikawa
1990s	Internet, supply chain management	Numerous
2000s	Applications service providers and outsourcing	Numerous

THE INFLUENCE OF JAPANESE MANUFACTURERS

A number of Japanese manufacturers developed or refined management practices that increased the productivity of their operations and the quality of their products. This made them very competitive, sparking interest in their approaches by companies outside Japan. Their approaches emphasized quality and continual improvement, worker teams and empowerment, and achieving customer satisfaction. The Japanese can be credited with spawning the "quality revolution" that occurred in industrialized countries, and with generating widespread interest in time-based management (just-in-time production).

The influence of the Japanese on U.S. manufacturing and service companies has been enormous and promises to continue for the foreseeable future. Because of that influence, this book will provide considerable information about Japanese methods and successes.
Table 1.4 provides a chronological summary of some of the key developments in the evolution of operations management.

KEY TRENDS AND ISSUES IN BUSINESS

Business organizations must be cognizant of current trends and take them into account in their strategic planning. Advances in information technology and global competition have influenced the major trends. Although different organizations have different priorities, and hence are differently affected by various trends, a representative list of major trends includes

The Internet, e-commerce, and e-business.

Management of technology.

Globalization.

Management of supply chains.

Outsourcing.

Agility.

Ethical behavior.

The *Internet* offers great potential for business organizations, but the potential as well as the risks must be clearly understood in order to determine if and how to exploit this potential. In many cases, the Internet has altered the way companies compete in the marketplace.

E-business

E-commerce

Electronic business, or e-business, involves the use of the Internet to transact business. E-business is changing the way business organizations interact with their customers and their suppliers. Most familiar to the general public is e-commerce, consumer–business transactions such as buying online or requesting information. However, business-to-business transactions such as e-procurement represent an increasing share of e-business. E-business is receiving increased attention from business owners and managers in developing strategies, planning, and decision making.

Technology

The word technology has several definitions, depending on the context. Generally, *technology* refers to the application of scientific discoveries to the development and improvement of goods and services. It can involve knowledge, materials, methods, and equipment. The term *high technology* refers to the most advanced and developed machines and methods. Operations management is primarily concerned with three kinds of technology: product and service technology, process technology, and information technology (IT). All three can have a major impact on costs, productivity, and competitiveness.

Product and service technology refers to the discovery and development of new products and services. This is done mainly by researchers and engineers, who use the scientific approach to develop new knowledge and translate that into commercial applications.

Process technology refers to methods, procedures, and equipment used to produce goods and provide services. They include not only processes within an organization but also supply chain processes.

Information technology (IT) refers to the science and use of computers and other electronic equipment to store, process, and send information. Information technology is heavily ingrained in today's business operations. This includes electronic data processing, the use of bar codes to identify and track goods, obtaining point-of-sale information, data transmission, the Internet, e-commerce, e-mail, and more.

Management of technology is high on the list of major trends, and it promises to be high well into the future. For example, computers have had a tremendous impact on businesses in many ways, including new product and service features, process management, medical diagnosis, production planning and scheduling, data processing, and communication. Advances in materials, methods, and equipment also have had an impact on competition and productivity. Advances in information technology also have had a major impact on businesses. Obviously there have been—and will continue to be—many benefits from technological advances. However, technological advance also places a burden on management. For example, management must keep abreast of changes and quickly assess both their benefits and risks. Predicting advances can be tricky at best, and new technologies often carry a high price tag and usually a high cost to operate or repair. And in the case of computer operating systems, as new systems are introduced, support for older versions is discontinued, making periodic upgrades necessary. Conflicting technologies can exist that make technological choices even more difficult. Technological innovations in both *products* and *processes* will continue to change the way businesses operate, and hence require continuing attention.

The North American Free Trade Agreement (NAFTA) opened borders for trade between the United States and Canada and Mexico. The General Agreement on Tariffs and Trade (GATT) of 1994 reduced tariffs and subsidies in many countries, expanding world trade. The resulting global competition and global markets have had an impact on the strategies and operations of businesses large and small around the world. One effect is the importance business organizations are giving to management of their *supply chains.*

Globalization and the need for global supply chains have broadened the scope of supply chain management. However, tightened border security in certain instances has slowed some movement of goods and people. Moreover, in some cases, organizations are reassessing their use of offshore outsourcing.

The threat of global warming and increasing pollution will have a significant impact on business organizations and health care. Stricter environmental regulations, particularly in developed nations, will put additional constraints on operations. Furthermore, business organizations are coming under increasing pressure to reduce their carbon footprint (the amount of carbon dioxide generated by their operations and their supply chains) and to generally operate sustainable processes. Sustainability refers to service and production processes that use resources in ways that do not harm ecological systems that support both current and future human existence. Sustainability measures often go beyond traditional environmental and economic measures to include measures that incorporate social criteria in decision making.

Sustainability

All areas of business will be affected by this. Areas that will be most affected include product and service design, consumer education programs, disaster preparation and response, supply chain waste management, and outsourcing decisions. Note that outsourcing of goods production increases not only transportation costs, but also fuel consumption and carbon released into the atmosphere. Consequently, sustainability thinking may have implications for outsourcing decisions.

Agility refers to the ability of an organization to respond quickly to demands or opportunities. It is a strategy that involves maintaining a flexible system that can quickly respond to changes in either the volume of demand or changes in product/service offerings. This is particularly important as organizations scramble to remain competitive and cope with increasingly shorter product life cycles and strive to achieve shorter development times for new or improved products and services.

Agility

Ethical behavior is commanding increased attention from management at all levels. Accounting scandals, stock brokers releasing misleading information, product liability claims, and breaches in privacy and security of computer files are just some of the behaviors that have led to public outcries and congressional investigations.

While the preceding issues are getting much needed attention, there are also other important issues that must be addressed. These include greater emphasis on

Operations strategy.

Working with fewer resources.

Revenue management.

Process analysis and improvement, and quality improvement.

Increased regulation and product liability issues.

Lean production.

READING: UNIVERSITIES EMBRACE SUSTAINABILITY

Universities and colleges are increasingly embracing sustainability, linking it to global warming, biodiversity, and global commerce. Some are building sustainability into existing courses, while others are offering new courses, certificate programs, or degree programs. And some, such as Arizona State University and the Rochester Institute of Technology, are offering advanced degree programs.

Some universities are also "practicing what they preach," by applying sustainable practices in their operations. Among

them are Dartmouth College, Harvard University, Stanford, Williams College, and the University of British Columbia, which was named by the environmental magazine Grist as one of the top 15 universities in the world in reducing greenhouse gas emissions and being energy efficient.

SOURCE: BASED ON "THE SUSTAINABLE UNIVERSITY: SAVING THE PLANET BY DEGREES," CHRONICLE OF HIGHER EDUCATION, SPECIAL REPORT, OCTOBER 20, 2006, STANFORD NEWS SERVICE, JANUARY 2007, AND "B.C.'S SCHOOL OF GREENER LEARNING," TORONTO GLOBE AND MAIL, AUGUST 25, 2007, P. A6.

During the 1970s and 1980s, many companies neglected to include *operations strategy* in their corporate strategy. Some of them paid dearly for that neglect. Now more and more companies are recognizing the importance of operations strategy on the overall success of their business as well as the necessity for relating it to their overall business strategy.

Working with fewer resources due to layoffs, corporate downsizing, and general cost cutting is forcing managers to make trade-off decisions on resource allocation, and to place increased emphasis on cost control and productivity improvement.

Revenue management is a method used by some companies to maximize the revenue they receive from fixed operating capacity by influencing demand through price manipulation. Also known as yield management, it has been successfully used in the travel and tourism industries by airlines, cruise lines, hotels, amusement parks, and rental car companies, and in other industries such as trucking and public utilities.

Process analysis and improvement includes cost and time reduction, productivity improvement, process yield improvement, and quality improvement and increasing customer satisfaction. This is sometimes referred to as a six sigma process.

Six sigma

Given a boost by the "quality revolution" of the 1980s and 1990s, *quality* is now ingrained in business. Some businesses use the term *total quality management (TQM)* to describe their quality efforts. A quality focus emphasizes *customer satisfaction* and often involves *teamwork*. *Process improvement* can result in improved quality, cost reduction, and *time reduction*. Time relates to costs and to competitive advantage, and businesses seek ways to reduce the time to bring new products and services to the marketplace to gain a competitive edge. If two companies can provide the same product at the same price and quality, but one can deliver it four weeks earlier than the other, the quicker company will invariably get the sale. Time reductions are being achieved in many companies now. Kodak was able to cut in half the time needed to bring a new camera to market; Union Carbide was able to cut $400 million of fixed expenses; and Bell Atlantic was able to cut the time needed to hook up long-distance carriers from 15 days to less than 1, at a savings of $82 million.

Increased *regulation* and some very costly *product liability* claims have continued to make these issues important management issues.

Lean production, a new approach to production, emerged in the 1990s. It incorporates a number of the recent trends listed here, with an emphasis on quality, flexibility, time reduction, and teamwork. This has led to a *flattening* of the organizational structure, with fewer levels of management.

Lean system

Lean systems are so named because they use much less of certain resources than typical mass production systems use—space, inventory, and workers—to produce a comparable amount of output. Lean systems use a highly skilled workforce and flexible equipment. In effect, they incorporate advantages of both mass production (high volume, low unit cost) and craft production (variety and flexibility). And quality is higher than in mass production. This approach has now spread to services, including health care, offices, and shipping and delivery.

The skilled workers in lean production systems are more involved in maintaining and improving the system than their mass production counterparts. They are taught to stop an operation if they discover a defect, and to work with other employees to find and correct the cause of the defect so that it won't recur. This results in an increasing level of quality over time and eliminates the need to inspect and rework at the end of the line.

Because lean production systems operate with lower amounts of inventory, additional emphasis is placed on anticipating when problems might occur *before* they arise and avoiding those problems through planning. Even so, problems can still occur at times, and quick resolution is important. Workers participate in both the planning and correction stages.

Compared to workers in traditional systems, much more is expected of workers in lean production systems. They must be able to function in teams, playing active roles in operating and improving the system. Individual creativity is much less important than team success. Responsibilities also are much greater, which can lead to pressure and anxiety not present in traditional systems. Moreover, a flatter organizational structure means career paths are not as steep in lean production organizations. Workers tend to become generalists rather than specialists, another contrast to more traditional organizations.

THE NEED TO MANAGE THE SUPPLY CHAIN

Supply chain management is being given increasing attention as business organizations face mounting pressure to improve management of their supply chains. In the past, most organizations did little to manage their supply chains. Instead, they tended to concentrate on their own operations and on their immediate suppliers. Moreover, the planning, marketing, production and inventory management functions in organizations in supply chains have often operated independently of each other. As a result, supply chains experienced a range of problems that were seemingly beyond the control of individual organizations. The problems included large oscillations of inventories, inventory stockouts, late deliveries, and quality problems. These and other issues now make it clear that management of supply chains is essential to business success. The other issues include the following:

1. *The need to improve operations.* During the last decade, many organizations adopted practices such as lean operation and total quality management (TQM). As a result, they were able to achieve improved quality while wringing much of the excess costs out of their systems. Although there is still room for improvement, for many organizations, the major gains have been realized. Opportunity now lies largely with procurement, distribution, and logistics—the supply chain.

2. *Increasing levels of outsourcing.* Organizations are increasing their levels of outsourcing, buying goods or services instead of producing or providing them themselves. As outsourcing increases, organizations are spending increasing amounts on supply-related activities (wrapping, packaging, moving, loading and unloading, and sorting). A significant amount of the cost and time spent on these and other related activities may be unnecessary. Issues with imported products, including tainted food products, toothpaste, and pet foods, as well as unsafe tires and toys, have led to questions of liability and the need for companies to take responsibility for monitoring the safety of outsourced goods.

   Outsourcing

3. *Increasing transportation costs.* Transportation costs are increasing, and they need to be more carefully managed.

CHINESE-MADE MR. COOL TAINTED TOOTHPASTE IS DISPLAYED AT THE MINISTRY OF HEALTH IN SAN JOSE, COSTA RICA. CHINA SAID IT WAS INVESTIGATING REPORTS THAT TOOTHPASTE CONTAINING A POTENTIALLY DEADLY CHEMICAL HAD BEEN EXPORTED TO CENTRAL AMERICA, ONE IN A SERIES OF SCANDALS INVOLVING TAINTED CHINESE PRODUCTS. COSTA RICA HAS ORDERED THE REMOVAL OF CHINESE TOOTHPASTE AND OTHER BRANDS FROM STORE SHELVES.

4. *Competitive pressures.* Competitive pressures have led to an increasing number of new products, shorter product development cycles, and increased demand for customization. And in some industries, most notably consumer electronics, product life cycles are relatively short. Added to this are adoption of quick-response strategies and efforts to reduce lead times.

5. *Increasing globalization.* Increasing globalization has expanded the physical length of supply chains. A global supply chain increases the challenges of managing a supply chain. Having far-flung customers and/or suppliers means longer lead times and greater opportunities for disruption of deliveries. Often currency differences and monetary fluctuations are factors, as well as language and cultural differences. Also, tightened border security in some instances has slowed shipments of goods.

6. *Increasing importance of e-business.* The increasing importance of e-business has added new dimensions to business buying and selling and has presented new challenges.

7. *The complexity of supply chains.* Supply chains are complex; they are dynamic, and they have many inherent uncertainties that can adversely affect the supply chain, such as inaccurate forecasts, late deliveries, substandard quality, equipment breakdowns, and canceled or changed orders.

8. *The need to manage inventories.* Inventories play a major role in the success or failure of a supply chain, so it is important to coordinate inventory levels throughout a supply chain. Shortages can severely disrupt the timely flow of work and have far-reaching impacts, while excess inventories add unnecessary costs. It would not be unusual to find inventory shortages in some parts of a supply chain and excess inventories in other parts of the same supply chain.

ELEMENTS OF SUPPLY CHAIN MANAGEMENT

Supply chain management involves coordinating activities across the supply chain. Central to this is taking customer demand and translating it into corresponding activities at each level of the supply chain.

The key elements of supply chain management are listed in Table 1.5. The first element, customers, is the driving element. Typically, marketing is responsible for determining what customers want as well as forecasting the quantities and timing of customer demand. Product and service design must match customer wants with operations capabilities.

Processing occurs in each component of the supply chain: it is the core of each organization. The major portion of processing occurs in the organization that produces the product or service for the final customer (the organization that assembles the computer, services the car, etc.). A major aspect of this for both the internal and external portions of a supply chain is scheduling.

Inventory is a staple in most supply chains. Balance is the main objective; too little causes delays and disrupts schedules, but too much adds unnecessary costs and limits flexibility.

Purchasing is the link between an organization and its suppliers. It is responsible for obtaining goods and or services that will be used to produce products or provide services for the organization's customers. Purchasing selects suppliers, negotiates contracts, establishes alliances, and acts as liaison between suppliers and various internal departments.

The supply portion of a value chain is made up of one or more suppliers, all links in the chain, and each one capable of having an impact on the effectiveness—or the ineffectiveness— of the supply chain. Moreover, it is essential that the planning and execution be carefully coordinated between suppliers and all members of the demand portion of their chains.

Location can be a factor in a number of ways. Where suppliers are located can be important, as can location of processing facilities. Nearness to market, nearness to sources of supply, or nearness to both may be critical. Also, delivery time and cost are usually affected by location.

Two types of decisions are relevant to supply chain management—strategic and operational. The strategic decisions are the design and policy decisions. The operational decisions relate to day-to-day activities: managing the flow of material and product and other aspects of the supply chain in accordance with strategic decisions.

Elements of Supply Chain Management

table 1.5

ELEMENT	TYPICAL ISSUES	CHAPTER(S)
Customers	Determining what products and/or services customers want.	
Forecasting	Predicting the quantity and timing of customer demand.	
Design	Incorporating customers, wants, manufacturability, and time to market.	
Capacity planning	Matching supply and demand.	4
Processing	Controlling quality, scheduling work.	
Inventory	Meeting demand requirements while managing the costs of holding inventory.	4, 5
Purchasing	Evaluating potential suppliers, supporting the needs of operations on purchased goods and services.	
Suppliers	Monitoring supplier quality, on-time delivery, and flexibility; maintaining supplier relations.	
Location	Determining the location of facilities.	
Logistics	Deciding how to best move information and materials.	

The major decision areas in supply chain management are location, production, distribution, and inventory. The *location* decision relates to the choice of locations for both production and distribution facilities. Production and transportation costs and delivery lead times are important. *Production* and *distribution* decisions focus on what customers want, when they want it, and how much is needed. Outsourcing can be a consideration. Distribution decisions are strongly influenced by transportation cost and delivery times, because transportation costs often represent a significant portion of total cost. Moreover, shipping alternatives are closely tied to production and inventory decisions. For example, using air transport means higher costs but faster deliveries and less inventory in transit than sea, rail, or trucking options. Distribution decisions must also take into account capacity and quality issues. Operational decisions focus on scheduling, maintaining equipment, and meeting customer demand. Quality control and workload balancing are also important considerations. *Inventory* decisions relate to determining inventory needs and coordinating production and stocking decisions throughout the supply chain. Logistics management plays the key role in inventory decisions.

LOOKING AHEAD

In addition to the key trends and issues just mentioned, you will learn about other important aspects of management in today's businesses. Among them are the following:

Operations strategy.

Working with fewer resources.

Revenue management.

Process analysis and improvement, and quality improvement.

Increased regulation and product liability issues.

Lean operation.

During the 1970s and 1980s, many companies neglected to include *operations strategy* in their corporate strategy. Some of them paid dearly for that neglect. Now more and more companies are recognizing the importance of operations strategy on the overall success of their business as well as the necessity for relating it to their overall business strategy.

Working with fewer resources due to layoffs, corporate downsizing, and general cost cutting is forcing managers to make trade-off decisions on resource allocation, and to place increased emphasis on cost control and productivity improvement.

Revenue management is a method used by some companies to maximize the revenue they receive from fixed operating capacity by influencing demand through price manipulation. Also known as yield management, it has been successfully used in the travel and tourism industries by airlines, cruise lines, hotels, amusement parks, and rental car companies, and in other industries such as trucking and public utilities.

Process analysis and improvement includes cost and time reduction, productivity improvement, process yield improvement and quality improvement and increasing customer satisfaction. One approach is *six sigma,* which involves the application of statistical analysis to improve processes.

Given a boost by the "quality revolution" of the 1980s and 1990s, *quality* is now ingrained in business. Some businesses use the term *total quality management (TQM)* to describe their quality efforts. A quality focus emphasizes *customer satisfaction* and often involves *teamwork. Process improvement* can result in improved quality, cost reduction, and *time reduction.* Time relates to costs and to competitive advantage, and businesses seek ways to reduce the time to bring new products and services to the marketplace to gain a competitive edge. If two companies can provide the same product at the same price and quality, but one can deliver it four weeks earlier than the other, the quicker company will invariably get the sale.

OPERATIONS TOURS

Throughout the book you will discover operations tours that describe operations in all sorts of companies. The tour you are about to read is Wegmans Food Markets, a major regional supermarket chain and one of the largest privately held companies in the United States. Wegmans has been consistently ranked high on *Fortune* magazine's list of the 100 Best Companies to Work For since the inception of the survey a decade ago. In 2005 Wegmans was ranked number one on the list.

OPERATIONS TOUR: WEGMANS FOOD MARKETS

www.wegmans.com

Wegmans Food Markets, Inc., is one of the premier grocery chains in the United States. Headquartered in Rochester, New York, Wegmans operates over 70 stores, mainly in Rochester, Buffalo, and Syracuse. There are also a handful of stores elsewhere in New York State and in New Jersey, Pennsylvania, and Virginia. The company employs over 37,000 people, and has annual sales of over $3 billion.

Wegmans has a strong reputation for offering its customers high product quality and excellent service. Through a combination of market research, trial and error, and listening to its customers, Wegmans has evolved into a very successful organization. Its sales per square foot are 50 percent higher than the industry average.

Superstores: Many of the company's stores are giant 100,000-square-foot superstores, double or triple the size of average supermarkets. You can get an idea about the size of these stores from this: they usually have between 25 and 35 checkout lanes, and during busy periods, all of the checkouts are in operation. A superstore typically employs from 500 to 600 people.

Individual stores differ somewhat in terms of actual size and some special features. Aside from the features normally found in supermarkets, they generally have a full-service deli (typically a 40-foot display case), a 500-square-foot fisherman's wharf that has perhaps 10 different fresh fish offerings most days, a large bakery section (each store bakes its own bread, rolls, cakes, pies, and pastries), and extra-large produce sections. They also offer film processing, a complete pharmacy, a card shop, video rentals, and an Olde World Cheese section. In-store floral shops range in size up to 800 square feet of floor space and offer a wide variety of fresh-cut flowers, flower arrangements, vases, and plants. In-store card shops cover over 1,000 square feet of floor space. The bulk foods department provides customers with the opportunity to select the quantities they desire from a vast array of foodstuffs and some nonfood items such as birdseed and pet food.

Each store is a little different. Among the special features in some stores are a dry cleaning department, a wokery, and a salad bar. Some stores feature a Market Café that has different food stations, each devoted to preparing and serving a certain type of food. For example, one station will have pizza and other Italian specialties, and another oriental food, and still another chicken or fish. There also will be a sandwich bar, a salad bar, and a dessert station. Customers often wander among stations as they decide what to order. In some Market Cafés, diners can have wine with their meals and have brunch on Sundays. In several affluent locations, customers can stop in on their way home from work and choose from a selection of freshly prepared dinner entrees such as medallions of beef with herb butter, chicken Marsala, stuffed flank steak with mushrooms, Cajun tuna, crab cakes, and accompaniments such as roasted red potatoes, grilled vegetables, and Caesar salad. Many Wegmans stores offer ready-made sandwiches as well as made-to-order sandwiches. Some stores have a coffee-shop section with tables and chairs where shoppers can enjoy regular or specialty coffees and a variety of tempting pastries.

Produce Department: The company prides itself on fresh produce. Produce is replenished as often as 12 times a day. The larger stores have produce sections that are four to five times the size of a produce section in an average supermarket. Wegmans offers locally grown produce in season. Wegmans uses a "farm to market" system whereby some local growers deliver their produce directly to individual stores, bypassing the main warehouse. That reduces the company's inventory holding costs and gets the produce into the stores as quickly as possible. Growers may use specially designed containers that go right onto the store floor instead of large bins. This avoids the bruising that often occurs when fruits and vegetables are transferred from bins to display shelves and the need to devote labor to transfer the produce to shelves.

Meat Department: In addition to large display cases of both fresh and frozen meat products, many stores have a full-service butcher shop that offers a variety of fresh meat products and where butchers are available to provide customized cuts of meat for customers.

Meat department employees attend Wegmans' "Meat University," where they learn about different cuts of meat and how to best prepare them. They also learn about other items to pair with various meats, and suggest side dishes, breads, and wine. This helps instill a "selling culture" among employees, who often spend 75 percent of their time talking with customers.

Wegmans continually analyzes store operations to improve processes. In the meat department, a change from in-store cutting and traditional packaging to using a centralized meat processing facility and vacuum packaging extended the shelf life of meats and reduced staffing requirements in meat departments, reducing costs and providing customers with an improved product.

Ordering: Each department handles its own ordering. Although sales records are available from records of items scanned at the checkouts, they are not used directly for replenishing stock. Other factors—such as pricing, special promotions, and local circumstances (e.g., festivals, weather conditions)—must all be taken into account. However, for seasonal periods, such as holidays, managers often check scanner records to learn what past demand was during a comparable period.

The superstores typically receive one truckload of goods per day from the main warehouse. During peak periods, a store may receive two truckloads from the main warehouse. The short lead time greatly reduces the length of time an item

WEGMANS' PATTISSERIE IS AN AUTHENTIC FRENCH PASTRY SHOP.

(continued)

(concluded)

might be out of stock, unless the main warehouse is also out of stock.

The company exercises strict control over suppliers, insisting on product quality and on-time deliveries.

Inventory Management: Wegmans uses a companywide system to keep track of inventory. Departments take a monthly inventory count to verify the amount shown in the companywide system. Departments receive a periodic report indicating how many days of inventory the department has on hand. Having an appropriate amount on hand is important to department managers: If they have too much inventory on hand, that will add to their department's costs, whereas having too little inventory will result in shortages and thus lost sales and dissatisfied customers.

Employees: The company recognizes the value of good employees. It typically invests an average of $7,000 to train each new employee. In addition to learning about store operations, new employees learn the importance of good customer service and how to provide it. The employees are helpful, cheerfully answering customer questions or handling complaints. Employees are motivated through a combination of compensation, profit sharing, and benefits. Employee turnover for full-time workers is about 6 percent, compared to the industry average of about 20 percent.

Quality: Quality and customer satisfaction are utmost in the minds of Wegmans, management and its employees. Private-label food items as well as name brands are regularly evaluated in test kitchens, along with potential new products. Managers are responsible for checking and maintaining product and service quality in their departments. Moreover, employees are encouraged to report problems to their managers.

If a customer is dissatisfied with an item, and returns it, or even a portion of the item, the customer is offered a choice of a replacement or a refund. If the item is a Wegmans brand food item, it is then sent to the test kitchen to determine the cause of the problem. If the cause can be determined, corrective action is taken.

Technology: Wegmans continues to adopt new technologies to maintain its competitive edge, including new approaches to tracking inventory and managing its supply chain, and new ways to maintain freshness in the meat and produce departments.

Sustainability: Wegmans began replacing incandescent light bulbs with compact fluorescent bulbs in 2007, and the company expects this will result in generating 3,000 fewer tons of carbon dioxide each year. Also the company installed sensors in its dairy cases that reduced the time the cooling systems run by 50 percent.

Questions

1. How do customers judge the quality of a supermarket?
2. Indicate how and why each of these factors is important to the successful operation of a supermarket:
   a. Customer satisfaction.
   b. Forecasting.
   c. Capacity planning.
   d. Location.
   e. Inventory management.
   f. Layout of the store.
   g. Scheduling.
3. What are some of the ways Wegmans uses technology to gain an edge over its competition?

FRESH SEAFOOD IS DELIVERED DAILY, OFTEN DIRECT FROM BOAT TO STORE THE SAME DAY IT WAS CAUGHT.

WEGMANS' CHEFS FILL THE CHEF'S CASE WITH READY-TO-EAT AND READY-TO-HEAT ENTREES, SIDE DISHES, AND SALADS.

SUMMARY

The operations function in business organizations is responsible for producing goods and providing services. It is a core function of every business. Supply chains are the sequential system of suppliers and customers that begins with basic sources of inputs and ends with final customers of the system. Operations and supply chains are interdependent—one couldn't exist without the other, and no business organization could exist without both.

The focus of both operations management and supply chain management is on managing processes to meet demand in a cost-effective manner. Variations in those processes as well as variations in demand, and product and service variety, add to the challenge of managing those processes to achieve desired results.

Operations management involves system design and operating decisions related to product and service design, capacity planning, process selection, location selection, work management, inventory and supply management, production planning, quality assurance, scheduling, and project management.

The historical evolution of operations management provides interesting background information on the continuing evolution of this core business function.

Key trends in business relate to the Internet, e-commerce and e-business, management of technology, globalization, sustainability, supply chain management, outsourcing, agility, and ethical behavior.

The Operations Tours and Readings included in this and subsequent chapters provide insights into actual business operations.

KEY TERMS

Goods Physical items produced by business organizations.

Services Activities that provide some combination of time, location, form, and psychological value.

Operations management The management of systems or processes that *create goods and/or provide services.*

Supply chain A sequence of activities and organizations involved in producing and delivering a good or service.

Value-added The difference between the cost of inputs and the value or price of outputs.

Process One or more actions that transform inputs into outputs.

Lead time The time between ordering a good or service and receiving it.

Model An abstraction of reality; a simplified representation of something.

System A set of interrelated parts that must work together.

Pareto phenomenon A few factors account for a high percentage of the occurrence of some event(s).

Craft production System in which highly skilled workers use simple, flexible tools to produce small quantities of customized goods.

Mass production System in which low-skilled workers use specialized machinery to produce high volumes of standardized goods.

Interchangeable parts Parts of a product made to such precision that they do not have to be custom fitted.

Division of labor The breaking up of a production process into small tasks, so that each worker performs a small portion of the overall job.

E-business Use of the Internet to transact business.

E-commerce Consumer- to-business transactions.

Technology The application of scientific discoveries to the development and improvement of goods and services.

Sustainability Using resources in ways that do not harm ecological systems that support human existence.

Agility The ability of an organization to respond quickly to demands or opportunities.

Six sigma A process for reducing costs, improving quality, and increasing customer satisfaction.

Lean system System that uses minimal amounts of resources to produce a high volume of high-quality goods with some variety.

Outsourcing Buying goods or services instead of producing or providing them in-house.

DISCUSSION AND REVIEW QUESTIONS

1. Briefly describe the term *operations management*.
2. Identify the three major functional areas of business organizations and briefly describe how they interrelate.
3. Describe the operations function and the nature of the operations manager's job.
4. List five important differences between goods production and service operations; then list five important similarities.
5. Briefly discuss each of these terms related to the historical evolution of operations management:
   a. Industrial Revolution
   b. Scientific management
   c. Interchangeable parts
   d. Division of labor
6. Why are services important? Why is manufacturing important? What are nonmanufactured goods?
7. What are models and why are they important?
8. Why is the degree of customization an important consideration in process planning?
9. List the trade-offs you would consider for each of these decisions:
   a. Driving your own car versus public transportation.
   b. Buying a computer now versus waiting for an improved model.
   c. Buying a new car versus buying a used car.
   d. Speaking up in class versus waiting to get called on by the instructor.
   e. A small business owner having a Web site versus newspaper advertising.
10. Describe each of these systems: craft production, mass production, and lean production.
11. Why might some workers prefer not to work in a lean production environment?
12. Discuss the importance of each of the following:
    a. Matching supply and demand
    b. Managing a supply chain
13. List and briefly explain the four basic sources of variation, and explain why it is important for managers to be able to effectively deal with variation.
14. Why do people do things that are unethical?
15. Explain the term *value-added*.
16. Discuss the various impacts of outsourcing.
17. Discuss the term sustainability, and its relevance for business organizations.

TAKING STOCK

This item appears at the end of each chapter. It is intended to focus your attention on three key issues for business organizations in general, and operations management in particular. Those issues are trade-off decisions, collaboration among various functional areas of the organization, and the impact of technology. You will see three or more questions relating to these issues. Here is the first set of questions:

1. What are trade-offs? Why is careful consideration of trade-offs important in decision making?
2. Why is it important for the various functional areas of a business organization to collaborate?
3. In what general ways does technology have an impact on operations management decision making?

CRITICAL THINKING EXERCISES

This item also will appear in every chapter. It allows you to critically apply information you learned in the chapter to a practical situation. Here is the first set of exercises:

1. Many organizations offer a combination of goods and services to their customers. As you learned in this chapter, there are some key differences between production of goods and delivery of services. What are the implications of these differences relative to managing operations?
2. Why is it important to match supply and demand? If a manager believes that supply and demand will not be equal, what actions could the manager take to increase the probability of achieving a match?
3. One way that organizations compete is through technological innovation. However, there can be downsides for both the organization and the consumer. Explain.

CASE: HAZEL

Hazel had worked for the same Fortune 500 company for almost 15 years. Although the company had gone through some tough times, things were starting to turn around. Customer orders were up, and quality and productivity had improved dramatically from what they had been only a few years earlier due to a company-wide quality improvement program. So it came as a real shock to Hazel and about 400 of her coworkers when they were suddenly terminated following the new CEO's decision to downsize the company.

After recovering from the initial shock, Hazel tried to find employment elsewhere. Despite her efforts, after eight months of searching she was no closer to finding a job than the day she started. Her funds were being depleted and she was getting more discouraged. There was one bright spot, though: She was able to bring in a little money by mowing lawns for her neighbors. She got involved quite by chance when she heard one neighbor remark that now that his children were on their own, nobody was around to cut the grass. Almost jokingly, Hazel asked him how much he'd be willing to pay. Soon Hazel was mowing the lawns of five neighbors. Other neighbors wanted her to work on their lawns, but she didn't feel that she could spare any more time from her job search.

However, as the rejection letters began to pile up, Hazel knew she had to make a decision. On a sunny Tuesday morning, she decided, like many others in a similar situation, to go into business for herself—taking care of neighborhood lawns. She was relieved to give up the stress of job hunting, and she was excited about the prospect of being her own boss. But she was also fearful of being completely on her own. Nevertheless, Hazel was determined to make a go of it.

At first, business was a little slow, but once people realized Hazel was available, many asked her to take care of their lawns. Some people were simply glad to turn the work over to her; others switched from professional lawn care services. By the end of her first year in business, Hazel knew she could earn a living this way. She also performed other services such as fertilizing lawns, weeding gardens, and trimming shrubbery. Business became so good that Hazel hired two part-time workers to assist her and, even then, she believed she could expand further if she wanted to.

QUESTIONS

1 In what ways are Hazel's customers most likely to judge the quality of her lawn care services?

2 Hazel is the operations manager of her business. Among her responsibilities are forecasting, inventory management, scheduling, quality assurance, and maintenance.
   a What kinds of things would likely require forecasts?
   b What inventory items does Hazel probably have? Name one inventory decision she has to make periodically.
   c What scheduling must she do? What things might occur to disrupt schedules and cause Hazel to reschedule?
   d How important is quality assurance to Hazel's business? Explain.
   e What kinds of maintenance must be performed?

3 What are some of the trade-offs that Hazel probably considered relative to:
   a Working for a company instead of for herself?
   b Expanding the business?
   c Launching a Web site?

4 The town is considering an ordinance that would prohibit putting grass clippings at the curb for pickup because local landfills cannot handle the volume. What options might Hazel consider if the ordinance is passed? Name two advantages and two drawbacks of each option.

5 Hazel decided to offer the students who worked for her a bonus of $25 for ideas on how to improve the business, and they provided several good ideas. One idea that she initially rejected now appears to hold great promise. The student who proposed the idea has left, and is currently working for a competitor. Should Hazel send that student a check for the idea? What are the possible trade-offs?

6 All managers have to cope with variation.
   a What are the major sources of variation that Hazel has to contend with?
   b How might these sources of variation impact Hazel's ability to match supply and demand?
   c What are some ways she can cope with variation?

7 Hazel is thinking of making some of her operations sustainable. What are some ideas she might consider?

SELECTED BIBLIOGRAPHY AND FURTHER READING

Bowie, Norman E., ed. *The Blackwell Guide to Business Ethics*. Malden, MA: Blackwell, 2002.

Colvin, Geoffrey. "Managing in the Info Era." *Fortune,* March 6, 2000, pp. F6–F9.

Crainer, Stuart. *The Management Century.* New York: Jossey-Bass, 2000.

Fitzsimmons, James, and Mona Fitzsimmons. *Service Management,* 4th ed. New York: McGrawHill/Irwin, 2004.

Shinn, Sharon. "What About the Widgets?" *BizEd,* November–December 2004, pp. 30–35.

Womack, James P., Daniel Jones, and Daniel Roos. *The Machine That Changed the World.* New York: Harper Perennial, 1991, 2007.

Wisner. Joel D. and Linda L. Stanley. Process Management: Creating Value Along the Supply Chain. Mason, OH: Thomson South-Western, 2008.

PROCESS ANALYSIS

chapter 2

CUSTOMER-DRIVEN SERVICE FOR McDONALD'S

SELF-ORDERING KIOSKS

IDEO collaborated with McDonald's on the first generation of a new service system in their Lone Tree restaurant, south of Denver. The new system allows McDonald's customers to place their orders without assistance, providing improved flexibility, **Service** speed, accuracy, and convenience to McDonald's customers as well as its crews. The system consists of touch-screen self-order kiosks at the front counter and in the children's PlayPlace area that have been fully integrated into the McDonald's physical environment, operational flow, and brand message.

After reading this chapter you will:

1. Recognize three basic types of processes: a serial flow process, parallel processes (such as what happens in a restaurant), and logistics processes.
2. Understand basic flowcharting of processes.
3. Explain how to analyze processes using Little's law.
4. Understand how to calculate process performance measures.

Customers place their orders using an icon-based system and pay at the kiosk or at the pick-up counter. After placing their orders, customers pick up their food at the counter by showing the order number on their printed receipts. In the PlayPlace area, parents can place and pay for their orders while supervising their children. A McDonald's crewmember then delivers the food to their table.

This new model needed to work within the popular and highly efficient system in use today. The completed design spanned the entire ordering experience and not just the kiosks themselves. The team updated the restaurant's graphics, signage, counters, and crew uniforms, and created nine self-order kiosks with a fully developed icon-based menu system. All design elements plus the in-store layout of the new service experience were arranged to complement the traditional experience of ordering at the counter.

The work began with a national survey of all kinds of quick-serve and self-serve experiences and distilled behavioral patterns of McDonald's customers to guide the design work. Since its launch and after thousands of transactions, the new service has had a high customer adoption rate with virtually no lines.

PROCESS ANALYSIS

Understanding how processes work is essential to ensuring the competitiveness of a company. A process that does not match the needs of the firm will punish the firm every minute that the firm operates. Take, for example, two fast-food restaurants. If one restaurant can deliver a quarter-pound hamburger to the customer for $0.50 in direct costs and a second restaurant costs $0.75, no matter what the second restaurant does, it will lose $0.25 in profit for every hamburger it sells compared to the first restaurant. Many factors need to be considered when one sets up the process to make those hamburgers. These factors include the cost of the raw materials, the costs associated with how the hamburger is prepared, and the cost of taking the order and delivering it to the customer.

Process

What is a process? A process is any part of an organization that takes inputs and transforms them into outputs that, it is hoped, are of greater value to the organization than the original inputs. Consider some examples of processes. Honda Motors assembles the Accord in a plant in Marysville, Ohio. The assembly plant takes in parts and components that have been fabricated for the plant. Using labor, equipment along an assembly line, and energy, these parts and components are transformed into automobiles. McDonald's, at each of its restaurants, uses inputs such as hamburger meat, lettuce, tomatoes, and potatoes. To these inputs, trained labor is added in the form of cooks and order takers, and capital equipment is used to transform the inputs into hamburgers, french fries, and other foods.

Service

In both of these examples, the process produces products as output. However, the outputs of many processes are services. In a hospital, for example, specialized equipment and highly trained doctors, nurses, and technicians are combined with another input, the patient. The patient is transformed through proper treatment and care into a healthy patient. An airline is another example of a service organization. The airline uses airplanes, ground equipment, flight crews, ground crews, reservation personnel, and fuel to transport customers between locations all over the world.

This chapter describes how to analyze a process. Analyzing a process allows some important questions to be answered, such as these: How many customers can the process handle per hour? How long will it take to serve a customer? What change is needed in the process to expand capacity? How much does the process cost? A difficult, but important, first step in process analysis is to clearly define the purpose of the analysis. Is the purpose to solve a problem? Is it to better understand the impact of a change in how business will be done in the future?

Clearly understanding the purpose of the analysis is critical to setting the level of detail in modeling the process. The analysis must be kept as simple as possible. The following sections of this chapter discuss the details of constructing flowcharts and measures that are appropriate for different types of processes. But first, consider a simple example.

ANALYZING A LAS VEGAS SLOT MACHINE

The slot machine is common in casinos around the world. Let's use this machine to illustrate how a simple process is analyzed.

Assume that we work for the casino and management is considering a new type of electronic slot machine that is much faster than the current mechanical machine. Management has asked how much we can expect to make from the new electronic machine over a 24-hour period compared to the old mechanical machine.

Step 1. Analyzing the Mechanical Slot Machine   Begin by analyzing a mechanical slot machine. The slot machine is activated when the customer puts one or more coins in the machine and then pulls the arm on the machine (slot machines are often called "one-armed bandits"). Three wheels spin, and after a time each wheel stops and displays a particular symbol. The machine pays money when certain combinations of symbols simultaneously appear. For those not familiar with how a slot machine works, we have included a slot machine simulation program on the text Web site. Sorry, but it does not pay real money.

Service

Slot machines are designed to pay back a certain percentage of what they take in. Typical paybacks would be 90 to 95 percent of what is taken in; the casino keeps 5 to 10 percent. These payback percentages are a function of the number of different symbols that are on each wheel. Each symbol is repeated on each wheel a certain number of times. For example, if a wheel has 10 symbols, one might be a single bar, one a double bar, and one a lemon; two might be cherries, three lucky sevens, and two liberty bells. Because the wheels stop on a random symbol, the probability of lucky sevens coming up on all three wheels is $\frac{3}{10} \times \frac{3}{10} \times \frac{3}{10} = 0.027$, or 2.7 percent of the time. The probability of certain combinations of symbols coming up, combined with the payout for each combination, sets the average percentage that the machine is expected to pay out.

Consider a mechanical slot machine that pays out 95 percent of the coins played. With this machine, assume the average player feeds coins into the machine at a pace of one coin each 15 seconds. This 15-second interval is called the *cycle time* of the process. The cycle time of a repetitive process is the average time between completions of successive units. In the case of the slot machine, the unit is a silver dollar. With a 15-second cycle time, our

Cycle time

mechanical slot machine can process $4 (60 seconds/15 seconds) per minute, or $240 ($4/minute $\times$ 60 minutes) per hour. Because our slot machine has a payout of 95 percent, we would expect the machine to give the customer 228 (240 $\times$ 0.95) of the silver dollars that it took in and keep $12 for the casino for each hour that it is in operation. If we started with $100, we could expect to play for about 8.3 hours ($100/$12 per hour) before we would run out of silver dollars. We might be lucky and win the jackpot, or we might be unlucky and lose it all in the first hour; but, on average, we would expect to lose the entire $100 in 8.3 hours.

Step 2. Analyzing the New Electronic Slot Machine   Now consider the new electronic slot machine. It operates in exactly the same manner; the only difference is that it uses "electronic" coins and it takes only 10 seconds to process each bet. With a 10-second cycle time, the machine processes $6 (60 seconds/10 seconds) per minute, or $360 ($6/minute $\times$ 60 minutes) per hour. With a 95 percent payout, the machine would give the customer back 342 (360 $\times$ 0.95) silver dollars and keep $18 for the casino each hour. This machine would take our $100 in only 5.5 hours ($100/$18 per hour).

Step 3. Comparison   So how much does the electronic slot machine make for the casino in 24 hours compared to the mechanical slot machine? One more critical piece of information is needed to answer this question: How long will the slot machine operate over the 24 hours? The casino feels that the machine will be used 12 out of the 24 hours; this 12 out of 24 hours is the expected utilization of the machine. Utilization is the ratio of the time that a resource is actually activated relative to the time that it is available for use. Adjusting for utilization, the expected revenue from the mechanical machine is $144/day ($12/hour $\times$ 24 hours $\times$ 0.5) compared to revenue of $216/day ($18/hour $\times$ 24 hours $\times$ 0.5) for the electronic machine. When an analysis is performed, it is important to qualify the analysis with

Utilization

the assumptions made. In this comparison, we assumed that the operator only bets one silver dollar at a time and that the utilization would be the same for the mechanical and electronic slot machines.

Step 4. The Slot Machine Is One of Many Casino Processes The speed of the slot machine can have a major impact on the casino's revenue. The single slot machine is only a small part of the casino. To really understand how much revenue the casino can generate, we need to consider all of the other revenue-generating processes, such as the blackjack and poker tables, keno games, craps, and the other games in the casino. Many times analyzing an enterprise involves evaluating a number of independent activities, like our slot machine. The aggregate performance of each individual activity may be all that is needed to understand the overall process. On the other hand, often there is significant interaction between individual activities or processes that must be considered.

Think about our gambling casino. Many casinos offer great deals on food, which is served right in the casino. What do you think would be the main priority of the food operation manager in one of these casinos? Would great-tasting food be important? How important is the cost of the food? Is speed of service important? Good food certainly is important. If the food is unpleasant, the customer will not even consider eating at the casino. This is bad for the casino because if the customers leave, they take their money with them. Remember, the casino makes money based on how long the customers gamble. The more time spent gambling, the more money the casino makes. What about cost? If the customers think the meals are too expensive, they might leave. So it is important to keep the cost of the meals down so that they can be priced inexpensively. Many casinos even give meals away. How important is it to serve the customer quickly? Think about it this way: Every minute that the customers are sitting in the restaurant, they are not feeding silver dollars into a slot machine. So speed is important because it impacts the revenue generated at the games in the casino.

PROCESS FLOWCHARTING

Often the activities associated with a process affect one another so that it is important to consider the simultaneous performance of a number of activities, all operating at the same time. A good way to start analyzing a process is with a diagram showing the basic elements of a process—typically tasks, flows, and storage areas. Tasks are shown as rectangles, flows as arrows, and the storage of goods or other items as inverted triangles. Sometimes flows through a process can be diverted in multiple directions depending on some condition. Decision points are depicted as a diamond with the different flows running from the points on the diamond. Exhibit 2.1 displays examples of these symbols. Separating a diagram into different horizontal or vertical bands sometimes is useful because it allows the separation of tasks that are part of the process. For example, with the slot machine, the tasks performed by the customer can be separated from the tasks performed by the slot machine.

In the slot machine example, the level of abstraction considers the slot machine as a simple black box that takes in silver dollars and either keeps them or returns some of them during each cycle. Viewing the slot machine as a black box might be fine if the purpose is just to analyze how much the machine is expected to make for the casino each hour. In reality, more activities are required to support the slot machine. Inside an old style mechanical slot machine are two buckets of silver dollars. One bucket stores coins needed for internal use by the slot machine. When a customer wins, the payout comes from this payout bucket. The slot machine is designed to automatically keep this payout bucket filled during play. When the payout bucket is full, the silver dollars are deposited in a second winnings bucket. The winnings bucket must be periodically emptied to claim the winnings for the casino. The flowchart in Exhibit 2.1 depicts the external activities of the player and the internal movement of the coins within the machine.

Process Flowchart Example

exhibit 2.1

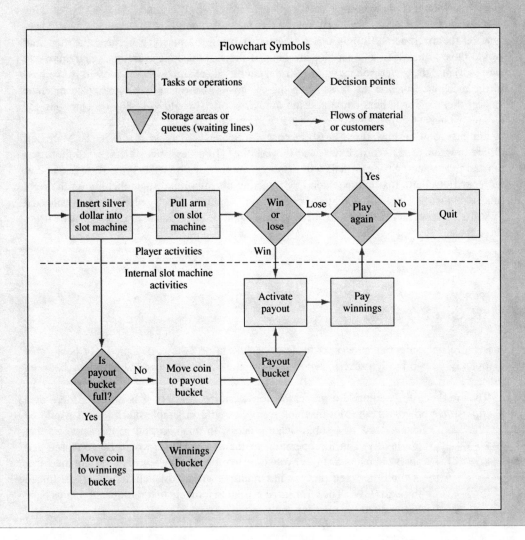

Probably the most interesting thing about the payout bucket is how big it should be. The slot machine is programmed so that if the payout bucket empties, the machine stops and lights on the top of the machine flash, thus notifying casino personnel that a lucky customer has emptied the machine. The payout bucket would be sized to keep this a rare occurrence. Think of the payout bucket as a buffer or intermediate storage area for silver dollars that allows the slot machine to operate on its own. The smaller the payout bucket, the more the casino personnel need to attend to the machine, and the more time the machine is idle for lack of silver dollars. On the other hand, with a larger bucket more money is tied up.

The situation with the winnings bucket in the machine is similar. A small winnings bucket will need to be emptied more often. On the other hand, a large winnings bucket means that the casino does not deposit the money into its bank account as quickly. The advantage of buffering operations with the slot machine is easily seen. Large buffers allow the process to operate independently, whereas small buffers require more attention. In the case of the slot machine, the buffer is composed of the silver dollars. In other situations, where the buffer is other items such as a raw material, these items have a value, so they also represent money.

Consider a slot machine that we expect to deposit $12 into the winnings bucket every hour. If our winnings bucket can hold 1,000 silver dollars, then we expect to need to empty the winnings bucket every 83.3 hours ($1,000/$12 per hour) if the slot machine is used 100 percent of the time. What happens when the winnings bucket fills up? If the slot machine is smart enough to know that the winnings bucket is full, it might be programmed to just stop working with its lights flashing as they do when the payout bucket empties. This would cause downtime on the machine and might upset a customer using the machine because the customer would have to move to another slot machine. If the slot machine were not programmed to stop working, the silver dollars would fill the cavity where the bucket is located in the base of the machine. Imagine the mess when the casino worker opens that overflowed machine and all those silver dollars come pouring out. How often would you plan on emptying the winnings bucket?

An easy way to draw flowcharts is to use the Shapes gallery available in the Microsoft Office programs (i.e., Word, Excel, and PowerPoint). To access this gallery, go to the Insert tab and then select "Shapes." This will display a number of flowchart symbols to use to create your flowchart. Text can be added by selecting a symbol and then clicking on the right mouse button. Select "Add text" to insert text in the symbol. The symbols can be connected by using "Connectors" available from the Shapes gallery. Nice flowcharts can be made using these tools.

TYPES OF PROCESSES

It is useful to categorize processes to describe how a process is designed. By being able to quickly categorize a process, we can show the similarities and differences between processes.

The first way to categorize a process is to determine whether it is a *single-stage* or a *multiple-stage* process. If the slot machine were viewed as a simple black box, it would be

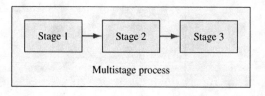
Multistage process

categorized as a single-stage process. In this case, all of the activities that are involved in the operation of the slot machine would be collapsed and analyzed using a single cycle time to represent the speed of the slot machine. A multiple-stage process has multiple groups of activities that are linked through flows. The term *stage* is used to indicate that multiple activities have been pulled together for analysis purposes.

BUFFERING, BLOCKING, AND STARVING

Buffering

A multiple-stage process may be buffered internally. Buffering refers to a storage area between stages where the output of a stage is placed prior to being used in a downstream stage. Buffering allows the stages to operate independently. If one stage feeds a second stage with no intermediate buffer, then the assumption is that the two stages are directly linked. When a process is designed this way, the most common problems that can happen are blocking and starving. Blocking occurs when the activities in the stage must stop because there is no place to deposit the item just completed. Starving occurs when the activities in a stage must stop because there is no work.

Blocking
Starving

Consider a two-stage process where the first stage has a cycle time of 30 seconds and the second a cycle time of 45 seconds. If this process needs to produce 100 units, then for each unit produced, the first stage would be blocked for 15 seconds.

What would happen if an inventory buffer were placed between the two stages? In this case, the first stage would complete the 100 units in 3,000 seconds (30 seconds/unit $\times$ 100 units). During these 3,000 seconds, the second stage would complete only 66 units ((3,000 − 30) seconds/45 seconds/unit). The 30 seconds are subtracted from the 3,000 seconds because the second stage is starved for the first 30 seconds. This would mean that the inventory would build to 34 units (100 units − 66 units) over that first 3,000 seconds. All of the units would be produced in 4,530 seconds. The second stage in this case is called a bottleneck because it limits the capacity of the process.

Bottleneck

What would happen if the first stage required 45 seconds and the second stage had the 30-second cycle time? In this case, the first stage would be the bottleneck, and each unit would go directly from the first stage to the second. The second stage would be starved for 15 seconds waiting for each unit to arrive; however, it would still take 4,530 seconds to complete all 100 units. All of this assumes that there is no variability in the cycle time. With the relatively low 67 percent utilization on the second stage, variability would have little impact on the performance of this system, but if the cycle times were closer, some inventory might collect in the buffer.

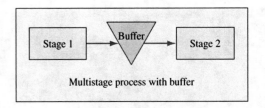

Multistage process with buffer

Often activities, stages, and even entire processes are operated in parallel. For example, operating two identical activities in parallel would theoretically double capacity. Or perhaps two different sets of activities can be done at the same time on the unit being produced. In analyzing a system with parallel activities or stages, it is important to understand the context. In the case where parallel processes represent alternatives, for example, a diamond should show that flows divert and what percentage of the flow moves in each direction. Sometimes two or more processes terminate in a common inventory buffer. This normally indicates that the two processes make identical items that are going into this inventory. Separate inventories should be used in the diagram if the outputs of the parallel processes are different.

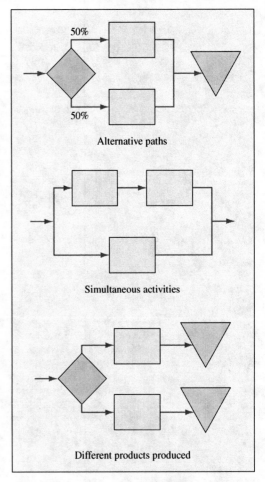

Alternative paths

Simultaneous activities

Different products produced

MAKE-TO-STOCK VERSUS MAKE-TO-ORDER

Another useful way to characterize a process is whether the process *makes to stock* or *makes to order*. To illustrate these concepts, consider the processes used to make hamburgers at the three major fast-food restaurant chains in the United States: McDonald's, Burger King, and Wendy's. In the case of McDonald's, in 1999 the company converted to a new make-to-order process, but the company has now revised that into a "hybrid" system. We begin our tour of the approaches used by the top fast-food restaurants by first reviewing the traditional approach.

Consider a traditional restaurant making hamburgers. Before the era of fast food, hamburgers were always made to order. In the traditional process, the customer places an order specifying the degree of doneness (medium or well done) and requests specific condiments (pickles, cheese, mustard, onions, catsup). Using this specification, the cook takes raw hamburger meat from inventory (typically this inventory is refrigerated and the patties have already been made), cooks the hamburger, and warms the bun. The hamburger is then assembled and delivered to the customer. The quality of the hamburger is highly dependent on the skill of the cook.

Service

This make-to-order process is activated only in response to an actual order. Inventory (both work-in-process and finished goods) is kept to a minimum. Theoretically, one would expect that response time would be slow because all the activities need to be completed before the product is delivered to the customer. Services by their very nature often use make-to-order processes.

Make-to-order

McDonald's revolutionized the hamburger-making process by developing a high-volume approach. A diagram of McDonald's traditional process is shown in Exhibit 2.2A. With the old process, hamburgers were grilled in batches. Standard hamburgers (for example, the "Big Mac" consists of two beef patties, sauce, lettuce, cheese, pickles, and onion on a sesame seed bun) were then prepared and stored in a holding bin for immediate delivery to the customer. A person that judged current demand and placed orders to keep inventory in the bin at an appropriate level controlled the whole process. This is a highly efficient make-to-stock process that produces standard products that can be delivered quickly to the

Make-to-stock

exhibit 2.2   Making Hamburgers at McDonald's, Burger King, and Wendy's

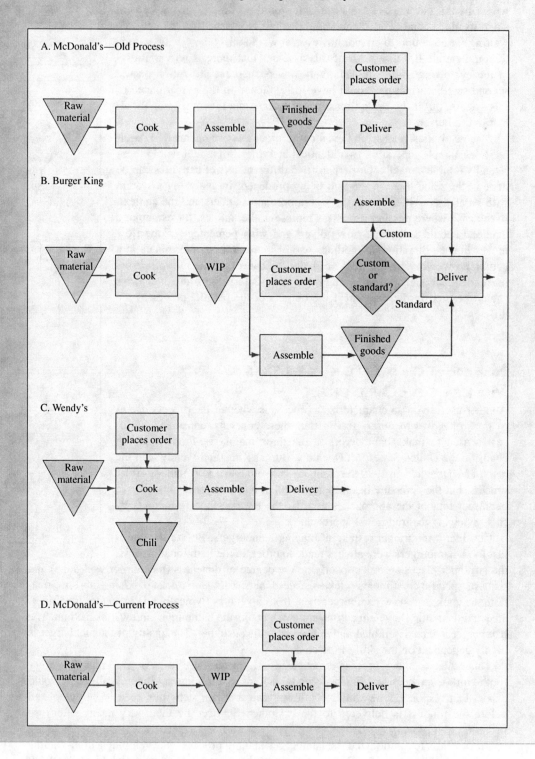

A. McDonald's—Old Process

B. Burger King

C. Wendy's

D. McDonald's—Current Process

customer. This quick process appeals to families with small children, for whom speed of delivery is important.

In general, a make-to-stock process ends with finished goods inventory; customer orders are then served from this inventory. A make-to-stock process can be controlled based on the actual or anticipated amount of finished goods inventory. A target stocking level, for example, might be set, and the process would be periodically activated to maintain that target stocking level. Make-to-stock processes are also used when demand is seasonal. In this case, inventory can be built during the slow season and used during the peak season, thus allowing the process to run at a constant rate throughout the year.

The unique feature of the Burger King process, shown in Exhibit 2.2B, is a highly specialized conveyor–broiler. Raw hamburger patties are placed on a moving conveyor that runs through a flaming broiler. In exactly 90 seconds, the patties are cooked on both sides with a unique broiler taste. To move a patty through the conveyor–broiler in a fixed time, the thickness of the patties must be the same for all the hamburger products. The buns are also warmed on a conveyor. This system results in a unique, highly consistent product. The cooked patties are stored in a warmed storage container. During periods of high demand, some standard hamburgers are prepared and inventoried for immediate delivery. Custom hamburgers with unique combinations of condiments are prepared to order. This *hybrid* process provides flexibility to respond to customer preferences through the assemble-to-order backend process—thus, the Burger King "have it your way" slogan. In general, hybrid processes combine the features **Hybrid** of both make-to-order and make-to-stock. Here two types of process are parallel alternatives at the end of the Burger King process. In the most common hybrid form, a generic product is made and stocked at some point in the process. These generic units are then finished in a final process based on actual orders.

WENDY'S MAKE-TO-ORDER PROCESS.

Continuing with our tour, Wendy's uses a make-to-order process (as shown in Exhibit 2.2C) that is in full view of the customer. Hamburger patties are cooked on a grill. During high-volume times, the cook tries to get a little ahead and anticipates the arrival of customers. Patties that are on the grill too long are used in the chili soup. On arrival of a customer order, a patty is taken from the grill and the hamburger is assembled to the exact specifications of the customer. Because the process starts with the cooking of the patty, it is a little slower. The customer can see what is going on, and the perception is of a high-quality custom product.

Finally, the current McDonald's process introduced in 1999 (Exhibit 2.2D) is a hybrid process. Cooked hamburger patties are inventoried in a special storage device that maintains the moistness of the cooked patties for up to 30 minutes. The process makes extensive use of the latest cooking technologies. Hamburger patties are cooked in less than 45 seconds. Buns are toasted in only 11 seconds. Individual items on each customer order are transmitted immediately to the area where the hamburgers are assembled using a specially designed computer system. The assembly process that includes toasting the buns is designed to respond to a customer order in only 15 seconds. By combining the latest technology and clever process engineering, McDonald's has developed a very quick response process. The product is fresh, delivered quickly, and made to the exact specifications of the customer.

McDONALD'S ASSEMBLY PROCESS.

Each of the processes used by these companies has its strengths and weaknesses. McDonald's is the high-volume leader, catering to families with young children. Burger King has its unique taste. Wendy's appeals to those who want their hamburgers prepared the old-fashioned way. Each company focuses advertising and promotional efforts toward attracting the segment of the market its process characteristics best support.

One final method for categorizing a process is by whether it is paced or nonpaced. Recall that Burger King uses the conveyor–broiler to cook hamburgers in exactly 90 seconds. Pacing refers to the fixed timing of the movement of items through the process. In a serial **Pacing** process, the movement of items through each activity (or stage) is often paced in some mechanical way in order to coordinate the line. An assembly line may, for example, move every 45 seconds. Another mechanism used is a clock that counts down the amount of time left in each cycle. When the clock reaches zero, the parts are manually moved to the next activity. Dividing the time available to produce a certain product by customer demand for the product calculates the required cycle time for a process. For example, if an automobile manufacturer needs to produce 1,000 automobiles during a shift where the assembly line operates 420 minutes, the cycle time is 25.2 seconds (420 minutes/1,000 automobiles $\times$ 60 seconds/minute = 25.2 seconds/automobile).

MEASURING PROCESS PERFORMANCE

There is much variation in the way performance metrics are calculated in practice. This section defines metrics in a manner consistent with the most common use in practice. It is vital, though, to understand exactly how a metric coming from a particular company or industry is calculated prior to making any decisions. This would be easier if metrics were calculated more consistently, but this just is not the case. So if a manager says that his utilization is 90 percent or her efficiency is 115 percent, a standard follow-up question is "How did you calculate that?" Metrics often are calculated in the context of a particular process. Metrics used in cases that you are studying may be defined slightly differently from what is given here. It is important to understand, within the context of the case, how a term is being used.

Comparing the metrics of one company to another, often referred to as *benchmarking,* is an important activity. Metrics tell a firm if progress is being made toward improvement. Similar to the value of financial measures to accountants, process performance metrics give the operations manager a gauge on how productively a process currently is operating and how productivity is changing over time. Often operations managers need to improve the performance of a process or project the impact of a proposed change. The metrics described in this section are important for answering these questions. To help in understanding these calculations, Exhibit 2.3 shows how these metrics relate to one another.

exhibit 2.3 Process Performance Metrics

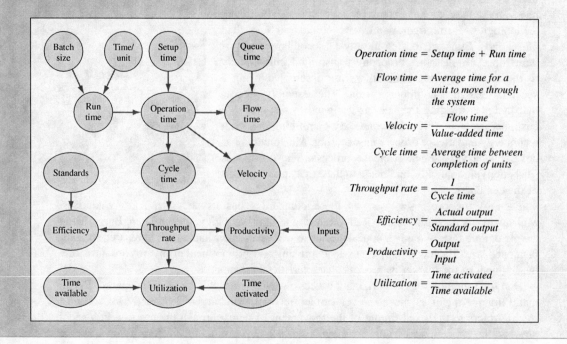

$Operation\ time = Setup\ time + Run\ time$

$Flow\ time = Average\ time\ for\ a\ unit\ to\ move\ through\ the\ system$

$Velocity = \dfrac{Flow\ time}{Value\text{-}added\ time}$

$Cycle\ time = Average\ time\ between\ completion\ of\ units$

$Throughput\ rate = \dfrac{1}{Cycle\ time}$

$Efficiency = \dfrac{Actual\ output}{Standard\ output}$

$Productivity = \dfrac{Output}{Input}$

$Utilization = \dfrac{Time\ activated}{Time\ available}$

Possibly the most common process metric is utilization. As discussed earlier in the chapter, utilization is the ratio of the time that a resource is actually being used relative to the time that it is available for use. Utilization is always measured in reference to some resource—for example, the utilization of direct labor or the utilization of a machine resource. The distinction between productivity and utilization is important. Productivity is the ratio of output to input. Total factor productivity is usually measured in monetary units, dollars, for example, by taking the dollar value of the output (such as goods and services sold) and dividing by the cost of all the inputs (that is, material, labor, and capital investment). Alternatively, *partial factor productivity* is measured based on an individual input, labor being the most common. Partial factor productivity answers the question of how much output we can get from a given level of input; for example, how many computers are made per employee working in the computer manufacturing plant? Utilization measures the actual activation of the resource. For example, what is the percentage of time that an expensive machine is actually operating?

Productivity

Efficiency is a ratio of the actual output of a process relative to some standard. For example, consider a machine designed to package cereal at a rate of 30 boxes per minute. If during a shift the operators actually produce at a rate of 36 boxes per minute, then the efficiency of the machine is 120 percent (36/30). An alternative way that the term *efficiency* is used is to measure the loss or gain in a process. For example, if 1,000 units of energy are put into a process designed to convert that energy to some alternative form, and the process produces only 800 units of energy in the new form, then the process is 80 percent efficient.

Efficiency

Run time is the time required to produce a batch of parts. This is calculated by multiplying the time required to produce each unit by the batch size. The setup time is the time required to prepare a machine to make a particular item. Machines that have significant setup time will typically run parts in batches. The operation time is the sum of the setup time and run time for a batch of parts that are run on a machine. Consider the cereal-boxing machine that is designed to produce at a rate of 30 boxes per minute. The run time for each box is 2 seconds. To switch the machine from 16-ounce boxes to 12-ounce boxes requires a setup time of 30 minutes. The operation time to make a batch of 10,000 12-ounce boxes is 21,800 seconds (30 minutes' setup $\times$ 60 seconds/minute + 2 seconds/box $\times$ 10,000 boxes), or 363.33 minutes.

Run time
Setup time
Operation time

In practice, often setup time is not included in the utilization of the process. In essence, setup time is categorized like the downtime caused by repair or some other disruption to the process. This assumption can vary from company to company, so it is important when comparing the utilization of a machine or other resource to understand exactly how the company categorizes setup time.

The cycle time (also defined earlier in this chapter) is the elapsed time between starting and completing a job.[1] Another related term is flow time. Flow time includes the time that the unit spends actually being worked on together with the time spent waiting in a queue. As a simple example, consider a paced assembly line that has six stations and runs with a cycle time of 30 seconds. If the stations are located one right after another and every 30 seconds parts move from one station to the next, then the throughput time is three minutes (30 seconds $\times$ 6 stations/60 seconds per minute). The throughput rate is the output rate that the process is expected to produce over a period of time. The throughput rate of the assembly line is 120 units per hour (60 minutes/hour $\times$ 60 seconds/minute $\div$ 30 seconds/unit). In this case, the throughput rate is the mathematical inverse of the cycle time.

Flow time

Throughput rate

Often units are not worked on 100 percent of the time as they move through a process. Because there often is some variability in the cycle time of a process, buffers are incorporated in the process to allow individual activities to operate independently, at least to some

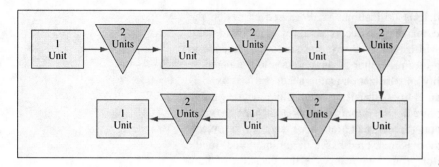

extent. In the six-station assembly line just described, consider the impact of having 10 additional buffer positions along the line. Assume that two of these positions are between the first and second workstations, two are between stations 2 and 3, and so forth. If these positions are always occupied, then the throughput time would be eight minutes (assuming a total of 16 positions along the assembly line and an average cycle time of 30 seconds).

Process velocity (throughput ratio)

Value-added time

Process velocity (also known as throughput ratio) is the ratio of the total throughput time to the value-added time. Value-added time is the time in which useful work is actually being done on the unit. Assuming that all of the activities that are included in the process are value-added activities, value-added time should be the sum of the activity operation times in the process. The process velocity (or throughput ratio) for our assembly line with the 10 additional buffer positions, assuming the positions are used 100 percent of the time, is 2.66 (8 minutes/3 minutes).

PRODUCTION PROCESS MAPPING AND LITTLE'S LAW

Supply Chain

Next, we look at how to quickly develop a high-level map of a process, which can be useful to understand how material flows and where inventory is held. The approach used here should be the first step in analyzing the flow of material through a production process. This idea will be further developed in "Value Stream Mapping" in Chapter 8.

Consider a simple system that might be typical of many make-to-stock companies. As shown in Exhibit 2.4, material is purchased from a set of suppliers and initially staged in raw material inventory. The material is used in a manufacturing process where the product is fabricated. After fabrication, the product is put into finished goods inventory and from here it is shipped according to orders received from customers.

Focusing on the Make part of the process, it is useful to analyze how this step operates using performance measures that relate to the inventory investment and also how quickly material flows through the process. A simplified way of thinking about material in a process is that it is in one of two states. The first state is where material is moving or "in-transit."

exhibit 2.4   Make-to-Stock Process Map

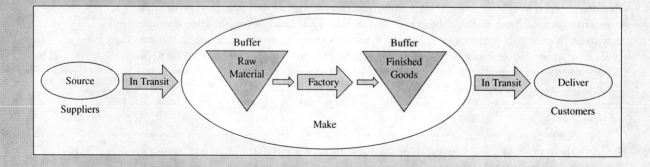

The second state is material that is sitting in inventory and acting as a "buffer" waiting to be used.

In the first state, material is moving in the process. This is material that is in-transit between entities in the process, for example, between the vendor and the raw material inventory at the manufacturer. Material that is in a manufacturing process in a factory can also be considered in-transit. Actually, we refer to this material as "work-in-process" inventory. In the second state, material is held in a storage area and waits until it is needed. In the case of raw material inventory, the need is dependent on the factory usage of the item. This "buffer" inventory allows different entities in the process to operate relatively independently.

A common measure is the total average value of inventory in the process. From an accounting view this would be the sum of the value (at cost) of the raw material, work-in-process, and finished goods inventory. This is commonly tracked in accounting systems and reported in the firm's financial statements. In addition to the total value of this inventory, another measure is the firm's inventory turn, which is the cost of goods sold divided by the average inventory value. Although useful for accounting purposes, these measures are not particularly useful for evaluating the performance of a process. Consider the total average value of inventory. What is better, a firm that has $2 million worth of inventory on average or one that has $4 million? This depends greatly on the size of the firm, the type of strategy being used (make-to-order or make-to-stock, for example), and the relative cost of the product being produced.

Total average value of inventory

Inventory turn

A better measure than the total value of inventory is inventory turn. Since inventory turn scales the amount of inventory by dividing by the cost of goods sold, this provides a relative measure that has some comparability, at least across similar firms. For two similar consumer products manufacturers, an inventory turn of six times per year is certainly much better than a firm turning inventory two times per year. A measure directly related is days-of-supply, which is the inverse of inventory turn scaled to days. For example, if a firm turns inventory six times per year, the days of supply is equal to one-sixth times per year or approximately every 61 days (this is calculated as 1/6 year × 365 days/year = 60.8 days).

Days-of-supply

Simple systems can be analyzed quickly using a principle known as Little's law. Little's law says there is a long-term relationship between the inventory, throughput, and flow time of a production system in steady state. The relationship is:

Little's law

$$Inventory = Throughput\ rate \times Flow\ time \qquad [2.1]$$

As noted earlier, throughput rate is the long-term average rate that items are flowing through the process and flow time is the time that it takes a unit to flow through the process from beginning to end. Consider the Factory process in Exhibit 2.4. Raw material is brought into the factory and is transformed and then stored in finished goods inventory. The analysis assumes that the process is operating in "steady state," meaning that over a long enough period of time the amount that is produced by the factory is equal to the amount shipped to customers. The throughput rate of the process is equal to average demand, and the process is not producing any excess or shortage. If this was not true and the amount produced by the manufacturing process was greater than demand, for example, the finished goods inventory would build over time. So if demand averages 1,000 units per day and 20 days are needed for a unit to flow through the factory, then the expected work-in-process in the factory would be 20,000 units.

We can think of Little's law as a relationship between units and time. Inventory is measured in pieces, flow time in days, and throughput in pieces per day. Therefore, if we divide inventory by throughput we get flow time. For example, 20,000 units divided by 1,000 units per day is 20 days. We can also take inventory and divide by flow time and get throughput rate. Here 20,000 units divided by 20 days is equal to 1,000 units a day. This conversion is useful when diagnosing a plant's performance.

To appreciate a major limitation, suppose that a process has just started with no inventory on hand. Some of the initial production will be used to fill the system, thus limiting initial throughput. In this case Little's law will not hold, but after the process has been operating for a while, and there is inventory at every step, the process stabilizes, and then the relationship holds.

Little's law is actually much more general than a simple way to convert between units. It can be applied to single work stations, multistep production lines, factories, or even entire supply chains. Further, it applies to processes with variability in the arrival rate (or demand rate) and processing time. It can be applied to single or multiple product systems. It even applies to nonproduction systems where inventory represents people, financial orders, or other entities.

Supply Chain

For our factory, it is common for accounting systems to capture average work-in-process in terms of the value (at cost) of the inventory that is being worked on in the factory. For our example, say that work-in-process averages $200,000 and that each unit is valued at cost at $10.00. This would imply that there are 20,000 units in the factory (calculated $200,000 ÷ $10.00 per unit = 20,000 units).

The following example shows how these concepts can be applied to quickly analyze simple processes.

Global

Step by Step

EXAMPLE 2.1

An automobile company assembles cars in a plant and purchases batteries from a vendor in China. The average cost of each battery is $45. The automobile company takes ownership of the batteries when they arrive at the plant. It takes exactly 12 hours to make a car in the plant and the plant assembles 200 cars per 8-hour shift (currently the plant operates one shift per day). Each car uses one battery. The company holds on average 8,000 batteries in raw material inventory at the plant as a buffer. Assignment: Find the total number of batteries in the plant on average (in work-in-process at the plant and in raw material inventory). How much are these batteries worth? How many days of supply are held in raw material inventory on average?

SOLUTION

We can split this into two inventories, work-in-process and raw material. For the work-in-process, Little's law can be directly applied to find the amount of work-in-process inventory:

$$Inventory = Throughput \times Flow\ time$$

Throughput is the production rate of the plant, 200 cars per 8-hour shift, or 25 cars per hour. Since we use one battery per car, our throughput rate for the batteries is 25 per hour. Flow time is 12 hours, so the work-in-process is:

$$Work\text{-}in\text{-}process\ inventory = 25\ batteries/hour \times 12\ hours = 300\ batteries$$

We know from the problem there are 8,000 batteries in raw material inventory, so the total number of batteries in the pipeline on average is:

$$Total\ inventory = 8,000 + 300 = 8,300\ batteries$$

These batteries are worth $8,300 \times \$45 = \$373,500$.

The days of supply in raw material inventory is the "flow time" for a battery in raw material inventory (or the average amount of time that a battery spends in raw material inventory). Here, we need to assume that they are used in the same order they arrive. Rearranging our Little's law formula:

$$Flow\ time = Inventory/Throughput$$

So, Flow time = 8,000 batteries/(200 batteries/day) = 40 days, which represents a 40-day supply of inventory. ●

In the next section, we look at how the production processes are organized in different environments. This is largely dependent on the variety of products being produced and on the volume. How a company produces airplanes is very different when compared to building computers or making ink pens.

PROCESS ANALYSIS EXAMPLES

In this section, the concepts described thus far in the chapter are illustrated with three examples. These examples are typical of the types of analysis that are performed in manufacturing, services, and logistics businesses. Keep in mind that the analysis used in each example can be applied to many different contexts. Be creative in applying something that you have seen in another context to the problem at hand. The first example analyzes a bread-making process. Following this, a restaurant operation is evaluated. Finally, a typical logistics operation is appraised.

A BREAD-MAKING OPERATION[2]

EXAMPLE 2.2: Bread Making

For the manager of a bakery, a first priority is to understand the products that are made and the process steps required. Exhibit 2.5A is a simplified diagram of the bread-making process. Two steps are required to prepare the bread. The first is preparing the dough and baking the loaves, here referred to as bread making. The second is packaging the loaves. Due to the size of the mixers in the bakery, bread is made in batches of 100 loaves. Bread making completes a batch of 100 loaves every hour, which is the cycle time for the activity. Packaging needs only 0.75 hour to place the 100 loaves in bags.

Step by Step

From this we see that bread making is the bottleneck in the process. A bottleneck is the activity in a process that limits the overall capacity of the process. So if we assume that the bread-making and packaging activities both operate the same amount of time each day, then the bakery has a capacity of 100 loaves per hour. Notice that over the course of the day the packaging operation will be idle for quarter-hour periods in which the next batch of bread is still being made but packaging has already completed bagging the previous batch. One would expect that the packaging operation would be utilized only 75 percent of the time under this scenario.

Bread-Making Processes

exhibit 2.5

A. Bread making on one line

Raw material → Bread making / **Cycle time:** 1 hour/100 loaves → WIP → Pack / **Cycle time:** $\frac{3}{4}$ hour/100 loaves → Finished Goods

B. Bread making on two parallel lines

Raw material → Bread making / **Cycle time:** 1 hour/100 loaves and Bread making / **Cycle time:** 1 hour/100 loaves → WIP → Pack / **Cycle time:** $\frac{3}{4}$ hour/100 loaves → Finished Goods

Suppose that instead of having only one bread-making operation we now have two, as shown in Exhibit 2.5B. The cycle time for each individual bread-making operation is still one hour per 100 loaves. The cycle time for the two bread-making lines operating together is half an hour. Because the packaging operation takes 0.75 hour to bag 100 loaves, the packaging operation now is the bottleneck. If both bread making and packaging were operated the same number of hours each day, it would be necessary to limit how much bread was made because we do not have the capacity to package it. However, if we operated the packaging operation for three eight-hour shifts and bread making for two shifts each day, then the daily capacity of each would be identical at 3,200 loaves a day (this assumes that the packaging operation starts up one hour after the bread-making operation). Doing this requires building up a shift's worth of inventory each day as work-in-process. Packaging would bag this during the third shift. So what is the flow time of our bakery?

SOLUTION

In the original operation with just the single bread-making process, this is easy to calculate because inventory would not build between the bread-making and packaging processes. In this case the flow time would be 1.75 hours. In the case where we operate the packaging operation for three shifts, the average wait in work-in-process inventory needs to be considered. If both bread-making operations start at the same time, then at the end of the first hour the first 100 loaves move immediately into packaging while the second 100 loaves wait. The waiting time for each 100-loaf batch increases until the baking is done at the end of the second shift.

This is a case where Little's law can estimate the time that the bread is sitting in work-in-process. To apply Little's law, we need to estimate the average work-in-process between bread making and packaging. During the first two shifts, inventory builds from 0 to 1,200 loaves. We can estimate the average work-in-process over this 16-hour period to be 600 loaves (half the maximum). Over the last eight-hour shift inventory drops from the 1,200-loaf maximum down to 0. Again the average work-in-process is 600 loaves. Given this, the overall average over the 24-hour period is simply 600 loaves of bread. The packing process limits the cycle time for the process to 0.75 hour per 100 loaves (assume that the loaves are packaged in a batch), and this is equivalent to a throughput rate of 133.3 loaves/hour (100/0.75 = 133.3). Little's law calculates that the average time that loaves are in work-in-process is 4.5 hours (600 loaves/133.3 loaves/hour).

The total flow time is the time that the loaves are in work-in-process plus the operations time for the bread-making and packaging processes. The total flow time then is 6.25 hours (1 hour for bread making + 4.5 hours in inventory + 0.75 hour packaging). ●

A RESTAURANT OPERATION

EXAMPLE 2.3: A Restaurant

Service

Step by Step

Our bakery operates in what is referred to as *steady state,* meaning that the operation is started up and runs at a steady rate during the entire time that it is in operation. The output of this steady state process is adjusted by setting the amount of time that the operation is run. In the case of the bakery, we assumed that bread making worked for three shifts and packaging for two shifts.

A restaurant cannot run in this manner. The restaurant must respond to varying customer demand throughout the day. During some peak times, it may be impossible to serve all customers immediately, and some customers may have to wait to be seated. The restaurant, because of this varying demand, is a *non–steady state* process. Keep in mind that many of the menu items in a restaurant can be pre-prepared. The pre-prepared items, salads and desserts, for example, help speed the processes that must be performed when customers are at the restaurant being served.

Consider the restaurant in the casino that we discussed earlier. Because it is important that customers be served quickly, the managers have set up a buffet arrangement where customers serve themselves. The buffet is continually replenished to keep items fresh. To further speed service, a fixed amount is charged for the meal, no matter what the customer eats. Assume that we have designed our buffet so customers take an average of 30 minutes to get their food and eat. Further, assume that they typically eat in groups (or customer parties) of two or three to a table. The restaurant has 40 tables. Each table can accommodate four people. What is the maximum capacity of this restaurant?

SOLUTION

It is easy to see that the restaurant can accommodate 160 people seated at tables at a time. Actually, in this situation, it might be more convenient to measure the capacity in terms of customer parties because this is how the capacity will be used. If the average customer party is 2.5 individuals, then the average seat utilization is 62.5 percent (2.5 seats/party ÷ 4 seats/table) when the restaurant is operating at capacity. The cycle time for the restaurant, when operating at capacity, is 0.75 minute (30 minutes/table ÷ 40 tables). So, on average, a table would become available every 45 seconds. The restaurant could handle 80 customer parties per hour (60 minutes ÷ 0.75 minute/party).

The problem with this restaurant is that everyone wants to eat at the same time. Management has collected data and expects the following profile for customer parties arriving during lunch, which runs from 11:30 A.M. until 1:30 P.M. Customers are seated only until 1:00 P.M.

TIME	PARTIES ARRIVING
11:30–11:45	15
11:45–12:00	35
12:00–12:15	30
12:15–12:30	15
12:30–12:45	10
12:45–1:00	5
Total parties	110

Because the restaurant operates for two hours for lunch and the capacity is 80 customer parties per hour, the restaurant does not appear to have a problem. In reality, though, the uneven flow of customers into the restaurant is a problem. A simple way to analyze the situation is to calculate how we expect the system to look in terms of number of customers being served and number waiting in line at the end of each 15-minute interval. Think of this as taking a snapshot of the restaurant every 15 minutes.

The key to understanding the analysis is to look at the cumulative numbers. The difference between cumulative arrivals and cumulative departures gives the number of customer parties in the restaurant (those seated at tables and those waiting). Because there are only 40 tables, when the cumulative difference through a time interval is greater than 40, a waiting line forms. When all 40 tables are busy, the system is operating at capacity; and, from the previous calculation, we know the cycle time for the entire restaurant is 45 seconds per customer party at this time (this means that on average a table empties every 45 seconds or 20 tables empty during each 15-minute interval). The last party will need to wait for all of the earlier parties to get a table, so the expected waiting time is the number of parties in line multiplied by the cycle time.

TIME PERIOD	PARTIES ARRIVING DURING PERIOD (CUMULATIVE)	PARTIES DEPARTING DURING PERIOD (CUMULATIVE)	PARTIES EITHER AT TABLE OR WAITING TO BE SERVED (AT END OF PERIOD)	TABLES USED (AT END OF PERIOD)	CUSTOMER PARTIES WAITING (AT END OF PERIOD)	EXPECTED WAITING TIME (AT END OF PERIOD)
11:30–11:45	15	0	15	15		
11:45–12:00	35 (50)	0	50	40	10	7.5 minutes
12:00–12:15	30 (80)	15	65	40	25	18.75 minutes
12:15–12:30	15 (95)	20 (35)	60	40	20	15 minutes
12:30–12:45	10 (105)	20 (55)	50	40	10	7.5 minutes
12:45–1:00	5 (110)	20 (75)	35	35		
1:00–1:30	0 (110)	35 (110)				

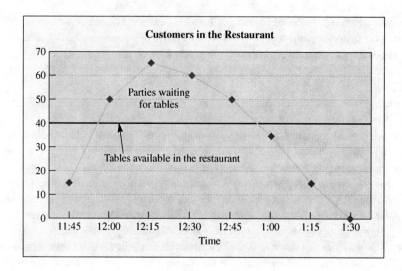

The analysis shows that by 12 noon, 10 customer parties are waiting in line. This line builds to 25 parties by 12:15. The waiting line shortens to only 10 parties by 12:45.

So what can we do to solve our waiting line problem? One idea might be to shorten the cycle time for a single table, but customers are unlikely to be rushed through their lunch in less than 30 minutes. Another idea would be to add tables. If the restaurant could add 25 tables, then a wait would not be expected. Of course, this would eat into the space used for slot machines, so this alternative might not be attractive to casino management. A final idea might be to double up parties at the tables, thus getting a higher seat utilization. Doubling up might be the easiest thing to try. If 25 out of the 40 tables were doubled up, our problem would be solved. ●

PLANNING A TRANSIT BUS OPERATION

EXAMPLE 2.4: Transit Bus Operation

Service

Step by Step

Global

The final example involves a *logistics* system. The term *logistics* refers to the movement of things such as materials, people, or finished goods. Our example involves a bus route that would be typical of one used on campus or in a metropolitan area. A similar analysis could be used for analyzing plane routes, truck routes, or ships. Similar to the restaurant, a bus transit route does not operate in steady state. There are definite peaks in demand during the day and evening. A good approach to take, the same as was done with the restaurant, is to analyze distinct periods of time that represent the different types of demand patterns placed on the service. These distinct analyses can be referred to as *scenarios*. Depending on the situation, it might be reasonable to develop either a single solution that covers all the relevant scenarios or a set of solutions for the different scenarios.

A great bus route is the Balabus, or "tourist bus," in Paris. This route loops past all the major attractions in Paris. Some of the sights along the route include Notre-Dame, the Louvre, Concorde, Champs-Elysées, the Arc de Triomphe, the Eiffel Tower, and others.

Consider the problem of planning the number of buses needed to service this route. A number of factors need to be considered. Let's assume that a single bus takes exactly two hours to traverse the route during peak traffic. The bus company has designed delays in the route so that even though traffic is busy, the bus can keep on schedule. The route has 60 stops, although the bus stops only when passengers on the bus request a stop or when the driver sees customers waiting to board at a stop. Each bus has seating capacity of about 50 passengers, and another 30 passengers can stand. This route is busy much of the day because visitors to the city tend to start visiting the sites early and continue until dark. Finally, the transit authority wants to give good service and have enough capacity to handle peak customer loads. The following is an analysis of the situation.

SOLUTION

A key measure of service is how long a customer must wait prior to the arrival of a bus. Consider initially the case of only a single bus serving the route. If a person at a random time comes to a bus stop, we know that the maximum time that the customer needs to wait is two hours. Here we assume that the bus is able to cover the route in exactly two hours. If this cycle time varies significantly, the waiting time goes up. This would be the case when the unlucky customer just missed the bus. If the bus was halfway through the route (relative to where the customer is waiting), then the customer needs to wait one hour. Continuing with this logic, we can estimate the average wait time for the customer to be one hour. In general, we can say that the average wait time would be half the cycle time of the process. If two buses are used, the cycle time is one hour and the average wait is 30 minutes. If we want the average wait to be two minutes, then the required cycle time is four minutes, and 30 buses are needed (120 minutes ÷ 4 minutes/bus = 30 buses).

The next issue relates to the capacity of the system. If we have 30 buses on the route and each bus seats 50 passengers with another 30 standing, we know that we can accommodate 1,500 seated or 2,400 passengers in total at one point in time.

Assume that the following table is an estimate of the number of passengers that travel the route during a typical tourist season day. The table shows calculations of the amount of bus capacity required during each hour. If a customer rides the bus for 45 minutes, then one seat is needed for 45 minutes, or 0.75 hour, to handle that passenger. Of course, 60 minutes, or a full hour's worth of capacity, is available for each seat that we have. At maximum utilization including standing, each bus can handle 80 passenger-hours' worth of load. Dividing the expected passenger load during the hour by the maximum load for a single bus calculates the minimum number of buses needed. Similarly, dividing the expected passenger load by the number of seats on each bus calculates the number of buses needed so that all passengers can be seated.

TIME	NUMBER OF CUSTOMERS	AVERAGE TIME ON BUS	LOAD (PASSENGER HOURS)	MINIMUM NUMBER OF BUSES NEEDED	BUSES NEEDED FOR ALL PASSENGERS TO BE SEATED
8:00–9:00 A.M.	2,000	45 minutes	1,500	18.75	30
9:00–10:00 A.M.	4,000	30 minutes	2,000	25	40
10:00–11:00 A.M.	6,000	30 minutes	3,000	37.5	60
11:00 A.M.–12:00 NOON	5,000	30 minutes	2,500	31.25	50
12:00–1:00 P.M.	4,000	30 minutes	2,000	25	40
1:00–2:00 P.M.	3,500	30 minutes	1,750	21.875	35
2:00–3:00 P.M.	3,000	45 minutes	2,250	28.125	45
3:00–4:00 P.M.	3,000	45 minutes	2,250	28.125	45
4:00–5:00 P.M.	3,000	45 minutes	2,250	28.125	45
5:00–6:00 P.M.	4,000	45 minutes	3,000	37.5	60
6:00–7:00 P.M.	3,000	45 minutes	2,250	28.125	45
7:00–8:00 P.M.	1,500	45 minutes	1,125	14.0625	22.5
TOTALS	42,000		25,875		

From the analysis, if the Paris transit authority uses only 30 buses throughout the day, many people will need to stand. Further, during the morning rush between 10 and 11 A.M. and the evening rush between 5 and 6 P.M., not all of the customers can be accommodated. It would seem reasonable that at least 40 buses should be used between 9 A.M. and 7 P.M. Even with this number of buses, one would expect passengers to be standing most of the time.

If the transit authority decided to use 40 buses between the extended hours of 8 A.M. through 8 P.M., what would be the average utilization of the buses in terms of seats occupied? Over this 12-hour period, 24,000 seat-hours of capacity would be available (40 buses × 12 hours × 50 seats/bus). The table indicates that 25,875 seat-hours are needed. The utilization would be 107.8 percent (25,875/24,000 × 100). What this means is that, on average, 7.8 percent of the customers must stand. Of course, this average value significantly understates the severe capacity problem that occurs during the peak times of the day. ●

Consider in the preceding example how useful this type of analysis is to the Paris transit authority. Data can be collected for each day of the week, and the analysis performed. Interesting questions concerning the design of the route or the capacity of the buses can be evaluated. Consider, for example, what would happen if the route were split into two parts. What if larger buses that could carry 120 passengers were put into service? The analysis can be extended to include the cost of providing the service by considering the wages paid the operators, the cost to maintain and operate the vehicles, and depreciation of the buses. As seen from the above example, designing a transit system involves a trade-off between the convenience of the service, or how frequently buses arrive at each stop, and the capacity utilization of the buses.

PROCESS FLOW TIME REDUCTION

Critical processes are subject to the well-known rule that time is money. For example, the longer a customer waits, the more likely the customer is to switch to a different vendor. The longer material is kept in inventory, the higher the investment cost. There are exceptions in services, where more time in process can lead to more money. See the box "Efficiency Meets Corporate Goals: A Love Story."

Unfortunately, critical processes often depend on specific limited resources, resulting in bottlenecks. Flow time can sometimes be reduced without purchasing additional equipment. The following are some suggestions for reducing the flow time of a process that do not require the purchase of new equipment. Often a combination of ideas is appropriate.[3]

1. **Perform activities in parallel.**   Most of the steps in an operations process are performed in sequence. A serial approach results in the flow time for the entire process being the sum of the individual steps plus transport and waiting time between steps. Using a parallel approach can reduce flow time by as much as 80 percent and produces a better result.

   A classic example is product development, where the current trend is toward concurrent engineering. Instead of forming a concept, making drawings, creating a bill of materials, and mapping processes, all activities are performed in parallel by integrated teams. Development time is reduced dramatically, and the needs of all those involved are addressed during the development process.

2. **Change the sequence of activities.**   Documents and products are often transported back and forth between machines, departments, buildings, and so forth. For instance, a document might be transferred between two offices a number of times for inspection and signing. If the sequence of some of these activities can be altered, it may be possible to perform much of the document's processing when it comes to a building the first time.

3. **Reduce interruptions.**   Many processes are performed with relatively large time intervals between the activities. For example, purchase orders may be issued only every other day. Individuals preparing reports that result in purchase orders should be aware of deadlines to avoid missing them, because improved timing in these processes can save many days of flow time.

To illustrate these ideas, consider an electronics manufacturer that has been receiving customer complaints about a long order lead time of 29 days. As assessment of the order-processing system revealed 12 instances where managers had to approve employees' work.

EFFICIENCY MEETS CORPORATE GOALS: A LOVE STORY

Due to my lack of patience, I gave birth to a beautiful process improvement idea at a local coffee shop. It came to me as I stood in front of coffee servers with pupils the size of bowling balls owing to the high-octane java they had been drinking for six straight hours.

The process improvement idea was to improve the efficiency with which they provide value to their customers. Or, in brew-guy terms, reduce the wait time, reducing the line, delivering coffee faster.

The Problem: Why is it that regular coffee drinkers wait in the same line as drinkers of a double latte cinnamon frappuccino, which takes eons to prepare?

Idea: Give the straight joe Joes and Josephines their own line. Simple, yet brilliant.

So, armed with good intentions and a righteous buzz, I approached the entrepreneurial spirit disguised as the coffee shop owner, ordered my regular drip, and pitched my idea.

Watching him dervish around, it was clear that I underestimated my sponsor's passion for process. As he slung beans, brew, and bucks to their containers, I thought to myself: he would have made a lovely ballerina. And he knew *exactly* what he was doing.

"Mr. Process Analyst," said he, "it is the goal of my corporation to make money. And it is during this pregnant pause provided prior to pouring coffee that patrons peer into the pleasantly populated pastry case, and decide they want a coffee *and* a pastry!" I was amazed, as I hadn't heard such alliteration since Muhammad Ali was in his prime, and equally amazed at his perfect logic and very effective process. It was, in fact, a beautiful thing. We embraced, and I devoured a wedge of pound cake the size of a cat.

So, consultants, managers, process analysts, and general do-gooders alike, take heed. The most efficient process does not always attain your corporate goals; thus, it is imperative that the process and goal be aligned. Also, learn to appreciate the process in front of you, and the business people that designed it. They (whomever "they" may be) do know their stuff much of the time. And it is essential you *listen* and *learn* from these subject matter experts before you open your mouth and propose possible process nonsense.

SOURCE: ADAPTED FROM "EFFICIENCY MEETS CORPORATE GOALS: A LOVE STORY," ANONYMOUS, POSTED JULY 21, 2006, ON www.pavilion.com.

It was determined that the first 10 approvals were not needed. This saved an average of seven to eight days in the order processing.

Many subsystems—each performing the same or similar tasks—had interfered with the process. The logical step was to eliminate redundancy, and a detailed flowchart of the process was created. At close inspection, 16 steps proved very similar to one another. Changing the sequence of activities and creating one companywide order document removed 13 of these steps.

Over four months, the order system was totally redesigned to allow information to be entered once and become available to the entire organization. Due to this adjustment, activities could be handled in a parallel manner. After a value-added analysis (focused on eliminating the non–value-adding activities), the manufacturer was able to reduce the customer order lead time from 29 days to 9 days, save cost and employee time per order, and increase customer satisfaction.

SUMMARY

Process analysis is a basic skill needed to understand how a business operates. Great insight is obtained by drawing a simple flowchart showing the flow of materials or information through an enterprise. The diagram should include all the operating elements and show how they fit together. Be sure to indicate where material is stored or where orders are queued. Often 90 percent or more of the time that is required to serve a customer is spent just waiting. Hence, merely eliminating the waiting time can dramatically improve the performance of the process.

Remember this fundamental concept when analyzing a process: What goes into the process must come out of the process. A process taken as a whole is like the funnel shown in Exhibit 2.6. The outlet of the funnel restricts the amount that can flow through. In a real business process, certain resources limit output. If liquid is poured into the funnel at a rate greater than it can exit, the level in the funnel will continue to grow. As the level of liquid in the funnel grows, the time needed for the liquid to flow through the funnel increases. If too much liquid is poured into the funnel, it just spills over the top and never flows through.

The same is true of a real process. If too many jobs are pumped into the process, the time that it takes to complete a job will increase because the waiting time will increase. At some point, customers will go somewhere else and the business will be lost. When a process is operating at capacity, the only way to take on more work without increasing the waiting time is to add more capacity. This requires finding what activity is limiting the output of the process and increasing the capacity of that activity. In essence, the tube leading out of the funnel needs to be made larger.

exhibit 2.6   What Goes into a Process Must Come Out of the Process. Input Rate Must Be Less Than or Equal to the Output Rate; Otherwise, the System Will Overflow.

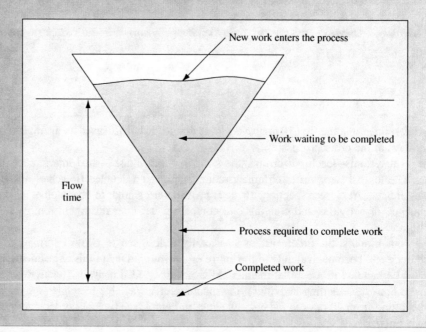

KEY TERMS

Process Any set of activities performed by an organization that takes inputs and transforms them into outputs ideally of greater value to the organization than the original inputs.

Cycle time The average time between completions of successive units in a process (this is the definition used in this book). The term is sometimes used to mean the elapsed time between starting and completing a job.

Utilization The ratio of the time that a resource is actually activated relative to the time that it is available for use.

Buffering A storage area between stages where the output of a stage is placed prior to being used in a downstream stage. Buffering allows the stages to operate independently.

Blocking The activities in the stage must stop because there is no place to deposit the item just completed.

Starving The activities in a stage must stop because there is no work.

Bottleneck A resource that limits the capacity or maximum output of the process.

Make-to-order A process that is activated only in response to an actual order.

Make-to-stock A process that produces standard products that are stored in finished goods inventory. The product is delivered quickly to the customer from the finished goods inventory.

Hybrid Combines the features of both make-to-order and make-to-stock. Typically, a generic product is made and stocked at some point in the process. These generic units are customized in a final process to meet actual orders.

Pacing Movement of items through a process is coordinated through a timing mechanism. Most processes are not paced, but assembly lines usually are paced.

Productivity The ratio of output to input. Taking the dollar value of the output and dividing by the dollar value of the inputs usually measures total factor productivity. Alternatively, *partial factor productivity* is measured based on an individual input and often is not calculated using dollar values (an example would be units/person).

Efficiency A ratio of the actual output of a process relative to some standard.

Run time The time required to produce a batch of parts.

Setup time The time required to prepare a machine to make a particular item.

Operation time The sum of the setup time and run time for a batch of parts that are run on a machine.

Flow time The average time that it takes a unit to move through an entire process. Usually the term *lead time* is used to refer to the total time that it takes a customer to receive an order (includes time to process the order, throughput time, and delivery time).

Throughput rate The output rate that the process is expected to produce over a period of time.

Process velocity or throughput ratio The ratio of the total flow time to the value-added time.

Value-added time The time in which useful work is actually being done on the unit.

Total average value of inventory The total average investment in raw material, work-in-process, and finished goods inventory. This is valued at the cost to the firm.

Inventory turn The cost of goods sold divided by the total average value of inventory.

Days-of-supply The number of days of inventory of an item. If an item were not replenished, this would be the numbers of days until the firm would run out of the item (on average). Also, the inverse of inventory turn expressed in days.

Little's law States a mathematical relationship between throughput rate, flow time, and the amount of work-in-process inventory. Flow time is equal to work-in-process divided by the throughput rate.

FORMULA REVIEW

Little's law

$$Inventory = Throughput\ rate \times Flow\ time \qquad [2.1]$$

SOLVED PROBLEMS

SOLVED PROBLEM 1

Suppose we schedule shipments to our customers so that we expect each shipment to wait for two days in finished goods inventory (in essence we add two days to when we expect to be able to ship). We do this as protection against system variability to ensure a high on-time delivery service. If we ship approximately 2,000 units each day, how many units do we expect to have in finished goods inventory due to allowing this extra time? If the item is valued at $4.50 each, what is the expected value of this inventory?

Solution

Using Little's law the expected finished goods inventory is:

$$\text{Inventory} = 2{,}000 \text{ units per day} \times 2 \text{ days} = 4{,}000 \text{ units}$$

This would be valued at 4,000 units $\times$ $4.50 per unit = $18,000

SOLVED PROBLEM 2

Daffy Dave's Sub Shop makes custom submarine sandwiches to order. They are analyzing the processes at their shop. The general flow of the process is shown below. A different person is working at each of the steps in the process.

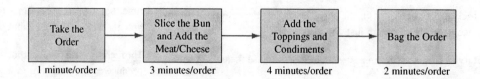

Take the Order — 1 minute/order → Slice the Bun and Add the Meat/Cheese — 3 minutes/order → Add the Toppings and Condiments — 4 minutes/order → Bag the Order — 2 minutes/order

Daffy Dave wants to figure out the following for a typical 8-hour work day.
a. What is the current maximum output of the process?
b. If we add another person, where would we add him or her and what is the benefit?
c. Is there a benefit if we can shift 1 minute from Bun and Meat to Order Taking? Assume we do not make the change in part *b* above.
d. Is there a benefit if we shift 1 minute of work from Condiments to Bagging? Assume we do not make the changes in parts *b* and *c* above.

Solution

a. Maximum output is 120 subs per day.

OPERATION	OUTPUT
Take Orders	(60 min. per hour/1 min. per order) * 8 hours = 480 subs per day
Bun and Meat	(60 min. per hour/3 min. per order) * 8 hours = 160 subs per day
Toppings/Condiments	(60 min. per hour/4 min. per order) * 8 hours = 120 subs per day
Bag the Order	(60 min. per hour/2 min. per order) * 8 hours = 240 subs per day

Output per day is determined by the slowest station; therefore, we can only produce 120 per day because that is the limit of the Toppings/Condiments station.

b. Dave should add the person to the slowest station (Condiments/Toppings) since it is the bottleneck.

OPERATION	OUTPUT
Take Orders	480 subs per day
Bun and Meat	160 subs per day
Toppings/Condiments	120 * 2 = 240 subs per day
Bag the Order	240 subs per day

The impact is not a very big one. Even though the Toppings/Condiments station now can do 240 subs per day, the Bun and Meat station can only do 160, so that is the maximum output.

c. Order Taking station will go from 1 minute to 2 minutes, and Bun and Meat goes from 3 minutes to 2 minutes.

OPERATION	OUTPUT
Take Orders	(60 min. per hour/2 min. per order) * 8 hours = 240 subs per day
Bun and Meat	(60 min. per hour/2 min. per order) * 8 hours = 240 subs per day
Toppings/Condiments	(60 min. per hour/4 min. per order) * 8 hours = 120 subs per day
Bag the Order	(60 min. per hour/2 min. per order) * 8 hours = 240 subs per day

There is no benefit to this change. Dave can still only make 120 subs per day since we can only produce 120 per day because that is the limit of the Toppings/Condiments station.

d. Toppings/Condiments station will go from 4 minutes to 3 minutes, and Bagging goes from 2 minutes to 3 minutes.

OPERATION	OUTPUT
Take Orders	(60 min. per hour/1 min. per order) * 8 hours = 480 subs per day
Bun and Meat	(60 min. per hour/3 min. per order) * 8 hours = 160 subs per day
Toppings/Condiments	(60 min. per hour/3 min. per order) * 8 hours = 160 subs per day
Bag the Order	(60 min. per hour/3 min. per order) * 8 hours = 160 subs per day

There is a benefit to this change. Dave can now make 160 subs per day. This will provide the same benefit as hiring another worker. However, if Dave wants to increase output further, he will have to hire some additional staff.

REVIEW AND DISCUSSION QUESTIONS

1. Compare McDonald's old and current processes for making hamburgers. How valid is McDonald's claim that the new process will produce fresher hamburgers for the customer? Comparing McDonald's current process to the processes used by Burger King and Wendy's, which process would appear to produce the freshest hamburgers?

2. State in your own words what Little's law means. Describe an example that you have observed where Little's law applies.

3. Explain how having more work-in-process inventory can improve the efficiency of a process. How can this be bad?

4. Recently some operations management experts have begun insisting that simply minimizing process velocity, which actually means minimizing the time that it takes to process something through the system, is the single most important measure for improving a process. Can you think of a situation in which this might not be true?

PROBLEMS[4]

1. You are in a line at the bank drive-through and 10 cars are in front of you. You estimate that the clerk is taking about five minutes per car to serve. How long do you expect to wait in line?

2. A firm has redesigned its production process so that it now takes 10 hours for a unit to be made. Using the old process, it took 15 hours to make a unit. If the process makes one unit each hour on average and each unit is worth $1,500, what is the reduction in work-in-process value?

3. An enterprising student has set up an internship clearinghouse for business students. Each student who uses the service fills out a form and lists up to 10 companies that he or she would like to have contacted. The clearinghouse has a choice of two methods to use for processing the forms. The traditional method requires about 20 minutes to review the form and arrange the information in the proper order for processing. Once this setup is done, it takes only two minutes per company requested to complete the processing. The other alternative uses an optical scan/retrieve system, which takes only a minute to prepare but requires five minutes per company for completing the processing. If it costs about the same amount per minute for processing with either of the two methods, when should each be used?

4 Rockness Recycling refurbishes rundown business students. The process uses a moving belt, which carries each student through the five steps of the process in sequence. The five steps are as follows:

STEP	DESCRIPTION	TIME REQUIRED PER STUDENT
1	Unpack and place on belt	1.0 minute
2	Strip off bad habits	1.5 minutes
3	Scrub and clean mind	0.8 minute
4	Insert modern methods	1.0 minute
5	Polish and pack	1.2 minutes

One faculty member is assigned to each of these steps. Faculty members work a 40-hour week and rotate jobs each week. Mr. Rockness has been working on a contract from General Eclectic, which requires delivery of 2,000 refurbished students per week. A representative of the human resources department has just called complaining that the company hasn't been receiving the agreed-upon number of students. A check of finished goods inventory by Mr. Rockness reveals that there is no stock left. What is going on?

5 The bathtub theory of operations management is being promoted as the next breakthrough for global competitiveness. The factory is a bathtub with 50 gallons of capacity. The drain is the outlet to the market and can output three gallons per hour when wide open. The faucet is the raw material input and can let material in at a rate of four gallons per hour. Now, to test your comprehension of the intricacies of operations (assume the bathtub is empty to begin with):

a. Draw a diagram of the factory and determine the maximum rate at which the market can be served if all valves are set to maximum. What happens to the system over time?

b. Suppose that instead of a faucet, a five-gallon container is used for filling the bathtub (assume a full container is next to the tub to begin with); it takes two hours to refill the container and return it to the bathtub. What happens to the system over time?

6 A local market research firm has just won a contract for several thousand small projects involving data gathering and statistical analysis. In the past, the firm has assigned each project to a single member of its highly trained professional staff. This person would both gather and analyze the data. Using this approach, an experienced person can complete an average of 10 such projects in an eight-hour day.

The firm's management is thinking of assigning two people to each project in order to allow them to specialize and become more efficient. The process would require the data gatherer to fill out a matrix on the computer, check it, and transmit it to the statistical analysis program for the analyst to complete. Data can be gathered on one project while the analysis is being completed on another, but the analysis must be complete before the statistical analysis program can accept the new data. After some practice, the new process can be completed with a standard time of 20 minutes for the data gathering and 30 minutes for the analysis.

a. What is the production (output per hour) for each alternative? What is the productivity (output per labor hour)?

b. How long would it take to complete 1,000 projects with each alternative? What would be the labor content (total number of labor hours) for 1,000 projects for each alternative?

7 A processor makes two components, A and B, which are then packaged together as the final product (each product sold contains one A and one B). The processor can do only one component at a time: either it can make As or it can make Bs. There is a setup time when switching from A to B.

Current plans are to make 100 units of component A, then 100 units of component B, then 100 units of component A, then 100 units of component B, and so forth, where the setup and run times for each component are given below.

COMPONENT	SETUP/CHANGEOVER TIME	RUN TIME/UNIT
A	5 minutes	0.2 minute
B	10 minutes	0.1 minute

Assume the packaging of the two components is totally automated and takes only two seconds per unit of the final product. This packaging time is small enough that you can ignore it. What is the average hourly output, in terms of the number of units of packaged product (which includes one component A and one component B)?

8 The following represents a process used to assemble a chair with an upholstered seat. Stations A, B, and C make the seat; stations J, K, and L assemble the chair frame; station X is where the two subassemblies are brought together; and some final tasks are completed in stations Y and Z. One worker is assigned to each of the stations. Generally there is no inventory kept anywhere in the system, although there is room for one unit between each of the stations that might be used for a brief amount of time.

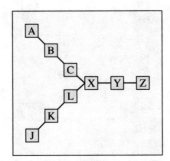

Given the following amount of work in seconds required at each station:

A	38	J	32	X	22
B	34	K	30	Y	18
C	35	L	34	Z	20

a. What is the possible daily output of this "process" if 8 hours of processing time is available each day?

b. Given your output rate in part *a*, what is the efficiency of the process?

c. What is the flow time of the process?

9 Wally's Widget Warehouse takes orders from 7 A.M. to 7 P.M. The manager wants to analyze the process and has provided the process flow diagram shown below. There are three steps required to ship a customer order. The first step is to take the order from a customer. The second step is to pick the order for the customer, and then they have to pack the order ready for shipping. Wally promises that every order placed today gets shipped tomorrow. That means that the picking and packing operations must finish all orders before they go home.

Wally wants to figure out the following.

a. What is the current maximum output of the process assuming that no one works overtime?

b. How long will the picking and packing operations have to work if we have a day where the order taker works at his maximum capacity?

c. Given *b*, what is the maximum number of orders waiting to be picked?

d. Given *b*, what is the maximum number of orders waiting to be packed?

e. If we double the packing capacity (from 60 to 120 orders per hour), what impact does this have on your answers in parts *b*, *c*, and *d*?

10 The National State Bank is trying to make sure that they have enough tellers to handle the Friday afternoon rush of workers wanting to cash their paychecks. They are only concerned

with the last hour of the day from 4:00 to 5:00 P.M. It takes 5 minutes per customer to be processed by the tellers. The average customer arrivals are shown in the table below.

TIME	CUSTOMERS ARRIVING
4:00–4:05	2
4:05–4:10	5
4:10–4:15	6
4:15–4:20	8
4:20–4:25	10
4:25–4:30	12
4:30–4:35	16
4:35–4:40	12
4:40–4:45	10
4:45–4:50	6
4:50–4:55	4
4:55–5:00	2
5:00–5:05	0
Total	93

The bank currently has 8 teller stations, and all are staffed during the Friday afternoon rush hour.
     a. What is the current maximum output at the bank during rush hour?
     b. Can the bank process all the customers by 5:00 P.M.?
     c. What is the maximum waiting time for customers, and what time period does it occur in?

11   I-mart is a discount optical shop that can fill most prescription orders in around 1 hour. The management is analyzing the processes at the store. There currently is one person assigned to each task below. The optometrist assigned to task "B" takes an hour off for lunch and the other employees work the entire day.

TASK	TIME
A. Greet/register the patient	2 minutes/patient
B. Optometrist conducts eye exam	25 minutes/patient
C. Frame/lenses selection	20 minutes/patient
D. Glasses made (process can run 6 pairs of glasses at the same time)	60 minutes/patient
E. Final fitting	5 minutes/patient

For a typical 10-hour retail day (10 A.M.–8 P.M.), the manager would like to calculate the following:
     a. What is the current maximum output of the process per day (assuming every patient requires glasses)?
     b. If another person was added, where is the logical place?
     c. What effect would a mail order lab (where the glasses are made off site and returned in 5–7 days) have on the process?

12   A quoting department for a custom publishing house can complete 4 quotes per day, and there are 20 quotes in various stages in the department. Applying Little's law, the current lead time for a quote is how many days?

13   A small barber shop has a single chair and an area for waiting, where only one person can be in the chair at a time, and no one leaves without getting their hair cut. So the system is roughly:

$$Entrance \rightarrow Wait \rightarrow Haircut \rightarrow Exit$$

Assume customers arrive at the rate of 10 per hour and stay an average of 0.5 hour.
What is the average number of customers in the barber shop?

ADVANCED PROBLEM

14   Remember Mr. Rockness in Problem 4? He now retrains college professors. It is a much more challenging task but still involves five steps. He has worked hard to balance the line; however, there is a lot of variability. Each stage in the process now handles between one and six faculty

members per hour depending on how bad the case is. If there is some inventory available for every position (do not worry about the start-up), what is the expected output per hour? (Assume that each stage is independent and that it is equally likely that one, two, three, four, five, or six faculty members get processed each hour at each stage.)[5]

CASE: ANALYZING CASINO MONEY-HANDLING PROCESSES

Retrieving money from a mechanical slot machine is referred to as the *drop process*. The drop process begins with a security officer and the slot drop team leader obtaining the slot cabinet keys from the casino cashier's cage. Getting the keys takes about 15 minutes. The slot drop team consists of employees from the hard count coin room, security, and accounting. The slot drop leader, under the observation of a security officer and a person from accounting, actually removes the drop bucket from the slot machine cabinet. When the drop bucket is pulled from the slot cabinet, a tag with the proper slot machine number is placed on top of the coins to identify where that bucket came from when the weigh process begins. Retrieving the drop bucket takes about 10 minutes per slot machine. Once a cart is filled with buckets from 20 different slot machines, the drop team leader and security and accounting people deliver the buckets to the hard count room. The buckets are securely locked in the hard count room to await the start of the hard count process. Delivering and securing the buckets takes about 30 minutes per cart.

The hard count process is performed at a designated time known to gaming regulatory authorities. The hard count team first tests the weigh scale, which takes 10 minutes. The scale determines the dollar value, by denomination, for set weights of 10 and 25 pounds. These results are compared to calibration results, calculated when the scale was last serviced, to determine if a significant variance exists. If one does exist, the hard count supervisor must contact the contractor responsible for maintaining the scale and the controller's office. If no significant variance is found, the weigh process can continue.

Following the scale check, each drop bucket is emptied into the weigh scale holding hopper. Using information from the identification tag, the specific slot machine number from which the bucket originated is entered into the weigh scale computer. The weigh scale computer is programmed to convert the weight of coins, by denomination, into specific dollar values, which are recorded in the weigh journal along with the slot machine number. This weighing and recording process takes seven minutes per bucket. Once the scale has weighed the contents of the drop bucket, the coins automatically drop onto a conveyor belt, which transports them to wrapping machines. As the coins are wrapped, the rolls of coins drop onto another conveyor belt, which takes them to a canning station. Twenty-five silver dollars are wrapped in each roll at a rate of 10 rolls per minute.

At the canning station, the coin rolls are placed in metal or plastic cans that hold specific dollar amounts based on coin denomination. The cans are stacked to facilitate counting the wrapped coins. Silver dollar cans hold $1,000, or 40 rolls, and take five minutes to fill and stack. When the weigh process is completed, the weigh scale computer runs a summary report totaling the weight by denomination. These totals are recorded on the weigh/wrap verification report, which takes five minutes to produce.

When the wrap portion of the count is completed and all of the rolled coins have been canned and stacked, they are manually counted by denomination. These totals are also recorded on the weigh/wrap verification report. The variance in both dollar amounts and percentages, for each denomination, is calculated. Variances that exceed plus or minus 2 percent or are $1,000 or greater (whichever is less) must be investigated by the hard count supervisor, who writes an explanatory report. If no significant variances exist, all members of the hard count team sign the weigh/wrap verification report. To complete the hard count process, the casino cashier's cage is then notified that the slot drop is ready to be transferred into cage accountability. Manually counting and verifying the counts take on average two minutes per can.

In a process separate from the hard count, a cage cashier performs an independent count and verification, by denomination, of the wrap. If everything balances, the main bank cashier signs the weigh/wrap verification report, accepting the slot drop into cage accountability. It is at this point that the actual slot gross gaming revenue is recognized.

QUESTIONS

1 Draw a diagram of the drop process. How long should it take to empty 300 silver dollar slot machines?
2 Draw a diagram of the hard count process. How long should this process take to complete for 300 silver dollar slot machines? Assume that each slot machine has an average of 750 silver dollars when it is emptied.
3 The casino is considering the purchase of a second coin-wrapping machine. What impact would this have on the hard count process? Is this the most desirable machine to purchase?
4 What would be the impact of purchasing "electronic" slot machines that do not use coins?

CASE: KRISTEN'S COOKIE COMPANY (A)

You and your roommate are preparing to start Kristen's Cookie Company in your on-campus apartment. The company will provide fresh cookies to starving students late at night. You need to evaluate the preliminary design for the company's production process to figure out many variables, including what prices to charge, whether you will be able to make a profit, and how many orders to accept.

BUSINESS CONCEPT

Your idea is to bake fresh cookies to order, using any combination of ingredients that the buyer wants. The cookies will be ready for pickup at your apartment within an hour.

Several factors will set you apart from competing products such as store-bought cookies. First, your cookies will be completely fresh. You will not bake any cookies before receiving the order; therefore, the buyer will be getting cookies that are literally hot out of the oven.

Second, like Steve's Ice Cream,[6] you will have a variety of ingredients available to add to the basic dough, including chocolate chips, M&M's, chopped Heath bars, coconut, walnuts, and raisins. Buyers will telephone in their orders and specify which of these ingredients they want in their cookies. You guarantee completely fresh cookies. In short, you will have the freshest, most exotic cookies anywhere, available right on campus.

THE PRODUCTION PROCESS

Baking cookies is simple: mix all the ingredients in a food processor; spoon out the cookie dough onto a tray; put the cookies into the oven; bake them; take the tray of cookies out of the oven; let the cookies cool; and, finally, take the cookies off the tray and carefully pack them in a box. You and your roommate already own all the necessary capital equipment: one food processor, cookie trays, and spoons. Your apartment has a small oven that will hold one tray at a time. Your landlord pays for all the electricity. The variable costs, therefore, are merely the cost of the ingredients (estimated to be $0.60/dozen), the cost of the box in which the cookies are packed ($0.10 per box; each box holds a dozen cookies), and your time (what value do you place on your time?).

A detailed examination of the production process, which specifies how long each of the steps will take, follows. The first step is to take an order, which your roommate has figured out how to do quickly and with 100 percent accuracy. (Actually, you and your roommate devised a method using the campus electronic mail system to accept orders and to inform customers when their orders will be ready for pickup. Because this runs automatically on your personal computer, it does not take any of your time.) Therefore, this step will be ignored in further analysis.

You and your roommate have timed the necessary physical operations. The first physical production step is to wash out the mixing bowl from the previous batch, add all of the ingredients, and mix them in your food processor. The mixing bowls hold ingredients for up to 3 dozen cookies. You then dish up the cookies, one dozen at a time, onto a cookie tray. These activities take six minutes for the washing and mixing steps, regardless of how many cookies are being made in the batch. That is, to mix enough dough and ingredients for two dozen cookies takes the same six minutes as one dozen cookies. However, dishing up the cookies onto the tray takes two minutes per tray.

The next step, performed by your roommate, is to put the cookies in the oven and set the thermostat and timer, which takes about one minute. The cookies bake for the next nine minutes. So total baking time is 10 minutes, during the first minute of which your roommate is busy setting the oven. Because the oven holds only one tray, a second dozen takes an additional 10 minutes to bake.

Your roommate also performs the last steps of the process by first removing the cookies from the oven and putting them aside to cool for 5 minutes, then carefully packing them in a box and accepting payment. Removing the cookies from the oven takes only a negligible amount of time, but it must be done promptly. It takes two minutes to pack each dozen and about one minute to accept payment for the order.

That is the process for producing cookies by the dozen in Kristen's Cookie Company. As experienced bakers know, a few simplifications were made in the actual cookie production process.

For example, the first batch of cookies for the night requires preheating the oven. However, such complexities will be put aside for now. Begin your analysis by developing a process flow diagram of the cookie-making process.

KEY QUESTIONS TO ANSWER BEFORE YOU LAUNCH THE BUSINESS

To launch the business, you need to set prices and rules for accepting orders. Some issues will be resolved only after you get started and try out different ways of producing the cookies. Before you start, however, you at least want a preliminary plan, with as much as possible specified, so that you can do a careful calculation of how much time you will have to devote to this business each night, and how much money you can expect to make. For example, when you conduct a market survey to determine the likely demand, you will want to specify exactly what your order policies will be. Therefore, answering the following operational questions should help you:

1. How long will it take you to fill a rush order?
2. How many orders can you fill in a night, assuming you are open four hours each night?
3. How much of your own and your roommate's valuable time will it take to fill each order?
4. Because your baking trays can hold exactly one dozen cookies, you will produce and sell cookies by the dozen. Should you give any discount for people who order two dozen cookies, three dozen cookies, or more? If so, how much? Will it take you any longer to fill a two-dozen cookie order than a one-dozen cookie order?
5. How many food processors and baking trays will you need?
6. Are there any changes you can make in your production plans that will allow you to make better cookies or more cookies in less time or at lower cost? For example, is there a bottleneck operation in your production process that you can expand cheaply? What is the effect of adding another oven? How much would you be willing to pay to rent an additional oven?

PROBLEMS FOR FURTHER THOUGHT

1. What happens if you are trying to do this by yourself without a roommate?
2. Should you offer special rates for rush orders? Suppose you have just put a tray of cookies into the oven and someone calls up with a "crash priority" order for a dozen cookies of a different flavor. Can you fill the priority order while still fulfilling the order for the cookies that are already in the oven? If not, how much of a premium should you charge for filling the rush order?
3. When should you promise delivery? How can you look quickly at your order board (list of pending orders) and tell a caller when his or her order will be ready? How much of a safety margin for timing should you allow?
4. What other factors should you consider at this stage of planning your business?
5. Your product must be made to order because each order is potentially unique. If you decide to sell standard cookies instead, how should you change the production system? The order-taking process?

KRISTEN'S COOKIE COMPANY (A), CASE 9-686-093, WRITTEN BY ROGER BOHN. COPYRIGHT © 1986 BY THE HARVARD BUSINESS SCHOOL PUBLISHING CORPORATION. ALL RIGHTS RESERVED.

SUPER QUIZ

1 This is a part of an organization that takes inputs and transforms them into outputs.

2 This is the ratio of the time that a resource is activated relative to the time it is available for use.

3 This is when one or more activities stop because of a lack of work.

4 This is when an activity stops because there is no place to put the work that was just completed.

5 This is a step in a process that is the slowest compared to the other steps. This step limits the capacity of the process.

6 What is the difference between McDonald's old and current processes?

7 This refers to the fixed timing of the movement of items through a process.

8 This is when one company compares itself to another relative to operations performance.

9 This is the time that it takes a unit to flow through the process from beginning to end. It includes time waiting in queues and buffers.

10 The relationship between time and units in a process is call this.

11 What is the mathematical relationship between time and units in a process?

12 What is the major assumption about how a process is operating for Little's law to be valid.

1. A process 2. Utilization 3. Starving 4. Blocking 5. Bottleneck 6. Make-to-stock versus make-to-order 7. Pacing 8. Benchmarking 9. Flow time 10. Little's law 11. Inventory = Throughput rate × Flow time 12. Process is operating in steady state

SELECTED BIBLIOGRAPHY

Anupindai, R.; S. Chopra; S. D. Deshmukh; J. A. van Mieghem; and E. Zemel. *Managing Business Process Flows.* 2nd ed. Upper Saddle River, NJ: Prentice Hall, 2005.

Gray, A. E., and J. Leonard. "Process Fundamentals." Harvard Business School 9-696-023.

Jeston, J., and J. Nelis. *Business Process Management: Practical Guidelines to Successful Implementation.* Burlington, MA: Butterworth-Heinemann, 2006.

FOOTNOTES

1 Often the term *cycle time* is used to mean *flow time*. It is important to carefully determine how the term is being used in the context of the process being studied.

2 This example is similar to one given by A. E. Gray in "Capacity Analysis: Sample Problems," Harvard Business School 9-696-058.

3 B. Andersen, "Process Cycle Time Reduction," *Quality Progress*, July 1999, p. 120. For some additional guidelines for improving process, also see Chapter 17.

4 The authors are indebted to D. Clay Whybark of the University of North Carolina for contributing Problems 3–6 and Problem 11.

5 The idea for this problem came from an exercise developed by Dr. Eli Goldratt titled "The Great Manufacturing Crapshoot."

6 Steve's Ice Cream was started in the Boston area by a young entrepreneur to provide make-to-order ice cream, using mix-ins.

chapter 3

PROCESS SELECTION AND FACILITY LAYOUT

Learning Objectives

After completing this chapter, you should be able to:

1. Explain the strategic importance of process selection.
2. Explain the influence that process selection has on an organization.
3. Describe the basic processing types.
4. Discuss automated approaches to processing.
5. Explain the need for management of technology.
6. List some reasons for redesign of layouts.
7. Describe the basic layout types.
8. List the main advantages and disadvantages of product layouts and process layouts.
9. Solve simple line-balancing problems.
10. Develop simple process layouts.

Product and service choices, capacity planning, process selection, and layout of facilities are among the most basic decisions managers make because they have long-term consequences for business organizations.

This chapter is about process selection and facility layout (i.e., the arrangement of the workplace). Processes convert inputs into outputs; they are at the core of operations management. But the impact of process selection goes beyond operations management: It affects the entire organization and its ability to achieve its mission, and it affects the organization's supply chain. So process selection choices very often have strategic significance. Different process types have different capacity ranges, and once a process type is functioning, changing it can be difficult, time consuming, and

costly. Obviously, long-term forecasts as well as an organization's mission and goals are important in developing a process strategy.

Process selection has operational and supply chain implications. Operational implications include equipment and labor requirements, operations costs, and both the ability to meet demand and the ability to respond to variations in demand. Supply chain implications relate to the volume and variety of inputs and outputs and the degree of flexibility that is required.

Technology is often a factor in process selection and layout. Three aspects of technology can be factors: product technology, processing technology, and information technology.

Process selection and facility layout are closely tied, and for that reason, these two topics are presented in a single chapter. The first part of the chapter covers the basic options for processing work. This is followed by a discussion of how processes and layout are linked. The remainder of the chapter is devoted to layout design.

INTRODUCTION

Process selection refers to deciding on the way production of goods or services will be organized. It has major implications for capacity planning, layout of facilities, equipment, and design of work systems. Process selection occurs as a matter of course when new products or services are being planned. However, it also occurs periodically due to technological changes in products or equipment, as well as competitive pressures. Figure 3.1 provides an overview of where process selection and capacity planning fit into system design. Forecasts, product and service design, and technological considerations all influence capacity planning and process selection. Moreover, capacity and process selection are interrelated, and are often done in concert. They, in turn, affect facility and equipment choices, layout, and work design.

How an organization approaches process selection is determined by the organization's *process strategy.* Key aspects include

- Capital intensity: the mix of equipment and labor that will be used by the organization.
- Process flexibility: the degree to which the system can be adjusted to changes in processing requirements due to such factors as changes in product or service design, changes in volume processed, and changes in technology.

TECHNOLOGY

Technological innovation

Technology

Technology and technological innovation often have a major influence on business processes. Technological innovation refers to the discovery and development of new or improved products, services, or processes for producing or providing them. Technology refers to applications of scientific discoveries to the development and improvement of goods and services and/or the processes that produce or provide them. It can involve such factors as knowledge, materials, methods, and equipment. The term *high technology* refers to the most advanced and developed equipment and methods.

There are different kinds of technology. Operations management is primarily concerned with three kinds of technology, all of which can have a major impact on costs, productivity, and competitiveness:

1. *Product and service technology* is the discovery and development of new products and services. This is done mainly by researchers and engineers, who use the scientific approach to develop new knowledge and translate that into commercial applications.

figure 3.1   Process Selection and Capacity Planning Influence System Design

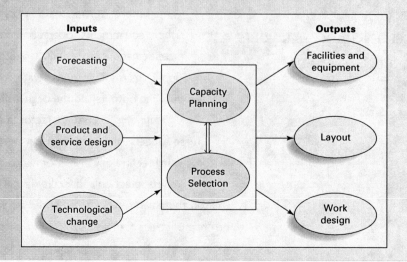

2. *Process technology* includes methods, procedures, and equipment used to produce goods and provide services. This not only involves processes within an organization, it also extends to supply chain processes.

3. *Information technology (IT)* is the science and use of computers and other electronic equipment to store, process, and send information. IT is heavily ingrained in today's business operations. This includes electronic data processing, the use of bar codes and radio frequency tags to identify and track goods, devices used to obtain point-of-sale information, data transmission, the Internet, e-commerce, e-mail, and more.

TECHNOLOGY AS A COMPETITIVE ADVANTAGE

Technological innovation in products and services and in processing technology can produce tremendous benefits for organizations.

Technological advances in products can yield competitive advantages for companies that are quick to market them, often helping to increase market share and generate substantial profits. Examples include products such as cell phones and personal digital assistants (PDAs), wireless computing and wireless e-mail, digital cameras, satellite radio, and global positioning system devices. Many technological advances in production and service can be attributed to NASA's space program. Examples include advances in food processing, robotics, and medical telemetry.

Technological advances in processes can also yield competitive advantages for companies by increasing quality, lowering costs, increasing productivity, and expanding processing capabilities. Among the examples are laser technology used in surgery and laser measuring devices, advances in medical diagnostic equipment, high-speed Internet connections, high-definition television, online banking, information retrieval systems, and high-speed search engines. Processing technologies often come through acquisition rather than through internal efforts of an organization.

TECHNOLOGY ACQUISITION

While process technology can have enormous benefits, it also carries substantial risk unless a significant effort is made to fully understand both the downside as well as the upside of a particular technology. It is essential to understand what the technology will and won't do. Also, there are economic considerations (initial cost, space, cash flow, maintenance, consultants), integration considerations (cost, time, resources), and human considerations (training, safety, job loss).

PROCESS SELECTION

Three primary questions bear on process selection:

1. How much *variety* in products or services will the system need to handle?
2. What degree of equipment *flexibility* will be needed?
3. What is the expected volume of output?

Answers to these questions will serve as a guide to selecting an appropriate process.

PROCESS TYPES

There are five basic process types: job shop, batch, repetitive, continuous, and project. The first four types can be described as follows:

Job shop. A job shop usually operates on a relatively small scale. It is used when a low volume of high-variety goods or services will be needed. Processing is *intermittent;* work includes small jobs, each with somewhat different processing requirements. High flexibility using general-purpose equipment and skilled workers are important characteristics

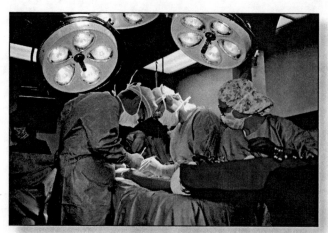

A JOB SHOP PROCESS: A MIDWESTERN HOSPITAL MEDICAL TEAM PERFORMS A DIAGNOSTIC PROCEDURE INVOLVING A CARDIAC CATHETERIZATION.

A BATCH PROCESS: MENU ITEMS ARE PREPARED IN BATCHES, IN THE KITCHEN OF THE SPAGO RESTAURANT IN THE FORUM AT CAESAR'S PALACE, LAS VEGAS, NEVADA.

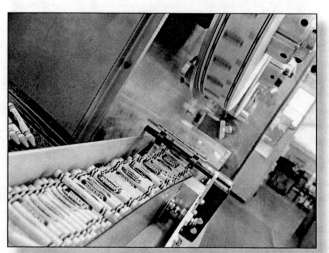

A REPETITIVE PROCESS: CRAYOLA LLC, MAKER OF CRAYOLA PRODUCTS, PRODUCES NEARLY 3 BILLION CRAYONS EACH YEAR IN ITS EASTON, PA, MANUFACTURING FACILITY.

A CONTINUOUS PROCESS: AN OIL REFINERY PERFORMS A CONTINUOUS PROCESS, MIXING AND SEPARATING CRUDE OIL INTO GAS, FUEL OIL, CHEMICALS, AND MANY OTHER PRODUCTS.

of a job shop. A manufacturing example of a job shop is a tool and die shop that is able to produce one-of-a-kind tools. A service example is a veterinarian's office, which is able to process a variety of animals and a variety of injuries and diseases.

Batch. Batch processing is used when a moderate volume of goods or services is desired, and it can handle a moderate variety in products or services. The equipment need not be as flexible as in a job shop, but processing is still intermittent. The skill level of workers doesn't need to be as high as in a job shop because there is less variety in the jobs being processed. Examples of batch systems include bakeries, which make bread, cakes, or cookies in batches; movie theaters, which show movies to groups (batches) of people; and airlines, which carry planeloads (batches) of people from airport to airport. Other examples of products that lend themselves to batch production are paint, ice cream, soft drinks, beer, magazines, and books. Other examples of services include plays, concerts, music videos, radio and television programs, and public address announcements.

Repetitive. When higher volumes of more standardized goods or services are needed, repetitive processing is used. The standardized output means only slight flexibility of equipment is needed. Skill of workers is generally low. Examples of this type of system include production lines and assembly lines. In fact, this type of process is sometimes referred to as *assembly*. Familiar products made by these systems include automobiles, television sets, pencils, and computers. An example of a service system is an automatic carwash. Other examples of service include cafeteria lines and ticket collectors at sports events and concerts.

Continuous. When a very high volume of nondiscrete, highly standardized output is desired, a continuous system is used. These systems have almost no variety in output and, hence, no need for equipment flexibility. Workers' skill requirements can range from low to high, depending on the complexity of the system and the expertise workers need. Generally, if equipment is highly specialized, worker skills can be lower. Examples of nondiscrete products made in continuous systems include petroleum products, steel, sugar, flour, and salt. Continuous services include air monitoring, supplying electricity to homes and businesses, and the Internet.

These process types are found in a wide range of manufacturing and service settings. The ideal is to have process capabilities match product or service requirements. Failure to do so can result in inefficiencies and higher costs than are necessary, perhaps creating a competitive disadvantage. Table 3.1 provides a brief description of each process type along with advantages and disadvantages of each.

Figure 3.2 provides an overview of the four process types in the form of a matrix, with an example for each process type. Note that job variety, process flexibility, and unit cost are highest for a job shop and get progressively lower moving from job shop to continuous processing. Conversely, volume of output is lowest for a job shop and gets progressively higher moving from job shop to continuous processing. Note, too, that the examples fall along the diagonal. The implication is that the diagonal represents the ideal choice of processing system for a given set of circumstances. For example, if the goal is to be able to process a small volume of jobs that will involve high variety, job shop processing is most appropriate. For less variety and a higher volume, a batch system would be most appropriate, and so on. Note that combinations far from the diagonal would not even be considered, such as using a job shop for high-volume, low-variety jobs, or continuous processing for low-volume, high-variety jobs, because that would result in either higher than necessary costs or lost opportunities.

Another consideration is that products and services often go through *life cycles* that begin with low volume, which increases as products or services become better known. When that happens, a manager must know when to shift from one type of process (e.g., job shop) to the next (e.g., batch). Of course, some operations remain at a certain level (e.g., magazine publishing), while others increase (or decrease as markets become saturated) over time. Again, it is important for a manager to assess his or her products and services and make a judgment on whether to plan for changes in processing over time.

All of these process types (job shop, batch, repetitive, and continuous) are typically ongoing operations. However, some situations are not ongoing but instead are of limited durations. In such instances, the work is often organized as a *project*.

A project is used for work that is nonroutine, with a unique set of objectives to be accomplished in a limited time frame. Examples range from simple to complicated, including such

Project

Types of Processing

table 3.1

	JOB SHOP	BATCH	REPETITIVE/ASSEMBLY	CONTINUOUS
Description	Customized goods or services	Semi-standardized goods or services	Standardized goods or services	Highly standardized goods or services
Advantages	Able to handle a wide variety of work	Flexibility	Low unit cost, high volume, efficient	Very efficient, very high volume
Disadvantages	Slow, high cost per unit, complex planning and scheduling	Moderate cost per unit, moderate scheduling complexity	Low flexibility, high cost of downtime	Very rigid, lack of variety, costly to change, very high cost of downtime

things as putting on a play, consulting, making a motion picture, launching a new product or service, publishing a book, building a dam, and building a bridge. Equipment flexibility and worker skills can range from low to high.

The type of process or processes used by an organization influences a great many activities of the organization. Table 3.2 briefly describes some of those influences.

figure 3.2   Product and Service Processes

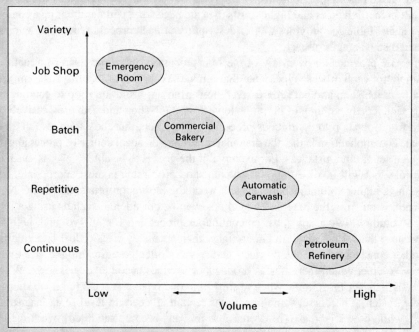

SOURCE: ADAPTED FROM R. HAYES AND S. WHEELWRIGHT, *RESTORING OUR COMPETITIVE EDGE* (NEW YORK: WILEY, 1984), P. 209. © 1984 JOHN WILEY & SONS. USED WITH PERMISSION.

table 3.2   Process Choice Affects Numerous Activities/Functions

ACTIVITY/ FUNCTION	JOB SHOP	BATCH	REPETITIVE	CONTINUOUS	PROJECTS
Cost estimation	Difficult	Somewhat routine	Routine	Routine	Simple to complex
Cost per Unit	High	Moderate	Low	Low	Very high
Equipment used	General purpose	General purpose	Special purpose	Special purpose	Varied
Fixed costs	Low	Moderate	High	Very high	Varied
Variable costs	High	Moderate	Low	Very low	High
Labor skills	High	Moderate	Low	Low to high	Low to high
Marketing	Promote capabilities	Promote capabilities; semi-standardized goods and services	Promote standardized goods/ services	Promote standardized goods/ services	Promote capabilities
Scheduling	Complex	Moderately complex	Routine	Routine	Complex, subject to change
Work-in-process inventory	High	High	Low	Low	Varied

The processes discussed do not always exist in their "pure" forms. It is not unusual to find hybrid processes—processes that have elements of other process types embedded in them. For instance, companies that operate primarily in a repetitive mode, or a continuous mode, will often have repair shops (i.e., job shops) to fix or make new parts for equipment that fails. Also, if volume increases for some items, an operation that began, say, in a job shop or as a batch mode may evolve into a batch or repetitive operation. This may result in having some operations in a job shop or batch mode, and others in a repetitive mode.

OPERATIONS TOUR: MORTON SALT

www.mortonintl.com

Introduction: Morton Salt is a subsidiary of Morton International, a manufacturer of specialty chemicals, air bags, and salt products. The Morton salt-processing facility in Silver Springs, New York, between Buffalo and Rochester, is one of six similar Morton salt-processing facilities in the United States. The Silver Springs plant employs about 200 people, ranging from unskilled to skilled. It produces salt products for water conditioning, grocery, industrial, and agricultural markets. The grocery business consists of 26-oz. round cans of iodized salt. Although the grocery business represents a relatively small portion of the total output (approximately 15 percent), it is the most profitable.

Salt Production: The basic raw material, salt, is obtained by injecting water into salt caverns that are located some 2,400 feet below the surface. There, the salt deposits dissolve in the water. The resulting brine is pumped to the surface where it is converted into salt crystals. The brine is boiled, and much of the liquid evaporates, leaving salt crystals and some residual moisture, which is removed in a drying process. This process is run continuously for about six weeks at a time. Initially, salt is produced at the rate of 45 tons per hour. But the rate of output decreases due to scale buildup, so that by the sixth week, output is only 75 percent of the initial rate. At that point, the process is halted to perform maintenance on the equipment and remove the scale, after which, salt production resumes.

The salt is stored in silos until it is needed for production, or it is shipped in bulk to industrial customers. Conveyors move the salt to each of the four dedicated production areas, one of which is round can production. (See diagram.) The discussion here focuses exclusively on round can production.

Round Can Production: Annual round can production averages roughly 3.8 million cans. Approximately 70 percent of the output is for the Morton label, and the rest is for private label. There are two parallel, high-speed production lines. The two lines share common processes at the beginning of the lines, and then branch out into two identical lines. Each line is capable of producing 9,600 cans per hour (160 cans per minute). The equipment is not flexible, so the production rate is fixed. The operations are completely standardized; the only variable is the brand label that is applied. One line requires 12 production workers, while both lines together can be operated by 18 workers because of the common processes. Workers on the line perform low-skilled, repetitive tasks.

The plant produces both the salt and the cans the salt is packaged in. The cans are essentially a cylinder with a top and a bottom; they are made of cardboard, except for a plastic pour spout in the top. The cylinder portion is formed from two sheets of chip board that are glued together and then rolled into a continuous tube. The glue not only binds the material, it also provides a moisture barrier. The tube is cut in a two-step process: it is first cut into long sections, and those sections are then cut into can-size pieces. The top and bottom pieces for the cans are punched from a continuous strip of cardboard. The separate pieces move along conveyor belts to the lines where the components are assembled into cans and glued. The cans are then filled with salt and the pour spout is added. Finally, the cans are loaded onto pallets and placed into inventory, ready to be shipped to distributors.

Quality: Quality is checked at several points in the production process. Initially, the salt is checked for purity when it is obtained from the wells. Iodine and an anti-caking compound are added to the salt, and their levels are verified using chemical analysis. Crystal size is important. In order to achieve the desired size and to remove lumps, the salt is forced through a scraping screen, which can cause very fine pieces of metal to mix with the salt. However, these pieces are effectively removed by magnets that are placed at appropriate points in the process. If, for any reason, the salt is judged to be contaminated, it is diverted to a nonfood product.

Checking the quality of the cans is done primarily by visual inspection, including verifying the assembly operation is correct, checking filled cans for correct weight, inspecting cans to see that labels are properly aligned, and checking to see that metal pour spouts are correctly attached.

(continued)

(concluded)

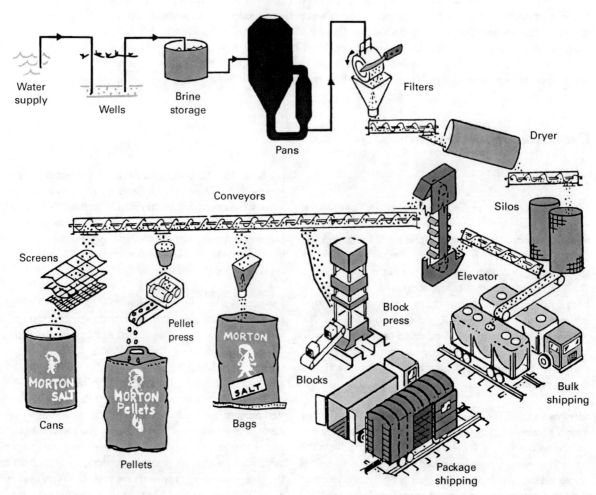

The equipment on the production line is sensitive to misshapen or damaged cans, and frequently jams, causing production delays. This greatly reduces the chance of a defective can getting through the process, but it reduces productivity, and the salt in the defective cans must be scrapped. The cost of quality is fairly high, owing to the amount of product that is scrapped, the large number of inspectors, and the extensive laboratory testing that is needed.

Production Planning and Inventory: The plant can sell all of the salt it produces. The job of the production scheduler is to distribute the salt that is stored in the silos to the various production areas, taking into account production capacities in each area and available inventory levels of those products. A key consideration is to make sure there is sufficient storage capacity in the silos to handle the incoming salt from brine production.

Equipment Maintenance and Repair: The equipment is 1950s vintage, and it requires a fair amount of maintenance to

keep it in good working order. Even so, breakdowns occur as parts wear out. The plant has its own tool shop where skilled workers repair parts or make new parts because replacement parts are no longer available for the old equipment.

Questions

1   Briefly describe salt production, from brine production to finished round cans.

2   Briefly describe quality assurance efforts in round can production.

3   What are some of the possible reasons why the company continues to use the old processing equipment instead of buying new, more modern equipment?

4   Where would you place salt production in the product–process spectrum?

5   Determine the approximate number of tons of salt produced annually. Hints: one ton = 2,000 pounds, and one pound = 16 ounces.

6   What improvements can you suggest for the plant?

PRODUCT AND SERVICE PROFILING

Process selection can involve substantial investment in equipment and have a very specific influence on the layout of facilities, which also require heavy investment. Moreover, mismatches between operations capabilities and market demand and pricing or cost strategies can have a significant negative impact on the ability of the organization to compete or, in government agencies, to effectively service clients. Therefore, it is highly desirable to assess the degree of correlation between various process choices and market conditions *before* making process choices in order to achieve an appropriate matching.

Product or service profiling can be used to avoid any inconsistencies by identifying key product or service dimensions and then selecting appropriate processes. Key dimensions often relate to the range of products or services that will be processed, expected order sizes, pricing strategies, expected frequency of schedule changes, and order-winning requirements.

Product or service profiling

SUSTAINABLE PRODUCTION OF GOODS AND SERVICES

Business organizations are facing increasing pressure from a variety of sources to operate sustainable production processes. According to the Lowell Center for Sustainable Production (http://sustainableproduction.org), "Sustainable Production is the creation of goods and services using processes and systems that are: non-polluting; conserving of energy and natural resources; economically efficient; safe and healthful for workers, communities, and consumers; and, socially and creatively rewarding for all working people." To achieve this, the Lowell Center advocates designing and operating processes in ways that:

- "wastes and ecologically incompatible byproducts are reduced, eliminated or recycled on-site;
- chemical substances or physical agents and conditions that present hazards to human health or the environment are eliminated;
- energy and materials are conserved, and the forms of energy and materials used are most appropriate for the desired ends; and
- work spaces are designed to minimize or eliminate chemical, ergonomic and physical hazard."

To achieve these goals, business organizations must focus on a number of factors that include energy use and efficiency, CO_2 (carbon footprint) and toxic emissions, waste generation, lighting, heating, cooling, ventilation, noise and vibration, and worker health and safety.

LEAN PROCESS DESIGN

Lean process design is guided by general principles that are discussed more fully in a later chapter. One principle of particular interest here is waste reduction, which relates to sustainability objectives. Lean design also focuses on variance reduction in workload over the entire process to achieve level production and thereby improve process flow. Successful lean design results in reduced inventory and floor space; quicker response times and shorter lead times; reduced defects, rework, and scrap; and increased productivity. Lean design is often translated into practice using cellular layouts, which are discussed later in this chapter.

Lean process design has broad applications in seemingly diverse areas such as health care delivery systems, manufacturing, construction projects, and process reengineering.

AUTOMATION

A key question in process design is whether to automate. Automation is machinery that has sensing and control devices that enable it to operate automatically. If a company decides to automate, the next question is how much. Automation can range from factories that are completely automated to a single automated operation.

Automation

Automated services are also an option. Although not as plentiful as in manufacturing, automated services are becoming increasingly important. Examples range from automated teller machines (ATMs) to automated heating and air conditioning, and include automated inspection, automated storage and retrieval systems, package sorting, mail processing, e-mail, online banking, and E-Z pass.

Automation offers a number of advantages over human labor. It has low variability, whereas it is difficult for a human to perform a task in exactly the same way, in the same amount of time, and on a repetitive basis. In a production setting, variability is detrimental to quality and to meeting schedules. Moreover, machines do not get bored or distracted, nor do they go out on strike, ask for higher wages, or file labor grievances. Still another advantage of automation is reduction of variable costs. In order for automated processing to be an option, job-processing requirements must be *standardized* (i.e., have very little or no variety).

Automation is frequently touted as a strategy necessary for competitiveness. However, automation also has certain disadvantages and limitations compared to human labor. To begin with, it can be costly. Technology is expensive; usually it requires high volumes of output to offset high costs. In addition, automation is much less flexible than human labor. Once a process has been automated, there is substantial reason for not changing it. Moreover, workers sometimes fear automation because it might cause them to lose their jobs. That can have an adverse effect on morale and productivity.

Decision makers must carefully examine the issue of whether to automate or the degree to which to automate, so that they clearly understand all the ramifications. Also, much thought and careful planning are necessary to successfully *integrate* automation into a production system. Otherwise, it can lead to major problems. Automation has important implications not only for cost and flexibility, but also for the fit with overall strategic priorities. If the decision is made to automate, care must be taken to remove waste from the system prior to automating, to avoid building the waste into the automated system. Table 3.3 has a list of questions for organizations that are considering automation.

Generally speaking, there are three kinds of automation: fixed, programmable, and flexible.

Fixed automation is the most rigid of the three types. Sometimes referred to as Detroit-type automation, it uses high-cost, specialized equipment for a fixed sequence of operations. Low cost and high volume are its primary advantages; minimal variety and the high cost of making major changes in either product or process are its primary limitations.

Programmable automation is at the opposite end of the spectrum. It involves the use of high-cost, general-purpose equipment controlled by a computer program that provides both the sequence of operations and specific details about each operation. This type of automation has the capability of economically producing a fairly wide variety of low-volume products in small batches. Numerically controlled (N/C) machines and some robots are applications of programmable automation.

Computer-aided manufacturing (CAM)

Numerically controlled (N/C) machines

Computer-aided manufacturing (CAM) refers to the use of computers in process control, ranging from robots to automated quality control. Numerically controlled (N/C) machines are programmed to follow a set of processing instructions based on mathematical relationships that tell the machine the details of the operations to be performed. The instructions are stored on a device such as magnetic tape, or microprocessor. Although N/C machines have been used for many years, they are an important part of new approaches to manufacturing. Individual machines often have their own computer; this is referred to as *computerized numerical control (CNC)*. Or one computer may control a number of N/C machines, which is referred to as *direct numerical control (DNC)*.

table 3.3	Automation Questions

1. What level of automation is appropriate? (Some operations are more suited to being automated than others, so partial automation can be an option.)

2. How would automation affect the flexibility of an operation system?

3. How can automation projects be justified?

4. How should changes be managed?

5. What are the risks of automating?

6. What are some of the likely effects of implementing automation on market share, costs, quality, customer satisfaction, labor relations, and ongoing operations?

Computer numerical control (CNC) refers to a computer that reads instructions and drives a machine tool. CNC machines are controlled directly from files created by CAM software packages. With increased automation of manufacturing processes with CNC machining, considerable improvements in consistency and quality have been achieved. CNC automation reduced the frequency of errors and provided operators with time to perform additional tasks. The intelligence of CNC controllers has dramatically increased job shop cell production. Some machines might even make 1,000 parts on a weekend with no operator, checking each part with lasers and sensors.

N/C machines are best used in cases where parts are processed frequently and in small batches, where part geometry is complex, close tolerances are required, mistakes are costly, and there is the possibility of frequent changes in design. The main limitations of N/C machines are the higher skill levels needed to program the machines and their inability to detect tool wear and material variation.

The use of robots in manufacturing is sometimes an option. A robot consists of three parts: a mechanical arm, a power supply, and a controller. Unlike movie versions of robots, which vaguely resemble human beings, industrial robots are much less glamorous and much less mobile; most robots are stationary except for their movable arms. **Robot**

Robots can handle a wide variety of tasks, including welding, assembly, loading and unloading of machines, painting, and testing. They relieve humans from heavy or dirty work and often eliminate drudgery tasks.

Some uses of robots are fairly simple, others are much more complex. At the lowest level are robots that follow a fixed set of instructions. Next are programmable robots, which can repeat a set of movements after being led through the sequence. These robots "play back" a mechanical sequence much as a video recorder plays back a visual sequence. At the next level up are robots that follow instructions from a computer. At the top are robots that can recognize objects and make certain simple decisions.

"If you think robots are mainly the stuff of space movies, think again. Right now, all over the world, robots are on the move. They are painting cars at Ford plants, assembling Milano cookies for Pepperidge Farms, walking into live volcanoes, driving trains in Paris, and defusing bombs in Northern Ireland. As they grow tougher, nimbler, and smarter, today's robots are doing more and more things humans can't—or don't want to—do."

Source: www.thetech.org/robotics.

figure 3.3   Industrial Robot

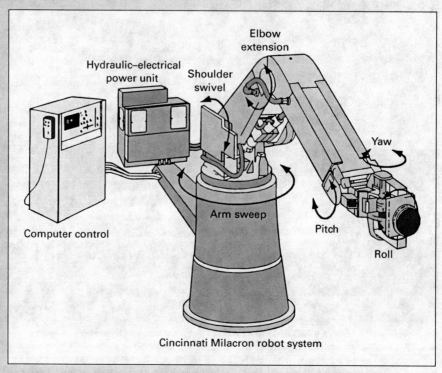

Cincinnati Milacron robot system

SOURCE: MORRIS A. COHEN AND UDAY M. APTE, *MANUFACTURING AUTOMATION* (BURR RIDGE, IL: IRWIN/MCGRAW-HILL, 1997), P. 138.

Figure 3.3 illustrates a robot.

Flexible automation evolved from programmable automation. It uses equipment that is more customized than that of programmable automation. A key difference between the two is that flexible automation requires significantly less changeover time. This permits almost continuous operation of equipment *and* product variety without the need to produce in batches.

In practice, flexible automation is used in several different formats.

READING: TOUR DE FORCE

Gerald Scott

www.chryslercorp.com

DaimlerChrysler's plant that builds Viper and Prowler is the Motor City's "hottest ticket."

The Viper-Prowler plant is not your typical Detroit assembly operation. Instead of mass production techniques using robots, it's "craftsman-style" production for hand-building Vipers and Prowlers. With mass production, DaimlerChrysler can produce up to 75 cars per hour. With late shifts DaimlerChrysler's nearby Jefferson North Assembly Plant can crank out 1,114 Jeep Grand Cherokees in a 24-hour workday. By comparison, the Viper plant produces 13 Vipers a day and has a capacity for 20 Prowlers.

At 392,000 square feet, the Viper plant is a boutique compared to most massive auto plants, such as Saturn Corp.'s Spring Hill, Tenn., manufacturing complex, which is 5 million square feet. The Jefferson North plant has 2.4 million square feet.

"We're not the biggest plant in the area, but we've got the best work force and build the most exciting products—the Plymouth Prowler and Dodge Viper," said Hinckley, who has spent 33 years working in various Detroit auto plants for General Motors and Chrysler and is known for building and driving "kit car" racers. "We're expanding our plant, too. We also are part of the revitalization of Detroit.

"Our plant was about 380,000 square feet and we've just added another 10,000 square feet to improve our process flow and improve our quality. And it provides a little more space since we added the Prowler.

"It will allow us to do a better job of reaching the Prowler's ultimate capacity. It's about a $1 million expansion—for other large plants, that's nothing but for a facility this size it's a lot of money.'

"For me it's a dream job. I've been a 'hot rodder' all my life and build race cars and racing engines, and how many hot rodders get to lead the team that runs the only hot-rod plant in the world?"

Conner Avenue is a throwback to early 20th Century, pre–mass assembly techniques. Vipers and Prowlers are built on parallel 720-foot assembly lines, each with a dozen or so workstations, where the cars are hand-assembled. In a rarity, there are no robots in this plant.

When each workstation completes its task, the entire line advances to the next station. So in those 45-minute stops, the employees are relatively free to grab a cup of coffee or talk to tour groups, something they could never do in a plant cranking out 73 units per hour.

The automaker's flexible labor agreement with UAW Local 212 means everybody working in the plant is a "craftsman" and can solve any problem anywhere on the line—in most plants, job categories are sharply defined and protected.

Most large auto assembly plants still require 2,000 or more workers, while the Viper plant needs only 260.

"We do everything from forklift driving to mopping and sweeping, we do it all," says Andrew Stokes, a UAW craftsman who works in underbody and heavy repair.

"I'm one of the first 12 to work on the Prowler," he added. "The Prowler is a little easier to assemble but a little harder to repair. The Viper seems to be a lot more open than the Prowler is—the car seems to be built around the engine and trans and that makes it a little harder to work on."

Thanks to such an interest from car buyers in this plant, Daimler Chrysler allows Viper customers to pick up their car as it comes out of final assembly, to meet the employees who built it and to drive it home from the plant instead of from the dealership.

Questions

1 What is different about this assembly plant compared to more typical auto assembly plants?

2 Why do you suppose there are no robots or other automation?

SOURCE: EXCERPTS FROM "TOUR DE FORCE" BY GERALD SCOTT, CHICAGO TRIBUNE. © 1998 GERALD SCOTT. USED WITH PERMISSION.

PROCESS STRATEGY

Throughout this book, the importance of *flexibility* as a competitive strategy is stressed. However, flexibility does not always offer the best choice in processing decisions. Flexible systems and equipment are often more expensive and not as efficient as less flexible alternatives. In certain instances, flexibility is unnecessary because products are in mature stages, requiring few design changes, and there is a steady volume of output. Ordinarily, this type of situation calls for specialized processing equipment, with no need for flexibility. The implication is clear: Flexibility should be adopted with great care; its applications should be matched with situations in which a *need* for flexibility clearly exists.

In practice, decision makers choose flexible systems for either of two reasons: Demand variety or uncertainty exists about demand. The second reason can be overcome through improved forecasting.

FACILITIES LAYOUT

Layout refers to the configuration of departments, work centers, and equipment, with particular emphasis on movement of work (customers or materials) through the system. This section describes the main types of layout designs and the models used to evaluate design alternatives.

As in other areas of system design, layout decisions are important for three basic reasons: (1) they require substantial investments of money and effort; (2) they involve long-term commitments, which makes mistakes difficult to overcome; and (3) they have a significant impact on the cost and efficiency of operations.

The need for layout planning arises both in the process of designing new facilities and in redesigning existing facilities. The most common reasons for redesign of layouts include inefficient operations (e.g., high cost, bottlenecks), accidents or safety hazards, changes in the design of products or services, introduction of new products or services, changes in the volume of output or mix of outputs, changes in methods or equipment, changes in environmental or other legal requirements, and morale problems (e.g., lack of face-to-face contact).

Poor layout design can adversely affect system performance. For example, a change in the layout at the Minneapolis–St. Paul International Airport solved a problem that had plagued travelers. In the former layout, security checkpoints were located in the boarding area. That meant that arriving passengers who were simply changing planes had to pass through a security checkpoint before being able to board their connecting flight, along with other passengers whose journeys were originating at Minneapolis–St. Paul. This created excessive waiting times for both sets of passengers. The new layout relocated the security checkpoints, moving them from the boarding area to a position close to the ticket counters. Thus, the need for passengers who were making connecting flights to pass through security was eliminated, and in the process, the waiting time for passengers departing from Minneapolis–St. Paul was considerably reduced.[1]

The basic objective of layout design is to facilitate a smooth flow of work, material, and information through the system. Supporting objectives generally involve the following:

1. To facilitate attainment of product or service quality.
2. To use workers and space efficiently.
3. To avoid bottlenecks.
4. To minimize material handling costs.
5. To eliminate unnecessary movements of workers or materials.
6. To minimize production time or customer service time.
7. To design for safety.

The three basic types of layout are product, process, and fixed-position. *Product layouts* are most conducive to repetitive processing, *process layouts* are used for intermittent processing, and *fixed-position layouts* are used when projects require layouts. The characteristics, advantages, and disadvantages of each layout type are described in this section, along with hybrid layouts, which are combinations of these pure types. These include cellular layouts and flexible manufacturing systems.

REPETITIVE PROCESSING: PRODUCT LAYOUTS

Product layout

Product layouts are used to achieve a smooth and rapid flow of large volumes of goods or customers through a system. This is made possible by highly standardized goods or services that allow highly standardized, repetitive processing. The work is divided into a series of standardized tasks, permitting specialization of equipment and division of labor. The large volumes handled by these systems usually make it economical to invest substantial sums of money in equipment and job design. Because only one or a few very similar items are involved, it is feasible to arrange an entire layout to correspond to the technological processing requirements of the product or service. For instance, if a portion of a manufacturing operation required the sequence of cutting, sanding, and painting, the appropriate pieces of equipment would be arranged in that same sequence. And because each item follows the same sequence of operations, it is often possible to utilize fixed-path material-handling equipment such as conveyors to transport items between operations. The resulting arrangement forms a line like the one depicted in Figure 3.4. In manufacturing environments, the

Production line

Assembly line

lines are referred to as production lines or assembly lines, depending on the type of activity involved. In service processes, the term *line* may or may not be used. It is common to refer to a cafeteria line as such but not a car wash, although from a conceptual standpoint the

A Flow Line for Production or Service

figure 3.4

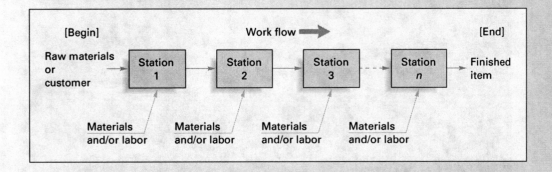

Cafeteria Line

figure 3.5

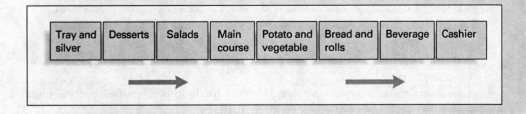

two are nearly identical. Figure 3.5 illustrates the layout of a typical cafeteria serving line. Examples of this type of layout are less plentiful in service environments because processing requirements usually exhibit too much variability to make standardization feasible. Without high standardization, many of the benefits of repetitive processing are lost. When lines are used, certain compromises may be made. For instance, an automatic car wash provides equal treatment to all cars—the same amount of soap, water, and scrubbing—even though cars may differ considerably in cleaning needs.

Product layouts achieve a high degree of labor and equipment utilization, which tends to offset their high equipment costs. Because items move quickly from operation to operation, the amount of work-in-process is often minimal. Consequently, operations are so closely tied to each other that the entire system is highly vulnerable to being shut down because of mechanical failure or high absenteeism. Maintenance procedures are geared to this. *Preventive maintenance*—periodic inspection and replacement of worn parts or those with high failure rates—reduces the probability of breakdowns during the operations. Of course, no amount of preventive activity can completely eliminate failures, so management must take measures to provide quick repair. These include maintaining an inventory of spare parts and having repair personnel available to quickly restore equipment to normal operation. These procedures are fairly expensive; because of the specialized nature of equipment, problems become more difficult to diagnose and resolve, and spare-part inventories can be extensive.

Repetitive processing can be machine paced (e.g., automatic car wash, automobile assembly), worker paced (e.g., fast-food restaurants such as McDonald's, Burger King), or even customer paced (e.g., cafeteria line).

The main advantages of product layouts are

1. A high rate of output.
2. Low unit cost due to high volume. The high cost of specialized equipment is spread over many units.

FACILITY LAYOUT AT FIRST CAPITAL FEDERAL CREDIT UNION. THE FLOOR PLAN ALLOCATES SPACE TO VARIOUS FUNCTIONAL AREAS, INCLUDING GREETING CUSTOMERS AND CONDUCTING FINANCIAL TRANSACTIONS. A WAITING AREA IS SPACIOUS AND CHILD FRIENDLY.

3. Labor specialization, which reduces training costs and time, and results in a wide span of supervision.
4. Low material-handling cost per unit. Material handling is simplified because units follow the same sequence of operations. Material handling is often automated.
5. A high utilization of labor and equipment.
6. The establishment of routing and scheduling in the initial design of the system. These activities do not require much attention once the system is operating.
7. Fairly routine accounting, purchasing, and inventory control.

The primary disadvantages of product layouts include the following:

1. The intensive division of labor usually creates dull, repetitive jobs that provide little opportunity for advancement and may lead to morale problems and to repetitive stress injuries.
2. Poorly skilled workers may exhibit little interest in maintaining equipment or in the quality of output.
3. The system is fairly inflexible in response to changes in the volume of output or changes in product or process design.
4. The system is highly susceptible to shutdowns caused by equipment breakdowns or excessive absenteeism because workstations are highly interdependent.
5. Preventive maintenance, the capacity for quick repairs, and spare-parts inventories are necessary expenses.
6. Incentive plans tied to individual output are impractical since they would cause variations among outputs of individual workers, which would adversely affect the smooth flow of work through the system.

U-Shaped Layouts. Although a straight production line may have intuitive appeal, a U-shaped line (see Figure 3.6) has a number of advantages that make it worthy of consideration. One disadvantage of a long, straight line is that it interferes with cross-travel of workers and vehicles. A U-shaped line is more compact; it often requires approximately half the length of a straight production line. In addition, a U-shaped line permits increased communication among workers on the line because workers are clustered, thus facilitating teamwork. Flexibility in work assignments is increased because workers can handle not only adjacent stations but also stations on opposite sides of the line. Moreover, if materials enter

A U-shaped Production Line

figure 3.6

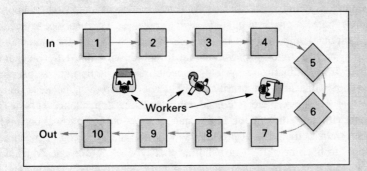

Comparison of Process and Product Layouts

figure 3.7

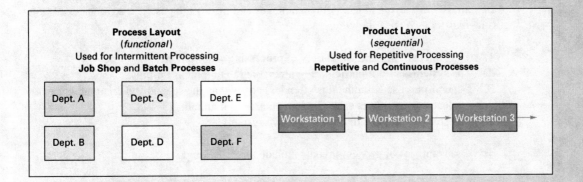

the plant at the same point that finished products leave it, a U-shaped line minimizes material handling.

Of course, not all situations lend themselves to U-shaped layouts: On highly automated lines there is less need for teamwork and communication. And entry and exit points may be on opposite sides of the building. Also, operations may need to be separated because of noise or contamination factors.

NONREPETITIVE PROCESSING: PROCESS LAYOUTS

Process layouts are designed to process items or provide services that involve a variety of processing requirements. The variety of jobs that are processed requires frequent adjustments to equipment. This causes a discontinuous work flow, which is referred to as intermittent processing. The layouts feature departments or other *functional* groupings in which similar kinds of activities are performed. A manufacturing example of a process layout is the *machine shop,* which has separate departments for milling, grinding, drilling, and so on. Items that require those operations are frequently moved in lots or batches to the departments in a sequence that varies from job to job. Consequently, variable-path material-handling equipment (forklift trucks, jeeps, tote boxes) is needed to handle the variety of routes and items. The use of *general-purpose equipment* provides the *flexibility* necessary to handle a wide range of processing requirements. Workers who operate the equipment are usually skilled or semiskilled. Figure 3.7 illustrates the departmental arrangement typical of a process layout.

Process layouts

Intermittent processing

Process layouts are quite common in service environments. Examples include hospitals, colleges and universities, banks, auto repair shops, airlines, and public libraries. For instance, hospitals have departments or other units that specifically handle surgery, maternity, pediatrics, psychiatric, emergency, and geriatric care. And universities have separate schools or departments that concentrate on one area of study such as business, engineering, science, or math.

Because equipment in a process layout is arranged by type rather than by processing sequence, the system is much less vulnerable to shutdown caused by mechanical failure or absenteeism. In manufacturing systems especially, idle equipment is usually available to replace machines that are temporarily out of service. Moreover, because items are often processed in lots (batches), there is considerably less interdependence between successive operations than with a product layout. Maintenance costs tend to be lower because the equipment is less specialized than that of product layouts, and the grouping of machinery permits repair personnel to become skilled in handling that type of equipment. Machine similarity reduces the necessary investment in spare parts. On the negative side, routing and scheduling must be done on a continual basis to accommodate the variety of processing demands typically imposed on these systems. Material handling is inefficient, and unit handling costs are generally much higher than in product layouts. In-process inventories can be substantial due to batch processing. Furthermore, it is not uncommon for such systems to have equipment utilization rates under 50 percent because of routing and scheduling complexities related to the variety of processing demands being handled.

In sum, process layouts have both advantages and disadvantages. The advantages of process layouts include the following:

1. The systems can handle a variety of processing requirements.
2. The systems are not particularly vulnerable to equipment failures.
3. General-purpose equipment is often less costly than the specialized equipment used in product layouts and is easier and less costly to maintain.
4. It is possible to use individual incentive systems.

The disadvantages of process layouts include the following:

1. In-process inventory costs can be high if batch processing is used in manufacturing systems.
2. Routing and scheduling pose continual challenges.
3. Equipment utilization rates are low.
4. Material handling is slow and inefficient, and more costly per unit than in product layouts.
5. Job complexities often reduce the span of supervision and result in higher supervisory costs than with product layouts.
6. Special attention necessary for each product or customer (e.g., routing, scheduling, machine setups) and low volumes result in higher unit costs than with product layouts.
7. Accounting, inventory control, and purchasing are much more involved than with product layouts.

FIXED-POSITION LAYOUTS

Fixed-position layout

In fixed-position layouts, the item being worked on remains stationary, and workers, materials, and equipment are moved about as needed. This is in marked contrast to product and process layouts. Almost always, the nature of the product dictates this kind of arrangement: Weight, size, bulk, or some other factor makes it undesirable or extremely difficult to move the product. Fixed-position layouts are used in large construction projects (buildings, power plants, dams), shipbuilding, and production of large aircraft and space mission rockets. In those instances, attention is focused on timing of material and equipment deliveries so as not to clog up the work site and to avoid having to relocate materials and equipment around the work site. Lack of storage space can present significant problems, for example, at construction sites in crowded urban locations. Because of the many diverse activities carried out on large projects and because of the wide range of skills required, special efforts are needed to coordinate the activities, and the span of control can be quite narrow. For these reasons, the administrative burden is often much higher than it would be under either of the other layout types. Material handling may or may not be a factor; in many cases, there is no tangible product involved (e.g., designing a computerized inventory system). When goods and materials are involved, material handling often resembles process-type, variable-path, general-purpose equipment. Projects might require use of earth-moving equipment and trucks to haul materials to, from, and around the work site, for example.

Fixed-position layouts are widely used in farming, firefighting, road building, home building, remodeling and repair, and drilling for oil. In each case, compelling reasons bring workers, materials, and equipment to the "product's" location instead of the other way around.

COMBINATION LAYOUTS

The three basic layout types are ideal models, which may be altered to satisfy the needs of a particular situation. It is not hard to find layouts that represent some combination of these pure types. For instance, supermarket layouts are essentially process layouts, yet we find that most use fixed-path material-handling devices such as roller-type conveyors in the stockroom and belt-type conveyors at the cash registers. Hospitals also use the basic process arrangement, although frequently patient care involves more of a fixed-position approach, in which nurses, doctors, medicines, and special equipment are brought to the patient. By the same token, faulty parts made in a product layout may require off-line reworking, which involves customized processing. Moreover, conveyors are frequently observed in both farming and construction activities.

Process layouts and product layouts represent two ends of a continuum from small jobs to continuous production. Process layouts are conducive to the production of a wider range of products or services than product layouts, which is desirable from a customer standpoint where customized products are often in demand. However, process layouts tend to be less efficient and have higher unit production costs than product layouts. Some manufacturers are moving away from process layouts in an effort to capture some of the benefits of product layouts. Ideally, a system is flexible and yet efficient, with low unit production costs. Cellular manufacturing, group technology, and flexible manufacturing systems represent efforts to move toward this ideal.

THE QUEEN MARY 2 WHEN UNDER CONSTRUCTION AT THE CHANTIERS DE L'ATLANTIQUE SHIPYARD IN ST. NAZAIRE, FRANCE. WHEN A LARGE PROJECT MUST REMAIN STATIONARY, WORKERS AND EQUIPMENT COME TO THE SITE. THE QM2 WEIGHS 150,000 TONS, IS 1,132 FEET LONG, AND IS 147.6 FEET WIDE. ITS CAPACITY IS 2,620 PASSENGERS AND 1,253 OFFICERS WAND CREW.

CELLULAR LAYOUTS

Cellular production

Cellular Production. Cellular production is a type of layout in which workstations are grouped into what is referred to as a *cell.* Groupings are determined by the operations needed to perform work for a set of similar items, or *part families,* that require similar processing. The cells become, in effect, miniature versions of product layouts. The cells may have no conveyorized movement of parts between machines, or may have a flow line connected by a conveyor (automatic transfer). All parts follow the same route although minor variations (e.g., skipping an operation) are possible. In contrast, the functional layout involves multiple paths for parts. Moreover, there is little effort or need to identify part families.

Cellular manufacturing enables companies to produce a variety of products with as little waste as possible. A cell layout provides a smooth flow of work through the process with minimal transport or delay. Benefits frequently associated with cellular manufacturing include minimal work in process, reduced space requirements and lead times, productivity and quality improvement, and increased flexibility.

Figure 3.8 provides a comparison between a traditional process layout (3.8A) and a cellular layout (3.8B). To get a sense of the advantage of the cellular layout, trace the movement

figure 3.8   Comparison of Process and Cellular Layouts

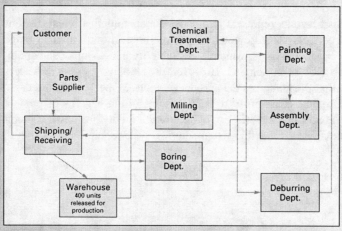

A. Example of an order processed in a traditional process layout.

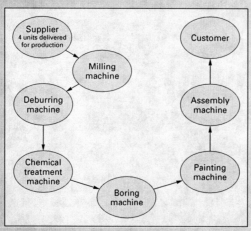

B. The same example of an order processed in a cellular layout.

SOURCE: ADAPTED FROM R. HAYES AND S. WHEELWRIGHT, *RESTORING OUR COMPETITIVE EDGE* (NEW YORK: WILEY, 1984), P. 209. © 1984 JOHN WILEY & SONS. USED WITH PERMISSION.

of an order in the traditional layout (3.8A) that is depicted by the path of the arrow. Begin on the bottom left at Shipping/Receiving, then follow the arrow to Warehouse, where a batch of raw material is released for production. Follow the path (shown by the arrows) that the batch takes as it moves through the system to Shipping/Receiving and then to the Customer. Now turn to Figure 3.8B. Note the simple path the order takes as it moves through the system.

Several techniques facilitate effective cellular layout design. Among them are the following two:

> *Single-minute exchange of die (SMED)* enables an organization to quickly convert a machine or process to produce a different (but similar) product type. Thus, a single cell can produce a variety of products without the time-consuming equipment changeover associated with large batch processes, enabling the organization to quickly respond to changes in customer demand.
>
> *Right-sized equipment* is often smaller than equipment used in traditional process layouts, and mobile, so that it can quickly be reconfigured into a different cellular layout in a different location.

Table 3.4 lists the benefits of cellular layouts compared to functional layouts.

The biggest challenges of implementing cellular manufacturing involve issues of equipment and layout and issues of workers and management. Equipment and layout issues relate to design and cost. The costs of work stoppages during implementation can be considerable, as can the costs of new or modified equipment and the rearrangement of the layout. The costs to implement cellular manufacturing must be weighed against the cost savings that can be expected from using cells. Also, the implementation of cell manufacturing often requires employee training and the redefinition of jobs. Each of the workers in each cell should ideally be able to complete the entire range of tasks required in that cell, and often this means being more multiskilled than they were previously. In addition, cells are often expected to be self-managing, and therefore workers will have to be able to work effectively in teams. Managers have to learn to be less involved than with more traditional work methods.

Group Technology. Effective cellular manufacturing must have groups of identified items with similar processing characteristics. This strategy for product and process design is known as group technology and involves identifying items with similarities in either *design characteristics* or *manufacturing characteristics,* and grouping them into *part families.* Design characteristics include size, shape, and function; manufacturing or processing characteristics involve the type and sequence of operations required. In many cases, design and processing characteristics are correlated, although this is not always the case. Thus, design families may be different from processing families. Figure 3.9 illustrates a group of parts with similar processing characteristics but different design characteristics.

Group technology

A Comparison of Functional (Process) Layouts and Cellular Layouts   **table 3.4**

DIMENSION	FUNCTIONAL	CELLULAR
Number of moves between departments	Many	Few
Travel distances	Longer	Shorter
Travel paths	Variable	Fixed
Job waiting time	Greater	Shorter
Throughput time	Higher	Lower
Amount of work in process	Higher	Lower
Supervision difficulty	Higher	Lower
Scheduling complexity	Higher	Lower
Equipment utilization	Lower	Higher

figure 3.9

A Group of Parts with Similar Manufacturing Process Requirements but Different Design Attributes

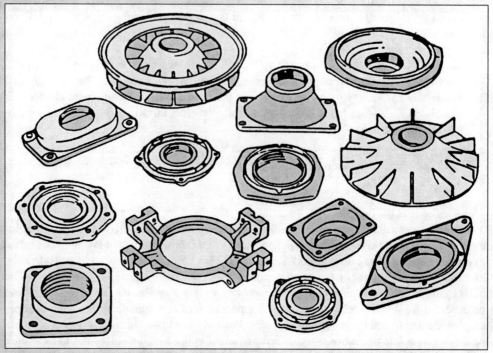

SOURCE: MIKELL P. GROOVER, AUTOMATION, PRODUCTION SYSTEMS, AND COMPUTER-AIDED MANUFACTURING © 1980, P. 540. REPRINTED BY PERMISSION OF PEARSON EDUCATION INC., UPPER SADDLE RIVER, N.J.

Once similar items have been identified, items can be classified according to their families; then a system can be developed that facilitates retrieval from a database for purposes of design and manufacturing. For instance, a designer can use the system to determine if there is an existing part similar or identical to one that needs to be designed. It may happen that an existing part, with some modification, is satisfactory. This greatly enhances the productivity of design. Similarly, planning the manufacturing of a new part can include matching it with one of the part families in existence, thereby alleviating much of the burden of specific processing details.

The conversion to group technology and cellular production requires a systematic analysis of parts to identify the part families. This is often a major undertaking; it is a time-consuming job that involves the analysis of a considerable amount of data. Three primary methods for accomplishing this are visual inspection, examination of design and production data, and production flow analysis.

Visual inspection is the least accurate of the three but also the least costly and the simplest to perform. Examination of design and production data is more accurate but much more time-consuming; it is perhaps the most commonly used method of analysis. Production flow analysis has a manufacturing perspective and not a design perspective, because it examines operations sequences and machine routings to uncover similarities. Moreover, the operation sequences and routings are taken as givens; in reality the existing procedures may be far from optimal.

Conversion to cellular production can involve costly realignment of equipment. Consequently, a manager must weigh the benefits of a switch from a process layout to a cellular one against the cost of moving equipment as well as the cost and time needed for grouping parts.

Flexible manufacturing systems (FMSs) are more fully automated versions of cellular manufacturing.

FLEXIBLE MANUFACTURING SYSTEMS

A flexible manufacturing system (FMS) is a group of machines that include supervisory computer control, automatic material handling, and robots or other automated processing equipment. Reprogrammable controllers enable these systems to produce a variety of *similar* products. Systems may range from three or four machines to more than a dozen. They are designed to handle intermittent processing requirements with some of the benefits of automation and some of the flexibility of individual, or stand-alone, machines (e.g., N/C machines). Flexible manufacturing systems offer reduced labor costs and more consistent quality compared with more traditional manufacturing methods, lower capital investment and higher flexibility than "hard" automation, and relatively quick changeover time. Flexible manufacturing systems often appeal to managers who hope to achieve both the flexibility of job shop processing and the productivity of repetitive processing systems.

Flexible manufacturing system (FMS)

Although these are important benefits, an FMS also has certain limitations. One is that this type of system can handle a relatively narrow range of part variety, so it must be used for a family of similar parts, which all require similar machining. Also, an FMS requires longer planning and development times than more conventional processing equipment because of its increased complexity and cost. Furthermore, companies sometimes prefer a gradual approach to automation, and FMS represents a sizable chunk of technology.

Computer-integrated manufacturing (CIM) is a system that uses an integrating computer system to link a broad range of manufacturing activities, including engineering design, flexible manufacturing systems, purchasing, order processing, and production planning and control. Not all elements are absolutely necessary. For instance, CIM might be as simple as linking two or more FMSs by a host computer. More encompassing systems can link scheduling, purchasing, inventory control, shop control, and distribution. In effect, a CIM system integrates information from other areas of an organization with manufacturing.

Computer-integrated manufacturing (CIM)

The overall goal of using CIM is to link various parts of an organization to achieve rapid response to customer orders and/or product changes, to allow rapid production, and to reduce *indirect* labor costs.

A shining example of how process choices can lead to competitive advantages can be found at Allen-Bradley's computer-integrated manufacturing process in Milwaukee, Wisconsin. The company converted a portion of its factory to a fully automated "factory within a factory" to assemble contactors and relays for electrical motors. A handful of humans operate the factory, although once an order has been entered into the system, the machines do virtually all the work, including packaging and shipping, and quality control. Any defective items are removed from the line, and replacement parts are automatically ordered and scheduled to compensate for the defective items. The humans program the machines, monitor operations, and attend to any problems signaled by a system of warning lights.

As orders come into the plant, computers determine production requirements and schedules and order the necessary parts. Bar-coded labels that contain processing instructions are automatically placed on individual parts. As the parts approach a machine, a sensing device reads the bar code and communicates the processing instructions to the machine. The factory can produce 600 units an hour.

The company has realized substantial competitive advantages from the system. Orders can be completed and shipped within 24 hours of entry into the system, indirect labor costs and inventory costs have been greatly reduced, and quality is very high.

SERVICE LAYOUTS

As is the case with manufacturing, service layouts can often be categorized as product layouts, process layout, or fixed-position layouts. In a fixed-position service layout (e.g., appliance repair, roofing, landscaping, home remodeling, copier service), materials, labor, and equipment are brought to the customer's residence or office). Process layouts are common in services due mainly to the high degree of variety in customer processing requirements. Examples include hospitals, supermarkets and department stores, vehicle repair centers, and banks. If the service is organized sequentially, with all customers or work following the same or similar sequence, as it is in a car wash or a cafeteria line, a product layout is used.

However, service layout requirements are somewhat different from manufacturing layout requirements. The degree of customer contact and the degree of customization are two key factors in service layout design. If contact and customization are both high, as in health care and personal care, the service environment is a job shop, usually with high labor content and flexible equipment, and a layout that supports this. If customization is high but contact low (e.g., picture framing, tailoring), the layout can be arranged to facilitate workers and equipment. If contact is high but customization is low (e.g., supermarkets, gas stations), self-service is a possibility, in which case layout must take into account ease of obtaining the service as well as customer safety. If the degree of contact and the need for customization are low, the core service and the customer can be separated, making it easier to achieve a high degree of efficiency in operations. Highly standardized services may lend themselves to automation (e.g., Web services, online banking, ATM machines).

Let's consider some of these layouts.

Warehouse and Storage Layouts. The design of storage facilities presents a different set of factors than the design of factory layouts. Frequency of order is an important consideration; items that are ordered frequently should be placed near the entrance to the facility, and those ordered infrequently should be placed toward the rear of the facility. Any correlations between items are also significant (i.e., item A is usually ordered with item B), suggesting that placing those two items close together would reduce the cost and time of *picking* (retrieving) those items. Other considerations include the number and widths of aisles, the height of storage racks, rail and/or truck loading and unloading, and the need to periodically make a physical count of stored items.

Retail Layouts. The objectives that guide design of manufacturing layouts often pertain to cost minimization and product flow. However, with retail layouts such as department stores, supermarkets, and specialty stores, designers must take into account the presence of customers and the opportunity to influence sales volume and customer attitudes through carefully designed layouts. Traffic patterns and traffic flow are important factors to consider. Some large retail chains use standard layouts for all or most of their stores. This has several advantages. Most obvious is the ability to save time and money by using one layout instead of custom designing one for each store. Another advantage is to avoid confusing consumers who visit more than one store. In the case of service retail outlets, especially small ones such as dry cleaners, shoe repair, and auto service centers, layout design is much simpler.

Office Layouts. Office layouts are undergoing transformations as the flow of paperwork is replaced with the increasing use of electronic communications. This lessens the need to

KIOSKS BENEFIT CUSTOMERS BY SPEEDING UP TEDIOUS PROCESSES AND REDUCING WAITING TIME. AT MCDONALD'S, KIOSKS ACTUALLY INCREASE SALES BY AN AVERAGE OF $1 OVER FACE-TO-FACE PURCHASES. MANAGERS EXPLAIN THIS BY THE KIOSK'S ABILITY TO PROMPT CUSTOMERS FOR MORE PURCHASES BY SHOWING PICTURES OF PRODUCTS THEY MIGHT WANT TO BUY.

Scott Adams's Dilbert chronicles the impersonal "cubicle farms" of the modern office. IDEO designers created and lived in their own "Dilbertville" for several weeks to experience firsthand the challenges workers face. The result is a cubicle that allows workers to select from a "kit of parts" and create a space based on their own tastes and lifestyles. (www.ideo.com)

place office workers in a layout that optimizes the physical transfer of information or paperwork. Another trend is to create an image of openness; office walls are giving way to low-rise partitions, which also facilitate commication among workers.

Automation in Services. One way to improve productivity and reduce costs in services is to remove the customer from the process as much as possible. Automated services is one increasingly used alternative. For example, financial services use ATMs, automated call answering, online banking, and electronic funds transfers; retail stores use optical scanning to process sales; and the travel industry uses electronic reservation systems. Other examples of automated services include shipping, mail processing, communication, and health care services.

Automating services means more-standardized services and less need to involve the customer directly. However, service standardization brings trade-off. Generally costs are reduced and productivity increases, but the lack of customization and the inability to deal with a real person raise the risk of customer dissatisfaction.

Reading: Designing Supermarkets

David Schardt: The produce is over here, the dairy's over there. The soft drink specials are at the end of the aisles, the candy's at the checkout. Always.

A visit to your local supermarket isn't as haphazard as it seems. It's been laid out so that you spend as much as possible on what the store wants you to buy. And that's often more than you came in for, as we learned when we spoke to supermarket industry insiders.

Here's how a typical supermarket is designed to maximize sales.

On the Edge: The more time you spend shopping along the sides and back of the supermarket, the more money the store makes. About half its profits come from perimeter items like fruits and veggies, milk and cheese, and meat, poultry, and fish. That's also where you'll find the bakery, the salad bar, and the deli. If a store wants to distinguish itself from its competitors, it's got to be here.

Space Eaters: Some foods are so profitable that they command their own aisles. Breakfast cereals bring in more dollars per foot of shelf space than any other product in the interior of the store. So most supermarkets give cereals plenty of space.

(continued)

(concluded)

Soft drinks aren't as profitable . . . at least not on paper. But beverage manufacturers sweeten the pot with so much free merchandise and cash rebates that carbonated soft drinks end up being one of the biggest moneymakers in a typical store.

The Meating Place: TWhy are the meat, poultry, and seafood displays almost always along the back of the supermarket? So that you'll see them every time you emerge from an aisle. Not a bad place to put the most profitable sections of the store.

Going to the Dairy: Why are the dairy products usually as far away from the entrance as possible? Most everybody buys milk when they shop. To reach it, they've got to walk through a good chunk of the supermarket, often along the perimeter. That's right where the store wants shoppers.

Also, stores like to "anchor" a display by putting popular items at each end. That's why milk, for example, is often at one end of the dairy case and margarine and butter at the other. You've got to run the gauntlet of cheese, yogurts, dips, etc. to get what you came for.

Paying for Space: Every year, grocery chains are offered more than 15,000 new products, nearly all of which will fail. How do stores decide which ones to stock?

Moolah, in some cases. Large supermarkets often require manufacturers to pay for shelf space. "Slotting fees," as they're called, can range from $5,000 to $25,000 per supermarket chain for each new food. The small local tofu cheese plant seldom has that kind of money to throw around.

In "Prison": Some supermarket insiders call the aisles of the store the "prison." Once you're in one, you're stuck until you come out the other end. The "prison" is where most of the less-profitable (for the store) national and regional name brands are, so the more time you spend there, the less time you'll spend along the perimeter . . . buying higher-profit items.

Productive Produce: Think it's a coincidence that you almost always have to walk through the produce department when you enter a supermarket? The look of those shiny, neatly stacked fruits and vegetables is the most important influence on where people decide to shop.

It also doesn't hurt that produce is the second most profitable section (meat is first). While it occupies a little over 10 percent of the typical supermarket, it brings in close to 20 percent of the store's profits.

SOURCE: COPYRIGHT 1994, CSPI. REPRINTED FROM *NUTRITION ACTION HEALTHLETTER* (1875 CONNECTICUT AVENUE, N.W., SUITE 300, WASHINGTON, D.C. 10009-5728). USED WITH PERMISSION.

DESIGNING PRODUCT LAYOUTS: LINE BALANCING

www.ford.com

The goal of a product layout is to arrange workers or machines in the sequence that operations need to be performed. The sequence is referred to as a production line or an assembly line. These lines range from fairly short, with just a few operations, to long lines that have a large number of operations. Automobile assembly lines are examples of long lines. At the assembly line for Ford Mustangs, a Mustang travels about nine miles from start to finish!

Many of the benefits of a product layout relate to the ability to divide required work into a series of elemental tasks (e.g., "assemble parts C and D") that can be performed quickly and routinely by low-skilled workers or specialized equipment. The durations of these elemental tasks typically range from a few seconds to 15 minutes or more. Most time requirements are so brief that it would be impractical to assign only one task to each worker. For one thing, most workers would quickly become bored by the limited job scope. For another, the number of workers required to complete even a simple product or service would be enormous. Instead, tasks are usually grouped into manageable bundles and assigned to workstations staffed by one or two operators.

Line balancing

The process of deciding how to assign tasks to workstations is referred to as line balancing. The goal of line balancing is to obtain task groupings that represent approximately equal time requirements. This minimizes the idle time along the line and results in a high utilization of labor and equipment. Idle time occurs if task times are not equal among workstations; some stations are capable of producing at higher rates than others. These "fast" stations will experience periodic waits for the output from slower stations or else be forced into idleness to avoid buildups of work between stations. Unbalanced lines are undesirable in terms of inefficient utilization of labor and equipment and because they may create morale problems at the slower stations for workers who must work continuously.

Lines that are perfectly balanced will have a smooth flow of work as activities along the line are synchronized to achieve maximum utilization of labor and equipment. The major obstacle to attaining a perfectly balanced line is the difficulty of forming task bundles that have the same duration. One cause of this is that it may not be feasible to combine certain activities into the same bundle, either because of differences in equipment requirements or because the activities are not compatible (e.g., risk of contamination of paint from sanding). Another cause of difficulty is that differences among elemental task lengths cannot always be overcome by grouping tasks. A third cause of an inability to perfectly balance a line is that a required technological sequence may prohibit otherwise desirable task combinations. Consider a series of three operations that have durations of two minutes, four minutes, and two minutes, as shown in the following diagram. Ideally, the first and third operations could be combined at one workstation and have a total time equal to that of the second operation. However, it may not be possible to combine the first and third operations. In the case of an automatic car wash, scrubbing and drying operations could not realistically be combined at the same workstation due to the need to rinse cars between the two operations.

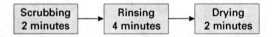

Line balancing involves assigning tasks to workstations. Usually, each workstation has one worker who handles all of the tasks at that station, although an option is to have several workers at a single workstation. For purposes of illustration, however, all of the examples and problems in this chapter have workstations with one worker. A manager could decide to use anywhere from one to five workstations to handle five tasks. With one workstation, all tasks would be done at that station; with five stations, one task would be assigned to each station. If two, three, or four workstations are used, some or all of the stations will have multiple tasks assigned to them. How does a manager decide how many stations to use?

The primary determinant is what the line's cycle time will be. The cycle time is the *maximum* time allowed at each workstation to perform assigned tasks before the work moves on. The cycle time also establishes the output rate of a line. For instance, if the cycle time is two minutes, units will come off the end of the line at the rate of one every two minutes. Hence, the line's capacity is a function of its cycle time.

Cycle time

We can gain some insight into task groupings and cycle time by considering a simple example.

Suppose that the work required to fabricate a certain product can be divided up into five elemental tasks, with the task times and precedence relationships as shown in the following diagram:

$$\rightarrow \boxed{\text{0.1 min.}} \rightarrow \boxed{\text{0.7 min.}} \rightarrow \boxed{\text{1.0 min.}} \rightarrow \boxed{\text{0.5 min.}} \rightarrow \boxed{\text{0.2 min.}} \rightarrow$$

The task times govern the range of possible cycle times. The *minimum* cycle time is equal to the *longest* task time (1.0 minute), and the *maximum* cycle time is equal to the sum of the task times ($0.1 + 0.7 + 1.0 + 0.5 + 0.2 = 2.5$ minutes). The minimum cycle time would apply if there were five workstations. The maximum cycle time would apply if all tasks were performed at a single workstation. The minimum and maximum cycle times are important because they establish the potential range of output for the line, which we can compute using the following formula:

$$\text{Output rate} = \frac{\text{Operating time per day}}{\text{Cycle time}} \qquad [3.1]$$

Assume that the line will operate for eight hours per day (480 minutes). With a cycle time of 1.0 minute, output would be

$$\frac{480 \text{ minutes per day}}{1.0 \text{ minute per unit}} = 480 \text{ units per day}$$

With a cycle time of 2.5 minutes, the output would be

$$\frac{480 \text{ minutes per day}}{2.5 \text{ minutes per unit}} = 192 \text{ units per day}$$

Assuming that no parallel activities are to be employed (e.g., two lines), the output selected for the line must fall in the range of 192 units per day to 480 units per day.

As a general rule, the cycle time is determined by the desired output; that is, a desired output level is selected, and the cycle time is computed. If the cycle time does not fall between the maximum and minimum bounds, the desired output rate must be revised. We can compute the cycle time using this equation:

$$\text{Cycle time} = \frac{\text{Operating time per day}}{\text{Desired output rate}} \qquad [3.2]$$

For example, suppose that the desired output rate is 480 units. Using Formula 3.2, the necessary cycle time is

$$\frac{480 \text{ minutes per day}}{480 \text{ units per day}} = 1.0 \text{ minute per unit}$$

The number of workstations that will be needed is a function of both the desired output rate and our ability to combine elemental tasks into workstations. We can determine the *theoretical minimum* number of stations necessary to provide a specified rate of output as follows:

$$N_{min} = \frac{\Sigma t}{\text{Cycle time}} \qquad [3.3]$$

where

N_{min} = Theoretical minimum number of stations

Σt = Sum of task times

Suppose the desired rate of output is the maximum of 480 units per day.[2] (This will require a cycle time of 1.0 minute.) The minimum number of stations required to achieve this goal is

$$N_{min} = \frac{2.5 \text{ minutes per unit}}{1 \text{ minute per unit per station}} = 2.5 \text{ stations}$$

Because 2.5 stations is not feasible, it is necessary to *round up* (because 2.5 is the minimum) to three stations. Thus, the actual number of stations used will equal or exceed three, depending on how successfully the tasks can be grouped into work stations.

Precedence diagram   A very useful tool in line balancing is a precedence diagram. Figure 3.10 illustrates a simple precedence diagram. It visually portrays the tasks that are to be performed along with the *sequential* requirements, that is, the *order* in which tasks must be performed. The diagram is read from left to right, so the initial task(s) are on the left and the final task is on the right. In terms of precedence requirements, we can see from the diagram, for example, that the only requirement to begin task *b* is that task *a* must be finished. However, in order to begin task *d,*

A Simple Precedence Diagram

figure 3.10

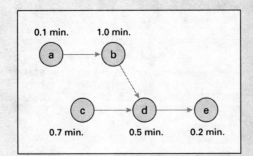

Line Balancing Procedure

table 3.5

1. Determine the cycle time and the minimum number of workstations.

2. Make assignments to workstations in order, beginning with Station 1. Tasks are assigned to workstations moving from left to right through the precedence diagram.

3. Before each assignment, use the following criteria to determine which tasks are eligible to be assigned to a workstation:
   a. All preceding tasks in the sequence have been assigned.
   b. The task time does not exceed the time remaining at the workstation.
   If no tasks are eligible, move on to the next workstation.

4. After each task assignment, determine the time remaining at the current workstation by subtracting the sum of times for tasks already assigned to it from the cycle time.

5. Break ties that occur using one of these rules:
   a. Assign the task with the longest task time.
   b. Assign the task with the greatest number of followers.
   If there is still a tie, choose one task arbitrarily.

6. Continue until all tasks have been assigned to workstations.

7. Compute appropriate measures (e.g., percent idle time, efficiency) for the set of assignments.

tasks b and c must *both* be finished. Note that the elemental tasks are the same ones that we have been using.

Now let's see how a line is balanced. This involves assigning tasks to workstations. Generally, no techniques are available that guarantee an optimal set of assignments. Instead, managers employ *heuristic (intuitive) rules,* which provide good and sometimes optimal sets of assignments. A number of line-balancing heuristics are in use, two of which are described here for purposes of illustration:

1. Assign tasks in order of most following tasks.
2. Assign tasks in order of greatest positional weight. Positional weight is the sum of each task's time and the times of all following tasks.

The general procedure used in line balancing is described in Table 3.5.

EXAMPLE 3.1

Arrange the tasks shown in Figure 3.10 into three workstations. Use a cycle time of 1.0 minute. Assign tasks in order of the most number of followers.

SOLUTION

WORKSTATION	TIME REMAINING	ELIGIBLE	ASSIGN TASK	REVISED TIME REMAINING	STATION IDLE TIME
1	1.0	a, c	a	0.9	
	0.9	c	c	0.2	
	0.2	none	—		0.2
2	1.0	b	b	0.0	0.0
3	1.0	d	d	0.5	
	0.5	e	e	0.3	
	0.3	—	—		0.3
					0.5

Comment: The initial "time remaining" for each workstation is equal to the cycle time. For a task to be eligible, tasks preceding it must have been assigned, and the task's time must not exceed the station's remaining time.

Example 3.1 is purposely simple; it is designed to illustrate the basic procedure. Later examples will illustrate tiebreaking, constructing precedence diagrams, and the positional weight method. Before considering those examples, let us first consider some measures of effectiveness that can be used for evaluating a given set of assignments.

Two widely used measures of effectiveness are

Balance delay

1. The *percentage of idle time* of the line. This is sometimes referred to as the balance delay. It can be computed as follows:

$$\text{Percentage of idle time} = \frac{\text{Idle time per cycle}}{N_{\text{actual}} \times \text{Cycle time}} \times 100 \qquad [3.4]$$

where

N_{actual} = Actual number of stations.

For the preceding example, the value is

$$\text{Percentage of idle time} = \frac{.5}{3 \times 1.0} \times 100 = 16.7\%$$

In effect, this is the average idle time divided by the cycle time, multiplied by 100. Note that cycle time refers to the actual cycle time that is achieved.

2. The *efficiency* of the line. This is computed as follows:

$$\text{Efficiency} = 100\% - \text{Percent idle time} \qquad [3.5]$$

Here,

$$\text{Efficiency} = 100\% - 16.7\% = 83.3\%$$

Now let's consider the question of whether the selected level of output should equal the maximum output possible. The minimum number of workstations needed is a function of the desired output rate and, therefore, the cycle time. Thus, a lower rate of output (hence, a longer cycle time) may result in a need for fewer stations. Hence, the manager must consider whether the potential savings realized by having fewer workstations would be greater than the decrease in profit resulting from producing fewer units.

The preceding examples serve to illustrate some of the fundamental concepts of line balancing. They are rather simple; in most real-life situations, the number of branches and tasks is often much greater. Consequently, the job of line balancing can be a good deal more complex. In many instances, the number of alternatives for grouping tasks is so great that it is virtually impossible to conduct an exhaustive review of all possibilities. For this reason, many real-life problems of any magnitude are solved using heuristic approaches. The purpose of a heuristic approach is to reduce the number of alternatives that must be considered, but it does not guarantee an optimal solution.

SOME GUIDELINES FOR LINE BALANCING

In balancing an assembly line, tasks are assigned *one at a time* to the line, starting at the first workstation. At each step, the unassigned tasks are checked to determine which are eligible for assignment. Next, the eligible tasks are checked to see which of them will fit in the workstation being loaded. A heuristic is used to select one of the tasks that will fit, and the task is assigned. This process is repeated until there are no eligible tasks that will fit. Then the next workstation can be loaded. This continues until all tasks are assigned. The objective is to minimize the idle time for the line subject to technological and output constraints.

Technological constraints tell us which elemental tasks are *eligible* to be assigned at a particular position on the line. Technological constraints can result from the precedence or ordering relationships among the tasks. The precedence relationships require that certain tasks must be performed before others (and so, must be assigned to workstations before others). Thus, in a car wash, the rinsing operation must be performed before the drying operation. The drying operation is not eligible for assignment until the rinsing operation has been assigned. Technological constraints may also result from two tasks being incompatible (e.g., space restrictions or the nature of the operations may prevent their being placed in the same work center). For example, sanding and painting operations would not be assigned to the same work center because dust particles from the sanding operation could contaminate the paint.

Output constraints, on the other hand, determine the maximum amount of work that a manager can assign to each workstation, and this determines whether an eligible task *will fit* at a workstation. The desired output rate determines the cycle time, and the sum of the task times assigned to any workstation must not exceed the cycle time. If a task can be assigned to a workstation without exceeding the cycle time, then the task will fit.

Once it is known which tasks are *eligible* and *will fit*, the manager can select the task to be assigned (if there is more than one to choose from). This is where the heuristic rules help us decide which task to assign from among those that are eligible and will fit.

To clarify the terminology, *following tasks* are all tasks that you would encounter by following all paths from the task in question through the precedence diagram. *Preceding tasks* are all tasks you would encounter by tracing all paths *backward* from the task in question. In the precedence diagram below, tasks *b, d, e,* and *f* are followers of task *a.* Tasks *a, b,* and *c* are preceding tasks for *e.*

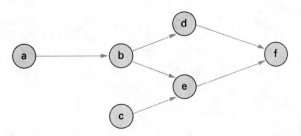

The *positional weight* for a task is the sum of the task times for itself and all its following tasks.

Neither of the heuristics *guarantees* the *best* solution, or even a good solution to the line-balancing problem, but they do provide guidelines for developing a solution. It may be useful to apply several different heuristics to the same problem and pick the best (least idle time) solution out of those developed.

EXAMPLE 3.2

Using the information contained in the table shown, do each of the following:

1. Draw a precedence diagram.
2. Assuming an eight-hour workday, compute the cycle time needed to obtain an output of 400 units per day.
3. Determine the minimum number of workstations required.
4. Assign tasks to workstations using this rule: Assign tasks according to greatest number of following tasks. In case of a tie, use the tiebreaker of assigning the task with the longest processing time first.

TASK	IMMEDIATE FOLLOWER	TASK TIME (IN MINUTES)
a	b	0.2
b	e	0.2
c	d	0.8
d	f	0.6
e	f	0.3
f	g	1.0
g	h	0.4
h	end	0.3
		$\Sigma t = 3.8$

5. Compute the resulting percent idle time and efficiency of the system.

SOLUTION

1. Drawing a precedence diagram is a relatively straightforward task. Begin with activities with no predecessors. We see from the list of Immediate Followers that tasks a and c do not appear. Hence, they have no immediate predecessors. We build from here.

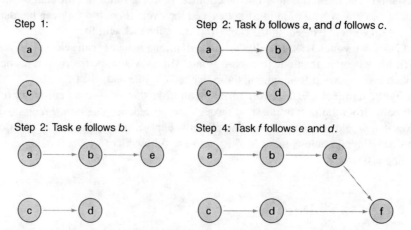

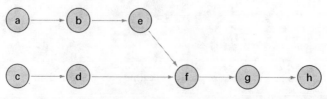

2. Cycle time $= \dfrac{\text{Operating time}}{\text{Desired output rate}} = \dfrac{480 \text{ minutes per day}}{400 \text{ units per day}} = 1.2 \text{ minutes per cycle}$

3. $N_{min} = \dfrac{\Sigma t}{\text{Cycle time}} = \dfrac{3.8 \text{ minutes per unit}}{1.2 \text{ minutes per cycle per station}} = 3.17$ stations (round to 4)

4. Beginning with station 1, make assignments following this procedure: Determine from the precedence diagram which tasks are eligible for assignment. Then determine which of the eligible tasks will fit the time remaining for the station. Use the tiebreaker if necessary. Once a task has been assigned, remove it from consideration. When a station cannot take any more assignments, go on to the next station. Continue until all tasks have been assigned.

Station	Time Remaining	Eligible	Will Fit	Assign (task time)	Revised Time Remaining	Idle
1	1.2	a, c*	a, c*	a (0.2)	1.0	
	1.0	c, b**	c, b**	c (0.8)	0.2	
	0.2	b, d	b	b (0.2)	0.0	
	0	e, d	None	—		0.0
2	1.2	e, d	e, d	d (0.6)	0.6	
	0.6	e	e	e (0.3)	0.3	
	0.3***	f	None	—		0.3
3	1.2	f	f	f (1.0)	0.2	
	0.2	g	None	—		0.2
4	1.2	g	g	g (0.4)	0.8	
	0.8	h	h	h (0.3)	0.5	
	0.5	—	—	—		0.5
						1.0 min.

*Neither a nor c has any predecessors, so both are eligible. Task a was assigned since it has more followers.

**Once a is assigned, b and c are now eligible. Both will fit in the time remaining of 1.0 minute. The tie cannot be broken by the "most followers" rule, so the longer task is assigned.

***Although f is eligible, this task will not fit, so station 2 is left with 0.3 minute of idle time per 1.2-minute cycle.

These assignments are shown in the following diagram. Note: One should not expect that heuristic approaches will always produce optimal solutions; they merely provide a practical way to deal with complex problems that may not lend themselves to optimizing techniques. Moreover, different heuristics often yield different answers.

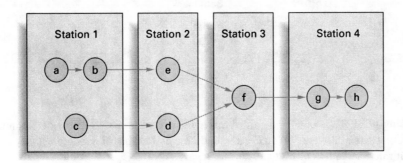

5. Percent idle time $= \dfrac{1.0 \text{ min.}}{4 \times 1.2 \text{ min.}} \times 100 = 20.83\%.$

Efficiency $= 100\% - 20.83\% = 79.17\%.$

OTHER FACTORS

The preceding discussion on line balancing presents a relatively straightforward approach to approximating a balanced line. In practice, the ability to do this usually involves additional considerations, some of which are technical.

Technical considerations include skill requirements of different tasks. If skill requirements of tasks are quite different, it may not be feasible to place the tasks in the same workstation. Similarly, if the tasks themselves are incompatible (e.g., the use of fire and flammable liquids), it may not be feasible even to place them in stations that are near to each other.

Developing a workable plan for balancing a line may also require consideration of human factors as well as equipment and space limitations.

Although it is convenient to treat assembly operations as if they occur at the same rate time after time, it is more realistic to assume that whenever humans are involved, task completion times will be variable. The reasons for the variations are numerous, including fatigue, boredom, and failure to concentrate on the task at hand. Absenteeism also can affect line balance. Minor variability can be dealt with by allowing some slack along the line. However, if more variability is inherent in even a few tasks, that will severely impact the ability to achieve a balanced line.

For these reasons, lines that involve human tasks are more of an ideal than a reality. In practice, lines are rarely perfectly balanced. However, this is not entirely bad, because some unbalance means that slack exists at points along the line, which can reduce the impact of brief stoppages at some workstations. Also, workstations that have slack can be used for new workers who may not be "up to speed."

OTHER APPROACHES

Companies use a number of other approaches to achieve a smooth flow of production. One approach is to use *parallel workstations*. These are beneficial for bottleneck operations which would otherwise disrupt the flow of product as it moves down the line. The bottlenecks may be the result of difficult or very long tasks. Parallel workstations increase the work flow and provide flexibility.

Consider this example.[3] A job has four tasks; task times are 1 minute, 1 minute, 2 minutes, and 1 minute. The cycle time for the line would be 2 minutes, and the output rate would be 30 units per hour:

$$\frac{60 \text{ minutes per hour}}{2 \text{ minutes per unit}} = 30 \text{ units per hour}$$

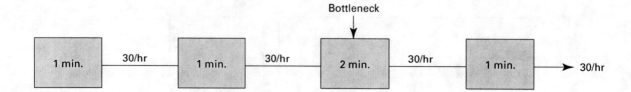

Using parallel stations for the third task would result in a cycle time of 1 minute because the output rate at the parallel stations would be equal to that of a single station and allow an output rate for the line of 60 units per hour:

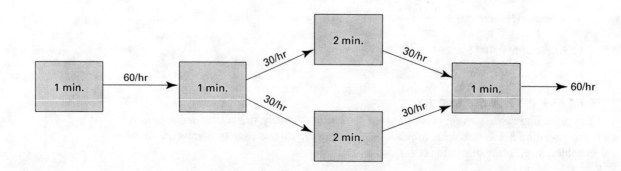

Another approach to achieving a balanced line is to *cross-train* workers so that they are able to perform more than one task. Then, when bottlenecks occur, the workers with temporarily increased idle time can assist other workers who are temporarily overburdened, thereby maintaining an even flow of work along the line. This is sometimes referred to as *dynamic line balancing,* and it is used most often in lean production systems.

Still another approach is to design a line to handle more than one product on the same line. This is referred to as a *mixed model line.* Naturally, the products have to be fairly similar, so that the tasks involved are pretty much the same for all products. This approach offers great flexibility in varying the amount of output of the products. The following reading describes one such line.

READING: BMW'S STRATEGY: FLEXIBILITY

The assembly line in Dingolfing, Germany, where BMW assembles its 7-Series, has built-in flexibility that allows it to easily produce multiple models. Rival car producers typically configure their assembly lines to produce just a single model at a time. In order for them to produce a different model, the line must be shut down so that it can be changed over to be able to produce the different model. BMW's production flexibility enables its line to easily respond to market fluctuations while avoiding the costly changeovers that its rivals' more rigid lines require.

SOURCE: BASED ON "BETTING ON THE S" *THE WALL STREET JOURNAL,* JULY 11, 2005, P. B1.

DESIGNING PROCESS LAYOUTS

The main issue in designing process layouts concerns the relative positioning of the departments involved. As illustrated in Figure 3.11, departments must be assigned to locations. The problem is to develop a reasonably good layout; some combinations will be more desirable than others. For example, some departments may benefit from adjacent locations whereas others should be separated. A lab with delicate equipment would not be located near a department that had equipment with strong vibrations. Conversely, two departments that share some of the same equipment would benefit from being close together.

Layouts can also be influenced by external factors such as the location of entrances, loading docks, elevators, windows, and areas of reinforced flooring. Also important are noise levels, safety, and the size and locations of restrooms.

In some instances (e.g., the layouts of supermarkets, gas stations, and fast-food chains), a sufficient number of installations having similar characteristics justify the development of standardized layouts. For example, the use of the same basic patterns in McDonald's fast-food locations facilitates construction of new structures and employee training. Food preparation, order taking, and customer service follow the same pattern throughout the chain. Installation and service of equipment are also standardized. This same concept has been successfully employed in computer software products such as Microsoft Windows and the Macintosh Operating System. Different applications are designed with certain basic features in common, so that a user familiar with one application can readily use other applications without having to start from scratch with each new application.

www.mcdonalds.com

The majority of layout problems involve single rather than multiple locations, and they present unique combinations of factors that do not lend themselves to a standardized approach. Consequently, these layouts require customized designs.

A major obstacle to finding the most efficient layout of departments is the large number of possible assignments. For example, there are more than 87 billion different ways that 14 departments can be assigned to 14 locations if the locations form a single line. Different location configurations (e.g., 14 departments in a two-by-seven grid) often reduce the number of possibilities, as do special requirements (e.g., the stamping department may have to be assigned to a location with reinforced flooring). Still, the remaining number of layout

figure 3.11   Work Centers must be Assigned to Locations

	Locations			Work centers to be assigned
	A	B	C	1
				2
				3
	D	E	F	4
				5
				6

THE IGUS MANUFACTURING PLANT IN COLOGNE, GERMANY, CAN SHRINK OR EXPAND IN A FLASH. ITS FLEXIBLE DESIGN KEEPS IT COMPETITIVE IN A FAST-CHANGING MARKET. BECAUSE THE LAYOUT OF THE PLANT CHANGES SO OFTEN, SOME EMPLOYEES USE SCOOTERS TO MORE EFFICIENTLY PROVIDE NEEDED SKILLS, SUPPLIES, AND SERVICES TO MULTIPLE WORKSTATIONS. (WWW.IGUS.COM)

possibilities is quite large. Unfortunately, no algorithms exist to identify the best layout arrangement under all circumstances. Often planners must rely on heuristic rules to guide trial-and-error efforts for a satisfactory solution to each problem.

MEASURES OF EFFECTIVENESS

One advantage of process layouts is their ability to satisfy a variety of processing requirements. Customers or materials in these systems require different operations and different sequences of operations, which causes them to follow different paths through the system. Material-oriented systems necessitate the use of variable-path material-handling equipment to move materials from work center to work center. In customer-oriented systems, people must travel or be transported from work center to work center. In both cases, transportation costs or time can be significant. Because of this factor, one of the major objectives in process layout is to minimize transportation cost, distance, or time. This is usually accomplished by locating departments with relatively high interdepartmental work flow as close together as possible.

Other concerns in choosing among alternative layouts include initial costs in setting up the layout, expected operating costs, the amount of effective capacity created, and the ease of modifying the system.

In situations that call for improvement of an existing layout, costs of relocating any work center must be weighed against the potential benefits of the move.

INFORMATION REQUIREMENTS

The design of process layouts requires the following information:

1. A list of departments or work centers to be arranged, their approximate dimensions, and the dimensions of the building or buildings that will house the departments.
2. A projection of future work flows between the various work centers.
3. The distance between locations and the cost per unit of distance to move loads between locations.
4. The amount of money to be invested in the layout.
5. A list of any special considerations (e.g., operations that must be close to each other or operations that must be separated).
6. The location of key utilities, access and exit points, loading docks, and so on, in existing buildings.

The ideal situation is to first develop a layout and then design the physical structure around it, thus permitting maximum flexibility in design. This procedure is commonly followed when new facilities are constructed. Nonetheless, many layouts must be developed in existing structures where floor space, the dimensions of the building, location of entrances and elevators, and other similar factors must be carefully weighed in designing the layout. Note that multilevel structures pose special problems for layout planners.

MINIMIZING TRANSPORTATION COSTS OR DISTANCES

The most common goals in designing process layouts are minimization of transportation costs or distances traveled. In such cases, it can be very helpful to summarize the necessary data in *from-to charts* like those illustrated in Tables 3.6 and 3.7. Table 3.6 indicates the distance between each of the locations, and Table 3.7 indicates actual or projected work flow between each pair. For instance, the distance chart reveals that a trip from location A to location B will

Distance Between Locations (Meters)   **table 3.6**

		LOCATION		
FROM	TO	A	B	C
A			20	40
B				30
C				

Interdepartmental Work Flow (Loads per Day)   **table 3.7**

		DEPARTMENT		
		1	2	3
	1		30	170
Dept.	2			100
	3			

involve a distance of 20 meters. (Distances are often measured between department centers.) Oddly enough, the length of a trip between locations A and B may differ depending on the *direction* of the trip, due to one-way routes, elevators, or other factors. To simplify the discussion, assume a constant distance between any two locations regardless of direction. However, it is not realistic to assume that interdepartmental work flows are equal—there is no reason to suspect that department 1 will send as much work to department 2 as department 2 sends to 1. For example, several departments may send goods to packaging, but packaging may send only to the shipping department.

Transportation costs can also be summarized in from-to charts, but we shall avoid that complexity, assuming instead that costs are a direct, linear function of distance.

mhhe.com/stevenson10e

EXAMPLE 3.3

Assign the three departments shown in Table 3.7 to locations A, B, and C, which are separated by the distances shown in Table 3.6, in such a way that transportation cost is minimized. Note that Table 3.7 summarizes the flows in both directions. Use this heuristic: Assign departments with the greatest interdepartmental work flow first to locations that are closest to each other.

SOLUTION

Ranking departments according to highest work flow and locations according to highest interlocation distances helps in making assignments.

Trip	Distance (meters)	Department Pair	Work Flow
A–B	20	1–3	170
B–C	30	2–3	100
A–C	40	1–2	30

From these listings, you can see that departments 1 and 3 have the highest interdepartmental work flow, and that locations A and B are the closest. Thus, it seems reasonable to consider assigning 1 and 3 to locations A and B, although it is not yet obvious which department should be assigned to which location. Further inspection of the work flow list reveals that 2 and 3 have higher work flow than 1 and 2, so 2 and 3 should probably be located more closely than 1 and 2. Hence, it would seem reasonable to place 3 between 1 and 2, or at least centralize that department with respect to the other two. The resulting assignments might appear as illustrated in Figure 3.12.

figure 3.12   Interdepartmental Work Flows for Assigned Departments

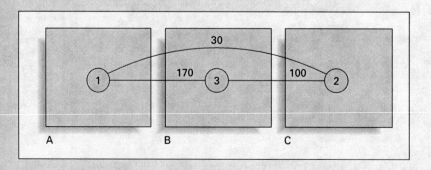

If the cost per meter to move any load is $1, you can compute the total daily transportation cost for this assignment by multiplying each department's number of loads by the trip distance, and summing those quantities:

DEPARTMENT	NUMBER OF LOADS BETWEEN	LOCATION	DISTANCE TO:	LOADS × DISTANCE
1	2: 30	A	C: 40	30 × 40 = 1,200
	3: 170		B: 20	170 × 20 = 3,400
2	3: 100			
3		B	C: 30	100 × 30 = 3,000
				7,600

At $1 per load meter, the cost for this plan is $7,600 per day. Even though it might appear that this arrangement yields the lowest transportation cost, you cannot be absolutely positive of that without actually computing the total cost for every alternative and comparing it to this one. Instead, rely on the choice of reasonable heuristic rules such as those demonstrated above to arrive at a satisfactory, if not optimal, solution. ●

CLOSENESS RATINGS

Although the preceding approach is widely used, it suffers from the limitation of focusing on only one objective, and many situations involve multiple criteria. Richard Muther developed a more general approach to the problem, which allows for subjective input from analysis or managers to indicate the relative importance of each combination of department pairs.[4] That information is then summarized in a grid like that shown in Figure 3.13. Read the grid in the same way as you would read a mileage chart on a road map, except that letters rather than distances appear at the intersections. The letters represent the importance of closeness for each department pair, with A being the most important and X being an undesirable pairing. Thus, in the grid it is "absolutely necessary" to locate 1 and 2 close to each other because there is an A at the intersection of those departments on the grid. On the other hand, 1 and 4 should not be close together because their intersection has an X. In practice, the letters on the grid are often accompanied by numbers that indicate the reason for each assignment; they are omitted here to simplify the illustration. Muther suggests the following list:

1. Use same equipment or facilities.
2. Share the same personnel or records.

A Muther Grid

figure 3.13

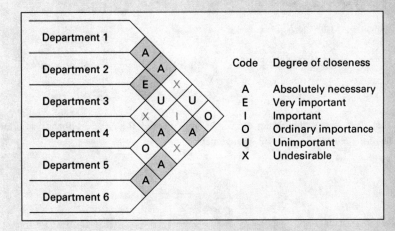

3. Sequence of work flow.
4. Ease of communication.
5. Unsafe or unpleasant conditions.
6. Similar work performed.

EXAMPLE 3.4

Assign the six departments in Figure 3.13 to a 2×3 set of locations using the heuristic rule: Assign critical departments first, because they are the most important.

SOLUTION

Critical pairs of departments are those with A or X ratings. Prepare a list of those by referring to the grid:

A LINKS	X LINKS
1–2	1–4
1–3	3–6
2–6	3–4
3–5	
4–6	
5–6	

Next, form a cluster of A links, beginning with the department that appears most frequently in the A list (in this case, 6). For instance:

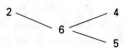

Take the remaining A links in order, and add them to this main cluster where possible, rearranging the cluster as necessary. Form separate clusters for departments that do not link with the main cluster. In this case, all link with the main cluster.

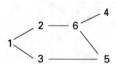

Next, graphically portray the X links:

Observe that, as it stands, the cluster of A links also satisfies the X separations. It is a fairly simple exercise to fit the cluster into a 2×3 arrangement:

1	2	6
3	5	4

Note that the lower-level ratings have also been satisfied with this arrangement, even though no attempt was made to explicitly consider the E and I ratings. Naturally, not every problem will yield the same results, so it may be necessary to do some additional adjusting to see if improvements can be made, keeping in mind that the A and X assignments deserve the greatest consideration.

Note that departments are considered close not only when they touch side to side but also when they touch corner to corner. ●

The value of this rating approach is that it permits the use of multiple objectives and subjective inputs. Its limitations relate to the use of subjective inputs in general: They are imprecise and unreliable.

SUMMARY

Process selection choices often have strategic implications for organizations. They can affect cost, quality, productivity, customer satisfaction, and competitive advantage. Process types include job shop, batch processing, repetitive processing, continuous processing, and projects. Process type determines how work is organized, and it has implications for the entire organization and its supply chain. Process type and layout are closely related.

Layout decisions are an important aspect of the design of operations systems, affecting operating costs and efficiency. Layout decisions are often closely related to process selection decisions.

Product layouts are geared to high-volume output of standardized items. Workers and equipment are arranged according to the technological sequence required by the product or service involved. Emphasis in design is on work flow through the system, and specialized processing and handling equipment is often used. Product layouts are highly vulnerable to breakdowns. Preventive maintenance is used to reduce the occurrence of breakdowns.

Process layouts group similar activities into departments or other work centers. These systems can handle a wide range of processing requirements and are less susceptible to breakdowns. However, the variety of processing requirements necessitates continual routing and scheduling and the use of variable-path material-handling equipment. The rate of output is generally much lower than that of product layouts.

Fixed-position layouts are used when size, fragility, cost, or other factors make it undesirable or impractical to move a product through a system. Instead, workers, equipment, and materials are brought to the product.

The main design efforts in product layout development focus on dividing up the work required to produce a product or service into a series of tasks that are as nearly equal as possible. The goal is to achieve a high degree of utilization of labor and equipment. In process layout, design efforts often focus on the relative positioning of departments to minimize transportation costs or to meet other requirements concerning the proximity of certain department pairs.

The large number of possible alternatives to layout problems prevents an examination of each one. Instead, heuristic rules guide discovery of alternatives. The solutions thus obtained are usually satisfactory although not necessarily optimal. Computer packages are available to reduce the effort required to obtain solutions to layout problems, but these too rely largely on heuristic methods.

KEY TERMS

Technological innovation The discovery and development of new or improved products, services, or processes for producing or providing them.

Technology The application of scientific discoveries to the development and improvement of products and services and operations processes.

Project A nonrepetitive set of activities directed toward a unique goal within a limited time frame.

Product or service profiling Linking key product or service requirements to process capabilities.

Automation Machinery that has sensing and control devices that enable it to operate automatically.

Computer-aided manufacturing (CAM) The use of computers in process control.

Numerically controlled (N/C) machines Machines that perform operations by following mathematical processing instructions.

Robot A machine consisting of a mechanical arm, a power supply, and a controller.

Product layout Layout that uses standardized processing operations to achieve smooth, rapid, high-volume flow.

Production line Standardized layout arranged according to a fixed sequence of production tasks.

Assembly line Standardized layout arranged according to a fixed sequence of assembly tasks.

Process layouts Layouts that can handle varied processing requirements.

Intermittent processing Nonrepetitive processing.

Fixed-position layout Layout in which the product or project remains stationary, and workers, materials, and equipment are moved as needed.

Cellular production Layout in which workstations are grouped into a cell that can process items that have similar processing requirements.

Group technology The grouping into part families of items with similar design or manufacturing characteristics.

Flexible manufacturing system (FMS) A group of machines designed to handle intermittent processing requirements and produce a variety of similar products.

Computer-integrated manufacturing (CIM) A system for linking a broad range of manufacturing activities through an integrating computer system.

Line balancing The process of assigning tasks to workstations in such a way that the workstations have approximately equal time requirements.

Cycle time The maximum time allowed at each workstation to complete its set of tasks on a unit.

Precedence diagram A diagram that shows elemental tasks and their precedence requirements.

Balance delay Percentage of idle time of a line.

SOLVED PROBLEMS

PROBLEM 1

The tasks shown in the following precedence diagram are to be assigned to workstations with the intent of minimizing idle time. Management has designed an output rate of 275 units per day. Assume 440 minutes are available per day.

a. Determine the appropriate cycle time.
b. What is the minimum number of stations possible?
c. Assign tasks using the "positional weight" rule: Assign tasks with highest following times (including a task's own time) first. Break ties using greatest number of following tasks.
d. Compute efficiency.

Solution

a. Cycle time $= \dfrac{\text{Operating time}}{\text{Desired output}} = \dfrac{440 \text{ minutes per day}}{275 \text{ units per day}} = 1.6 \text{ minutes}$

b. $N = \dfrac{\Sigma t}{\text{Cycle time}} = \dfrac{4.2}{1.6 \text{ minutes}} = 2.625$ (round to 3)

c. Add positional weights (task time plus the sum of all following times) to the diagram. Start at the right end and work backward:

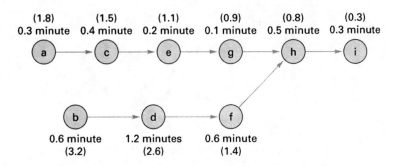

STATION	TIME REMAINING*	ELIGIBLE	WILL FIT	ASSIGN TASK/TIME	STATION IDLE TIME
1	1.6	a, b	a, b	b/0.6	
	1.0	a, d	a	a/0.3	
	0.7	c, d	c	c/0.4	
	0.3	e, d	e	e/0.2	
	0.1	g, d	g	g/0.1	
	0	—	—	—	0
2	1.6	d	d	d/1.2	
	0.4	f	none	none	0.4
3	1.6	f	f	f/0.6	
	1.0	h	h	h/0.5	
	0.5	i	i	i/0.3	
	0.2	—	—	—	0.2
					0.6

*The initial time for each station is the cycle time computed in part *a.*

The resulting assignments are shown below.

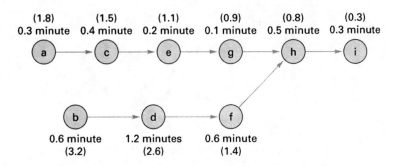

d. Efficiency $= 100\% - \text{Percent idle time} = 100\% - \dfrac{0.6 \text{ min.}}{3 \times 1.6 \text{ min.}}100 = 87.5\%.$

PROBLEM 2

Assign nine automobile service departments to bays in a 3×3 grid so that the closeness ratings in the following matrix are satisfied. (The unimportant and ordinary-importance ratings have been omitted to simplify the example.) The location of department 4 must be in the upper right-hand corner of the grid to satisfy a town ordinance.

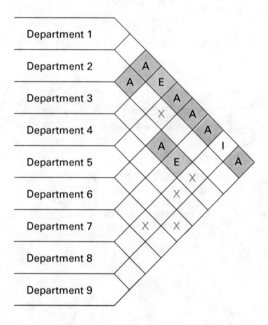

Solution

Note that department 1 has many A ratings, making it a strong candidate for the center position in the grid. We can form a cluster of departments that should be close together:

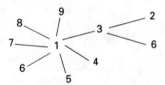

Next, we can identify departmental pairings that should be avoided:

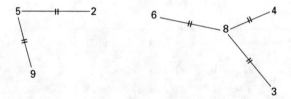

These departments should be spaced around the perimeter of the grid. After a bit of trial and error, the final grid shown below emerged. Check it against the rating matrix to see if it satisfies the ratings.

2	3	4
9	1	6
8	7	5

PROBLEM 3

Five departments are to be assigned to locations B–F in the grid. (For technical reasons, department 6 must be assigned to location A.) Transportation cost is $2 per foot. The objective is to minimize total transportation cost. Information on interdepartmental work flows and distances between locations is shown in the following tables. Assign departments with the greatest interdepartmental work flow first.

		DISTANCE BETWEEN LOCATIONS (FEET)					
FROM	TO	A	B	C	D	E	F
A		—	50	100	50	80	130
B			—	50	90	40	70
C				—	140	60	50
D					—	50	120
E						—	50
F							—

		NUMBER OF TRIPS PER DAY BETWEEN CENTERS					
FROM	TO	1	2	3	4	5	6
1		—	125	62	64	25	50
2			—	10	17	26	54
3				—	2	0	20
4					—	13	2
5						—	5
6							—

A Dept. 6	B	C
D	E	F

Solution

First either rank or arrange the work flows from high to low. Here they have been arranged from high to low.

DEPT.	WORK FLOW	DEPT.	WORK FLOW
1–2	125	2–4	17
1–4	64	4–5	13
1–3	62	2–3	10
2–6	54	5–6	5
1–6	50	3–4	2
2–5	26	4–6	2
1–5	25	3–5	0
3–6	20		

From this, we can see that departments 1 and 2 have the greatest interdepartmental work flow, so they should be close, perhaps at B and E. Next, work flows for 1–3 and 1–4 are high. Note, though, that the work flow for 3–4 is low, suggesting that they need not be close. Instead, we would place them on either side of department 1. Note also that 3–4 is only 2, 3–5 is 0, while 3–6 is 20 and 4–5 is 13. Hence, place department 3 at location D, department 4 at location F, and department 5 at location C.

A Dept. 6	B Dept. 2	C Dept. 5
D Dept. 3	E Dept. 1	F Dept. 4

Total cost:

TRIP		b DISTANCE	c FREQUENCY	(b × c × \$2) COST
1–2	(B–E)	40	125	\$10,000
1–3	(D–E)	50	62	6,200
1–4	(F–E)	50	64	6,400
1–5	(E–C)	60	25	3,000
1–6	(A–E)	80	50	8,000
2–3	(B–D)	90	10	1,800
2–4	(B–F)	70	17	2,380
2–5	(B–C)	50	26	2,600
2–6	(A–B)	50	54	5,400
3–4	(F–D)	120	2	480
3–5	(D–C)	140	0	0
3–6	(A–D)	50	20	2,000
4–5	(C–F)	50	13	1,300
4–6	(A–F)	130	2	520
5–6	(A–C)	100	5	1,000
				\$51,080

DISCUSSION AND REVIEW QUESTIONS

1 Explain the importance of process selection in system design.
2 Briefly describe the five process types, and indicate the kinds of situations in which each would be used.
3 Briefly discuss the advantages and disadvantages of automation.
4 Briefly describe computer-assisted approaches to production.
5 What is a flexible manufacturing system, and under what set of circumstances is it most appropriate?
6 Why is management of technology important?
7 Why might the choice of equipment that provides flexibility sometimes be viewed as a management copout?
8 What are the trade-offs that occur when a process layout is used? What are the trade-offs that occur when a product layout is used?
9 List some common reasons for redesigning layouts.
10 Briefly describe the two main layout types.
11 What are the main advantages of a product layout? The main disadvantages?
12 What are the main advantages of a process layout? The main disadvantages?
13 What is the goal of line balancing? What happens if a line is unbalanced?
14 Why are routing and scheduling continual problems in process layouts?
15 Compare equipment maintenance strategies in product and process layouts.
16 Briefly outline the impact that job sequence has on each of the layout types.
17 The City Transportation Planning Committee must decide whether to begin a long-term project to build a subway system or to upgrade the present bus service. Suppose you are an expert in fixed-path and variable-path material-handling equipment, and the committee seeks your counsel on this matter. What are the advantages and limitations of the subway and bus systems?
18 Identify the fixed-path and variable-path material-handling equipment commonly found in supermarkets.
19 What are heuristic approaches, and why are they used in designing layouts?
20 Why are product layouts atypical in service environments?
21 According to a study by the Alliance of American Insurers, it costs more than three times the original purchase price in parts and labor to reconstruct a wrecked Chevrolet. Explain the reasons for this large discrepancy in terms of the processes used to assemble the original car and those required to reconstruct the wrecked car.
22 Name some ways that a layout can help or hinder productivity.
23 What is cellular manufacturing? What are its main benefits and limitations?

24 What is group technology?

25 Explain the consequences of task time variability on line balancing.

TAKING STOCK

1 Name three major trade-offs in process selection.

2 What trade-offs are involved when deciding how often to rebalance an assembly line?

3 Who needs to be involved in process selection?

4 Who needs to be involved in layout design?

5 In what ways does technology have an impact on process selection? How can technology impact layout decisions?

CRITICAL THINKING EXERCISES

1 There are several factors that must exist in order to make automation feasible. Name the two or three most important factors and briefly explain their importance.

2 Layout decisions affect a wide range of facilities, from factories, supermarkets, offices, department stores, and warehouses, to malls, parking lots and garages, and kitchens. Layout is also important in the design of some products such as the interiors of automobiles and the arrangement of components inside computers and other electronic devices. Select three different items from this list, or other similar items, and explain for each what the four or five key considerations for layout design are.

PROBLEMS

1 An assembly line with 17 tasks is to be balanced. The longest task is 2.4 minutes, and the total time for all tasks is 18 minutes. The line will operate for 450 minutes per day.

a. What are the minimum and maximum cycle times?

b. What range of output is theoretically possible for the line?

c. What is the minimum number of workstations needed if the maximum output rate is to be sought?

d. What cycle time will provide an output rate of 125 units per day?

e. What output potential will result if the cycle time is (1) 9 minutes? (2) 15 minutes?

2 A manager wants to assign tasks to workstations as efficiently as possible, and achieve an hourly output of 33⅓ units. Assume the shop works a 60-minute hour. Assign the tasks shown in the accompanying precedence diagram (times are in minutes) to workstations using the following rules:

a. In order of most following tasks. Tiebreaker: greatest positional weight.

b. In order of greatest positional weight.

c. What is the efficiency?

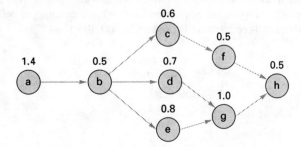

3 A manager wants to assign tasks to workstations as efficiently as possible, and achieve an hourly output of 4 units. The department uses a working time of 56 minutes per hour. Assign the tasks shown in the accompanying precedence diagram (times are in minutes) to workstations using the following rules:

a. In order of most following tasks. Tiebreaker: greatest positional weight.

b. In order of greatest positional weight.

c. What is the efficiency?

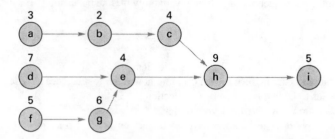

4   A producer of inkiet copiers is planning to add a new line of copiers, and you have been asked to balance the process, given the following task times and precedence relationships. Assume that cycle time is to be the minimum possible.

Task	Length (minutes)	Immediate Follower
a	0.2	b
b	0.4	d
c	0.3	d
d	1.3	g
e	0.1	f
f	0.8	g
g	0.3	h
h	1.2	end

a. Do each of the following:
   (1) Draw the precedence diagram.
   (2) Assign tasks to stations in order of greatest number of following tasks.
   (3) Determine the percentage of idle time.
   (4) Compute the rate of output in copiers per day that could be expected for this line assuming a 420-minute working day.
b. Answer these questions:
   (1) What is the shortest cycle time that will permit use of only two workstations? Is this cycle time feasible? Identify the tasks you would assign to each station.
   (2) Determine the percentage of idle time that would result if two stations were used.
   (3) What is the daily output under this arrangement?
   (4) Determine the output rate that would be associated with the maximum cycle time.

5   As part of a major plant renovation project, the industrial engineering department has been asked to balance a revised assembly operation to achieve an output of 240 units per eight-hour day. Task times and precedence relationships are as follows:

Task	Duration (minutes)	Precedes Task
a	0.2	b
b	0.4	c
c	0.2	f
d	0.4	e
e	1.2	g
f	1.2	g
g	1.0	end

Do each of the following:
a. Draw the precedence diagram.
b. Determine the minimum cycle time, the maximum cycle time, and the calculated cycle time.

c. Determine the minimum number of stations needed.

d. Assign tasks to workstations on the basis of greatest number of following tasks. Use longest processing time as a tiebreaker. If ties still exist, assume indifference in choice.

e. Compute the percentage of idle time for the assignment in part *d.*

6 Twelve tasks, with times and precedence requirements as shown in the following table, are to be assigned to workstations using a cycle time of 1.5 minutes. Two heuristic rules will be tried: (1) greatest positional weight, and (2) greatest number of following tasks.

In each case, the tiebreaker will be shortest task time.

TASK	LENGTH (MINUTES)	FOLLOWS TASK
a	0.1	—
b	0.2	a
c	0.9	b
d	0.6	c
e	0.1	—
f	0.2	d, e
g	0.4	f
h	0.1	g
i	0.2	h
j	0.7	i
k	0.3	j
l	0.2	k

a. Draw the precedence diagram for this line.

b. Assign tasks to stations under each of the two rules.

c. Compute the percentage of idle time for each rule.

7 For the set of tasks given below, do the following:

a. Develop the precedence diagram.

b. Determine the minimum and maximum cycle times in seconds for a desired output of 500 units in a 7-hour day. Why might a manager use a cycle time of 50 seconds?

c. Determine the minimum number of workstations for output of 500 units per day.

d. Balance the line using the *largest positional weight* heuristic. Break ties with the *most following tasks* heuristic. Use a cycle time of 50 seconds.

e. Calculate the percentage idle time for the line.

TASK	TASK TIME (SECONDS)	IMMEDIATE PREDECESSORS
A	45	—
B	11	A
C	9	B
D	50	—
E	26	D
F	11	E
G	12	C
H	10	C
I	9	F, G, H
J	10	I
	193	

8 A shop works a 400-minute day. The manager of the shop wants an output of 200 units per day for the assembly line that has the elemental tasks shown in the table. Do the following:

a. Construct the precedence diagram.

b. Assign tasks according to the *most following tasks* rule.

c. Assign tasks according to the *greatest positional weight* rule.

d. Compute the balance delay for each rule. Which one yields the better set of assignments in this instance?

TASK	IMMEDIATELY PRECEDES TASK(S)	TASK TIME
a	b, c, d	0.5
b	e	1.4
c	e	1.2
d	f	0.7
e	g, j	0.5
f	i	1.0
g	h	0.4
h	k	0.3
i	j	0.5
j	k	0.8
k	m	0.9
m	End	0.3

9 Arrange six departments into a 2×3 grid so that these conditions are satisfied: 1 close to 2, 5 close to 2 and 6, 2 close to 5, and 3 not close to 1 or 2.

10 Using the information given in the preceding problem, develop a Muther-type grid using the letters A, O, and X. Assume that any pair of combinations not mentioned have an O rating.

11 Using the information in the following grid, determine if the department locations shown are appropriate. If not, modify the assignments so that the conditions are satisfied.

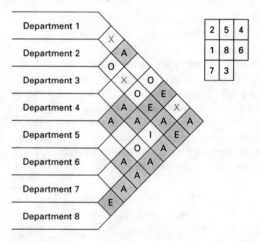

12 Arrange the eight departments shown in the accompanying Muther grid into a 2×4 format. *Note:* Department 1 must be in the location shown.

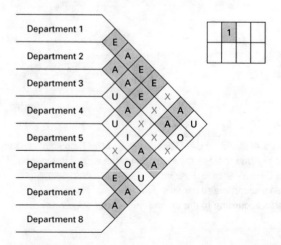

13   Arrange the departments so they satisfy the conditions shown in the following rating grid into a 3×3 format. Place department 5 in the lower left corner of the 3×3 grid.

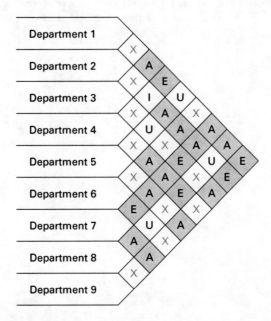

14   *a.* Determine the placement of departments for a newly designed facility that will minimize total transportation costs using the data in the following tables. Assume that reverse distances are the same. The locations are shown in the grid. Use a cost of $1 per trip yard.

Location A	Location B	Location C
	Location D	

	DISTANCE BETWEEN LOCATIONS (YARDS)						NUMBER OF TRIPS PER DAY BETWEEN DEPARTMENTS			
FROM \ TO	A	B	C	D	FROM \ TO	1	2	3	4
A	—	40	80	70	1	—	10	20	80
B		—	40	50	2		—	40	90
C			—	60	3			—	55
D				—	4				—

b. Suppose the company has revised its plans for the processes described in part *a* to accommodate technological process changes. Determine the placement of departments that will now minimize total travel cost. Use the distances shown in part *a*, but use the following new matrix of daily trips between departments.

	NUMBER OF TRIPS PER DAY BETWEEN DEPARTMENTS			
FROM \ TO	A	B	C	D
1	—	20	20	40
2		—	10	50
3			—	60
4				—

15   Eight work centers must be arranged in an L-shaped building. The locations of centers 1 and 3 are assigned as shown in the accompanying diagram. Assuming transportation costs are $1 per load per meter, develop a suitable layout that minimizes transportation costs using the given information. Compute the total cost. (Assume the reverse distances are the same.)

DISTANCE (METERS)

FROM \ TO	A	B	C	D	E	F	G	G
A	—	40	40	60	120	80	100	110
B		—	60	40	60	140	120	130
C			—	45	85	40	70	90
D				—	40	50	40	45
E					—	90	50	40
F						—	40	60
G							—	40
H								—

LOADS PER DAY

FROM \ TO	1	2	3	4	5	6	7	8
1	—	10	5	90	370	135	125	0
2		—	360	120	40	115	45	120
3			—	350	110	40	20	200
4				—	190	70	50	190
5					—	10	40	10
6						—	50	20
7							—	20
8								—

16.   Develop a process layout that will minimize the total distance traveled by patients at a medical clinic, using the following information on projected departmental visits by patients and distance between locations. Assume a distance of 35 feet between the reception area and each potential location. Use the format shown.

DISTANCE BETWEEN LOCATIONS (FEET)

FROM \ TO	A	B	C	D	E	F
A	—	40	80	100	120	160
B		—	40	60	80	120
C			—	20	40	80
D				—	20	40
E					—	40
F						—

TRIPS BETWEEN DEPARTMENTS (PER DAY)

TO \	RECEPTION	1	2	3	4	5	6
RECEPTION	—	20	50	210	20	10	130
1	10	—	0	40	110	80	50
2	40		—	0	50	40	120
3	10		0	—	10	250	10
4	0				—	40	90
5	10					—	20
6	30						—

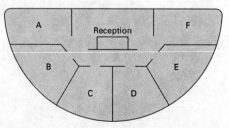

17. Ten labs will be assigned to the circular layout shown. Recalling a similar layout's congestion in the halls, the new lab manager has requested an assignment that will minimize traffic between offices. In addition, movement in the halls is restricted to a counterclockwise route. Develop a suitable layout using the following information.

NUMBER OF TRIPS PER DAY BETWEEN DEPARTMENTS

FROM \ To	1	2	3	4	5	6	7	8	9	10
1	—	40	51	26	23	9	20	12	11	35
2		—	37	16	27	15	18	18	18	36
3			—	18	20	14	50	18	25	36
4				—	35	14	14	22	23	31
5					—	24	14	13	21	25
6						—	17	44	42	25
7							—	14	33	40
8								—	43	35
9									—	47
10										—

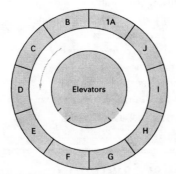

18. Rebalance the assembly line in Problem 7. This time, use the *longest operation time* heuristic. Break ties with the *most following tasks* heuristic. What is the percentage idle time for your line?

SELECTED BIBLIOGRAPHY AND FURTHER READINGS

Cohen, Morris, and Uday M. Apte. *Manufacturing Automation.* Burr Ridge, IL: Richard D. Irwin, 1997.

Francis, Richard L., Leon F. McGinnis Jr., and John A. White. *Facility Layout and Location: An Analytical Approach.* 3rd ed. Upper Saddle River, NJ: Prentice Hall, 1998.

Groover, Mikell P. *Automation, Production Systems, and Computer-Aided Manufacturing.* 2nd ed. Upper Saddle River, NJ: Prentice Hall, 2001.

Hill, Terry. *Manufacturing Strategy.* 3rd ed. Burr Ridge, IL: Richard D. Irwin, 2001.

Kilbridge, M. D., and L. Wester. "A Heuristic Method of Assembly Line Balancing." *Journal of Industrial Engineering* 12 (July–August 1961).

Milas, Gene H. "Assembly Line Balancing . . . Let's Remove the Mystery." *Industrial Engineering,* May 1990, pp. 31–36.

Upton, David. "The Management of Manufacturing Flexibility." *California Management Review* 36, no. 2 (1994), pp. 72–89.

Upton, David. "What Really Makes Factories Flexible." *Harvard Business Review,* July–August 1995, pp. 74–84.

FOOTNOTES

1 Based on "Airport Checkpoints Moved to Help Speed Travelers on Their Way," *Minneapolis–St. Paul Star Tribune,* January 13, 1995, p. 1B.

2 At first glance, it might seem that the desired output would logically be the maximum possible output. However, you will see why that is not always the best alternative.

3 Adapted from Mikell P. Groover, *Automation, Production Systems, and Computer-Aided Manufacturing,* 2nd ed. © 1987. Reprinted by permission of Pearson Education, Inc., Upper Saddle River, N.J.

4 Richard Muther and John Wheeler, "Simplified Systematic Layout Planning," *Factory* 120, nos. 8, 9, and 10 (August, September, October 1962), pp. 68–77, 111–119, 101–113, respectively.

Supplement to

chapter 3

LINEAR PROGRAMMING

Learning Objectives

After completing this supplement, you should be able to:

1. Describe the type of problem that would lend itself to solution using linear programming.
2. Formulate a linear programming model from a description of a problem.
3. Solve simple linear programming problems using the graphical method.
4. Interpret computer solutions of linear programming problems.
5. Do sensitivity analysis on the solution of a linear programming problem.

Linear programming is a powerful quantitative tool used by operations managers and other managers to obtain optimal solutions to problems that involve restrictions or limitations, such as budgets and available materials, labor, and machine time. These problems are referred to as *constrained optimization* problems. There are numerous examples of linear programming applications to such problems, including

- Establishing locations for emergency equipment and personnel that will minimize response time.
- Determining optimal schedules for airlines for planes, pilots, and ground personnel.
- Developing financial plans.
- Determining optimal blends of animal feed mixes.
- Determining optimal diet plans.
- Identifying the best set of worker–job assignments.
- Developing optimal production schedules.
- Developing shipping plans that will minimize shipping costs.
- Identifying the optimal mix of products in a factory.
- Performing production and service planning.

INTRODUCTION

Linear programming (LP) techniques consist of a sequence of steps that will lead to an optimal solution to linear-constrained problems, if an optimum exists. There are a number of different linear programming techniques; some are special-purpose (i.e., used to find solutions for specific types of problems) and others are more general in scope. This supplement covers the two general-purpose solution techniques: graphical linear programming and computer solutions. Graphical linear programming provides a visual portrayal of many of the important concepts of linear programming. However, it is limited to problems with only two variables. In practice, computers are used to obtain solutions for problems, some of which involve a large number of variables.

LINEAR PROGRAMMING MODELS

mhhe.com/stevenson10e

ScreenCam
Tutorial

Linear programming models are mathematical representations of constrained optimization problems. These models have certain characteristics in common. Knowledge of these characteristics enables us to recognize problems that can be solved using linear programming. In addition, it also can help us formulate LP models. The characteristics can be grouped into two categories: components and assumptions. First, let's consider the components.

Four components provide the structure of a linear programming model:

1. Objective function.
2. Decision variables.
3. Constraints.
4. Parameters.

Linear programming algorithms require that a single goal or *objective*, such as the maximization of profits, be specified. The two general types of objectives are maximization and minimization. A maximization objective might involve profits, revenues, efficiency, or rate of return. Conversely, a minimization objective might involve cost, time, distance traveled, or scrap. The objective function is a mathematical expression that can be used to determine the total profit (or cost, etc., depending on the objective) for a given solution.

Objective function

Decision variables represent choices available to the decision maker in terms of amounts of either inputs or outputs. For example, some problems require choosing a combination of inputs to minimize total costs, while others require selecting a combination of outputs to maximize profits or revenues.

Constraints are limitations that restrict the alternatives available to decision makers. The three types of constraints are less than or equal to ($\leq$), greater than or equal to ($\geq$), and simply equal to ($=$). A $\leq$ constraint implies an upper limit on the amount of some scarce resource (e.g., machine hours, labor hours, materials) available for use. A $\geq$ constraint specifies a minimum that must be achieved in the final solution (e.g., must contain at least 10 percent real fruit juice, must get at least 30 MPG on the highway). The $=$ constraint is more restrictive in the sense that it specifies *exactly* what a decision variable should equal (e.g., make 200 units of product A). A linear programming model can consist of one or more constraints. The constraints of a given problem define the set of all feasible combinations of decision variables; this set is referred to as the **feasible solution space**. Linear programming algorithms are designed to search the feasible solution space for the combination of decision variables that will yield an optimum in terms of the objective function.

An LP model consists of a mathematical statement of the objective and a mathematical statement of each constraint. These statements consist of symbols (e.g., x_1, x_2) that represent

the decision variables and numerical values, called parameters. The parameters are fixed   Parameters
values; the model is solved *given* those values.

Example 3S–1 illustrates an LP model.

Example 3S–1

Here is an LP model of a situation that involves the production of three possible products, each of which
will yield a certain profit per unit, and each requires a certain use of two resources that are in limited
supply: labor and materials. The objective is to determine how much of each product to make to achieve
the greatest possible profit while satisfying all constraints.

Decision variables
$$\begin{cases} x_1 = \text{Quantity of product 1 to produce} \\ x_2 = \text{Quantity of product 2 to produce} \\ x_3 = \text{Quantity of product 3 to produce} \end{cases}$$

Maximize $\quad 5x_1 + 8x_2 + 4x_3$ (profit) $\quad$ (Objective function)

Subject to

Labor	$2x_1 + 4x_2 + 8x_3 \le 250$ hours	
Material	$7x_1 + 6x_2 + 5x_3 \le 100$ pounds	(Constraints)
Product 1	$x_1 \qquad\qquad\quad \ge 10$ units	

$$x_1, x_2, x_3 \ge 0 \quad \text{(Nonnegativity constraints)}$$

First, the model lists and defines the decision variables. These typically represent *quantities.*
In this case, they are quantities of three different products that might be produced.

Next, the model states the objective function. It includes every decision variable in the model and the
contribution (profit per unit) of each decision variable. Thus, product x_1 has a profit of $5 per unit. The
profit from product x_1 for a given solution will be 5 times the value of x_1 specified by the solution; the
total profit from all products will be the sum of the individual product profits. Thus, if $x_1 = 10$, $x_2 = 0$,
and $x_3 = 6$, the value of the objective function would be

$$5(10) + 8(0) + 4(6) = 74$$

The objective function is followed by a list (in no particular order) of three constraints. Each constraint has a right-side numerical value (e.g., the labor constraint has a right-side value of 250) that
indicates the amount of the constraint and a relation sign that indicates whether that amount is a maximum ($\le$), a minimum ($\ge$), or an equality ($=$). The left side of each constraint consists of the variables
subject to that particular constraint and a coefficient for each variable that indicates how much of the
right-side quantity *one unit* of the decision variable represents. For instance, for the labor constraint,
one unit of x_1 will require two hours of labor. The sum of the values on the left side of each constraint
represents the amount of that constraint used by a solution. Thus, if $x_1 = 10$, $x_2 = 0$, and $x_3 = 6$, the
amount of labor used would be

$$2(10) + 4(0) + 8(6) = 68 \text{ hours}$$

Because this amount does not exceed the quantity on the right-hand side of the constraint, it is said
to be *feasible.*

Note that the third constraint refers to only a single variable; x_1 must be at least 10 units. Its implied
coefficient is 1, although that is not shown.

Finally, there are the nonnegativity constraints. These are listed on a single line; they reflect the
condition that no decision variable is allowed to have a negative value.

In order for LP models to be used effectively, certain *assumptions* must be satisfied:

1. *Linearity:* The impact of decision variables is linear in constraints and the objective function.
2. *Divisibility:* Noninteger values of decision variables are acceptable.
3. *Certainty:* Values of parameters are known and constant.
4. *Nonnegativity:* Negative values of decision variables are unacceptable.

MODEL FORMULATION

An understanding of the components of linear programming models is necessary for model formulation. This helps provide organization to the process of assembling information about a problem into a model.

Naturally, it is important to obtain valid information on what constraints are appropriate, as well as on what values of the parameters are appropriate. If this is not done, the usefulness of the model will be questionable. Consequently, in some instances, considerable effort must be expended to obtain that information.

In formulating a model, use the format illustrated in Example 3S–1. Begin by identifying the decision variables. Very often, decision variables are "the quantity of" something, such as x_1 = the quantity of product 1. Generally, decision variables have profits, costs, times, or a similar measure of value associated with them. Knowing this can help you identify the decision variables in a problem.

Constraints are restrictions or requirements on one or more decision variables, and they refer to available amounts of resources such as labor, material, or machine time, or to minimal requirements, such as "Make at least 10 units of product 1." It can be helpful to give a name to each constraint, such as "labor" or "material 1." Let's consider some of the different kinds of constraints you will encounter.

1. A constraint that refers to one or more decision variables. This is the most common kind of constraint. The constraints in Example 3S–1 are of this type.

2. A constraint that specifies a ratio. For example, "The ratio of x_1 to x_2 must be at least 3 to 2." To formulate this, begin by setting up the following ratio:

$$\frac{x_1}{x_2} \geq \frac{3}{2}$$

Then, cross multiply, obtaining

$$2x_1 \geq 3x_2$$

This is not yet in a suitable form because all variables in a constraint must be on the left side of the inequality (or equality) sign, leaving only a constant on the right side. To achieve this, we must subtract the variable amount that is on the right side from both sides. That yields

$$2x_1 - 3x_2 \geq 0$$

[Note that the direction of the inequality remains the same.]

3. A constraint that specifies a percentage for one or more variables relative to one or more other variables. For example, "x_1 cannot be more than 20 percent of the mix." Suppose that the mix consists of variables x_1, x_2, and x_3. In mathematical terms, this would be

$$x_1 \leq .20(x_1 + x_2 + x_3)$$

As always, all variables must appear on the left side of the relationship. To accomplish that, we can expand the right side, and then subtract the result from both sides. Expanding yields

$$x_1 \leq .20x_1 + .20x_2 + .20x_3$$

Subtracting yields

$$.80x_1 - .20x_2 - .20x_3 \leq 0$$

Once you have formulated a model, the next task is to solve it. The following sections describe two approaches to problem solution: graphical solutions and computer solutions.

GRAPHICAL LINEAR PROGRAMMING

Graphical linear programming is a method for finding optimal solutions to two-variable problems. This section describes that approach.

Graphical linear programming

OUTLINE OF GRAPHICAL PROCEDURE

The graphical method of linear programming plots the constraints on a graph and identifies an area that satisfies all of the constraints. The area is referred to as the *feasible solution space*. Next, the objective function is plotted and used to identify the optimal point in the feasible solution space. The coordinates of the point can sometimes be read directly from the graph, although generally an algebraic determination of the coordinates of the point is necessary.

The general procedure followed in the graphical approach is as follows:

1. Set up the objective function and the constraints in mathematical format.
2. Plot the constraints.
3. Identify the feasible solution space.
4. Plot the objective function.
5. Determine the optimum solution.

The technique can best be illustrated through solution of a typical problem. Consider the problem described in Example 3S–2.

Example 3S–2

General description: A firm that assembles computers and computer equipment is about to start production of two new types of microcomputers. Each type will require assembly time, inspection time, and storage space. The amounts of each of these resources that can be devoted to the production of the microcomputers is limited. The manager of the firm would like to determine the quantity of each microcomputer to produce in order to maximize the profit generated by sales of these microcomputers.

Additional information: In order to develop a suitable model of the problem, the manager has met with design and production personnel. As a result of those meetings, the manager has obtained the following information:

	TYPE 1	TYPE 2
Profit per unit	$60	$50
Assembly time per unit	4 hours	10 hours
Inspection time per unit	2 hours	1 hour
Storage space per unit	3 cubic feet	3 cubic feet

The manager also has acquired information on the availability of company resources. These (daily) amounts are as follows:

RESOURCE	AMOUNT AVAILABLE
Assembly time	100 hours
Inspection time	22 hours
Storage space	39 cubic feet

The manager met with the firm's marketing manager and learned that demand for the microcomputers was such that whatever combination of these two types of microcomputers is produced, all of the output can be sold.

In terms of meeting the assumptions, it would appear that the relationships are *linear:* The contribution to profit per unit of each type of computer and the time and storage space per unit of each type of computer are the same regardless of the quantity produced. Therefore, the total impact of each type of computer on the profit and each constraint is a linear function of the quantity of that variable. There may be a question of *divisibility* because, presumably, only whole units of computers will be sold. However, because this is a recurring process (i.e., the computers will be produced daily; a noninteger solution such as 3.5 computers per day will result in 7 computers every other day), this does not seem to pose a problem. The question of *certainty* cannot be explored here; in practice, the manager could be questioned to determine if there are any other possible constraints and whether the values shown for assembly times, and so forth, are known with certainty. For the purposes of discussion, we will assume certainty. Last, the assumption of *nonnegativity* seems justified; negative values for production quantities would not make sense.

Because we have concluded that linear programming is appropriate, let us now turn our attention to constructing a model of the microcomputer problem. First, we must define the decision variables. Based on the statement "The manager . . . would like to determine the quantity of each microcomputer to produce," the decision variables are the quantities of each type of computer. Thus,

$$x_1 = \text{quantity of type 1 to produce}$$
$$x_2 = \text{quantity of type 2 to produce}$$

Next, we can formulate the objective function. The profit per unit of type 1 is listed as \$60, and the profit per unit of type 2 is listed as \$50, so the appropriate objective function is

$$\text{Maximize } Z = 60x_1 + 50x_2$$

where Z is the value of the objective function, given values of x_1 and x_2. Theoretically, a mathematical function requires such a variable for completeness. However, in practice, the objective function often is written without the Z, as sort of a shorthand version. (That approach is underscored by the fact that computer input does not call for Z: It is understood. The output of a computerized model does include a Z, though.)

Now for the constraints. There are three resources with limited availability: assembly time, inspection time, and storage space. The fact that availability is limited means that these constraints will all be $\leq$ constraints. Suppose we begin with the assembly constraint. The type 1 microcomputer requires 4 hours of assembly time per unit, whereas the type 2 microcomputer requires 10 hours of assembly time per unit. Therefore, with a limit of 100 hours available, the assembly constraint is

$$4x_1 + 10x_2 \leq 100 \text{ hours}$$

Similarly, each unit of type 1 requires 2 hours of inspection time, and each unit of type 2 requires 1 hour of inspection time. With 22 hours available, the inspection constraint is

$$2x_1 + 1x_2 \leq 22$$

(Note: The coefficient of 1 for x_2 need not be shown. Thus, an alternative form for this constraint is $2x_1 + x_2 \leq 22$.) The storage constraint is determined in a similar manner:

$$3x_1 + 3x_2 \leq 39$$

There are no other system or individual constraints. The nonnegativity constraints are

$$x_1, x_2 \geq 0$$

In summary, the mathematical model of the microcomputer problem is

$$x_1 = \text{quantity of type 1 to produce}$$
$$x_2 = \text{quantity of type 2 to produce}$$
$$\text{Maximize } 60x_1 + 50x_2$$

Subject to

Assembly	$4x_1 + 10x_2 \leq 100$ hours	
Inspection	$2x_1 + 1x_2 \leq 22$ hours	
Storage	$3x_1 + 3x_2 \leq 39$ cubic feet	
	$x_1, x_2 \geq 0$	

The next step is to plot the constraints.

PLOTTING CONSTRAINTS

Begin by placing the nonnegativity constraints on a graph, as in Figure 3S.1. The procedure for plotting the other constraints is simple:

1. Replace the inequality sign with an equal sign. This transforms the constraint into an *equation of a straight line.*
2. Determine where the line intersects each axis.
   a. To find where it crosses the x_2 axis, set x_1 equal to zero and solve the equation for the value of x_2.
   b. To find where it crosses the x_1 axis, set x_2 equal to zero and solve the equation for the value of x_1.
3. Mark these intersections on the axes, and connect them with a straight line. (Note: If a constraint has only one variable, it will be a vertical line on a graph if the variable is x_1, or a horizontal line if the variable is x_2.)
4. Indicate by shading (or by arrows at the ends of the constraint line) whether the inequality is greater than or less than. (A general rule to determine which side of the line satisfies the inequality is to pick a point that is not on the line, such as 0,0, solve the equation using these values, and see whether it is greater than or less than the constraint amount.)
5. Repeat steps 1–4 for each constraint.

Graph Showing the Nonnegativity Constraints   **figure 3S.1**

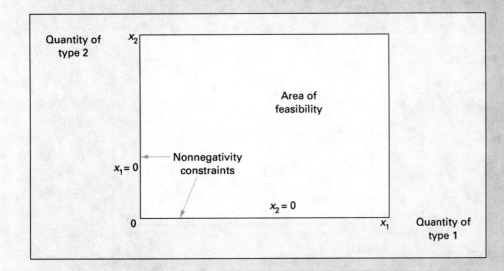

Consider the assembly time constraint:

$$4x_1 + 10x_2 \leq 100$$

Removing the inequality portion of the constraint produces this straight line:

$$4x_1 + 10x_2 = 100$$

Next, identify the points where the line intersects each axis, as step 2 describes. Thus with $x_2 = 0$, we find

$$4x_1 + 10(0) = 100$$

Solving, we find that $4x_1 = 100$, so $x_1 = 25$ when $x_2 = 0$. Similarly, we can solve the equation for x_2 when $x_1 = 0$:

$$4(0) + 10x_2 = 100$$

Solving for x_2, we find $x_2 = 10$ when $x_1 = 0$.

Thus, we have two points: $x_1 = 0$, $x_2 = 10$, and $x_1 = 25$, $x_2 = 0$. We can now add this line to our graph of the nonnegativity constraints by connecting these two points (see Figure 3S.2).

Next we must determine which side of the line represents points that are less than 100. To do this, we can select a test point that is not on the line, and we can substitute the x_1 and x_2 values of that point into the left side of the equation of the line. If the result is less than 100, this tells us that all points on that side of the line are less than the value of the line (e.g., 100). Conversely, if the result is greater than 100, this indicates that the other side of the line represents the set of points that will yield values that are less than 100. A relatively simple test point to use is the origin (i.e., $x_1 = 0$, $x_2 = 0$). Substituting these values into the equation yields

$$4(0) + 10(0) = 0$$

Obviously this is less than 100. Hence, the side of the line closest to the origin represents the "less than" area (i.e., the feasible region).

The feasible region for this constraint and the nonnegativity constraints then becomes the shaded portion shown in Figure 3S.3.

figure 3S.2   Plot of the First Constraint (Assembly Time)

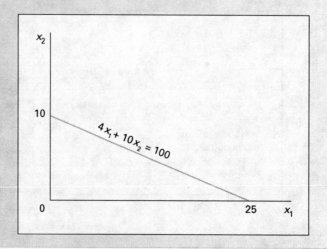

The Feasible Region, Given the First Constraint and the Nonnegativity Constraints

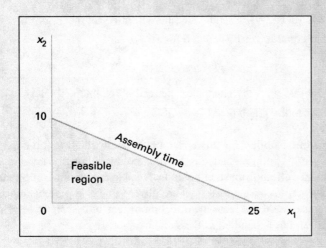

The Point 10, 10 is Above the Constraint Line

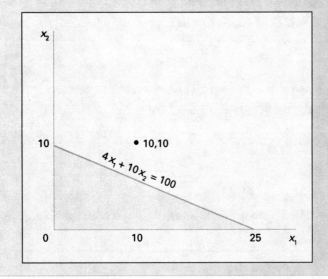

For the sake of illustration, suppose we try one other point, say $x_1 = 10, x_2 = 10$. Substituting these values into the assembly constraint yields

$$4(10) + 10(10) = 140$$

Clearly this is greater than 100. Therefore, all points on this side of the line are greater than 100 (see Figure 3S.4).

Continuing with the problem, we can add the two remaining constraints to the graph. For the inspection constraint:

1. Convert the constraint into the equation of a straight line by replacing the inequality sign with an equality sign:

$$2x_1 + 1x_2 \leq 22 \quad \text{becomes} \quad 2x_1 + 1x_2 = 22$$

2. Set x_1 equal to zero and solve for x_2:

$$2(0) + 1x_2 = 22$$

Solving, we find $x_2 = 22$. Thus, the line will intersect the x_2 axis at 22.

3. Next, set x_2 equal to zero and solve for x_1:

$$2x_1 + 1(0) = 22$$

Solving, we find $x_1 = 11$. Thus, the other end of the line will intersect the x_1 axis at 11.

4. Add the line to the graph (see Figure 3S.5).

Note that the area of feasibility for this constraint is below the line (Figure 3S.5). Again the area of feasibility at this point is shaded in for illustration, although when graphing problems, it is more practical to refrain from shading in the feasible region until all constraint lines have been drawn. However, because constraints are plotted one at a time, using a small arrow at the end of each constraint to indicate the direction of feasibility can be helpful.

The storage constraint is handled in the same manner:

1. Convert it into an equality:

$$3x_1 + 3x_2 = 39$$

2. Set x_1 equal to zero and solve for x_2:

$$3(0) + 3x_2 = 39$$

Solving, $x_2 = 13$. Thus, $x_2 = 13$ when $x_1 = 0$.

3. Set x_2 equal to zero and solve for x_1:

$$3x_1 + 3(0) = 39$$

Solving, $x_1 = 13$. Thus, $x_1 = 13$ when $x_2 = 0$.

4. Add the line to the graph (see Figure 3S.6).

figure 3S.5   Partially Completed Graph, Showing the Assembly, Inspection, and Nonnegativity Constraints

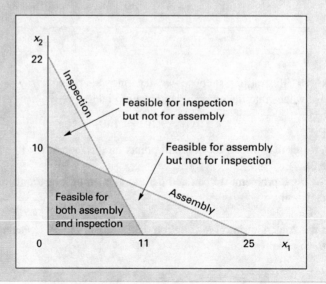

Completed Graph of the Microcomputer Problem Showing All Constraints and the Feasible Solution Space

figure 3S.6

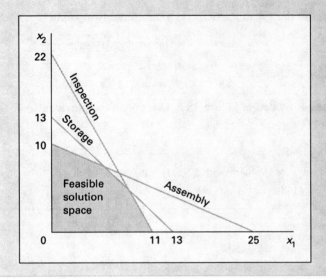

IDENTIFYING THE FEASIBLE SOLUTION SPACE

The feasible solution space is the set of all points that satisfies *all* constraints. (Recall that the x_1 and x_2 axes form nonnegativity constraints.) The heavily shaded area shown in Figure 3S.6 is the feasible solution space for our problem.

The next step is to determine which point in the feasible solution space will produce the optimal value of the objective function. This determination is made using the objective function.

PLOTTING THE OBJECTIVE FUNCTION LINE

Plotting an objective function line involves the same logic as plotting a constraint line: Determine where the line intersects each axis. Recall that the objective function for the microcomputer problem is

$$60x_1 + 50x_2$$

This is not an equation because it does not include an equal sign. We can get around this by simply setting it equal to some quantity. Any quantity will do, although one that is evenly divisible by both coefficients is desirable.

Suppose we decide to set the objective function equal to 300. That is,

$$60x_1 + 50x_2 = 300$$

We can now plot the line on our graph. As before, we can determine the x_1 and x_2 intercepts of the line by setting one of the two variables equal to zero, solving for the other, and then reversing the process. Thus, with $x_1 = 0$, we have

$$60(0) + 50x_2 = 300$$

Solving, we find $x_2 = 6$. Similarly, with $x_2 = 0$, we have

$$60x_1 + 50(0) = 300$$

Solving, we find $x_1 = 5$. This line is plotted in Figure 3S.7.

The profit line can be interpreted in the following way. It is an *isoprofit* line; every point on the line (i.e., every combination of x_1 and x_2 that lies on the line) will provide a profit of $300. We can see from the graph many combinations that are both on the $300 profit line and within the feasible solution space. In fact, considering noninteger as well as integer solutions, the possibilities are infinite.

Suppose we now consider another line, say the $600 line. To do this, we set the objective function equal to this amount. Thus,

$$60x_1 + 50x_2 = 600$$

Solving for the x_1 and x_2 intercepts yields these two points:

x_1 intercept	x_2 intercept
$x_1 = 10$	$x_1 = 0$
$x_2 = 0$	$x_2 = 12$

This line is plotted in Figure 3S.8, along with the previous $300 line for purposes of comparison.

figure 3S.7   Microcomputer Problem with $300 Profit Line Added

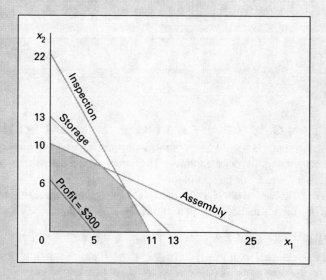

figure 3S.8   Microcomputer Problem with Profit Lines Of $300 and $600

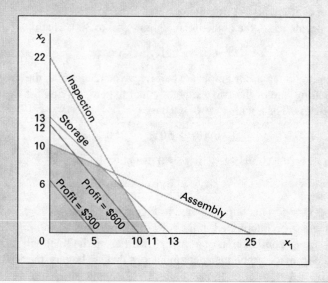

Two things are evident in Figure 3S.8 regarding the profit lines. One is that the $600 line is *farther* from the origin than the $300 line; the other is that the two lines are *parallel.* The lines are parallel because they both have the same slope. The slope is not affected by the right side of the equation. Rather, it is determined solely by the coefficients 60 and 50. It would be correct to conclude that regardless of the quantity we select for the value of the objective function, the resulting line will be parallel to these two lines. Moreover, if the amount is greater than 600, the line will be even farther away from the origin than the $600 line. If the value is less than 300, the line will be closer to the origin than the $300 line. And if the value is between 300 and 600, the line will fall between the $300 and $600 lines. This knowledge will help in determining the optimal solution.

Consider a third line, one with the profit equal to $900. Figure 3S.9 shows that line along with the previous two profit lines. As expected, it is parallel to the other two, and even farther away from the origin. However, the line does not touch the feasible solution space at all. Consequently, there is no feasible combination of x_1 and x_2 that will yield that amount of profit. Evidently, the maximum possible profit is an amount between $600 and $900, which we can see by referring to Figure 3S.9. We could continue to select profit lines in this manner, and eventually, we could determine an amount that would yield the greatest profit. However, there is a much simpler alternative. We can plot just one line, say the $300 line. We know that all other lines will be parallel to it. Consequently, by moving this one line parallel to itself we can "test" other profit lines. We also know that as we move away from the origin, the profits get larger. What we want to know is how far the line can be moved out from the origin and still be touching the feasible solution space, and the values of the decision variables at that point of greatest profit (i.e., the optimal solution). Locate this point on the graph by placing a straight edge along the $300 line (or any other convenient line) and sliding it away from the origin, being careful to keep it parallel to the line. This approach is illustrated in Figure 3S.10.

Once we have determined where the optimal solution is in the feasible solution space, we must determine the values of the decision variables at that point. Then, we can use that information to compute the profit for that combination.

Note that the optimal solution is at the intersection of the inspection boundary and the storage boundary (see Figure 3S.10). In other words, the optimal combination of x_1 and x_2

Microcomputer Problem with Profit Lines of $300, $600, and $900

figure 3S.9

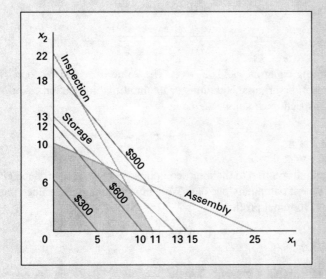

figure 3S.10   Finding the Optimal Solution to the Microcomputer Problem

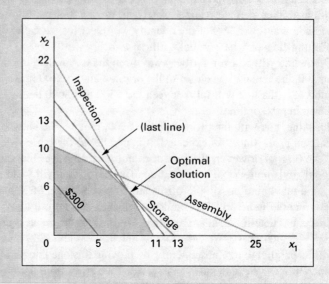

must satisfy both boundary (equality) conditions. We can determine those values by solving the two equations *simultaneously*. The equations are

$$\text{Inspection} \quad 2x_1 + 1x_2 = 22$$
$$\text{Storage} \quad 3x_1 + 3x_2 = 39$$

The idea behind solving two *simultaneous equations* is to algebraically eliminate one of the unknown variables (i.e., to obtain an equation with a single unknown). This can be accomplished by multiplying the constants of one of the equations by a fixed amount and then adding (or subtracting) the modified equation from the other. (Occasionally, it is easier to multiply each equation by a fixed quantity.) For example, we can eliminate x_2 by multiplying the inspection equation by 3 and then subtracting the storage equation from the modified inspection equation. Thus,

$$3(2x_1 + 1x_2 = 22) \quad \text{becomes} \quad 6x_1 + 3x_2 = 66$$

Subtracting the storage equation from this produces

$$6x_1 + 3x_2 = 66$$
$$-(3x_1 + 3x_2 = 39)$$
$$\overline{3x_1 + 0x_2 = 27}$$

Solving the resulting equation yields $x_1 = 9$. The value of x_2 can be found by substituting $x_1 = 9$ into either of the original equations or the modified inspection equation. Suppose we use the original inspection equation. We have

$$2(9) + 1x_2 = 22$$

Solving, we find $x_2 = 4$.

Hence, the optimal solution to the microcomputer problem is to produce nine type 1 computers and four type 2 computers per day. We can substitute these values into the objective function to find the optimal profit:

$$\$60(9) + \$50(4) = \$740$$

Hence, the last line—the one that would last touch the feasible solution space as we moved away from the origin parallel to the $300 profit line—would be the line where profit equaled $740.

In this problem, the optimal values for both decision variables are integers. This will not always be the case; one or both of the decision variables may turn out to be noninteger. In some situations noninteger values would be of little consequence. This would be true if the decision variables were measured on a continuous scale, such as the amount of water, sand, sugar, fuel oil, time, or distance needed for optimality, or if the contribution per unit (profit, cost, etc.) were small, as with the number of nails or ball bearings to make. In some cases, the answer would simply be rounded down (maximization problems) or up (minimization problems) with very little impact on the objective function. Here, we assume that noninteger answers are acceptable as such.

Let's review the procedure for finding the optimal solution using the objective function approach:

1. Graph the constraints.
2. Identify the feasible solution space.
3. Set the objective function equal to some amount that is divisible by each of the objective function coefficients. This will yield integer values for the x_1 and x_2 intercepts and simplify plotting the line. Often, the product of the two objective function coefficients provides a satisfactory line. Ideally, the line will cross the feasible solution space close to the optimal point, and it will not be necessary to slide a straight edge because the optimal solution can be readily identified visually.
4. After identifying the optimal point, determine which two constraints intersect there. Solve their equations simultaneously to obtain the values of the decision variables at the optimum.
5. Substitute the values obtained in the previous step into the objective function to determine the value of the objective function at the optimum.

REDUNDANT CONSTRAINTS

In some cases, a constraint does not form a unique boundary of the feasible solution space. Such a constraint is called a redundant constraint. Two such constraints are illustrated in Figure 3S.11. Note that a constraint is redundant if it meets the following test: Its removal would not alter the feasible solution space.

Redundant constraint

Examples of Redundant Constraints

figure 3S.11

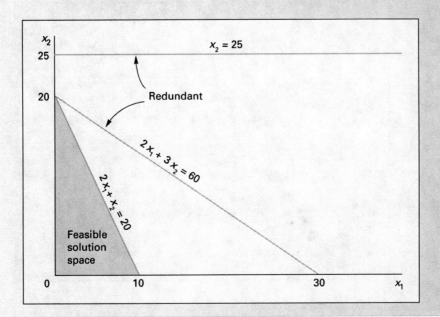

When a problem has a redundant constraint, at least one of the other constraints in the problem is more restrictive than the redundant constraint.

SOLUTIONS AND CORNER POINTS

The feasible solution space in graphical linear programming is typically a polygon. Moreover, the solution to any problem will be at one of the corner points (intersections of constraints) of the polygon. It is possible to determine the coordinates of each corner point of the feasible solution space, and use those values to compute the value of the objective function at those points. Because the solution is always at a corner point, comparing the values of the objective function at the corner points and identifying the best one (e.g., the maximum value) is another way to identify the optimal corner point. Using the graphical approach, it is much easier to plot the objective function and use that to identify the optimal corner point. However, for problems that have more than two decision variables, and the graphical method isn't appropriate, the "enumeration" approach is used to find the optimal solution.

Enumeration approach

With the enumeration approach, the coordinates of each corner point are determined, and then each set of coordinates is substituted into the objective function to determine its value at that corner point. After all corner points have been evaluated, the one with the maximum or minimum value (depending on whether the objective is to maximize or minimize) is identified as the optimal solution.

Thus, in the microcomputer problem, the corner points are $x_1 = 0$, $x_2 = 10$, $x_1 = 11$, $x_2 = 0$ (by inspection; see Figure 3S.10), and $x_1 = 9$, $x_2 = 4$ and $x_1 = 5$, $x_2 = 8$ (using simultaneous equations, as illustrated on page 134). Substituting into the objective function, the values are $500 for (0,10); $740 for (9,4); $660 for (11,0), and $700 for (5,8). Because (9,4) yields the highest value, that corner point is the optimal solution.

In some instances, the objective function will be *parallel* to one of the constraint lines that forms a *boundary of the feasible solution space.* When this happens, *every* combination of x_1 and x_2 on the segment of the constraint that touches the feasible solution space represents an optimal solution. Hence, there are multiple optimal solutions to the problem. Even in such a case, the solution will also be a corner point—in fact, the solution will be at *two* corner points: those at the ends of the segment that touches the feasible solution space. Figure 3S.12 illustrates an objective function line that is parallel to a constraint line.

figure 3S.12   Some LP Problems Have Multiple Optimal Solutions

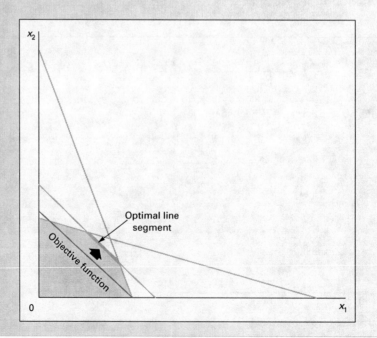

MINIMIZATION

Graphical minimization problems are quite similar to maximization problems. There are, however, two important differences. One is that at least one of the constraints must be of the $=$ or $\geq$ variety. This causes the feasible solution space to be away from the origin. The other difference is that the optimal point is the one closest to the origin. We find the optimal corner point by sliding the objective function (which is an *isocost* line) *toward* the origin instead of away from it.

Example 3S–3

Solve the following problem using graphical linear programming.

$$\text{Minimize} \quad Z = 8x_1 + 12x_2$$
$$\text{Subject to} \quad 5x_1 + 2x_2 \geq 20$$
$$4x_1 + 3x_2 \geq 24$$
$$x_2 \geq 2$$
$$x_1, x_2 \geq 0$$

SOLUTION

1. Plot the constraints (shown in Figure 3S.13).
   a. Change constraints to equalities.
   b. For each constraint, set $x_1 = 0$ and solve for x_2, then set $x_2 = 0$ and solve for x_1.
   c. Graph each constraint. Note that $x_2 = 2$ is a horizontal line parallel to the x_1 axis and 2 units above it.
2. Shade the feasible solution space (see Figure 3S.13).
3. Plot the objective function.
   a. Select a value for the objective function that causes it to cross the feasible solution space. Try $8 \times 12 = 96$; $8x_1 + 12x_2 = 96$ (acceptable).
   b. Graph the line (see Figure 3S.14).

The Constraints Define the Feasible Solution Space

figure 3S.13

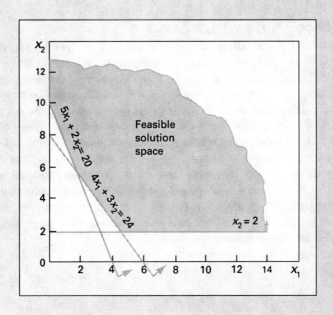

figure 3S.14   The Optimum is the Last Point the Objective Function Touches as it is Moved Toward the Origin

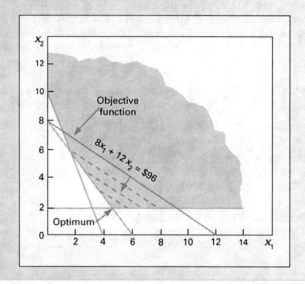

4. Slide the objective function toward the origin, being careful to keep it parallel to the original line.

5. The optimum (last feasible point) is shown in Figure 3S.14. The x_2 coordinate ($x_2 = 2$) can be determined by inspection of the graph. Note that the optimum point is at the intersection of the line $x_2 = 2$ and the line $4x_1 + 3x_2 = 24$. Substituting the value of $x_2 = 2$ into the latter equation will yield the value of x_1 at the intersection:

$$4x_1 + 3(2) = 24 \qquad x_1 = 4.5$$

Thus, the optimum is $x_1 = 4.5$ units and $x_2 = 2$.

6. Compute the minimum cost:

$$8x_1 + 12x_2 = 8(4.5) + 12(2) = 60 \; \bullet$$

SLACK AND SURPLUS

Binding constraint

If a constraint forms the optimal corner point of the feasible solution space, it is called a binding constraint. In effect, it limits the value of the objective function; if the constraint could be relaxed (less restrictive), an improved solution would be possible. For constraints that are not binding, making them less restrictive will have no impact on the solution.

If the optimal values of the decision variables are substituted into the left side of a binding constraint, the resulting value will exactly equal the right-hand value of the constraint. However, there will be a difference with a nonbinding constraint. If the left side is greater than the right side, we say that there is *surplus*; if the left side is less than the right side,

Surplus
Slack

we say that there is *slack*. Slack can only occur in a $\leq$ constraint; it is the amount by which the left side is less than the right side when the optimal values of the decision variables are substituted into the left side. And surplus can only occur in a $\geq$ constraint; it is the amount by which the left side exceeds the right side of the constraint when the optimal values of the decision variables are substituted into the left side.

For example, suppose the optimal values for a problem are $x_1 = 10$ and $x_2 = 20$. If one of the constraints is

$$3x_1 + 2x_2 \leq 100$$

substituting the optimal values into the left side yields

$$3(10) + 2(20) = 70$$

Because the constraint is $\leq$, the difference between the values of 100 and 70 (i.e., 30) is *slack*. Suppose the optimal values had been $x_1 = 20$ and $x_2 = 20$. Substituting these values into the left side of the constraint would yield $3(20) + 2(20) = 100$. Because the left side equals the right side, this is a binding constraint; slack is equal to zero.

Now consider this constraint:

$$4x_1 + x_2 \geq 50$$

Suppose the optimal values are $x_1 = 10$ and $x_2 = 15$; substituting into the left side yields

$$4(10) + 15 = 55$$

Because this is a $\geq$ constraint, the difference between the left- and right-side values is *surplus*. If the optimal values had been $x_1 = 12$ and $x_2 = 2$, substitution would result in the left side being equal to 50. Hence, the constraint would be a binding constraint, and there would be no surplus (i.e., surplus would be zero).

THE SIMPLEX METHOD

The simplex method is a general-purpose linear programming algorithm widely used to solve large-scale problems. Although it lacks the intuitive appeal of the graphical approach, its ability to handle problems with more than two decision variables makes it extremely valuable for solving problems often encountered in operations management.

    Although manual solution of linear programming problems using simplex can yield a number of insights on how solutions are derived, space limitations preclude describing it here. However, it is available on the Web site that accompanies this book. The discussion here will focus on computer solutions.

Simplex

COMPUTER SOLUTIONS

The microcomputer problem will be used to illustrate computer solutions. We repeat it here for ease of reference.

$$\text{Maximize} \quad 60x_1 + 50x_2 \quad \text{where } x_1 = \text{the number of type 1 computers}$$
$$x_2 = \text{the number of type 2 computers}$$

Subject to

Assembly	$4x_1 + 10x_2 \leq 100$ hours	
Inspection	$2x_1 + 1x_2 \leq 22$ hours	
Storage	$3x_1 + 3x_2 \leq 39$ cubic feet	
	$x_1, x_2 \geq 0$	

SOLVING LP MODELS USING MS EXCEL

Solutions to linear programming models can be obtained from spreadsheet software such as Microsoft's Excel. Excel has a routine called Solver that performs the necessary calculations.

    To use Solver:

1. First, enter the problem in a worksheet, as shown in Figure 3S.15. What is not obvious from the figure is the need to enter a formula for each cell where there is a zero (Solver automatically inserts the zero after you input the formula). The formulas are for the value

ScreenCam Tutorial

figure 3S.15   MS Excel Worksheet for Microcomputer Problem

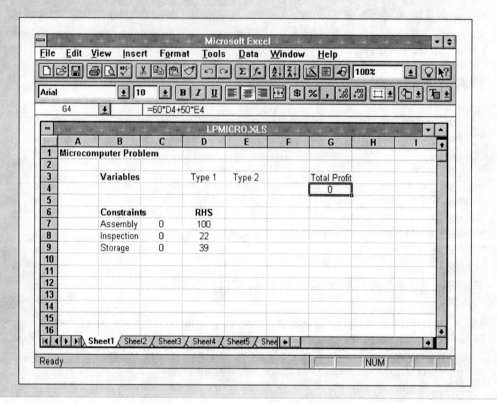

of the objective function and the constraints, in the appropriate cells. Before you enter the formulas, designate the cells where you want the optimal values of x_1 and x_2. Here, cells D4 and E4 are used. To enter a formula, click on the cell that the formula will pertain to, and then enter the formula, starting with an equal sign. We want the optimal value of the objective function to appear in cell G4. For G4, enter the formula

$$=60*D4+50*E4$$

The constraint formulas, using cells C7, C8, and C9, are

for C7:   =4*D4+10*E4

for C8:   =2*D4+1*E4

for C9:   =3*D4+3*E4

2. Now, to access Solver in Excel 2003, click on Tools on the top of the worksheet, and in that menu, click on Solver. In Excel 2007, click Data at the top of the worksheet, and in that ribbon, click on Solver in the Analysis group. The Solver menu will appear as illustrated in Figure 3S.16. Begin by setting the Target Cell (i.e., indicating the cell where you want the optimal value of the objective function to appear). Note, if the activated cell is the cell designated for the value of Z when you click on the Tools menu, Solver will automatically set that cell as the target cell.

Highlight Max if it isn't already highlighted. The Changing Cells are the cells where you want the optimal values of the decision variables to appear. Here, they are cells D4 and E4. We indicate this by the range D4:E4 (Solver will add the $signs).

Finally, add the constraints by clicking on Add ... When that menu appears, for each constraint, enter the cell that contains the formula for the left side of the constraint, then select

MS Excel Solver Parameters for Microcomputer Problem

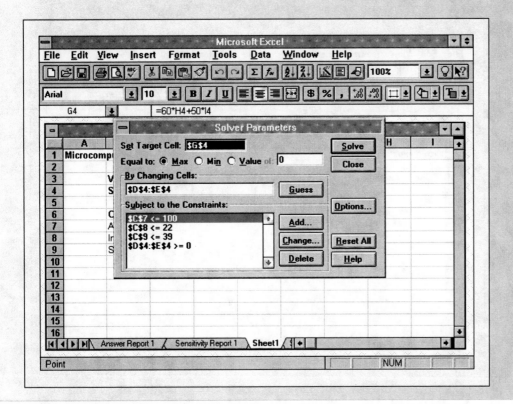

the appropriate inequality sign, and then enter either the right-side amount or the cell that has the right-side amount. Here, the right-side amounts are used. After you have entered each constraint, click on Add, and then enter the next constraint. (Note, constraints can be entered in any order.) For the nonnegativity constraints, enter the range of cells designated for the optimal values of the decision variables. Then, click on OK rather than Add, and you will return to the Solver menu. Click on Options . . . , and in the Options menu, click on Assume Linear Model, and then click on OK. This will return you to the Solver Parameters menu. Click on Solve.

3. The Solver Results menu will then appear, indicating that a solution has been found, or that an error has occurred. If there has been an error, go back to the Solver Parameters menu and check to see that your constraints refer to the correct changing cells, and that the inequality directions are correct. Make the corrections and click on Solve.

Assuming everything is correct, in the Solver Results menu, in the Reports box, highlight both Answer and Sensitivity, and then click on OK.

4. Solver will incorporate the optimal values of the decision variables and the objective function in your original layout on your worksheet (see Figure 3S.17). We can see that the optimal values are type $1 = 9$ units and type $2 = 4$ units, and the total profit is 740. The answer report will also show the optimal values of the decision variables (upper part of Figure 3S.18), and some information on the constraints (lower part of Figure 3S.18). Of particular interest here is the indication of which constraints have slack and how much slack. We can see that the constraint entered in cell C7 (assembly) has a slack of 24, and that the constraints entered in cells C8 (inspection) and C9 (storage) have slack equal to zero, indicating that they are binding constraints.

figure 3S.17   MS Excel Worksheet Solution for Microcomputer Problem

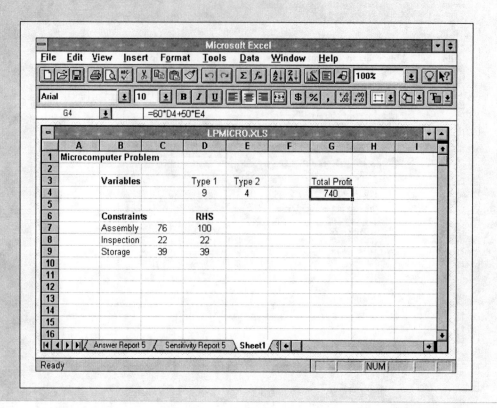

figure 3S.18   MS Excel Answer Report for Microcomputer Problem

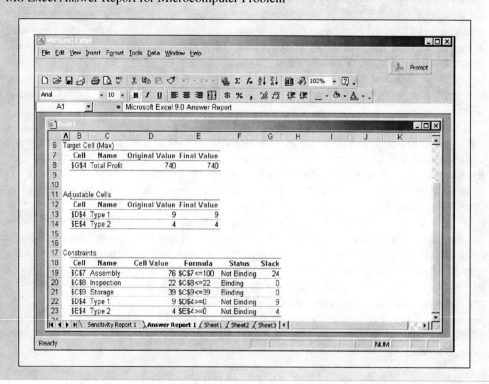

SENSITIVITY ANALYSIS

Sensitivity analysis is a means of assessing the impact of potential changes to the parameters (the numerical values) of an LP model. Such changes may occur due to forces beyond a manager's control; or a manager may be contemplating making the changes, say, to increase profits or reduce costs.

Sensitivity analysis

There are three types of potential changes:

1. Objective function coefficients.
2. Right-hand values of constraints.
3. Constraint coefficients.

We will consider the first two of these here. We begin with changes to objective function coefficients.

ScreenCam
Tutorial

OBJECTIVE FUNCTION COEFFICIENT CHANGES

A change in the value of an objective function coefficient can cause a change in the optimal solution of a problem. In a graphical solution, this would mean a change to another corner point of the feasible solution space. However, not every change in the value of an objective function coefficient will lead to a changed solution; generally there is a *range of values for which the optimal values of the decision variables will not change.* For example, in the microcomputer problem, if the profit on type 1 computers increased from $60 per unit to, say, $65 per unit, the optimal solution would still be to produce nine units of type 1 and four units of type 2 computers. Similarly, if the profit per unit on type 1 computers decreased from $60 to, say, $58, producing nine of type 1 and four of type 2 would still be optimal. These sorts of changes are not uncommon; they may be the result of such things as price changes in raw materials, price discounts, cost reductions in production, and so on. Obviously, when a change does occur in the value of an objective function coefficient, it can be helpful for a manager to know if that change will affect the optimal values of the decision variables. The manager can quickly determine this by referring to that coefficient's range of optimality, which is the range in possible values of that objective function coefficient over which the optimal values of the decision variables will not change. Before we see how to determine the range, consider the implication of the range. The range of optimality for the type 1 coefficient in the microcomputer problem is 50 to 100. That means that as long as the coefficient's value is in that range, the optimal values will be 9 units of type 1 and 4 units of type 2. Conversely, *if a change extends beyond the range of optimality, the solution will change.*

Range of optimality

Similarly, suppose, instead, the coefficient (unit profit) of type 2 computers was to change. Its range of optimality is 30 to 60. As long as the change doesn't take it outside of this range, nine and four will still be the optimal values. Note, however, even for changes that are *within* the range of optimality, the optimal value of the objective function *will* change. If the type 1 coefficient increased from $60 to $61, and nine units of type 1 is still optimum, profit would increase by $9: nine units times $1 per unit. Thus, for a change that is within the range of optimality, a revised value of the objective function must be determined.

Now let's see how we can determine the range of optimality using computer output.

Using MS Excel. There is a table for the Changing Cells (see Figure 3S.19). It shows the value of the objective function that was used in the problem for each type of computer (i.e., 60 and 50), and the allowable increase and allowable decrease for each coefficient. By subtracting the allowable decrease from the original value of the coefficient, and adding the allowable increase to the original value of the coefficient, we obtain the range of optimality for each coefficient. Thus, we find for type 1:

$$60 - 10 = 50 \quad \text{and} \quad 60 + 40 = 100$$

Hence, the range for the type 1 coefficient is 50 to 100. For type 2:

$$50 - 20 = 30 \quad \text{and} \quad 50 + 10 = 60$$

figure 3S.19   MS Excel Sensitivity Report for Microcomputer Problem

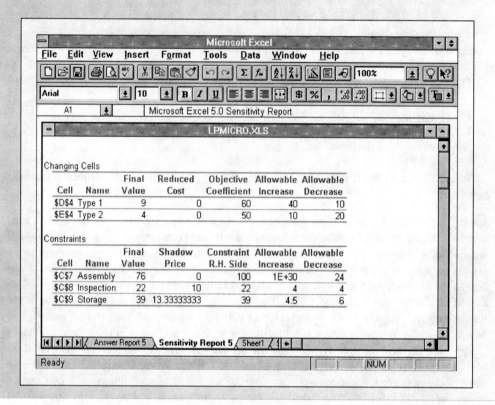

Hence the range for the type 2 coefficient is 30 to 60.

In this example, both of the decision variables are *basic* (i.e., nonzero). However, in other problems, one or more decision variables may be *nonbasic* (i.e., have an optimal value of zero). In such instances, unless the value of that variable's objective function coefficient increases by more than its *reduced cost,* it won't come into solution (i.e., become a basic variable). Hence, the range of optimality (sometimes referred to as the *range of insignificance*) for a nonbasic variable is from negative infinity to the sum of its current value and its reduced cost.

Now let's see how we can handle multiple changes to objective function coefficients, that is, a change in more than one coefficient. To do this, divide each coefficient's change by the allowable change in the same direction. Thus, if the change is a decrease, divide that amount by the allowable decrease. Treat all resulting fractions as positive. Sum the fractions. If the sum does not exceed 1.00, then multiple changes are within the range of optimality and will not result in any change to the optimal values of the decision variables.

CHANGES IN THE RIGHT-HAND SIDE (RHS) VALUE OF A CONSTRAINT

In considering right-hand side (RHS) changes, it is important to know if a particular constraint is binding on a solution. A constraint is binding if substituting the values of the decision variables of that solution into the left side of the constraint results in a value that is equal to the RHS value. In other words, that constraint stops the objective function from achieving a better value (e.g., a greater profit or a lower cost). Each constraint has a corresponding shadow price, which is a marginal value that indicates the amount by which

Shadow price

the value of the objective function would change if there were a one-unit change in the RHS value of that constraint. If a constraint is nonbinding, its shadow price is zero, meaning that increasing or decreasing its RHS value by one unit will have no impact on the value of the objective function. Nonbinding constraints have either slack (if the constraint is ≤) or surplus (if the constraint is ≥). Suppose a constraint has 10 units of slack in the optimal solution, which means 10 units that are unused. If we were to increase or decrease the constraint's RHS value by one unit, the only effect would be to increase or decrease its slack by one unit. But there is no profit associated with slack, so the value of the objective function wouldn't change. On the other hand, if the change is to the RHS value of a binding constraint, then the optimal value of the objective function would change. Any change in a binding constraint will cause the optimal values of the decision variables to change, and hence, cause the value of the objective function to change. For example, in the microcomputer problem, the inspection constraint is a binding constraint; it has a shadow price of 10. That means if there was one hour less of inspection time, total profit would decrease by $10, or if there was one more hour of inspection time available, total profit would increase by $10. In general, multiplying the amount of change in the RHS value of a constraint by the constraint's shadow price will indicate the change's impact on the optimal value of the objective function. However, this is only true over a limited range called the range of   **Range of feasibility** feasibility. In this range, the value of the shadow price remains constant. Hence, as long as a change in the RHS value of a constraint is within its range of feasibility, the shadow price will remain the same, and one can readily determine the impact on the objective function.

Let's see how to determine the range of feasibility from computer output.

Using MS Excel. In the sensitivity report there is a table labeled "Constraints" (see Figure 3S.19). The table shows the shadow price for each constraint, its RHS value, and the allowable increase and allowable decrease. Adding the allowable increase to the RHS value and subtracting the allowable decrease will produce the range of feasibility for that constraint. For example, for the inspection constraint, the range would be

$$22 + 4 = 26; \quad 22 - 4 = 18$$

Hence, the range of feasibility for inspection is 18 to 26 hours. Similarly, for the storage constraint, the range is

$$39 - 6 = 33 \quad \text{to} \quad 39 + 4.5 = 43.5$$

The range for the assembly constraint is a little different; the assembly constraint is nonbinding (note the shadow price of 0) while the other two are binding (note their nonzero shadow prices). The assembly constraint has a slack of 24 (the difference between its RHS value of 100 and its final value of 76). With its slack of 24, its RHS value could be decreased by as much as 24 (to 76) before it would become binding. Conversely, increasing its right-hand side will only produce more slack. Thus, no amount of increase in the RHS value will make it binding, so there is no upper limit on the allowable increase. Excel indicates this by the large value (1E + 30) shown for the allowable increase. So its range of feasibility has a lower limit of 76 and no upper limit.

If there are changes to more than one constraint's RHS value, analyze these in the same way as multiple changes to objective function coefficients. That is, if the change is an increase, divide that amount by that constraint's allowable increase; if the change is a decrease, divide the decrease by the allowable decrease. Treat all resulting fractions as positives. Sum the fractions. As long as the sum does not exceed 1.00, the changes are within the range of feasibility for multiple changes, and the shadow prices won't change.

Table 3S.1 summarizes the impacts of changes that fall within either the range of optimality or the range of feasibility.

Now let's consider what happens if a change goes beyond a particular range. In a situation involving the range of optimality, a change in an objective function that is beyond the range of optimality will result in a new solution. Hence, it will be necessary to recompute the solution. For a situation involving the range of feasibility, there are two cases to consider.

table 3S.1   Summary of the Impact of Changes within their Respective Ranges

CHANGES TO OBJECTIVE FUNCTION COEFFICIENTS THAT ARE WITHIN THE RANGE OF OPTIMALITY	
COMPONENT	RESULT
Values of decision variables	No change
Value of objective function	Will change

CHANGES TO RHS VALUES OF CONSTRAINTS THAT ARE WITHIN THE RANGE OF FEASIBILITY	
COMPONENT	RESULT
Value of shadow price	No change
List of basic variables	No change
Values of basic variables	Will change
Value of objective function	Will change

The first case would be increasing the RHS value of a $\leq$ constraint to beyond the upper limit of its range of feasibility. This would produce slack equal to the amount by which the upper limit is exceeded. Hence, if the upper limit is 200, and the increase is 220, the result is that the constraint has a slack of 20. Similarly, for a $\geq$ constraint, going below its lower bound creates a surplus for that constraint. The second case for each of these would be exceeding the opposite limit (the lower bound for a $\leq$ constraint, or the upper bound for a $\geq$ constraint). In either instance, a new solution would have to be generated.

KEY TERMS

Objective function Mathematical statement of profit (or cost, etc.) for a given solution.

Decision variables Amounts of either inputs or outputs.

Constraints Limitations that restrict the available alternatives.

Feasible solution space The set of all feasible combinations of decision variables as defined by the constraints.

Parameters Numerical constants.

Graphical linear programming Graphical method for finding optimal solutions to two-variable problems.

Redundant constraint A constraint that does not form a unique boundary of the feasible solution space.

Enumeration approach Substituting the coordinates of each corner point into the objective function to determine which corner point is optimal.

Binding constraint A constraint that forms the optimal corner point of the feasible solution space.

Surplus When the values of decision variables are substituted into a $\geq$ constraint the amount by which the resulting value exceeds the right-side value.

Slack When the values of decision variables are substituted into a $\leq$ constraint the amount by which the resulting value is less than the right-side value.

Simplex A linear programming algorithm that can solve problems having more than two decision variables.

Sensitivity analysis Assessing the impact of potential changes to the numerical values of an LP model.

Range of optimality Range of values over which the solution quantities of all the decision variables remain the same.

Shadow price Amount by which the value of the objective function would change with a one-unit change in the RHS value of a constraint.

Range of feasibility Range of values for the RHS of a constraint over which the shadow price remains the same.

SOLVED PROBLEMS

PROBLEM 1

A small construction firm specializes in building and selling single-family homes. The firm offers two basic types of houses, model A and model B. Model A houses require 4,000 labor hours, 2 tons of stone, and 2,000 board feet of lumber. Model B houses require 10,000 labor hours, 3 tons of stone, and 2,000 board feet of lumber. Due to long lead times for ordering supplies and the scarcity of skilled and semiskilled workers in the area, the firm will be forced to rely on its present resources for the upcoming building season. It has 400,000 hours of labor, 150 tons of stone, and 200,000 board feet of lumber. What mix of model A and B houses should the firm construct if model A yields a profit of $3,000 per unit and model B yields $6,000 per unit? Assume that the firm will be able to sell all the units it builds.

Solution

1 Formulate the objective function and constraints:[1]

$$\text{Maximize} \quad Z = 3,000A + 6,000B$$

Subject to

Labor	$4,000A + 10,000B$	$\leq$	400,000 labor hours
Stone	$2A + 3B$	$\leq$	150 tons
Lumber	$2,000A + 2,000B$	$\leq$	200,000 board feet
	A, B	$\geq$	0

2 Graph the constraints and objective function, and identify the optimum corner point (see graph). Note that the lumber constraint is *redundant:* It does not form a boundary of the feasible solution space.

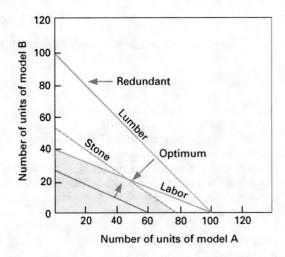

3 Determine the optimal quantities of models A and B, and compute the resulting profit. Because the optimum point is at the intersection of the stone and labor constraints, solve those two equations for their common point:

$$
\begin{array}{rl}
\text{Labor } 4,000A + 10,000B & = 400,000 \\
-2,000 \times (\text{Stone } 2A + 3B & = 150) \\
\hline
4,000B & = 100,000 \\
B & = 25
\end{array}
$$

Substitute $B = 25$ in one of the equations, and solve for A:

$$2A + 3(25) = 150 \qquad A = 37.5$$
$$Z = 3,000(37.5) + 6,000(25) = 262,500$$

4   We could have used the enumeration approach to find the optimal corner point. The corner points and the value of the objective function at each corner point are:

$A = 0, B = 40$ (found by inspection); $Z = 3,000(0) + 6,000(40) = 240,000$

$A = 37.5, B = 25$ (found using simultaneous equations); $Z = 262,500$ (see step 3)

$A = 80, B = 0$ (found by inspection); $Z = 3,000(80) + 6,000(0) = 240,000$

The best value of Z is 262,500 (because this is a maximization problem), so that indicates that the optimal corner point is $A = 37.5, B = 25$.

PROBLEM 2

This LP model was solved by computer:

Maximize $15x_1 + 20x_2 + 14x_3$

where x_1 = quantity of product 1
x_2 = quantity of product 2
x_3 = quantity of product 3

Subject to

Labor	$5x_1 + 6x_2 + 4x_3 \leq 210$ hours	
Material	$10x_1 + 8x_2 + 5x_3 \leq 200$ pounds	
Machine	$4x_1 + 2x_2 + 5x_3 \leq 170$ minutes	
	$x_1, x_2, x_3 \geq 0$	

The following information was obtained from the output. The ranges were also computed based on the output, and they are shown as well.

```
Total profit = 548.00

Variable      Value     Reduced Cost    Range of Optimality
Product 1       0          10.6          unlimited to 25.60
Product 2       5           0                 9.40 to 22.40
Product 3      32           0                12.50 to 50.00

Constraint    Slack     Shadow Price    Range of Feasibility
Labor          52          0.0           158.00 to unlimited
Material        0          2.4           170.00 to 270.91
Machine         0          0.4            50.00 to 200.00
```

a. Which decision variables are basic (i.e., in solution)?

b. By how much would the profit per unit of product 1 have to increase in order for it to have a nonzero value (i.e., for it to become a basic variable)?

c. If the profit per unit of product 2 increased by $2 to $22, would the optimal production quantities of products 2 and 3 change? Would the optimal value of the objective function change?

d. If the available amount of labor decreased by 12 hours, would that cause a change in the optimal values of the decision variables or the optimal value of the objective function? Would anything change?

e. If the available amount of material increased by 10 pounds to 210 pounds, how would that affect the optimal value of the objective function?

f. If profit per unit on product 2 increased by $1 and profit per unit on product 3 decreased by $.50, would that fall within the range of multiple changes? Would the values of the decision variables change? What would be the revised value of the objective function?

Solution

a. Products 2 and 3 are in solution (i.e., have nonzero values); the optimal value of product 2 is 5 units, and the optimal value of product 3 is 32 units.

b. The amount of increase would have to equal its *reduced cost* of $10.60.

c. No, because the change would be within its range of optimality, which has an upper limit of $22.40. The objective function value would increase by an amount equal to the quantity of product 2 and its increased unit profit. Hence, it would increase by 5($2) = $10 to $558.

d. Labor has a slack of 52 hours. Consequently, the only effect would be to decrease the slack to 40 hours.

e. The change is within the range of feasibility. The objective function value will increase by the amount of change multiplied by material's shadow price of $2.40. Hence, the objective function value would increase by 10($2.40) = $24.00. (Note: If the change had been a *decrease* of 10 pounds, which is also within the range of feasibility, the value of the objective function would have *decreased* by this amount.)

f. To determine if the changes are within the range for multiple changes, we first compute the ratio of the amount of each change to the end of the range *in the same direction*. For product 2, it is $1/$2.40 = .417; for product 3, it is $-$.50/ $- $1.50 = .333. Next, we compute the sum of these ratios: .417 + .333 = .750. Because this does not exceed 1.00, we conclude that these changes are within the range. This means that the optimal values of the decision variables will not change. We can compute the change to the value of the objective function by multiplying each product's optimal quantity by its changed profit per unit: 5($1) + 32($- $.50) = 2$11. Hence, with these changes, the value of the objective function would decrease by $11; its new value would be $548 $- $11 = $537.

DISCUSSION AND REVIEW QUESTIONS

1 For which decision environment is linear programming most suited?
2 What is meant by the term *feasible solution space?* What determines this region?
3 Explain the term *redundant constraint.*
4 What is an isocost line? An isoprofit line?
5 What does sliding an objective function line toward the origin represent? Away from the origin?
6 Briefly explain these terms:
   a. Basic variable.
   b. Shadow price.
   c. Range of feasibility.
   d. Range of optimality.

PROBLEMS

1 Solve these problems using graphical linear programming and answer the questions that follow. Use simultaneous equations to determine the optimal values of the decision variables.

   a. Maximize $Z = 4x_1 + 3x_2$
      Subject to

Material	$6x_1 + 4x_2 \leq 48$ lb	
Labor	$4x_1 + 8x_2 \leq 80$ hr	
	$x_1, x_2 \geq 0$	

   b. Maximize $Z = 2x_1 + 10x_2$
      Subject to

Durability	$10x_1 + 4x_2 \geq 40$ wk	
Strength	$1x_1 + 6x_2 \geq 24$ psi	
Time	$1x_1 + 2x_2 \leq 14$ hr	
	$x_1, x_2 \geq 0$	

   c. Maximize $Z = 6A + 3B$ (revenue)
      Subject to

Material	$20A + 6B \leq 600$ lb	
Machinery	$25A + 20B \leq 1{,}000$ hr	
Labor	$20A + 30B \leq 1{,}200$ hr	
	A, B ≥ 0	

   (1) What are the optimal values of the decision variables and Z?
   (2) Do any constraints have (nonzero) slack? If yes, which one(s) and how much slack does each have?
   (3) Do any constraints have (nonzero) surplus? If yes, which one(s) and how much surplus does each have?
   (4) Are any constraints redundant? If yes, which one(s)? Explain briefly.

2 Solve these problems using graphical linear programming and then answer the questions that follow. Use simultaneous equations to determine the optimal values of the decision variables.

a. Minimize $Z = 1.80S + 2.20T$
     Subject to

Potassium	$5S + 8T$	≥ 200 gr
Carbohydrate	$15S + 6T$	≥ 240 gr
Protein	$4S + 12T$	≥ 180 gr
T	T	≥ 10 gr
	S, T	≥ 0

b. Minimize $Z = 2x_1 + 3x_2$
     Subject to

D	$4x_1 + 2x_2$	≥ 20
E	$2x_1 + 6x_2$	≥ 18
F	$1x_1 + 2x_2$	≤ 12
	x_1, x_2	≥ 0

(1) What are the optimal values of the decision variables and Z?

(2) Do any constraints have (nonzero) slack? If yes, which one(s) and how much slack does each have?

(3) Do any constraints have (nonzero) surplus? If yes, which one(s) and how much surplus does each have?

(4) Are any constraints redundant? If yes, which one(s)? Explain briefly.

3. An appliance manufacturer produces two models of microwave ovens: H and W. Both models require fabrication and assembly work; each H uses four hours of fabrication and two hours of assembly, and each W uses two hours of fabrication and six hours of assembly. There are 600 fabrication hours available this week and 480 hours of assembly. Each H contributes $40 to profits, and each W contributes $30 to profits. What quantities of H and W will maximize profits?

     a. Use the objective function approach.

     b. Use the enumeration approach.

4. A small candy shop is preparing for the holiday season. The owner must decide how many bags of deluxe mix and how many bags of standard mix of Peanut/Raisin Delite to put up. The deluxe mix has ⅔ pound raisins and ⅓ pound peanuts, and the standard mix has ½ pound raisins and ½ pound peanuts per bag. The shop has 90 pounds of raisins and 60 pounds of peanuts to work with.

     Peanuts cost $.60 per pound and raisins cost $1.50 per pound. The deluxe mix will sell for $2.90 per pound, and the standard mix will sell for $2.55 per pound. The owner estimates that no more than 110 bags of one type can be sold.

     a. If the goal is to maximize profits, how many bags of each type should be prepared?

     b. What is the expected profit?

5. A retired couple supplement their income by making fruit pies, which they sell to a local grocery store. During the month of September, they produce apple and grape pies. The apple pies are sold for $1.50 to the grocer, and the grape pies are sold for $1.20. The couple is able to sell all of the pies they produce owing to their high quality. They use fresh ingredients. Flour and sugar are purchased once each month. For the month of September, they have 1,200 cups of sugar and 2,100 cups of flour. Each apple pie requires 1½ cups of sugar and 3 cups of flour, and each grape pie requires 2 cups of sugar and 3 cups of flour.

     a. Determine the number of grape and the number of apple pies that will maximize revenues if the couple working together can make an apple pie in six minutes and a grape pie in three minutes. They plan to work no more than 60 hours.

     b. Determine the amounts of sugar, flour, and time that will be unused.

6. Solve each of these problems by computer and obtain the optimal values of the decision variables and the objective function.

     a. Maximize $4x_1 + 2x_2 + 5x_3$
        Subject to

$$1x_1 + 2x_2 + 1x_3 \leq 25$$
$$1x_1 + 4x_2 + 2x_3 \leq 40$$
$$3x_1 + 3x_2 + 1x_3 \leq 30$$
$$x_1, x_2, x_3 \geq 0$$

b. Maximize $\quad 10x_1 + 6x_2 + 3x_3$

Subject to

$$1x_1 + 1x_2 + 2x_3 \leq 25$$
$$2x_1 + 1x_2 + 4x_3 \leq 40$$
$$1x_1 + 2x_2 + 3x_3 \leq 40$$
$$x_1, x_2, x_3 \geq 0$$

7 For Problem 6*a*, determine the following:

a. The range of feasibility for each constraint.

b. The range of optimality for the coefficients of the objective function.

8 For Problem 6*b:*

a. Find the range of feasibility for each constraint, and interpret your answers.

b. Determine the range of optimality for each coefficient of the objective function. Interpret your results.

9 A small firm makes three similar products, which all follow the same three-step process, consisting of milling, inspection, and drilling. Product A requires 12 minutes of milling, 5 minutes for inspection, and 10 minutes of drilling per unit; product B requires 10 minutes of milling, 4 minutes for inspection, and 8 minutes of drilling per unit; and product C requires 8 minutes of milling, 4 minutes for inspection, and 16 minutes of drilling. The department has 20 hours available during the next period for milling, 15 hours for inspection, and 24 hours for drilling. Product A contributes $2.40 per unit to profit, product B contributes $2.50 per unit, and product C contributes $3.00 per unit. Determine the optimal mix of products in terms of maximizing contribution to profits for the period. Then, find the range of optimality for the profit coefficient of each variable.

10 Formulate and then solve a linear programming model of this problem, to determine how many containers of each product to produce tomorrow to maximize profits. The company makes four juice products using orange, grapefruit, and pineapple juice.

PRODUCT	RETAIL PRICE PER QUART
Orange juice	$1.00
Grapefruit juice	.90
Pineapple juice	.80
All-in-One	1.10

The All-in-One juice has equal parts of orange, grapefruit, and pineapple juice. Each product is produced in a one-quart size (there are four quarts in a gallon). On hand are 400 gallons of orange juice, 300 gallons of grapefruit juice, and 200 gallons of pineapple juice. The cost per gallon is $2.00 for orange juice, $1.60 for grapefruit juice, and $1.40 for pineapple juice.

In addition, the manager wants grapefruit juice to be used for no more than 30 percent of the number of containers produced. She wants the ratio of the number of containers of orange juice to the number of containers of pineapple juice to be at least 7 to 5.

11 A wood products firm uses available time at the end of each week to make goods for stock. Currently, two products on the list of items are produced for stock: a chopping board and a knife holder. Both items require three operations: cutting, gluing, and finishing. The manager of the firm has collected the following data on these products:

		TIME PER UNIT (MINUTES)		
ITEM	PROFIT/UNIT	CUTTING	GLUING	FINISHING
Chopping board	$2	1.4	5	12
Knife holder	$6	0.8	13	3

The manager has also determined that, during each week, 56 minutes are available for cutting, 650 minutes are available for gluing, and 360 minutes are available for finishing.

a. Determine the optimal quantities of the decision variables.

b. Which resources are not completely used by your solution? How much of each resource is unused?

12   The manager of the deli section of a grocery superstore has just learned that the department has 112 pounds of mayonnaise, of which 70 pounds is approaching its expiration date and must be used. To use up the mayonnaise, the manager has decided to prepare two items: a ham spread and a deli spread. Each pan of the ham spread will require 1.4 pounds of mayonnaise, and each pan of the deli spread will require 1.0 pound. The manager has received an order for 10 pans of ham spread and 8 pans of the deli spread. In addition, the manager has decided to have at least 10 pans of each spread available for sale. Both spreads will cost $3 per pan to make, but ham spread sells for $5 per pan and deli spread sells for $7 per pan.
 a. Determine the solution that will minimize cost.
 b. Determine the solution that will maximize profit.

13   A manager wants to know how many units of each product to produce on a daily basis in order to achieve the highest contribution to profit. Production requirements for the products are shown in the following table.

PRODUCT	MATERIAL 1 (POUNDS)	MATERIAL 2 (POUNDS)	LABOR (HOURS)
A	2	3	3.2
B	1	5	1.5
C	6	—	2.0

Material 1 costs $5 a pound, material 2 costs $4 a pound, and labor costs $10 an hour. Product A sells for $80 a unit, product B sells for $90 a unit, and product C sells for $70 a unit. Available resources each day are 200 pounds of material 1; 300 pounds of material 2; and 150 hours of labor.

  The manager must satisfy certain output requirements: The output of product A should not be more than one-third of the total number of units produced; the ratio of units of product A to units of product B should be 3 to 2; and there is a standing order for 5 units of product A each day. Formulate a linear programming model for this problem, and then solve.

14   A chocolate maker has contracted to operate a small candy counter in a fashionable store. To start with, the selection of offerings will be intentionally limited. The counter will offer a regular mix of candy made up of equal parts of cashews, raisins, caramels, and chocolates, and a deluxe mix that is one-half cashews and one-half chocolates, which will be sold in one-pound boxes. In addition, the candy counter will offer individual one-pound boxes of cashews, raisins, caramels, and chocolates.

  A major attraction of the candy counter is that all candies are made fresh at the counter. However, storage space for supplies and ingredients is limited. Bins are available that can hold the amounts shown in the table:

INGREDIENT	CAPACITY (POUNDS PER DAY)
Cashews	120
Raisins	200
Caramels	100
Chocolates	160

In order to present a good image and to encourage purchases, the counter will make at least 20 boxes of each type of product each day. Any leftover boxes at the end of the day will be removed and given to a nearby nursing home for goodwill.

  The profit per box for the various items has been determined as follows:

ITEM	PROFIT PER BOX
Regular	$.80
Deluxe	.90
Cashews	.70
Raisins	.60
Caramels	.50
Chocolates	.75

 a. Formulate the LP model.
 b. Solve for the optimal values of the decision variables and the maximum profit.

15. Given this linear programming model, solve the model and then answer the questions that follow.

Maximize $12x_1 + 18x_2 + 15x_3$ where x_1 = the quantity of product 1 to make etc.

Subject to

Machine	$5x_1 + 4x_2 + 3x_3 \leq 160$ minutes
Labor	$4x_1 + 10x_2 + 4x_3 \leq 288$ hours
Materials	$2x_1 + 2x_2 + 4x_3 \leq 200$ pounds
Product 2	$x_2 \leq 16$ units
	$x_1, x_2, x_3 \geq 0$

a. Are any constraints binding? If so, which one(s)?

b. If the profit on product 3 was changed to $22 a unit, what would the values of the decision variables be? The objective function? Explain.

c. If the profit on product 1 was changed to $22 a unit, what would the values of the decision variables be? The objective function? Explain.

d. If 10 hours less of labor time were available, what would the values of the decision variables be? The objective function? Explain.

e. If the manager decided that as many as 20 units of product 2 could be produced (instead of 16), how much additional profit would be generated?

f. If profit per unit on each product increased by $1, would the optimal values of the decision variables change? Explain. What would the optimal value of the objective function be?

16. A garden store prepares various grades of pine bark for mulch: nuggets (x_1), mini-nuggets (x_2), and chips (x_3). The process requires pine bark, machine time, labor time, and storage space. The following model has been developed.

Maximize $9x_1 + 9x_2 + 6x_3$ (profit)

Subject to

Bark	$5x_1 + 6x_2 + 3x_3 \leq 600$ pounds
Machine	$2x_1 + 4x_2 + 5x_3 \leq 600$ minutes
Labor	$2x_1 + 4x_2 + 3x_3 \leq 480$ hours
Storage	$1x_1 + 1x_2 + 1x_3 \leq 150$ bags
	$x_1, x_2, x_3 \geq 0$

a. What is the marginal value of a pound of pine bark? Over what range is this price value appropriate?

b. What is the maximum price the store would be justified in paying for additional pine bark?

c. What is the marginal value of labor? Over what range is this value in effect?

d. The manager obtained additional machine time through better scheduling. How much additional machine time can be effectively used for this operation? Why?

e. If the manager can *obtain* either additional pine bark or additional storage space, which one should she choose and how much (assuming additional quantities cost the same as usual)?

f. If a change in the chip operation increased the profit on chips from $6 per bag to $7 per bag, would the optimal quantities change? Would the value of the objective function change? If so, what would the new value(s) be?

g. If profits on chips increased to $7 per bag and profits on nuggets decreased by $.60, would the optimal quantities change? Would the value of the objective function change? If so, what would the new value(s) be?

h. If the amount of pine bark available decreased by 15 pounds, machine time decreased by 27 minutes, and storage capacity increased by five bags, would this fall in the range of feasibility for multiple changes? If so, what would the value of the objective function be?

CASE: SON, LTD.

Son, Ltd., manufactures a variety of chemical products used by photoprocessors. Son was recently bought out by a conglomerate, and managers of the two organizations have been working together to improve the efficiency of Son's operations.

Managers have been asked to adhere to weekly operating budgets and to develop operating plans using quantitative methods whenever possible. The manager of one department has been given a weekly operating budget of $11,980 for production of three chemical products, which for convenience shall be referred to as Q, R, and W. The budget is intended to pay for direct labor and materials. Processing requirements for the three products, on a per unit basis, are shown in the table.

The company has a contractual obligation for 85 units of product R per week.

Material A costs $4 per pound, as does material B. Labor costs $8 an hour.

Product Q sells for $122 a unit, product R sells for $115 a unit, and product W sells for $76 a unit.

The manager is considering a number of different proposals regarding the quantity of each product to produce. The manager is primarily interested in maximizing contribution. Moreover, the manager wants to know how much labor will be needed, as well as the amount of each material to purchase.

Questions

Prepare a report that addresses the following issues:

1 The optimal quantities of products and the necessary quantities of labor and materials.

2 One proposal is to make equal amounts of the products. What amount of each will maximize contribution, and what quantities of labor and materials will be needed? How much less will total contribution be if this proposal is adopted?

3 How would you formulate the constraint for material A if it was determined that there is a 5 percent waste factor for material A and equal quantities of each product are required?

Product	Labor (hours)	Material A (pounds)	Material B (pounds)
Q	5	2	1
R	4	2	—
W	2	½	2

Case: Custom Cabinets, Inc.©

Custom Cabinets, Inc. (CCI), manufactures two major lines of kitchen and bathroom cabinets. The SemiCustom Line consists of cabinets that are variations on a standard design. These cabinets are made to order. The StandardLine is a lower priced line of cabinets that use standardized designs and materials. StandardLine cabinets are made to stock. The company has been in business for many years and has consistently performed well financially.

It was obvious that something big was up as the management staff began to gather for a meeting called by CCI General Manager John Fleming. There was little of the usual light banter, and more significantly, there were no coffee and donuts. The CCI culture celebrates even small achievements with coffee and donuts. Their absence was not a good omen.

John began rather somberly. "As you know we are almost 2 months into our second fiscal quarter. Frankly, the financial results don't look very good. You are aware, I'm sure, of how the stock market has been punishing companies that fail to at least meet their sales and profit targets. We are in danger of having to announce that we met our sales goals but fell short of our profit goals. This will be a real jolt to our shareholders, and since, except for the interns, we are all in the company's stock purchase plan, that means it will hurt us too. We only have one month to turn this around. We don't want to take any shortcut approaches to meeting our goals—we want the results to reflect the real results of our operation.

The headquarters brass talked with a consultant who analyzed our records. Her opinion is that we need to address operations efficiency. In her words, we have to learn to get more out of our existing resources. She leaves the details to us to figure out. Our biggest personnel resource to assign to this problem is our group of management interns from Nearby University. I've talked to the interns and alerted them that for the next month or so they are to work directly with Bill Chavez, our Operations Manager, on this project. The goal is to be sure that we get the maximum bang for our resource buck during the next month's operations. We have to get the most profit possible to make the quarter's results look at least respectable. Needless to say, I want each of you to give the intern group your fullest cooperation."

Now you understand why the interns were invited to the staff meeting. You've just been on board for a few weeks and have just begun to understand the company's operations. That means the boss can't be looking to you for engineering solutions. Your expertise is operations management, not engineering.

As the meeting broke up, Bill Chavez asked you (the interns) to stay for a follow-up meeting with him. "I've been very impressed with the work that you have done in your short time with CCI. You obviously get an excellent education at Nearby U. I asked Tom to assign you to me because I think you are our best hope of pulling out some really good profit numbers. You don't have any preconceived ideas about what will and will not work, so I expect you to come up with ideas that are more innovative than the old hands.

"I spent most of the morning with the other department heads gathering information that I think you might need (that information is enclosed with this case). If you need additional information send me an e-mail or stop in my office. If I can get the information you need, I will do so. We're counting on you. Don't let us down. I'll let you guys figure out when and where to meet. Needless to say you have full access to all our computer resources should you need them.

"There are a few things you need to keep in mind. Our Semi-Custom Line is hot because of our excellent customer service. We never fail to deliver a SemiCustom unit on time. We also need to meet our customer orders on the StandardLine units, but we can cut the stockage levels if necessary. We can't, however, exceed the stockage levels. Making excess inventory is no way to be more efficient. If necessary, we could work 10 percent overtime in assembly and 5 percent overtime in finishing. Each overtime hour will add $5.00 per hour to our labor cost. I've checked with all our suppliers. We can get up to 50,000 additional board-feet of wood by paying a $0.50 per board-foot upcharge and 10,000 additional square feet of laminate for an upcharge of $0.15 per square foot. There is no reasonable prospect of obtaining more of the other materials at any price. Because of the way our profit center is set up, we get credit for building to the authorized stockage level as if it were a final sale."

As you were leaving the meeting, Barbara Wilson invited you to the break room for a cup of coffee. Barbara is the Lead Production Scheduler and has worked for Custom Cabinets for a long time. You have been told that she knows everything about how things work

ENCLOSURE A
BILLS OF MATERIALS AND LABOR

	WOOD BD.-FT.	TRIM LIN. FT.	GRANITE SQ. FT.	SOLID SURFACE SQ. FT.	LAMINATE SQ. FT.	ASSBLY. LABOR HRS.	FINISH LABOR HRS.
SEMICUSTOM LINE							
SC-A	125	27	175	0	0	37	7
SC-B	160	42	243	0	0	57	12
SC-C	140	35	0	160	0	30	5
SC-D	200	52	0	140	0	35	7
STANDARDLINE							
S-10	60	21	0	112	0	21	3
S-20	110	28	0	0	135	25	5
S-30	200	50	0	0	254	30	7
S-40	180	43	0	0	176	27	5
AVAILABLE	400,000	140,000	45,000	150,000	400,000	100,000	25,000

ENCLOSURE B
ORDERS AND PROFITS

	PROFIT/UNIT @ STANDARD	CUSTOMER ORDERS NEXT MONTH	BUILD-TO-STOCK AUTHORIZATION NEXT MONTH
SEMICUSTOM LINE			
SC-A	$325	117	0
SC-B	$575	92	0
SC-C	$257	130	0
SC-D	$275	150	0
STANDARDLINE			
S-10	$175	475	400
S-20	$210	363	350
S-30	$260	510	450
S-40	$230	412	475

SOURCE: © VICTOR E. SOWER, 2006.

here and is a good person to know. "I heard about your assignment," she began. "Let me tell you

some things about your boss, Bill Chavez. He is a great guy to work for and he really knows his stuff. He is not one of the college guys who act as if they know everything—no offense. He worked his way up. He is very intelligent, but doesn't have the educational background that you do. In the past, new college graduates have made some mistakes in writing reports for Bill. He likes for everything in the report to be written in words he can understand. He likes you to include computer printouts in an appendix to the report (he likes to see all the backup detail), but wants you to explain in the body of the report why they are necessary and what they mean. If he doesn't understand what you are recommending and why, he won't ask questions. He will just discard the report, and that will be the last assignment you will ever do for him. I figured that the least I could do would be to buy you a cup of coffee and try to help you get off to a good start on this project."

SELECTED BIBLIOGRAPHY AND FURTHER READINGS

Bierman, Harold, Charles P. Bonini, and Warren H. Hausman. *Quantitative Analysis for Business Decisions*. 9th ed. Burr Ridge, IL: Richard D. Irwin, 1997.

Hillier, Frederick S., Mark S. Hillier, and Gerald Lieberman. *Introduction to Management Science*. Burr Ridge, IL: Irwin/McGraw-Hill, 2000.

Ragsdale, Cliff T. *Spreadsheet Modeling and Decision Analysis: A Practical Introduction to Management Science*. Cambridge, MA: Course Technology, 1995.

Stevenson, W. J., and Ceyhun Ozgur. *Introduction to Management Science with Spreadsheets*. New York: McGraw-Hill, 2006.

Taylor, Bernard. *Introduction to Management Science*. 6th ed. Upper Saddle River, NJ: Prentice Hall, 1999.

FOOTNOTE

1 For the sake of consistency, we will assign to the horizontal axis the first decision variable mentioned in the problem. In this case, variable *A* will be represented on the horizontal axis and variable *B* on the vertical axis.

AGGREGATE PLANNING

chapter 4

Seasonal variations in demand are quite common in many industries and public services, such as air-conditioning, fuel, public utilities, police and fire protection, and travel. And these are just a few examples of industries and public services that have to deal with uneven demands. Generally speaking, organizations cannot predict exactly the quantity and timing of demands for specific products or services months in advance under these conditions. Even so, they typically must assess their capacity needs (e.g., labor, inventories) and costs months in advance in order to be able to handle demand. How do they do it? They use a process often referred to as aggregate planning. That is the subject of this chapter.

Learning Objectives

After completing this chapter, you should be able to:

1. Explain what aggregate planning is and how it is useful.
2. Identify the variables decision makers have to work with in aggregate planning and some of the possible strategies they can use.
3. Describe some of the graphical and quantitative techniques planners use.
4. Prepare aggregate plans and compute their costs.

In the spectrum of production planning, aggregate planning is intermediate-range capacity planning that typically covers a time horizon of 2 to 12 months, although in some companies it may extend to as much as 18 months. It is particularly useful for organizations that experience seasonal or other fluctuations in demand or capacity. The goal of aggregate planning is to achieve a production plan that will effectively utilize the organization's resources to match expected demand. Planners must make decisions on output rates, employment levels and changes, inventory levels and changes, back orders, and subcontracting in or out.

Some organizations use the term "sales and operations planning" instead of aggregate planning for intermediate-range planning. Similarly, sales and operations planning is defined as making intermediate-range decisions to balance supply and demand, integrating financial and operations planning. Because the plan affects functions throughout the organization, it is typically prepared with inputs from sales (demand forecasts), finance (financial constraints), and operations (capacity

Aggregate planning

Sales and operations planning

constraints). Note that the sales and operations plan is important planning information that will have impacts throughout the supply chain, and it should be shared with supply chain partners, who might also have valuable inputs.

INTRODUCTION

INTERMEDIATE PLANNING IN PERSPECTIVE

Organizations make capacity decisions on three levels: long term, intermediate term, and short term. Long-term decisions relate to product and service selection (i.e., determining which products or services to offer), facility size and location, equipment decisions, and layout of facilities. These long-term decisions essentially establish the capacity constraints within which intermediate planning must function. Intermediate decisions, as noted above, relate to general levels of employment, output, and inventories, which in turn establish boundaries within which short-range capacity decisions must be made. Thus, short-term decisions essentially consist of deciding the best way to achieve desired results within the constraints resulting from long-term and intermediate-term decisions. Short-term decisions involve scheduling jobs, workers and equipment, and the like. The three levels of capacity decisions are depicted in Table 4.1.

Many business organizations develop a *business plan* that encompasses both long-term and intermediate-term planning. The business plan establishes guidelines for the organization, taking into account the organization's strategies and policies; forecasts of demand for the organization's products or services; and economic, competitive, and political conditions. A key objective in business planning is to coordinate the intermediate plans of various organization functions, such as marketing, operations, and finance. In manufacturing companies, coordination also includes engineering and materials management. Consequently, all of these functional areas must work together to formulate the aggregate plan. Aggregate planning decisions are strategic decisions that define the framework within which operating decisions will be made. They are the starting point for scheduling and production control systems. They provide input for financial plans; they involve forecasting input and demand management, and they may require changes in employment levels. And if the organization is involved in *time-based competition*, it will be important to incorporate some flexibility in the aggregate plan to be able to handle changing requirements promptly. As noted, the plans must fit into the framework established by the organization's long-term goals and strategies, and the limitations established by long-term facility and capital budget decisions. The aggregate plan will guide the more detailed planning that eventually leads to a *master schedule*. Figure 4.1 illustrates the planning sequence.

table 4.1   Overview of Planning Levels (Chapter Number are Shown)

Long-Range Plans	Intermediate Plans
Layout }3	(This chapter)
	General levels of:
	Employment
	Output
	Finished-goods inventories
	Subcontracting
	Back orders

Planning Sequence

figure 4.1

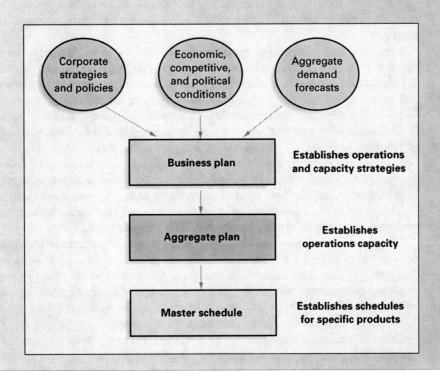

PRODUCT LINES, SUCH AS THESE FOUR MODELS IN THE IPAQ POCKET PC FROM HEWLETT-PACKARD, MAY SHARE COMMON PARTS. IN THIS CASE THREE MODELS SHARE THE SAME HOUSING. IN AGGREGATE PLANNING, HP WOULD CONSIDER THESE AS AIMED AT ONE AGGREGATE MARKET, AND WOULD ALSO ROLL UP COSTS OF COMMON PARTS AND PROCESSES. (WWW.HP.COM)

Aggregate planning also can serve as an important input to other strategic decisions; for example, management may decide to add capacity when aggregate planning alternatives for temporarily increasing capacity, such as working overtime and subcontracting, are too costly.

THE CONCEPT OF AGGREGATION

Aggregate planning is essentially a "big-picture" approach to planning. Planners usually try to avoid focusing on individual products or services—unless the organization has only one major product or service. Instad, they focus on a group of similar products or services, or sometimes an entire product or service line. For example, planners in a company producing television sets would not concern themselves with 21-inch sets versus 25-inch or 27-inch sets. Instead, planners would lump all models together and deal with them as though they were a single product, hence the term *aggregate* planning. Thus, when fast-food companies such as McDonald's, Burger King, or Wendy's plan employment and output levels, they don't try to determine how demand will be broken down into the various menu options they offer; they focus on overall demand and the overall capacity they want to provide.

Now consider how aggregate planning might work in a large department store. Space allocation is often an aggregate decision. That is, a manager might decide to allocate 20 percent of the available space in the clothing department to women's sportswear, 30 percent to juniors, and so on, without regard for what brand names will be offered or how much of juniors will be jeans. The aggregate measure might be square feet of space or racks of clothing.

For purposes of aggregate planning, it is often convenient to think of capacity in terms of labor hours or machine hours per period, or output rates (barrels per period, units per period), without worrying about how much of a particular item will actually be involved. This approach frees planners to make general decisions about the use of resources without having to get into the complexities of individual product or service requirements. Product groupings make the problem of obtaining an acceptable unit of aggregation easier because product groupings may lend themselves to the same aggregate measures.

Why do organizations need to do aggregate planning? The answer is twofold. One part is related to *planning:* It takes time to implement plans. For instance, if plans call for hiring (and training) new workers, that will take time. The second part is strategic: *Aggregation* is important because it is not possible to predict with any degree of accuracy the timing and volume of demand for individual items. So if an organization were to "lock in" on individual items, it would lose the flexibility to respond to the market.

Generally speaking, aggregate planning is connected to the budgeting process. Most organizations plan their financial requirements annually on a department-by-department basis.

Finally, aggregate planning is important because it can help synchronize flow throughout the supply chain; it affects costs, equipment utilization, employment levels, and customer satisfaction.

Two key issues in aggregate planning are how to handle variations in demand and how to handle changes.

DEALING WITH VARIATIONS

As in other areas of business management, variations in either supply or demand can occur. Minor variations are usually not a problem, but large variations generally have a major impact on the ability to match supply and demand, so they must be dealt with. Most organizations use rolling 3-, 6-, 9-, and 12-month forecasts—forecasts that are updated periodically—rather than relying on a once-a-year forecast. This allows planners to take into account any changes in either expected demand or expected supply and to develop revised plans.

Some businesses tend to exhibit a fair degree of stability, whereas in others, variations are more the norm. In those instances, a number of strategies are used to counter variations. One is to maintain a certain amount of excess capacity to handle increases in demand. This strategy makes sense when the opportunity cost of lost revenue greatly exceeds the cost of maintaining excess capacity. Another strategy is to maintain a degree of flexibility in dealing with changes. That might involve hiring temporary workers and/or working overtime when needed. Organizations that experience seasonal demands typically use this approach. Such as delayed differentiation and modular design, may also be options. Still another strategy is to wait as long as possible before committing to a certain level of supply capability. This might involve scheduling products or services with known demands first, which allows some time to pass, shortening the time horizon, and perhaps enabling demands for the remaining products or services to become less uncertain.

AN OVERVIEW OF AGGREGATE PLANNING

Aggregate planning begins with a forecast of aggregate demand for the intermediate range. This is followed by a general plan to meet demand requirements by setting output, employment, and finished-goods inventory levels or service capacities. Managers might consider a number of plans, each of which must be examined in light of feasibility and cost. If a plan is reasonably good but has minor difficulties, it may be reworked. Conversely, a poor plan should be discarded and alternative plans considered until an acceptable one is uncovered. The production plan is essentially the output of aggregate planning.

Aggregate plans are updated periodically, often monthly, to take into account updated forecasts and other changes. This results in a *rolling planning horizon* (i.e., the aggregate plan always covers the next 12–18 months).

Demand and Supply. Aggregate planners are concerned with the *quantity* and the *timing* of expected demand. If total expected demand for the planning period is much different from available capacity over that same period, the major approach of planners will be to try to achieve a balance by altering capacity, demand, or both. On the other hand, even if capacity and demand are approximately equal for the planning horizon as a whole, planners may still be faced with the problem of dealing with uneven demand *within* the planning interval. In some periods, expected demand may exceed projected capacity, in others expected demand may be less than projected capacity, and in some periods the two may be equal. The task of aggregate planners is to achieve rough equality of demand and capacity over the entire planning horizon. Moreover, planners are usually concerned with minimizing the cost of the aggregate plan, although cost is not the only consideration.

Inputs to Aggregate Planning. Effective aggregate planning requires good *information*. First, the available resources over the planning period must be known. Then, a forecast of expected demand must be available. Finally, planners must take into account any policies regarding changes in employment levels (e.g., some organizations view layoffs as extremely undesirable, so they would use that only as a last resort).

Table 4.2 lists the major inputs to aggregate planning.

Companies in the travel industry and some other industries often experience duplicate orders from customers who make multiple reservations but only intend to keep at most one of them. This makes capacity planning all the more difficult.

Aggregate Planning Inputs and Outputs

table 4.2

INPUTS	OUTPUTS
Resources	Total cost of a plan
Workforce/production rates	Projected levels of
Facilities and equipment	Inventory
Demand forecast	Output
Policies on workforce changes	Employment
Subcontracting	Subcontracting
Overtime	Backordering
Inventory levels/changes	
Back orders	
Costs	
Inventory carrying cost	
Back orders	
Hiring/firing	
Overtime	
Inventory changes	
Subcontracting	

READING: DUPLICATE ORDERS CAN LEAD TO EXCESS CAPACITY

We've all heard about someone who booked seats on two airlines, or reserved two hotel rooms, usually because travel plans weren't firmed up, but the person didn't want to miss out on the trip. Later, the person canceled one set of reservations. This sort of duplicate ordering isn't just limited to the travel industry. The trouble is, companies base their capacity planning on demand estimates, and when there are numerous duplicate orders, it is easy to overestimate demand and end up with excess capacity. In some instances, this has led companies to expand at a time when demand was actually leveling off or even decreasing! The problem is further compounded if companies conclude that canceled orders reflect customers' reluctance to wait, and respond by *adding* capacity when, in fact, order cancellation may actually reflect duplicate ordering.

Some semiconductor companies downplay data on bookings because it is too difficult to distinguish between duplicate orders and actual demand.

Yet it is important to account for double orders. Otherwise, by counting duplicate orders as true demand, you overestimate the demand rate, and by counting the cancellations of duplicate orders as lost sales, you overestimate customers' sensitivity to delay, and then you wind up with excess capacity.

"The optimal level of capacity increases with customers' sensitivity to delay, so estimating customers' sensitivity to delay is a very important part of the puzzle."

Duplicate orders can make capacity planning very difficult. The key is to carefully estimate both the rate of duplicate ordering and the degree of order cancellation that can be attributed to duplicate ordering.

SOURCE: BASED ON MOR ARMONY AND ERICA L. PLAMBECK, "THE IMPACT OF DUPLICATE ORDERS ON DEMAND ESTIMATION AND CAPACITY INVESTMENT," GSB RESEARCH PAPER #1740, GRADUATE SCHOOL OF BUSINESS, STANFORD UNIVERSITY, JUNE 2002.

DEMAND AND SUPPLY OPTIONS

Aggregate planning strategies can be described as proactive, reactive, or mixed. *Proactive* strategies involve demand options: They attempt to alter demand so that it matches capacity. *Reactive* strategies involve capacity options: They attempt to alter capacity so that it matches demand. *Mixed* strategies involve an element of each of these approaches.

Demand Options.   Demand options include pricing, promotions, using back orders (delaying order filling), and creating new demand.

1. **Pricing.**   Pricing differentials are commonly used to shift demand from peak periods to off-peak periods. Some hotels, for example, offer lower rates for weekend stays, and some airlines offer lower fares for night travel. Movie theaters may offer reduced rates for matinees, and some restaurants offer "early bird specials" in an attempt to shift some of the heavier dinner demand to an earlier time that traditionally has less traffic. Some restaurants also offer smaller portions at reduced rates, and most have smaller portions and prices for children. To the extent that pricing is effective, demand will be shifted so that it corresponds more closely to capacity, albeit for an *opportunity cost* that represents the lost profit stemming from capacity insufficient to meet demand during certain periods.

   An important factor to consider is the *degree* of price elasticity for the product or service: The more the elasticity, the more effective pricing will be in influencing demand patterns.

2. **Promotion.**   Advertising and other forms of promotion, such as displays and direct marketing, can sometimes be very effective in shifting demand so that it conforms more closely to capacity. Obviously, timing of these efforts and knowledge of response rates and response patterns will be needed to achieve the desired results. Unlike pricing policy, there is much less control over the timing of demand, so there is the risk that promotion can worsen the condition it was intended to improve, by bringing in demand at the wrong time, further stressing capacity.

3. **Back orders.** An organization can shift demand to other periods by allowing back orders. That is, orders are taken in one period and deliveries promised for a later period. The success of this approach depends on how willing customers are to wait for delivery. Moreover, the costs associated with back orders can be difficult to pin down since they would include lost sales, annoyed or disappointed customers, and perhaps additional paperwork.

4. **New demand.** Many organizations are faced with the problem of having to provide products or services for peak demand in situations where demand is very uneven. For instance, demand for bus transportation tends to be more intense during the morning and late afternoon rush hours but much lighter at other times. Creating new demand for buses at other times (e.g., trips by schools, clubs, and senior citizen groups) would make use of the excess capacity during those slack times. Similarly, many fast-food restaurants are open for breakfast to use their capacities more fully, and some landscaping firms in northern climates use their equipment during the winter months for snow removal. Manufacturing firms that experience seasonal demands for certain products (e.g., snowblowers) are sometimes able to develop a demand for a complementary product (e.g., lawn mowers, garden equipment) that makes use of the same production processes. They thereby achieve a more consistent use of labor, equipment, and facilities. Another option may be "insourcing" work from another organization.

Supply Options. Supply options include hiring/laying off workers, overtime/slack time, part-time or temporary workers, inventories, and subcontractors.

1. **Hire and lay off workers.** The extent to which operations are labor intensive determines the impact that changes in the workforce level will have on capacity. The resource requirements of each worker also can be a factor. For instance, if a supermarket usually has 10 of 14 checkout lines operating, an additional four checkout workers could be added. Hence, the ability to add workers is constrained at some point by other resources needed to support the workers. Conversely, there may be a lower limit on the number of workers needed to maintain a viable operation (e.g., a skeleton crew).

   Union contracts may restrict the amount of hiring and laying off a company can do. Moreover, because laying off can present serious problems for workers, some firms have policies that either prohibit or limit downward adjustments to a workforce. On the other hand, hiring presumes an available supply of workers. This may change from time to time and, at times of low supply, have an impact on the ability of an organization to pursue this approach.

   Another consideration is the skill level of workers. Highly skilled workers are generally more difficult to find than lower-skilled workers, and recruiting them involves greater costs. So the usefulness of this option may be limited by the need for highly skilled workers.

   Use of hiring and laying off entails certain costs. Hiring costs include recruitment, screening, and training to bring new workers "up to speed." And quality may suffer. Some savings may occur if workers who have recently been laid off are rehired. Layoff costs include severance pay, the cost of realigning the remaining workforce, potential bad feelings toward the firm on the part of workers who have been laid off, and some loss of morale for workers who are retained (i.e., in spite of company assurances, some workers will believe that in time they too will be laid off).

   An increasing number of organizations view workers as assets rather than as variable costs, and would not consider this approach. Instead, they might use slack time for other purposes.

2. **Overtime/slack time.** Use of overtime or slack time is a less severe method for changing capacity than hiring and laying off workers, and it can be used across the board or selectively as needed. It also can be implemented more quickly than hiring and laying off and allows the firm to maintain a steady base of employees. The use of

overtime can be especially attractive in dealing with seasonal demand peaks by reducing the need to hire and train people who will have to be laid off during the off-season. Overtime also permits the company to maintain a skilled workforce and employees to increase earnings, and companies may save money because fringe and other benefits are generally fixed. Moreover, in situations with crews, it is often necessary to use a full crew rather than to hire one or two additional people. Thus, having the entire crew work overtime would be preferable to hiring extra people.

It should be noted that some union contracts allow workers to refuse overtime. In those cases, it may be difficult to muster a full crew to work overtime or to get an entire production line into operation after regular hours. Although workers often like the additional income overtime can generate, they may not appreciate having to work on short notice or the fluctuations in income that result. Still other considerations relate to the fact that overtime often results in lower productivity, poorer quality, more accidents, and increased payroll costs, whereas idle time results in less efficient use of machines and other fixed assets.

The use of slack when demand is less than capacity can be an important consideration. Some organizations use this time for training. It also can give workers time for problem solving and process improvement, while retraining skilled workers.

3. **Part-time workers.** In certain instances, the use of part-time workers is a viable option—much depends on the nature of the work, training and skills needed, and union agreements. Seasonal work requiring low-to-moderate job skills lends itself to part-time workers, who generally cost less than regular workers in hourly wages and fringe benefits. However, unions may regard such workers unfavorably because they typically do not pay union dues and may lessen the power of unions. Department stores, restaurants, and supermarkets make use of part-time workers. So do parks and recreation departments, resorts, travel agencies, hotels, and other service organizations with seasonal demands. In order to be successful, these organizations must be able to hire part-time employees when they are needed.

Some companies use contract workers, also called *independent contractors,* to fill certain needs. Although they are not regular employees, often they work alongside regular workers. In addition to having different pay scales and no benefits, they can be

AMAZON IS VERY AGGRESSIVE ABOUT MANAGING ITS INVENTORY LEVELS. THIS MAY MEAN THAT RARELY ORDERED ITEMS ARE NOT KEPT IN INVENTORY AND MAY REQUIRE TIME TO SOURCE FROM A SUPPLIER. IT ALSO MEANS THAT AMAZON TRIES TO MOVE INVENTORY OUT TO CUSTOMERS AS QUICKLY AS POSSIBLE. (WWW.AMAZON.COM)

added or subtracted from the workforce with greater ease than regular workers, giving companies great flexibility in adjusting the size of the workforce.

4. **Inventories.**   The use of finished-goods inventories allows firms to produce goods in one period and sell or ship them in another period, although this involves holding or carrying those goods as inventory until they are needed. The cost includes not only storage costs and the cost of money tied up that could be invested elsewhere, but also the cost of insurance, obsolescence, deterioration, spoilage, breakage, and so on. In essence, inventories can be built up during periods when production capacity exceeds demand and drawn down in periods when demand exceeds production capacity.

This method is more amenable to manufacturing than to service industries since manufactured goods can be stored whereas services generally cannot. However, an analogous approach used by services is to make efforts to streamline services (e.g., standard forms) or otherwise do a portion of the service during slack periods (e.g., organize the workplace). In spite of these possibilities, services tend not to make much use of inventories to alter capacity requirements.

5. **Subcontracting.**   Subcontracting enables planners to acquire temporary capacity, although it affords less control over the output and may lead to higher costs and quality problems. The question of whether to make or buy (i.e., in manufacturing) or to perform a service or hire someone else to do the work generally depends on factors such as available capacity, relative expertise, quality considerations, cost, and the amount and stability of demand.

Conversely, in periods of excess capacity, an organization may subcontract *in,* that is, conduct work for another organization. As an alternative to subcontracting, an organization might consider *outsourcing:* contracting with another organization to supply some portion of the goods or services on a regular basis.

BASIC STRATEGIES FOR MEETING UNEVEN DEMAND

As you see, managers have a wide range of decision options they can consider for achieving a balance of demand and capacity in aggregate planning. Since the options that are most suited to influencing demand fall more in the realm of marketing than in operations (with the exception of backlogging), we shall concentrate on the capacity options, which are in the realm of operations but include the use of back orders.

ScreenCam Tutorial

Aggregate planners might adopt a number of strategies. Some of the more prominent ones are the following:

1. Maintain a level workforce.
2. Maintain a steady output rate.
3. Match demand period by period.
4. Use a combination of decision variables.

While other strategies might be considered, these will suffice to give you a sense of how aggregate planning operates in a vast number of organizations. The first three strategies are "pure" strategies because each has a single focal point; the last strategy is "mixed" because it lacks the single focus. Under a level capacity strategy, variations in demand are met by using some combination of inventories, overtime, part-time workers, subcontracting, and back orders while maintaining a steady rate of output. Matching capacity to demand implies a chase demand strategy; the planned output for any period would be equal to expected demand for that period.

Level capacity strategy

Chase demand strategy

Many organizations regard a level workforce as very appealing. Since workforce changes through hiring and laying off can have a major impact on the lives and morale of employees and can be disruptive for managers, organizations often prefer to handle uneven demand in other ways. Moreover, changes in workforce size can be very costly, and there is always the risk that there will not be a sufficient pool of workers with the appropriate skills when needed. Aside from these considerations, such changes can involve a significant amount of paperwork. Unions tend to favor a level workforce because the freedom to hire and lay off workers diminishes union strengths.

To maintain a constant level of output and still satisfy varying demand, an organization must resort to some combination of subcontracting, backlogging, and use of inventories to absorb fluctuations. Subcontracting requires an investment in evaluating sources of supply as well as possible increased costs, less control over output, and perhaps quality considerations. Backlogs can lead tolost sales, increased record keeping, and lower levels of customer service. Allowing inventories to absorb fluctuations can entail substantial costs by having money tied up in inventories, having to maintain relatively large storage facilities, and incurring other costs related to inventories. Furthermore, inventories are not usually an alternative for service-oriented organizations. However, there are certain advantages, such as minimum costs of recruitment and training, minimum overtime and idle-time costs, fewer morale problems, and stable use of equipment and facilities.

A chase demand strategy presupposes a great deal of ability and willingness on the part of managers to be flexible in adjusting to demand. A major advantage of this approach is that inventories can be kept relatively low, which can yield substantial savings for an organization. A major disadvantage is the lack of stability in operations—the atmosphere is one of dancing to demand's tune. Also, when forecast and reality differ, morale can suffer, since it quickly becomes obvious to workers and managers that efforts have been wasted. Figure 4.2 provides a comparison of the two strategies, using a varying demand pattern to highlight the differences in the two approaches. The same demand pattern is used for each approach. In the upper portion of the figure the pattern is shown. Notice that there are three situations: (1) demand and capacity are equal; (2) demand is less than capacity; and (3) demand exceeds capacity.

The middle portion of the figure illustrates what happens with a chase approach. When normal capacity would exceed demand, capacity is cut back to match demand. Then, when demand exceeds normal capacity, the chase approach is to temporarily increase capacity to match demand.

The bottom portion of the figure illustrates the level-output strategy. When demand is less than capacity, output continues at normal capacity, and the excess output is put into inventory in anticipation of the time when demand exceeds capacity. When demand exceeds capacity, inventory is used to offset the shortfall in output.

Organizations may opt for a strategy that involves some combination of the pure strategies. This allows managers greater flexibility in dealing with uneven demand and perhaps in experimenting with a wide variety of approaches. However, the absence of a clear focus may lead to an erratic approach and confusion on the part of employees.

CHOOSING A STRATEGY

Whatever strategy an organization is considering, three important factors are *company policy, flexibility,* and *costs.* Company policy may set constraints on the available options or the extent to which they can be used. For instance, company policy may discourage layoffs except under extreme conditions. Subcontracting may not be a viable alternative due to the desire to maintain secrecy about some aspect of the manufacturing of the product (e.g., a secret formula or blending process). Union agreements often impose restrictions. For example, a union contract may specify both minimum and maximum numbers of hours part-time workers can be used. The degree of flexibility needed to use the chase approach may not be present for companies designed for high, steady output, such as refineries and auto assembly plants.

As a rule, aggregate planners seek to match supply and demand within the constraints imposed on them by policies or agreements and at minimum cost. They usually evaluate alternatives in terms of their overall costs. Table 4.3 compares reactive strategies. In the next section, a number of techniques for aggregate planning are described and presented with some examples of cost evaluation of alternative plans.

A Varying Demand Pattern and a Comparison of a Chase Demand Strategy Versus a Level Strategy

figure 4.2

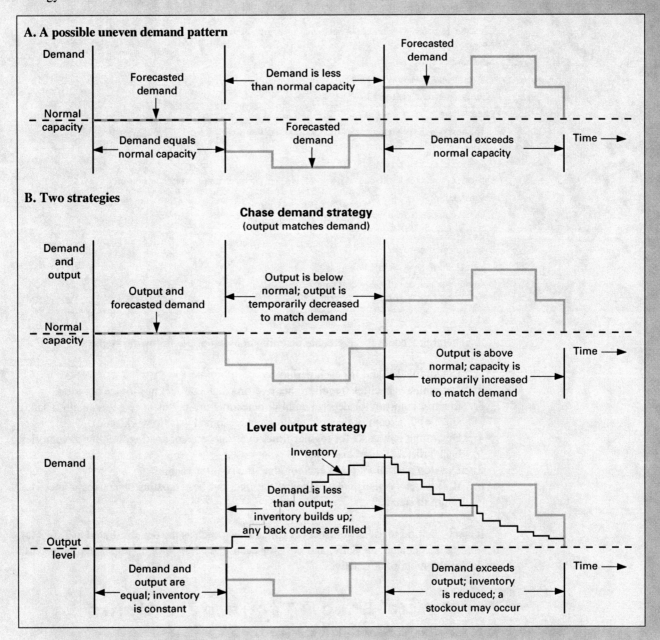

TECHNIQUES FOR AGGREGATE PLANNING

Numerous techniques are available to help with the task of aggregate planning. Generally, they fall into one of two categories: Informal trial-and-error techniques and mathematical techniques. In practice, informal techniques are more frequently used. However, a considerable amount of research has been devoted to mathematical techniques, and even though they are not as widely used, they often serve as a basis for comparing the effectiveness of alternative techniques for aggregate planning. Thus, it will be instructive to briefly examine them as well as the informal techniques.

ScreenCam
Tutorial

table 4.3   Comparison of Reactive Strategies

CHASE APPROACH

Capacities (workforce levels, output rates, etc.) are adjusted to match demand requirements over the planning horizon.

Advantages:

    Investment in inventory is low

    Labor utilization is kept high

Disadvantage:

    The cost of adjusting output rates and/or workforce levels

LEVEL APPROACH

Capacities (workforce levels, output rates, etc.) are kept constant over the planning horizon.

Advantage:

    Stable output rates and workforce levels

Disadvantages:

    Greater inventory costs

    Increased overtime and idle time

    Resource utilizations that vary over time

A general procedure for aggregate planning consists of the following steps:

1. Determine demand for each period.
2. Determine capacities (regular time, overtime, subcontracting) for each period.
3. Identify company or departmental policies that are pertinent (e.g., maintain a safety stock of 5 percent of demand, maintain a reasonably stable workforce).
4. Determine unit costs for regular time, overtime, subcontracting, holding inventories, back orders, layoffs, and other relevant costs.
5. Develop alternative plans and compute the cost for each.
6. If satisfactory plans emerge, select the one that best satisfies objectives. Otherwise, return to step 5.

It can be helpful to use a worksheet or spreadsheet, such as the one illustrated in Table 4.4, to summarize demand, capacity, and cost for each plan. In addition, graphs can be used to guide development of alternatives.

TRIAL-AND-ERROR TECHNIQUES USING GRAPHS AND SPREADSHEETS

Trial-and-error approaches consist of developing simple tables or graphs that enable planners to visually compare projected demand requirements with existing capacity. Alternatives are usually evaluated in terms of their overall costs. The chief disadvantage of such techniques is that they do not necessarily result in the optimal aggregate plan.

Two examples illustrate the development and comparison of aggregate plans. In the first example, regular output is held steady, with inventory absorbing demand variations. In the second example, a lower rate of regular output is used, supplemented by use of overtime. In both examples, some backlogs are allowed to build up.

These examples and other examples and problems in this chapter are based on the following assumptions:

1. The regular output capacity is the same in all periods. No allowance is made for holidays, different numbers of workdays in different months, and so on. This assumption simplifies computations.

Worksheet/Spreadsheet

table 4.4

Period	1	2	3	4	5		Total
Forecast							
Output							
Regular time							
Overtime							
Subcontract							
Output – Forecast							
Inventory							
Beginning							
Ending							
Average							
Backlog							
Costs							
Output							
Regular							
Overtime							
Subcontract							
Hire/Lay off							
Inventory							
Back orders							
Total							

2. Cost (back order, inventory, subcontracting, etc.) is a linear function composed of unit cost and number of units. This often has a reasonable approximation to reality, although there may be only narrow ranges over which this is true. Cost is sometimes more of a step function.

3. Plans are feasible; that is, sufficient inventory capacity exists to accommodate a plan, subcontractors with appropriate quality and capacity are standing by, and changes in output can be made as needed.

4. All costs associated with a decision option can be represented by a lump sum or by unit costs that are independent of the quantity involved. Again, a step function may be more realistic; but for purposes of illustration and simplicity, this assumption is appropriate.

5. Cost figures can be reasonably estimated and are constant for the planning horizon.

6. Inventories are built up and drawn down at a uniform rate and output occurs at a uniform rate throughout each period. However, backlogs are treated as if they exist for an entire period, even though in periods where they initially appear, they would tend to build up toward the end of the period. Hence, this assumption is a bit unrealistic for some periods, but it simplifies computations.

In the examples and problems in this chapter, we use the following relationships to determine the number of workers, the amount of inventory, and the cost of a particular plan.

The number of workers available in any period is calculated as follows:

Number of workers in a period = Number of workers at end of the previous period + Number of new workers at start of the period − Number of laid-off workers at start of the period

Note: An organization would not hire and lay off simultaneously, so at least one of the last two terms will equal zero.

The amount of inventory at the end of a given period is calculated as follows:

$$\begin{array}{c}\text{Inventory}\\\text{at the end of}\\\text{a period}\end{array} = \begin{array}{c}\text{Inventory}\\\text{at end of the}\\\text{previous period}\end{array} + \begin{array}{c}\text{Production}\\\text{in the}\\\text{current period}\end{array} - \begin{array}{c}\text{Amount used to}\\\text{satisfy demand in the}\\\text{current period}\end{array}$$

The average inventory for a period is equal to

$$\frac{\text{Beginning inventory} + \text{Ending inventory}}{2}$$

The cost of a particular plan for a given period can be determined by summing the appropriate costs:

$$\begin{array}{c}\text{Cost for}\\\text{a period}\end{array} = \begin{array}{c}\text{Output cost}\\\text{(Reg + OT + Subcontract)}\end{array} + \begin{array}{c}\text{Hire/lay-off}\\\text{cost}\end{array} + \begin{array}{c}\text{Inventory}\\\text{cost}\end{array} + \begin{array}{c}\text{Back-order}\\\text{cost}\end{array}$$

The appropriate costs are calculated as follows:

TYPE OF COST	HOW TO CALCULATE
Output	
Regular	Regular cost per unit × Quantity of regular output
Overtime	Overtime cost per unit × Overtime quantity
Subcontract	Subcontract cost per unit × Subcontract quantity
Hire/lay off	
Hire	Cost per hire × Number hired
Lay off	Cost per layoff × Number laid off
Inventory	Carrying cost per unit × Average inventory
Back order	Back-order cost per unit × Number of back-order units

The following examples are only two of many possible options that could be tried. Perhaps some of the others would result in a lower cost. With trial and error, you can never be completely sure you have identified the lowest-cost alternative unless every possible alternative is evaluated. Of course, the purpose of these examples is to illustrate the process of developing and evaluating an aggregate plan rather than to find the lowest-cost plan.

In practice, successful achievement of a good plan depends on the resourcefulness and persistence of the planner. Computer software such as the Excel templates that accompany this book can eliminate the computational burden of trial-and-error techniques.

EXAMPLE 4.1

mhhe.com/stevenson10e

Planners for a company that makes several models of skateboards are about to prepare the aggregate plan that will cover six periods. They have assembled the following information:

PERIOD	1	2	3	4	5	6	TOTAL
Forecast	200	200	300	400	500	200	1,800
Costs							
Output							
Regular time	= $2 per skateboard						
Overtime	= $3 per skateboard						
Subcontract	= $6 per skateboard						
Inventory	= $1 per skateboard per period on average inventory						
Back orders	= $5 per skateboard per period						

They now want to evaluate a plan that calls for a steady rate of regular-time output, mainly using inventory to absorb the uneven demand but allowing some backlog. Overtime and subcontracting are not used because they want steady output. They intend to start with zero inventory on hand in the first period. Prepare an aggregate plan and determine its cost using the preceding information. Assume a level output rate of 300 units (skateboards) per period with regular time (i.e., 1,800/6 = 300). Note that the planned ending inventory is zero. There are 15 workers, and each can produce 20 skateboards per period.

SOLUTION

PERIOD	1	2	3	4	5	6	TOTAL
Forecast	200	200	300	400	500	200	1,800
Output							
Regular	300	300	300	300	300	300	1,800
Overtime	—	—	—	—	—	—	
Subcontract	—	—	—	—	—	—	
Output − Forecast	100	100	0	(100)	(200)	100	0
Inventory							
Beginning	0	100	200	200	100	0	
Ending	100	200	200	100	0	0	
Average	50	150	200	150	50	0	600
Backlog	0	0	0	0	100	0	100
Costs							
Output							
Regular	$600	600	600	600	600	600	$3,600
Overtime	—	—	—	—	—	—	
Subcontract	—	—	—	—	—	—	
Hire/Lay off	—	—	—	—	—	—	
Inventory	$ 50	150	200	150	50	0	$ 600
Back orders	$ 0	0	0	0	500	0	$ 500
Total	$650	750	800	750	1,150	600	$4,700

Note that the total regular-time output of 1,800 units equals the total expected demand. Ending inventory equals beginning inventory plus or minus the quantity Output − Forecast. If Output − Forecast is negative, inventory is decreased in that period by that amount. If insufficient inventory exists, a backlog equal to the shortage amount appears, as in period 5. This is taken care of using the excess output in period 6.

The costs were computed as follows. Regular cost in each period equals 300 units $\times$ $2 per unit or $600. Inventory cost equals average inventory $\times$ $1 per unit. Back-order cost is $5 per unit. The total cost for this plan is $4,700.

Note that the first two quantities in each column are givens. The remaining quantities in the upper portion of the table were determined working down each column, beginning with the first column. The costs were then computed based on the quantities in the upper part of the table. ●

Very often, graphs can be used to guide the development of alternatives. Some planners prefer cumulative graphs while others prefer to see a period-by-period breakdown of a plan. For instance, Figure 4.3 shows a cumulative graph for a plan with steady output (the slope of the dashed line represents the production rate) and inventory absorption of demand variations. Figure 4.2 is an example of a period-by-period graph. The obvious advantage of a graph is that it provides a visual portrayal of a plan. The preference of the planner determines which of these two types of graphs is chosen.

EXAMPLE 4.2

After reviewing the plan developed in the preceding example, planners have decided to develop an alternative plan. They have learned that one person is about to retire from the company. Rather than replace that person, they would like to stay with the smaller workforce and use overtime to make up for the lost output. The reduced regular-time output is 280 units per period. The maximum amount of overtime output per period is 40 units. Develop a plan and compare it to the previous one.

SOLUTION

PERIOD	1	2	3	4	5	6	TOTAL
Forecast	200	200	300	400	500	200	1,800
Output							
Regular	280	280	280	280	280	280	1,680
Overtime	0	0	40	40	40	0	120
Subcontract	—	—	—	—	—	—	
Output – Forecast	80	80	20	(80)	(180)	80	0
Inventory							
Beginning	0	80	160	180	100	0	
Ending	80	160	180	100	0	0	
Average	40	120	170	140	50	0	520
Backlog	0	0	0	0	80	0	80
Costs							
Output							
Regular	$560	560	560	560	560	560	$3,360
Overtime	0	0	120	120	120	0	$ 360
Subcontract	—	—	—	—	—	—	
Hire/Lay off	—	—	—	—	—	—	
Inventory	40	120	170	140	50	0	$ 520
Back orders	$ 0	0	0	0	400	0	$ 400
Total	$600	680	850	820	1,130	560	$4,640

The amount of overtime that must be scheduled has to make up for lost output of 20 units per period for six periods, which is 120. This is scheduled toward the center of the planning horizon since that is where the bulk of demand occurs. Scheduling it earlier would increase inventory carrying costs; scheduling it later would increase the backlog cost.

Overall, the total cost for this plan is $4,640, which is $60 less than the previous plan. Regular-time production cost and inventory cost are down, but there is overtime cost. However, this plan achieves savings in backorder cost, making it somewhat less costly overall than the plan in Example 4.1.

MATHEMATICAL TECHNIQUES

A number of mathematical techniques have been developed to handle aggregate planning. They range from mathematical programming models to heuristic and computer search models. This section briefly describes some of the better-known techniques.

Linear Programming. Linear programming (LP) models are methods for obtaining optimal solutions to problems involving the allocation of scarce resources in terms of cost minimization or profit maximization. With aggregate planning, the goal is usually to minimize the sum of costs related to regular labor time, overtime, subcontracting, carrying inventory, and costs associated

eXcel
mhhe.com/stevenson10e

ScreenCam
Tutorial

A Cumulative Graph

figure 4.3

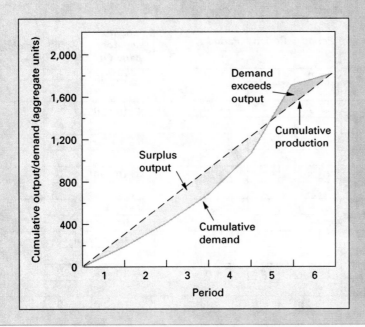

with changing the size of the workforce. Constraints involve the capacities of the workforce, inventories, and subcontracting.

The problem can be formulated as a transportation-type programming model as a way to obtain aggregate plans that would match capacities with demand requirements and minimize costs. In order to use this approach, planners must identify capacity (supply) of regular time, overtime, subcontracting, and inventory on a period-by-period basis, as well as related costs of each variable.

Table 4.5 shows the notation and setup of a transportation table. Note the systematic way that costs change as you move across a row from left to right. Regular cost, overtime cost, and subcontracting cost are at their lowest when the output is consumed (i.e., delivered, etc.) in the same period it is produced (at the intersection of period 1 row and column for regular cost, at the intersection of period 2 row and column for regular cost, and so on). If goods are made available in one period but carried over to later periods (i.e., moving across a row), holding costs are incurred at the rate of h per period. Thus, holding goods for two periods results in a unit cost of $2h$, whether or not the goods came from regular production, overtime, or subcontracting. Conversely, with back orders, the unit cost increases as you move across a row from right to left, beginning at the intersection of a row and column for the same period (e.g., period 3). For instance, if some goods are produced in period 3 to satisfy back orders from period 2, a unit back-order cost of b is incurred. And if goods in period 3 are used to satisfy back orders two periods earlier (e.g., from period 1), a unit cost of $2b$ is incurred. Unused capacity is generally given a unit cost of 0, although it is certainly possible to insert an actual cost if that is relevant. Finally, beginning inventory is given a unit cost of 0 if it is used to satisfy demand in period 1. However, if it is held over for use in later periods, a holding cost of h per unit is added for each period. If the inventory is to be held for the entire planning horizon, a total unit cost of h times the number of periods, n, will be incurred.

Example 4.3 illustrates the setup and final solution of a transportation model of an aggregate planning problem.

table 4.5   Transportation Notation for Aggregate Planning

		Period 1	Period 2	Period 3	. . .	Ending inventory period n	Unused capacity	Capacity
Period	Beginning inventory	0	h	$2h$	. . .	$(n-1)h$	0	I_0
1	Regular time	r	$r+h$	$r+2h$	. . .	$r+(n-1)h$	0	R_1
	Overtime	t	$t+h$	$t+2h$	. . .	$t+(n-1)h$	0	O_1
	Subcontract	s	$s+h$	$s+2h$	. . .	$s+(n-1)h$	0	S_1
2	Regular time	$r+b$	r	$r+h$	. . .	$r+(n-2)h$	0	R_2
	Overtime	$t+b$	t	$t+h$	. . .	$t+(n-2)h$	0	O_2
	Subcontract	$s+b$	s	$s+h$	. . .	$s+(n-2)h$	0	S_2
3	Regular time	$r+2b$	$r+b$	r	. . .	$r+(n-3)h$	0	R_3
	Overtime	$t+2b$	$t+b$	t	. . .	$t+(n-3)h$	0	O_3
	Subcontract	$s+2b$	$s+b$	s	. . .	$s+(n-3)h$	0	S_3
	Demand				. . .			Total

r = Regular production cost per unit h = Holding cost per unit period
t = Overtime cost per unit b = Back order cost per unit per period
s = Subcontracting cost per unit n = Number of periods in planning horizon

mhhe.com/stevenson10e

EXAMPLE 4.3

Given the following information set up the problem in a transportation table and solve for the minimum-cost plan:

	PERIOD		
	1	2	3
Demand	550	700	750
Capacity			
Regular	500	500	500
Overtime	50	50	50
Subcontract	120	120	100
Beginning inventory	100		
Costs			
Regular time		$60 per unit	
Overtime		$80 per unit	
Subcontract		$90 per unit	
Inventory carrying cost		$1 per unit per month	
Back-order cost		$3 per unit per month	

SOLUTION

The transportation table and solution are shown in Table 4.6. Some of the entries require additional explanation:

 a. In this example, inventory carrying costs are $1 per unit per period (costs are shown in the upper right-hand corner of each cell in the table). Hence, units produced in one period and carried over to a later period will incur a holding cost that is a linear function of the length of time held.

 b. Linear programming models of this type require that supply (capacity) and demand be equal. A dummy column has been added (nonexistent capacity) to satisfy that requirement. Since it does not "cost" anything extra to not use capacity in this case, cell costs of $0 have been assigned.

 c. No backlogs were needed in this example.

 d. The quantities (e.g., 100 and 450 in column 1) are the amounts of output or inventory that will be used to meet demand requirements. Thus, the demand of 550 units in period 1 will be met using 100 units from inventory and 450 obtained from regular-time output. ◉

Where backlogs are not permitted, the cell costs for the backlog positions can be made prohibitively high so that no backlogs will appear in the solution.

Transportation Solution

table 4.6

	Supply from	Demand for				Total capacity available (supply)
		Period 1	Period 2	Period 3	Unused capacity (dummy)	
Period 1	Beginning inventory	[0] 100	[1]	[2]	[0]	100
	Regular time	[60] 450	[61] 50	[62]	[0]	500
	Overtime	[80]	[81] 50	[82]	[0]	50
	Subcontract	[90]	[91] 30	[92]	[0] 90	120
Period 2	Regular time	[63]	[60] 500	[61]	[0]	500
	Overtime	[83]	[80] 50	[81]	[0]	50
	Subcontract	[93]	[90] 20	[91] 100	[0]	120
Period 3	Regular time	[66]	[63]	[60] 500	[0]	500
	Overtime	[86]	[83]	[80] 50	[0]	50
	Subcontract	[96]	[93]	[90] 100	[0]	100
	Demand	550	700	750	90	2,090

table 4.7   Summary of Planning Techniques

TECHNIQUE	SOLUTION APPROACH	CHARACTERISTICS
Spreadsheet	Heuristic (trial and error)	Intuitively appealing, easy to understand; solution not necessarily optimal
Linear programming	Optimizing	Computerized; linear assumptions not always valid
Simulation	Heuristic (trial and error)	Computerized models can be examined under a variety of conditions

The main limitations of LP models are the assumptions of linear relationships among variables, the inability to continuously adjust output rates, and the need to specify a single objective (e.g., minimize costs) instead of using multiple objectives (e.g., minimize cost while stabilizing the workforce).

Simulation models

Simulation Models. A number of simulation models have been developed for aggregate planning. (Simulation is described in detail on the textbook Web site.) The essence of simulation is the development of computerized models that can be tested under a variety of conditions in an attempt to identify reasonably acceptable (although not always optimal) solutions to problems.

Table 4.7 summarizes planning techniques.

Aggregate planning techniques other than trial and error do not appear to be widely used. Instead, in the majority of organizations, aggregate planning seems to be accomplished more on the basis of experience along with trial-and-error methods. It is difficult to say exactly why some of the mathematical techniques mentioned are not used to any great extent. Perhaps the level of mathematical sophistication discourages greater use, or the assumptions required in certain models appear unrealistic, or the models may be too narrow in scope. Whatever the reasons, none of the techniques to date have captured the attention of aggregate planners on a broad scale. Simulation is one technique that seems to be gaining favor. Research on improved approaches to aggregate planning is continuing.

AGGREGATE PLANNING IN SERVICES

Aggregate planning for services takes into account projected customer demands, equipment capacities, and labor capabilities. The resulting plan is a time-phased projection of service staff requirements.

Here are examples of service organizations that use aggregate planning:

Hospitals: Hospitals use aggregate planning to allocate funds, staff, and supplies to meet the demands of patients for their medical services. For example, plans for bed capacity, medications, surgical supplies, and personnel needs are based on patient load forecasts.

Airlines: Aggregate planning in the airline industry is fairly complex due to the need to take into account a wide range of factors (planes, flight personnel, ground personnel) and multiple routes and landing/departure sites. Also, capacity decisions must take into account the percentage of seats to be allocated to various fare classes in order to maximize profit or yield.

Restaurants: Aggregate planning in the case of a high-volume product output business such as a restaurant is directed toward smoothing the service rate, determining the size of the workforce, and managing demand to match a fixed capacity. The general approach usually involves building inventory during slack periods and depleting it during peak periods.

Because this is very similar to manufacturing, traditional aggregate planning methods can be applied, although two differences must be taken into account. One difference is that in restaurants, inventory is perishable: Cooked food can be held for only a very short time. Another difference, particularly in fast-food restaurants, is that peak and slack periods occur often and are relatively short-lived.

Other services: Financial, hospitality, transportation, and recreation services provide a high-volume, intangible output. Aggregate planning for these and similar services involves managing demand and planning for human resource requirements. The main goals are to accommodate peak demand and to find ways to effectively use labor resources during periods of low demand.

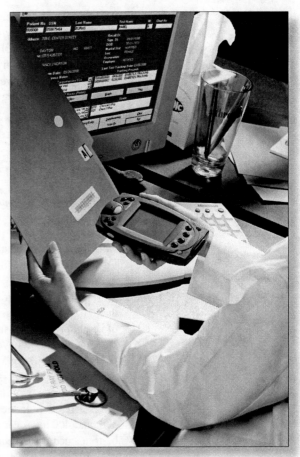

Aggregate planning for manufacturing and aggregate planning for services share similarities in some respects, but there are some important differences—related in general to the differences between manufacturing and services:

1. *Demand for service can be difficult to predict.* The volume of demand for services is often quite variable. In some situations, customers may *need* prompt service (e.g., police, fire, medical emergency), while in others, they simply *want* prompt service and may be willing to go elsewhere if their wants are not met. These factors place a greater burden on service providers to anticipate demand. Consequently, service providers must pay careful attention to planned capacity levels.

2. *Capacity availability can be difficult to predict.* Processing requirements for services can sometimes be quite variable, similar to the variability of work in a job shop setting. Moreover, the variety of tasks required of servers can be great, again similar to the variety of tasks in a job shop. However, in services, the types of variety are more pervasive than they are in manufacturing. This makes it more difficult to establish simple measures of capacity. For example, what would be the capacity of a person who paints interiors of houses? The number of rooms per day or the number of square feet per hour are possible measures, but rooms come in many different sizes, and because the level of detail (and, thus, the painting implements that can be used) vary tremendously, a suitable measure for planning purposes can be quite difficult to arrive at. Similarly, bank tellers are called upon to handle a wide variety of transactions and requests for information, again making it difficult to establish a suitable measure of their capacity.

3. *Labor flexibility can be an advantage in services.* Labor often comprises a significant portion of service compared to manufacturing. That, coupled with the fact that service providers are often able to handle a fairly wide variety of service requirements, means that to some extent, planning is easier than it is in manufacturing. Of course, manufacturers recognize this advantage, and many are cross-training their employees to achieve the same flexibility. Moreover, in both manufacturing and service systems, the use of part-time workers can be an important option. Note that in self-service systems, the (customer) labor automatically adjusts to changes in demand!

4. *Services occur when they are rendered.* Unlike manufacturing output, most services can't be inventoried. Services such as financial planning, tax counseling, and oil changes can't be stockpiled. This removes the option of building up inventories during a slow period in anticipation of future demand. Moreover, service capacity that goes unused is essentially wasted. Consequently, it becomes even more important to be able to match capacity and demand.

Because service capacity is perishable (e.g., an empty seat on an airplane flight can't be saved for use on another flight), aggregate planners need to take that into account when

Yield management

deciding how to match supply and demand. Yield management is an approach that seeks to maximize revenue by using a strategy of variable pricing; prices are set relative to capacity availability. Thus, during periods of low demand, price discounts are offered to attract a wider population. Conversely, during peak periods, higher prices are posted to take advantage of limited supply relative to demand. Users of yield management include airlines, restaurants, theaters, hotels, resorts, cruise lines, and parking lots.

DISAGGREGATING THE AGGREGATE PLAN

For the production plan to be translated into meaningful terms for production, it is necessary to *disaggregate* the aggregate plan. This means breaking down the aggregate plan into specific product requirements in order to determine labor requirements (skills, size of workforce), materials, and inventory requirements. At this stage, however, it will be helpful for you to have some understanding of the need for disaggregation and what the term implies.

Working with aggregate units facilitates intermediate planning. However, to put the production plan into operation, one must convert, or decompose, those aggregate units into units of actual products or services that are to be produced or offered. For example, a lawn mower manufacturer may have an aggregate plan that calls for 200 lawn mowers in January, 300 in February, and 400 in March. That company may produce push mowers, self-propelled mowers, and riding mowers. Although all the mowers probably contain some of the same parts and involve some similar or identical operations for fabrication and assembly, there would be some differences in the materials, parts, and operations that each type requires. Hence, the 200, 300, and 400 aggregate lawn mowers that are to be produced during those three months must be translated into specific numbers of mowers of each type prior to actually purchasing the appropriate materials and parts, scheduling operations, and planning inventory requirements.

Master schedule

The result of disaggregating the aggregate plan is a master schedule showing the quantity and timing of *specific* end items for a scheduled horizon, which often covers about six to eight weeks ahead. A master schedule shows the planned output for individual products rather than an entire product group, along with the timing of production. The master schedule contains important information for marketing as well as for production. It reveals when orders are scheduled for production and when completed orders are to be shipped.

Figure 4.4 shows an overview of the context of disaggregation.

figure 4.4   Moving from the Aggregate Plan to a Master Schedule

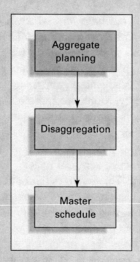

Disaggregating the Aggregate Plan

figure 4.5

AGGREGATE PLAN	MONTH PLANNED OUTPUT *	JAN.	FEB.	MAR.
		200	300	400

*Aggregate units

MASTER SCHEDULE	MONTH PLANNED OUTPUT *	JAN.	FEB.	MAR.
	Push	100	100	100
	Self-propelled	75	150	200
	Riding	25	50	100
	Total	200	300	400

*Actual units

Figure 4.5 illustrates disaggregating the aggregate plan. The illustration makes a simple assumption in order to clearly show the concept of disaggregation: The totals of the aggregate and the disaggregated units are equal. In reality, that is not always true. As a consequence, disaggregating the aggregate plan may require considerable effort.

Figure 4.5 shows the aggregate plan broken down by units. However, it also can be useful to show the breakdown in *percentages* for different products or product families.

MASTER SCHEDULING

The master schedule is the heart of production planning and control. It determines the quantities needed to meet demand from all sources, and that governs key decisions and activities throughout the organization.

The master schedule interfaces with marketing, capacity planning, production planning, and distribution planning: It enables marketing to make valid delivery commitments to warehouses and final customers; it enables production to evaluate capacity requirements; it provides the necessary information for production and marketing to negotiate when customer requests cannot be met by normal capacity; and it provides senior management with the opportunity to determine whether the business plan and its strategic objectives will be achieved.

The central person in the master scheduling process is the master scheduler.

THE MASTER SCHEDULER

Most manufacturing organizations have (or should have) a master scheduler. The duties of the master scheduler generally include

1. Evaluating the impact of new orders.
2. Providing delivery dates for orders.
3. Dealing with problems:
   a. Evaluating the impact of production delays or late deliveries of purchased goods.
   b. Revising the master schedule when necessary because of insufficient supplies or capacity.
   c. Bringing instances of insufficient capacity to the attention of production and marketing personnel so that they can participate in resolving conflicts.

THE MASTER SCHEDULING PROCESS

A master schedule indicates the quantity and timing (i.e., delivery times) for a product, or a group of products, but it does not show planned *production*. For instance, a master schedule may call for delivery of 50 cases of cranberry-apple juice to be delivered on May 1. But this may not require any production; there may be 200 cases in inventory. Or it may require *some* production: If there were 40 cases in inventory, an additional 10 cases would be needed to achieve the specified delivery amount. Or it may involve production of 50 or more cases: In some instances, it is more economical to produce large amounts rather than small amounts, with the excess temporarily placed in inventory until needed. Thus, the *production lot size* might be 70 cases, so if additional cases were needed (e.g., 50 cases), a run of 70 cases would be made.

Master production schedule (MPS)

The master production schedule (MPS) indicates the quantity and timing of planned production, taking into account desired delivery quantity and timing as well as on-hand inventory. The master production schedule is one of the primary outputs of the master scheduling process, as illustrated in Figure 4.6.

Rough-cut capacity planning (RCCP)

Once a *tentative* master schedule has been developed, it must be validated. This is an extremely important step. Validation is referred to as rough-cut capacity planning (RCCP). It involves testing the feasibility of a proposed master schedule relative to available capacities, to assure that no obvious capacity constraints exist. This means checking capacities of production and warehouse facilities, labor, and vendors to ensure that no gross deficiencies exist that will render the master schedule unworkable. The master production schedule then serves as the basis for *short-range* planning. It should be noted that whereas the aggregate plan covers an interval of, say, 12 months, the master schedule covers only a portion of this. In other words, the aggregate plan is disaggregated in stages, or phases, that may cover a few weeks to two or three months. Moreover, the master schedule may be updated monthly, even though it covers two or three months. For instance, the lawn mower master schedule would probably be updated at the end of January to include any revisions in planned output for February and March as well as new information on planned output for April.

TIME FENCES

Changes to a master schedule can be disruptive, particularly changes to the early, or near, portions of the schedule. Typically, the further out in the future a change is, the less the tendency to cause problems.

High-performance organizations have an effective master scheduling process. A key component of effective scheduling is the use of *time fences* to facilitate order promising and the entry of orders into the system. Time fences divide a scheduling time horizon into three sections or phases, sometimes referred to as *frozen, slushy,* and *liquid,* in reference to the firmness of the schedule (see Figure 4.7).

Time fences

Frozen is the near-term phase that is so soon that delivery of a new order would be impossible, or only possible using very costly or extraordinary options such as delaying another order. Authority for new-order entry in this phase usually lies with the VP of manufacturing.

figure 4.6 The Master Scheduling Process

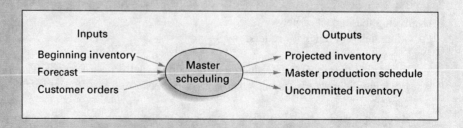

Time Fences in an MPS

figure 4.7

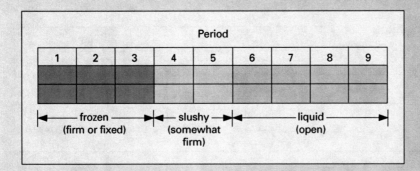

The length of the frozen phase is often a function of the total time needed to produce a product, from procuring materials to shipping the order. There is a high degree of confidence in order-promise dates.

Slushy is the next phase, and its time fence is usually a few periods beyond the frozen phase. Order entry in this phase necessitates trade-offs, but is less costly or disruptive than in the frozen phase. Authority for order entry usually lies with the master scheduler. There is relative confidence in order-promise dates, and capacity planning becomes very specific.

Liquid is the farthest out on the time horizon. New orders or cancellations can be entered with ease. Order promise dates are tentative, and will be firmed up with the passage of time when orders are in the firm phase of the schedule horizon.

A key element in the success of the master scheduling process is strict adherence to time fence policies and rules. It is essential that they be adhered to and communicated throughout the organization.

INPUTS

The master schedule has three inputs: the beginning inventory, which is the actual quantity on hand from the preceding period; forecasts for each period of the schedule; and customer orders, which are quantities already *committed* to customers.

OUTPUTS

The master scheduling process uses this information on a period-by-period basis to determine the projected inventory, production requirements, and the resulting uncommitted inventory, which is referred to as available-to-promise (ATP) inventory. Knowledge of the uncommitted inventory can enable marketing to make realistic promises to customers about deliveries of new orders.

Available-to-promise (ATP) inventory

The master scheduling process begins with a preliminary calculation of projected on-hand inventory. This reveals when additional inventory (i.e., production) will be needed. Consider this example. A company that makes industrial pumps wants to prepare a master production schedule for June and July. Marketing has forecasted demand of 120 pumps for June and 160 pumps for July. These have been evenly distributed over the four weeks in each month: 30 per week in June and 40 per week in July, as illustrated in Figure 4.8A.

Now, suppose that there are currently 64 pumps in inventory (i.e., beginning inventory is 64 pumps), and that there are customer orders that have been committed (booked) and must be filled (see Figure 4.8B).

Figure 4.8B contains the three primary inputs to the master scheduling process: the beginning inventory, the forecast, and the customer orders that have been booked or committed. This information is necessary to determine three quantities: the projected on-hand inventory, the master production schedule, and the uncommitted (ATP) inventory. The first step is to

figure 4.8a   Weekly Forecast Requirements for Industrial Pumps

	June				July			
	1	**2**	**3**	**4**	**5**	**6**	**7**	**8**
Forecast	30	30	30	30	40	40	40	40

figure 4.8b   Eight-Week Schedule Showing Forecasts, Customer Orders, and Beginning Inventory

Beginning inventory	June				July			
64	**1**	**2**	**3**	**4**	**5**	**6**	**7**	**8**
Forecast	30	30	30	30	40	40	40	40
Customer orders (committed)	33	20	10	4	2			

calculate the projected on-hand inventory, one week at a time, until it falls below a specified limit. In this example, the specified limit will be zero. Hence, we will continue until the projected on-hand inventory becomes negative.

The projected on-hand inventory is calculated as follows:

$$\text{Projected on-hand inventory} = \text{Inventory from previous week} - \text{Current week's requirements} \tag{4.1}$$

where the current week's requirements are the *larger* of forecast and customer orders (committed).

For the first week, projected on-hand inventory equals beginning inventory minus the larger of forecast and customer orders. Because customer orders (33) are larger than the forecast (30), the customer orders amount is used. Thus, for the first week, we obtain

$$\text{Projected on-hand inventory} = 64 - 33 = 31$$

Projected on-hand inventories are shown in Figure 4.9 for the first three weeks (i.e., until the projected on-hand amount becomes negative).

When the projected on-hand inventory becomes negative, this is a signal that production will be needed to replenish inventory. Hence, a negative projected on-hand inventory will require planned production. Suppose that a production lot size of 70 pumps is used, so that whenever production is called for, 70 pumps will be produced. (The determination of lot size

Projected On-Hand Inventory is Computed Week by Week Until it Becomes Negative

figure 4.9

Beginning inventory	June				July			
64	1	2	3	4	5	6	7	8
Forecast	30	30	30	30	40	40	40	40
Customer orders (committed)	33	20	10	4	2			
Projected on-hand inventory	31	1	−29					

Customer orders are larger than forecast in week 1; projected on-hand inventory is 64 − 33 = 31

Forecast is larger than customer orders in week 2; projected on-hand inventory is 31 − 30 = 1

Forecast is larger than customer orders in week 3; projected on-hand inventory is 1 − 30 = −29

Determining the MPS and Projected On-Hand Inventory

figure 4.10

WEEK	INVENTORY FROM PREVIOUS WEEK	REQUIREMENTS*	NET INVENTORY BEFORE MPS	(70) MPS	PROJECTED INVENTORY
1	64	33	31		31
2	31	30	1		1
3	1	30	−29	+ 70 =	41
4	41	30	11		11
5	11	40	−29	+ 70 =	41
6	41	40	1		1
7	1	40	−39	+ 70 =	31
8	31	40	−9	+ 70 =	61

*Requirements equals the larger of forecast and customer orders in each week.

was described in Chapter 5.) Hence, the negative projected on-hand inventory in the third week will require production of 70 pumps, which will meet the projected shortfall of 29 pumps and leave 41 (i.e., $70 - 29 = 41$) pumps for future demand.

These calculations continue for the entire schedule. Every time projected inventory becomes negative, another production lot of 70 pumps is added to the schedule. Figure 4.10 illustrates the calculations. The result is the master schedule and projected on-hand inventory for each week of the schedule. These can now be added to the master schedule (see Figure 4.11).

It is now possible to determine the amount of inventory that is uncommitted and, hence, available to promise. Several methods are used in practice. The one we shall employ involves

figure 4.11   Projected On-Hand Inventory and MPS are Added to the Master Schedule

64	June				July			
	1	2	3	4	5	6	7	8
Forecast	30	30	30	30	40	40	40	40
Customer orders (committed)	33	20	10	4	2			
Projected on-hand inventory	31	1	41	11	41	1	31	61
MPS			70		70		70	70

figure 4.12   The Available-To-Promise Inventory Quantities have been Added to the Master Schedule

64	June				July			
	1	2	3	4	5	6	7	8
Forecast	30	30	30	30	40	40	40	40
Customer orders (committed)	33	20	10	4	2			
Projected on-hand inventory	31	1	41	11	41	1	31	61
MPS			70		70		70	70
Available-to-promise inventory (uncommitted)	11		56		68		70	70

a "look-ahead" procedure: Sum booked customer orders week by week until (but not including) a week in which there is an MPS amount. For example, in the first week, this procedure results in summing customer orders of 33 (week 1) and 20 (week 2) to obtain 53. In the first week, this amount is subtracted from the beginning inventory of 64 pumps plus the MPS (zero in this example) to obtain the amount that is available to promise. Thus,

$$64 + 0 - (33 + 20) = 11$$

This inventory is uncommitted, and it can be delivered in either week 1 or 2, or part can be delivered in week 1 and part in week 2. (Note that the ATP quantity is only calculated for the first week and for other weeks in which there is an MPS quantity. Hence, it is calculated for weeks 1, 3, 5, 7, 8.) See Figure 4.12.

For weeks other than the first week, the beginning inventory drops out of the computation, and ATP is the look-ahead quantity subtracted from the MPS quantity.

Thus, for week 3, the promised amounts are $10 + 4 = 14$, and the ATP is $70 - 14 = 56$.

For week 5, customer orders are 2 (future orders have not yet been booked). The ATP is $70 - 2 = 68$.

For weeks 7 and 8, there are no customer orders, so for the present, all of the MPS amount is available to promise.

As additional orders are booked, these would be entered in the schedule, and the ATP amounts would be updated to reflect those orders. Marketing can use the ATP amounts to provide realistic delivery dates to customers.

SUMMARY

Aggregate planning establishes general levels of employment, output, and inventories for periods of 2 to 12 months. In the spectrum of planning, it falls between the broad decisions of long-range planning and the very specific and detailed short-range planning decisions. It begins with an overall forecast for the planning horizon and ends with preparations for applying the plans to specific products and services.

The essence of aggregate planning is the aggregation of products or services into one "product" or "service." This permits planners to consider overall levels of employment and inventories without having to become involved with specific details that are better left to short-range planning. Planners often use informal graphic and charting techniques to develop plans, although various mathematical techniques have been suggested. It appears that the complexity and the restrictive assumptions of these techniques limit their widespread use in practice.

After the aggregate plan has been developed, it is disaggregated or broken down into specific product requirements. This leads to a master schedule, which indicates the planned quantities and timing of specific outputs. Inputs to the master schedule are on-hand inventory amounts, forecasts of demand, and customer orders. The outputs are projected production and inventory requirements, and the projected uncommitted inventory, which is referred to as available-to-promise (ATP) inventory.

The aggregate planning process is summarized in Table 4.8.

Summary of Aggregate Planning

table 4.8

PURPOSE

Decide on the combination of
   Output rates
   Employment levels
   On-hand inventory levels

OBJECTIVES

   Minimize cost
   Others, may include
      Maintain a desirable level of customer service
      Minimize workforce fluctuations

POSSIBLE STRATEGIES

A. Supply Management (reactive)

Level Production
Allow inventory to absorb variations in demand
Use back ordering during periods of high demand

(Continued)

table 4.8   Summary of Aggregate Planning *(Continued)*

Chase Production
Vary output by varying the number of workers by hiring or layoffs to track demand
Vary output throughout the use of overtime or idle time
Vary output using part-time workers
Use subcontracting to supplement output

Mixed Strategy
Use a combination of level and chase approaches

B. Demand Management (proactive)

Influence demand through promotion, pricing, etc.
Produce goods or services that have complementary demand patterns

MANAGERIAL IMPORTANCE OF AGGREGATE PLANNING

Has an effect on
    Costs
    Equipment utilization
    Customer satisfaction
    Employment levels
    Synchronization of flow throughout the supply chain

KEY TERMS

Aggregate planning Intermediate-range capacity planning, usually covering 2 to 12 months.

Sales and operations planning Intermediate-range decisions to balance supply and demand, integrating financial and operations planning.

Level capacity strategy Maintaining a steady rate of regular-time output while meeting variations in demand by a combination of options.

Chase demand strategy Matching capacity to demand; the planned output for a period is set at the expected demand for that period.

Simulation models Computerized models that can be tested under different scenarios to identify acceptable solutions to problems.

Yield management The application of pricing strategies to allocate capacity among various categories of demand.

Master schedule Shows quantity and timing of specific end items for a scheduled horizon.

Master production schedule (MPS) This schedule indicates the quantity and timing of planned completed production.

Rough-cut capacity planning (RCCP) Approximate balancing of capacity and demand to test the feasibility of a master schedule.

Time fences Points in time that separate phases of a master schedule planning horizon.

Available-to-promise (ATP) inventory Uncommitted inventory.

SOLVED PROBLEMS

PROBLEM 1

A manager is attempting to put together an aggregate plan for the coming nine months. She has obtained a forecast of expected demand for the planning horizon. The plan must deal with highly seasonal demand; demand is relatively high in periods 3 and 4 and again in period 8, as can be seen from the following forecasts:

PERIOD	1	2	3	4	5	6	7	8	9	TOTAL
Forecast	190	230	260	280	210	170	160	260	180	1,940

The department now has 20 full-time employees, each of whom can produce 10 units of output per period at a cost of $6 per unit. Inventory carrying cost is $5 per unit per period, and backlog cost is $10 per unit per period. The manager is considering a plan that would involve hiring two people to start working in period 1, one on a temporary basis who would work only through period 5. This would cost $500 in addition to unit production costs.

a. What is the rationale for this plan?

b. Determine the total cost of the plan, including production, inventory, and back-order costs.

Solution

a. With the current workforce of 20 people each producing 10 units per period, regular capacity is 1,800 units. That is 140 units less than expected demand. Adding one worker would increase regular capacity to $1,800 + 90 = 1,890$ units. That would still be 50 units short, or just the amount one temporary worker could produce in five periods. Since one of the two seasonal peaks is quite early, it would make sense to start the temporary worker right away to avoid some of the back-order cost.

b. The production plan for this strategy is as follows:

PERIOD	1	2	3	4	5	6	7	8	9	TOTAL
Forecast	190	230	260	280	210	170	160	260	180	1,940
Output										
Regular	220	220	220	220	220	210	210	210	210	1,940
Overtime	—	—	—	—	—	—	—	—	—	—
Subcontract	—	—	—	—	—	—	—	—	—	—
Output − Forecast	30	(10)	(40)	(60)	10	40	50	(50)	30	0
Inventory										
Beginning	0	30	20	0	0	0	0	20	0	
Ending	30	20	0	0	0	0	20	0	0	
Average	15	25	10	0	0	0	10	10	0	70
Backlog	0	0	20	80	70	30	0	30	0	230
Costs										
Output										
Regular @ $6	$1,320	1,320	1,320	1,320	1,320	1,260	1,260	1,260	1,260	$11,640
Overtime										
Subcontract										
Inventory @ $5	$ 75	125	50	0	0	0	50	50	0	$350
Back order @ $10	0	0	200	800	700	300	0	300	0	$ 2,300
Total	$1,395	1,445	1,570	2,120	2,020	1,560	1,310	1,610	1,260	$14,290

The total cost for this plan is $14,290, plus the $500 cost for hiring and for the layoff, giving a total of $14,790. This plan may or may not be good. The manager would need information on other costs and options before settling on one plan.

Although the calculations are relatively straightforward, the backlogs can sometimes seem difficult to obtain. Consider these rules for computing the backlog:

1. Start with the Output − Forecast value. If this is positive and there was a backlog in the preceding period, reduce the backlog by this amount. If the amount exceeds the backlog, the difference becomes the ending inventory for the period. If they are exactly equal, the backlog and the ending inventory will both be equal to zero.

2. If Output − Forecast is negative, subtract it from the beginning inventory. If this produces a negative value, that value becomes the backlog for that period.

You also can use the appropriate Excel template to obtain the solution:

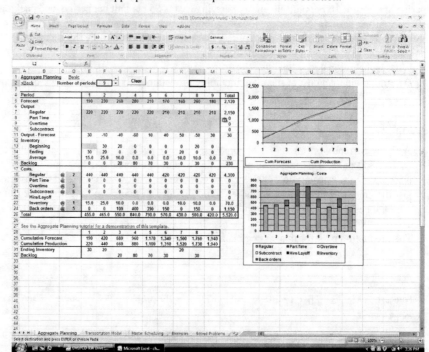

PROBLEM 2

Spring and Summer Fashions, a clothing producer, has generated a forecast for the next eight weeks. Demand is expected to be fairly steady, except for periods 3 and 4, which have higher demands:

PERIOD	1	2	3	4	5	6	7	8	TOTAL
Forecast	1,200	1,200	1,400	3,000	1,200	1,200	1,200	1,200	11,600

The company typically hires seasonal workers to handle the extra workload in periods 3 and 4. The cost for hiring and training a seasonal worker is $50 per worker, and the company plans to hire two additional workers and train them in period 3, for work in period 4, and then lay them off (no cost for layoff). Develop an aggregate plan that uses steady output from regular workers with added output from the two seasonal workers in period 4. The output rate for the seasonal workers is slightly less than that of regular workers, so their cost per unit is higher. The cost per unit for regular workers is $4 per hour, while cost per unit for the seasonal workers is $5 per unit. Backlog cost is $1 per unit per period.

Solution

Period			1	2	3	4	5	6	7	8	Total
Forecast			1,200	1,200	1,400	3,000	1,200	1,200	1,200	1,200	11,600
Output											
Regular			1,200	1,200	1,200	1,200	1,200	1,200	1,200	1,200	9,600
Part Time						2,000					2,000
Overtime											0
Subcontract											0
Output - Forecast			0	0	−200	200	0	0	0	0	0
Inventory											
Beginning			0	0	0	0	0	0	0	0	
Ending			0	0	0	0	0	0	0	0	
Average			0.0	0.0	0.0	0.0	0.0	0.0	0.0	0.0	0
Backlog			0	0	200	0	0	0	0	0	200
Costs :											
Regular	@	4	4,800	4,800	4,800	4,800	4,800	4,800	4,800	4,800	38,800
Part Time	@	5	0	0	0	10,000	0	0	0	0	10,800
OverTime	@		0	0	0	0	0	0	0	0	0
Subcontract	@		0	0	0	0	0	0	0	0	0
Hire/Layoff		50				100					100
Inventory	@		0.0	0.0	0.0	0.0	0.0	0.0	0.0	0.0	0.0
Back orders	@	1	0	0	200	0	0	0	0	0	200
Total			4,800.0	4,800.0	5,100.0	14,800	4,800.0	4,800.0	4,800.0	4,800.0	48,700.0

PROBLEM 3

Prepare a schedule like that shown in Figure 4.11 for the following situation. The forecast for each period is 70 units. The starting inventory is zero. The MPS rule is to schedule production if the projected inventory on hand is negative. The production lot size is 100 units. The following table shows committed orders.

PERIOD	CUSTOMER ORDERS
1	80
2	50
3	30
4	10

PERIOD	(A) INVENTORY FROM PREVIOUS PERIOD	(B) REQUIREMENTS*	(C = A − B) NET INVENTORY BEFORE MPS	MPS	(MPS + C) PROJECTED INVENTORY
1	0	80	(80)	100	20
2	20	70	(50)	100	50
3	50	70	(20)	100	80
4	80	70	10	0	10

*Requirements equal the larger of forecast and customer orders in each period.

STARTING INV. = 0	1	2	3	4
FORECAST	70	70	70	70
CUSTOMER ORDERS	80	50	30	10
PROJECTED ON-HAND INVENTORY	20	50	80	10
MPS	100	100	100	0
ATP	20	50	60	0

DISCUSSION AND REVIEW QUESTIONS

1 What three levels of planning involve operations managers? What kinds of decisions are made at the various levels?
2 What are the three phases of intermediate planning?
3 What is aggregate planning? What is its purpose?
4 Why is there a need for aggregate planning?
5 What are the most common decision variables for aggregate planning in a manufacturing setting? In a service setting?
6 What aggregate planning difficulty that might confront an organization offering a variety of products and/or services would not confront an organization offering one or a few similar products or services?
7 Briefly discuss the advantages and disadvantages of each of these planning strategies:
   a. Maintain a level rate of output and let inventories absorb fluctuations in demand.
   b. Vary the size of the workforce to correspond to predicted changes in demand requirements.
   c. Maintain a constant workforce size, but vary hours worked to correspond to predicted demand requirements.
8 What are the primary advantages and limitations of informal graphic and charting techniques for aggregate planning?
9 Briefly describe the planning techniques listed below, and give an advantage and disadvantage for each:
   a. Spreadsheet
   b. Linear programming
   c. Simulation
10 What are the inputs to master scheduling? What are the outputs?
11 Explain the managerial significance of aggregate planning.

TAKING STOCK

1 What general trade-offs are involved in master scheduling in terms of the frozen portion of the schedule?
2 Who needs to interface with the master schedule and why?
3 How has technology had an impact on master scheduling?

CRITICAL THINKING EXERCISE

Service operations often face more difficulty in planning than their manufacturing counterparts. However, service does have certain advantages that manufacturing often does not. Explain service planning difficulty, and the advantages and disadvantages.

PROBLEMS

1 Refer to Example 1. The president of the firm has decided to shut down the plant for vacation and installation of new equipment in period 4. After installation, the cost per unit will remain the same, but the output rate for regular time will be 450. Regular output is the same as in Example 1 for periods 1, 2,and 3; 0 for period 4; and 450 for each of the remaining periods. Note, though, that the forecast of 400 units in period 4 must be dealt with. Prepare the aggregate plan, and compute its total cost.

2 Refer to Example 1. Suppose that the regular output rate will drop to 290 units per period due to an expected change in production requirements. Costs will not change. Prepare an aggregate plan and compute its total cost for each of these alternatives:
   a. Use overtime at a fixed rate of 20 units per period as needed. Plan for an ending inventory of zero for period 6. Backlogs cannot exceed 90 units per period.
   b. Use subcontracting at a maximum rate of 50 units per period; the usage need not be the same in every period. Have an ending inventory of zero in the last period. Again backlogs cannot exceed 90 units in any period. Compare these two plans.

3 Refer to Example 2. Suppose you can use a combination of overtime and subcontracting, but you cannot use subcontracting in more than two periods. Up to 50 units of subcontracting and either 0 or 40 units of overtime are allowed per period. Subcontracting is $6 per unit, and overtime is $3 per unit. (Hint: Use subcontracting only when overtime units are not sufficient to decrease backlogs to 80 units or less.) Plan for an ending inventory balance of 0 for period 6. Prepare a plan that will minimize total cost.

4 Refer to Example 2. Determine whether a plan to use subcontracting at a maximum rate of 50 units per period as needed with no overtime would achieve a lower total cost than the plan shown in Example 2. Again, plan for a zero inventory balance at the end of period 6.

5 Manager T. C. Downs of Plum Engines, a producer of lawn mowers and leaf blowers, must develop an aggregate plan given the forecast for engine demand shown in the table. The department has a normal capacity of 130 engines per month. Normal output has a cost of $60 per engine. The beginning inventory is zero engines. Overtime has a cost of $90 per engine.

   a. Develop a chase plan that matches the forecast and compute the total cost of your plan.

   b. Compare the costs to a level plan that uses inventory to absorb fluctuations. Inventory carrying cost is $2 per engine per month. Backlog cost is $90 per engine per month.

MONTH	1	2	3	4	5	6	7	8	TOTAL
Forecast	120	135	140	120	125	125	140	135	1,040

6 Manager Chris Channing of Fabric Mills, Inc., has developed the forecast shown in the table for bolts of cloth. The figures are in hundreds of bolts. The department has a normal capacity of 275(00) bolts per month, except for the seventh month, when capacity will be 250(00) bolts. Normal output has a cost of $40 per hundred bolts. Workers can be assigned to other jobs if production is less than normal. The beginning inventory is zero bolts.
   a. Develop a chase plan that matches the forecast and compute the total cost of your plan. Overtime is $60 per hundred bolts.

b. Would the total cost be less with regular production with no overtime, but using a subcontractor to handle the excess above normal capacity at a cost of $50 per hundred bolts? Backlogs are not allowed. The inventory carrying cost is $2 per hundred bolts.

MONTH	1	2	3	4	5	6	7	TOTAL
Forecast	250	300	250	300	280	275	270	1,925

7 SummerFun, Inc., produces a variety of recreation and leisure products. The production manager has developed an aggregate forecast:

MONTH	MAR	APR	MAY	JUN	JUL	AUG	SEP	TOTAL
Forecast	50	44	55	60	50	40	51	350

Use the following information to develop aggregate plans.

Regular production cost	$80 per unit	Back-order cost	$20 per unit
Overtime production cost	$120 per unit	Beginning inventory	0 units
Regular capacity	40 units per month		
Overtime capacity	8 units per month		
Subcontracting cost	$140 per unit		
Subcontracting capacity	12 units per month		
Holding cost	$10 per unit per month		

Develop an aggregate plan using each of the following guidelines and compute the total cost for each plan. Which plan has the lowest total cost?
a. Use regular production. Supplement using inventory, overtime, and subcontracting as needed. No backlogs allowed.
b. Use a level strategy. Use a combination of backlogs, subcontracting, and inventory to handle variations in demand.

8 Nowjuice, Inc., produces bottled pomogranate juice. A planner has developed an aggregate forecast for demand (in cases) for the next six months.

MONTH	MAY	JUN	JUL	AUG	SEP	OCT
Forecast	4,000	4,800	5,600	7,200	6,400	5,000

Use the following information to develop aggregate plans.

Regular production cost	$10 per case
Regular production capacity	5,000 cases
Overtime production cost	$16 per case
Subcontracting cost	$20 per case
Holding cost	$1 per case per month
Beginning inventory	0

Develop an aggregate plan using each of the following guidelines and compute the total cost for each plan. Which plan has the lowest total cost?
a. Use level production. Supplement using overtime as needed.
b. Use a combination of overtime (500 cases per period maximum), inventory, and subcontracting (500 cases per period maximum) to handle variations in demand.
c. Use overtime up to 750 cases per period and inventory to handle variations in demand.

9 Wormwood, Ltd., produces a variety of furniture products. The planning committee wants to prepare an aggregate plan for the next six months using the following information:

	MONTH							COST PER UNIT	
	1	2	3	4	5	6		Regular time	$50
DEMAND	160	150	160	180	170	140		Overtime	75
CAPACITY								Subcontract	80
REGULAR	150	150	150	150	160	160		Inventory, per period	4
OVERTIME	10	10	0	10	10	10			

Subcontracting can handle a maximum of 10 units per month. Beginning inventory is zero. Develop a plan that minimizes total cost. No back orders are allowed.

10 Refer to Solved Problem 1. Prepare two additional aggregate plans. Call the one in the solved problem plan A. For plan B, hire one more worker at a cost of $200. Make up any shortfall using subcontracting at $8 per unit, with a maximum of 20 units per period (i.e., use subcontracting to reduce back orders when the forecast exceeds regular output). Note that the ending inventory in period 9 should be zero. Therefore, Total forecast − Total output = Quantity subcontracted. An additional constraint is that back orders cannot exceed 80 units in any period. For plan C, assume no workers are hired (so regular output is 200 units per period instead of 210 as in plan B). Use subcontracting as needed, but no more than 20 units per period. Compute the total cost of each plan. Which plan has the lowest cost?

11 Refer to Solved Problem 1. Suppose another option is to use part-time workers to assist during seasonal peaks. The cost per unit, including hiring and training, is $11. The output rate is 10 units per worker per period for all workers. A maximum of 10 part-time workers can be used, and the same number of part-time workers must be used in all periods that have part-time workers. The ending inventory in period 9 should be 10 units. The limit on backlogs is 20 units per period. Try to make up backlogs as soon as possible. Compute the total cost for this plan, and compare it to the cost of the plan used in the solved problem. Assume 20 full-time workers.

12 Refer to Solved Problem 1. Prepare an aggregate plan that uses overtime ($9 per unit, maximum output 25 units per period) and inventory variation. Try to minimize backlogs. The ending inventory in period 9 should be zero, and the limit on backlogs is 60 units per period. Note that Total output = Total regular output + Overtime quantity. Compute the total cost of your plan, and compare it to the total cost of the plan used in the solved problem. Assume 20 full-time workers.

13 Refer to Solved Problem 1. Prepare an aggregate plan that uses some combination of laying off ($100 per worker), subcontracting ($8 per unit, maximum of 20 units per period, must use for three consecutive periods), and overtime ($9 per unit, maximum of 25 per period, maximum of 60 for the planning horizon). Compute the total cost, and compare it with any of the other plans you have developed. Which plan has the lowest total cost? Assume you start with 21 workers.

14 Verify the transportation solution shown in Example 3.

15 Refer to Example 3. Suppose that an increase in warehousing costs and other costs brings inventory carrying costs to $2 per unit per month. All other costs and quantities remain the same. Determine a revised solution to this transportation problem.

16 Refer to Example 3. Suppose that regular-time capacity will be reduced to 440 units in period 3 to accommodate a companywide safety inspection of equipment. What will the additional cost of the optimal plan be as compared to the one shown in Example 3? Assume all costs and quantities are the same as given in Example 3 except for the regular-time output in period 3.

17 Solve Problem 16 using an inventory carrying cost of $2 per unit per period.

18 Dundas Bike Components Inc. of Wheelville, Illinois, manufactures bicycle wheels in two different sizes for the Big Bike Co. assembly plant located across town. David Dundas, the firm's owner-manager, has just received Big Bike's order for the next six months.

	NOV.	DEC.	JAN.	FEB.	MAR.	APR.
20-INCH WHEELS	1,000 units	900	600	700	1,100	1,100
24-INCH WHEELS	500 units	500	300	500	400	600

a. Under what circumstances will it be possible for David to develop just one aggregate plan rather than two (one for each size wheel)? Explain in two to three sentences without calculations.

b. Currently Dundas employs 28 full-time, highly skilled employees, each of whom can produce 50 wheels per month. Because skilled labor is in short supply in the Wheelville area, David would like to develop a pure level-output plan. There is no inventory of finished wheels on hand at present, but David would like to have 300 on hand at the end of April. Big Bike will tolerate back orders of up to 200 units per month. Show your level plan in tabular form.

c. Calculate the total annual cost of your plan using these costs:

Regular	$5.00	Hiring	$300
OVERTIME	$7.50	LAYOFF	$400
PART-TIME	NA	INVENTORY	$1.00
SUBCONTRACT	NA	BACK ORDER	$6.00

19 Prepare a master production schedule for industrial pumps in the manner of Figure 4.11 in the chapter. Use the same inputs as the example, but change the MPS rule from "schedule production when the projected on-hand inventory would be negative without production" to "schedule production when the projected on-hand inventory would be less than 10 without production."

20 Update the master schedule shown in Figure 4.11 given these updated inputs: It is now the end of week 1; customer orders are 25 for week 2, 16 for week 3, 11 for week 4, 8 for week 5, and 3 for week 6. Use the MPS rule of ordering production when projected on-hand inventory would be negative without production.

21 Prepare a master schedule like that shown in Figure 4.11 given this information: The forecast for each week of an eight-week schedule is 50 units. The MPS rule is to schedule production if the projected on-hand inventory would be negative without it. Customer orders (committed) are as follows:

WEEK	CUSTOMER ORDERS
1	52
2	35
3	20
4	12

Use a production lot size of 75 units and no beginning inventory.

22 Determine the available-to-promise (ATP) quantities for each period for Problem 21.

23 Prepare a schedule like that shown in Figure 4.12 for the following situation: The forecast is 80 units for each of the first two periods and 60 units for each of the next three periods. The starting inventory is 20 units. The company uses a chase strategy for determining the production lot size, except there is an upper limit on the lot size of 70 units. Also, the desired safety stock is 10 units. *Note:* The ATP quantities are based on maximum allowable production and do not include safety stock. Committed orders are as follows:

PERIOD	CUSTOMER ORDERS
1	82
2	80
3	60
4	40
5	20

CASE: EIGHT GLASSES A DAY (EGAD)

The EGAD Bottling Company has decided to introduce a new line of premium bottled water that will include several "designer" flavors. Marketing manager Georgianna Mercer is predicting an upturn in demand based on the new offerings and the increased public awareness of the health benefits of drinking more water. She has prepared aggregate forecasts for the next six months, as shown in the following table (quantities are in tankloads):

MONTH	MAY	JUN	JUL	AUG	SEPT	OCT	TOTAL
Forecast	50	60	70	90	80	70	420

Production manager Mark Mercer (no relation to Georgianna) has developed the following information. (Note that one unit equals 100 bottles, and there are 10,000 bottles per tankload.)

Regular production cost	$10 per unit
Regular production capacity	60 units
Overtime production cost	$16 per unit
Subcontracting cost	$18 per unit
Holding cost	$2 per unit per month
Back-ordering cost	$50 per month per unit
Beginning inventory	0 units

AMONG THE STRATEGIES BEING CONSIDERED ARE THE FOLLOWING:

1 Level production supplemented by up to 10 tankloads a month from overtime.

2 A combination of overtime, inventory, and subcontracting.

3 Using overtime for up to 15 tankloads a month, along with inventory to handle variations.

QUESTIONS

1 The objective is to choose the plan that has the lowest cost. Which plan would you recommend?

2 Presumably, information about the new line has been shared with supply chain partners. Explain what information should be shared with various partners, and why sharing that information is important.

SELECTED BIBLIOGRAPHY AND FURTHER READING

Brandimarte, P., and A. Villa (Eds). *Modeling Manufacturing Systems: From Aggregate Planning to Real-Time Control.* New York: Springer, 1999.

Buxey, G. "Production Planning for Seasonal Demand." *International Journal of Operations and Production Management* 13, no. 7 (July 1993), pp. 4–21.

Hopp, Wallace J., and Mark L. Spearman. *Factory Physics.* 2nd ed. New York: Irwin/McGraw-Hill, 2001.

Silver, E. A., D. F. Pyke, and R. Peterson. *Inventory Management and Production Planning and Scheduling.* New York: Wiley, 1998.

Sipper, Daniel, and Robert Bulfin Jr. *Production: Planning, Control, and Integration.* New York: McGraw-Hill, 1997.

Vollmann, Thomas E., William L. Berry, and D. Clay Whybark. *Manufacturing Planning and Control Systems.* 4th ed. Burr Ridge, IL: Richard D. Irwin, 1997.

Ware, Norman, and Donald Fogarty. "Master Schedule/ Master Production Schedule: The Same or Different?" *Production and Inventory Management Journal,* First Quarter 1990, pp. 34–37.

part 2

INVENTORY MANAGEMENT AND SCHEDULING

The chapters in this part relate to the management and control of inventories and to scheduling, often key factors in the success or failure of operations management to achieve profit and/or cost objectives while satisfying customers. The basic issues are how to best manage resources to effectively match supply and demand.

The chapters in this part cover the following topics:

1. Inventory Management, Chapter 5
2. Aggregate Planning, Chapter 4

chapter 5

INVENTORY MANAGEMENT

Learning Objectives

After completing this chapter, you should be able to:

1. Define the term *inventory*, list the major reasons for holding inventories, and list the main requirements for effective inventory management.

2. Discuss the nature and importance of service inventories.

3. Discuss periodic and perpetual review systems.

4. Discuss the objectives of inventory management.

5. Describe the A-B-C approach and explain how it is useful.

6. Describe the basic EOQ model and its assumptions and solve typical problems.

7. Describe the economic production quantity model and solve typical problems.

8. Describe the quantity discount model and solve typical problems.

9. Describe reorder point models and solve typical problems.

10. Describe situations in which the single-period model would be appropriate, and solve typical problems.

nventory management is a core operations management activity. Good inventory management is important for the successful operation of most businesses and their supply chains. Operations, marketing, and finance have interests in good inventory management. Poor inventory management hampers operations, diminishes customer satisfaction, and increases operating costs.

Some organizations have excellent inventory management, and many have satisfactory inventory management. Too many, however, have unsatisfactory inventory management, which sometimes is a sign that management does not recognize the importance of inventories. More often than not, though, the recognition is there. What is lacking is an understanding of

what needs to be done and how to do it. This chapter presents the concepts that underlie good inventory management. Topics include functions of inventories, requirements for effective inventory management, objectives of inventory control, and techniques for determining *how much* to order and *when* to order.

INTRODUCTION

Inventory

An inventory is a stock or store of goods. Firms typically stock hundreds or even thousands of items in inventory, ranging from small things such as pencils, paper clips, screws, nuts, and bolts to large items such as machines, trucks, construction equipment, and airplanes. Naturally, many of the items a firm carries in inventory relate to the kind of business it engages in. Thus, manufacturing firms carry supplies of raw materials, purchased parts, partially finished items, and finished goods, as well as spare parts for machines, tools, and other supplies. Department stores carry clothing, furniture, carpeting, stationery, cosmetics, gifts, cards, and toys. Some also stock sporting goods, paints, and tools. Hospitals stock drugs, surgical supplies, life-monitoring equipment, sheets and pillow cases, and more. Supermarkets stock fresh and canned foods, packaged and frozen foods, household supplies, magazines, baked goods, dairy products, produce, and other items.

The inventory models described in this chapter relate primarily to what are referred to as *independent-demand* items, that is, items that are ready to be sold or used. Thus, a computer would be an independent-demand item, while the components that are used to assemble a computer would be dependent-demand items: The demand for those items would depend on how many of each item is needed for a computer, as well as how many computers are going to be made.

Managing dependent-demand inventory is described in a different chapter because there are basic differences in assumptions and in the character of inventory decisions.

READING: $$$

We proceed as follows. First look for a five-by-five-by-three-foot bin of gears or parts that looks like it has been there awhile. Pick up a gear and ask, casually, "How much is this worth?" You then ask, "How many of these are in the bin?" followed by, "How long has this bin been here?" and, "What's your cost of money for this company?" I recall one case in a nameless South American country where the unit cost times the number of parts times the time it had been there times the interest rate resulted in a cost-per-day figure that would insure comfortable retirement for the plant manager on the bank of the Rio de la Plata at one of the better resorts to be found there. The plant manager suddenly realized that what he was holding was not just a chunk of high-test steel, but was *real money*. He then pointed out that *he* now understood the value of the inventory but could I suggest a way to drive the point home to upper management? I suggested that he go to the accounting department and borrow enough money to be equal to the bin's value for as long as it had been sitting there, and pile it on the top of the bin. I further suggested that he do that for every bin on the production line. We rapidly figured out that by the time we had the money piled up on the bin, you would not even be able to *see* the bin. My opinion was that if the upper managers were given a tour of the line with the money piled up, they would *never* forget it.

SOURCE: GENE WOOLSEY, "ON DOING GOOD THINGS AND DUMB THINGS IN PRODUCTION AND INVENTORY CONTROL," *INTERFACES*, VOL. 5, NO. 3, (MAY 1975). COPYRIGHT © 1975 THE INSTITUTE FOR OPERATIONS RESEARCH AND THE MANAGEMENT SCIENCES (INFORMS). REPRINTED BY PERMISSION.

THE NATURE AND IMPORTANCE OF INVENTORIES

Inventories are a vital part of business. Not only are they necessary for operations, but they also contribute to customer satisfaction. To get a sense of the significance of inventories, consider the following: Some very large firms have tremendous amounts of inventory. For example, General Motors was at one point reported to have as much as $40 billion worth of materials, parts, cars, and trucks in its supply chain! Although the amounts and dollar values of inventories carried by different types of firms vary widely, a typical firm probably has about 30 percent of its current assets and perhaps as much as 90 percent of its working capital

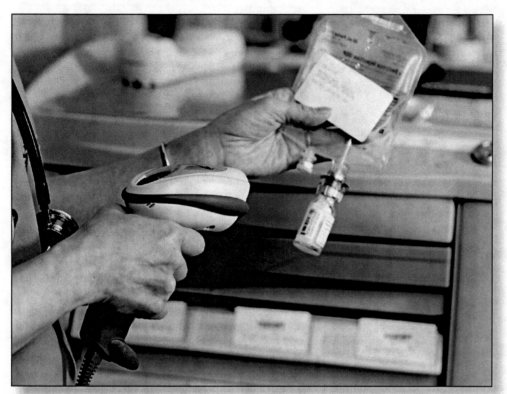

BY INITIATING A PROGRAM THAT UTILIZES BARCODES AND SCANNERS, SUCH AS THIS ONE BY MOTOROLA, HOSPITALS CAN CONTROL INVENTORY SUPPLY AREAS, AS WELL AS KEEP TRACK OF ALL EQUIPMENT IN USE ACROSS THE ENTERPRISE. STOCKROOM INVENTORY APPLICATIONS TRACK CONSUMABLE ITEMS SUCH AS MEDICATION AND SUPPLIES, WHILE CHECK IN/OUT APPLICATIONS TRACK SHARED OR RE-USABLE ITEMS SUCH AS X-RAYS, LAB RESULTS, DIAGNOSTIC TOOLS, AND OTHER MEDICAL EQUIPMENT.

invested in inventory. One widely used measure of managerial performance relates to *return on investment* (ROI), which is profit after taxes divided by total assets. Because inventories may represent a significant portion of total assets, a reduction of inventories can result in a significant increase in ROI. Furthermore, the ratio of inventories to sales in the manufacturing, wholesale, and retail sectors is one measure that is used to gauge the health of the U.S. economy.

Inventory decisions in service organizations can be especially critical. Hospitals, for example, carry an array of drugs and blood supplies that might be needed on short notice. Being out of stock on some of these could imperil the well-being of a patient. However, many of these items have a limited shelf life, so carrying large quantities would mean having to dispose of unused, costly supplies. On-site repair services for computers, printers, copiers, and fax machines also have to carefully consider which parts to bring to the site to avoid having to make an extra trip to obtain parts. The same goes for home repair services such as electricians, appliance repairers, and plumbers.

The major source of revenues for retail and wholesale businesses is the sale of merchandise (i.e., inventory). In fact, in terms of dollars, the inventory of goods held for sale is one of the largest assets of a merchandising business. Retail stores that sell clothing wrestle with decisions about which styles to carry, and how much of each to stock, knowing full well that fast-selling items will mean greater profits than having to heavily discount goods that didn't sell.

The different kinds of inventories include the following:

Raw materials and purchased parts.
Partially completed goods, called *work-in-process (WIP)*.
Finished-goods inventories (manufacturing firms) or merchandise (retail stores).
Tools and supplies.
Maintenance and repairs (MRO) inventory.
Goods-in-transit to warehouses, distributors, or customers (pipeline inventory).

Both manufacturing and service organizations have to take into consideration the space requirements of inventory. In some cases, space limitations may pose restrictions on inventory storage capability, thereby adding another dimension to inventory decisions.

To understand why firms have inventories at all, you need to be aware of the various functions of inventory.

FUNCTIONS OF INVENTORY

Inventories serve a number of functions. Among the most important are the following:

1. *To meet anticipated customer demand.* A customer can be a person who walks in off the street to buy a new stereo system, a mechanic who requests a tool at a tool crib, or a manufacturing operation. These inventories are referred to as *anticipation stocks* because they are held to satisfy expected (i.e., *average*) demand.

2. *To smooth production requirements.* Firms that experience seasonal patterns in demand often build up inventories during preseason periods to meet overly high requirements during seasonal periods. These inventories are aptly named *seasonal inventories.* Companies that process fresh fruits and vegetables deal with seasonal inventories. So do stores that sell greeting cards, skis, snowmobiles, or Christmas trees.

3. *To decouple operations.* Historically, manufacturing firms have used inventories as buffers between successive operations to maintain continuity of production that would otherwise be disrupted by events such as breakdowns of equipment and accidents that cause a portion of the operation to shut down temporarily. The buffers permit other operations to continue temporarily while the problem is resolved. Similarly, firms have used buffers of raw materials to insulate production from disruptions in deliveries from suppliers, and finished goods inventory to buffer sales operations from manufacturing disruptions. More recently, companies have taken a closer look at buffer inventories, recognizing the cost and space they require, and realizing that finding and eliminating sources of disruptions can greatly decrease the need for decoupling operations.

   Inventory buffers are also important in supply chains. Careful analysis can reveal both points where buffers would be most useful and points where they would merely increase costs without adding value.

4. *To protect against stockouts.* Delayed deliveries and unexpected increases in demand increase the risk of shortages. Delays can occur because of weather conditions, supplier stockouts, deliveries of wrong materials, quality problems, and so on. The risk of shortages can be reduced by holding *safety stocks,* which are stocks in excess of average demand to compensate for *variabilities* in demand and lead time.

5. *To take advantage of order cycles.* To minimize purchasing and inventory costs, a firm often buys in quantities that exceed immediate requirements. This necessitates storing some or all of the purchased amount for later use. Similarly, it is usually economical to produce in large rather than small quantities. Again, the excess output must be stored for later use. Thus, inventory storage enables a firm to buy and produce in *economic lot sizes* without having to try to match purchases or production with demand requirements in the short run. This results in *periodic* orders, or order *cycles.* The resulting stock is known as *cycle stock.* Order cycles are not always based on economic lot sizes. In some instances, it is practical or economical to group orders and/or to order at fixed intervals.

6. *To hedge against price increases.* Occasionally a firm will suspect that a substantial price increase is about to occur and purchase larger-than-normal amounts to beat the increase. The ability to store extra goods also allows a firm to take advantage of price discounts for larger orders.

7. *To permit operations.* The fact that production operations take a certain amount of time (i.e., they are not instantaneous) means that there will generally be some work-in-process inventory. In addition, intermediate stocking of goods—including raw materials, semifinished items, and finished goods at production sites, as well as goods stored in warehouses—leads to *pipeline* inventories throughout a production-distribution system.

Little's Law can be useful in quantifying pipeline inventory. It states that the average amount of inventory in a system is equal to the product of the average rate at which inventory units leave the system (i.e., the average demand rate) and the average time a unit is in the system. Thus, if a unit is in the system for an average of 10 days, and the demand rate is 5 units per day, the average inventory is 50 units: 5 units/day $\times$ 10 days = 50 units.

Little's Law

8. *To take advantage of quantity discounts.* Suppliers may give discounts on large orders.

OBJECTIVES OF INVENTORY CONTROL

Inadequate control of inventories can result in both under- and overstocking of items. Understocking results in missed deliveries, lost sales, dissatisfied customers, and production bottlenecks; overstocking unnecessarily ties up funds that might be more productive elsewhere. Although overstocking may appear to be the lesser of the two evils, the price tag for excessive overstocking can be staggering when inventory holding costs are high—as illustrated by the little story about the bin of gears at the beginning of the chapter—and matters can easily get out of hand. It is not unheard of for managers to discover that their firm has a 10-year supply of some item. (No doubt the firm got a good buy on it!)

Inventory management has two main concerns. One is the *level of customer service,* that is, to have the right goods, in sufficient quantities, in the right place, at the right time. The other is the *costs of ordering and carrying inventories.*

The overall objective of inventory management is to achieve satisfactory levels of customer service while keeping inventory costs within reasonable bounds. Toward this end, the decision maker tries to achieve a balance in stocking. He or she must make two fundamental decisions: the *timing* and *size* of orders (i.e., when to order and how much to order). The greater part of this chapter is devoted to models that can be applied to assist in making those decisions.

Managers have a number of measures of performance they can use to judge the effectiveness of inventory management. The most obvious, of course, is customer satisfaction, which they might measure by the number and quantity of backorders and/or customer complaints. A widely used measure is inventory turnover, which is the ratio of annual cost of goods sold to average inventory investment. The turnover ratio indicates how many times a year the inventory is sold. Generally, the higher the ratio, the better, because that implies more efficient use of inventories. However, the desirable number of turns depends on the industry and what the profit margins are. The higher the profit margins, the lower the acceptable number of inventory turns, and vice versa. Also, a product that takes a long time to manufacture, or a long time to sell, will have a low turnover rate. This is often the case with high-end retailers (high profit margins). Conversely, supermarkets (low profit margins) have a fairly high turnover rate. Note, though, that there should be a balance between inventory investment and maintaining good customer service. Managers often use inventory turnover to evaluate inventory management performance; monitoring this metric over time can yield insights into changes in performance.

Inventory turnover

Another useful measure is days of inventory on hand, a number that indicates the expected number of days of sales that can be supplied from existing inventory. Here, a balance is desirable; a high number of days might imply excess inventory, while a low number might imply a risk of running out of stock.

REQUIREMENTS FOR EFFECTIVE INVENTORY MANAGEMENT

Management has two basic functions concerning inventory. One is to establish a system of keeping track of items in inventory, and the other is to make decisions about how much and when to order. To be effective, management must have the following:

1. A system to *keep track of the inventory* on hand and on order.
2. A reliable *forecast of demand* that includes an indication of possible *forecast error.*

3. Knowledge of *lead times* and *lead time variability.*
4. Reasonable estimates of inventory *holding costs, ordering costs,* and *shortage costs.*
5. A *classification system* for inventory items.

Let's take a closer look at each of these requirements.

INVENTORY COUNTING SYSTEMS

Periodic system

Inventory counting systems can be periodic or perpetual. Under a periodic system, a physical count of items in inventory is made at periodic intervals (e.g., weekly, monthly) in order to decide how much to order of each item. Many small retailers use this approach: A manager periodically checks the shelves and stockroom to determine the quantity on hand. Then the manager estimates how much will be demanded prior to the next delivery period and bases the order quantity on that information. An advantage of this type of system is that orders for many items occur at the same time, which can result in economies in processing and shipping orders. There are also several disadvantages of periodic reviews. One is a lack of control between reviews. Another is the need to protect against shortages between review periods by carrying extra stock.

Perpetual inventory system

A perpetual inventory system (also known as a *continual* system) keeps track of removals from inventory on a continuous basis, so the system can provide information on the current level of inventory for each item. When the amount on hand reaches a predetermined minimum, a fixed quantity, Q, is ordered. An obvious advantage of this system is the control provided by the continuous monitoring of inventory withdrawals. Another advantage is the fixed-order quantity; management can determine an optimal order quantity. One disadvantage of this approach is the added cost of record keeping. Moreover, a physical count of inventories must still be performed periodically to verify records because of possible errors, pilferage, spoilage, and other factors that can reduce the effective amount of inventory. Bank transactions such as customer deposits and withdrawals are examples of continuous recording of inventory changes.

Two-bin system

Perpetual systems range from very simple to very sophisticated. A two-bin system, a very elementary system, uses two containers for inventory. Items are withdrawn from the first bin until its contents are exhausted. It is then time to reorder. Sometimes an order card is placed at the bottom of the first bin. The second bin contains enough stock to satisfy expected demand until the order is filled, plus an extra cushion of stock that will reduce the chance of a stockout if the order is late or if usage is greater than expected. The advantage of this system is that there is no need to record each withdrawal from inventory; the disadvantage is that the reorder card may not be turned in for a variety of reasons (e.g., misplaced, the person responsible forgets to turn it in).

Perpetual systems can be either *batch* or *online.* In batch systems, inventory records are collected periodically and entered into the system. In online systems, the transactions are recorded immediately. The advantage of online systems is that they are always up-to-date. In batch systems, a sudden surge in demand could result in reducing the amount of inventory below the reorder point between the periodic read-ins. Frequent batch collections can minimize that problem.

Universal product code (UPC)

Supermarkets, discount stores, and department stores have always been major users of periodic counting systems. Today, most have switched to computerized checkout systems using a laser scanning device that reads a universal product code (UPC), or *bar code,* printed on an item tag or on packaging. A typical grocery product code is illustrated here.

The zero on the left of the bar code identifies this as a grocery item, the first five numbers (14800) indicate the manufacturer (Mott's), and the last five numbers (23208) indicate the specific item (natural-style applesauce). Items in small packages, such as candy and gum, use a six-digit number.

UPC scanners represent major benefits to supermarkets. In addition to their increase in speed and accuracy, these systems give managers continuous information on inventories, reduce the need for periodic inventories and order-size determinations, and improve the level of customer service by indicating the price and quantity of each item on the customer's receipt, as in the following illustration:

```
BRACO CAPELLINI            .79
BUB YUM DBL LIME           .30 T
2/LO FAT MILK H G         1.03
EUROP ROLLS                .91
HUNTS TOMATO               .55
NEWSPAPER                  .35
KR CAS BRICK CHEES        1.59
GRAPES-GREEN
   .91 LB @ .89 PER LB     .81
TAX DUE                    .02
TOTAL                     6.35

CASH                     20.00*
CHANGE                   13.65

8/07/08 18:01 21  16  23100  2570
```

Bar coding is important for other sectors of business besides retailing. Manufacturing and service industries benefit from the simplified production and inventory control it provides. In manufacturing, bar codes attached to parts, subassemblies, and finished goods greatly facilitate counting and monitoring activities. Automatic routing, scheduling, sorting, and packaging can also be done using bar codes. In health care, use of bar codes can help to reduce drug dispensing errors.

Radio frequency identification (RFID) tags are also used to keep track of inventory in certain applications.

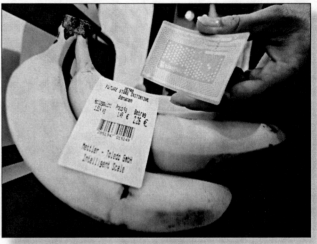

HERE ARE A TRADITIONAL BAR CODE LABEL AND RFID TAG WITH A MICROCHIP. INFORMATION SPECIFIC TO THIS PARTICULAR BUNCH OF BANANAS CAN BE STORED AND MODIFIED EVERY TIME THE BANANAS PASS BY A SCANNER. RFID IS USED FOR IDENTIFICATION, INVENTORY AND PRODUCT FLOW TRACKING.

READING: RADIO FREQUENCY IDENTIFICATION (RFID) TAGS

Keeping track of inventories in-house and throughout a supply chain is vitally important for manufacturing, service, and retail operations. Bar codes have long been used for that purpose, but they carry only a limited amount of information and require direct line-of-sight to be scanned. Radio frequency identification (RFID) tags are a technological breakthrough in inventory management, providing real-time information that increases the ability to track and process shipping containers, parts in warehouses, items on supermarket shelves, and a whole lot more. They carry much more information than bar codes, and they don't require line-of-sight to be scanned.

RFID tags transmit product information or other data to network-connected RFID readers via radio waves. Tags attached to pallets, boxes, or individual items can enable a business to identify, track, monitor, or locate any object that is within range of a reader. For example, the tags are used in "speed passes" for toll roads.

In agriculture, fruit growers might use RFID tags to constantly monitor temperatures around fruit during shipping. This ensures that the fruit is kept at appropriate temperature. The tags can be used for a wide range of agricultural products, containing information such as cultivation history, as well as whether the fruit is organically grown and what fertilizers or chemicals have been used.

Because major retail chains, such as Wal-Mart and Target, and governmental agencies now require their suppliers to use RFID tags, many companies have already made RFID a priority in their business strategies.

Although RFID technology holds the potential for improved safety, convenience, and inventory management, widespread adoption, particularly in retail operations, could take several years. Until a global standard is established and cheap disposable tags are developed, the main areas of growth continue to be in nonretail operations.

DEMAND FORECASTS AND LEAD-TIME INFORMATION

Inventories are used to satisfy demand requirements, so it is essential to have reliable estimates of the amount and timing of demand. Similarly, it is essential to know how long it will take for orders to be delivered. In addition, managers need to know the extent to which demand and lead time (the time between submitting an order and receiving it) might vary; the greater the potential variability, the greater the need for additional stock to reduce the risk of a shortage between deliveries. Thus, there is a crucial link between forecasting and inventory management.

Point-of-sale (POS) systems electronically record actual sales. Knowledge of actual sales can greatly enhance forecasting and inventory management: By relaying information about actual demand in real time, these systems enable management to make any necessary changes to restocking decisions. These systems are being increasingly emphasized as an important input to effective supply chain management by making this information available to suppliers.

INVENTORY COSTS

Three basic costs are associated with inventories: holding, transaction (ordering), and shortage costs.

Holding, or carrying, costs relate to physically having items in storage. Costs include interest, insurance, taxes (in some states), depreciation, obsolescence, deterioration, spoilage, pilferage, breakage, and warehousing costs (heat, light, rent, security). They also include opportunity costs associated with having funds that could be used elsewhere tied up in inventory. Note that it is the *variable* portion of these costs that is pertinent.

The significance of the various components of holding cost depends on the type of item involved, although taxes, interest, and insurance are generally based on the dollar value of an inventory. Items that are easily concealed (e.g., pocket cameras, transistor radios, calculators) or fairly expensive (cars, TVs) are prone to theft. Fresh seafood, meats and poultry, produce, and baked goods are subject to rapid deterioration and spoilage. Dairy products, salad dressings, medicines, batteries, and film also have limited shelf lives.

Holding costs are stated in either of two ways: as a percentage of unit price or as a dollar amount per unit. Typical annual holding costs range from 20 percent to 40 percent of the value of an item. In other words, to hold a $100 item in inventory for one year could cost from $20 to $40.

Ordering costs are the costs of ordering and receiving inventory. They are the costs that vary with the actual placement of an order. Besides shipping costs, they include determining how much is needed, preparing invoices, inspecting goods upon arrival for quality and quantity, and moving the goods to temporary storage. Ordering costs are generally expressed as a fixed dollar amount per order, regardless of order size.

When a firm produces its own inventory instead of ordering it from a supplier, the costs of machine setup (e.g., preparing equipment for the job by adjusting the machine, changing cutting tools) are analogous to ordering costs; that is, they are expressed as a fixed charge per production run, regardless of the size of the run.

Shortage costs result when demand exceeds the supply of inventory on hand. These costs can include the opportunity cost of not making a sale, loss of customer goodwill, late charges, and similar costs. Furthermore, if the shortage occurs in an item carried for internal use (e.g., to supply an assembly line), the cost of lost production or downtime is considered a shortage cost. Such costs can easily run into hundreds of dollars a minute or more. Shortage costs are sometimes difficult to measure, and they may be subjectively estimated.

CLASSIFICATION SYSTEM

An important aspect of inventory management is that items held in inventory are not of equal importance in terms of dollars invested, profit potential, sales or usage volume, or stockout penalties. For instance, a producer of electrical equipment might have electric generators,

Lead time

Point-of-sale (POS) systems

Holding (carrying) cost

Ordering costs

Shortage costs

coils of wire, and miscellaneous nuts and bolts among the items carried in inventory. It would be unrealistic to devote equal attention to each of these items. Instead, a more reasonable approach would be to allocate control efforts according to the *relative importance* of various items in inventory.

A-B-C approach

The A-B-C approach classifies inventory items according to some measure of importance, usually annual dollar value (i.e., dollar value per unit multiplied by annual usage rate), and then allocates control efforts accordingly. Typically, three classes of items are used: A (very important), B (moderately important), and C (least important). However, the actual number of categories may vary from organization to organization, depending on the extent to which a firm wants to differentiate control efforts. With three classes of items, A items generally account for about 10 to 20 percent of the *number* of items in inventory but about 60 to 70 percent of the *annual dollar value.* At the other end of the scale, C items might account for about 50 to 60 percent of the number of items but only about 10 to 15 percent of the dollar value of an inventory. These percentages vary from firm to firm, but in most instances a relatively small number of items will account for a large share of the value or cost associated with an inventory, and these items should receive a relatively greater share of control efforts. For instance, A items should receive close attention through frequent reviews of amounts on hand and control over withdrawals, where possible, to make sure that customer service levels are attained. The C items should receive only loose control (two-bin system, bulk orders), and the B items should have controls that lie between the two extremes.

Note that C items are not necessarily *un*important; incurring a stockout of C items such as the nuts and bolts used to assemble manufactured goods can result in a costly shutdown of an assembly line. However, due to the low annual dollar value of C items, there may not be much additional cost incurred by ordering larger quantities of some items, or ordering them a bit earlier.

ONE WAY TO LOWER INVENTORY HOLDING COSTS IS TO IMPROVE SPACE UTILIZATION THROUGH NARROW AISLE HANDLING EQUIPMENT, MEZZANINES, LAYOUT, OR OTHER APPROPRIATE STORAGE MODES. ANOTHER IS AN INVENTORY MANAGEMENT SYSTEM THAT ALLOWS COMPANIES TO MAINTAIN TIGHT CONTROL OVER INVENTORY LEVELS. THIS ALLOWS PROCESS PLANNERS TO OPTIMIZE MATERIAL AND MAINTAIN ACCURATE QUANTITIES.

EXAMPLE 5.1

A manager has obtained a list of unit costs and estimated annual demands for 10 inventory items and now wants to categorize the items on an A-B-C basis. Multiplying each item's annual demand by its unit cost yields its annual dollar value:

mhhe.com/stevenson10e

ITEM NUMBER	ANNUAL DEMAND	×	UNIT COST	=	ANNUAL DOLLAR VALUE
1	2,500		$ 360		$ 900,000
2	1,000		70		70,000
3	2,400		500		1,200,000
4	1,500		100		150,000
5	700		70		49,000
6	1,000		1,000		1,000,000
7	200		210		42,000
8	1,000		4,000		4,000,000
9	8,000		10		80,000
10	500		200		100,000
					7,591,000

SOLUTION

Arranging the annual dollars values in descending order can facilitate assigning items to categories:

Item Number	Annual Dollar Value	Classification	Percentage of Items	Percentage of Annual Dollar Value
8	$4,000,000	A	10	52.7
3	1,200,000	B		
6	1,000,000	B	30	40.8
1	900,000	B		
4	150,000	C		
10	100,000	C		
9	80,000	C	60	6.5
2	70,000	C		
5	49,000	C		
7	42,000	C		
			100	100

Note that category A has the fewest number of items but the highest percentage of annual dollar value, while category C has the most items but only a small percentage of the annual dollar value. ●

Although annual dollar value may be the primary factor in classifying inventory items, a manager may take other factors into account in making exceptions for certain items (e.g., changing the classification of a B item to an A item). Factors may include the risk of obsolescence, the risk of a stockout, the distance of a supplier, and so on.

Figure 5.1 illustrates the A-B-C concept.

Managers use the A-B-C concept in many different settings to improve operations. One key use occurs in customer service, where a manager can focus attention on the most important aspects of customer service by categorizing different aspects as very important, important, or of only minor importance. The point is to not overemphasize minor aspects of customer service at the expense of major aspects.

Cycle counting

Another application of the A-B-C concept is as a guide to cycle counting, which is a physical count of items in inventory. The purpose of cycle counting is to reduce discrepancies between the amounts indicated by inventory records and the actual quantities of inventory on hand. Accuracy is important because inaccurate records can lead to disruptions in operations, poor customer service, and unnecessarily high inventory carrying costs. The counts are conducted more frequently than once a year, which reduces the costs of inaccuracies compared to only doing an annual count, by allowing for investigation and correction of the causes of inaccuracies.

The key questions concerning cycle counting for management are

1. How much accuracy is needed?
2. When should cycle counting be performed?
3. Who should do it?

APICS recommends the following guidelines for inventory record accuracy: ± 0.2 percent for A items, ± 1 percent for B items, and ± 5 percent for C items. A items are counted frequently, B items are counted less frequently, and C items are counted the least frequently.

Some companies use certain events to trigger cycle counting, whereas others do it on a periodic (scheduled) basis. Events that can trigger a physical count of inventory include an

A Typical A-B-C Breakdown in Relative Annual Dollar Value of Items and Number of Items by Category

figure 5.1

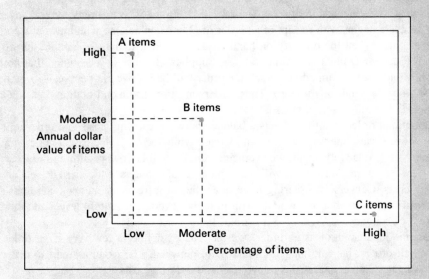

out-of-stock report written on an item indicated by inventory records to be in stock, an inventory report that indicates a low or zero balance of an item, and a specified level of activity (e.g., every 2,000 units sold).

Some companies use regular stockroom personnel to do cycle counting during periods of slow activity while others contract with outside firms to do it on a periodic basis. Use of an outside firm provides an independent check on inventory and may reduce the risk of problems created by dishonest employees. Still other firms maintain full-time personnel to do cycle counting.

HOW MUCH TO ORDER: ECONOMIC ORDER QUANTITY MODELS

The question of how much to order is frequently determined by using an economic order quantity (EOQ) model. EOQ models identify the optimal order quantity by minimizing the sum of certain annual costs that vary with order size. Three order size models are described here:

Economic order quantity (EOQ)

ScreenCam
Tutorial

1. The basic economic order quantity model.
2. The economic production quantity model.
3. The quantity discount model.

BASIC ECONOMIC ORDER QUANTITY (EOQ) MODEL

The basic EOQ model is the simplest of the three models. It is used to identify a *fixed* order size that will minimize the sum of the annual costs of holding inventory and ordering inventory. The unit purchase price of items in inventory is not generally included in the total cost because the unit cost is unaffected by the order size unless quantity discounts are a factor. If holding costs are specified as a percentage of unit cost, then unit cost is indirectly included in the total cost as a part of holding costs.

The basic model involves a number of assumptions. They are listed in Table 5.1.

Inventory ordering and usage occur in cycles. Figure 5.2 illustrates several inventory cycles. A cycle begins with receipt of an order of Q units, which are withdrawn at a constant rate over time. When the quantity on hand is just sufficient to satisfy demand during lead time, an order for Q units is submitted to the supplier. Because it is assumed that both the usage rate and the lead time do not vary, the order will be received at the precise instant that the inventory on hand falls to zero. Thus, orders are timed to avoid both excess stock and stockouts (i.e., running out of stock).

The optimal order quantity reflects a balance between carrying costs and ordering costs: As order size varies, one type of cost will increase while the other decreases. For example, if the order size is relatively small, the average inventory will be low, resulting in low carrying costs. However, a small order size will necessitate frequent orders, which will drive up annual ordering costs. Conversely, ordering large quantities at infrequent intervals can hold down annual ordering costs, but that would result in higher average inventory levels and therefore increased carrying costs. Figure 5.3 illustrates these two extremes.

Thus, the ideal solution is an order size that causes neither a few very large orders nor many small orders, but one that lies somewhere between. The exact amount to order will depend on the relative magnitudes of carrying and ordering costs.

Annual carrying cost is computed by multiplying the average amount of inventory on hand by the cost to carry one unit for one year, even though any given unit would not necessarily be held for a year. The average inventory is simply half of the order quantity: The amount on hand decreases steadily from Q units to 0, for an average of $(Q + 0)/2$, or $Q/2$. Using the symbol H to represent the average annual carrying cost per unit, the *total annual carrying cost* is

$$\text{Annual carrying cost} = \frac{Q}{2}H$$

where

Q = Order quantity in units

H = Holding (carrying) cost per unit

Carrying cost is thus a linear function of Q: Carrying costs increase or decrease in direct proportion to changes in the order quantity Q, as Figure 5.4A illustrates.

On the other hand, annual ordering cost will decrease as order size increases because, for a given annual demand, the larger the order size, the fewer the number of orders needed. For instance, if annual demand is 12,000 units and the order size is 1,000 units per order, there must be 12 orders over the year. But if Q = 2,000 units, only six orders will be needed; if Q = 3,000 units, only four orders will be needed. In general, the number of orders per

table 5.1   Assumptions of the Basic EOQ Model

1. Only one product is involved.
2. Annual demand requirements are known.
3. Demand is spread evenly throughout the year so that the demand rate is reasonably constant.
4. Lead time does not vary.
5. Each order is received in a single delivery.
6. There are no quantity discounts.

The Inventory Cycle: Profile of Inventory Level Over Time

figure 5.2

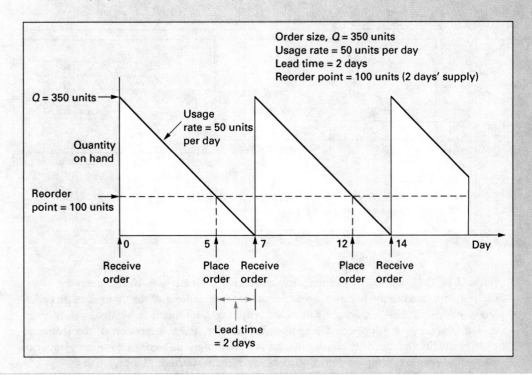

Average Inventory Level and Number of Orders Per Year are Inversely Related: As One Increases, the Other Decreases

figure 5.3

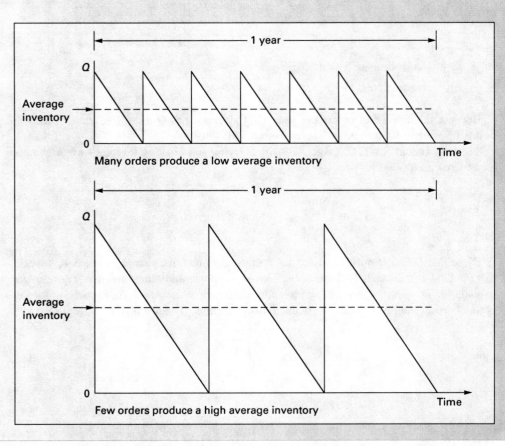

figure 5.4   Carrying Cost, Ordering Cost, and Total Cost Curve

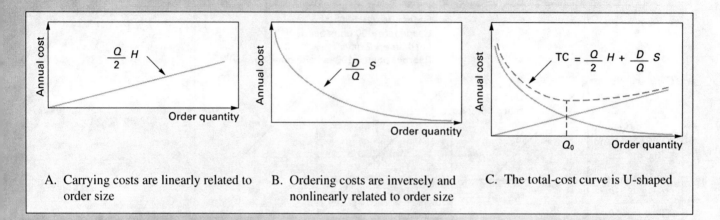

A. Carrying costs are linearly related to order size

B. Ordering costs are inversely and nonlinearly related to order size

C. The total-cost curve is U-shaped

year will be D/Q, where D = Annual demand and Q = Order size. Unlike carrying costs, ordering costs are relatively insensitive to order size; regardless of the amount of an order, certain activities must be done, such as determining how much is needed, periodically evaluating sources of supply, and preparing the invoice. Even inspection of the shipment to verify quality and quantity characteristics is not strongly influenced by order size since large shipments are sampled rather than completely inspected. Hence, ordering cost is treated as a constant. *Annual ordering cost* is a function of the number of orders per year and the ordering cost per order:

$$\text{Annual ordering cost} = \frac{D}{Q}S$$

where

D = Demand, usually in units per year

S = Ordering cost

Because the number of orders per year, D/Q, decreases as Q increases, annual ordering cost is inversely related to order size, as Figure 5.4B illustrates.

The total annual cost (TC) associated with carrying and ordering inventory when Q units are ordered each time is

$$\text{TC} = \begin{array}{c} \text{Annual} \\ \text{carrying} \\ \text{cost} \end{array} + \begin{array}{c} \text{Annual} \\ \text{ordering} \\ \text{cost} \end{array} = \frac{Q}{2}H + \frac{D}{Q}S \qquad [5.1]$$

(Note that D and H must be in the same units, e.g., months, years.) Figure 5.4C reveals that the total-cost curve is U-shaped (i.e., convex, with one minimum) and that *it reaches its minimum at the quantity where carrying and ordering costs are equal.* An expression for the optimal order quantity, Q_0, can be obtained using calculus.[1] The result is the formula

$$Q_0 = \sqrt{\frac{2DS}{H}} \qquad [5.2]$$

Thus, given annual demand, the ordering cost per order, and the annual carrying cost per unit, one can compute the optimal (economic) order quantity. The minimum total cost is then found by substituting Q_0 for Q in Formula 5.1.

The length of an order cycle (i.e., the time between orders) is

$$\text{Length of order cycle} = \frac{Q}{D} \qquad [5.3]$$

EXAMPLE 5.2

A local distributor for a national tire company expects to sell approximately 9,600 steel-belted radial tires of a certain size and tread design next year. Annual carrying cost is $16 per tire, and ordering cost is $75. The distributor operates 288 days a year.

mhhe.com/stevenson10e

a. What is the EOQ?
b. How many times per year does the store reorder?
c. What is the length of an order cycle?
d. What is the total annual cost if the EOQ quantity is ordered?

SOLUTION

$D = 9,600$ tires per year
$H = \$16$ per unit per year
$S = \$75$

a. $Q_0 = \sqrt{\dfrac{2DS}{H}} = \sqrt{\dfrac{2(9,600)75}{16}} = 300$ tires

b. Number of orders per year: $D/Q = \dfrac{9,600 \text{ tires}}{300 \text{ tires}} = 32.$

c. Length of order cycle: $Q/D = \dfrac{300 \text{ tires}}{9,600 \text{ tires/yr}} = \frac{1}{32}$ of a year, which is $\frac{1}{32} \times 288,$ or nine workdays.

d. $TC = $ Carrying cost $+$ Ordering cost
$= (Q/2)H + (D/Q)S$
$= (300/2)16 + (9,600/300)75$
$= \$2,400 + \$2,400$
$= \$4,800$

Note that the ordering and carrying costs are equal at the EOQ, as illustrated in Figure 5.4C.

Carrying cost is sometimes stated as a percentage of the purchase price of an item rather than as a dollar amount per unit. However, as long as the percentage is converted into a dollar amount, the EOQ formula is still appropriate.

mhhe.com/stevenson10e

EXAMPLE 5.3

Piddling Manufacturing assembles security monitors. It purchases 3,600 black-and-white cathode ray tubes a year at $65 each. Ordering costs are $31, and annual carrying costs are 20 percent of the purchase price. Compute the optimal quantity and the total annual cost of ordering and carrying the inventory.

SOLUTION

$$D = 3{,}600 \text{ cathode ray tubes per year}$$
$$S = \$31$$
$$H = .20(\$65) = \$13$$
$$Q_0 = \sqrt{\frac{2DS}{H}} = \sqrt{\frac{2(3{,}600)(31)}{13}} \approx 131 \text{ cathode ray tubes}$$

$$
\begin{aligned}
TC &= \text{Carrying costs} + \text{Ordering costs} \\
&= (Q_{0/2})H \;+\; (D/Q_0)S \\
&= (131/2)13 \;+\; (3{,}600/131)31 \\
&= \quad \$852 \quad + \quad \$852 \quad = \$1{,}704
\end{aligned}
$$

Comment Holding and ordering costs, and annual demand, are typically estimated values rather than values that can be precisely determined, say, from accounting records. Holding costs are sometimes *designated* by management rather than computed. Consequently, the EOQ should be regarded as an *approximate* quantity rather than an exact quantity. Thus, rounding the calculated value is perfectly acceptable; stating a value to several decimal places would tend to give an unrealistic impression of the precision involved. An obvious question is: How good is this "approximate" EOQ in terms of minimizing cost? The answer is that the EOQ is fairly robust; the total cost curve is relatively flat near the EOQ, especially to the right of the EOQ. In other words, even if the resulting EOQ differs from the actual EOQ, total costs will not increase much at all. This is particularly true for quantities larger than the real EOQ, because the total cost curve rises very slowly to the right of the EOQ. (See Figure 5.5.)

figure 5.5   The Total Cost Curve is Relatively Flat Near the EOQ

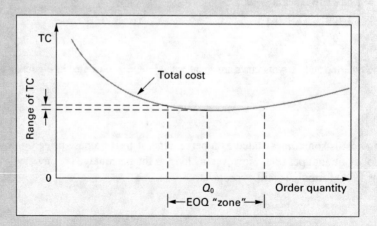

Because the total cost curve is relatively flat around the EOQ, there can be some flexibility to modify the order quantity a bit from the EOQ (say, to achieve a round lot or full truckload) without incurring much of an increase in total cost.

ECONOMIC PRODUCTION QUANTITY (EPQ)

The batch mode of production is widely used in production. Even in assembly operations, portions of the work are done in batches. The reason for this is that in certain instances, the capacity to produce a part exceeds the part's usage or demand rate. As long as production continues, inventory will continue to grow. In such instances, it makes sense to periodically produce such items in batches, or *lots,* instead of producing continually.

The assumptions of the EPQ model are similar to those of the EOQ model, except that instead of orders received in a single delivery, units are received incrementally during production. The assumptions are

1. Only one item is involved.
2. Annual demand is known.
3. The usage rate is constant.
4. Usage occurs continually, but production occurs periodically.
5. The production rate is constant.
6. Lead time does not vary.
7. There are no quantity discounts.

Figure 5.6 illustrates how inventory is affected by periodically producing a batch of a particular item.

During the production phase of the cycle, inventory builds up at a rate equal to the difference between production and usage rates. For example, if the daily production rate is 20 units and the daily usage rate is 5 units, inventory will build up at the rate of $20 - 5 = 15$ units per day. As long as production occurs, the inventory level will continue to build; when production ceases, the inventory level will begin to decrease. Hence, the inventory level will be maximum at the point where production ceases. When the amount of inventory on hand is exhausted, production is resumed, and the cycle repeats itself.

Because the company makes the product itself, there are no ordering costs as such. Nonetheless, with every production run (batch) there are setup costs—the costs required

EOQ With Incremental Inventory Replenishment

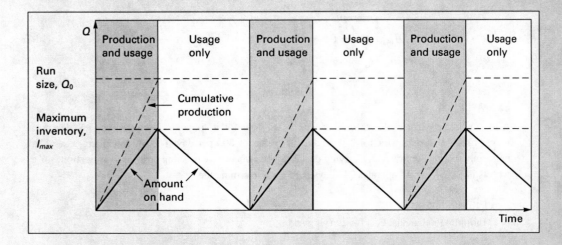

figure 5.6

to prepare the equipment for the job, such as cleaning, adjusting, and changing tools and fixtures. Setup costs are analogous to ordering costs because they are independent of the lot (run) size. They are treated in the formula in exactly the same way. The larger the run size, the fewer the number of runs needed and, hence, the lower the annual setup cost. The number of runs or batches per year is D/Q, and the annual setup cost is equal to the number of runs per year times the setup cost, S, per run: $(D/Q)S$.

The total cost is

$$TC_{min} = \text{Carrying cost} + \text{Setup cost} = \left(\frac{I_{max}}{2}\right)H + (D/Q)S \qquad [5.4]$$

where

$$I_{max} = \text{Maximum inventory}$$

The economic run quantity is

$$Q_p = \sqrt{\frac{2DS}{H}}\sqrt{\frac{p}{p-u}} \qquad [5.5]$$

where

$$p = \text{Production or delivery rate}$$
$$u = \text{Usage rate}$$

The cycle time (the time between orders or between the beginnings of runs) for the economic run size model is a function of the run size and usage (demand) rate:

$$\text{Cycle time} = \frac{Q_p}{u} \qquad [5.6]$$

Similarly, the run time (the production phase of the cycle) is a function of the run (lot) size and the production rate:

$$\text{Run time} = \frac{Q_p}{p} \qquad [5.7]$$

The maximum and average inventory levels are

$$I_{max} = \frac{Q_p}{p}(p-u) \quad \text{and} \quad I_{average} = \frac{I_{max}}{2} \qquad [5.8]$$

mhhe.com/stevenson10e

EXAMPLE 5.4

A toy manufacturer uses 48,000 rubber wheels per year for its popular dump truck series. The firm makes its own wheels, which it can produce at a rate of 800 per day. The toy trucks are assembled uniformly over the entire year. Carrying cost is $1 per wheel a year. Setup cost for a production run of wheels is $45. The firm operates 240 days per year. Determine the

a. Optimal run size.
b. Minimum total annual cost for carrying and setup.

c. Cycle time for the optimal run size.

d. Run time.

SOLUTION

$$D = 48,000 \text{ wheels per year}$$
$$S = \$45$$
$$H = \$1 \text{ per wheel per year}$$
$$p = 800 \text{ wheels per day}$$
$$u = 48,000 \text{ wheels per 240 days, or 200 wheels per day}$$

a. $$Q_p = \sqrt{\frac{2DS}{H}}\sqrt{\frac{p}{p-u}} = \sqrt{\frac{2(48,000)45}{1}}\sqrt{\frac{800}{800-200}} = 2,400 \text{ wheels}$$

b. $$TC_{min} = \text{Carrying cost} + \text{Setup cost} = \left(\frac{I_{max}}{2}\right)H + (D/Q_p)S$$

Thus, you must first compute I_{max}:

$$I_{max} = \frac{Q_p}{p}(p-u) = \frac{2,400}{800}(800-200) = 1,800 \text{ wheels}$$

$$TC = \frac{1,800}{2} \times \$1 + \frac{48,000}{2,400} \times \$45 = \$900 + \$900 = \$1,800$$

Note again the equality of cost (in this example, setup and carrying costs) at the EOQ.

c. $$\text{Cycle time} = \frac{Q_p}{u} = \frac{2,400 \text{ wheels}}{200 \text{ wheels per day}} = 12 \text{ days}$$

Thus, a run of wheels will be made every 12 days.

d. $$\text{Run time} = \frac{Q_p}{p} = \frac{2,400 \text{ wheels}}{800 \text{ wheels per day}} = 3 \text{ days}$$

Thus, each run will require three days to complete. ●

QUANTITY DISCOUNTS

Quantity discounts are price reductions for large orders offered to customers to induce them to buy in large quantities. For example, a Chicago surgical supply company publishes the price list shown in Table 5.2 for boxes of gauze strips. Note that the price per box decreases as order quantity increases.

Quantity discounts

If quantity discounts are offered, the buyer must weigh the potential benefits of reduced purchase price and fewer orders that will result from buying in large quantities against the increase in carrying costs caused by higher average inventories. The buyer's goal with quantity discounts is to select the order quantity that will minimize total cost, where total cost is the sum of carrying cost, ordering cost, *and* purchasing (i.e., product) cost:

$$TC = \text{Carrying cost} + \text{Ordering cost} + \text{Purchasing cost} \qquad [5.9]$$

$$= \left(\frac{Q}{2}\right)H + \left(\frac{D}{Q}\right)S + PD$$

where

$$P = \text{Unit price}$$

table 5.2   Price List for Extra-Wide Gauze Strips

ORDER QUANTITY	PRICE PER BOX
1 to 44	$2.00
45 to 69	1.70
70 or more	1.40

figure 5.7   Adding *PD* Doesn't Change the EOQ

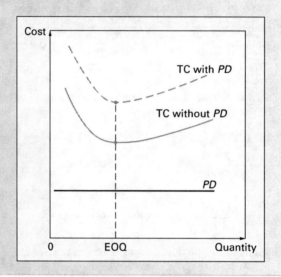

Recall that in the basic EOQ model, determination of order size does not involve the purchasing cost. The rationale for not including unit price is that under the assumption of no quantity discounts, price per unit is the same for all order sizes. Inclusion of unit price in the total-cost computation in that case would merely increase the total cost by the amount P times D. A graph of total annual purchase cost versus quantity would be a horizontal line. Hence, including purchasing costs would merely raise the total-cost curve by the same amount (PD) at every point. That would not change the EOQ. (See Figure 5.7.)

When quantity discounts are offered, there is a separate U-shaped total-cost curve for each unit price. Again, including unit prices merely raises each curve by a constant amount. However, because the unit prices are all different, each curve is raised by a different amount: Smaller unit prices will raise a total-cost curve less than larger unit prices. Note that no one curve applies to the entire range of quantities; each curve applies to only a *portion* of the range. (See Figure 5.8.) Hence, the applicable or *feasible* total cost is initially on the curve with the highest unit price and then drops down, curve by curve, at the *price breaks,* which are the minimum quantities needed to obtain the discounts. Thus, in Table 5.2, the price breaks for gauze strips are at 45 and 70 boxes. The result is a total-cost curve with *steps* at the price breaks.

Even though each curve has a minimum, those points are not necessarily feasible. For example, the minimum point for the $1.40 curve in Figure 5.8 appears to be about 65 units. However, the price list shown in Table 5.2 indicates that an order size of 65 boxes will involve a unit price of $1.70. The actual total-cost curve is denoted by the solid lines; only those price–quantity combinations are feasible. The objective of the quantity discount model is to identify the order quantity that will represent the lowest total cost for the entire set of curves.

There are two general cases of the model. In one, carrying costs are constant (e.g., $2 per unit); in the other, carrying costs are stated as a percentage of purchase price (e.g., 20 percent of unit price). When carrying costs are constant, there will be a single minimum point. All curves will have their minimum point at the same quantity. Consequently, the total-cost curves line up vertically, differing only in that the lower unit prices are reflected

The Total-Cost Curve with Quantity Discounts is Composed of a Portion of The Total-Cost Curve for Each Price

figure 5.8

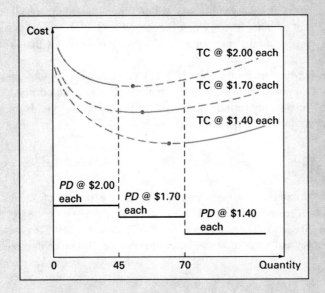

Comparison of TC Curves for Constant Carrying Costs and Carrying Costs that are a Percentage of Unit Costs

figure 5.9

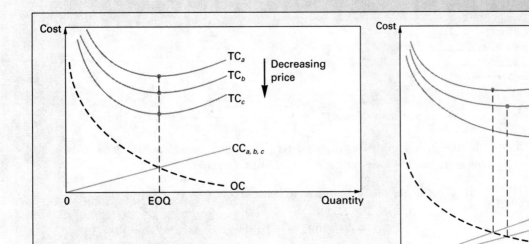

A. When carrying costs are constant, all curves have their minimum points at the same quantity.

B. When carrying costs are stated as a percentage of unit price, the minimum points do not line up.

by lower total-cost curves as shown in Figure 5.9A. (For purposes of illustration, the horizontal purchasing cost lines have been omitted.)

When carrying costs are specified as a percentage of unit price, each curve will have a different minimum point. Because carrying costs are a percentage of price, lower prices will mean lower carrying costs and larger minimum points. Thus, as price decreases, each curve's minimum point will be to the right of the next higher curve's minimum point. (See Figure 5.9B.)

The procedure for determining the overall EOQ differs slightly, depending on which of these two cases is relevant. For carrying costs that are constant, the procedure is as follows:

1. Compute the common minimum point.
2. Only one of the unit prices will have the minimum point in its feasible range since the ranges do not overlap. Identify that range.
   a. If the feasible minimum point is on the lowest price range, that is the optimal order quantity.
   b. If the feasible minimum point is in any other range, compute the total cost for the minimum point and for the price breaks of all *lower* unit costs. Compare the total costs; the quantity (minimum point or price break) that yields the lowest total cost is the optimal order quantity.

mhhe.com/stevenson10e

EXAMPLE 5.5

The maintenance department of a large hospital uses about 816 cases of liquid cleanser annually. Ordering costs are $12, carrying costs are $4 per case a year, and the new price schedule indicates that orders of less than 50 cases will cost $20 per case, 50 to 79 cases will cost $18 per case, 80 to 99 cases will cost $17 per case, and larger orders will cost $16 per case. Determine the optimal order quantity and the total cost.

SOLUTION

See Figure 5.10:

$$D = 816 \text{ cases per year} \qquad S = \$12 \qquad H = \$4 \text{ per case per year}$$

RANGE	PRICE
1 to 49	$20
50 to 79	18
80 to 99	17
100 or more	16

1. Compute the common minimum Q: $= \sqrt{\dfrac{2DS}{H}} = \sqrt{\dfrac{2(816)12}{4}} = 69.97 \approx 70 \text{ cases}$

2. The 70 cases can be bought at $18 per case because 70 falls in the range of 50 to 79 cases. The total cost to purchase 816 cases a year, at the rate of 70 cases per order, will be

$$
\begin{aligned}
TC_{70} &= \text{Carrying cost} + \text{Order cost} + \text{Purchase cost} \\
&= (Q/2)H + (D/Q)S + PD \\
&= (70/2)4 + (816/70)12 + 18(816) = \$14,968
\end{aligned}
$$

Because lower cost ranges exist, each must be checked against the minimum cost generated by 70 cases at $18 each. In order to buy at $17 per case, at least 80 cases must be purchased. (Because the TC curve is rising, 80 cases will have the lowest TC for that curve's feasible region.) The total cost at 80 cases will be

$$TC_{80} = (80/2)4 + (816/80)12 + 17(816) = \$14,154$$

To obtain a cost of $16 per case, at least 100 cases per order are required, and the total cost at that price break will be

$$TC_{100} = (100/2)4 + (816/100)12 + 16(816) = \$13,354$$

Therefore, because 100 cases per order yields the lowest total cost, 100 cases is the overall optimal order quantity.

Total-Cost Curves for Example 5

figure 5.10

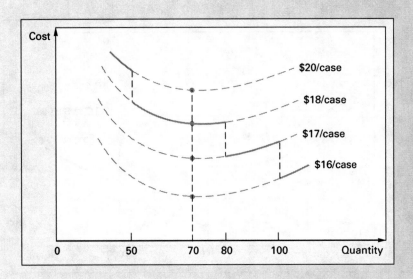

When carrying costs are expressed as a percentage of price, determine the best purchase quantity with the following procedure:

1. Beginning with the lowest unit price, compute the minimum points for each price range until you find a feasible minimum point (i.e., until a minimum point falls in the quantity range for its price).
2. If the minimum point for the lowest unit price is feasible, it is the optimal order quantity. If the minimum point is not feasible in the lowest price range, compare the total cost at the price break for all *lower* prices with the total cost of the feasible minimum point. The quantity that yields the lowest total cost is the optimum.

EXAMPLE 5.6

Surge Electric uses 4,000 toggle switches a year. Switches are priced as follows: 1 to 499, 90 cents each; 500 to 999, 85 cents each; and 1,000 or more, 80 cents each. It costs approximately $30 to prepare an order and receive it, and carrying costs are 40 percent of purchase price per unit on an annual basis. Determine the optimal order quantity and the total annual cost.

SOLUTION

See Figure 5.11:

$$D = 4,000 \text{ switches per year} \qquad S = \$30 \qquad H = .40P$$

RANGE	UNIT PRICE	H
1 to 499	$0.90	.40(0.90) = .36
500 to 999	$0.85	.40(0.85) = .34
1,000 or more	$0.80	.40(0.80) = .32

Find the minimum point for each price, starting with the lowest price, until you locate a feasible minimum point.

$$\text{Minimum point}_{0.80} = \sqrt{\frac{2DS}{H}} = \sqrt{\frac{2(4,000)30}{.32}} = 866 \text{ switches}$$

figure 5.11   Total-Cost Curves for Example 6

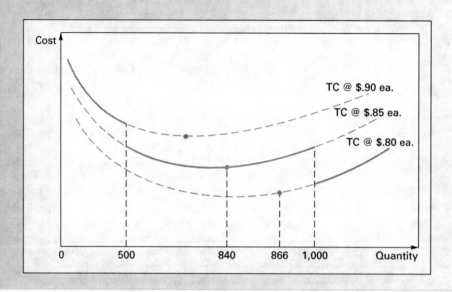

Because an order size of 866 switches will cost $0.85 each rather than $0.80 each, 866 is not a feasible minimum point for $0.80 per switch. Next, try $0.85 per unit.

$$\text{Minimum point}_{0.85} = \sqrt{\frac{2(4,000)30}{.34}} = 840 \text{ switches}$$

This is feasible; it falls in the $0.85 per switch range of 500 to 999.

Now compute the total cost for 840, and compare it to the total cost of the minimum quantity necessary to obtain a price of $0.80 per switch.

$$TC = \text{Carrying costs} + \text{Ordering costs} + \text{Purchasing costs}$$

$$= \left(\frac{Q}{2}\right)H \quad + \quad \left(\frac{D}{Q}\right)S \quad + \quad PD$$

$$TC_{840} = \frac{840}{2}(.34) \quad + \quad \frac{4,000}{840}(30) \quad + \quad 0.85(4,000) \quad = \$3,686$$

$$TC_{1,000} = \frac{1,000}{2}(.32) \quad + \quad \frac{4,000}{1,000}(30) \quad + \quad 0.80(4,000) \quad = \$3,480$$

Thus, the minimum-cost order size is 1,000 switches. ●

WHEN TO REORDER WITH EOQ ORDERING

Reorder point (ROP)

EOQ models answer the question of how much to order, but not the question of when to order. The latter is the function of models that identify the reorder point (ROP) in terms of a *quantity:* The reorder point occurs when the quantity on hand drops to a predetermined amount. That amount generally includes expected demand during lead time and perhaps an extra cushion of stock, which serves to reduce the probability of experiencing a stockout during lead time. Note that in order to know when the reorder point has been reached, a *perpetual* inventory is required.

The goal in ordering is to place an order when the amount of inventory on hand is sufficient to satisfy demand during the time it takes to receive that order (i.e., lead time). There are four determinants of the reorder point quantity:

1. The rate of demand (usually based on a forecast).
2. The lead time.
3. The extent of demand and/or lead time variability.
4. The degree of stockout risk acceptable to management.

If demand and lead time are both constant, the reorder point is simply

$$ROP = d \times LT \qquad [5.10]$$

where

$$d = \text{Demand rate (units per day or week)}$$
$$LT = \text{Lead time in days or weeks}$$

Note: Demand and lead time must be expressed in the same time units.

ScreenCam
Tutorial

EXAMPLE 5.7

Tingly takes Two-a-Day vitamins, which are delivered to his home by a routeman seven days after an order is called in. At what point should Tingly reorder?

mhhe.com/stevenson10e

SOLUTION

$$\text{Usage} = 2 \text{ vitamins a day}$$
$$\text{Lead time} = 7 \text{ days}$$
$$\text{ROP} = \text{Usage} \times \text{Lead time}$$
$$= 2 \text{ vitamins per day} \times 7 \text{ days} = 14 \text{ vitamins}$$

Thus, Tingly should reorder when 14 vitamin tablets are left.

When variability is present in demand or lead time, it creates the possibility that actual demand will exceed expected demand. Consequently, it becomes necessary to carry additional inventory, called safety stock, to reduce the risk of running out of inventory (a stockout) during lead time. The reorder point then increases by the amount of the safety stock:

Safety stock

$$ROP = \frac{\text{Expected demand}}{\text{during lead time}} + \text{Safety stock} \qquad [5.11]$$

For example, if expected demand during lead time is 100 units, and the desired amount of safety stock is 10 units, the ROP would be 110 units.

Figure 5.12 illustrates how safety stock can reduce the risk of a stockout during lead time (LT). Note that stockout protection is needed only during lead time. If there is a sudden surge at any point during the cycle, that will trigger another order. Once that order is received, the danger of an imminent stockout is negligible.

Because it costs money to hold safety stock, a manager must carefully weigh the cost of carrying safety stock against the reduction in stockout risk it provides. The customer *service level* increases as the risk of stockout decreases. Order cycle service level can be defined as the probability that demand will not exceed supply during lead time (i.e., that the amount of stock on hand will be sufficient to meet demand). Hence, a service level of 95 percent implies a probability of 95 percent that demand will not exceed supply during lead time. An equivalent statement that demand will be satisfied in 95 percent of such instances does *not* mean that 95 percent of demand will be satisfied. The risk of a stockout is the complement of service level; a customer service level of 95 percent implies a stockout risk of 5 percent. That is,

Service level

$$\text{Service level} = 100 \text{ percent} - \text{Stockout risk}$$

figure 5.12   Safety Stock Reduces Risk of Stockout During Lead Time

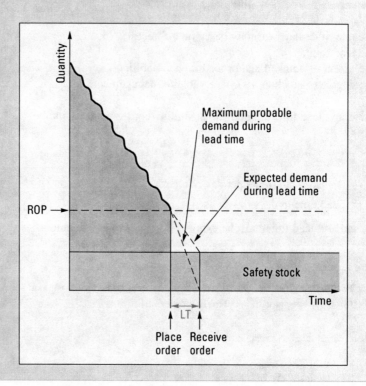

Later you will see how the order cycle service level relates to the *annual* service level.

Consider for a moment the importance of stockouts. When a stockout occurs, demand cannot be satisfied at that time. In manufacturing operations, stockouts mean that jobs will be delayed and additional costs will be incurred. If the stockout involves parts for an assembly line, or spare parts for a machine or conveyor belt on the line, the line will have to shut down, typically at a very high cost per hour, until parts can be obtained. For service operations, stockouts mean that services cannot be completed on time. Aside from the added cost that results from the time delay, there is not only the matter of customer dissatisfaction but also the fact that schedules will be disrupted, sometimes creating a "domino effect" on following jobs. In the retail sector, stockouts create a competitive *disadvantage* that can result in customer dissatisfaction and, ultimately, the loss of customers.

The amount of safety stock that is appropriate for a given situation depends on the following factors:

1. The average demand rate and average lead time.
2. Demand and lead time variability.
3. The desired service level.

For a given order cycle service level, the greater the variability in either demand rate or lead time, the greater the amount of safety stock that will be needed to achieve that service level. Similarly, for a given amount of variation in demand rate or lead time, achieving an increase in the service level will require increasing the amount of safety stock. Selection of a service level may reflect stockout costs (e.g., lost sales, customer dissatisfaction) or it might simply be a policy variable (e.g., the manager wants to achieve a specified service level for a certain item).

Let us look at several models that can be used in cases when variability is present. The first model can be used if an estimate of expected demand during lead time and its standard deviation are available. The formula is

$$\text{ROP} = \frac{\text{Expected demand}}{\text{during lead time}} + z\sigma_{d\text{LT}} \qquad [5.12]$$

The ROP Based on a Normal Distribution of Lead Time Demand

figure 5.13

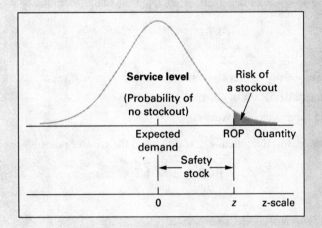

where

z = Number of standard deviations

$\sigma_{d\text{LT}}$ = The standard deviation of lead time demand

The models generally assume that any variability in demand rate or lead time can be adequately described by a normal distribution. However, this is not a strict requirement; the models provide approximate reorder points even where actual distributions depart from normal.

The value of z (see Figure 5.13) used in a particular instance depends on the stockout risk that the manager is willing to accept. Generally, the smaller the risk the manager is willing to accept, the greater the value of z. Use Appendix B, Table B, to obtain the value of z, given a desired service level for lead time.

EXAMPLE 5.8

mhhe.com/stevenson10e

Suppose that the manager of a construction supply house determined from historical records that demand for sand during lead time averages 50 tons. In addition, suppose the manager determined that demand during lead time could be described by a normal distribution that has a mean of 50 tons and a standard deviation of 5 tons. Answer these questions, assuming that the manager is willing to accept a stockout risk of no more than 3 percent:

a. What value of z is appropriate?
b. How much safety stock should be held?
c. What reorder point should be used?

SOLUTION

Expected lead time demand = 50 tons

$\sigma_{d\text{LT}}$ = 5 tons
Risk = 3 percent

a. From Appendix B, Table B, using a service level of $1 - .03 = .9700$, you obtain a value of $z = +1.88$.
b. Safety stock = $z\sigma_{d\text{LT}}$ = 1.88(5) = 9.40 tons
c. ROP = Expected lead time demand + Safety stock = 50 + 9.40 = 59.40 tons

When data on lead time demand are not readily available, Formula 5.12 cannot be used. Nevertheless, data are generally available on daily or weekly demand, and on the length of lead time. Using those data, a manager can determine whether demand and/or lead time is variable, if variability exists in one or both, and the related standard deviation(s). For those situations, one of the following formulas can be used:

If only demand is variable, then $\sigma_{dLT} = \sigma_d\sqrt{LT}$, and the reorder point is

$$ROP = \bar{d} \times LT + z\sigma_d\sqrt{LT} \qquad [5.13]$$

where

$\bar{d}$ = *Average* daily or weekly demand

σ_d = Standard deviation of demand per day or week

LT = Lead time in days or weeks

If only lead time is variable, then $\sigma_{dLT} = d\sigma_{LT}$, and the reorder point is

$$ROP = d \times \overline{LT} + zd\sigma_{LT} \qquad [5.14]$$

where

d = Daily or weekly demand

$\overline{LT}$ = *Average* lead time in days or weeks

σ_{LT} = Standard deviation of lead time in days or weeks

If both demand and lead time are variable, then

$$\sigma_{dLT} = \sqrt{\overline{LT}\sigma_d^2 + \bar{d}^2\sigma_{LT}^2}$$

and the reorder point is

$$ROP = \bar{d} \times \overline{LT} + z\sqrt{\overline{LT}\sigma_d^2 + \bar{d}^2\sigma_{LT}^2} \qquad [5.15]$$

Note: Each of these models assumes that demand and lead time are *independent*.

mhhe.com/stevenson10e

EXAMPLE 5.9

A restaurant uses an average of 50 jars of a special sauce each week. Weekly usage of sauce has a standard deviation of 3 jars. The manager is willing to accept no more than a 10 percent risk of stockout during lead time, which is two weeks. Assume the distribution of usage is normal.

   a. Which of the above formulas is appropriate for this situation? Why?
   b. Determine the value of z.
   c. Determine the ROP.

SOLUTION

$\bar{d}$ = 50 jars per week   LT = 2 weeks
σ_d = 3 jars per week   Acceptable risk = 10 percent, so service level is .90

   a. Because only demand is variable (i.e., has a standard deviation), Formula 5.13 is appropriate.
   b. From Appendix B, Table B, using a service level of .9000, you obtain $z = +1.28$.
   c. $ROP = \bar{d} \times LT + z\sigma_d\sqrt{LT} = 50 \times 2 + 1.28(3)\sqrt{2} = 100 + 5.43 = 105.43$.

     Because the inventory is discrete units (jars), we round this amount to 106. (Generally, round up.)

Note that a 2-bin ordering system (see p. 207) involves ROP reordering: The quantity in the second bin is equal to the ROP.

The logic of the three formulas for the reorder point may not be immediately obvious. The first part of each formula is the expected demand, which is the product of daily (or weekly) demand and the number of days (or weeks) of lead time. The second part of the formula is z times the standard deviation of lead time demand. For the formula in which only demand is variable, daily (or weekly) demand is assumed to be normally distributed and has the same mean and standard deviation (see Figure 5.14). The standard deviation of demand for the entire lead time is found by summing the *variances* of daily (or weekly) demands, and then finding the square root of that number because, unlike variances, standard deviations are not additive. Hence, if the daily standard deviation is σ_d, the *variance* is σ_d^2, and if lead time is four days, the variance of lead time demand will equal the sum of the four variances, which is $4\sigma_d^2$. The standard deviation of lead time demand will be the square root of this, which is equal to $2\sigma_d$. In general, this becomes $\sqrt{LT}\sigma_d$ and, hence, the last part of Formula 5.13.

When only lead time is variable, the explanation is much simpler. The standard deviation of lead time demand is equal to the constant daily demand multiplied by the standard deviation of lead time.

When both demand and lead time are variable, the formula appears truly impressive. However, it is merely the result of squaring the standard deviations of the two previous formulas to obtain their variances, summing them, and then taking the square root.

SHORTAGES AND SERVICE LEVELS

The ROP computation does not reveal the expected *amount* of shortage for a given lead time service level. The expected number of units short can, however, be very useful to a manager. This quantity can easily be determined from the same information used to compute the ROP, with one additional piece of information (see Table 5.3). Use of the table assumes that the distribution of lead time demand can be adequately represented by a normal distribution. If it can, the expected number of units short in each order cycle is given by this formula:

$$E(n) = E(z)\sigma_{dLT} \qquad [5.16]$$

where

$E(n)$ = Expected number of units short per order cycle

$E(z)$ = Standardized number of units short obtained from Table 5.3

σ_{dLT} = Standard deviation of lead time demand

Lead Time Demand   figure 5.14

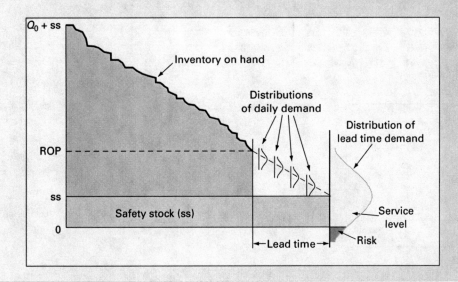

table 5.3   Normal Distribution Service Levels and Unit Normal Loss Function

LEAD TIME SERVICE LEVEL	z	$E(z)$	LEAD TIME SERVICE LEVEL	z	$E(z)$	LEAD TIME SERVICE LEVEL	z	$E(z)$	LEAD TIME SERVICE LEVEL	z	$E(z)$
.0082	−2.40	2.403	.2119	−.80	.920	.7881	0.80	.120	.9918	2.40	.0030
.0091	−2.36	2.363	.2236	−.76	.889	.7995	0.84	.112	.9927	2.44	.0020
.0102	−2.32	2.323	.2358	−.72	.858	.8106	0.88	.104	.9934	2.48	.0020
.0113	−2.28	2.284	.2483	−.68	.828	.8212	0.92	.097	.9941	2.52	.0020
.0125	−2.24	2.244	.2611	−.64	.798	.8315	0.96	.089	.9948	2.56	.0020
.0139	−2.20	2.205	.2743	−.60	.769	.8413	1.00	.083	.9953	2.60	.0010
.0154	−2.16	2.165	.2877	−.56	.740	.8508	1.04	.077	.9959	2.64	.0010
.0170	−2.12	2.126	.3015	−.52	.712	.8599	1.08	.071	.9963	2.68	.0010
.0188	−2.08	2.087	.3156	−.48	.684	.8686	1.12	.066	.9967	2.72	.0010
.0207	−2.04	2.048	.3300	−.44	.657	.8770	1.16	.061	.9971	2.76	.0010
.0228	−2.00	2.008	.3446	−.40	.630	.8849	1.20	.056	.9974	2.80	.0008
.0250	−1.96	1.969	.3594	−.36	.597	.8925	1.24	.052	.9977	2.84	.0007
.0274	−1.92	1.930	.3745	−.32	.576	.8997	1.28	.048	.9980	2.88	.0006
.0301	−1.88	1.892	.3897	−.28	.555	.9066	1.32	.044	.9982	2.92	.0005
.0329	−1.84	1.853	.4052	−.24	.530	.9131	1.36	.040	.9985	2.96	.0004
.0359	−1.80	1.814	.4207	−.20	.507	.9192	1.40	.037	.9987	3.00	.0004
.0392	−1.76	1.776	.4364	−.16	.484	.9251	1.44	.034	.9988	3.04	.0003
.0427	−1.72	1.737	.4522	−.12	.462	.9306	1.48	.031	.9990	3.08	.0003
.0465	−1.68	1.699	.4681	−.08	.440	.9357	1.52	.028	.9991	3.12	.0002
.0505	−1.64	1.661	.4840	−.04	.419	.9406	1.56	.026	.9992	3.16	.0002
.0548	−1.60	1.623	.5000	.00	.399	.9452	1.60	.023	.9993	3.20	.0002
.0594	−1.56	1.586	.5160	.04	.379	.9495	1.64	.021	.9994	3.24	.0001
.0643	−1.52	1.548	.5319	.08	.360	.9535	1.68	.019	.9995	3.28	.0001
.0694	−1.48	1.511	.5478	.12	.342	.9573	1.72	.017	.9995	3.32	.0001
.0749	−1.44	1.474	.5636	.16	.324	.9608	1.76	.016	.9996	3.36	.0001
.0808	−1.40	1.437	.5793	.20	.307	.9641	1.80	.014	.9997	3.40	.0001
.0869	−1.36	1.400	.5948	.24	.290	.9671	1.84	.013			
.0934	−1.32	1.364	.6103	.28	.275	.9699	1.88	.012			
.1003	−1.28	1.328	.6255	.32	.256	.9726	1.92	.010			
.1075	−1.24	1.292	.6406	.36	.237	.9750	1.96	.009			
.1151	−1.20	1.256	.6554	.40	.230	.9772	2.00	.008			
.1230	−1.16	1.221	.6700	.44	.217	.9793	2.04	.008			
.1314	−1.12	1.186	.6844	.48	.204	.9812	2.08	.007			
.1401	−1.08	1.151	.6985	.52	.192	.9830	2.12	.006			
.1492	−1.04	1.117	.7123	.56	.180	.9846	2.16	.005			
.1587	−1.00	1.083	.7257	.60	.169	.9861	2.20	.005			
.1685	−.96	1.049	.7389	.64	.158	.9875	2.24	.004			
.1788	−.92	1.017	.7517	.68	.148	.9887	2.28	.004			
.1894	−.88	0.984	.7642	.72	.138	.9898	2.32	.003			
.2005	−.84	0.952	.7764	.76	.129	.9909	2.36	.003			

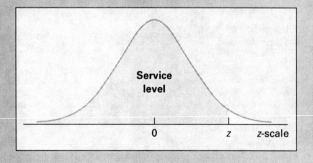

EXAMPLE 5.10

Suppose the standard deviation of lead time demand is known to be 20 units. Lead time demand is approximately normal.

a. For a lead time service level of 90 percent, determine the expected number of units short for any order cycle.
b. What lead time service level would an expected shortage of 2 units imply?

SOLUTION

$\sigma_{d\text{LT}} = 20$ units

a. Lead time (cycle) service level = .90. From Table 5.3, $E(z) = 0.048$. Using Formula 5.16, $E(n) = 0.048(20 \text{ units}) = 0.96$, or about 1 unit.
b. For the case where $E(n) = 2$, you must solve for $E(z)$ and then use Table 5.3 to determine the lead time service that implies. Thus, $E(n) = E(z)\sigma_{d\text{LT}}$, so $E(z) = E(n)/\sigma_{d\text{LT}} = 2/20 = 0.100$. From Table 5.3, this implies a service level of approximately 81.7 percent (interpolating). ●

The expected number of units short is just that—an expected or *average* amount; the exact number of units short in any given cycle will be an amount close to that. Moreover, if discrete items are involved, the actual number of units short in any cycle will be an integer.

Having determined the expected number of units short for an order cycle, you can determine the expected number of units short per year. It is simply the expected number of units short per cycle multiplied by the number of cycles (orders) per year. Thus,

$$E(N) = E(n)\frac{D}{Q} \qquad [5.17]$$

where

$E(N)$ = Expected number of units short per year

EXAMPLE 5.11

Given the following information, determine the expected number of units short per year.

$$D = 1{,}000 \quad Q = 250 \quad E(n) = 2.5$$

SOLUTION

Using the formula $E(N) = E(n)\dfrac{D}{Q}$,

$$E(N) = 2.5\left(\frac{1{,}000}{250}\right) = 10.0 \text{ units per year} \quad ●$$

It is sometimes convenient to think of service level in annual terms. One definition of annual service level is the percentage of demand filled directly from inventory. This is also known as the *fill rate*. Thus, if $D = 1{,}000$, and 990 units were filled directly from inventory (shortages totaling 10 units over the year were recorded), the annual service level (fill rate) would be $990/1{,}000 = 99$ percent. The annual service level and the lead time service level can be related using the following formula:

$$\text{SL}_{\text{annual}} = 1 - \frac{E(N)}{D} \qquad [5.18]$$

Using Formulas 5.17 and 5.16,

$$E(N) = E(n)D/Q = E(z)\sigma_{dLT}D/Q$$

Thus,

$$SL_{annual} = 1 - \frac{E(z)\sigma_{dLT}}{Q} \qquad [5.19]$$

EXAMPLE 5.12

Given a lead time service level of .90, $D = 1,000$, $Q = 250$, and $\sigma_{dLT} = 16$, determine (*a*) the annual service level, and (*b*) the amount of cycle safety stock that would provide an annual service level of .98. From Table 5.3, $E(z) = .048$ for a 90 percent lead time service level.

SOLUTION

    a.   Using Formula 5.19:

$$SL_{annual} = 1 - .048(16)/250 = .997$$

    b.   Using Formula 5.19 and an annual service level of .98, solve for $E(z)$:

$$.98 = 1 - E(z)(16)/250$$

Solving, $E(z) = .312$. From Table 5.3, with $E(z) = .312$, you can see that this value of $E(z)$ is a little more than the value of .307. So it appears that an acceptable value of z might be .19. The necessary safety stock to achieve the specified annual service level is equal to $z\sigma_{dLT}$. Hence, the safety stock is .19(16) = 3.04, or approximately 3 units. ⬤

Note that in the preceding example, a lead time service level of 90 percent provided an annual service level of 99.7 percent. Naturally, different values of D, Q, and σ_{dLT} will tend to produce different results for a cycle service level of 90 percent. Nonetheless, the annual service level will usually be greater than the cycle service level. In addition, since the annual service level as defined relates to the percentage of units short per year, it makes sense to base cycle service levels on a specified annual service level. This means setting the annual level, using Formula 5.19 to solve for $E(z)$, and then using that value to obtain the service level for the order cycles.

Fill rate

It should be mentioned that suppliers of service organizations are sometimes more concerned with the *fill rate* than with the number of units short. The fill rate is the percentage of demand filled by stock on hand.

HOW MUCH TO ORDER: FIXED-ORDER-INTERVAL MODEL

Fixed-order-interval (FOI) model

The fixed-order-interval (FOI) model is used when orders must be placed at fixed time intervals (weekly, twice a month, etc.): The timing of orders is set. The question, then, at each order point, is how much to order. Fixed-interval ordering systems are widely used by retail businesses. If demand is variable, the order size will tend to vary from cycle to cycle. This is quite different from an EOQ/ROP approach in which the order size generally remains fixed from cycle to cycle, while the length of the cycle varies (shorter if demand is above average, and longer if demand is below average).

REASONS FOR USING THE FIXED-ORDER-INTERVAL MODEL

In some cases, a supplier's policy might encourage orders at fixed intervals. Even when that is not the case, grouping orders for items from the same supplier can produce savings in shipping costs. Furthermore, some situations do not readily lend themselves to continuous monitoring of inventory levels. Many retail operations (e.g., drugstores, small grocery stores) fall into this category. The alternative for them is to use fixed-interval ordering, which requires only periodic checks of inventory levels.

DETERMINING THE AMOUNT TO ORDER

If both the demand rate and lead time are constant, the fixed-interval model and the fixed-quantity model function identically. The differences in the two models become apparent only when examined under conditions of variability. Like the ROP model, the fixed-interval model can have variations in demand only, in lead time only, or in both demand and lead time. However, for the sake of simplicity and because it is perhaps the most frequently encountered situation, the discussion here will focus only on *variable demand* and *constant lead time.*

Figure 5.15 provides a comparison of the fixed-quantity and fixed-interval systems. In the fixed-quantity arrangement, orders are triggered by a *quantity* (ROP), while in the fixed-interval arrangement orders are triggered by a *time.* Therefore, the fixed-interval system must have stockout protection for lead time plus the next order cycle, but the fixed-quantity system needs protection only during lead time because additional orders can be placed at any time and will be received shortly (lead time) thereafter. Consequently, there is a greater need for safety stock in the fixed-interval model than in the fixed-quantity model. Note, for example, the large dip into safety stock during the second order cycle with the fixed-interval model.

Both models are sensitive to demand experience just prior to reordering, but in somewhat different ways. In the fixed-quantity model, a higher-than-normal demand causes a *shorter time* between orders, whereas in the fixed-interval model, the result is *a larger order size.* Another difference is that the fixed-quantity model requires close monitoring of inventory levels in order to know *when* the amount on hand has reached the reorder point. The fixed-interval model requires only a periodic review (i.e., physical count) of inventory levels just prior to placing an order to determine how much is needed.

Order size in the fixed-interval model is determined by the following computation:

$$\begin{array}{c} \text{Amount} \\ \text{to order} \end{array} = \begin{array}{c} \text{Expected demand} \\ \text{during protection} \\ \text{interval} \end{array} + \begin{array}{c} \text{Safety} \\ \text{stock} \end{array} - \begin{array}{c} \text{Amount on hand} \\ \text{at reorder time} \end{array} \qquad [5.20]$$

$$= \bar{d}(\text{OI} + \text{LT}) + z\sigma_d\sqrt{\text{OI} + \text{LT}} - A$$

where

$\text{OI} = $ Order interval (length of time between orders)

$A = $ Amount on hand at reorder time

As in previous models, we assume that demand during the protection interval is normally distributed.

figure 5.15   Comparison of Fixed-Quantity and Fixed-Interval Ordering

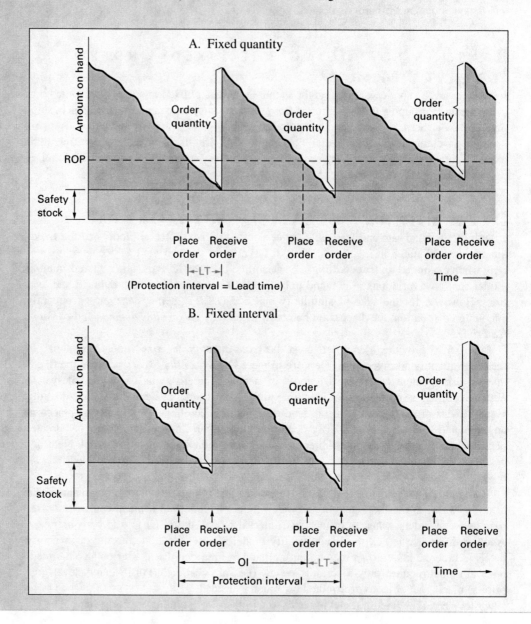

mhhe.com/stevenson10e

EXAMPLE 5.13

Given the following information, determine the amount to order.

$\bar{d}$ = 30 units per day	Desired service level = 99 percent
σ_d = 3 units per day	Amount on hand at reorder time = 71 units
LT = 2 days	OI = 7 days

SOLUTION

$z = 2.33$ for 99 percent service level

$$\text{Amount to order} = \bar{d}(OI + LT) + z\sigma_d\sqrt{OI + LT} - A$$

$$= 30(7 + 2) + 2.33(3)\sqrt{7 + 2} - 71 = 220 \text{ units}$$

An issue related to fixed-interval ordering is the risk of a stockout. From the perspective (i.e., the point in time) of placing an order, there are two points in the order cycle at which a stockout could occur. One is shortly after the order is placed, while waiting to receive the current order (refer to Figure 5.15). The second point is near the end of the cycle, while waiting to receive the next order.

To find the initial risk of a stockout, use the ROP formula (5.13), setting ROP equal to the quantity on hand when the order is placed, and solve for z, then obtain the service level for that value of z from Appendix B, Table B and subtract it from 1.0000 to get the risk of a stockout.

To find the risk of a stockout at the end of the order cycle, use the fixed-interval formula (5.20) and solve for z. Then obtain the service level for that value of z from Appendix B, Table B and subtract it from 1.0000 to get the risk of a stockout.

Let's look at an example.

EXAMPLE 5.14

Given the following information:

$$LT = 4 \text{ days} \qquad A = 43 \text{ units}$$
$$OI = 12 \text{ days} \qquad Q = 171 \text{ units}$$
$$\bar{d} = 10 \text{ units/day}$$
$$\sigma_d = 2 \text{ units/day}$$

Determine the risk of a stockout at

a. The end of the initial lead time.

b. The end of the second lead time.

SOLUTION

a. For the risk of stockout for the first lead time, we use Formula 5.13. Substituting the given values, we get $43 = 10 \times 4 + z(2)(2)$. Solving, $z = +.75$. From Appendix B, Table B, the service level is .7734. The risk is $1 - .7734 = .2266$, which is fairly high.

b. For the risk of a stockout at the end of the second lead time, we use Formula 5.20. Substituting the given values we get $171 = 10 \times (4 + 12) + z(2)(4) - 43$. Solving, $z = +6.75$. This value is way out in the right tail of the normal distribution, making the service level virtually 100 percent, and, thus, the risk of a stockout at this point is essentially equal to zero.

BENEFITS AND DISADVANTAGES

The fixed-interval system results in tight control. In addition, when multiple items come from the same supplier, grouping orders can yield savings in ordering, packing, and shipping costs. Moreover, it may be the only practical approach if inventory withdrawals cannot be closely monitored.

On the negative side, the fixed-interval system necessitates a larger amount of safety stock for a given risk of stockout because of the need to protect against shortages during an entire order interval plus lead time (instead of lead time only), and this increases the carrying cost. Also, there are the costs of the periodic reviews.

THE SINGLE-PERIOD MODEL

The single-period model (sometimes referred to as the *newsboy problem*) is used to handle ordering of perishables (fresh fruits, vegetables, seafood, cut flowers) and items that have a limited useful life (newspapers, magazines, spare parts for specialized equipment). The *period* for spare parts is the life of the equipment, assuming that the parts cannot be used

Single-period model

for other equipment. What sets unsold or unused goods apart is that they are not typically carried over from one period to the next, at least not without penalty. Day-old baked goods, for instance, are often sold at reduced prices; leftover seafood may be discarded; and out-of-date magazines may be offered to used book stores at bargain rates. There may even be some cost associated with disposal of leftover goods.

Analysis of single-period situations generally focuses on two costs: shortage and excess. Shortage cost may include a charge for loss of customer goodwill as well as the opportunity cost of lost sales. Generally, shortage cost is simply unrealized profit per unit. That is,

Shortage cost

$$C_{\text{shortage}} = C_s = \text{Revenue per unit} - \text{Cost per unit}$$

If a shortage or stockout relates to an item used in production or to a spare part for a machine, then shortage cost refers to the actual cost of lost production.

Excess cost

Excess cost pertains to items left over at the end of the period. In effect, excess cost is the difference between purchase cost and salvage value. That is,

$$C_{\text{excess}} = C_e = \text{Original cost per unit} - \text{Salvage value per unit}$$

If there is cost associated with disposing of excess items, the salvage will be negative and will therefore *increase* the excess cost per unit.

The goal of the single-period model is to identify the order quantity, or stocking level, that will minimize the long-run excess and shortage costs.

There are two general categories of problems that we will consider: those for which demand can be approximated using a continuous distribution (perhaps a theoretical one such as a uniform or normal distribution) and those for which demand can be approximated using a discrete distribution (say, historical frequencies or a theoretical distribution such as the Poisson). The kind of inventory can indicate which type of model might be appropriate. For example, demand for petroleum, liquids, and gases tends to vary over some *continuous scale,* thus lending itself to description by a continuous distribution. Demand for tractors, cars, and computers is expressed in terms of the *number of units* demanded and lends itself to description by a discrete distribution.

CONTINUOUS STOCKING LEVELS

The concept of identifying an optimal stocking level is perhaps easiest to visualize when demand is *uniform.* Choosing the stocking level is similar to balancing a seesaw, but instead of a person on each end of the seesaw, we have excess cost per unit (C_e) on one end of the distribution and shortage cost per unit (C_s) on the other. The optimal stocking level is analogous to the fulcrum of the seesaw; the stocking level equalizes the cost weights, as illustrated in Figure 5.16.

figure 5.16   The Optimal Stocking Level Balances Unit Shortage and Excess Costs

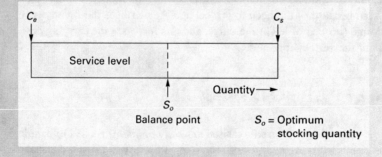

The *service level* is the *probability* that demand will not exceed the stocking level, and computation of the service level is the key to determining the optimal stocking level, S_o.

$$\text{Service level} = \frac{C_s}{C_s + C_e} \qquad [5.21]$$

where

C_s = Shortage cost per unit

C_e = Excess cost per unit

If actual demand exceeds S_o, there is a shortage; hence, C_s is on the right end of the distribution. Similarly, if demand is less than So, there is an excess, so C_e is on the left end of the distribution. When $C_e = C_s$, the optimal stocking level is halfway between the endpoints of the distribution. If one cost is greater than the other, S_o will be closer to the larger cost.

EXAMPLE 5.15

mhhe.com/stevenson10e

Sweet cider is delivered weekly to Cindy's Cider Bar. Demand varies uniformly between 300 liters and 500 liters per week. Cindy pays 20 cents per liter for the cider and charges 80 cents per liter for it. Unsold cider has no salvage value and cannot be carried over into the next week due to spoilage. Find the optimal stocking level and its stockout risk for that quantity.

SOLUTION

C_e = Cost per unit − Salvage value per unit

    = \$0.20   − \$0

    = \$0.20 per unit

C_s = Revenue per unit − Cost per unit

    = \$0.80   − \$0.20

    = \$0.60 per unit

$$\text{SL} = \frac{C_s}{C_s + C_e} = \frac{\$0.60}{\$0.60 + \$0.20} = .75$$

Thus, the optimal stocking level must satisfy demand 75 percent of the time. For the uniform distribution, this will be at a point equal to the minimum demand plus 75 percent of the difference between maximum and minimum demands:

$$S_o = 300 + .75(500 - 300) = 450 \text{ liters}$$

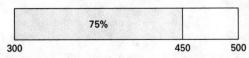

The stockout risk is $1.00 - .75 = .25$.

A similar approach applies when demand is normally distributed.

EXAMPLE 5.16

mhhe.com/stevenson10e

Cindy's Cider Bar also sells a blend of cherry juice and apple cider. Demand for the blend is approximately normal, with a mean of 200 liters per week and a standard deviation of 10 liters per week. C_s = 60 cents per liter, and C_e = 20 cents per liter. Find the optimal stocking level for the apple-cherry blend.

SOLUTION

$$SL = \frac{C_s}{C_s + C_e} = \frac{\$0.60}{\$0.60 + \$0.20} = .75$$

This indicates that 75 percent of the area under the normal curve must be to the left of the stocking level. Appendix B, Table B, shows that a value of z between $+0.67$ and $+0.68$, say, $+0.675$, will satisfy this. The optimal stocking level is $So = $ mean $+ z\sigma$. Thus,

$$S_o = 200 \text{ liters} + 0.675(10 \text{ liters}) = 206.75 \text{ liters}$$

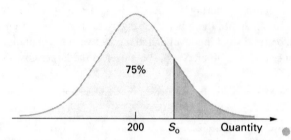

DISCRETE STOCKING LEVELS

When stocking levels are discrete rather than continuous, the service level computed using the ratio $C_s /(C_s + C_e)$ usually does not coincide with a feasible stocking level (e.g., the optimal amount may be *between* five and six units). The solution is to stock at the *next higher level* (e.g., six units). In other words, choose the stocking level so that the desired service level is equaled or *exceeded*. Figure 5.17 illustrates this concept.

The next example illustrates the use of an empirical distribution, followed by an example that illustrates the use of a Poisson distribution.

figure 5.17   The Service Level Achievement Must Equal or Exceed the Ratio *Cs/Cs + Ce*

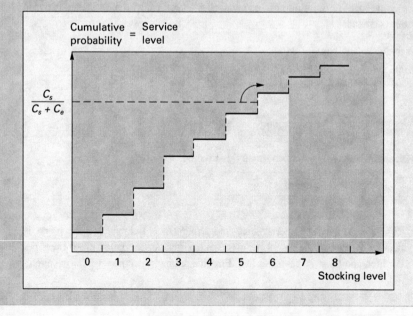

EXAMPLE 5.17

mhhe.com/stevenson10e

Historical records on the use of spare parts for several large hydraulic presses are to serve as an estimate of usage for spares of a newly installed press. Stockout costs involve downtime expenses and special ordering costs. These average $4,200 per unit short. Spares cost $800 each, and unused parts have zero salvage. Determine the optimal stocking level.

Number of Spares Used	Relative Frequency	Cumulative Frequency
0 -------------	.20	.20
1 -------------	.40	.60
2 -------------	.30	.90
3 -------------	.10	1.00
4 or more	.00	
	1.00	

SOLUTION

$$C_s = \$4,200 \qquad C_e = \$800 \qquad SL = \frac{C_s}{C_s + C_e} = \frac{\$4,200}{\$4,200 + \$800} = .84$$

The cumulative-frequency column indicates the percentage of time that demand did not exceed (was equal to or less than) some amount. For example, demand does not exceed one spare 60 percent of the time, or two spares 90 percent of the time. Thus, in order to achieve a service level of *at least* 84 percent, it will be necessary to stock two spares (i.e., to go to the next higher stocking level). ●

EXAMPLE 5.18

mhhe.com/stevenson10e

Demand for long-stemmed red roses at a small flower shop can be approximated using a Poisson distribution that has a mean of four dozen per day. Profit on the roses is $3 per dozen. Leftover flowers are marked down and sold the next day at a loss of $2 per dozen. Assume that all marked-down flowers are sold. What is the optimal stocking level?

SOLUTION

$$C_s = \$3 \qquad C_e = \$2 \qquad SL = \frac{C_s}{C_s + C_e} = \frac{\$3}{\$3 + \$2} = .60$$

Obtain the cumulative frequencies from the Poisson table (Appendix B, Table C) for a mean of 4.0:

Demand (dozen per day)	Cumulative Frequency
0	.018
1	.092
2	.238
3	.433
4	.629
5	.785
⋮	⋮

Compare the service level to the cumulative frequencies. In order to attain a service level of at least .60, it is necessary to stock four dozen. ●

One final point about discrete stocking levels: If the computed service level is *exactly* equal to the cumulative probability associated with one of the stocking levels, there are *two* equivalent stocking levels in terms of minimizing long-run cost—the one with equal probability and the next higher one. In the preceding example, if the ratio had been equal to .629, we would be indifferent between stocking four dozen and stocking five dozen roses each day.

POOR INVENTORY ACCURACY LEADS TO MORE INVENTORY AND REQUIRES MORE CAPITAL. SOFTWARE SYSTEMS MAINTAIN ENORMOUS AMOUNTS OF DATA AND HAVE A GREAT AMOUNT OF FUNCTIONALITY. SYSTEMS CAN ANALYZE INVENTORY LEVELS, ALLOCATE STOCK PLAN PURCHASES, AND ALLOCATE DELIVERIES ACCORDINGLY. THEY CAN IDENTIFY KEY SUPPLIERS OF EACH STOCKED ITEM AND CAN GIVE LEAD TIMES AND DOCK-TO-STOCK TIMES FOR REALISTIC TIME-PHASING.

OPERATIONS STRATEGY

Inventories often represent a substantial investment. More important, improving inventory processes can offer significant benefits in terms of cost reduction and customer satisfaction. Among the areas that have potential are the following:

Record keeping. It is important to have inventory records that are accurate and up-to-date, so that inventory decisions are based on correct information. Estimates of holding, ordering, and setup costs, as well as demand and lead times, should be reviewed periodically and updated when necessary.

Variation reduction. Lead time variations and forecast errors are two key factors that impact inventory management, and variation reduction in these areas can yield significant improvement in inventory management.

Lean operation. Lean systems are demand driven, which means that goods are pulled through the system to match demand instead of being pushed through without a direct link to demand. Moreover, lean systems feature smaller lot sizes than more traditional systems, based in part on the belief that holding costs are higher than those assigned by traditional systems, and partly as a deliberate effort to reduce ordering and setup costs by simplifying and standardizing

necessary activities. An obvious benefit is a decrease in average inventory on hand and, hence, lower carrying costs. Other benefits include fewer disruptions of work flow, reduction in space needs, enhanced ability to spot problems, and increased feasibility to place machines and workers closer together, which allows more opportunities for socialization, communication, and cooperation.

Supply chain management. Working more closely with suppliers to coordinate shipments, reduce lead times, and reduce supply chain inventories can reduce the size and frequency of stockouts while lowering inventory carrying costs. Blanket orders and vendor-managed inventories can reduced transaction costs. Also, consignment agreements, where buyers are not charged for inventory items until the items are sold, may be an option. Storage costs can sometimes be reduced by using cross-docking, whereby inbound trucks with goods arriving at distributor warehouses from suppliers are directly loaded onto outbound trucks for store or dealer delivery, avoiding warehouse handling and storage costs.

SUMMARY

Inventory management is a core operations management activity. Good inventory management is often the mark of a well-run organization. Inventory levels must be planned carefully in order to balance the cost of holding inventory and the cost of providing reasonable levels of customer service. Successful inventory management requires a system to keep track of inventory transactions, accurate information about demand and lead times, realistic estimates of certain inventory-related costs, and a priority system for classifying the items in inventory and allocating control efforts.

Four classes of models are described: EOQ, ROP, fixed-order-interval, and single-period models. The first three are appropriate if unused items can be carried over into subsequent periods. The single-period model is appropriate when items cannot be carried over. EOQ models address the question of how much to order. The ROP models address the question of when to order and are particularly helpful in dealing with situations that include variations in either demand rate or lead time. ROP models involve service level and safety stock considerations. When the time between orders is fixed, the FOI model is useful for determining the order quantity. The single-period model is used for items that have a "shelf life" of one period. The models presented in this chapter are summarized in Table 5.4.

KEY TERMS

Inventory A stock or store of goods.

Little's Law The average amount of inventory in a system is equal to the product of the average demand rate and the average time a unit is in the system.

Inventory turnover Ratio of average cost of goods sold to average inventory investment.

Periodic system Physical count of items in inventory made at periodic intervals (weekly, monthly).

Perpetual inventory system System that keeps track of removals from inventory continuously, thus monitoring current levels of each item.

Two-bin system Two containers of inventory; reorder when the first is empty.

Universal product code (UPC) Bar code printed on a label that has information about the item to which it is attached.

Lead time Time interval between ordering and receiving the order.

Point-of-sale (POS) systems Record items at time of sale.

Holding (carrying) cost Cost to carry an item in inventory for a length of time, usually a year.198

Ordering costs Costs of ordering and receiving inventory.

Shortage costs Costs resulting when demand exceeds the supply of inventory; often unrealized profit per unit.

A-B-C approach Classifying inventory according to some measure of importance, and allocating control efforts accordingly.

Cycle counting A physical count of items in inventory.

Economic order quantity (EOQ) The order size that minimizes total annual cost.

Quantity discounts Price reductions for large orders.

Reorder point (ROP) When the quantity on hand of an item drops to this amount, the item is reordered.

Safety stock Stock that is held in excess of expected demand due to variable demand and/or lead time.

Service level Probability that demand will not exceed supply during lead time.

Fill rate The percentage of demand filled by the stock on hand.

Fixed-order-interval (FOI) model Orders are placed at fixed time intervals.

Single-period model Model for ordering of perishables and other items with limited useful lives.

Shortage cost Generally, the unrealized profit per unit.

Excess cost Difference between purchase cost and salvage value of items left over at the end of a period.

table 5.4   Summary of Inventory Formulas

MODEL	FORMULA		SYMBOLS
1. Basic EOQ	$Q_0 = \sqrt{\dfrac{2DS}{H}}$	(5.2)	Q_o = Economic order quantity D = Annual demand S = Order cost H = Annual carrying cost per unit Q = Order quantity
	$TC = \dfrac{Q}{2}H + \dfrac{D}{Q}S$	(5.1)	
	Length of order cycle $= \dfrac{Q}{D}$	(5.3)	
2. Economic production quantity	$Q_p = \sqrt{\dfrac{2DS}{H}}\sqrt{\dfrac{p}{p-u}}$	(5.5)	Q_p = Optimal run or order size p = Production or delivery rate u = Usage rate I_{MAX} = Maximum inventory level
	$TC = \dfrac{I_{max}}{2}H + \dfrac{D}{Q}S$	(5.4)	
	Cycle time $= \dfrac{Q}{u}$	(5.6)	
	Run time $= \dfrac{Q}{p}$	(5.7)	
	$I_{max} = \dfrac{Q_0}{p}(p-u)$	(5.8)	
3. Quantity discounts	$TC = \dfrac{Q}{2}H + \dfrac{D}{Q}S + PD$	(5.9)	P = Unit price

4. Reorder point under:
  a. Constant demand and lead time
  b. Variable demand rate
  c. Variable lead time
  d. Variable lead time and demand
	$ROP = d(LT)$	(5.10)	ROP = Quantity on hand at reorder point
			d = Demand rate
			LT = Lead time
			$\bar{d}$ = Average demand rate
			σd = Standard deviation of demand rate
			z = Standard normal deviation
			$\overline{LT}$ = Average lead time
			σLT = Standard deviation of lead time

	$ROP = \bar{d}LT + z(\sigma_d)\sqrt{LT}$	(5.13)	
	$ROP = d\overline{LT} + z(\sigma_{LT})d$	(5.14)	
	$ROP = \bar{d}\overline{LT} + z\sqrt{\overline{LT}\sigma_d^2 + \bar{d}^2\sigma_{LT}^2}$	(5.15)	

5. ROP shortages
  a. Units short per cycle
  b. Units short per year
  c. Annual service level
	$E(n) = E(z)\sigma_{dLT}$	(5.16)	$E(n)$ = Expected number short per cycle
			$E(z)$ = Standardized number short
			$\sigma_d LT$ = Standard deviation of lead time demand
			$E(N)$ = Expected number short per year
			SL_{annual} = Annual service level

	$E(N) = E(n)\dfrac{D}{Q}$	(5.17)	
	$SL_{annual} = 1 - \dfrac{E(z)\sigma_{dLT}}{Q}$	(5.19)	
6. Fixed interval	$Q = \bar{d}(OI + LT)$ $\quad + z\sigma_d\sqrt{OI + LT} - A$	(5.20)	OI = Time between orders A = Amount on hand at order time
7. Single period	$SL = \dfrac{C_s}{C_s + C_e}$	(5.21)	SL = Service level C_s = Shortage cost per unit C_e = Excess cost per unit

SOLVED PROBLEMS

PROBLEM 1

Basic EOQ. A toy manufacturer uses approximately 32,000 silicon chips annually. The chips are used at a steady rate during the 240 days a year that the plant operates. Annual holding cost is $3 per chip, and ordering cost is $120. Determine
a. The optimal order quantity.
b. The number of workdays in an order cycle.

Solution

$$D = 32,000 \text{ chips per year} \qquad S = \$120$$
$$H = \$3 \text{ per unit per year}$$

a. $\quad Q_0 = \sqrt{\dfrac{2DS}{H}} = \sqrt{\dfrac{2(32,000)120}{3}} = 1,600 \text{ chips.}$

b. $\quad \dfrac{Q}{D} = \dfrac{1,600 \text{ chips}}{32,000 \text{ chips/yr.}} = \dfrac{1}{20}\text{year} \text{ (i.e., } \frac{1}{20} \times 240 \text{ days), or 12 days.}$

PROBLEM 2

Economic production quantity. The Dine Corporation is both a producer and a user of brass couplings. The firm operates 220 days a year and uses the couplings at a steady rate of 50 per day. Couplings can be produced at a rate of 200 per day. Annual storage cost is $2 per coupling, and machine setup cost is $70 per run.
a. Determine the economic run quantity.
b. Approximately how many runs per year will there be?
c. Compute the maximum inventory level.
d. Determine the length of the *pure consumption* portion of the cycle.

Solution

$$D = 50 \text{ units per day} \times 220 \text{ days per year} = 11,000 \text{ units per year}$$
$$S = \$70$$
$$H = \$2 \text{ per unit per year}$$
$$p = 200 \text{ units per day}$$
$$u = 50 \text{ units per day}$$

a. $\quad Q_p = \sqrt{\dfrac{2DS}{H}}\sqrt{\dfrac{p}{p-u}} = \sqrt{\dfrac{2(11,000)70}{2}}\sqrt{\dfrac{200}{200-50}} \approx 1,013 \text{ units.}$

b. Number of runs per year: $D/Q_0 = 11,000/1,013 = 10.86$, or approximately 11.

c. $\quad I_{max} = \dfrac{Q_p}{p}(p-u) = \dfrac{1,013}{200}(200-50) = 759.75 \text{ or } 760 \text{ units.}$

d.

$$\text{Length of cycle} = \dfrac{Q_p}{u} = \dfrac{1,013 \text{ units}}{50 \text{ units per day}} = 20.26 \text{ days}$$

$$\text{Length of run} = \dfrac{Q_p}{p} = \dfrac{1,013 \text{ units}}{200 \text{ units per day}} = 5.065 \text{ days}$$

$$\text{Length of pure consumption portion} = \text{Length of cycle} - \text{Length of run}$$

$$= 20.26 - 5.065 = 15.20 \text{ days.}$$

PROBLEM 3

Quantity discounts. A small manufacturing firm uses roughly 3,400 pounds of chemical dye a year. Currently the firm purchases 300 pounds per order and pays $3 per pound. The supplier has just announced that orders of 1,000 pounds or more will be filled at a price of $2 per pound. The manufacturing firm incurs a cost of $100 each time it submits an order and assigns an annual holding cost of 17 percent of the purchase price per pound.

a. Determine the order size that will minimize the total cost.

b. If the supplier offered the discount at 1,500 pounds instead of 1,000 pounds, what order size would minimize total cost?

Solution

$$D = 3{,}400 \text{ pounds per year} \qquad S = \$100 \qquad H = 0.17P$$

a. Compute the EOQ for $2 per pound:

The quantity ranges are

RANGE	UNIT PRICE
1 to 999	$3
1,000 +	$2

$$Q_{\$2/pound} = \sqrt{\frac{2DS}{H}} = \sqrt{\frac{2(3{,}400)100}{0.17(2)}} = 1{,}414 \text{ pounds}$$

Because this quantity is feasible at $2 per pound, it is the optimum.

b. When the discount is offered at 1,500 pounds, the EOQ for the $2 per pound range is no longer feasible. Consequently, it becomes necessary to compute the EOQ for $3 per pound and compare the total cost for that order size with the total cost using the price break quantity (i.e., 1,500).

$$Q_{\$3/pound} = \sqrt{\frac{2DS}{H}} = \sqrt{\frac{2(3{,}400)100}{0.17(3)}} \approx 1{,}155 \text{ pounds}$$

$$TC = \left(\frac{Q}{2}\right)H + \left(\frac{D}{Q}\right)S + PD$$

$$TC_{1,155} = \left(\frac{1{,}155}{2}\right)0.17(3) + \left(\frac{3{,}400}{1{,}155}\right)100 + 3(3{,}400)$$

$$= \$294.53 + \$294.37 + \$10{,}200 = \$10{,}789$$

$$TC_{1,500} = \left(\frac{1{,}500}{2}\right)0.17(2) + \left(\frac{3{,}400}{1{,}500}\right)100 + 2(3{,}400)$$

$$= \$255 + \$226.67 + \$6{,}800 = \$7{,}282$$

Hence, because it would result in a lower total cost, 1,500 is the optimal order size.

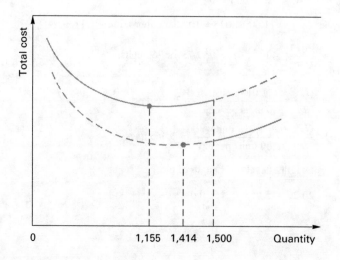

PROBLEM 4

ROP for variable demand and constant lead time. The housekeeping department of a motel uses approximately 400 washcloths per day. The actual number tends to vary with the number of guests on any given night. Usage can be approximated by a normal distribution that has a mean of 400 and a standard deviation of 9 washcloths per day. A linen supply company delivers towels and washcloths with a lead time of three days. If the motel policy is to maintain a stockout risk of 2 percent, what is the minimum number of washcloths that must be on hand at reorder time, and how much of that amount can be considered safety stock?

Solution

$\bar{d}$ = 400 washcloths per day　　LT = 3 days

σ_d = 9 washcloths per day　　Risk = 2 percent, so service level = 98 percent

From Appendix B, Table B, the z value that corresponds to an area under the normal curve to the left of z for 98 percent is about +2.055.

$$ROP = \bar{d}LT + z\sigma_d\sqrt{LT} = 400(3) + 2.055(9)\sqrt{3}$$
$$= 1,200 + 32.03, \text{ or approximately } 1,232 \text{ washcloths}$$

Safety stock is approximately 32 washcloths.

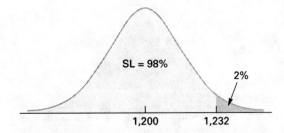

PROBLEM 5

ROP for constant demand and variable lead time. The motel in the preceding example uses approximately 600 bars of soap each day, and this tends to be fairly constant. Lead time for soap delivery is normally distributed with a mean of six days and a standard deviation of two days. A service level of 90 percent is desired.

a. Find the ROP.

b. How many days of supply are on hand at the ROP?

$$d = 600 \text{ bars per day}$$
$$SL = 90 \text{ percent, so } z = +1.28 \text{ (from Appendix B, Table B)}$$
$$\overline{LT} = 6 \text{ days}$$
$$\sigma_{LT} = 2 \text{ days}$$

a.　$ROP = d\overline{LT} + z(\sigma_{LT})d = 600(6) + 1.28(2)(600)$
　　$= 5,136 \text{ bars of soap}$

b.　$\dfrac{ROP}{d} = \dfrac{5,136}{600} = 8.56 \text{ days}$

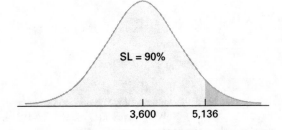

PROBLEM 6

ROP for variable demand rate and variable lead time. The motel replaces broken glasses at a rate of 25 per day. In the past, this quantity has tended to vary normally and have a standard deviation of 3 glasses per day. Glasses are ordered from a Cleveland supplier. Lead time is normally distributed with an average of 10 days and a standard deviation of 2 days. What ROP should be used to achieve a service level of 95 percent?

Solution

$$\bar{d} = 25 \text{ glasses per day} \qquad \overline{LT} = 10 \text{ days}$$
$$\sigma_d = 3 \text{ glasses per day} \qquad \sigma_{LT} = 2 \text{ days}$$
$$SL = 95 \text{ percent, so } z = +1.65 \text{ (Appendix B, Table B)}$$
$$ROP = \bar{d}\overline{LT} + z\sqrt{\overline{LT}\sigma_d^2 + \bar{d}^2\sigma_{LT}^2}$$
$$= 25(10) + 1.65\sqrt{10(3)^2 + (25)^2(2)^2} = 334 \text{ glasses}$$

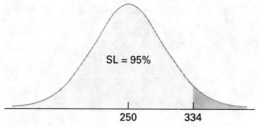

SL = 95%

250　　334

PROBLEM 7

Shortages and service levels. The manager of a store that sells office supplies has decided to set an annual service level of 96 percent for a certain model of telephone answering equipment. The store sells approximately 300 of this model a year. Holding cost is $5 per unit annually, ordering cost is $25, and $\sigma_{dLT} = 7$.

a. What average number of units short per year will be consistent with the specified annual service level?
b. What average number of units short per cycle will provide the desired annual service level?
c. What lead time service level is necessary for the 96 percent annual service level?

Solution

$$SL_{annual} = 96 \text{ percent} \qquad D = 300 \text{ units} \qquad H = \$5 \qquad S = \$25 \qquad \sigma_{dLT} = 7$$

a. $E(N) = (1 - SL_{annual})D = (1 - .96)(300) = 12 \text{ units}$

b. $E(N) = E(n)\dfrac{D}{Q}$. Solving for $E(n)$, you have

$$E(n) = E(N) \div \left(\frac{D}{Q}\right) = 12 \div \left(\frac{300}{Q}\right)$$

$$Q = \sqrt{\frac{2DS}{H}} = \sqrt{\frac{2(300)(25)}{5}} = 54.77 \text{ (round to 55)}$$

Then $E(n) = 12 \div \left(\dfrac{300}{55}\right) = 2.2.$

c. In order to find the lead time service level, you need the value of $E(z)$. Because the value of $E(n)$ is 2.2 and $E(n) = E(z)\sigma_{dLT}$, you have $2.2 = E(z)(7)$. Solving gives $E(z) = 2.2 \div 7 = 0.314$. Interpolating in Table 5.3 gives the approximate lead time service level. Thus,

$$\frac{.307 - .314}{.307 - .324} = \frac{.5793 - x}{.5793 - .5636}$$

Solving,

$$x = .5728$$

[To interpolate, find the two values between which the computed number falls in the $E(z)$ column. Then find the difference between the computed value and one end of the range, and divide by the difference between the two ends of the range. Perform the corresponding calculation on the two service levels using x for the unknown value, and solve for x. Often, simply "eyeballing" the unknown value will suffice.]

PROBLEM 8

Fixed-order-interval model. A lab orders a number of chemicals from the same supplier every 30 days. Lead time is five days. The assistant manager of the lab must determine how much of one of these chemicals to order. A check of stock revealed that eleven 25-milliliter (ml) jars are on hand. Daily usage of the chemical is approximately normal with a mean of 15.2 ml per day and a standard deviation of 1.6 ml per day. The desired service level for this chemical is 95 percent.
a. How many jars of the chemical should be ordered?
b. What is the average amount of safety stock of the chemical?

Solution

$\bar{d}$ = 15.2 ml per day   OI = 30 days   SL = 95% requires z = 1.65

σ_d = 1.6 ml per day   LT = 5 days   A = 11 jars $\times$ 25 ml per jar = 275 ml

a. Amount to order = $\bar{d}$(OI + LT) + $z\sigma_d \sqrt{\text{OI} + \text{LT}}$ − A

$\qquad\qquad\qquad$ = 15.2(30 + 5) + 1.65(1.6)$\sqrt{30 + 5}$ − 275 = 272.62 ml

Convert this to number of jars:

$$\frac{272.62 \text{ ml}}{25 \text{ ml per jar}} = 10.90 \text{ or } 11 \text{ jars}$$

b. Safety stock = $z\sigma_d \sqrt{\text{OI} + \text{LT}}$ = 1.65(1.6)$\sqrt{30 + 5}$ = 15.62 ml.

PROBLEM 9

Single-period model. A firm that installs cable TV systems uses a certain piece of equipment for which it carries two spare parts. The parts cost $500 each and have no salvage value. Part failures can be modeled by a Poisson distribution with a mean of two failures during the useful life of the equipment. Holding and disposal costs are negligible. Estimate the apparent range of shortage cost.

Solution

$$C_s \text{ is unknown} \qquad C_e = \$500$$

The Poisson table (Appendix B, Table C) provides these values for a mean of 2.0:

NUMBER OF FAILURES	CUMULATIVE PROBABILITY
0	.135
1	.406
2	.677
3	.857
4	.947
5	.983
⋮	⋮

For the optimal stocking level, the service level must usually be rounded up to a feasible stocking level. Hence, you know that the service level must have been between .406 and .677 in order to make two units the optimal level. By setting the service level equal first to .406 and then to .677, you can establish bounds on the possible range of shortage costs.

$$\frac{C_s}{C_s + \$500} = .406, \text{ so } C_s = .406(\$500 + C_s)$$

Solving, you find Cs = $341.75.

    Similarly,

$$\frac{C_s}{C_s + \$500} = .677, \text{ so } C_s = .677(\$500 + C_s)$$

Solving, you find $C_s = \$1,047.99$. Hence, the apparent range of shortage cost is \$341.75 to \$1,047.99.

DISCUSSION AND REVIEW QUESTIONS

1. What are the primary reasons for holding inventory?
2. What are the requirements for effective inventory management?
3. Briefly describe each of the costs associated with inventory.
4. What potential benefits and risks do RFID tags have for inventory management?
5. Why might it be inappropriate to use inventory turnover ratios to compare inventory performance of companies that are in different industries?
6. List the major assumptions of the EOQ model.
7. How would you respond to the criticism that EOQ models tend to provide misleading results because values of D, S, and H are, at best, educated guesses?
8. Explain briefly how a higher carrying cost can result in a decrease in inventory.
9. What is safety stock, and what is its purpose?
10. Under what circumstances would the amount of safety stock held be
    a. Large?   b. Small?   c. Zero?
11. What is meant by the term *service level?* Generally speaking, how is service level related to the amount of safety stock held?
12. Describe briefly the A-B-C approach to inventory control.
13. The purchasing agent for a company that assembles and sells air-conditioning equipment in a Latin American country noted that the cost of compressors has increased significantly each time they have been reordered. The company uses an EOQ model to determine order size. What are the implications of this price escalation with respect to order size? What factors other than price must be taken into consideration?
14. Explain how a decrease in setup time can lead to a decrease in the average amount of inventory a firm holds, and why that would be beneficial.
15. What is the single-period model, and under what circumstances is it appropriate?
16. Can the optimal stocking level in the single-period model ever be less than expected demand? Explain briefly.
17. What are some ways in which a company can reduce the need for inventories?

TAKING STOCK

1. What trade-offs are involved in each of these aspects of inventory management?
   a. Buying additional amounts to take advantage of quantity discounts.
   b. Treating holding cost as a percentage of unit price instead of as a constant amount.
   c. Conducting cycle counts once a quarter instead of once a year.
2. Who needs to be involved in inventory decisions involving holding costs? Setting inventory levels? Quantity discount purchases?
3. How has technology aided inventory management? How have technological improvements in products such as automobiles and computers impacted inventory decisions?

CRITICAL THINKING EXERCISES

1   To be competitive, many fast-food chains began to expand their menus to include a wider range of foods. Although contributing to competitiveness, this has added to the complexity of operations, including inventory management. Specifically, in what ways does the expansion of menu offerings create problems for inventory management?

2   As a supermarket manager, how would you go about evaluating the criticalness of an inventory shortage?

3   Sam is at the post office to mail a package. After he pays for mailing the package, the clerk asks if he would like to buy some stamps. Sam pauses to think before he answers. He doesn't have a credit card with him. After paying for the package, he has about $30 in his pocket. Analyze this from an inventory standpoint. Identify the relevant considerations.

PROBLEMS

1   The manager of an automobile repair shop hopes to achieve a better allocation of inventory control efforts by adopting an A-B-C approach to inventory control.

   a. Given the monthly usages in the following table, classify the items in A, B, and C categories according to dollar usage:

ITEM	USAGE	UNIT COST
4021	90	$1,400
9402	300	12
4066	30	700
6500	150	20
9280	10	1,020
4050	80	140
6850	2,000	10
3010	400	20
4400	5,000	5

   b. Determine the percentage of items in each category and the annual dollar value for each category.

2   The following table contains figures on the monthly volume and unit costs for a random sample of 16 items from a list of 2,000 inventory items at a health care facility:

ITEM	UNIT COST	USAGE	ITEM	UNIT COST	USAGE
K34	$10	200	F99	20	60
K35	25	600	D45	10	550
K36	36	150	D48	12	90
M10	16	25	D52	15	110
M20	20	80	D57	40	120
Z45	80	200	N08	30	40
F14	20	300	P05	16	500
F95	30	800	P09	10	30

   a. Develop an A-B-C classification for these items.

   b. How could the manager use this information?

   c. After reviewing your classification scheme, suppose that the manager decides to place item P05 into the A category. What are some possible explanations for this decision?

3   A large bakery buys flour in 25-pound bags. The bakery uses an average of 4,860 bags a year. Preparing an order and receiving a shipment of flour involves a cost of $10 per order. Annual carrying costs are $75 per bag.

   a. Determine the economic order quantity.

   b. What is the average number of bags on hand?

   c. How many orders per year will there be?

   d. Compute the total cost of ordering and carrying flour.

   e. If ordering costs were to increase by $1 per order, how much would that affect the minimum total annual cost?

4   A large law firm uses an average of 40 boxes of copier paper a day. The firm operates 260 days a year. Storage and handling costs for the paper are $30 a year per box, and it costs approximately $60 to order and receive a shipment of paper.

   a. What order size would minimize the sum of annual ordering and carrying costs?

   b. Compute the total annual cost using your order size from part *a.*

   c. Except for rounding, are annual ordering and carrying costs always equal at the EOQ?

   d. The office manager is currently using an order size of 200 boxes. The partners of the firm expect the office to be managed "in a cost-efficient manner." Would you recommend that the office manager use the optimal order size instead of 200 boxes? Justify your answer.

5   Garden Variety Flower Shop uses 750 clay pots a month. The pots are purchased at $2 each. Annual carrying costs per pot are estimated to be 30 percent of cost, and ordering costs are $20 per order. The manager has been using an order size of 1,500 flower pots.

   a. What additional annual cost is the shop incurring by staying with this order size?

   b. Other than cost savings, what benefit would using the optimal order quantity yield?

6   A produce distributor uses 800 packing crates a month, which it purchases at a cost of $10 each. The manager has assigned an annual carrying cost of 35 percent of the purchase price per crate. Ordering costs are $28. Currently the manager orders once a month. How much could the firm save annually in ordering and carrying costs by using the EOQ?

7   A manager receives a forecast for next year. Demand is projected to be 600 units for the first half of the year and 900 units for the second half. The monthly holding cost is $2 per unit, and it costs an estimated $55 to process an order.

   a. Assuming that monthly demand will be level during each of the six-month periods covered by the forecast (e.g., 100 per month for each of the first six months), determine an order size that will minimize the sum of ordering and carrying costs for each of the six-month periods.

   b. Why is it important to be able to assume that demand will be level during each six-month period?

   c. If the vendor is willing to offer a discount of $10 *per order* for ordering in multiples of 50 units (e.g., 50, 100, 150), would you advise the manager to take advantage of the offer in either period? If so, what order size would you recommend?

8   A food processor uses approximately 27,000 glass jars a month for its fruit juice product. Because of storage limitations, a lot size of 4,000 jars has been used. Monthly holding cost is 18 cents per jar, and reordering cost is $60 per order. The company operates an average of 20 days a month.

   a. What penalty is the company incurring by its present order size?

   b. The manager would prefer ordering 10 times each month but would have to justify any change in order size. One possibility is to simplify order processing to reduce the ordering cost. What ordering cost would enable the manager to justify ordering every other day?

   c. Suppose that after investigating ordering cost, the manager is able to reduce it to $50. How else could the manager justify using an order size that would be consistent with ordering every other day?

9   The Friendly Sausage Factory (FSF) can produce hot dogs at a rate of 5,000 per day. FSF supplies hot dogs to local restaurants at a steady rate of 250 per day. The cost to prepare the equipment for producing hot dogs is $66. Annual holding costs are 45 cents per hot dog. The factory operates 300 days a year. Find

   a. The optimal run size.

   b. The number of runs per year.

   c. The length (in days) of a run.

10 A chemical firm produces sodium bisulfate in 100-pound bags. Demand for this product is 20 tons per day. The capacity for producing the product is 50 tons per day. Setup costs $100, and storage and handling costs are $5 per ton a year. The firm operates 200 days a year. (Note: 1 ton = 2,000 pounds.)

   a. How many bags per run are optimal?

   b. What would the average inventory be for this lot size?

   c. Determine the approximate length of a production run, in days.

d. About how many runs per year would there be?

e. How much could the company save annually if the setup cost could be reduced to $25 per run?

11 A company is about to begin production of a new product. The manager of the department that will produce one of the components for the product wants to know how often the machine used to produce the item will be available for other work. The machine will produce the item at a rate of 200 units a day. Eighty units will be used daily in assembling the final product. Assembly will take place five days a week, 50 weeks a year. The manager estimates that it will take almost a full day to get the machine ready for a production run, at a cost of $300. Inventory holding costs will be $10 a year.

a. What run quantity should be used to minimize total annual costs?

b. What is the length of a production run in days?

c. During production, at what rate will inventory build up?

d. If the manager wants to run another job between runs of this item, and needs a minimum of 10 days per cycle for the other work, will there be enough time?

e. Given your answer to part *d,* the manager wants to explore options that will allow this other job to be performed using this equipment. Name three options the manager can consider.

f. Suppose the manager decides to increase the run size of the new product. How many additional units would be needed to just accommodate the other job? How much will that increase the total annual cost?

12 A company manufactures hair dryers. It buys some of the components, but it makes the heating element, which it can produce at the rate of 800 per day. Hair dryers are assembled daily, 250 days a year, at a rate of 300 per day. Because of the disparity between the production and usage rates, the heating elements are periodically produced in batches of 2,000 units.

a. Approximately how many *batches* of heating elements are produced annually?

b. If production on a batch begins when there is no inventory of heating elements on hand, how much inventory will be on hand *two days later?*

c. What is the average inventory of elements, assuming each production cycle begins when there are none on hand?

d. The same equipment that is used to make the heating elements could also be used to make a component for another of the firm's products. That job would require four days, including setup. Setup time for making a batch of the heating elements is a half day. Is there enough time to do this job between production of batches of heating elements? Explain.

13 A mail-order house uses 18,000 boxes a year. Carrying costs are 60 cents per box a year, and ordering costs are $96. The following price schedule applies. Determine

a. The optimal order quantity.

b. The number of orders per year.

NUMBER OF BOXES	PRICE PER BOX
1,000 to 1,999	$1.25
2,000 to 4,999	1.20
5,000 to 9,999	1.15
10,000 or more	1.10

14 A jewelry firm buys semiprecious stones to make bracelets and rings. The supplier quotes a price of $8 per stone for quantities of 600 stones or more, $9 per stone for orders of 400 to 599 stones, and $10 per stone for lesser quantities. The jewelry firm operates 200 days per year. Usage rate is 25 stones per day, and ordering costs are $48.

a. If carrying costs are $2 per year for each stone, find the order quantity that will minimize total annual cost.

b. If annual carrying costs are 30 percent of unit cost, what is the optimal order size?

c. If lead time is six working days, at what point should the company reorder?

15 A manufacturer of exercise equipment purchases the pulley section of the equipment from a supplier who lists these prices: less than 1,000, $5 each; 1,000 to 3,999, $4.95 each; 4,000 to 5,999, $4.90 each; and 6,000 or more, $4.85 each. Ordering costs are $50, annual carrying costs per unit are 40 percent of purchase cost, and annual usage is 4,900 pulleys. Determine an order quantity that will minimize total cost.

16 A company will begin stocking remote control devices. Expected monthly demand is 800 units. The controllers can be purchased from either supplier A or supplier B. Their price lists are as follows:

SUPPLIER A		SUPPLIER B	
QUANTITY	UNIT PRICE	QUANTITY	UNIT PRICE
1–199	$14.00	1–149	$14.10
200–499	13.80	150–349	13.90
500 +	13.60	350 +	13.70

Ordering cost is $40 and annual holding cost is 25 percent of unit price per unit. Which supplier should be used and what order quantity is optimal if the intent is to minimize total annual costs?

17 A manager just received a new price list from a supplier. It will now cost $1.00 a box for order quantities of 801 or more boxes, $1.10 a box for 200 to 800 boxes, and $1.20 a box for smaller quantities. Ordering cost is $80 per order and carrying costs are $10 per box a year. The firm uses 3,600 boxes a year. The manager has suggested a "round number" order size of 800 boxes. The manager's rationale is that with a U-shaped cost curve that is fairly flat at its minimum, the difference in total annual cost between 800 and 801 units would be small anyway. How would you reply to the manager's suggestion? What order size would you recommend?

18 A newspaper publisher uses roughly 800 feet of baling wire each day to secure bundles of newspapers while they are being distributed to carriers. The paper is published Monday through Saturday. Lead time is six workdays. What is the appropriate reorder point quantity, given that the company desires a service level of 95 percent, if that stockout risk for various levels of safety stock are as follows: 1,500 feet, 0.10; 1,800 feet, 0.05; 2,100 feet, 0.02; and 2,400 feet, 0.01?

19 Given this information:
Expected demand during lead time = 300 units
Standard deviation of lead time demand = 30 units
Determine each of the following, assuming that lead time demand is distributed normally:
a. The ROP that will provide a risk of stockout of 1 percent during lead time.
b. The safety stock needed to attain a 1 percent risk of stockout during lead time.
c. Would a stockout risk of 2 percent require more or less safety stock than a 1 percent risk? Explain. Would the ROP be larger, smaller, or unaffected if the acceptable risk was 2 percent instead of 1 percent? Explain.

20 Given this information:
Lead-time demand = 600 pounds
Standard deviation of lead time demand = 52 pounds (Assume normality.)
Acceptable stockout risk during lead time = 4 percent
a. What amount of safety stock is appropriate?
b. When should this item be reordered?
c. What risk of stockout would result from a decision not to have any safety stock?

21 Demand for walnut fudge ice cream at the Sweet Cream Dairy can be approximated by a normal distribution with a mean of 21 gallons per week and a standard deviation of 3.5 gallons per week. The new manager desires a service level of 90 percent. Lead time is two days, and the dairy is open seven days a week. (Hint: Work in terms of weeks.)
a. If an ROP model is used, what ROP would be consistent with the desired service level? How many days of supply are on hand at the ROP, assuming average demand?
b. If a fixed-interval model is used instead of an ROP model, what order size would be needed for the 90 percent service level with an order interval of 10 days and a supply of 8 gallons on hand at the order time? What is the probability of experiencing a stockout before this order arrives?
c. Suppose the manager is using the ROP model described in part *a*. One day after placing an order with the supplier, the manager receives a call from the supplier that the order will be delayed because of problems at the supplier's plant. The supplier promises to have the order there in two days. After hanging up, the manager checks the supply of walnut fudge ice cream and finds that 2 gallons have been sold since the order was placed. Assuming the

supplier's promise is valid, what is the probability that the dairy will run out of this flavor before the shipment arrives?

22 The injection molding department of a company uses an average of 30 gallons of special lubricant a day. The supply of the lubricant is replenished when the amount on hand is 170 gallons. It takes four days for an order to be delivered. Safety stock is 50 gallons, which provides a stockout risk of 9 percent. What amount of safety stock would provide a stockout risk of 3 percent? Assume normality.

23 A company uses 85 circuit boards a day in a manufacturing process. The person who orders the boards follows this rule: Order when the amount on hand drops to 625 boards. Orders are delivered approximately six days after being placed. The delivery time is normal with a mean of six days and a standard deviation of 1.10 days. What is the probability that the supply of circuit boards will be exhausted before the order is received if boards are reordered when the amount on hand drops to 625 boards?

24 One item a computer store sells is supplied by a vendor who handles only that item. Demand for that item recently changed, and the store manager must determine when to replenish it. The manager wants a probability of at least 96 percent of not having a stockout during lead time. The manager expects demand to average a dozen units a day and have a standard deviation of 2 units a day. Lead time is variable, averaging four days with a standard deviation of one day. Assume normality and that seasonality is not a factor.

   a. When should the manager reorder to achieve the desired probability?

   b. Why might the model not be appropriate if seasonality was present?

25 The manager of a car wash received a revised price list from the vendor who supplies soap, and a promise of a shorter lead time for deliveries. Formerly the lead time was four days, but now the vendor promises a reduction of 25 percent in that time. Annual usage of soap is 4,500 gallons. The car wash is open 360 days a year. Assume that daily usage is normal, and that it has a standard deviation of 2 gallons per day. The ordering cost is $30 and annual carrying cost is $3 a gallon. The revised price list (cost per gallon) is shown in the following table:

QUANTITY	UNIT PRICE
1–399	$2.00
400–799	1.70
800 +	1.62

   a. What order quantity is optimal?

   b. What ROP is appropriate if the acceptable risk of a stockout is 1.5 percent?

26 A small copy center uses five 500-sheet boxes of copy paper a week. Experience suggests that usage can be well approximated by a normal distribution with a mean of five boxes per week and a standard deviation of one-half box per week. Two weeks are required to fill an order for letterhead stationery. Ordering cost is $2, and annual holding cost is 20 cents per box.

   a. Determine the economic order quantity, assuming a 52-week year.

   b. If the copy center reorders when the supply on hand is 12 boxes, compute the risk of a stockout.

   c. If a fixed interval of seven weeks instead of an ROP is used for reordering, what risk does the copy center incur that it will run out of stationery before this order arrives if it orders 36 boxes when the amount on hand is 12 boxes?

27 Ned's Natural Foods sells unshelled peanuts by the pound. Historically, Ned has observed that daily demand is normally distributed with a mean of 80 pounds and a standard deviation of 10 pounds. Lead time also appears normally distributed with a mean of eight days and a standard deviation of one day.

   a. What ROP would provide a stockout risk of 10 percent during lead time?

   b. What is the expected number of units (pounds) short per cycle?

28 Regional Supermarket is open 360 days per year. Daily use of cash register tape averages 10 rolls. Usage appears normally distributed with a standard deviation of 2 rolls per day. The cost of ordering tape is $1, and carrying costs are 40 cents per roll a year. Lead time is three days.

   a. What is the EOQ?

   b. What ROP will provide a lead time service level of 96 percent?

   c. What is the expected number of units short per cycle with 96 percent? Per year?

   d. What is the annual service level?

29 A service station uses 1,200 cases of oil a year. Ordering cost is $40, and annual carrying cost is $3 per case. The station owner has specified an *annual* service level of 99 percent.
   a. What level of safety stock is appropriate if lead time demand is normally distributed with a mean of 80 cases and a standard deviation of 5 cases?
   b. What is the risk of a stockout during lead time?

30 Weekly demand for diesel fuel at a department of parks depot is 250 gallons. The depot operates 52 weeks a year. Weekly usage is normal and has a standard deviation of 14 gallons. Holding cost for the fuel is $1 a month, and it costs $20 in administrative time to submit an order for more fuel. It takes one-half week to receive a delivery of diesel fuel. Determine the amount of safety stock that would be needed if the manager wants
   a. An annual service level of 98 percent. What is the implication of negative safety stock?
   b. The expected number of units short per order cycle to be no more than 5 gallons.

31 A drugstore uses fixed-order cycles for many of the items it stocks. The manager wants a service level of .98. The order interval is 14 days, and lead time is 2 days. Average demand for one item is 40 units per day, and the standard deviation of demand is 3 units per day. Given the on-hand inventory at the reorder time for each order cycle shown in the following table, determine the order quantities for cycles 1, 2, and 3:

CYCLE	ON HAND
1	42
2	8
3	103

32 A manager must set up inventory ordering systems for two new production items, P34 and P35. P34 can be ordered at any time, but P35 can be ordered only once every four weeks. The company operates 50 weeks a year, and the weekly usage rates for both items are normally distributed. The manager has gathered the following information about the items:

	ITEM P34	ITEM P35
Average weekly demand	60 units	70 units
Standard deviation	4 units per week	5 units per week
Unit cost	$15	$20
Annual holding cost	30%	30%
Ordering cost	$70	$30
Lead time	2 weeks	2 weeks
Acceptable stockout risk	2.5%	2.5%

   a. When should the manager reorder each item?
   b. Compute the order quantity for P34.
   c. Compute the order quantity for P35 if 110 units are on hand at the time the order is placed.

33 Given the following list of items,
   a. Classify the items as A, B, or C.
   b. Determine the economic order quantity for each item (round to the nearest whole unit).

ITEM	ESTIMATED ANNUAL DEMAND	ORDERING COST	HOLDING COST (%)	UNIT PRICE
H4-010	20,000	50	20	2.50
H5-201	60,200	60	20	4.00
P6-400	9,800	80	30	28.50
P6-401	14,500	50	30	12.00
P7-100	6,250	50	30	9.00
P9-103	7,500	50	40	22.00
TS-300	21,000	40	25	45.00
TS-400	45,000	40	25	40.00
TS-041	800	40	25	20.00
V1-001	33,100	25	35	4.00

34 Demand for jelly doughnuts on Saturdays at Don's Doughnut Shoppe is shown in the following table. Determine the optimal number of doughnuts, in dozens, to stock if labor, materials, and overhead are estimated to be $3.20 per dozen, doughnuts are sold for $4.80 per dozen, and leftover doughnuts at the end of each day are sold the next day at half price. What is the *resulting* service level?

DEMAND (DOZENS)	RELATIVE FREQUENCY	DEMAND (DOZENS)	RELATIVE FREQUENCY
19	.01	25	.10
20	.05	26	.11
21	.12	27	.10
22	.18	28	.04
23	.13	29	.02
24	.14		

35 A public utility intends to buy a turbine as part of an expansion plan and must now decide on the number of spare parts to order. One part, no. X135, can be purchased for $100 each. Carrying and disposal costs are estimated to be 145 percent of the purchase price over the life of the turbine. A stockout would cost roughly $88,000 due to downtime, ordering, and "special purchase" factors. Historical records based on the performance of similar equipment operating under similar conditions suggest that demand for spare parts will tend to approximate a Poisson distribution with a mean of 3.2 parts for the useful life of the turbine.

a. What is the optimal number of spares to order?

b. Carrying no spare parts would be the best strategy for what range of shortage cost?

36 Skinner's Fish Market buys fresh Boston bluefish daily for $4.20 per pound and sells it for $5.70 per pound. At the end of each business day, any remaining bluefish is sold to a producer of cat food for $2.40 per pound. Daily demand can be approximated by a normal distribution with a mean of 80 pounds and a standard deviation of 10 pounds. What is the optimal stocking level?

37 A small grocery store sells fresh produce, which it obtains from a local farmer. During the strawberry season, demand for fresh strawberries can be reasonably approximated using a normal distribution with a mean of 40 quarts per day and a standard deviation of 6 quarts per day. Excess costs run 35 cents per quart. The grocer orders 49 quarts per day.

a. What is the implied cost of shortage per quart?

b. Why might this be a reasonable figure?

38 Demand for devil's food whipped-cream layer cake at a local pastry shop can be approximated using a Poisson distribution with a mean of six per day. The manager estimates it costs $9 to prepare each cake. Fresh cakes sell for $12. Day-old cakes sell for $9 each. What stocking level is appropriate if one-half of the day-old cakes are sold and the rest thrown out?

39 Burger Prince buys top-grade ground beef for $1.00 per pound. A large sign over the entrance guarantees that the meat is fresh daily. Any leftover meat is sold to the local high school cafeteria for 80 cents per pound. Four hamburgers can be prepared from each pound of meat. Burgers sell for 60 cents each. Labor, overhead, meat, buns, and condiments cost 50 cents per burger. Demand is normally distributed with a mean of 400 pounds per day and a standard deviation of 50 pounds per day. What daily order quantity is optimal? (Hint: Shortage cost must be in dollars per pound.)

40 Demand for rug-cleaning machines at Clyde's U-Rent-It is shown in the following table. Machines are rented by the day only. Profit on the rug cleaners is $10 per day. Clyde has four rug-cleaning machines.

DEMAND	FREQUENCY
0	.30
1	.20
2	.20
3	.15
4	.10
5	.05
	1.00

a. Assuming that Clyde's stocking decision is optimal, what is the implied range of excess cost per machine?

b. Your answer from part *a* has been presented to Clyde, who protests that the amount is too low. Does this suggest an increase or a decrease in the number of rug machines he stocks? Explain.

c. Suppose now that the $10 mentioned as profit is instead the excess cost per day for each machine and that the shortage cost is unknown. Assuming that the optimal number of machines is four, what is the implied range of shortage cost per machine?

41 A manager is going to purchase new processing equipment and must decide on the number of spare parts to order with the new equipment. The spares cost $200 each, and any unused spares will have an expected salvage value of $50 each. The probability of usage can be described by this distribution:

NUMBER	0	1	2	3
PROBABILITY	.10	.50	.25	.15

If a part fails and a spare is not available, two days will be needed to obtain a replacement and install it. The cost for idle equipment is $500 per day. What quantity of spares should be ordered?

42 A Las Vegas supermarket bakery must decide how many wedding cakes to prepare for the upcoming weekend. Cakes cost $33 each to make, and they sell for $60 each. Unsold cakes are reduced to half-price on Monday, and typically one-third of those are sold. Any that remain are donated to a nearby senior center. Analysis of recent demand resulted in the following table:

DEMAND	0	1	2	3
PROBABILITY	.15	.35	.30	.20

How many cakes should be prepared to maximize expected profit?

43 Offwego Airlines has a daily flight from Chicago to Las Vegas. On average, 18 ticket holders cancel their reservations, so the company intentionally overbooks the flight. Cancellations can be described by a normal distribution with a mean of 18 passengers and a standard deviation of 4.55 passengers. Profit per passenger is $99. If a passenger arrives but cannot board due to overbooking, the company policy is to provide a cash payment of $200. How many tickets should be overbooked to maximize expected profit?

44 Caring Hospital's dispensary reorders doses of a drug when the supply on hand falls to 18 units. Lead time for resupply is three days. Given the typical usage over the last 10 days, what service level is achieved with the hospital's reorder policy? Hint: Use Formula 5.13.

DAY	1	2	3	4	5	6	7	8	9	10
UNITS	3	4	7	5	5	6	4	3	4	5

CASE: UPD MANUFACTURING

UPD Manufacturing produces a range of health care appliances for hospital as well as for home use. The company has experienced a steady demand for its products, which are highly regarded in the health care field. Recently the company has undertaken a review of its inventory ordering procedures as part of a larger effort to reduce costs.

One of the company's products is a blood pressure testing kit. UPD manufactures all of the components for the kit in-house except for the digital display unit. The display units are ordered at six-week intervals from the supplier. This ordering system began about five years ago, because the supplier insisted on it. However, that supplier was bought out by another supplier about a year ago, and the six-week ordering requirement is no longer in place. Nonetheless, UPD has continued to use the six-week ordering policy. According to purchasing manager Tom Chambers, "Unless somebody can give me a reason for changing, I'm going to stick with what we've been doing. I don't have time to reinvent the wheel."

Further discussions with Tom revealed a cost of $32 to order and receive a shipment of display units from the supplier. The company assembles 89 kits a week. Also, information from Sara James, in Accounting, indicated a weekly carrying cost of $.08 for each display unit.

The supplier has been quite reliable with deliveries; orders are received five working days after they are faxed to the supplier. Tom indicated that as far as he was concerned, lead-time variability is virtually nonexistent.

QUESTIONS

1 Would using an order interval other than every six weeks reduce costs? If so, what order interval would be best, and what order size would that involve?

2 Would you recommend changing to the optimal order interval? Explain.

CASE: HARVEY INDUSTRIES

BACKGROUND

Harvey Industries, a Wisconsin company, specializes in the assembly of high-pressure washer systems and in the sale of repair parts for these systems. The products range from small portable high-pressure washers to large industrial installations for snow removal from vehicles stored outdoors during the winter months. Typical uses for high-pressure water cleaning include:

Automobiles	Airplanes
Building maintenance	Barns
Engines	Ice cream plants
Lift trucks	Machinery
Swimming pools	

Industrial customers include General Motors, Ford, Chrysler, Delta Airlines, United Parcel Service, and Shell Oil Company.

Although the industrial applications are a significant part of its sales, Harvey Industries is primarily an assembler of equipment for coin operated self-service car wash systems. The typical car wash is of concrete block construction with an equipment room in the center, flanked on either side by a number of bays. The cars are driven into the bays where the owner can wash and wax the car, utilizing high-pressure hot water and liquid wax. A dollar bill changer is available to provide change for the use of the equipment and the purchase of various products from dispensers. The products include towels, tire cleaner, and upholstery cleaner.

In recent years Harvey Industries has been in financial difficulty. The company has lost money for three of the last four years, with the last year's loss being $17,174 on sales of $1,238,674. Inventory levels have been steadily increasing to their present levels of $124,324.

The company employs 23 people with the management team consisting of the following key employees: president, sales manager, manufacturing manager, controller, and purchasing manager. The abbreviated organization chart reflects the reporting relationship of the key employees and the three individuals who report directly to the manufacturing manager.

CURRENT INVENTORY CONTROL SYSTEM

The current inventory control "system" consists of orders for stock replenishment being made by the stockroom foreman, the purchasing manager, or the manufacturing manager whenever one of them notices that the inventory is low. An order for replenishment of inventory is also placed whenever someone (either a customer or an employee in the assembly area) wants an item and it is not in stock.

Some inventory is needed for the assembly of the high-pressure equipment for the car wash and industrial applications. There are current and accurate bills of material for these assemblies. The material needs to support the assembly schedule are generally known well in advance of the build schedule.

The majority of inventory transactions are for repair parts and for supplies used by the car washes, such as paper towels, detergent, and wax concentrate. Because of the constant and rugged use of the car wash equipment, there is a steady demand for the various repair parts.

The stockroom is well organized, with parts stored in locations according to each vendor. The number of vendors is relatively limited, with each vendor generally supplying many different parts. For example, the repair parts from Allen Bradley, a manufacturer of electrical motors, are stocked in the same location. These repair parts will be used to provide service for the many electrical motors that are part of the high-pressure pump and motor assembly used by all of the car washes.

Because of the heavy sales volume of repair parts, there are generally two employees working in the stockroom—a stockroom foreman who reports to the manufacturing manager and an assistant to the foreman. One of these two employees will handle customer orders. Many customers stop by and order the parts and supplies they need. Telephone orders are also received and are shipped by United Parcel Service the same day.

The assembly area has some inventory stored on the shop floor. This inventory consists of low-value items that are used every day, such as nuts, bolts, screws, and washers. These purchased items do not amount to very much dollar volume throughout the year. Unfortunately, oftentimes the assembly area is out of one of these basic items and this causes a significant amount of downtime for the assembly lines.

Paperwork is kept to a minimum. A sales slip listing the part numbers and quantities sold to a customer is generally made out for each sale. If the assembly department needs items that are not stocked on the assembly floor, someone from that department will enter the stockroom and withdraw the necessary material. There

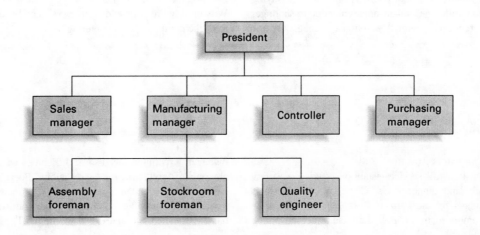

is no paperwork made out for the items needed on the assembly floor.

There were 973 different part numbers purchased for stock last year and those purchases amounted to $314,673. An analysis of inventory records shows that $220,684 was spent on just 179 of the part numbers.

Fortunately for Harvey Industries, most of the items they purchase are stocked by either the manufacturer or by a wholesaler. When it is discovered that the company is out of stock on an item, it generally takes only two or three days to replenish the stock.

Due to the company's recent losses, its auditing firm became concerned about the company's ability to continue in business.

Recently the company sold off excess vacant land adjoining its manufacturing facility to generate cash to meet its financial obligations.

NEW PRESIDENT

Because of the recent death of the owner, the trust department of a Milwaukee Bank (as trustee for the state) has taken over the company's affairs and has appointed a new company president. The new president has identified many problem areas—one of which is improper inventory control. He has retained you as a consultant to make specific recommendations concerning a revised inventory control system. What are your recommendations and their rationale?

SOURCE: CASE "HARVEY INDUSTRIES" BY DONALD CONDIT PRESENTED AT MIDWEST CASE WRITER'S ASSOCIATION WORKSHOP, 1984. COPYRIGHT © 1984 DONALD CONDIT. REPRINTED BY PERMISSION.

CASE: GRILL RITE

Grill Rite is an old-line company that started out making wooden matches. As that business waned, the company entered the electric barbecue grill market, with five models of grills it sells nationally. For many years the company maintained a single warehouse from which it supplied its distributors.

The plant where the company produces barbecue sets is located in a small town, and many workers have been with the company for many years. During the transition from wooden matches to barbecue grills, many employees gave up their weekends to help with changing over the plant and learning the new skills they would need, without pay. In fact, Mac Wilson, the company president, can reel off a string of such instances of worker loyalty. He has vowed to never lay off any workers, and to maintain a full employment, steady rate of output. "Yes, I know demand for these babies (barbecue grills) is seasonal, but the inventory boys will just have to deal with it. On an annual basis, our output matches sales."

Inventory is handled by a system of four warehouses. There is a central warehouse located near the plant that supplies some customers directly, and the three regional warehouses.

The vice president for sales, Julie Berry, is becoming increasingly frustrated with the inventory system that she says "is antiquated and unresponsive." She points to increasing complaints from regional sales managers about poor customer service, saying customer orders go unfilled or are late, apparently due to shortages at the regional warehouse. Regional warehouse managers, stung

by complaints from sales managers, have responded by increasing their order sizes from the main warehouse, and maintaining larger amounts of safety stock. This has resulted in increased inventory holding costs, but it hasn't eliminated the problem. Complaints are still coming in from salespeople about shortages and lost sales. According to managers of the regional warehouses, their orders to the main warehouse aren't being shipped, or when they are, they are smaller quantities than requested. The manager of the main warehouse, Jimmy Joe ("JJ") Sorely, says his policy is to give preference to "filling direct orders from actual customers, rather than warehouse orders that might simply reflect warehouses trying to replenish their safety stock. And besides, I never know when I'll get hit with an order from one of the regional warehouses. I guess they think we've got an unlimited supply." Then he adds, "I thought when we added the warehouses, we could just divide our inventory among the warehouses, and everything would be okay."

When informed of the "actual customers" remark, a regional warehouse manager exclaimed, "We're their biggest customer!"

Julie Berry also mentioned that on more than one occasion she has found that items that were out of stock at one regional warehouse were in ample supply in at least one other regional warehouse.

Take the position of a consultant called in by president Mac Wilson. What recommendations can you make to alleviate the problems the company is encountering?

CASE: FARMERS RESTAURANT

SARAH LUBBERS AND CHRIS RUSCHE
Farmers Restaurant is a full service restaurant offering a variety of breakfast, lunch, and dinner items. Currently, Kristin Davis is the general manager for the Farmers Restaurant located in the Grand Rapids/Wyoming metro area of Michigan. Since becoming

manager, Kristin has faced some difficulties with ordering the right amounts of food items for the restaurant. Because of this, there are some weeks the restaurant has a surplus of menu items that are no longer fresh, and must be discarded. At other times, the restaurant has experienced shortages of some items. The fact that inventory accounts for an average cost of 26% of the restaurant's total revenues underscores the importance of managing inventory. Kristin would like to find a way to ensure that she is maintaining the proper amount of inventory. Customer counts at Kristin's restaurant have been declining recently, so one of Kristin's greatest focuses is to keep current customers and attract new customers. She believes that a key aspect of this is having all of the items on the menu in stock.

The restaurant industry is competitive. In the Grand Rapids/Wyoming metro area alone there are over 1,600 restaurants. Some of Farmers Restaurant's most serious competitors are IHOP, Applebee's, and Big Boy, all of which are located within 20 miles of the Farmers Restaurant, so customers have many alternatives from which to choose.

Online inventory systems are used to assist restaurant managers in determining on-hand inventory and gauging how well the restaurant is controlling food costs. The fiscal week for Farmers Restaurant starts on Thursday and ends on Wednesday of the following week. Each Wednesday, the manager physically counts the inventory on hand and enters the data into the online inventory system. The computer software system then compares the on-hand inventory for that week, the amount of food ordered, and the inventory on hand for the end of the previous week with the sales for the current week. By doing so, it is able to determine a total food cost. The manager compares this cost with the benchmark cost to see how well the restaurant has been managing its inventory. This is one of the most important numbers to managers at the Farmers Restaurant because it accounts for approximately 30% of total costs in terms of a store's cost structure.

The computer software system also compares the total cost of food on hand with the total amount of sales for that week and computes a percentage of on-hand inventories. As a guideline, the company has set a standard of having between 29% and 36% for its on-hand inventory level. The company feels that this level of inventory is an appropriate average to ensure quality food that is fresh and within expiration. Lastly, it is better to keep the inventory at a minimum level to ensure the accuracy and ease of inventory counts.

The Farmers Restaurant Kristin manages has been running above average in terms of food costs. For this reason, her boss has become concerned with the performance of the ordering system she is using at her restaurant. Kristen has been using her intutition to decide how much product to order despite the fact that the product order sheets provide a moving average usage of each product. Kristin bases her inventory management on her intuition because she does not understand how to utilize the moving average forecasting technique when placing orders. An additional complication with ordering inventory is that each item is packed in multiple quantities, so she cannot order the exact amount that she needs. Her boss requested that she create a more accurate way of ordering food and to report back to him in one month. Kristin is worried that if she cuts inventory levels too low she will run out of products which may result in a decrease in customer counts.

After Kristin met with her boss, she began to think about what changes she could make. She knows that inventory has been a weak point for her, but she remembers one of her employees talking about inventory management from one of his college courses. Kristin decides to ask the employee if he would be willing to help her try and come up with a better way for her to order products. Kristin tells him how the ordering system works, shows him the ordering form, and relates the above information.

Suppose you have been asked to work with Kristen to improve inventory ordering.

QUESTIONS

1   Describe the importance of inventory management as it relates to the Farmers Restaurant.
2   What ordering system would be best for this situation?
3   Given the following information, provide an example of how much of Farmers Sausage Gravy Mix should be ordered. You are doing the order for Thursday. Also, Kristen would like a service level of 95%, and you have found that there is a standard deviation of 3.5 units per week, and a moving average weekly demand of 35 servings. The gravy mix comes in packs of two servings. There are currently three packs in inventory.
4   Given the above information and an on-hand inventory of 12, determine the risk of stock out at the end of initial lead time and at the end of the second lead time.
5   The supplier Kristen uses is located in Ohio. Why might Kristen consider dealing with a nearby supplier instead of the one in Ohio? What reasons might there be for not switching suppliers?

OPERATIONS TOUR: BRUEGGER'S BAGEL BAKERY

www.brueggers.com

Bruegger's Bagel Bakery makes and sells a variety of bagels, including plain, onion, poppyseed, and cinnamon raisin, as well as assorted flavors of cream cheese. Bagels are the major source of revenue for the company.

The bagel business is a $3 billion industry. Bagels are very popular with consumers. Not only are they relatively low in fat, they are filling, and they taste good! Investors like the bagel industry because it can be highly profitable: it only costs about $.10 to make a bagel, and they can be sold for $.50 each or more. Although some bagel companies have done poorly in recent years, due mainly to poor management, Bruegger's business is booming; it is number one nationally, with over 450 shops that sell bagels, coffee, and bagel sandwiches for takeout or on-premise consumption. Many stores in the Bruegger's chain generate an average of $800,000 in sales annually.

Production of bagels is done in batches, according to flavor, with each flavor being produced on a daily basis. Production of bagels at Bruegger's begins at a processing plant, where the

(continued)

(concluded)

basic ingredients of flour, water, yeast, and flavorings are combined in a special mixing machine. After the dough has been thoroughly mixed, it is transferred to another machine that shapes the dough into individual bagels. Once the bagels have been formed, they are loaded onto refrigerated trucks for shipping to individual stores. When the bagels reach a store, they are unloaded from the trucks and temporarily stored while they rise. The final two steps of processing involve boiling the bagels in a kettle of water and malt for one minute, and then baking the bagels in an oven for approximately 15 minutes.

The process is depicted in the figure.

Quality is an important feature of a successful business. Customers judge the quality of bagels by their appearance (size, shape, and shine), taste, and consistency. Customers are also sensitive to the service they receive when they make their purchases. Bruegger's devotes careful attention to quality at every stage of operation, from choosing suppliers of ingredients, careful monitoring of ingredients, and keeping equipment in good operating condition to monitoring output at each step in the process. At the stores, employees are instructed to watch for deformed bagels and to remove them when they find them. (Deformed bagels are returned to a processing plant where they are sliced into bagel chips, packaged, and then taken back to the stores for sale, thereby reducing the scrap rate.) Employees who work in the stores are carefully chosen and then trained so that they are competent to operate the necessary equipment in the stores and to provide the desired level of service to customers.

The company operates with minimal inventories of raw materials and inventories of partially completed bagels at the plant and very little inventory of bagels at the stores. One reason for this is to maintain a high degree of freshness in the final product by continually supplying fresh product to the stores. A second reason is to keep costs down; minimal inventories mean less space is needed for storage.

Questions

1   Bruegger's maintains relatively little inventory at either its plants or its retail stores. List the benefits and risks of this policy.

2   Quality is very important to Bruegger's.

   a. What features of bagels do customers look at to judge their quality?

   b. At what points in the production process do workers check bagel quality?

   c. List the steps in the production process, beginning with purchasing ingredients, and ending with the sale, and state how quality can be positively affected at each step.

3   Which inventory models could be used for ordering the ingredients for bagels? Which model do you think would be most appropriate for deciding how many bagels to make in a given batch?

4   Bruegger's has bagel-making machines at its plants. Another possibility would be to have a bagel-making machine at each store. What advantages does each alternative have?

Processing plant   A retail store

OPERATIONS TOUR: PSC, INC.

www.pscnet.com

PSC designs and produces a variety of laser bar code scanning devices. The products include handheld bar code readers, high-speed fixed-position industrial scanners, and retail checkout scanners as well as a full line of accessories, software, and supplies to support its products. Headquartered in Eugene, Oregon, the company has manufacturing facilities in Eugene and Paris, France, with roughly 1,200 employees worldwide.

PRODUCTS

Bar code scanners are designed for a variety of situations that can involve long-range scanning, reading small bar codes, and performing high-speed scans. They are used extensively in industry, business, and government to manage and control the entire supply chain, which includes suppliers, production, warehousing, distribution, retail sales, and service. Examples of bar code readers include the familiar point-of-sale scanners encountered at supermarkets and other retail stores. They come in a variety of forms, ranging from handheld to built-in models. High-speed, unattended scanners are used for automated material handling and sorting. Typical installations include high-volume distribution centers such as JC Penney's catalog operation and airport baggage handling systems. The company also produces "reader engines" that it supplies to other companies for use in their products. These may be as small as 1.2 cubic inches. One application for an "engine product" is found in lottery ticket validation machines. Use of bar code readers has greatly increased the speed and accuracy of data collection, resulting in increased productivity, improved production and inventory tracking and control, and improved market information.

OPERATIONS

Forecasting Forecasting is not a significant activity at PSC due to several factors. There is high standardization of scanner components, which creates stability in usage requirements. Supplier lead times are relatively short, often only a few days. Orders are typically small; 70 percent of all orders are for 10 units or less. There is a fair degree of production flexibility, particularly in terms of product customization. As a result of these factors, the company relies mainly on short-term, moving average forecasts.

Product Design PSC has developed a robust design in many of its products, enabling them to perform effectively under a broad range of operating conditions. For example, many of its handheld scanners can operate at temperatures ranging from $-22°F$ to $120°F$, and can withstand drops onto concrete surfaces from heights up to six feet and still function. This has enabled the company to offer warranties ranging from 24 to 36 months, far exceeding the industry standard of 3 to 12 months.

Layout PSC has developed an efficient production layout that consists of assembly lines and work centers. The assembly lines handle standardized production and subassemblies and the work centers handle final assembly and customization of products. Assembly lines are U-shaped to facilitate communication among workers. The work centers are designed for production flexibility; they can be reconfigured in about four hours. Work centers are staffed by teams of three to six cross-trained workers who are responsible for an order from start to finish.

The Production Process Production involves a combination of assembly line and batch processing that provides high volume and flexibility to customized individual orders. Because of the high standardization among the internal components of different scanners, many of the subassemblies can be produced on assembly lines. Customization is done primarily on the external portion of various products according to customer specification.

The production process for scanner engines is depicted in the process flowchart shown in the figure. The process begins when an order is received from a customer. The order is then configured according to customer specifications. Next it is entered into the computer to obtain a bill of materials (BOM), and the order is transmitted to production control so that it can be scheduled for production. A "traveler" packet containing product specifications and the BOM is created. It will accompany the order throughout the process.

The traveler is sent to the "kitting" area where standard parts and any customized parts are obtained and placed into a bin ("kit") and then placed in a flow rack until the assigned work center is ready for the job (i.e., a pull system).

The next phase of the process transforms unprogrammed, panelized circuit boards into programmed boards. The boards first pass through a screen printer which uses a stencil to coat the boards with a solder paste. Next the boards pass through a chip mounter which enters values for the smaller, passive components of the circuit board at a rate of 25,000 parts per hour. A second mounter enters values for the larger, programmable components at a rate of 7,000 parts per hour. The slower rate for the larger components is offset by the fact that there are fewer of those components. The process ends up being balanced, and no bottlenecks occur.

The programmed boards move by conveyor to a station for visual inspection. Rejects are returned to the chip mounter area, and boards that pass are sent through an oven to solidify the solder, making the programming permanent. The circuit boards are then removed from the panels and placed into the kit. The kits are then taken to designated work centers for customization and placement in scanner engines.

Work centers typically have builders, computer operators, and a tester. A builder mounts the laser diodes on the circuit board and passes it to a computer operator who downloads the customer specifications into the microprocessor of the scan engine. The operator also mounts the optical components and adjusts them for the design of the scanner (e.g., long-range scanning). Next, the engine goes to the tester, who checks to make sure that the scanner is capable of reading bar codes and laser characteristics. Engines that fail are sent for repair and later retested. If the engine fails a second time, it is either returned for further repair or scrapped. Engines which pass are placed in an electrostatic bag which protects them from static electricity that could damage the programming.

Engines are then sent to Audit for another check for performance quality.

(continued)

(concluded)

PSC Inc. Scanner Engine Production Process Flowchart

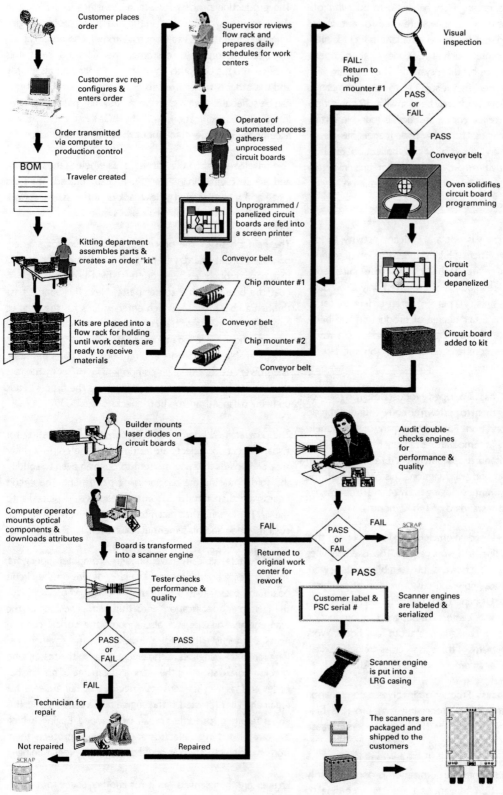

Engines that pass are incorporated into the final product, a serial number is added, along with a label, and the product is sent to the packing area and then shipped to the customer.

Inventory The company uses a variety of methods for inventory management, and it attempts to minimize the amount of inventory. A computer determines component requirements and generates purchase orders for the components for each order, and then appropriate orders for various components from vendors are prepared. However, the company maintains a stock of standard components that are replenished using a reorderpoint system. The company has adopted point-of-use replenishment for some areas of operations, having deliveries come directly to the production floor. Finished products are immediately shipped to the customer, which enhances the company's delivery performance and avoids finished goods inventory.

Suppliers Approximately 40 vendors supply parts and materials to PSC, each of which has been subjected to a multiple-step supplier certification program that includes the supplier completing a self-evaluation questionnaire; an on-site visit of supplier facilities by a team from PSC made up of people from engineering, purchasing, and operations; a probation period; and rating of products using government MIL-STD 105 specifications. Vendor performance is tracked on product quality, delivery, and service.

When an item is removed from inventory, it is scanned into the computer, and this information is transmitted directly to suppliers, along with purchase orders to restock components.

Quality Quality is strongly emphasized at PSC. Employees are trained in quality concepts and the use of quality tools. Training is incorporated on-the-job so that employees can see the practical applications of what they are learning. Employees are responsible for performing in-process quality checks (quality at the source), and to report any defects they discover to their supervisor. Defects are assigned to one of three categories for problem solving:

- Operator/training error. The supervisor notifies a trainer who then provides appropriate retraining.
- Process/equipment problem. The supervisor notifies the manufacturing engineer who is then responsible for diagnosing the cause and correcting the problem.
- Parts/material problem. The supervisor notifies quality assurance, who then notifies the vendor to correct the problem. Defective parts are either scrapped or returned to the vendor.

LEAN PRODUCTION

PSC strives to operate on lean production principles. In addition to emphasizing high levels of quality, production flexibility, low levels of inventories, and having some deliveries come right to the production floor, its organization structure is fairly flat, and it uses a team approach. Still another feature of lean production is that many of PSC's workers are multiskilled. The company encourages employees to master new skills through a pay-for-skill program, and bases hourly pay rates on the number of skills a worker can perform.

BUSINESS STRATEGY

The company has developed what it believes is a strong strategy for success. Strategic initiatives include anticipating customer demand for miniaturization and the ability to customize products; expanding its proprietary technology; and expanding internationally into Western Europe (now accounts for about 35 percent of sales) and the Pacific rim (now accounts for about 10 percent of sales). Several plants or groups are ISO certified, which has been important for European sales. The company intends to continue to expand its product lines through acquisition of other companies.

SELECTED BIBLIOGRAPHY AND FURTHER READING

Hopp, Wallace J., and Mark L. Spearman. *Factory Physics.* 2nd ed. New York: Irwin/McGraw-Hill, 2001.

Peterson, R., and E. A. Silver. *Decision Systems for Inventory Management and Production Planning.* 2nd ed. New York: John Wiley & Sons, 1998.

Zipkin, Paul. *Foundations of Inventory Management.* New York: Irwin/McGraw-Hill, 2000.

FOOTNOTE

1 We can find the minimum point of the total-cost curve by differentiating TC with respect to Q, setting the result equal to zero, and solving for Q. Thus,

1. $\dfrac{dTC}{dQ} = \dfrac{dQ}{2}H + d(D/Q)S = H/2 - DS/Q^2$

2. $0 = H/2 - DS/Q^2$, so $Q^2 = \dfrac{2DS}{H}$ and $Q = \sqrt{\dfrac{2DS}{H}}$

Note that the second derivative is positive, which indicates a minimum has been obtained.a

chapter 6

SIX-SIGMA QUALITY

eneral Electric (GE) has been a major promoter of Six Sigma for more than 10 years. Jack Welch, the legendary and now retired CEO, declared that "the big myth is that Six Sigma is about quality control and statistics. It is that—but it's much more. Ultimately, it drives leadership to be better by providing tools to think through tough issues. At Six Sigma's core is an idea that can turn a company inside out, focusing the organization outward on the customer." GE's commitment to quality centers on Six Sigma. Six Sigma is defined on the GE Web site as follows:

First, What is Six Sigma? First, what it is not. It is not a secret society, a slogan or a cliché. Six Sigma is a highly disciplined process that helps us focus on developing and delivering

After reading this chapter you will:

1. Understand total quality management.

2. Describe how quality is measured and be aware of the different dimensions of quality.

3. Explain the define, measure, analyze, improve, and control (DMAIC) quality improvement process.

4. Understand what ISO certification means.

near-perfect products and services. Why "Sigma"? The word is a statistical term that measures how far a given process deviates from perfection. The central idea behind Six Sigma is that if you can measure how many "defects" you have in a process, you can systematically figure out how to eliminate them and get as close to "zero defects" as possible. To achieve Six Sigma Quality, a process must produce no more than 3.4 defects per million opportunities. An "opportunity" is defined as a chance for nonconformance, or not meeting the required specifications. This means we need to be nearly flawless in executing our key processes.

At its core, Six Sigma revolves around a few key concepts.

Critical to Quality:	Attributes most important to the customer
Defect:	Failing to deliver what the customer wants
Process Capability:	What your process can deliver
Variation:	What the customer sees and feels

Stable Operations:	Ensuring consistent, predictable processes to improve what the customer sees and feels
Design for Six Sigma:	Designing to meet customer needs and process capability

In this chapter, we first review the general subject of total quality management and the quality movement. We then develop the basic features and concepts of the Six-Sigma approach to TQM. We then describe the Shingo system, which takes a unique approach to quality by focusing on preventing mistakes. This is followed by a review of ISO 9000 and 14000 standards for quality certification used by many companies throughout the world. Finally, we provide the major steps of external benchmarking for quality improvement.

TOTAL QUALITY MANAGEMENT

Total quality management

Total quality management may be defined as "managing the entire organization so that it excels on all dimensions of products and services that are important to the customer." It has two fundamental operational goals:

1. Careful design of the product or service.
2. Ensuring that the organization's systems can consistently produce the design.

Global

These two goals can only be achieved if the entire organization is oriented toward them—hence the term *total* quality management. TQM became a national concern in the United States in the 1980s primarily as a response to Japanese quality superiority in manufacturing automobiles and other durable goods such as room air conditioners. A widely cited study of Japanese and U.S. air-conditioning manufacturers showed that the best-quality American products had *higher* average defect rates than those of the poorest Japanese manufacturers.[1]

THE MALCOLM BALDRIGE NATIONAL QUALITY AWARD

The Award is given to organizations that have demonstrated outstanding quality in their products and processes. Three Awards may be given annually in each of these categories: manufacturing, service, small business, education, health care, and nonprofit.

Applicants for the Award must submit an application of 50 pages or less that details the processes and results of their activities under seven major categories: Leadership; Strategic Planning; Customer and Market Focus; Measurement, Analysis and Knowledge Management; Workforce Focus; Process Management; and Results. The applications are scored on total points out of 1,000 by the Baldrige Board of Examiners and Judges. High-scoring applications are selected for site visits and Award recipients are selected from this group. The president of the United States traditionally presents the Awards at a special ceremony in Washington, DC. A major benefit to all applicants is the feedback report prepared by Examiners that is based on their processes and practices. Many states have used the Baldrige criteria as the basis of their quality programs. A report, *Building on Baldrige: American Quality for the*

21st Century, by the private Council on Competitiveness, said, "More than any other program, the Baldrige Quality Award is responsible for making quality a national priority and disseminating best practices across the United States."

So severe was the quality shortfall in the United States that improving it throughout industry became a national priority, with the Department of Commerce establishing the Malcolm Baldrige National Quality Award in 1987 to help companies review and structure their quality programs. Also gaining major attention at this time was the requirement that suppliers demonstrate that they are measuring and documenting their quality practices according to specified criteria, called ISO standards, if they wished to compete for international contracts. We will have more to say about this later.

Malcolm Baldrige National Quality Award

The philosophical leaders of the quality movement, notably Philip Crosby, W. Edwards Deming, and Joseph M. Juran—the so-called Quality Gurus—had slightly different definitions of what quality is and how to achieve it (see Exhibit 6.1), but they all had the same general message: To achieve outstanding quality requires quality leadership from senior management, a customer focus, total involvement of the workforce, and continuous improvement based upon rigorous analysis of processes. Later in the chapter, we will discuss how these precepts are applied in the latest approach to TQM—Six Sigma. We will now turn to some fundamental concepts that underlie any quality effort: quality specifications and quality costs.

The Quality Gurus Compared

exhibit 6.1

	CROSBY	DEMING	JURAN
Definition of quality	Conformance to requirements	A predictable degree of uniformity and dependability at low cost and suited to the market	Fitness for use (satisfies customer's needs)
Degree of senior management responsibility	Responsible for quality	Responsible for 94% of quality problems	Less than 20% of quality problems are due to workers
Performance standard/ motivation	Zero defects	Quality has many "scales"; use statistics to measure performance in all areas; critical of zero defects	Avoid campaigns to do perfect work
General approach	Prevention, not inspection	Reduce variability by continuous improvement; cease mass inspection	General management approach to quality, especially human elements
Structure	14 steps to quality improvement	14 points for management	10 steps to quality improvement
Statistical process control (SPC)	Rejects statistically acceptable levels of quality (wants 100% perfect quality)	Statistical methods of quality control must be used	Recommends SPC but warns that it can lead to tool-driven approach
Improvement basis	A process, not a program; improvement goals	Continuous to reduce variation; eliminate goals without methods	Project-by-project team approach; set goals
Teamwork	Quality improvement teams; quality councils	Employee participation in decision making; break down barriers between departments	Team and quality circle approach
Costs of quality	Cost of nonconformance; quality is free	No optimum; continuous improvement	Quality is not free; there is not an optimum
Purchasing and goods received	State requirements; supplier is extension of business; most faults due to purchasers themselves	Inspection too late; sampling allows defects to enter system; statistical evidence and control charts required	Problems are complex; carry out formal surveys
Vendor rating	Yes; quality audits useless	No, critical of most systems	Yes, but help supplier improve

QUALITY SPECIFICATION AND QUALITY COSTS

Fundamental to any quality program is the determination of quality specifications and the costs of achieving (or *not* achieving) those specifications.

DEVELOPING QUALITY SPECIFICATIONS

Design quality

The quality specifications of a product or service derive from decisions and actions made relative to the quality of its design and the quality of its conformance to that design. Design quality refers to the inherent value of the product in the marketplace and is thus a strategic decision for the firm. The dimensions of quality are listed in Exhibit 6.2. These dimensions refer to features of the product or service that relate directly to design issues. A firm designs a product or service to address the need of a particular market.

A firm designs a product or service with certain performance characteristics and features based on what the intended market expects. Materials and manufacturing process attributes can greatly impact the reliability and durability of a product. Here the company attempts to design a product or service that can be produced or delivered at reasonable cost. The serviceability of the product may have a great impact on the cost of the product or service to the customer after the initial purchase is made. It also may impact the warranty and repair cost to the firm. Aesthetics may greatly impact the desirability of the product or service, in particular consumer products. Especially when a brand name is involved, the design often represents the next generation of an ongoing stream of products or services. Consistency in the relative performance of the product compared to the state of the art, for example, may have a great impact on how the quality of the product is perceived. This may be very important to the long-run success of the product or service.

Conformance quality

Conformance quality refers to the degree to which the product or service design specifications are met. The activities involved in achieving conformance are of a tactical, day-to-day nature. It should be evident that a product or service can have high design quality but low conformance quality, and vice versa.

Quality at the source

Quality at the source is frequently discussed in the context of conformance quality. This means that the person who does the work takes responsibility for making sure that his or her output meets specifications. Where a product is involved, achieving the quality specifications is typically the responsibility of manufacturing management; in a service firm, it is usually the responsibility of the branch operations management. Exhibit 6.3 shows two examples of the dimensions of quality. One is a laser printer that meets the pages-per-minute and print density standards; the second is a checking account transaction in a bank.

Dimensions of quality

Both quality of design and quality of conformance should provide products that meet the customer's objectives for those products. This is often termed the product's *fitness for use,* and it entails identifying the dimensions of the product (or service) that the customer wants (that is, the voice of the customer) and developing a quality control program to ensure that these dimensions are met.

exhibit 6.2   The Dimensions of Design Quality

DIMENSION	MEANING
Performance	Primary product or service characteristics
Features	Added touches, bells and whistles, secondary characteristics
Reliability/durability	Consistency of performance over time, probability of failing, useful life
Serviceability	Ease of repair
Aesthetics	Sensory characteristics (sound, feel, look, and so on)
Perceived quality	Past performance and reputation

Examples of Dimensions of Quality

exhibit 6.3

	MEASURES	
DIMENSION	PRODUCT EXAMPLE: LASER PRINTER	SERVICE EXAMPLE: CHECKING ACCOUNT AT A BANK
Performance	Pages per minute Print density	Time to process customer requests
Features	Multiple paper trays Color capability	Automatic bill paying
Reliability/durability	Mean time between failures Estimated time to obsolescence Expected life of major components	Variability of time to process requests Keeping pace with industry trends
Serviceability	Availability of authorized repair centers Number of copies per print cartridge Modular design	Online reports Ease of getting updated information
Aesthetics	Control button layout Case style Courtesy of dealer	Appearance of bank lobby Courtesy of teller
Perceived quality	Brand name recognition Rating in *Consumer Reports*	Endorsed by community leaders

COST OF QUALITY

Although few can quarrel with the notion of prevention, management often needs hard numbers to determine how much prevention activities will cost. This issue was recognized by Joseph Juran, who wrote about it in 1951 in his *Quality Control Handbook*. Today, cost of quality (COQ) analyses are common in industry and constitute one of the primary functions of QC departments.

Cost of quality

There are a number of definitions and interpretations of the term *cost of quality*. From the purist's point of view, it means all of the costs attributable to the production of quality that is not 100 percent perfect. A less stringent definition considers only those costs that are the difference between what can be expected from excellent performance and the current costs that exist.

How significant is the cost of quality? It has been estimated at between 15 and 20 percent of every sales dollar—the cost of reworking, scrapping, repeated service, inspections, tests, warranties, and other quality-related items. Philip Crosby states that the correct cost for a well-run quality management program should be under 2.5 percent.[2]

Three basic assumptions justify an analysis of the costs of quality: (1) failures are caused, (2) prevention is cheaper, and (3) performance can be measured.

The costs of quality are generally classified into four types:

1. **Appraisal costs.** Costs of the inspection, testing, and other tasks to ensure that the product or process is acceptable.
2. **Prevention costs.** The sum of all the costs to prevent defects such as the costs to identify the cause of the defect, to implement corrective action to eliminate the cause, to train personnel, to redesign the product or system, and to purchase new equipment or make modifications.

A GOODYEAR ASSOCIATE INSPECTS A RADIAL TIRE AT THE SAO PAULO, BRAZIL, FACTORY. GOODYEAR PRACTICES BOTH VISUAL AND INTERNAL INSPECTIONS OF TIRES, EVEN PULLING SOME TIRES FROM THE PRODUCTION LINE TO BE X-RAYED.

exhibit 6.4

Quality Cost Report

	CURRENT MONTH'S COST	PERCENTAGE OF TOTAL
Prevention costs		
Quality training	$ 2,000	1.3%
Reliability consulting	10,000	6.5
Pilot production runs	5,000	3.3
Systems development	8,000	5.2
Total prevention	25,000	16.3
Appraisal costs		
Materials inspection	6,000	3.9
Supplies inspection	3,000	2.0
Reliability testing	5,000	3.3
Laboratory testing	25,000	16.3
Total appraisal	39,000	25.5
Internal failure costs		
Scrap	15,000	9.8
Repair	18,000	11.8
Rework	12,000	7.8
Downtime	6,000	3.9
Total internal failure	51,000	33.3
External failure costs		
Warranty costs	14,000	9.2
Out-of-warranty repairs and replacement	6,000	3.9
Customer complaints	3,000	2.0
Product liability	10,000	6.5
Transportation losses	5,000	3.3
Total external failure	38,000	24.9
Total quality costs	$153,000	100.0

3. **Internal failure costs.** Costs for defects incurred within the system: scrap, rework, repair.
4. **External failure costs.** Costs for defects that pass through the system: customer warranty replacements, loss of customers or goodwill, handling complaints, and product repair.

Exhibit 6.4 illustrates the type of report that might be submitted to show the various costs by categories. Prevention is the most important influence. A rule of thumb says that for every dollar you spend in prevention, you can save $10 in failure and appraisal costs.

Often increases in productivity occur as a by-product of efforts to reduce the cost of quality. A bank, for example, set out to improve quality and reduce the cost of quality and found that it had also boosted productivity. The bank developed this productivity measure for the loan processing area: the number of tickets processed divided by the resources required (labor cost, computer time, ticket forms). Before the quality improvement program, the productivity index was 0.2660 [$2,080/($11.23 \times 640$ hours $+ \$0.05 \times 2,600$ forms $+ \$500$ for systems costs)]. After the quality improvement project was completed, labor time fell to 546 hours and the number of forms rose to 2,100, for a change in the index to 0.3088, an increase in productivity of 16 percent.

Service

FUNCTIONS OF THE QC DEPARTMENT

Although the focus of this chapter is on corporatewide quality programs, it is useful to comment on the functions of QC departments.

The typical manufacturing QC department has a variety of functions to perform. These include testing designs for their reliability in the lab and the field; gathering performance data on products in the field and resolving quality problems in the field; planning and budgeting the QC program in the plant; and, finally, designing and overseeing quality control systems and inspection procedures, and actually carrying out inspection activities requiring special

J. D. POWER AND ASSOCIATES INITIAL QUALITY STUDY OF NEW CARS

The J. D. Power and Associates Initial Quality Study[SM] serves as the industry benchmark for new-vehicle quality measured at 90 days of ownership. The study is used extensively by manufacturers worldwide to help them design and build higher quality vehicles and by consumers to help them in their purchase decisions. Initial quality has been shown over the years to be a good predictor of long-term durability, which can significantly impact consumer purchase decisions. The study captures problems experienced by owners in two distinct categories: 1) design-related problems and 2) defects and malfunctions.

1 Exterior
   a Design-related problems: front or sliding doors with handles that are difficult to operate.
   b Defects/Malfunctions: front or sliding doors that are difficult to open or close, excessive wind noise, or paint imperfections—including chips or scratches at delivery.

2 The Driving Experience
   a Design-related problem: too much play or looseness in the steering system, excessive brake dust, or foot pedals that are too close together.
   b Defects/Malfunctions: brakes that pull noticeably, are noisy, or emit excessive brake dust.

3 Features/Controls/Displays
   a Design-related problems: problems with the remote keyless entry system, door locks, or cruise control systems that are difficult to use. Controls that are awkwardly located.
   b Defects/Malfunctions: problems with remote keyless entry systems, door locks, or cruise control systems that are not working properly.

4 Audio/Entertainment/Navigation
   a Design-related problems: audio and entertainment systems with controls that are difficult to use or awkwardly located, or hands-free communication systems that don't recognize commands.
   b Defects/Malfunctions: CD players with loading problems or radios with poor/no reception on AM/FM stations.

5 Seats
   a Design-related problems: forward/backward seat adjustments or memory seat controls that are difficult to understand or use.
   b Defects/Malfunctions: forward/backward seat adjustment or memory seats that are broken or not working properly.

6 Heat, Ventilation and Air Conditioning
   a Design-related problems: a vehicle heater that doesn't get hot fast enough or windows that fog up too often.
   b Defects/Malfunctions: a fan/blower with excessive noise or vents that emit air with a moldy or stale smell.

7 Interior
   a Design-related problems: a glove box or center console that is difficult to use.
   b Defects/Malfunctions: instrument panel or dash lights that are not working or a glove box or center console that is broken or damaged.

8 Engine/Transmission
   a Design-related problems: an engine that loses power when the AC is on or a manual transmission that is hard to operate.
   b Defects/Malfunctions: an engine that runs and then dies/stalls or an automatic transmission that shifts at the wrong time.

SOURCE: DIRECT COMMUNICATION WITH J. D. POWER AND ASSOCIATES.

technical knowledge to accomplish. The tools of the QC department fall under the heading of statistical quality control (SQC) and consist of two main sections: acceptance sampling and process control. These topics are covered in Chapter 6.1.

SIX-SIGMA QUALITY

Six Sigma refers to the philosophy and methods companies such as General Electric and Motorola use to eliminate defects in their products and processes. A defect is simply any component that does not fall within the customer's specification limits. Each step or activity in a company represents an opportunity for defects to occur, and Six-Sigma programs seek to

Six Sigma

reduce the variation in the processes that lead to these defects. Indeed, Six-Sigma advocates see variation as the enemy of quality, and much of the theory underlying Six Sigma is devoted to dealing with this problem. A process that is in Six-Sigma control will produce no more than two defects out of every billion units. Often, this is stated as four defects per million units, which is true if the process is only running somewhere within one sigma of the target specification.

One of the benefits of Six-Sigma thinking is that it allows managers to readily describe the performance of a process in terms of its variability and to compare different processes using a common metric. This metric is defects per million opportunities (DPMO). This calculation requires three pieces of data:

DPMO

1. **Unit.** The item produced or being serviced.
2. **Defect.** Any item or event that does not meet the customer's requirements.
3. **Opportunity.** A chance for a defect to occur.

A straightforward calculation is made using the following formula:

$$DPMO = \frac{\text{Number of defects}}{\text{Number of opportunities for error per unit} \times \text{Number of units}} \times 1,000,000$$

Service

Step by Step

EXAMPLE 6.1

The customers of a mortgage bank expect to have their mortgage applications processed within 10 days of filing. This would be called a *critical customer requirement*, or CCR, in Six-Sigma terms. Suppose all defects are counted (loans in a monthly sample taking more than 10 days to process) and it is determined that there are 150 loans in the 1,000 applications processed last month that don't meet this customer requirement. Thus, the DPMO = 150/1,000 × 1,000,000, or 150,000 loans out of every million processed that fail to meet a CCR. Put differently, it means that only 850,000 loans out of a million are approved within time expectations. Statistically, 15 percent of the loans are defective and 85 percent are correct. This is a case where all the loans processed in less than 10 days meet our criteria. Often there are upper and lower customer requirements rather than just a single upper requirement as we have here. ●

There are two aspects to Six-Sigma programs: the methodology side and the people side. We will take these up in order.

SIX-SIGMA METHODOLOGY

DMAIC
PDCA cycle
Continuous improvement
kaizen

While Six Sigma's methods include many of the statistical tools that were employed in other quality movements, here they are employed in a systematic project-oriented fashion through the define, measure, analyze, improve, and control (DMAIC) cycle. The DMAIC cycle is a more detailed version of the Deming PDCA cycle, which consists of four steps—plan, do, check, and act—that underly continuous improvement. (Continuous improvement, also called kaizen, seeks continual improvement of machinery, materials, labor utilization, and production methods through applications of suggestions and ideas of company teams.) Like Six Sigma, it also emphasizes the scientific method, particularly hypothesis testing about the relationship between process inputs (X's) and outputs (Y's) using design of experiments (DOE) methods. The availability of modern statistical software has reduced the drudgery of analyzing and displaying data and is now part of the Six-Sigma tool kit. The overarching focus of the methodology, however, is understanding and achieving what the customer wants, since that is seen as the key to profitability of a production process. In fact, to get across this point, some use the DMAIC as an acronym for "Dumb Managers Always Ignore Customers."

The standard approach to Six-Sigma projects is the DMAIC methodology developed by General Electric, described below:[3]

1. Define (D)
   - Identify customers and their priorities.
   - Identify a project suitable for Six-Sigma efforts based on business objectives as well as customer needs and feedback.
   - Identify CTQs (critical-to-quality characteristics) that the customer considers to have the most impact on quality.

2. Measure (M)
   - Determine how to measure the process and how it is performing.
   - Identify the key internal processes that influence CTQs and measure the defects currently generated relative to those processes.
3. Analyze (A)
   - Determine the most likely causes of defects.
   - Understand why defects are generated by identifying the key variables that are most likely to create process variation.
4. Improve (I)
   - Identify means to remove the causes of defects.
   - Confirm the key variables and quantify their effects on the CTQs.
   - Identify the maximum acceptance ranges of the key variables and a system for measuring deviations of the variables.
   - Modify the process to stay within an acceptable range.
5. Control (C)
   - Determine how to maintain the improvements.
   - Put tools in place to ensure that the key variables remain within the maximum acceptance ranges under the modified process.

ANALYTICAL TOOLS FOR SIX SIGMA AND CONTINUOUS IMPROVEMENT

The analytical tools of Six Sigma have been used for many years in traditional quality improvement programs. What makes their application to Six Sigma unique is the integration of these tools in a corporatewide management system. The tools common to all quality efforts, including Six Sigma, are flowcharts, run charts, Pareto charts, histograms, checksheets, cause-and-effect diagrams, and control charts. Examples of these, along with an opportunity flow diagram, are shown in Exhibit 6.5 arranged according to DMAIC categories where they commonly appear.

Flowcharts.   There are many types of flow charts. The one shown in Exhibit 6.5 depicts the process steps as part of a SIPOC (supplier, input, process, output, customer) analysis. SIPOC in essence is a formalized input-output model, used in the define stage of a project.

Run charts.   They depict trends in data over time, and thereby help to understand the magnitude of a problem at the define stage. Typically, they plot the median of a process.

Pareto charts.   These charts help to break down a problem into the relative contributions of its components. They are based on the common empirical finding that a large percentage of problems are due to a small percentage of causes. In the example, 80 percent of customer complaints are due to late deliveries, which are 20 percent of the causes listed.

Checksheets.   These are basic forms that help standardize data collection. They are used to create histograms such as shown on the Pareto chart.

Cause-and-effect diagrams.   Also called *fishbone diagrams,* they show hypothesized relationships between potential causes and the problem under study. Once the C&E diagram is constructed, the analysis would proceed to find out which of the potential causes were in fact contributing to the problem.

Opportunity flow diagram.   This is used to separate value-added from non-value-added steps in a process.

Control charts.   These are time-sequenced charts showing plotted values of a statistic, including a centerline average and one or more control limits. It is used here to assure that changes introduced are in statistical control. See Chapter 6.1 for a discussion of the various types and uses of charts for process control.

Other tools that have seen extensive use in Six-Sigma projects are failure mode and effect analysis (FMEA) and design of experiments (DOE).

Failure mode and effect analysis.   This is a structured approach to identify, estimate, prioritize, and evaluate risk of possible failures at each stage of a process. It begins with

exhibit 6.5   Analytical Tools for Six Sigma and Continuous Improvement

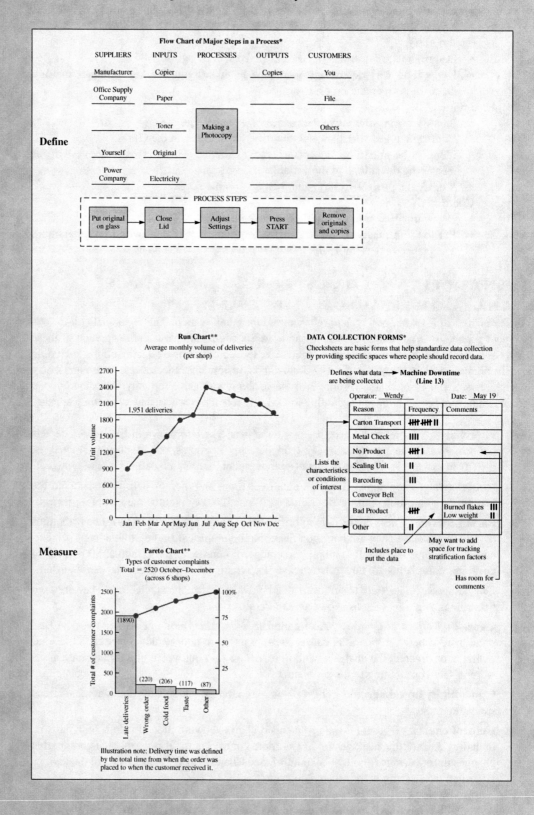

*SOURCE: RATH & STRONG, *RATH & STRONG'S SIX SIGMA POCKET GUIDE*, 2001.
**SOURCE: RAYTHEON SIX SIGMA, *THE MEMORY JOGGER*™ II, 2001.

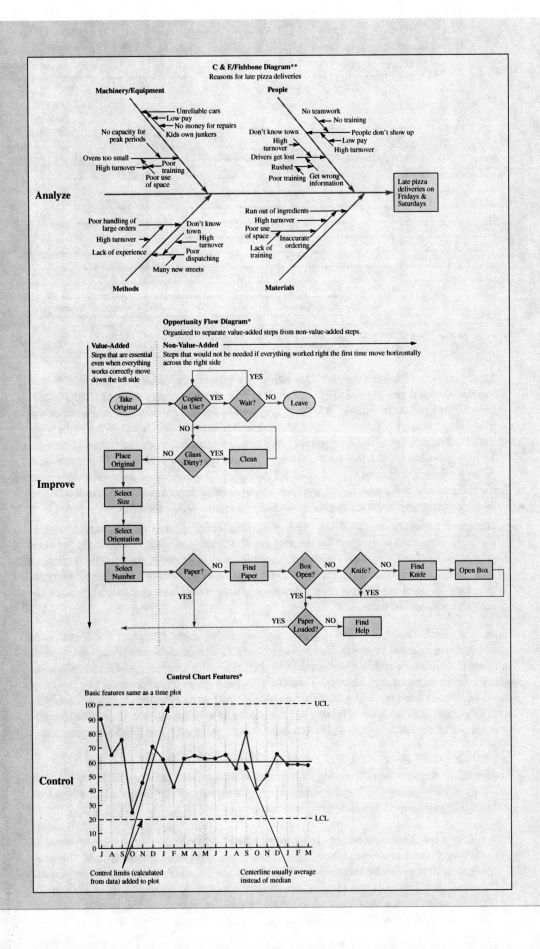

C & E/Fishbone Diagram**
Reasons for late pizza deliveries

Analyze

Opportunity Flow Diagram*
Organized to separate value-added steps from non-value-added steps.

Improve

Control Chart Features*
Basic features same as a time plot

Control

exhibit 6.6   FMEA Form

FMEA Analysis

Project: _____   Date: _____ (original)

Team: _____   _____ (revised)

Item or Process Step	Potential Failure Mode	Potential Effects of Failure	Severity	Potential Cause(s)	Occurrence	Current Controls	Detection	RPN	Recommended Action	Responsibility and Target Date	"After" → Action Taken	Severity	Occurrence	Detection	RPN

Total Risk Priority Number: _____   "After" Risk Priority Number: _____

SOURCE: RATH & STRONG, *RATH & STRONG'S SIX SIGMA POCKET GUIDE*: 2001, P. 31.

identifying each element, assembly, or part of the process and listing the potential failure modes, potential causes, and effects of each failure. A risk priority number (RPN) is calculated for each failure mode. It is an index used to measure the rank importance of the items listed in the FMEA chart. See Exhibit 6.6. These conditions include the probability that the failure takes place (occurrence), the damage resulting from the failure (severity), and the probability of detecting the failure in-house (detection). High RPN items should be targeted for improvement first. The FMEA suggests a recommended action to eliminate the failure condition by assigning a responsible person or department to resolve the failure by redesigning the system, design, or process and recalculating the RPN.

Design of experiments (DOE). DOE, sometimes referred to as *multivariate testing,* is a statistical methodology used for determining the cause-and-effect relationship between process variables (X's) and the output variable (Y). In contrast to standard statistical tests, which require changing each individual variable to determine the most influential one, DOE permits experimentation with many variables simultaneously through carefully selecting a subset of them.

Lean Six Sigma

Lean Six Sigma combines the implementation and quality control tools of Six Sigma with materials management concepts of *lean manufacturing.* Lean manufacturing (discussed in detail in Chapter 8) achieves high-volume production and minimal waste through the use of just-in-time inventory methods. The term *lean* in this context is a focus on reducing cost by lowering raw material, work-in-process, and finished goods inventory to an absolute minimum. Lowering inventory requires a high level of quality as processes need to be predictable since extra inventory is not available. Reducing variability is a key driver in successful lean Six-Sigma programs.

SIX-SIGMA ROLES AND RESPONSIBILITIES

Successful implementation of Six Sigma is based on using sound personnel practices as well as technical methodologies. The following is a brief summary of the personnel practices that are commonly employed in Six-Sigma implementation.

1. *Executive leaders,* **who are truly committed to Six Sigma and who promote it throughout the organization, and** *champions,* **who take ownership of the processes that are to be improved.** Champions are drawn from the ranks of the executives, and managers are expected to identify appropriate metrics early in the project and make certain that the improvement efforts focus on business results. (See the Breakthrough box "What Makes a Good Champion?")

BREAKTHROUGH

WHAT MAKES A GOOD CHAMPION?

At a manufacturing company implementing Six Sigma, a designated champion regularly met with his black belts. At one report-out meeting, a black belt informed him that she needed to purchase and install a table for sorting defects off-line. It would cost about $17,000, but it would provide an alternative to shutting down the entire line, which would cost far more. The controller told her to go through the normal requisition process and she'd have her table in about four months. That delay would have killed the project right then and there: to submit the project to "business as usual" would have shown little real commitment to supporting Six Sigma. So the champion asked for the data that backed up her request, analyzed it, agreed with it, and then got immediate executive sign-off on securing a table the following week.

This is the stuff of a good champion: removing barriers and sending a clear signal that he and upper management are aligned and committed to Six Sigma. The champion does whatever it takes to support the black belts.

SOURCE: GREG BRUE, *SIX SIGMA FOR MANAGERS* (NEW YORK: MCGRAW-HILL, 2002), P. 84.

2. **Corporatewide training in Six-Sigma concepts and tools.** GE spent over a billion dollars training its professional workforce in the concepts. Now, virtually every professional in the organization is qualified in Six-Sigma techniques. To convey the need to vigorously attack problems, professionals are given martial arts titles reflecting their skills and roles: black belts, who coach or actually lead a Six-Sigma improvement team; master black belts, who receive in-depth training on statistical tools and process improvement (they perform many of the same functions as black belts but for a larger number of teams); and green belts, who are employees who have received enough Six-Sigma training to participate in a team or, in some companies, to work individually on a small-scale project directly related to their own job. Different companies use these "belts" in different combinations with sponsors and champions to guide teams.

   Black belts
   Master black belts

   Green belts

3. **Setting of stretch objectives for improvement.**
4. **Continuous reinforcement and rewards.** At GE, before any savings from a project are declared, the black belt in charge must provide proof that the problems are fixed permanently.

THE SHINGO SYSTEM: FAIL-SAFE DESIGN

The Shingo system developed in parallel and in many ways in conflict with the statistically based approach to quality control. This system—or, to be more precise, philosophy of production management—is named after the codeveloper of the Toyota just-in-time system, Shigeo Shingo. Two aspects of the Shingo system in particular have received great attention. One is how to accomplish drastic cuts in equipment setup times by *single-minute exchange of die* (SMED) procedures. The other, the focus of this section, is the use of source inspection and the poka-yoke system to achieve zero defects.

Shingo has argued that SQC methods do not prevent defects. Although they provide information to tell us probabilistically when a defect will occur, they are after the fact. The way to prevent defects from coming out at the end of a process is to introduce controls within the process. Central to Shingo's approach is the difference between errors and defects. Defects arise because people make errors. Even though errors are inevitable, defects can be prevented if feedback leading to corrective action takes place immediately after the errors are made. Such feedback and action require inspection, which should be done on 100 percent of the items produced. This inspection can be one of three types: successive check, self-check, and source inspection. *Successive check* inspection is performed by the next person in the process or by an objective evaluator such as a group leader. Information on defects is immediate feedback for the worker who produced the

exhibit 6.7   Poka-Yoke Example (Placing labels on parts coming down a conveyor)

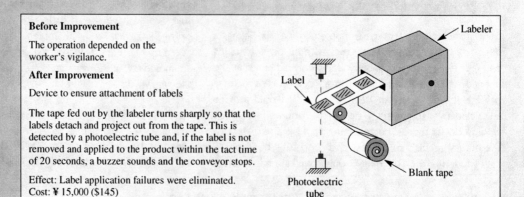

Before Improvement

The operation depended on the worker's vigilance.

After Improvement

Device to ensure attachment of labels

The tape fed out by the labeler turns sharply so that the labels detach and project out from the tape. This is detected by a photoelectric tube and, if the label is not removed and applied to the product within the tact time of 20 seconds, a buzzer sounds and the conveyor stops.

Effect: Label application failures were eliminated.
Cost: ¥ 15,000 ($145)

product, who then makes the repair. *Self-check* is done by the individual worker and is appropriate by itself on all but items that require sensory judgment (such as existence or severity of scratches, or correct matching of shades of paint). These require successive checks. *Source inspection* is also performed by the individual worker, except instead of checking for defects, the worker checks for the errors that will cause defects. This prevents the defects from ever occurring and, hence, requiring rework. All three types of inspection rely on controls consisting of fail-safe procedures or devices (called poka-yoke). Poka-yoke includes such things as checklists or special tooling that (1) prevents the worker from making an error that leads to a defect before starting a process or (2) gives rapid feedback of abnormalities in the process to the worker in time to correct them.

Fail-safe procedures
Poka-yoke

There are a wide variety of poka-yokes, ranging from kitting parts from a bin (to ensure that the right number of parts are used in assembly) to sophisticated detection and electronic signaling devices. An example taken from the writings of Shingo is shown in Exhibit 6.7.

There is a good deal more to say about the work of Shingo. Blasting industry's preoccupation with control charts, Shingo states they are nothing but a mirror reflecting current conditions. When a chemical plant QC manager proudly stated that it had 200 charts in a plant of 150 people, Shingo asked him if "they had a control chart for control charts."[4]

ISO 9000 AND ISO 14000

Global

ISO 9000

ISO 9000 and ISO 14000 are international standards for quality management and assurance. The standards are designed to help companies document that they are maintaining an efficient quality system. The standards were originally published in 1987 by the International Organization for Standardization (ISO), a specialized international agency recognized by affiliates in more than 160 countries. ISO 9000 has become an international reference for quality management requirements in business-to-business dealing, and ISO 14000 is primarily concerned with environmental management.

The idea behind the standards is that defects can be prevented through the planning and application of *best practices* at every stage of business—from design through manufacturing and then installation and servicing. These standards focus on identifying criteria by which any organization, regardless of whether it is manufacturing or service oriented, can ensure that product leaving its facility meets the requirements of its customers. These standards ask a company first to document and implement its systems for quality management and then to verify, by means of an audit conducted by an independent accredited third party, the compliance of those systems with the requirements of the standards.

The ISO 9000 standards are based on eight quality management principles that are defined in the ISO 9000:2000 document. These principles focus on business processes related to the following areas in the firm: (1) customer focus, (2) leadership, (3) involvement of people, (4) process approach, (5) system approach to management, (6) continual improvement, (7) factual approach to decision making, and (8) mutually beneficial supplier relationships. The ISO documents provide detailed requirements for meeting the standards and describe standard tools that are used for improving quality in the firm. These documents are intended to be generic and applicable to any organization producing products or services.

The ISO 14000 family of standards on environmental management addresses the need to be environmentally responsible. The standards define a three-pronged approach for dealing with environmental challenges. The first is the definition of more than 350 international standards for monitoring the quality of air, water, and soil. For many countries, these standards serve as the technical basis for environmental regulation. The second part of ISO 14000 is a strategic approach defining the requirements of an environmental management system that can be implemented using the monitoring tools. Finally, the environmental standard encourages the inclusion of environment aspects in product design and encourages the development of profitable environment-friendly products and services.

In addition to the generic ISO 9000 and ISO 14000 standards, many other specific standards have been defined. The following are some examples:

- QS-9000 is a quality management system developed by DaimlerChrysler, Ford, and General Motors for suppliers of production parts, materials, and services to the automotive industry.
- ISO/TS 16949, developed by the International Automotive Task Force, aligns existing American, German, French, and Italian automotive quality standards within the global automotive industry.
- ISO 14001 environmental standards are applied by automobile suppliers as a requirement from Ford and General Motors.
- ANSI/ASQ Z1.4-2003 provides methods for collecting, analyzing, and interpreting data for inspection by attributes, while Z1.9-2003 relates to inspection by variables.
- TL 9000 defines the telecommunications quality system requirements for the design, development, production, delivery, installation, and maintenance of products and services in the telecommunications industry.

The ISO standards provide accepted global guidelines for quality. Although certification is not required, many companies have found it is essential to be competitive in the global markets. Consider the situation where you need to purchase parts for your firm and several suppliers offer similar parts at similar prices. Assume that one of these firms has been ISO 9000–certified and the others have not. From whom would you purchase? There is no doubt that the ISO 9000–certified company would have the inside track in your decision making. Why? Because ISO 9000 specifies the way the supplier firm operates as well as its quality standards, delivery times, service levels, and so on.

Supply Chain

There are three forms of certification:

1. First party: A firm audits itself against ISO 9000 standards.
2. Second party: A customer audits its supplier.
3. Third party: A "qualified" national or international standards or certifying agency serves as an auditor.

The best certification of a firm is through a third party. Once passed by the third-party audit, a firm is certified and may be registered and recorded as having achieved ISO 9000 status and it becomes a part of a registry of certified companies. This third-party certification also has legal advantages in the European Community. For example, a manufacturer is liable for injury to a user of the product.

The firm, however, can free itself from any liability by showing that it has used the appropriate standards in its production process and carefully selected its suppliers as part of its purchasing requirements. For this reason, there is strong motivation to choose ISO 9000–certified suppliers.

EXTERNAL BENCHMARKING FOR QUALITY IMPROVEMENT

External benchmarking

Global

The quality improvement approaches described so far are more or less inward looking. They seek to make improvements by analyzing in detail the current practices of the company itself. External benchmarking, however, goes outside the organization to examine what industry competitors and excellent performers outside of the industry are doing. Benchmarking typically involves the following steps:

Identify processes needing improvement.   Identify a firm that is the world leader in performing the process. For many processes, this may be a company that is not in the same industry. Examples would be Procter & Gamble using L.L Bean as the benchmark in evaluating its order entry system, or ICL (a large British computer maker) benchmarking Marks and Spencer (a large U.K. clothing retailer) to improve its distribution system. A McKinsey study cited a firm that measured pit stops on a motor racing circuit as a benchmark for worker changes on its assembly line.[5] *Contact the managers of that company and make a personal visit to interview managers and workers.* Many companies select a team of workers from that process as part of the team of visitors.

Analyze data.   This entails looking at gaps between what your company is doing and what the benchmarking company is doing. There are two aspects of the study: one is comparing the actual processes; the other is comparing the performance of these processes according to a set of measures. The processes are often described using flowcharts and subjective evaluations of how workers relate to the process. In some cases, companies permit videotaping, although there is a tendency now for benchmarked companies to keep things under wraps for fear of giving away process secrets.

SUMMARY

How to achieve TQM is no secret any more. The challenge is to make certain that a quality program really does have a customer focus and is sufficiently agile to be able to make improvements quickly without losing sight of the real-time needs of the business. The quality system must be analyzed for its own quality. There is also a need for sustaining a quality culture over the long haul. Some companies (which will remain nameless) that gained a great reputation for quality in the 1980s and 90s simply ran out of gas in their quality efforts—their managers just couldn't sustain the level of enthusiasm necessary for quality to remain a top priority goal. As Tom Peters said, "Most Quality programs fail for one of two reasons: they have system without passion, or passion without system."[6]

KEY TERMS

Total quality management (TQM) Managing the entire organization so that it excels on all dimensions of products and services that are important to the customer.

Malcolm Baldrige National Quality Award An award established by the U.S. Department of Commerce and given annually to companies that excel in quality.

Design quality The inherent value of the product in the marketplace.

Conformance quality The degree to which the product or service design specifications are met.

Quality at the source The person who does the work is responsible for ensuring that specifications are met.

Dimensions of quality Criteria by which quality is measured.

Cost of quality Expenditures related to achieving product or service quality such as the costs of prevention, appraisal, internal failure, and external failure.

Six Sigma A statistical term to describe the quality goal of no more than four defects out of every million units. Also refers to a quality improvement philosophy and program.

DPMO (defects per million opportunities) A metric used to describe the variability of a process.

DMAIC An acronym for the **D**efine, **M**easure, **A**nalyze, **I**mprove, and **C**ontrol improvement methodology followed by companies engaging in Six-Sigma programs.

PDCA cycle Also called the "Deming cycle or wheel"; refers to the plan–do–check–act cycle of continuous improvement.

Continuous improvement The philosophy of continually seeking improvements in processes through the use of team efforts.

Kaizen Japanese term for continuous improvement.

Lean Six Sigma Combines the implementation and quality control tools of Six Sigma with the materials management concept of lean manufacturing with a focus on reducing cost by lowering inventory to an absolute minimum.

Black belts, master black belts, green belts Terms used to describe different levels of personal skills and responsibilities in Six-Sigma programs.

Fail-safe or poka-yoke procedures Simple practices that prevent errors or provide feedback in time for the worker to correct errors.

ISO 9000 Formal standards used for quality certification, developed by the International Organization for Standardization.

External benchmarking Looking outside the company to examine what excellent performers inside and outside the company's industry are doing in the way of quality.

REVIEW AND DISCUSSION QUESTIONS

1   Is the goal of Six Sigma realistic for services such as Blockbuster Video stores?
2   "If line employees are required to work on quality improvement activities, their productivity will suffer." Discuss.
3   "You don't inspect quality into a product; you have to build it in." Discuss the implications of this statement.
4   "Before you build quality in, you must think it in." How do the implications of this statement differ from those in question 3?
5   Business writer Tom Peters has suggested that in making process changes, we should "Try it, test it, and get on with it." How does this square with the DMAIC/continuous improvement philosophy?
6   Shingo told a story of a poka-yoke he developed to make sure that the operators avoided the mistake of putting fewer than the required four springs in a push-button device. The existing method involved assemblers taking individual springs from a box containing several hundred and then placing two of them behind an ON button and two more behind an OFF button. What was the poka-yoke Shingo created?
7   A typical word processing package is loaded with poka-yokes. List three. Are there any others you wish the packages had?

PROBLEMS

1   A manager states that his process is really working well. Out of 1,500 parts, 1,477 were produced free of a particular defect and passed inspection. Based upon Six-Sigma theory, how would you rate this performance, other things being equal?
2   Professor Chase is frustrated by his inability to make a good cup of coffee in the morning. Show how you would use a fishbone diagram to analyze the process he uses to make a cup of his evil brew.
3   Use the benchmarking process and as many DMAIC/CI analytical tools as you can to show how you can improve your performance in your weakest course in school.
4   Prepare a SIPOC flowchart (Exhibit 6.5) of the major steps in the process of boarding a commercial flight. Start the process with the passenger arriving curbside at your local airport.
5   Prepare an opportunity flow diagram for the same process of boarding a commercial flight.
6   The following table lists all costs of quality incurred by Sam's Surf Shop last year. What was Sam's appraisal cost for quality last year?

Annual inspection costs	$ 155,000
Annual cost of scrap materials	$ 286,000
Annual rework cost	$ 34,679
Annual cost of quality training	$ 456,000
Annual warranty cost	$1,546,000
Annual testing cost	$ 543,000

7   Below is a table of data collected over a six-month period in a local grocery store. Construct a Pareto analysis of the data and determine the percentage of total complaints represented by the two most common categories.

All Other	71
Checker	59
General	58
Service Level	55
Policy/Procedures	40
Price Marking	45
Product Quality	87
Product Request	105
Checkout Queue	33
Stock Condition	170

8   A common problem that many drivers encounter is a car that will not start. Create a fishbone diagram to assist in the diagnosis of the potential causes of this problem.

INTERNET ENRICHMENT EXERCISES

1   Visit the Baldrige Award Web site and see who won this year. What quality ideas did the winner demonstrate? What did the winner do that was particularly creative?
2   Visit the Six-Sigma Web site to see how companies are applying the concept.

CASE: HANK KOLB, DIRECTOR OF QUALITY ASSURANCE

Hank Kolb was whistling as he walked toward his office, still feeling a bit like a stranger since he had been hired four weeks before as director of quality assurance. All that week he had been away from the plant at a seminar given for quality managers of manufacturing plants by the corporate training department. He was now looking forward to digging into the quality problems at this industrial products plant employing 1,200 people.

Kolb poked his head into Mark Hamler's office, his immediate subordinate as the quality control manager, and asked him how things had gone during the past week. Hamler's muted smile and an "Oh, fine," stopped Kolb in his tracks. He didn't know Hamler very well and was unsure about pursuing this reply any further. Kolb was still uncertain of how to start building a relationship with him since Hamler had been passed over for the promotion to Kolb's job; Hamler's evaluation form had stated "superb technical knowledge; managerial skills lacking." Kolb decided to inquire a little further and asked Hamler what had happened; he replied, "Oh, just another typical quality snafu. We had a little problem on the Greasex line last week [a specialized degreasing solvent packed in a spray can for the high-technology sector]. A little high pressure was found in some cans on the second shift, but a supervisor vented them so that we could ship them out. We met our delivery schedule!" Because Kolb was still relatively unfamiliar with the plant and its products, he asked Hamler to elaborate; painfully, Hamler continued:

We've been having some trouble with the new filling equipment and some of the cans were pressurized beyond the upper specification limit.

The production rate is still 50 percent of standard, about 14 cases per shift, and we caught it halfway into the shift. Mac Evans [the inspector for that line] picked it up, tagged the cases "hold," and went on about his duties.

When he returned at the end of the shift to write up the rejects, Wayne Simmons, first-line supervisor, was by a pallet of finished goods finishing sealing up a carton of the rejected Greasex; the reject "hold" tags had been removed. He told Mac that he had heard about the high pressure from another inspector at coffee break, had come back, taken off the tags, individually turned the cans upside down and vented every one of them in the eight rejected cartons. He told Mac that production planning was really pushing for the stuff and they couldn't delay by having it sent through the rework area. He told Mac that he would get on the operator to run the equipment right next time. Mac didn't write it up but came in about three days ago to tell me about it. Oh, it happens every once in a while and I told him to make sure to check with maintenance to make sure the filling machine was adjusted; and I saw Wayne in the hall and told him that he ought to send the stuff through rework next time.

Kolb was a bit dumbfounded at this and didn't say much—he didn't know if this was a big deal or not. When he got to his office, he thought again what Morganthal, general manager, had said when he had hired him. He warned Kolb about the "lack of quality attitude" in the plant and said that Kolb "should try and do something about this." Morganthal further emphasized the quality problems in the plant: "We have to improve our quality; it's costing us a lot of money, I'm sure of it, but I can't prove it! Hank, you have my full support in this matter; you're in charge of these quality problems. This downward quality–productivity–turnover spiral has to end!"

The incident had happened a week before; the goods were probably out in the customers' hands by now, and everyone had forgotten about it (or wanted to). There seemed to be more pressing problems than this for Kolb to spend his time on, but this continued to nag him. He felt that the quality department was being treated as a joke, and he also felt that this was a personal slap from manufacturing. He didn't want to start a war with the production people, but what could he do? Kolb was troubled enough to cancel his appointments and spend the morning talking to a few people. After a long and very tactful morning, he learned the following information:

1 **From personnel.** The operator for the filling equipment had just been transferred from shipping two weeks ago. He had no formal training in this job but was being trained by Wayne, on the job, to run the equipment. When Mac had tested the high-pressure cans, the operator was nowhere to be found and had only learned of the rejected material from Wayne after the shift was over.

2 **From plant maintenance.** This particular piece of automated filling equipment had been purchased two years ago for use on another product. It had been switched to the Greasex line six months ago and maintenance completed 12 work orders during the last month for repairs or adjustments on it. The equipment had been adapted by plant maintenance for handling the lower viscosity of Greasex, which it had not originally been designed for. This included designing a special filling head. There was no scheduled preventive maintenance for this equipment and the parts for the sensitive filling head, replaced three times in the last six months, had to be made at a nearby machine shop. Nonstandard downtime was 15 percent of actual running time.

3 **From purchasing.** The plastic nozzle heads for the Greasex can, designed by a vendor for this new product on a rush order, were often found to have slight burrs on the inside rim, and this caused some trouble in fitting the top to the can. An increase in application pressure at the filling head by maintenance adjustment had solved the burr application problem or had at least forced the nozzle heads on despite burrs. Purchasing agents said that they were going to talk to the sales representative of the nozzle head supplier about this the next time he came in.

4 **From product design and packaging.** The can, designed especially for Greasex, had been contoured to allow better gripping by the user. This change, instigated by marketing research, set Greasex apart from the appearance of its competitors and was seen as significant by the designers. There had been no test of the effects of the contoured can on filling speed or filling hydrodynamics from a high-pressured filling head. Kolb had a hunch that the new design was acting as a venturi (carrier creating suction) when being filled, but the packaging designer thought that was unlikely.

5 **From the manufacturing manager.** He had heard about the problem; in fact, Simmons had made a joke about it, bragging about how he beat his production quota to the other foremen and shift supervisors. The manufacturing manager thought Simmons was one of the "best foremen we have . . . he always got his production out." His promotion papers were actually on the manufacturing manager's desk when Kolb dropped by. Simmons was being strongly considered for promotion to shift supervisor. The manufacturing manager, under pressure from Morganthal for cost improvements and reduced delivery times, sympathized with Kolb but said that the rework area would have vented with their pressure gauges what Wayne had done by hand. "But I'll speak with Wayne about the incident," he said.

6 **From marketing.** The introduction of Greasex had been rushed to market to beat competitors, and a major promotional advertising campaign was under way to increase consumer awareness. A deluge of orders was swamping the order-taking department and putting Greasex high on the back-order list. Production had to turn the stuff out; even being a little off spec was tolerable because "it would be better to have it on the shelf than not there at all. Who cares if the label is a little crooked or the stuff comes out with a little too much pressure? We need market share now in that high-tech segment."

What bothered Kolb most was the safety issue of the high pressure in the cans. He had no way of knowing how much of a hazard the high pressure was or if Simmons had vented them enough to effectively reduce the hazard. The data from the can manufacturer, which Hamler had showed him, indicated that the high pressure found by the inspector was not in the danger area. But, again, the inspector had used only a sample testing procedure to reject the eight cases. Even if he could morally accept that there was no product safety hazard, could Kolb make sure that this would never happen again?

Skipping lunch, Kolb sat in his office and thought about the morning's events. The past week's seminar had talked about the role of quality, productivity and quality, creating a new attitude, and the quality challenge; but where had they told him what to do when this happened? He had left a very good job to come here because he thought the company was serious about the importance of quality, and he wanted a challenge. Kolb had demanded and received a salary equal to the manufacturing, marketing, and R&D directors, and he was one of the direct reports to the general manager. Yet he still didn't know exactly what he should or shouldn't do, or even what he could or couldn't do under these circumstances.

QUESTIONS

1 What are the causes of the quality problems on the Greasex line? Display your answer on a fishbone diagram.

2 What general steps should Hank follow in setting up a continuous improvement program for the company? What problems will he have to overcome to make it work?

SOURCE: COPYRIGHT 1981 BY PRESIDENT AND FELLOWS OF HARVARD COLLEGE, HARVARD BUSINESS SCHOOL. CASE 681.083. THIS CASE WAS PREPARED BY FRANK S. LEONARD AS THE BASIS FOR CLASS DISCUSSION RATHER THAN TO ILLUSTRATE EITHER EFFECTIVE OR INEFFECTIVE HANDLING OF AN ADMINISTRATIVE SITUATION. REPRINTED BY PERMISSION OF THE HARVARD BUSINESS SCHOOL.

CASE: APPRECIATIVE INQUIRY—A DIFFERENT KIND OF FISHBONE

The standard cause-and-effect, or fishbone, diagram approach focuses on identifying the root cause of a problem. Finding this cause then becomes an input into developing a solution. On the other hand, improvements aren't always about finding out what went wrong; rather, they may be about identifying what was done right. This is what the AI approach is designed to do. The way it works is

exhibit 6.8   Identifying Excellence Drivers (the Hows of Excellence)

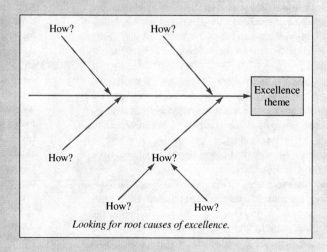

exhibit 6.9   Root Causes of Excellence

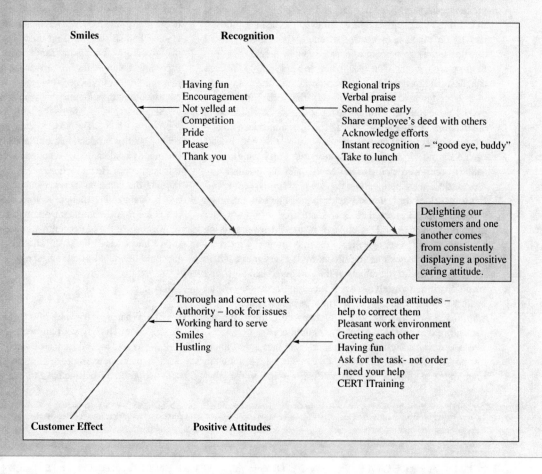

it solicits success stories from employees about how, for example, they delighted their customers. These are then put on the head of the fishbone diagram as the theme for study. (See Exhibit 6.8.) The approach then gathers the causes of success, which are entered on the fishbone as the "hows" of success. One of the particular benefits

of this is that it builds on the unique capabilities of the company rather than copying approaches taken by others.

This approach has been used successfully by Direct Discount Tires executive Steve Fornier Jr., who says, "AI is a simple tool that we can use to find out what and why things are done the way they are done. It gives our employees a chance to think for themselves, find solutions, and execute at higher levels rather than being recipients of a 'do this' 'do that' kind of speech. Because they are figuring out answers for themselves, it drives the entrepreneurial spirit, promotes innovation, and eventually creates new leaders and new best practices from the front line that will continue to keep us 'The Best.' Without this new innovation, we risk becoming stagnated." (The fishbone diagram for Direct Discount Tires is shown in Exhibit 6.9.)

QUESTIONS

1 From a worker's perspective, what do you see as the major benefit of appreciative inquiry compared to standard cause-and-effect analysis?
2 As an interesting exercise, think about your favorite instructor. Develop an appreciative inquiry fishbone diagram that identifies why you feel this instructor is so outstanding.

SOURCE: WILLIAM YOUNGDAHL AND CAREN SIEHL, LECTURE NOTES, AMERICAN GRADUATE SCHOOL OF INTERNATIONAL MANAGEMENT, 2006.

SUPER QUIZ

1 This refers to the inherent value of the product in the marketplace and is a strategic decision for the firm.
2 Relates to how well a product or services meets design specifications.
3 Relates to how the customer views quality dimensions of a product or service.

4 The series of international quality standards.
5 What is the enemy of good quality?
6 A Six-Sigma process that is running at the center of its control limits would expect this defect rate.
7 The standard quality improvement methodology developed by General Electric.

1. Design quality 2. Conformance quality 3. Fitness for use 4. ISO 9000 5. Variation 6. 2 parts per billion units 7. DMAIC cycle

SELECTED BIBLIOGRAPHY

Bemowski, K., and B. Stratton, eds. *101 Good Ideas: How to Improve Just About Any Process.* Washington, DC: American Society for Quality, 1999.

Blakeslee, J. A., Jr. "Implementing the Six Sigma Solution." *Quality Progress,* July 1999, pp. 77–85.

Brue, G. *Six Sigma for Managers.* New York: McGraw-Hill, 2002.

Chowdhury, S. *Design for Six Sigma.* Chicago: Dearborn Trade Publishing, 2002.

Chowdhury, S., and K. Zimmer. *QS-9000 Pioneers—Registered Companies Share Their Strategies for Success.* Burr Ridge, IL: Richard D. Irwin, 1996.

Crosby, P. B. *Quality Is Free.* New York: McGraw-Hill, 1979 (reissue 1992).

————. *Quality Is Still Free.* New York: McGraw-Hill, 1996.

Deming, W. E. *Quality, Productivity and Competitive Position.* Cambridge, MA: MIT Center for Advanced Engineering Study, 1982.

Eckes, G. *Six Sigma Revolution: How General Electric and Others Turned Process into Profits.* New York: John Wiley & Sons, 2001.

Evans, J. R., and W. M. Lindsay. *The Management and Control of Quality.* Cincinnati: South-Western/Thomson Learning, 2002.

Feigenbaum, A. V. *Total Quality Control.* New York: McGraw-Hill, 1991.

Gitlow, H.; A. Oppenheim; and R. Oppenheim. *Quality Management: Tools and Methods for Improvement.* 2nd ed. New York: Irwin/McGraw-Hill, 1995.

Juran, J. M. *Quality Control Handbook.* 3rd ed. New York: McGraw-Hill, 1979.

Juran, J. M., and F. M. Gryna. *Quality Planning and Analysis.* 2nd ed. New York: McGraw-Hill, 1980.

Pande, P. S.; R. P. Neuman; and R. R. Cavanagh. *The Six Sigma Way.* New York: McGraw-Hill, 2000.

————. *The Six Sigma Way Team Fieldbook.* New York: McGraw-Hill, 2002.

Robinson, A. *Modern Approaches to Manufacturing Improvement: The Shingo System.* Cambridge, MA: Productivity Press, 1990.

Shingo, S. *Zero Quality Control: Source Inspection and the Poka-Yoke System.* Stamford, CT: Productivity Press, 1986.

Taormina, T. *Virtual Leadership and the ISO 9000 Imperative.* Englewood Cliffs, NJ: Prentice Hall, 1996.

Welch, J. *Jack: Straight from the Gut.* New York: Warner Business Books, 2001.

FOOTNOTES

1 D. A. Garvin, *Managing Quality* (New York: Free Press, 1988).
2 P. B. Crosby, *Quality Is Free* (New York: New American Library, 1979), p. 15.
3 S. Walleck, D. O'Halloran, and C. Leader, "Benchmarking World-Class Performance," *McKinsey Quarterly,* no. 1 (1991), p. 7.
4 A. Robinson, *Modern Approaches to Manufacturing Improvement: The Shingo System* (Cambridge, MA: Productivity Press, 1990), p. 234.
5 Walleck, O'Halloran, and Leader, "Benchmarking World-Class Performance," p. 7.
6 T. Peters, *Thriving on Chaos* (New York: Knopf, 1987), p. 74.

chapter 6.1

PROCESS CAPABILITY AND SPC

BRIEFING OUTLINE

Assignable variation defined
Common variation defined

290 Variation Around Us
Upper and lower specification or tolerance limits defined

291 Process Capability
Capability index (C_{pk})
Capability index (C_{pk}) defined

296 Process Control Procedures
Statistical process control (SPC) defined
Attributes defined
Process control with attribute measurements:
using p charts
Process control with attribute measurements:
using c charts
Process control with variable measurements:
using $\bar{X}$ and R charts
Variables defined
How to construct $\bar{X}$ and R charts

304 Acceptance Sampling
Design of a single sampling plan for attributes
Operating characteristic curves

307 Summary

314 Case: Hot Shot Plastics Company

After reading this chapter you will:

1. Explain what statistical quality control is.
2. Calculate the capability of a process.
3. Understand how processes are monitored with control charts.
4. Recognize acceptance sampling concepts.

288

This chapter on statistical process control (SPC) covers the quantitative aspects of quality management. In general, SPC is a number of different techniques designed to evaluate quality from a conformance view. That is, how well are we doing at meeting the specifications that have been set during the design of the parts or services that we are providing? Managing quality performance using SPC techniques usually involves periodic sampling of a process and analysis of these data using statistically derived performance criteria.

As you will see, SPC can be applied to both manufacturing and service processes. Here are some examples of the types of situations where SPC can be applied:

- How many paint defects are there in the finish of a car? Have we improved our painting process by installing a new sprayer?
- How long does it take to execute market orders in our Web-based trading system? Has the installation of a new server improved the service? Does the performance of the system vary over the trading day?
- How well are we able to maintain the dimensional tolerance on our three-inch ball bearing assembly? Given the variability of our process for making this ball bearing, how many defects would we expect to produce per million bearings that we make?
- How long do customers wait to be served from our drive-through window during the busy lunch period?

Service

Processes that provide goods and services usually exhibit some variation in their output. This variation can be caused by many factors, some that we can control and others that are inherent in the process. Variation caused by factors that can be clearly identified and possibly even managed is called assignable variation. For example, variation caused by workers not being equally trained or by improper machine adjustment is assignable variation. Variation that is inherent in the process is called common variation. Common variation is often referred to as *random variation* and may be the result of the type of equipment used to complete a process, for example.

Assignable variation

Common variation

As the title of this chapter implies, this material requires an understanding of very basic statistics. Recall from your study of statistics involving numbers that are normally distributed the definition of the mean and standard deviation. The mean ($\overline{X}$) is just the average value of a set of numbers. Mathematically this is

$$\overline{X} = \sum_{i=1}^{N} x_i / N \qquad [6.1.1]$$

where:

x_i = Observed value

N = Total number of observed values

The standard deviation is

$$\sigma = \sqrt{\frac{\sum_{i=1}^{N}(x_i - \overline{X})^2}{N}}$$

[6.1.2]

In monitoring a process using SPC, samples of the process output would be taken and sample statistics calculated. The distribution associated with the samples should exhibit the same kind of variability as the actual distribution of the process, although the actual variance of the sampling distribution would be less. This is good because it allows the quick detection of changes in the actual distribution of the process. The purpose of sampling is to find when the process has changed in some nonrandom way, so that the reason for the change can be quickly determined.

In SPC terminology, *sigma* is often used to refer to the sample standard deviation. As you will see in the examples, sigma is calculated in a few different ways, depending on the underlying theoretical distribution (i.e., a normal distribution or a Poisson distribution).

VARIATION AROUND US

It is generally accepted that as variation is reduced, quality is improved. Sometimes that knowledge is intuitive. If a train is always on time, schedules can be planned more precisely. If clothing sizes are consistent, time can be saved by ordering from a catalog. But rarely are such things thought about in terms of the value of low variability. With engineers, the knowledge is better defined. Pistons must fit cylinders, doors must fit openings, electrical components must be compatible, and boxes of cereal must have the right amount of raisins—otherwise quality will be unacceptable and customers will be dissatisfied.

However, engineers also know that it is impossible to have zero variability. For this reason, designers establish specifications that define not only the target value of something but also acceptable limits about the target. For example, if the aim value of a dimension is 10 inches, the design specifications might then be 10.00 inches ± 0.02 inch. This would tell the manufacturing department that, while it should aim for exactly 10 inches, anything between 9.98 and 10.02 inches is OK. These design limits are often referred to as the upper and lower specification limits or the upper and lower tolerance limits.

Upper and lower specification or tolerance limits

A traditional way of interpreting such a specification is that any part that falls within the allowed range is equally good, whereas any part falling outside the range is totally bad. This is illustrated in Exhibit 6.1.1A. (Note that the cost is zero over the entire specification range, and then there is a quantum leap in cost once the limit is violated.)

Genichi Taguchi, a noted quality expert from Japan, has pointed out that the traditional view illustrated in Exhibit 6.1.1A is nonsense for two reasons:

1. From the customer's view, there is often practically no difference between a product just inside specifications and a product just outside. Conversely, there is a far greater difference in the quality of a product that is the target and the quality of one that is near a limit.
2. As customers get more demanding, there is pressure to reduce variability. However, Exhibit 6.1.1A does not reflect this logic.

Taguchi suggests that a more correct picture of the loss is shown in Exhibit 6.1.1B. Notice that, in this graph, the cost is represented by a smooth curve. There are dozens of illustrations of this notion: the meshing of gears in a transmission, the speed of photographic film, the temperature in a workplace or department store. In nearly anything that can be measured, the customer sees not a sharp line, but a gradation of acceptability away from the "Aim" specification. Customers see the loss function as Exhibit 6.1.1B rather than Exhibit 6.1.1A.

Of course, if products are consistently scrapped when they are outside specifications, the loss curve flattens out in most cases at a value equivalent to scrap cost in the ranges outside

Views of the Cost of Variability

exhibit 6.1.1

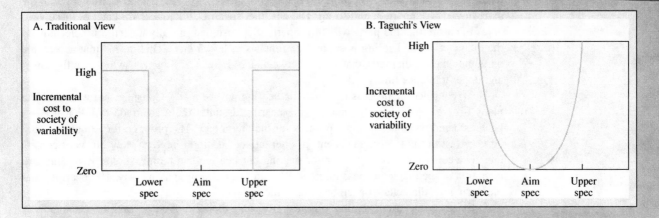

A. Traditional View

Incremental cost to society of variability: High — Zero

Lower spec — Aim spec — Upper spec

B. Taguchi's View

Incremental cost to society of variability: High — Zero

Lower spec — Aim spec — Upper spec

specifications. This is because such products, theoretically at least, will never be sold so there is no external cost to society. However, in many practical situations, either the process is capable of producing a very high percentage of product within specifications and 100 percent checking is not done, or if the process is not capable of producing within specifications, 100 percent checking is done and out-of-spec products can be reworked to bring them within specs. In any of these situations, the parabolic loss function is usually a reasonable assumption.

In the next two sections, we discuss two concepts—process capability and control charts. Process capability relates to how good the process is at making parts when it is running properly. Control charts are used to continuously check that the process is running properly.

PROCESS CAPABILITY

Taguchi argues that being within tolerance is not a yes/no decision, but rather a continuous function. The Motorola quality experts, on the other hand, argue that the process used to produce a good or deliver a service should be so good that the probability of generating a defect should be very, very low. Motorola made process capability and product design famous by adopting Six-Sigma limits. When we design a part, we specify that certain dimensions should be within the upper and lower specification limits.

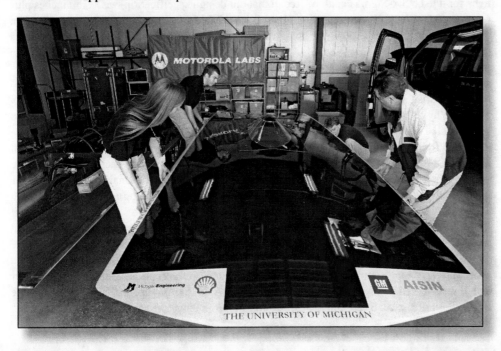

As a simple example, assume that we are designing a bearing for a rotating shaft—say an axle for the wheel of a car. Both the bearing and the axle are subject to many variables—for example, the width of the bearing, the size of the rollers, the size of the axle, the length of the axle, how it is supported, and so on. The designer specifies tolerances for each of these variables to ensure that the parts will fit properly. Suppose that initially a design is selected and the diameter of the bearing is set at 1.250 inches $\pm$ 0.005 inch. This means that acceptable parts may have a diameter that varies between 1.245 and 1.255 inches (which are the lower and upper tolerance limits).

Next, consider the process in which the bearing will be made. Consider that we can select many different processes for making the bearing. Usually there are trade-offs that need to be considered when designing a process for making a part. The process, for example, might be very fast but not very consistent, or alternatively it might be very slow but very consistent. The consistency of a process for making our bearing can be measured by the standard deviation of the diameter measurement. We can run a test by making, say, 100 bearings and measuring the diameter of each bearing in the sample.

Let's say that, after running our test, we find that the average or mean diameter is 1.250 inches. Another way to say this is that the process is "centered" right in the middle of the upper and lower specification limits. In reality, it may be very difficult to have a perfectly centered process like our example. Let's say that the diameter values have a standard deviation or sigma equal to 0.002 inch. What this means is that our process does not make each bearing exactly the same size.

As we will see later in this chapter, normally we monitor a process using control charts such that if the process starts making bearings that are more than three standard deviations (±0.006 inch) above or below 1.250 inches, we stop the process. This means that we will produce parts that vary between 1.244 [this is $1.250 - (3 \times .002)$] and 1.256 [this is $1.250 + (3 \times .002)$] inches. The 1.244 and 1.256 are referred to as the upper and lower process limits. Be careful and do not get confused with the terminology here. The "process" limits relate to how consistent our process is for making the bearing. Our goal in managing the process is to keep it within plus or minus three standard deviations of the process mean. The "specification" limits are related to the design of the part. Recall that, from a design view, acceptable parts have a diameter between 1.245 and 1.255 inches (which are the lower and upper specification limits).

As we can see, our process limits are slightly greater than the specification limits given to us by the designer. This is not good because we will produce some parts that do not meet specifications. Companies with Six-Sigma processes insist that a process making a part be capable of operating so that the design specification limits are six standard deviations away from the process mean. For our bearing process, how small would the process standard deviation need to be for it to be Six-Sigma capable? Recall that our design specification was 1.250 inches plus or minus 0.005 inch. When you think about it, that 0.005 inch must relate to the variation in the process. By dividing 0.005 inch by 6, which equals 0.00083, we can determine our process standard deviation for a Six-Sigma process. So for our process to be Six-Sigma capable, the mean diameter produced by the process would need to be exactly 1.250 inches and the process standard deviation would need to be less than or equal to 0.00083 inch.

We can imagine that some of you are really confused at this point with the whole idea of Six Sigma. Why doesn't our company, for example, just check the diameter of each bearing and throw out the ones with a diameter less than 1.245 or greater than 1.255? This could certainly be done, and for many, many parts 100 percent testing is done. The problem is for a company that is making thousands of parts each hour, testing each critical dimension of each part made can be very expensive. For our bearing, there could easily be 10 or more additional critical dimensions in addition to the diameter. These would all need to be checked. Using a 100 percent testing approach, the company would spend more time testing than it takes to actually make the part! This is why a company uses small samples to periodically check that the process is in statistical control. We discuss exactly how this statistical sampling works later in the chapter.

We say that a process is *capable* when the mean and standard deviation of the process are operating such that the upper and lower control limits are acceptable relative to the upper and lower specification limits. Consider diagram A in Exhibit 6.1.2. This represents the distribution of the bearing diameter dimension in our original process. The average or mean

Process Capability

exhibit 6.1.2

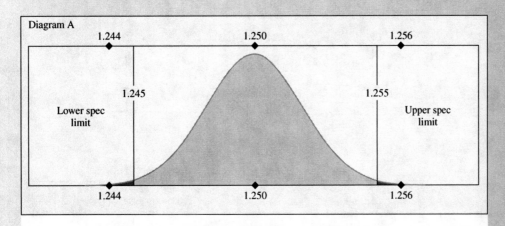

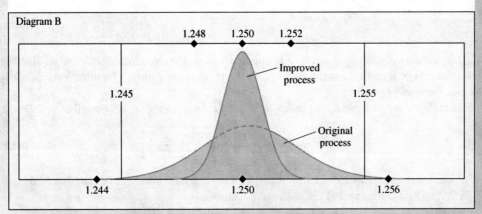

value is 1.250 and the lower and upper design specifications are 1.245 and 1.255, respectively. Process control limits are plus and minus three standard deviations (1.244 and 1.256). Notice that there is a probability (the red areas) of producing defective parts.

If we can improve our process by reducing the standard deviation associated with the bearing diameter, the probability can be reduced. Diagram B in Exhibit 6.1.2 shows a new process where the standard deviation has been reduced to 0.00083 (the orange area). Even though we cannot see it in the diagram, there is some probability that a defect could be produced by this new process, but that probability is very, very small.

Suppose that the central value or mean of the process shifts away from the mean. Exhibit 6.1.3 shows the mean shifted one standard deviation closer to the upper specification limit. This, of course, causes a slightly higher number of expected defects, but we can see that this is still very, very good. We use the *capability index* to measure how well our process is capable of producing relative to the design tolerances. We describe how to calculate this index in the next section.

CAPABILITY INDEX (C_{pk})

The capability index (C_{pk}) shows how well the parts being produced fit into the range specified by the design limits. If the design limits are larger than the three sigma allowed in the process, then the mean of the process can be allowed to drift off-center before readjustment, and a high percentage of good parts will still be produced.

Referring to Exhibits 6.1.2 and 6.1.3, the capability index (C_{pk}) is the position of the mean and tails of the process relative to design specifications. The more off-center, the greater the chance to produce defective parts.

Capability index (C_{pk})

Excel: SPC

exhibit 6.1.3   Process Capability with a Shift in the Process Mean

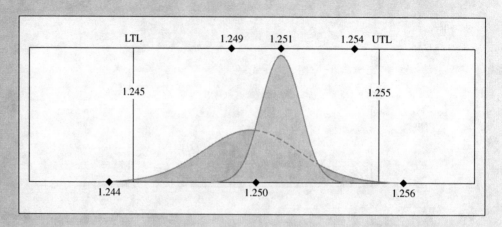

Because the process mean can shift in either direction, the direction of shift and its distance from the design specification set the limit on the process capability. The direction of shift is toward the smaller number.

Formally stated, the capability index (C_{pk}) is calculated as the smaller number as follows:

$$C_{pk} = \min\left[\frac{\overline{X} - \text{LTL}}{3\sigma} \quad \text{or} \quad \frac{\text{UTL} - \overline{X}}{3\sigma}\right] \qquad [6.1.3]$$

Working with our example in Exhibit 6.1.3, let's assume our process is centered at 1.251 and $\sigma = 0.00083$ (σ is the symbol for standard deviation).

$$C_{pk} = \min\left[\frac{1.251 - 1.245}{3(.00083)} \quad \text{or} \quad \frac{1.255 - 1.251}{3(.00083)}\right]$$

$$= \min\left[\frac{.006}{.00249} \quad \text{or} \quad \frac{.004}{.00249}\right]$$

$$C_{pk} = \min[2.4 \quad \text{or} \quad 1.6]$$

$C_{pk} = 1.6$, which is the smaller number.

This tells us that the process mean has shifted to the right similar to Exhibit 6.1.3, but parts are still well within design limits.

At times it is useful to calculate the actual probability of producing a defect. Assuming that the process is producing with a consistent standard deviation, this is a fairly straightforward calculation, particularly when we have access to a spreadsheet. The approach to use is to calculate the probability of producing a part outside the lower and upper design limits given the mean and standard deviation of the process.

Working with our example, where the process is not centered, with a mean of 1.251 inches, $\sigma = .00083$, LTL = 1.245, and UTL = 1.255, we first need to calculate the Z score associated with the upper and lower tolerance (specification) limits. Recall from your study of statistics that the Z score is the standard deviation either to the right or to the left of zero in a probability distribution.

$$Z_{\text{LTL}} = \frac{\text{LTL} - \overline{X}}{\sigma} \qquad Z_{\text{UTL}} = \frac{\text{UTL} - \overline{X}}{\sigma}$$

For our example,

$$Z_{\text{LTL}} = \frac{1.245 - 1.251}{.00083} = -7.2289 \qquad Z_{\text{UTL}} = \frac{1.255 - 1.251}{.00083} = 4.8193$$

An easy way to get the probabilities associated with these Z values is to use the NORMSDIST function built into Excel (you also can use the table in Appendix G). The format for this function is NORMSDIST(Z), where Z is the Z value calculated above. Excel returns the following values. (We have found that you might get slightly different results from those given here, depending on the version of Excel you are using.)

$$\text{NORMSDIST}(-7.2289) = 2.43461\text{E-}13 \quad \text{and} \quad \text{NORMSDIST}(4.8193) = .99999928$$

Interpreting this information requires understanding exactly what the NORMSDIST function is providing. NORMSDIST is giving the cumulative probability to the left of the given Z value. Since $Z = -7.2289$ is the number of standard deviations associated with the lower specification limit, the fraction of parts that will be produced lower than this is 2.43461E-13. This number is in scientific notation, and that E-13 at the end means we need to move the decimal over 13 places to get the real fraction defective. So the fraction defective is .00000000000024361, which is a very small number! Similarly, we see that approximately .99999928 of our parts will be below our upper specification limit. What we are really interested in is the fraction that will be above this limit since these are the defective parts. This fraction defective above the upper spec is $1 - .99999928 = .00000082$ of our parts.

Adding these two fraction defective numbers together we get .00000082000024361. We can interpret this to mean that we only expect about .82 part per million to be defective. Clearly, this is a great process. You will discover as you work the problems at the end of the chapter that this is not always the case.

EXAMPLE 6.1.1

The quality assurance manager is assessing the capability of a process that puts pressurized grease in an aerosol can. The design specifications call for an average of 60 pounds per square inch (psi) of pressure in each can with an upper tolerance limit of 65 psi and a lower tolerance limit of 55 psi. A sample is taken from production and it is found that the cans average 61 psi with a standard deviation of 2 psi. What is the capability of the process? What is the probability of producing a defect?

Step by Step

SOLUTION

Step 1—Interpret the data from the problem

$$\text{LTL} = 55 \quad \text{UTL} = 65 \quad \bar{X} = 61 \quad \sigma = 2$$

Step 2—Calculate the C_{pk}

$$C_{pk} = \min\left[\frac{\bar{X} - \text{LTL}}{3\sigma}, \frac{\text{UTL} - \bar{X}}{3\sigma}\right]$$

$$C_{pk} = \min\left[\frac{61 - 55}{3(2)}, \frac{65 - 61}{3(2)}\right]$$

$$C_{pk} = \min[1, .6667] = .6667$$

Step 3—Calculate the probability of producing a defect

Probability of a can with less than 55 psi

$$Z = \frac{X - \bar{X}}{\sigma} = \frac{55 - 61}{2} = -3$$

$$\text{NORMSDIST}(-3) = .001349898$$

Probability of a can with more than 65 psi

$$Z = \frac{X - \bar{X}}{\sigma} = \frac{65 - 61}{2} = 2$$

$$1 - \text{NORMSDIST}(2) = 1 - .977249868 = .022750132$$

Probability of a can less than 55 psi or more than 65 psi

$$Probability = .001349898 + .022750132 = .024100030$$

Or approximately 2.4 percent of the cans will be defective. ●

The following table is a quick reference for the fraction of defective units for various design limits (expressed in standard deviations). This table assumes that the standard deviation is constant and that the process is centered exactly between the design limits.

DESIGN LIMITS	DEFECTIVE PARTS	FRACTION DEFECTIVE
$\pm 1\sigma$	317 per thousand	.3173
$\pm 2\sigma$	45 per thousand	.0455
$\pm 3\sigma$	2.7 per thousand	.0027
$\pm 4\sigma$	63 per million	.000063
$\pm 5\sigma$	574 per billion	.000000574
$\pm 6\sigma$	2 per billion	.000000002

Motorola's design limit of six sigma with a shift of the process off the mean by 1.5σ ($C_{pk} = 1.5$) gives 3.4 defects per million. If the mean is exactly in the center ($C_{pk} = 2$), then 2 defects per *billion* are expected, as the table above shows.

PROCESS CONTROL PROCEDURES

Process control is concerned with monitoring quality *while the product or service is being produced.* Typical objectives of process control plans are to provide timely information on whether currently produced items are meeting design specifications and to detect shifts in the process that signal that future products may not meet specifications. Statistical process control (SPC) involves testing a random sample of output from a process to determine whether the process is producing items within a preselected range.

Statistical process control (SPC)

Attributes

The examples given so far have all been based on quality characteristics (or *variables*) that are measurable, such as the diameter or weight of a part. Attributes are quality characteristics that are classified as either conforming or not conforming to specification. Goods or services may be observed to be either good or bad, or functioning or malfunctioning. For example, a lawnmower either runs or it doesn't; it attains a certain level of torque and horsepower or it doesn't. This type of measurement is known as sampling by attributes. Alternatively, a lawnmower's torque and horsepower can be measured as an amount of deviation from a set standard. This type of measurement is known as sampling by variables. The following section describes some standard approaches to controlling processes: first an approach useful for attribute measures and then an approach for variable measures. Both of these techniques result in the construction of control charts. Exhibit 6.1.4 shows some examples of how control charts can be analyzed to understand how a process is operating.

PROCESS CONTROL WITH ATTRIBUTE MEASUREMENTS: USING p CHARTS

Measurement by attributes means taking samples and using a single decision—the item is good or it is bad. Because it is a yes or no decision, we can use simple statistics to create a p chart with an upper control limit (UCL) and a lower control limit (LCL). We can draw these control limits on a graph and then plot the fraction defective of each individual sample tested. The process is assumed to be working correctly when the samples, which are taken periodically during the day, continue to stay between the control limits.

Control Chart Evidence for Investigation

exhibit 6.1.4

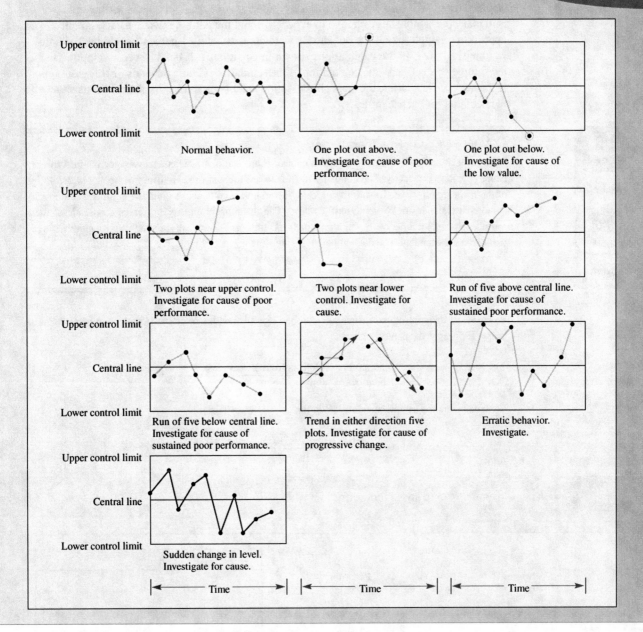

$$\bar{p} = \frac{\text{Total number of defects from all samples}}{\text{Number of samples} \times \text{Sample size}} \qquad [6.1.4]$$

$$s_p = \sqrt{\frac{\bar{p}(1-\bar{p})}{n}} \qquad [6.1.5]$$

$$\text{UCL} = \bar{p} + zs_p \qquad [6.1.6]$$

$$\text{LCL} = \bar{p} - zs_p \qquad [6.1.7]$$

where $\bar{p}$ is the fraction defective, s_p is the standard deviation, n is the sample size, and z is the number of standard deviations for a specific confidence. Typically, $z = 3$ (99.7 percent confidence) or $z = 2.58$ (99 percent confidence) is used.

Size of the Sample   The size of the sample must be large enough to allow counting of the attribute. For example, if we know that a machine produces 1 percent defects, then a sample size of five would seldom capture a defect. A rule of thumb when setting up a *p* chart is to make the sample large enough to expect to count the attribute twice in each sample. So an appropriate sample size if the defect rate were approximately 1 percent would be 200 units.

One final note: In the calculations shown in equations 6.1.4–6.1.7, the assumption is that the sample size is fixed. The calculation of the standard deviation depends on this assumption. If the sample size varies, the standard deviation and upper and lower control limits should be recalculated for each sample.

Step by Step

Service

EXAMPLE 6.1.2: Control Chart Design

An insurance company wants to design a control chart to monitor whether insurance claim forms are being completed correctly. The company intends to use the chart to see if improvements in the design of the form are effective. To start the process, the company collected data on the number of incorrectly completed claim forms over the past 10 days. The insurance company processes thousands of these forms each day, and due to the high cost of inspecting each form, only a small representative sample was collected each day. The data and analysis are shown in Exhibit 6.1.5.

SOLUTION

To construct the control chart, first calculate the overall fraction defective from all samples. This sets the centerline for the control chart.

$$\bar{p} = \frac{\text{Total number of defects from all samples}}{\text{Number of samples} \times \text{Sample size}} = \frac{91}{3000} = 0.03033$$

Next, calculate the sample standard deviation:

$$s_p = \sqrt{\frac{\bar{p}(1 - \bar{p})}{n}} = \sqrt{\frac{0.03033(1 - 0.03033)}{300}} = 0.00990$$

exhibit 6.1.5   Insurance Company Claim Form

Sample	Number Inspected	Number of Forms Completed Incorrectly	Fraction Defective
1	300	10	0.03333
2	300	8	0.02667
3	300	9	0.03000
4	300	13	0.04333
5	300	7	0.02333
6	300	7	0.02333
7	300	6	0.02000
8	300	11	0.03667
9	300	12	0.04000
10	300	8	0.02667
Totals	3000	91	0.03033
Sample standard deviation			0.00990

Finally, calculate the upper and lower control limits. A z-value of 3 gives 99.7 percent confidence that the process is within these limits.

$$\text{UCL} = \bar{p} + 3s_p = 0.03033 + 3(0.00990) = 0.06003$$

$$\text{LCL} = \bar{p} - 3s_p = 0.03033 - 3(0.00990) = 0.00063$$

The calculations in Exhibit 6.1.5, including the control chart, are included in the spreadsheet SPC. ●

Excel: SPC

PROCESS CONTROL WITH ATTRIBUTE MEASUREMENTS: USING c CHARTS

In the case of the p chart, the item was either good or bad. There are times when the product or service can have more than one defect. For example, a board sold at a lumber yard may have multiple knotholes and, depending on the quality grade, may or may not be defective. To monitor the number of defects per unit, the c chart is appropriate.

The underlying distribution for the c chart is the Poisson, which is based on the assumption that defects occur randomly on each unit. If c is the number of defects for a particular unit, then $\bar{c}$ is the average number of defects per unit, and the standard deviation is $\sqrt{\bar{c}}$. For the purposes of our control chart we use the normal approximation to the Poisson distribution and construct the chart using the following control limits.

$$\bar{c} = \text{Average number of defects per unit} \qquad [6.1.8]$$

$$s_p = \sqrt{\bar{c}} \qquad [6.1.9]$$

$$\text{UCL} = \bar{c} + z\sqrt{\bar{c}} \qquad [6.1.10]$$

$$\text{LCL} = \bar{c} - z\sqrt{\bar{c}} \quad \text{or} \quad 0 \text{ if less than } 0 \qquad [6.1.11]$$

Just as with the p chart, typically $z = 3$ (99.7 percent confidence) or $z = 2.58$ (99 percent confidence) is used.

Example 6.1.3

The owners of a lumber yard want to design a control chart to monitor the quality of 2×4 boards that come from their supplier. For their medium-quality boards they expect an average of four knotholes per 8 foot board. Design a control chart for use by the person receiving the boards using three-sigma (standard deviation) limits.

Step by Step

SOLUTION

For this problem, $\bar{c} = 4$, $s_p = \sqrt{\bar{c}} = 2$

$$\text{UCL} = \bar{c} + z\sqrt{\bar{c}} = 4 + 3(2) = 10$$

$$\text{LCL} = \bar{c} - z\sqrt{\bar{c}} = 4 - 3(2) = -2 \to 0 \qquad ●$$

PROCESS CONTROL WITH VARIABLE MEASUREMENTS: USING $\overline{X}$ AND R CHARTS

$\overline{X}$ and R (range) charts are widely used in statistical process control.

In attribute sampling, we determine whether something is good or bad, fits or doesn't fit—it is a go/no-go situation. In variables sampling, however, we measure the actual weight, volume, number of inches, or other variable measurements, and we develop control charts to determine the acceptability or rejection of the process based on those measurements.

Variables

For example, in attribute sampling, we might decide that if something is over 10 pounds we will reject it and under 10 pounds we will accept it. In variable sampling, we measure a sample and may record weights of 9.8 pounds or 10.2 pounds. These values are used to create or modify control charts and to see whether they fall within the acceptable limits.

The four main issues to address in creating a control chart are the size of the samples, number of samples, frequency of samples, and control limits.

Size of Samples   For industrial applications in process control involving the measurement of variables, it is preferable to keep the sample size small. There are two main reasons. First, the sample needs to be taken within a reasonable length of time; otherwise, the process might change while the samples are taken. Second, the larger the sample, the more it costs to take.

Sample sizes of four or five units seem to be the preferred numbers. The *means* of samples of this size have an approximately normal distribution, no matter what the distribution of the parent population looks like. Sample sizes greater than five give narrower control limits and thus more sensitivity. For detecting finer variations of a process, it may be necessary, in fact, to use larger sample sizes. However, when sample sizes exceed 15 or so, using $\overline{X}$ charts with standard deviation σ would be better than using $\overline{X}$ charts with the range R as in Example 6.1.4.

Number of Samples   Once the chart has been set up, each sample taken can be compared to the chart and a decision can be made about whether the process is acceptable. To set up the charts, however, prudence and statistics suggest that 25 or so samples be taken.

Frequency of Samples   How often to take a sample is a trade-off between the cost of sampling (along with the cost of the unit if it is destroyed as part of the test) and the benefit of adjusting the system. Usually, it is best to start off with frequent sampling of a process and taper off as confidence in the process builds. For example, one might start with a sample of five units every half hour and end up feeling that one sample per day is adequate.

Control Limits   Standard practice in statistical process control for variables is to set control limits three standard deviations above the mean and three standard deviations below. This means that 99.7 percent of the sample means are expected to fall within these control limits (that is, within a 99.7 percent confidence interval). Thus, if one sample mean falls outside this obviously wide band, we have strong evidence that the process is out of control.

HOW TO CONSTRUCT $\overline{X}$ AND R CHARTS

If the standard deviation of the process distribution is known, the $\overline{X}$ chart may be defined:

$$\text{UCL}_{\overline{X}} = \overline{\overline{X}} + zs_{\overline{X}} \qquad \text{and} \qquad \text{LCL}_{\overline{X}} = \overline{\overline{X}} - zs_{\overline{X}} \qquad \text{[6.1.12]}$$

where

$S_{\overline{X}} = s/\sqrt{n} = $ Standard deviation of sample means

$s = $ Standard deviation of the process distribution

$n = $ Sample size

$\overline{\overline{X}} = $ Average of sample means or a target value set for the process

$z = $ Number of standard deviations for a specific confidence level (typically, $z = 3$)

An $\overline{X}$ chart is simply a plot of the means of the sample s that were taken from a process. $\overline{\overline{X}}$ is the average of the means.

In practice, the standard deviation of the process is not known. For this reason, an approach that uses actual sample data is commonly used. This practical approach is described in the next section.

An R chart is a plot of the range within each sample. The range is the difference between the highest and the lowest numbers in that sample. R values provide an easily calculated measure of variation used like a standard deviation. An $\overline{R}$ chart is the average of the range of each sample. More specifically defined, these are

$$\overline{X} = \frac{\sum_{i=1}^{n} X_i}{n} \qquad \text{[Same as 6.1.1]}$$

where

$\overline{X} = $ Mean of the sample

$i = $ Item number

$n = $ Total number of items in the sample

$$\overline{\overline{X}} = \frac{\sum_{j=1}^{m} \overline{X}_j}{m} \qquad \text{[6.1.13]}$$

where

$\overline{\overline{X}} = $ The average of the means of the samples

$j = $ Sample number

$m = $ Total number of samples

$$\overline{R} = \frac{\sum_{j=1}^{m} R_j}{m} \qquad \text{[6.1.14]}$$

where

$R_j = $ Difference between the highest and lowest measurement in the sample

$\overline{R} = $ Average of the measurement differences R for all samples

E. L. Grant and R. Leavenworth computed a table (Exhibit 6.1.6) that allows us to easily compute the upper and lower control limits for both the $\overline{X}$ chart and the R chart.[1] These are defined as

$$\text{Upper control limit for } \overline{X} = \overline{\overline{X}} + A_2\overline{R} \qquad \text{[6.1.15]}$$

exhibit 6.1.6

Factor for Determining from $\bar{R}$ the Three-Sigma Control Limits for $\bar{X}$ and R Charts

Excel: SPC

NUMBER OF OBSERVATIONS IN SUBGROUP	FACTOR FOR $\bar{X}$ CHART	FACTORS FOR R CHART	
		LOWER CONTROL LIMIT	UPPER CONTROL LIMIT
n	A_2	D_3	D_4
2	1.88	0	3.27
3	1.02	0	2.57
4	0.73	0	2.28
5	0.58	0	2.11
6	0.48	0	2.00
7	0.42	0.08	1.92
8	0.37	0.14	1.86
9	0.34	0.18	1.82
10	0.31	0.22	1.78
11	0.29	0.26	1.74
12	0.27	0.28	1.72
13	0.25	0.31	1.69
14	0.24	0.33	1.67
15	0.22	0.35	1.65
16	0.21	0.36	1.64
17	0.20	0.38	1.62
18	0.19	0.39	1.61
19	0.19	0.40	1.60
20	0.18	0.41	1.59

Upper control limit for $\bar{X} = \text{UCL}_{\bar{X}} = \bar{\bar{X}} + A_2\bar{R}$
Lower control limit for $\bar{X} = \text{LCL}_{\bar{X}} = \bar{\bar{X}} - A_2\bar{R}$
Upper control limit for $R = \text{UCL}_R = D_4\bar{R}$
Lower control limit for $R = \text{LCL}_R = D_3\bar{R}$

Note: All factors are based on the normal distribution.

$$\text{Lower control limit for } \bar{X} = \bar{\bar{X}} - A_2\bar{R} \qquad [6.1.16]$$

$$\text{Upper control limit for } R = D_4\bar{R} \qquad [6.1.17]$$

$$\text{Lower control limit for } R = D_3\bar{R} \qquad [6.1.18]$$

Step by Step

EXAMPLE 6.1.4: $\bar{X}$ and R Charts

We would like to create $\bar{X}$ and R charts for a process. Exhibit 6.1.7 shows measurements for all 25 samples. The last two columns show the average of the sample $\bar{X}$ and the range R.

Values for A_2, D_3, and D_4 were obtained from Exhibit 6.1.6.

$$\text{Upper control limit for } \bar{X} = \bar{\bar{X}} + A_2\bar{R} = 10.21 + 0.58(0.60) = 10.56$$

$$\text{Lower control limit for } \bar{X} = \bar{\bar{X}} - A_2\bar{R} = 10.21 - 0.58(0.60) = 9.86$$

$$\text{Upper control limit for } R = D_4\bar{R} = 2.11(0.60) = 1.27$$

$$\text{Lower control limit for } R = D_3\bar{R} = 0(0.60) = 0$$

Measurements in Samples of Five from a Process

exhibit 6.1.7

SAMPLE NUMBER	EACH UNIT IN SAMPLE					AVERAGE $\overline{X}$	RANGE R
1	10.60	10.40	10.30	9.90	10.20	10.28	.70
2	9.98	10.25	10.05	10.23	10.33	10.17	.35
3	9.85	9.90	10.20	10.25	10.15	10.07	.40
4	10.20	10.10	10.30	9.90	9.95	10.09	.40
5	10.30	10.20	10.24	10.50	10.30	10.31	.30
6	10.10	10.30	10.20	10.30	9.90	10.16	.40
7	9.98	9.90	10.20	10.40	10.10	10.12	.50
8	10.10	10.30	10.40	10.24	10.30	10.27	.30
9	10.30	10.20	10.60	10.50	10.10	10.34	.50
10	10.30	10.40	10.50	10.10	10.20	10.30	.40
11	9.90	9.50	10.20	10.30	10.35	10.05	.85
12	10.10	10.36	10.50	9.80	9.95	10.14	.70
13	10.20	10.50	10.70	10.10	9.90	10.28	.80
14	10.20	10.60	10.50	10.30	10.40	10.40	.40
15	10.54	10.30	10.40	10.55	10.00	10.36	.55
16	10.20	10.60	10.15	10.00	10.50	10.29	.60
17	10.20	10.40	10.60	10.80	10.10	10.42	.70
18	9.90	9.50	9.90	10.50	10.00	9.96	1.00
19	10.60	10.30	10.50	9.90	9.80	10.22	.80
20	10.60	10.40	10.30	10.40	10.20	10.38	.40
21	9.90	9.60	10.50	10.10	10.60	10.14	1.00
22	9.95	10.20	10.50	10.30	10.20	10.23	.55
23	10.20	9.50	9.60	9.80	10.30	9.88	.80
24	10.30	10.60	10.30	9.90	9.80	10.18	.80
25	9.90	10.30	10.60	9.90	10.10	10.16	.70
						$\overline{\overline{X}} = 10.21$	
							$\overline{R} = 0.60$

Excel: SPC

$\overline{X}$ Chart and R Chart

exhibit 6.1.8

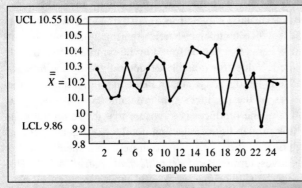

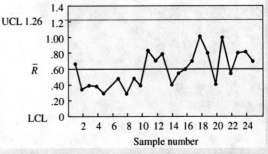

Excel: SPC

SOLUTION

Exhibit 6.1.8 shows the $\overline{X}$ chart and R chart with a plot of all the sample means and ranges of the samples. All the points are well within the control limits, although sample 23 is close to the $\overline{X}$ lower control limit. ●

ACCEPTANCE SAMPLING

DESIGN OF A SINGLE SAMPLING PLAN FOR ATTRIBUTES

Acceptance sampling is performed on goods that already exist to determine what percentage of products conform to specifications. These products may be items received from another company and evaluated by the receiving department, or they may be components that have passed through a processing step and are evaluated by company personnel either in production or later in the warehousing function. Whether inspection should be done at all is addressed in the following example.

Acceptance sampling is executed through a sampling plan. In this section, we illustrate the planning procedures for a single sampling plan—that is, a plan in which the quality is determined from the evaluation of one sample. (Other plans may be developed using two or more samples. See J. M. Juran and F. M. Gryna's *Quality Planning and Analysis* for a discussion of these plans.)

Step by Step

Excel: SPC

EXAMPLE 6.1.5: Costs to Justify Inspection

Total (100 percent) inspection is justified when the cost of a loss incurred by not inspecting is greater than the cost of inspection. For example, suppose a faulty item results in a $10 loss and the average percentage defective of items in the lot is 3 percent.

SOLUTION

If the average percentage of defective items in a lot is 3 percent, the expected cost of faulty items is 0.03 × $10, or $0.30 each. Therefore, if the cost of inspecting each item is less than $0.30, the economic decision is to perform 100 percent inspection. Not all defective items will be removed, however, because inspectors will pass some bad items and reject some good ones.

The purpose of a sampling plan is to test the lot to either (1) find its quality or (2) ensure that the quality is what it is supposed to be. Thus, if a quality control supervisor already knows the quality (such as the 0.03 given in the example), he or she does not sample for defects. Either all of them must be inspected to remove the defects or none of them should be inspected, and the rejects pass into the process. The choice simply depends on the cost to inspect and the cost incurred by passing a reject. ●

A single sampling plan is defined by n and c, where n is the number of units in the sample and c is the acceptance number. The size of n may vary from one up to all the items in the lot (usually denoted as N) from which it is drawn. The acceptance number c denotes the maximum number of defective items that can be found in the sample before the lot is rejected. Values for n and c are determined by the interaction of four factors (AQL, α, LTPD, and β) that quantify the objectives of the product's producer and its consumer. The objective of the producer is to ensure that the sampling plan has a low probability of rejecting good lots. Lots are defined as high quality if they contain no more than a specified level of defectives, termed the *acceptable quality level (AQL)*.[2] The objective of the consumer is to ensure that the sampling plan has a low probability of accepting bad lots. Lots are defined as low quality if the percentage of defectives is greater than a specified amount, termed *lot tolerance percent defective (LTPD)*. The probability associated with rejecting a high-quality lot is denoted by the Greek letter alpha (α) and is termed the *producer's risk*. The probability associated with

ALUMINUM SHEETS ARE EXAMINED UNDER QUALITY CONTROL LIGHTS ON THE ALUMINUM PRODUCTION LINE AT THE ALCOA SZÉKESFEHÉRVÁR, HUNGARY, EXTRUSION PLANT.

Excerpt from a Sampling Plan Table for $\alpha = 0.05$, $\beta = 0.10$

exhibit 6.1.9

c	LTPD ÷ AQL	$n \cdot$ AQL	c	LTPD ÷ AQL	$n \cdot$ AQL
0	44.890	0.052	5	3.549	2.613
1	10.946	0.355	6	3.206	3.286
2	6.509	0.818	7	2.957	3.981
3	4.890	1.366	8	2.768	4.695
4	4.057	1.970	9	2.618	5.426

accepting a low-quality lot is denoted by the letter beta (β) and is termed the *consumer's risk*. The selection of particular values for AQL, α, LTPD, and β is an economic decision based on a cost trade-off or, more typically, on company policy or contractual requirements.

There is a humorous story supposedly about Hewlett-Packard during its first dealings with Japanese vendors, who place great emphasis on high-quality production. HP had insisted on 2 percent AQL in a purchase of 100 cables. During the purchase agreement, some heated discussion took place wherein the Japanese vendor did not want this AQL specification; HP insisted that they would not budge from the 2 percent AQL. The Japanese vendor finally agreed. Later, when the box arrived, there were two packages inside. One contained 100 good cables. The other package had 2 cables with a note stating: "We have sent you 100 good cables. Since you insisted on 2 percent AQL, we have enclosed 2 defective cables in this package, though we do not understand why you want them."

The following example, using an excerpt from a standard acceptance sampling table, illustrates how the four parameters—AQL, α, LTPD, and β—are used in developing a sampling plan.

Step by Step

EXAMPLE 6.1.6: Values of n and c

Hi-Tech Industries manufactures Z-Band radar scanners used to detect speed traps. The printed circuit boards in the scanners are purchased from an outside vendor. The vendor produces the boards to an AQL of 2 percent defectives and is willing to run a 5 percent risk (α) of having lots of this level or fewer defectives rejected. Hi-Tech considers lots of 8 percent or more defectives (LTPD) unacceptable and wants to ensure that it will accept such poor-quality lots no more than 10 percent of the time (β). A large shipment has just been delivered. What values of n and c should be selected to determine the quality of this lot?

SOLUTION

The parameters of the problem are AQL = 0.02, α = 0.05, LTPD = 0.08, and β = 0.10. We can use Exhibit 6.1.9 to find c and n.

First, divide LTPD by AQL ($0.08 \div 0.02 = 4$). Then, find the ratio in column 2 that is equal to or just greater than that amount (4). This value is 4.057, which is associated with $c = 4$.

Finally, find the value in column 3 that is in the same row as $c = 4$ and divide that quantity by AQL to obtain n ($1.970 \div 0.02 = 98.5$).

The appropriate sampling plan is $c = 4$, $n = 99$. ●

OPERATING CHARACTERISTIC CURVES

While a sampling plan such as the one just described meets our requirements for the extreme values of good and bad quality, we cannot readily determine how well the plan discriminates between good and bad lots at intermediate values. For this reason, sampling plans are generally displayed graphically through the use of operating characteristic (OC) curves. These curves, which are unique for each combination of n and c, simply illustrate the probability of accepting lots with varying percentages of defectives. The procedure we have followed in

exhibit 6.1.10

Operating Characteristic Curve for AQL = 0.02, α = 0.05, LTPD = 0.08, β = 0.10

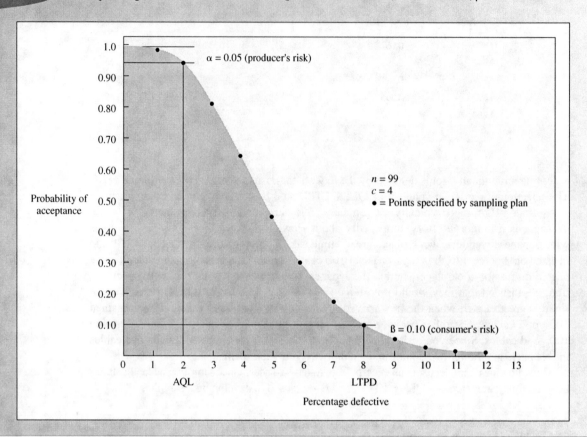

developing the plan, in fact, specifies two points on an OC curve: one point defined by AQL and $1 - \alpha$ and the other point defined by LTPD and β. Curves for common values of n and c can be computed or obtained from available tables.[3]

Shaping the OC Curve A sampling plan discriminating perfectly between good and bad lots has an infinite slope (vertical) at the selected value of AQL. In Exhibit 6.1.10, any percentage defective to the left of 2 percent would always be accepted, and those to the right, always rejected. However, such a curve is possible only with complete inspection of all units and thus is not a possibility with a true sampling plan.

An OC curve should be steep in the region of most interest (between the AQL and the LTPD), which is accomplished by varying n and c. If c remains constant, increasing the sample size n causes the OC curve to be more vertical. While holding n constant, decreasing c (the maximum number of defective units) also makes the slope more vertical, moving closer to the origin.

The Effects of Lot Size The size of the lot that the sample is taken from has relatively little effect on the quality of protection. Consider, for example, that samples—all of the same size of 20 units—are taken from different lots ranging from a lot size of 200 units to a lot size of infinity. If each lot is known to have 5 percent defectives, the probability of accepting the lot based on the sample of 20 units ranges from about 0.34 to about 0.36. This means that as long as the lot size is several times the sample size, it makes little difference how large the lot is. It seems a bit difficult to accept, but statistically (on the average in the long run) whether we have a carload or box full, we'll get about the same answer. It just seems that a carload should have a larger sample size. Of course, this assumes that the lot is randomly chosen and that defects are randomly spread through the lot.

SUMMARY

Statistical quality control is a vital topic. Quality has become so important that statistical quality procedures are *expected* to be part of successful firms. Sampling plans and statistical process control are taken as given with the emphasis shifting to broader aspects (such as eliminating dockside acceptance sampling because of reliable supplier quality, and employee empowerment transforming much of the process control). World-class manufacturing companies expect people to understand the basic concepts of the material presented in this chapter.

KEY TERMS

Assignable variation Deviation in the output of a process that can be clearly identified and managed.

Common variation Deviation in the output of a process that is random and inherent in the process itself.

Upper and lower specification or tolerance limits The range of values in a measure associated with a process that are allowable given the intended use of the product or service.

Capability index (C_{pk}) The ratio of the range of values produced by a process divided by the range of values allowed by the design specification.

Statistical process control (SPC) Techniques for testing a random sample of output from a process to determine whether the process is producing items within a prescribed range.

Attributes Quality characteristics that are classified as either conforming or not conforming to specification.

Variables Quality characteristics that are measured in actual weight, volume, inches, centimeters, or other measure.

FORMULA REVIEW

Mean or average

$$\overline{X} = \sum_{i=1}^{N} x_i / N \qquad [6.1.1]$$

Standard deviation

$$\sigma = \sqrt{\frac{\sum_{i=1}^{N}(x_i - \overline{X})^2}{N}} \qquad [6.1.2]$$

Capability index

$$C_{pk} = \min\left[\frac{\overline{X} - \text{LTL}}{3\sigma}, \quad \frac{\text{UTL} - \overline{X}}{3\sigma}\right] \qquad [6.1.3]$$

Process control charts using attribute measurements

$$\overline{p} = \frac{\text{Total number of defects from all samples}}{\text{Number of samples} \times \text{Sample size}} \qquad [6.1.4]$$

$$s_p = \sqrt{\frac{\overline{p}(1 - \overline{p})}{n}} \qquad [6.1.5]$$

$$\text{UCL} = \overline{p} + zs_p \qquad [6.1.6]$$

$$\text{LCL} = \overline{p} - zs_p \qquad [6.1.7]$$

Process control c charts

$$\overline{c} = \text{Average number of defects per unit} \qquad [6.1.8]$$

$$s_p = \sqrt{\overline{c}} \qquad [6.1.9]$$

$$\text{UCL} = \overline{c} + z\sqrt{\overline{c}} \qquad [6.1.10]$$

$$\text{LCL} = \overline{c} - z\sqrt{\overline{c}} \quad \text{or} \quad 0 \text{ if less than } 0 \qquad [6.1.11]$$

Process control $\overline{X}$ and R charts

$$\text{UCL}_{\overline{x}} = \overline{\overline{X}} + zs_{\overline{x}} \qquad \text{and} \qquad \text{LCL}_{\overline{x}} = \overline{\overline{X}} - zs_{\overline{x}} \qquad\qquad [6.1.12]$$

$$\overline{\overline{X}} = \frac{\sum\limits_{j=1}^{m} X_j}{m} \qquad\qquad [6.1.13]$$

$$\overline{R} = \frac{\sum\limits_{j=1}^{m} R_j}{m} \qquad\qquad [6.1.14]$$

$$\text{Upper control limit for } \overline{X} = \overline{\overline{X}} + A_2\overline{R} \qquad\qquad [6.1.15]$$

$$\text{Lower control limit for } \overline{X} = \overline{\overline{X}} - A_2\overline{R} \qquad\qquad [6.1.16]$$

$$\text{Upper control limit for } R = D_4\overline{R} \qquad\qquad [6.1.17]$$

$$\text{Lower control limit for } R = D_3\overline{R} \qquad\qquad [6.1.18]$$

SOLVED PROBLEMS

SOLVED PROBLEM 1

Excel: SPC

Completed forms from a particular department of an insurance company were sampled daily to check the performance quality of that department. To establish a tentative norm for the department, one sample of 100 units was collected each day for 15 days, with these results:

SAMPLE	SAMPLE SIZE	NUMBER OF FORMS WITH ERRORS	SAMPLE	SAMPLE SIZE	NUMBER OF FORMS WITH ERRORS
1	100	4	9	100	4
2	100	3	10	100	2
3	100	5	11	100	7
4	100	0	12	100	2
5	100	2	13	100	1
6	100	8	14	100	3
7	100	1	15	100	1
8	100	3			

a. Develop a p chart using a 95 percent confidence interval ($1.96s_p$).
b. Plot the 15 samples collected.
c. What comments can you make about the process?

Solution

a. $\bar{p} = \dfrac{46}{15(100)} = 0.0307$

$s_p = \sqrt{\dfrac{\bar{p}(1-\bar{p})}{n}} = \sqrt{\dfrac{0.0307(1-0.0307)}{100}} = \sqrt{0.0003} = 0.017$

$\text{UCL} = \bar{p} + 1.96s_p = 0.031 + 1.96(0.017) = 0.064$

$\text{LCL} = \bar{p} - 1.96s_p = 0.031 - 1.96(0.017) = -0.00232 \text{ or zero}$

b. The defectives are plotted below.

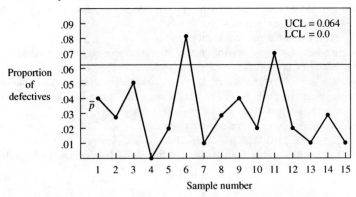

c. Of the 15 samples, 2 were out of the control limits. Because the control limits were established as 95 percent, or 1 out of 20, we would say that the process is out of control. It needs to be examined to find the cause of such widespread variation.

SOLVED PROBLEM 2

Management is trying to decide whether Part A, which is produced with a consistent 3 percent defective rate, should be inspected. If it is not inspected, the 3 percent defectives will go through a product assembly phase and have to be replaced later. If all Part A's are inspected, one-third of the defectives will be found, thus raising the quality to 2 percent defectives.

a. Should the inspection be done if the cost of inspecting is $0.01 per unit and the cost of replacing a defective in the final assembly is $4.00?

b. Suppose the cost of inspecting is $0.05 per unit rather than $0.01. Would this change your answer in *a*?

Solution

Should Part A be inspected?

0.03 defective with no inspection.

0.02 defective with inspection.

a. This problem can be solved simply by looking at the opportunity for 1 percent improvement.

Benefit = 0.01($4.00) = $0.04

Cost of inspection = $0.01

Therefore, inspect and save $0.03 per unit.

b. A cost of $0.05 per unit to inspect would be $0.01 greater than the savings, so inspection should not be performed.

REVIEW AND DISCUSSION QUESTIONS

1 The capability index allows for some drifting of the process mean. Discuss what this means in terms of product quality output.

2 Discuss the purposes of and differences between p charts, c charts and $\overline{X}$ and R charts.

3 In an agreement between a supplier and a customer, the supplier must ensure that all parts are within tolerance before shipment to the customer. What is the effect on the cost of quality to the customer?

4 In the situation described in Question 3, what would be the effect on the cost of quality to the supplier?

5 Discuss the trade-off between achieving a zero AQL (acceptable quality level) and a positive AQL (such as an AQL of 2 percent).

PROBLEMS

1 A company currently using an inspection process in its material receiving department is trying to install an overall cost reduction program. One possible reduction is the elimination of one inspection position. This position tests material that has a defective content on the average of 0.04. By inspecting all items, the inspector is able to remove all defects. The inspector can inspect 50 units per hour. The hourly rate including fringe benefits for this position is $9. If

the inspection position is eliminated, defects will go into product assembly and will have to be replaced later at a cost of $10 each when they are detected in final product testing.

a. Should this inspection position be eliminated?

b. What is the cost to inspect each unit?

c. Is there benefit (or loss) from the current inspection process? How much?

2   A metal fabricator produces connecting rods with an outer diameter that has a 1 ± 0.01 inch specification. A machine operator takes several sample measurements over time and determines the sample mean outer diameter to be 1.002 inches with a standard deviation of 0.003 inch.

a. Calculate the process capability index for this example.

b. What does this figure tell you about the process?

3   Ten samples of 15 parts each were taken from an ongoing process to establish a p chart for control. The samples and the number of defectives in each are shown in the following table:

SAMPLE	n	NUMBER OF DEFECTS IN SAMPLE	SAMPLE	n	NUMBER OF DEFECTS IN SAMPLE
1	15	3	6	15	2
2	15	1	7	15	0
3	15	0	8	15	3
4	15	0	9	15	1
5	15	0	10	15	0

a. Develop a p chart for 95 percent confidence (1.96 standard deviations).

b. Based on the plotted data points, what comments can you make?

4   Output from a process contains 0.02 defective unit. Defective units that go undetected into final assemblies cost $25 each to replace. An inspection process, which would detect and remove all defectives, can be established to test these units. However, the inspector, who can test 20 units per hour, is paid $8 per hour, including fringe benefits. Should an inspection station be established to test all units?

a. What is the cost to inspect each unit?

b. What is the benefit (or loss) from the inspection process?

5   There is a 3 percent error rate at a specific point in a production process. If an inspector is placed at this point, all the errors can be detected and eliminated. However, the inspector is paid $8 per hour and can inspect units in the process at the rate of 30 per hour.

     If no inspector is used and defects are allowed to pass this point, there is a cost of $10 per unit to correct the defect later on.

     Should an inspector be hired?

6   Resistors for electronic circuits are manufactured on a high-speed automated machine. The machine is set up to produce a large run of resistors of 1,000 ohms each.

     To set up the machine and to create a control chart to be used throughout the run, 15 samples were taken with four resistors in each sample. The complete list of samples and their measured values are as follows:

SAMPLE NUMBER	READINGS (IN OHMS)			
1	1010	991	985	986
2	995	996	1009	994
3	990	1003	1015	1008
4	1015	1020	1009	998
5	1013	1019	1005	993
6	994	1001	994	1005
7	989	992	982	1020
8	1001	986	996	996
9	1006	989	1005	1007
10	992	1007	1006	979
11	996	1006	997	989
12	1019	996	991	1011
13	981	991	989	1003
14	999	993	988	984
15	1013	1002	1005	992

Develop an $\overline{X}$ chart and an R chart and plot the values. From the charts, what comments can you make about the process? (Use three-sigma control limits as in Exhibit 6.1.6.)

7 In the past, Alpha Corporation has not performed incoming quality control inspections but has taken the word of its vendors. However, Alpha has been having some unsatisfactory experience recently with the quality of purchased items and wants to set up sampling plans for the receiving department to use.

For a particular component, X, Alpha has a lot tolerance percentage defective of 10 percent. Zenon Corporation, from which Alpha purchases this component, has an acceptable quality level in its production facility of 3 percent for component X. Alpha has a consumer's risk of 10 percent, and Zenon has a producer's risk of 5 percent.

a. When a shipment of Product X is received from Zenon Corporation, what sample size should the receiving department test?

b. What is the allowable number of defects in order to accept the shipment?

8 You are the newly appointed assistant administrator at a local hospital and your first project is to investigate the quality of the patient meals put out by the food-service department. You conducted a 10-day survey by submitting a simple questionnaire to the 400 patients with each meal, asking that they simply check off that the meal was either satisfactory or unsatisfactory. For simplicity in this problem, assume that the response was 1,000 returned questionnaires from the 1,200 meals each day. The results are as follows:

	NUMBER OF UNSATISFACTORY MEALS	SAMPLE SIZE
December 1	74	1,000
December 2	42	1,000
December 3	64	1,000
December 4	80	1,000
December 5	40	1,000
December 6	50	1,000
December 7	65	1,000
December 8	70	1,000
December 9	40	1,000
December 10	75	1,000
	600	10,000

a. Construct a p chart based on the questionnaire results, using a confidence interval of 95.5 percent, which is two standard deviations.

b. What comments can you make about the results of the survey?

9 Large-scale integrated (LSI) circuit chips are made in one department of an electronics firm. These chips are incorporated into analog devices that are then encased in epoxy. The yield is not particularly good for LSI manufacture, so the AQL specified by that department is 0.15 while the LTPD acceptable by the assembly department is 0.40.

a. Develop a sampling plan.

b. Explain what the sampling plan means; that is, how would you tell someone to do the test?

10 The state and local police departments are trying to analyze crime rates so they can shift their patrols from decreasing-rate areas to areas where rates are increasing. The city and county have been geographically segmented into areas containing 5,000 residences. The police recognize that not all crimes and offenses are reported: people do not want to become involved, consider the offenses too small to report, are too embarrassed to make a police report, or do not take the time, among other reasons. Every month, because of this, the police are contacting by phone a random sample of 1,000 of the 5,000 residences for data on crime. (Respondents are guaranteed anonymity.) Here are the data collected for the past 12 months for one area:

MONTH	CRIME INCIDENCE	SAMPLE SIZE	CRIME RATE
January	7	1,000	0.007
February	9	1,000	0.009
March	7	1,000	0.007
April	7	1,000	0.007

(continued)

MONTH	CRIME INCIDENCE	SAMPLE SIZE	CRIME RATE
May	7	1,000	0.007
June	9	1,000	0.009
July	7	1,000	0.007
August	10	1,000	0.010
September	8	1,000	0.008
October	11	1,000	0.011
November	10	1,000	0.010
December	8	1,000	0.008

Construct a p chart for 95 percent confidence (1.96) and plot each of the months. If the next three months show crime incidences in this area as

$$\text{January} = 10 \text{ (out of 1,000 sampled)}$$

$$\text{February} = 12 \text{ (out of 1,000 sampled)}$$

$$\text{March} = 11 \text{ (out of 1,000 sampled)}$$

what comments can you make regarding the crime rate?

11 Some citizens complained to city council members that there should be equal protection under the law against the occurrence of crimes. The citizens argued that this equal protection should be interpreted as indicating that high-crime areas should have more police protection than low-crime areas. Therefore, police patrols and other methods for preventing crime (such as street lighting or cleaning up abandoned areas and buildings) should be used proportionately to crime occurrence.

In a fashion similar to Problem 10, the city has been broken down into 20 geographic areas, each containing 5,000 residences. The 1,000 sampled from each area showed the following incidence of crime during the past month:

AREA	NUMBER OF CRIMES	SAMPLE SIZE	CRIME RATE
1	14	1,000	0.014
2	3	1,000	0.003
3	19	1,000	0.019
4	18	1,000	0.018
5	14	1,000	0.014
6	28	1,000	0.028
7	10	1,000	0.010
8	18	1,000	0.018
9	12	1,000	0.012
10	3	1,000	0.003
11	20	1,000	0.020
12	15	1,000	0.015
13	12	1,000	0.012
14	14	1,000	0.014
15	10	1,000	0.010
16	30	1,000	0.030
17	4	1,000	0.004
18	20	1,000	0.020
19	6	1,000	0.006
20	30	1,000	0.030
	300		

Suggest a reallocation of crime protection effort, if indicated, based on a p chart analysis. To be reasonably certain in your recommendation, select a 95 percent confidence level (that is, $Z = 1.96$).

12 The following table contains the measurements of the key length dimension from a fuel injector. These samples of size five were taken at one-hour intervals.

	OBSERVATIONS				
SAMPLE NUMBER	1	2	3	4	5
1	0.486	0.499	0.493	0.511	0.481
2	0.499	0.506	0.516	0.494	0.529
3	0.496	0.500	0.515	0.488	0.521
4	0.495	0.506	0.483	0.487	0.489
5	0.472	0.502	0.526	0.469	0.481
6	0.473	0.495	0.507	0.493	0.506
7	0.495	0.512	0.490	0.471	0.504
8	0.525	0.501	0.498	0.474	0.485
9	0.497	0.501	0.517	0.506	0.516
10	0.495	0.505	0.516	0.511	0.497
11	0.495	0.482	0.468	0.492	0.492
12	0.483	0.459	0.526	0.506	0.522
13	0.521	0.512	0.493	0.525	0.510
14	0.487	0.521	0.507	0.501	0.500
15	0.493	0.516	0.499	0.511	0.513
16	0.473	0.506	0.479	0.480	0.523
17	0.477	0.485	0.513	0.484	0.496
18	0.515	0.493	0.493	0.485	0.475
19	0.511	0.536	0.486	0.497	0.491
20	0.509	0.490	0.470	0.504	0.512

Construct a three-sigma $\overline{X}$ chart and R chart (use Exhibit 6.1.6) for the length of the fuel injector. What can you say about this process?

13 C-Spec, Inc., is attempting to determine whether an existing machine is capable of milling an engine part that has a key specification of 4 ± 0.003 inches. After a trial run on this machine, C-Spec has determined that the machine has a sample mean of 4.001 inches with a standard deviation of 0.002 inch.

   a. Calculate the C_{pk} for this machine.

   b. Should C-Spec use this machine to produce this part? Why?

14 The manager of an assembly line took five samples, each with six observations, under ideal conditions to develop control limits for an X-bar chart. The mean and range of each sample is shown in the table below:

SAMPLE NUMBER	SAMPLE MEAN	SAMPLE RANGE
1	2.18	0.33
2	2.12	0.38
3	1.86	0.40
4	1.98	0.38
5	2.02	0.35

What would be the 3 standard deviation lower control limit?

15 Interpret the following control chart and determine what action, if any, is appropriate.

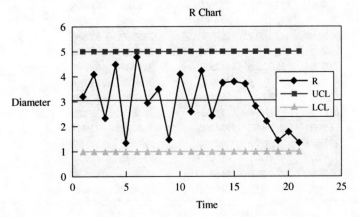

16 Below are the X-bar and R values for five samples. If the lower control limit for the X-bar chart is 8.34, what is the sample size?

SAMPLE	$\overline{X}$ BAR	R
1	8.51	0.44
2	8.37	0.58
3	8.42	0.66
4	8.61	0.47
5	8.54	0.60

ADVANCED PROBLEM

17 Design specifications require that a key dimension on a product measure 100 ± 10 units. A process being considered for producing this product has a standard deviation of four units.
   a. What can you say (quantitatively) regarding the process capability?
   b. Suppose the process average shifts to 92. Calculate the new process capability.
   c. What can you say about the process after the shift? Approximately what percentage of the items produced will be defective?

CASE: HOT SHOT PLASTICS COMPANY

Plastic keychains are being produced in a company named Hot Shot Plastics. The plastic material is first molded and then trimmed to the required shape. The curetimes (which is the time for the plastic to cool) during the molding process affect the edge quality of the keychains produced. The aim is to achieve statistical control of the curetimes using $\overline{X}$ and R charts.

Curetime data of 25 samples, each of size four, have been taken when the process is assumed to be in control. These are shown below (note: the spreadsheet "Hot Shot Plastics.xls" has these data).

SAMPLE No.	OBSERVATIONS				MEAN	RANGE
1	27.34667	27.50085	29.94412	28.21249	28.25103	2.59745
2	27.79695	26.15006	31.21295	31.33272	29.12317	5.18266
3	33.53255	29.32971	29.70460	31.05300	30.90497	4.20284
4	37.98409	32.26942	31.91741	29.44279	32.90343	8.54130
5	33.82722	30.32543	28.38117	33.70124	31.55877	5.44605
6	29.68356	29.56677	27.23077	34.00417	30.12132	6.77340
7	32.62640	26.32030	32.07892	36.17198	31.79940	9.85168
8	30.29575	30.52868	24.43315	26.85241	28.02750	6.09553
9	28.43856	30.48251	32.43083	30.76162	30.52838	3.99227
10	28.27790	33.94916	30.47406	28.87447	30.39390	5.67126
11	26.91885	27.66133	31.46936	29.66928	28.92971	4.55051
12	28.46547	28.29937	28.99441	31.14511	29.22609	2.84574
13	32.42677	26.10410	29.47718	37.20079	31.30221	11.09669
14	28.84273	30.51801	32.23614	30.47104	30.51698	3.39341
15	30.75136	32.99922	28.08452	26.19981	29.50873	6.79941
16	31.25754	24.29473	35.46477	28.41126	29.85708	11.17004
17	31.24921	28.57954	35.00865	31.23591	31.51833	6.42911
18	31.41554	35.80049	33.60909	27.82131	32.16161	7.97918
19	32.20230	32.02005	32.71018	29.37620	31.57718	3.33398
20	26.91603	29.77775	33.92696	33.78366	31.10110	7.01093
21	35.05322	32.93284	31.51641	27.73615	31.80966	7.31707
22	32.12483	29.32853	30.99709	31.39641	30.96172	2.79630
23	30.09172	32.43938	27.84725	30.70726	30.27140	4.59213
24	30.04835	27.23709	22.01801	28.69624	26.99992	8.03034
25	29.30273	30.83735	30.82735	31.90733	30.71869	2.60460
				Means	30.40289	5.932155

QUESTIONS

1 Prepare $\overline{X}$ and R charts using these data using the method described in the chapter.
2 Analyze the chart and comment on whether the process appears to be in control and stable.
3 Twelve additional samples of curetime data from the molding process were collected from an actual production run.

The data from these new samples are shown below. Update your control charts and compare the results with the previous data. The $\overline{X}$ and R charts are drawn with the new data using the same control limits established before. Comment on what the new charts show.

SAMPLE No.	OBSERVATIONS				MEAN	RANGE
1	31.65830	29.78330	31.87910	33.91250	31.80830	4.12920
2	34.46430	25.18480	37.76689	39.21143	34.15686	14.02663
3	41.34268	39.54590	29.55710	32.57350	35.75480	11.78558
4	29.47310	25.37840	25.04380	24.00350	25.97470	5.46960
5	25.46710	34.85160	30.19150	31.62220	30.53310	9.38450
6	46.25184	34.71356	41.41277	44.63319	41.75284	11.53828
7	35.44750	38.83289	33.08860	31.63490	34.75097	7.19799
8	34.55143	33.86330	35.18869	42.31515	36.47964	8.45185
9	43.43549	37.36371	38.85718	39.25132	39.72693	6.07178
10	37.05298	42.47056	35.90282	38.21905	38.41135	6.56774
11	38.57292	39.06772	32.22090	33.20200	35.76589	6.84682
12	27.03050	33.63970	26.63060	42.79176	32.52314	16.16116

SUPER QUIZ

1 Variation that can be clearly identified and possibly managed.
2 Variation inherent in the process itself.
3 If a process has a capability index of 1 and is running normally (centered between the design limits), what percentage of the units would one expect to be defective?
4 An alternative to viewing an item as simply good or bad due to its falling in or out of the tolerance range.
5 Quality characteristics that are classified as either conforming or not conforming to specification.

6 Quality characteristics that are actually measured, such as the weight of an item.
7 A quality chart suitable for when an item is either good or bad.
8 A quality chart suitable for when a number of blemishes are expected on each unit, such as a spool of yarn.
9 Useful for checking quality when we periodically purchase large quantities of an item and it would be very costly to check each unit individually.
10 A chart that depicts the manufacturer's and consumer's risk associated with a sampling plan.

1. Assignable variation 2. Common variation 3. Design limits are at $\pm 3\sigma$ or 2.7 defects per thousand 4. Taguchi loss function 5. Attributes 6. Variables 7. p-chart 8. c-chart 9. Acceptance sampling 10. Operating characteristic curve

SELECTED BIBLIOGRAPHY

Evans, J. R., and W. M. Lindsay. *Managing for Quality and Performance Excellence*. 7th ed. Mason, OH: South-Western College Publications, 2007.

Juran, J. M., and F. M. Gryna. *Quality Planning and Analysis*. 2nd ed. New York: McGraw-Hill, 1980.

Rath & Strong. *Rath & Strong's Six Sigma Pocket Guide*. Rath & Strong, Inc., 2000.

Small, B. B. (with committee). *Statistical Quality Control Handbook*. Western Electric Co., Inc., 1956.

Zimmerman, S. M., and M. L. Icenogel. *Statistical Quality Control; Using Excel*. 2nd ed. Milwaukee, WI: ASQ Quality Press, 2002.

FOOTNOTES

1 E. L. Grant and R. S. Leavenworth, *Statistical Quality Control* (New York: McGraw-Hill, 1996).

2 There is some controversy surrounding AQLs. This is based on the argument that specifying some acceptable percentage of defectives is inconsistent with the philosophical goal of zero defects. In practice, even in the best QC companies, there is an acceptable quality level. The difference is that it may be stated in parts per million rather than in parts per hundred. This is the case in Motorola's Six-Sigma quality standard, which holds that no more than 3.4 defects per million parts are acceptable.

3 See, for example, H. F. Dodge and H. G. Romig, *Sampling Inspection Tables—Single and Double Sampling* (New York: John Wiley & Sons, 1959); and *Military Standard Sampling Procedures and Tables for Inspection by Attributes* (MIL-STD-105D) (Washington, DC: U.S. Government Printing Office, 1983).

MATERIAL REQUIREMENTS PLANNING

chapter 7

FROM PUSH TO PULL

In the 1980s manufacturing led the national economy in the move from batch-oriented data processing systems to online transaction processing systems. The focus was MRP (initially material requirements planning, evolving to manufacturing resource planning), which later evolved into enterprise resource planning (ERP). It has been a long ride, and anyone who has been there for the duration deserves a rest.

However, the winds of change are blowing again as yet another new paradigm comes roaring through manufacturing. Specifically, we are speaking of the change in our economy from a build-to-stock to a build-to-order model of doing business.

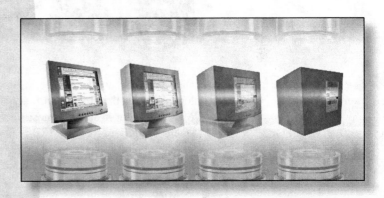

After reading the chapter you will:

1. Describe what MRP is and where it is best applied.

2. Understand the source of the information used by the system.

3. Demonstrate how to do an MRP "explosion."

4. Explain how order quantities are calculated in MRP systems.

The weak link in the build-to-stock model is inventory management, and this can be traced to an even weaker link, reliance upon sales forecasts. A build-to-order model begins with the order, not the forecast. The old problem of coordinating the procurement of parts, production of the product, and shipping the product still exists.

Today the term *flow management* is used to describe new hybrid production planning systems that combine the information integration and planning capability of MRP with the response of a JIT kanban system. Major ERP software vendors such as Oracle, SAP, and i2 Technologies are selling these new systems.

Essentially, the idea behind flow management is to produce a constantly changing mix of products, a mix that is based on current orders, using a stream of parts that are supplied just-in-time. It's important not to be tricked into thinking that all these new words really represent something new. Actually, flow manufacturing just combines things that have been used for years. In this case the combination is JIT kanban logic, MRP logic for planning material requirements, and client–server ERP.

Material requirements planning (MRP)

Our emphasis here is on material requirements planning (MRP), which is the key piece of logic that ties the production functions together from a material planning and control view. MRP has been installed almost universally in manufacturing firms, even those considered small. The reason is that MRP is a logical, easily understandable approach to the problem of determining the number of parts, components, and materials needed to produce each end item. MRP also provides the schedule specifying when each of these items should be ordered or produced.

MRP is based on dependent demand. Dependent demand is caused by the demand for a higher-level item. Tires, wheels, and engines are dependent demand items based on the demand for automobiles, for example.

Determining the number of dependent demand items needed is essentially a straightforward multiplication process. If one Part A takes five parts of B to make, then five parts of A require 25 parts of B. The basic difference in independent demand covered in the previous chapter and dependent demand covered in this chapter is as follows: If Part A is sold outside the firm, the amount of Part A that we sell is uncertain. We need to create a forecast using past data or do something like a market analysis. Part A is an independent item. However, Part B is a dependent part and its use depends on Part A. The number of B needed is simply the number of A times five. As a result of this type of multiplication, the requirements of other dependent demand items tend to become more and more lumpy as we go farther down into the product creation sequence. Lumpiness means that the requirements tend to bunch or lump rather than having an even dispersal. This is also caused by the way manufacturing is done. When manufacturing occurs in lots (or batches), items needed to produce the lot are withdrawn from inventory in quantities (perhaps all at once) rather than one at a time.

MASTER PRODUCTION SCHEDULING

Generally, the master schedule deals with end items and is a major input to the MRP process. If the end item is quite large or quite expensive, however, the master schedule may schedule major subassemblies or components instead.

All production systems have limited capacity and limited resources. This presents a challenging job for the master scheduler. Although the aggregate plan provides the general range of operation, the master scheduler must specify exactly what is to be produced. These decisions are made while responding to pressures from various functional areas such as the sales department (meet the customer's promised due date), finance (minimize inventory), management (maximize productivity and customer service, minimize resource needs), and manufacturing (have level schedules and minimize setup time).

To determine an acceptable feasible schedule to be released to the shop, trial master production schedules are run through the MRP program, which is described in the next section. The resulting planned order releases (the detailed production schedules) are checked to make sure that resources are available and that the completion times are reasonable. What appears to be a feasible master schedule may turn out to require excessive resources once the product explosion has taken place and materials, parts, and components from lower levels are determined. If this does happen (the usual case), the master production schedule is then modified with these limitations and the MRP program is run again. To ensure good master scheduling, the master scheduler (the human being) must

- Include all demands from product sales, warehouse replenishment, spares, and interplant requirements.
- Never lose sight of the aggregate plan.
- Be involved with customer order promising.
- Be visible to all levels of management.
- Objectively trade off manufacturing, marketing, and engineering conflicts.
- Identify and communicate all problems.

The upper portion of Exhibit 7.1 shows an aggregate plan for the total number of mattresses planned per month, without regard for mattress type. The lower portion shows a master production schedule specifying the exact type of mattress and the quantity planned for production by week. The next level down (not shown) would be the MRP program that develops detailed schedules showing when cotton batting, springs, and hardwood are needed to make the mattresses.

To again summarize the planning sequence, the aggregate operations plan specifies product groups. It does not specify exact items. The next level down in the planning process is the master production schedule. The master production schedule (MPS) is the time-phased plan specifying how many and when the firm plans to build each end item. For example, the aggregate plan for a furniture company may specify the total volume of mattresses it plans to produce over the next month or next quarter. The MPS goes

Master production schedule (MPS)

The Aggregate Plan and the Master Production Schedule for Mattresses

exhibit 7.1

Aggregate Production Plan for Mattresses

Month	1	2
Mattress production	900	950

Master Production Schedule for Mattress Models

	1	2	3	4	5	6	7	8
Model 327	200			400		200	100	
Model 538		100	100		150		100	
Model 749			100			200		200

exhibit 7.2   Master Production Schedule Time Fences

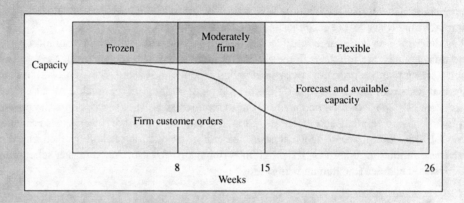

the next step down and identifies the exact size mattresses and their qualities and styles. All of the mattresses sold by the company would be specified by the MPS. The MPS also states period by period (usually weekly) how many and when each of these mattress types is needed.

Still further down the disaggregation process is the MRP program, which calculates and schedules all raw materials, parts, and supplies needed to make the mattress specified by the MPS.

TIME FENCES

The question of flexibility within a master production schedule depends on several factors: production lead time, commitment of parts and components to a specific end item, relationship between the customer and vendor, amount of excess capacity, and the reluctance or willingness of management to make changes.

The purpose of time fences is to maintain a reasonably controlled flow through the production system. Unless some operating rules are established and adhered to, the system could be chaotic and filled with overdue orders and constant expediting.

Exhibit 7.2 shows an example of a master production schedule time fence. Management defines *time fences* as periods of time having some specified level of opportunity for the customer to make changes. (The customer may be the firm's own marketing department, which may be considering product promotions, broadening variety, or the like.) Note in the exhibit that for the next eight weeks, this particular master schedule is frozen. Each firm has its own time fences and operating rules. Under these rules, *frozen* could be defined as anything from absolutely no changes in one company to only the most minor of changes in another. *Moderately firm* may allow changes in specific products within a product group so long as parts are available. *Flexible* may allow almost any variations in products, with the provisions that capacity remains about the same and that there are no long lead time items involved.

Available to promise

Some firms use a feature known as available to promise for items that are master scheduled. This feature identifies the difference between the number of units currently included in the master schedule and firm customer orders. For example, assume the master schedule indicates that 100 units of Model 538 mattress are going to be made during week seven. If firm customer orders now indicate that only 65 of those mattresses have actually been sold, the sales group has another 35 mattresses "available to promise" for delivery during that week. This can be a powerful tool for coordinating sales and production activities.

Industry Applications and Expected Benefits of MRP

exhibit 7.3

INDUSTRY TYPE	EXAMPLES	EXPECTED BENEFITS
Assemble-to-stock	Combines multiple component parts into a finished product, which is then stocked in inventory to satisfy customer demand. Examples: watches, tools, appliances.	High
Fabricate-to-stock	Items are manufactured by machine rather than assembled from parts. These are standard stock items carried in anticipation of customer demand. Examples: piston rings, electrical switches.	Low
Assemble-to-order	A final assembly is made from standard options that the customer chooses. Examples: trucks, generators, motors.	High
Fabricate-to-order	Items are manufactured by machine to customer order. These are generally industrial orders. Examples: bearings, gears, fasteners.	Low
Manufacture-to-order	Items are fabricated or assembled completely to customer specification. Examples: turbine generators, heavy machine tools.	High
Process	Includes industries such as foundries, rubber and plastics, specialty paper, chemicals, paint, drug, food processors.	Medium

WHERE MRP CAN BE USED

MRP is most valuable in industries where a number of products are made in batches using the same productive equipment. The list in Exhibit 7.3 includes examples of different industry types and the expected benefit from MRP. As you can see in the exhibit, MRP is most valuable to companies involved in assembly operations and least valuable to those in fabrication. One more point to note: MRP does not work well in companies that produce a low number of units annually. Especially for companies producing complex, expensive products requiring advanced research and design, experience has shown that lead times tend to be too long and too uncertain, and the product configuration too complex. Such companies need the control features that network scheduling techniques offer.

CATERPILLAR MANUFACTURES MORE THAN 300 PRODUCTS IN 23 COUNTRIES AND SERVES CUSTOMERS IN 200 COUNTRIES WORLDWIDE. "CAT" DEPENDS ON MRP FOR PLANNING ITS MANUFACTURING INVENTORY.

MATERIAL REQUIREMENTS PLANNING SYSTEM STRUCTURE

The material requirements planning portion of manufacturing activities most closely interacts with the master schedule, bill of materials file, inventory records file, and the output reports as shown in Exhibit 7.4.

Each facet of Exhibit 7.4 is detailed in the following sections, but essentially, the MRP system works as follows: the master production schedule states the number of items to be produced during specific time periods. A *bill of materials* file identifies the specific materials

exhibit 7.4   Overall View of the Inputs to a Standard Material Requirements Planning Program and the Reports Generated by the Program

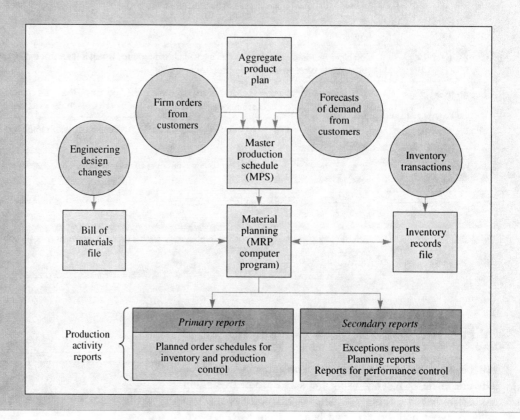

used to make each item and the correct quantities of each. The inventory records file contains data such as the number of units on hand and on order. These three sources—master production schedule, bill of materials file, and inventory records file—become the data sources for the material requirements program, which expands the production schedule into a detailed order scheduling plan for the entire production sequence.

DEMAND FOR PRODUCTS

Product demand for end items comes primarily from two main sources. The first is known customers who have placed specific orders, such as those generated by sales personnel, or from interdepartment transactions. These orders usually carry promised delivery dates. There is no forecasting involved in these orders—simply add them up. The second source is forecast demand. These are the normal independent-demand orders; the forecasting models used to predict the quantities. The demand from the known customers and the forecast demand are combined and become the input for the master production schedule, as described in the previous section.

In addition to the demand for end products, customers also order specific parts and components either as spares or for service and repair. These demands are not usually part of the master production schedule; instead, they are fed directly into the material requirements planning program at the appropriate levels. That is, they are added in as a gross requirement for that part or component.

BILL OF MATERIALS

Bill of materials (BOM)

The bill of materials (BOM) file contains the complete product description, listing not only the materials, parts, and components but also the sequence in which the product is created. This BOM file is one of the three main inputs to the MRP program. (The other two are the master schedule and the inventory records file.)

A. Bill of Materials (Product Structure Tree) for Product A

exhibit 7.5

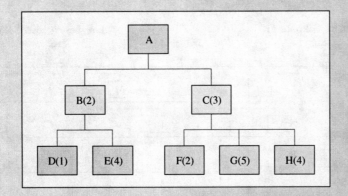

B. Parts List in an Indented Format and in a Single-Level List

INDENTED PARTS LIST
A
B(2)
D(1)
E(4)
C(3)
F(2)
G(5)
H(4)

SINGLE-LEVEL PARTS LIST
A
B(2)
C(3)
B
D(1)
E(4)
C
F(2)
G(5)
H(4)

The BOM file is often called the *product structure file* or *product tree* because it shows how a product is put together. It contains the information to identify each item and the quantity used per unit of the item of which it is a part. To illustrate this, consider Product A shown in Exhibit 7.5A. Product A is made of two units of Part B and three units of Part C. Part B is made of one unit of Part D and four units of Part E. Part C is made of two units of Part F, five units of Part G, and four units of Part H.

Bills of materials often list parts using an indented structure. This clearly identifies each item and the manner in which it is assembled because each indentation signifies the components of the item. A comparison of the indented parts in Exhibit 7.5B with the item structure in Exhibit 7.5A shows the ease of relating the two displays. From a computer standpoint, however, storing items in indented parts lists is very inefficient. To compute the amount of each item needed at the lower levels, each item would need to be expanded ("exploded") and summed. A more efficient procedure is to store parts data in simple single-level lists. That is, each item and component is listed showing only its parent and the number of units needed per unit of its parent. This avoids duplication because it includes each assembly only once. Exhibit 7.5B shows both the indented parts list and the single-level parts list for Product A.

A *modular* bill of materials is the term for a buildable item that can be produced and stocked as a subassembly. It is also a standard item with no options within the module. Many end items that are large and expensive are better scheduled and controlled as modules (or subassemblies). It is particularly advantageous to schedule subassembly modules when the same subassemblies appear in different end items. For example, a manufacturer of cranes can combine booms, transmissions, and engines in a variety of ways to meet a customer's needs. Using a modular bill of materials simplifies the scheduling and control and also makes it

exhibit 7.6   Product L Hierarchy in (A) Expanded to the Lowest Level of Each Item in (B)

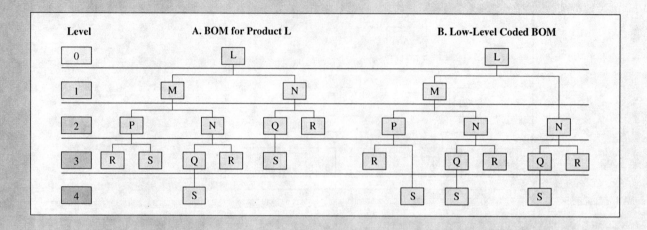

easier to forecast the use of different modules. Another benefit in using modular bills is that if the same item is used in a number of products, then the total inventory investment can be minimized.

A *super* bill of materials includes items with fractional options. (A super bill can specify, for example, 0.3 of a part. What that means is that 30 percent of the units produced contain that part and 70 percent do not.) Modular and super bills of materials are often referred to as planning bills of materials since they simplify the planning process.

Low-Level Coding   If all identical parts occur at the same level for each end product, the total number of parts and materials needed for a product can be computed easily. Consider Product L shown in Exhibit 7.6A. Notice that Item N, for example, occurs both as an input to L and as an input to M. Item N, therefore, needs to be lowered to level 2 (Exhibit 7.6B) to bring all Ns to the same level. If all identical items are placed at the same level, it becomes a simple matter for the computer to scan across each level and summarize the number of units of each item required.

INVENTORY RECORDS

The inventory records file can be quite lengthy. Exhibit 7.7 shows the variety of information contained in the inventory records. The MRP program accesses the *status* segment of the record according to specific time periods (called *time buckets* in MRP slang). These records are accessed as needed during the program run.

As we will see, the MRP program performs its analysis from the top of the product structure downward, calculating requirements level by level. There are times, however, when it is desirable to identify the parent item that caused the material requirement. The MRP program allows the creation of a *peg record* file either separately or as part of the inventory record file. Pegging requirements allows us to retrace a material requirement upward in the product structure through each level, identifying each parent item that created the demand.

Inventory Status File   The inventory status file is kept up to date by posting inventory transactions as they occur. These changes occur because of stock receipts and disbursements, scrap losses, wrong parts, canceled orders, and so forth.

MRP COMPUTER PROGRAM

The material requirements planning program operates using information from the inventory records, the master schedule, and the bill of materials. The process of calculating

The Inventory Status Record for an Item in Inventory

exhibit 7.7

Item master data segment	Part no.	Description		Lead time		Std. cost	Safety stock
	Order quantity		Setup	Cycle	Last year's usage		Class
	Scrap allowance		Cutting data	Pointers		Etc.	

			Control balance	Period 1 2 3 4 5 6 7 8	Totals
Inventory status segment	Allocated				
	Gross requirements				
	Scheduled receipts				
	Projected available balance				
	Planned order releases				
Subsidiary data segment	Order details				
	Pending action				
	Counters				
	Keeping track				

the exact requirements for each item managed by the system is often referred to as the "explosion" process. Working from the top level downward in the bill of materials, requirements from parent items are used to calculate the requirements for component items. Consideration is taken of current on-hand balances and orders that are scheduled for receipt in the future.

The following is a general description of the MRP explosion process:

1. The requirements for level 0 items, typically referred to as "end items," are retrieved from the master schedule. These requirements are referred to as "gross requirements" by the MRP program. Typically, the gross requirements are scheduled in weekly time buckets.

2. Next, the program uses the current on-hand balance together with the schedule of orders that will be received in the future to calculate the "net requirements." Net requirements are the amounts that are needed week by week in the future over and above what is currently on hand or committed to through an order already released and scheduled.

3. Using net requirements, the program calculates when orders should be received to meet these requirements. This can be a simple process of just scheduling orders to arrive according to the exact net requirements or a more complicated process where requirements are combined for multiple periods. This schedule of when orders should arrive is referred to as "planned-order receipts."

4. Since there is typically a lead time associated with each order, the next step is to find a schedule for when orders are actually released. Offsetting the "planned-order receipts" by the required lead time does this. This schedule is referred to as the "planned-order release."

5. After these four steps have been completed for all the level zero items, the program moves to level 1 items.

6. The gross requirements for each level 1 item are calculated from the planned-order release schedule for the parents of each level 1 item. Any additional independent demand also needs to be included in the gross requirements.

7. After the gross requirements have been determined, net requirements, planned-order receipts, and planned-order releases are calculated as described in steps 2–4 above.
8. This process is then repeated for each level in the bill of materials.

The process of doing these calculations is much simpler than the description, as you will see in the example that follows. Typically, the explosion calculations are performed each week or whenever changes have been made to the master schedule. Some MRP programs have the option of generating immediate schedules, called *net change* schedules. Net change

Net change systems

systems are "activity" driven and requirements and schedules are updated whenever a transaction is processed that has an impact on the item. Net change enables the system to reflect in "real time" the exact status of each item managed by the system.

AN EXAMPLE USING MRP

Ampere, Inc., produces a line of electric meters installed in residential buildings by electric utility companies to measure power consumption. Meters used on single-family homes are of two basic types for different voltage and amperage ranges. In addition to complete meters, some subassemblies are sold separately for repair or for changeovers to a different voltage or power load. The problem for the MRP system is to determine a production schedule to identify each item, the period it is needed, and the appropriate quantities. The schedule is then checked for feasibility, and the schedule is modified if necessary.

FORECASTING DEMAND

Demand for the meters and components originates from two sources: regular customers that place firm orders and unidentified customers that make the normal random demands for these items. Exhibit 7.8 shows the requirements for meters A and B and Subassembly D for a three-month period (months three through five). There are some "other parts" used to make the meters. In order to keep our example manageable, we are not including them in this example.

DEVELOPING A MASTER PRODUCTION SCHEDULE

For the meter and component requirements specified in Exhibit 7.8, assume that the quantities to satisfy the known and random demands must be available during the first week of the month. This assumption is reasonable because management (in our example) prefers to produce meters in a single batch each month rather than a number of batches throughout the month.

exhibit 7.8   Future Requirements for Meters A and B and Subassembly D Stemming from Specific Customer Orders and from Random Sources

	METER A		METER B		SUBASSEMBLY C	
MONTH	KNOWN	RANDOM	KNOWN	RANDOM	KNOWN	RANDOM
3	1,000	250	410	60	200	70
4	600	250	300	60	180	70
5	300	250	500	60	250	70

A Master Schedule to Satisfy Demand Requirements as Specified in Exhibit 7.8

exhibit 7.9

	Week								
	9	10	11	12	13	14	15	16	17
Meter A	1,250				850				550
Meter B	470				360				560
Subassembly D	270				250				320

Exhibit 7.9 shows the trial master schedule that we use under these conditions, with demand for months 3, 4, and 5 listed in the first week of each month, or as Weeks 9, 13, and 17. For brevity, we will work with demand through Week 9. The schedule we develop should be examined for resource availability, capacity availability, and so on, and then revised and run again. We will stop with our example at the end of this one schedule, however.

BILL OF MATERIALS (PRODUCT STRUCTURE)

The product structure for meters A and B is shown in Exhibit 7.10A in the typical way using low-level coding, in which each item is placed at the lowest level at which it appears in the

A. Product Structure for Meters A and B

exhibit 7.10

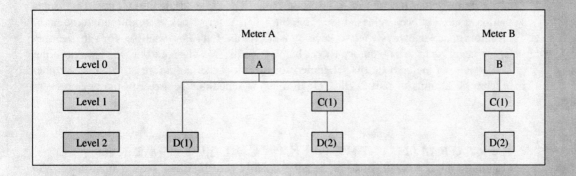

Tutorial: MRP

B. Indented Parts List for Meter A and Meter B, with the Required Number of Items per Unit of Parent Listed in Parentheses

METER A	
A	
D(1)	
C(1)	
	D(2)

METER B	
B	
C(1)	
	D(2)

Exhibit shows the subassemblies and parts that make up the meters and shows the numbers of units required per unit of parent in parentheses.

exhibit 7.11   Number of Units on Hand and Lead Time Data That Would Appear on the Inventory Record File

ITEM	ON-HAND INVENTORY	LEAD TIME (WEEKS)	SAFETY STOCK	ON ORDER
A	50	2	0	
B	60	2	0	10 (week 5)
C	40	1	5	
D	200	1	20	100 (week 4)

structure hierarchy. Meters A and B consist of a common subassembly C and some parts that include part D. To keep things simple, we will focus on only one of the parts, part D, which is a transformer.

From the product structure, notice that part D (the transformer) is used in subassembly C (which is used in both meters A and B). In the case of meter A, an additional part D (transformer) is needed. The "2" in parentheses next to D when used to make a C indicates that two D's are required for every C that is made. The product structure, as well as the indented parts list in Exhibit 7.10B, indicates how the meters are actually made. First, subassembly C is made, and potentially these are carried in inventory. In a final assembly process, meters A and B are put together, and in the case of meter A an additional part D is used.

INVENTORY RECORDS

The inventory records data would be similar to that shown in Exhibit 7.7. As shown earlier in the chapter, additional data such as vendor identity, cost, and lead time also would be included in these data. For this example, the pertinent data include the on-hand inventory at the start of the program run, safety stock requirements, and the current status of orders that have already been released (see Exhibit 7.11). Safety stock is a minimum amount of inventory that we always want to keep on hand for an item. For example, for subassembly C, we never want the inventory to get below 5 units. We also see that we have an order for 10 units of meter B that is scheduled for receipt at the beginning of Week 5. Another order for 100 units of part D (the transformer) is scheduled to arrive at the beginning of Week 4.

PERFORMING THE MRP CALCULATIONS

Conditions are now set to perform the MRP calculations: End-item requirements have been presented in the master production schedule, while the status of inventory and the order lead times are available, and we also have the pertinent product structure data. The MRP calculations (often referred to as an explosion) are done level by level, in conjunction with the inventory data and data from the master schedule.

Exhibit 7.12 shows the details of these calculations. The following analysis explains the logic in detail. We will limit our analysis to the problem of meeting the gross requirements for 1,250 units of meter A, 470 units of meter B, and 270 units of transformer D, all in Week 9.

An MRP record is kept for each item managed by the system. The record contains *gross requirements, scheduled receipts, projected available balance, net requirements, planned order receipts,* and *planned order releases* data. *Gross requirements* are the total amount required for a particular item. These requirements can be from external customer demand and also from demand calculated based on manufacturing requirements. *Scheduled receipts*

Material Requirements Planning Schedule for Meters A and B and Subassemblies C and D **exhibit 7.12**

Tutorial: MRP

Item		Week					
		4	5	6	7	8	9
A LT = 2 weeks On hand = 50 Safety stock = 0 Order qty = lot-for-lot	Gross requirements						1250
	Scheduled receipts						
	Projected available balance	50	50	50	50	50	50
	Net requirements						1200
	Planned order receipts						1200
	Planned order releases				1200		
B LT = 2 weeks On hand = 60 Safety stock = 0 Order qty = lot-for-lot	Gross requirements						470
	Scheduled receipts		10				
	Projected available balance	60	60	70	70	70	70
	Net requirements						400
	Planned order receipts						400
	Planned order releases				400		
C LT = 1 week On hand = 40 Safety stock = 5 Order qty = 2000	Gross requirements				400 + 1200		
	Scheduled receipts						
	Projected available balance	35	35	35	35	435	435
	Net requirements				1565		
	Planned order receipts				2000		
	Planned order releases			2000			
D LT = 1 week On hand = 200 Safety stock = 20 Order qty = 5000	Gross requirements			4000	1200		270
	Scheduled receipts	100					
	Projected available balance	180	280	280	1280	80	80
	Net requirements			3720			190
	Planned order receipts			5000			5000
	Planned order releases		5000			5000	

represent orders that have already been released and that are scheduled to arrive as of the beginning of the period. Once the paperwork on an order has been released, what was prior to that event a "planned" order now becomes a *scheduled receipt. Projected available balance* is the amount of inventory that is expected as of the end of a period. This can be calculated as follows:

$$\text{Projected available balance}_t = \text{Projected available balance}_{t-1} - \text{Gross requirements}_t + \text{Scheduled receipts}_t + \text{Planned order receipts}_t - \text{Safety stock}$$

A *net requirement* is the amount needed when the *projected available* balance plus the *scheduled receipts* in a period are not sufficient to cover the *gross requirement.* The *planned order receipt* is the amount of an order that is required to meet a net requirement in the period. Finally, the *planned order release* is the planned order receipt offset by the lead time.

Beginning with meter A, the projected available balance is 50 units and there are no net requirements until Week 9. In Week 9, an additional 1,200 units are needed to cover the demand of 1,250 generated from the order scheduled through the master schedule. The order quantity is designated "lot-for-lot," which means that we can order the exact quantity needed to meet net requirements. An order, therefore, is planned for receipt of 1,200 units for the beginning of Week 9. Since the lead time is two weeks, this order must be released at the beginning of Week 7.

Meter B is similar to A, although an order for 10 units is scheduled for receipt in period 5. We project that 70 units will be available at the end of week 5. There is a net requirement for 400 additional units to meet the gross requirement of 470 units in Week 9. This requirement is met with an order for 400 units that must be released at the beginning of Week 7.

Item C is the subassembly used in both meters A and B. We need additional C's only when either A or B is being made. Our analysis of A indicates that an order for 1,200 will be released in Week 7. An order for 400 B's also will be released in Week 7, so total demand for C is 1,600 units in Week 7. The projected available balance is the 40 units on hand minus the safety stock of 5 units that we have specified, or 35 units. In Week 7, the net requirement is 1,565 units. The order policy for C indicates an order quantity of 2,000 units, so an order receipt for 2,000 is planned for Week 7. This order needs to be released in Week 6 due to the one-week lead time. Assuming this order is actually processed in the future, the projected available balance is 435 units in Weeks 7, 8, and 9.

Item D, the transformer, has demand from three different sources. The demand in Week 6 is due to the requirement to put D's into subassembly C. In this case two D's are needed for every C, or 4,000 units (the product structure indicates this two-to-one relationship). In the seventh week, 1,200 D's are needed for the order for 1,200 A's that are scheduled to be released in Week 7. Another 270 units are needed in Week 9 to meet the independent demand that is scheduled through the master schedule. Projected available balance at the end of Week 4 is 280 units (200 on hand plus the scheduled receipt of 100 units minus the safety stock of 20 units) and 280 units in Week 5. There is a net requirement for an additional 3,720 units in Week 6, so we plan to receive an order for 5,000 units (the order quantity). This results in a projected balance of 80 in Week 7 since 1,200 are used to meet demand. Eighty units are projected to be available in Week 8. Due to the demand for 270 in Week 9, a net requirement of 190 units in Week 9 results in planning the receipt of an additional 5,000-unit order in Week 9.

Step by Step

EXAMPLE 7.1: MRP Explosion Calculations

Juno Lighting makes special lights that are popular in new homes. Juno expects demand for two popular lights to be the following over the next eight weeks.

	WEEK							
	1	2	3	4	5	6	7	8
VH1-234	34	37	41	45	48	48	48	48
VH2-100	104	134	144	155	134	140	141	145

A key component in both lights is a socket that the bulb is screwed into in the base fixture. Each light has one of these sockets. Given the following information, plan the production of the lights and purchases of the socket.

	VH1-234	VH2-100	LIGHT SOCKET
On hand	85	358	425
Q	200 (the production lot size)	400 (to production lot size)	500 (purchase quantity)
Lead time	1 week	1 week	3 weeks
Safety stock	0 units	0 units	20 units

SOLUTION

ITEM					WEEK				
		1	2	3	4	5	6	7	8
VH1-234	Gross requirement	34	37	41	45	48	48	48	48
Q = 200	Scheduled receipts								
LT = 1	Projected available balance	51	14	173	128	80	32	184	136
OH = 85	Net requirements			27				16	
SS = 0	Planned order receipts			200				200	
	Planned order releases		200				200		
VH2-100	Gross requirement	104	134	144	155	134	140	141	145
Q = 400	Scheduled receipts								
LT = 1	Projected available balance	254	120	376	221	87	347	206	61
OH = 358	Net requirements			24			53		
SS = 0	Planned order receipts			400			400		
	Planned order releases		400			400			
Socket	Gross requirement		600			400	200		
Q = 500	Scheduled receipts	500							
LT = 3	Projected available balance	905	305	305	305	405	205	205	205
OH = 425	Net requirements					95			
SS = 20	Planned order receipts					500			
	Planned order releases			500					

The best way to proceed is to work period by period by focusing on the projected available balance calculation. Whenever the available balance goes below zero, a net requirement is generated. When this happens, plan an order receipt to meet the requirement. For example, for VH1 we start with 85 units in inventory and need 34 to meet Week 1 production requirements. This brings our available balance at the end of Week 1 to 51 units. Another 37 units are used during Week 2, dropping inventory to 14. In Week 3, our project balance drops to 0 and we have a net requirement of 27 units that needs to be covered with an order scheduled to be received in Week 3. Since the lead time is one week, this order needs to be released in Week 2. Week 4 projected available balance is 128, calculated by taking the 200 units that are received in Week 3 and subtracting the Week 3 net requirement of 27 units and the 45 units needed for Week 4.

Since sockets are used in both VH1 and VH2, the gross requirements come from the planned order releases for these items: 600 are needed in Week 2 (200 for VH1s and 400 for VH2s), 400 in Week 5, and 200 in Week 6. Projected available balance is beginning inventory of 425 plus the scheduled receipts of 500 units minus the 20 units of safety stock. ●

LOT SIZING IN MRP SYSTEMS

The determination of lot sizes in an MRP system is a complicated and difficult problem. Lot sizes are the part quantities issued in the planned order receipt and planned order release sections of an MRP schedule. For parts produced in-house, lot sizes are the production quantities of batch sizes. For purchased parts, these are the quantities ordered from the supplier. Lot sizes generally meet part requirements for one or more periods.

Most lot-sizing techniques deal with how to balance the setup or order costs and holding costs associated with meeting the net requirements generated by the MRP planning process. Many MRP systems have options for computing lot sizes based on some of the more commonly used techniques. The use of lot-sizing techniques increases the complexity of running MRP schedules in a plant. In an attempt to save setup costs, the inventory generated with the larger lot sizes needs to be stored, making the logistics in the plant much more complicated.

Next we explain four lot-sizing techniques using a common example. The lot-sizing techniques presented are lot-for-lot (L4L), economic order quantity (EOQ), least total cost (LTC), and least unit cost (LUC).

Consider the following MRP lot-sizing problem; the net requirements are shown for eight scheduling weeks:

Cost per item	$10.00
Order or setup cost	$47.00
Inventory carrying cost/week	0.5%

Weekly net requirements:

1	2	3	4	5	6	7	8
50	60	70	60	95	75	60	55

LOT-FOR-LOT

Lot-for-lot (L4L) is the most common technique. It

- Sets planned orders to exactly match the net requirements.
- Produces exactly what is needed each week with none carried over into future periods.
- Minimizes carrying cost.
- Does not take into account setup costs or capacity limitations.

Exhibit 7.13 shows the lot-for-lot calculations. The net requirements are given in column 2. Because the logic of lot-for-lot says the production quantity (column 3) will exactly match the required quantity (column 2), no inventory will be left at the end (column 4). Without any inventory to carry over into the next week, there is zero holding cost (column 5). However, lot-for-lot requires a setup cost each week (column 6). Incidentally, there is a setup cost each week because this is a work center where a variety of items are worked on each week. This is not a case where the work center is committed to one product and sits idle when it is not working on that product (in which case only one setup would result). Lot-for-lot causes high setup costs.

ECONOMIC ORDER QUANTITY

In an EOQ model, either fairly constant demand must exist or safety stock must be kept to provide for demand variability. The EOQ model uses an estimate of total annual demand, the setup or order cost, and the annual holding cost. EOQ was not designed for a system with discrete time periods such as MRP. The lot-sizing techniques used for MRP assume that part requirements are satisfied at the start of the period. Holding costs are then charged only to

exhibit 7.13   Lot-for-Lot Run Size for an MRP Schedule

(1) WEEK	(2) NET REQUIREMENTS	(3) PRODUCTION QUANTITY	(4) ENDING INVENTORY	(5) HOLDING COST	(6) SETUP COST	(7) TOTAL COST
1	50	50	0	$0.00	$47.00	$ 47.00
2	60	60	0	0.00	47.00	94.00
3	70	70	0	0.00	47.00	141.00
4	60	60	0	0.00	47.00	188.00
5	95	95	0	0.00	47.00	235.00
6	75	75	0	0.00	47.00	282.00
7	60	60	0	0.00	47.00	329.00
8	55	55	0	0.00	47.00	376.00

Economic Order Quantity Run Size for an MRP Schedule   **exhibit 7.14**

WEEK	NET REQUIREMENTS	PRODUCTION QUANTITY	ENDING INVENTORY	HOLDING COST	SETUP COST	TOTAL COST
1	50	351	301	$15.05	$47.00	$ 62.05
2	60	0	241	12.05	0.00	74.10
3	70	0	171	8.55	0.00	82.65
4	60	0	111	5.55	0.00	88.20
5	95	0	16	0.80	0.00	89.00
6	75	351	292	14.60	47.00	150.60
7	60	0	232	11.60	0.00	162.20
8	55	0	177	8.85	0.00	171.05

the ending inventory for the period, not to the average inventory as in the case of the EOQ model. EOQ assumes that parts are used continuously during the period. The lot sizes generated by EOQ do not always cover the entire number of periods. For example, the EOQ might provide the requirements for 4.6 periods. Using the same data as in the lot-for-lot example, the economic order quantity is calculated as follows:

$$\text{Annual demand based on the 8 weeks} = D = \frac{525}{8} \times 52 = 3{,}412.5 \text{ units}$$

$$\text{Annual holding cost} = H = 0.5\% \times \$10 \times 52 \text{ weeks} = \$2.60 \text{ per unit}$$

$$\text{Setup cost} = S = \$47 \text{ (given)}$$

$$\therefore \text{EOQ} = \sqrt{\frac{2DS}{H}} = \sqrt{\frac{2(3{,}412.5)(\$47)}{\$2.60}} = 351 \text{ units}$$

Exhibit 7.14 shows the MRP schedule using an EOQ of 351 units. The EOQ lot size in Week 1 is enough to meet requirements for Weeks 1 through 5 and a portion of Week 6. Then, in Week 6 another EOQ lot is planned to meet the requirements for Weeks 6 through 8. Notice that the EOQ plan leaves some inventory at the end of Week 8 to carry forward into Week 9.

LEAST TOTAL COST

The least total cost method (LTC) is a dynamic lot-sizing technique that calculates the order quantity by comparing the carrying cost and the setup (or ordering) costs for various lot sizes and then selects the lot in which these are most nearly equal.

The top half of Exhibit 7.15 shows the least cost lot size results. The procedure to compute least total cost lot sizes is to compare order costs and holding costs for various numbers of weeks. For example, costs are compared for producing in Week 1 to cover the requirements for Week 1; producing in Week 1 for Weeks 1 and 2; producing in Week 1 to cover Weeks 1, 2, and 3, and so on. The correct selection is the lot size where the ordering costs and holding costs are approximately equal. In Exhibit 7.15 the best lot size is 335 because a $38 carrying cost and a $47 ordering cost are closer than $56.75 and $47 ($9 versus $9.75). This lot size covers requirements for Weeks 1 through 5. Unlike EOQ, the lot size covers only whole numbers of periods.

On the basis of the Week 1 decision to place an order to cover five weeks, we are now located in Week 6, and our problem is to determine how many weeks into the future we can provide for from here. Exhibit 7.15 shows that holding and ordering costs are closest in the quantity that covers requirements for Weeks 6 through 8. Notice that the holding and ordering costs here are far apart. This is because our example extends only to Week 8. If the planning horizon were longer, the lot size planned for Week 6 would likely cover more weeks into the

exhibit 7.15   Least Total Cost Run Size for an MRP Schedule

WEEKS	QUANTITY ORDERED	CARRYING COST	ORDER COST	TOTAL COST	
1	50	$0.00	$47.00	$47.00	
1–2	110	3.00	47.00	50.00	
1–3	180	10.00	47.00	57.00	
1–4	240	19.00	47.00	66.00	1st order
1–5	335	38.00	47.00	85.00	← Least total cost
1–6	410	56.75	47.00	103.75	
1–7	470	74.75	47.00	121.75	
1–8	525	94.00	47.00	141.00	
6	75	0.00	47.00	47.00	
6–7	135	3.00	47.00	50.00	2nd order
6–8	190	8.50	47.00	55.50	← Least total cost

WEEK	NET REQUIREMENTS	PRODUCTION QUANTITY	ENDING INVENTORY	HOLDING COST	SETUP COST	TOTAL COST
1	50	335	285	$14.25	$47.00	$ 61.25
2	60	0	225	11.25	0.00	72.50
3	70	0	155	7.75	0.00	80.25
4	60	0	95	4.75	0.00	85.00
5	95	0	0	0.00	0.00	85.00
6	75	190	115	5.75	47.00	137.75
7	60	0	55	2.75	0.00	140.50
8	55	0	0	0.00	0.00	140.05

future beyond Week 8. This brings up one of the limitations of both LTC and LUC (discussed below). Both techniques are influenced by the length of the planning horizon. The bottom half of Exhibit 7.15 shows the final run size and total cost.

LEAST UNIT COST

The least unit cost method is a dynamic lot-sizing technique that adds ordering and inventory carrying cost for each trial lot size and divides by the number of units in each lot size, picking the lot size with the lowest unit cost. The top half of Exhibit 7.16 calculates the unit cost for ordering lots to meet the needs of Weeks 1 through 8. Note that the minimum occurred when the quantity 410, ordered in Week 1, was sufficient to cover Weeks 1 through 6. The lot size planned for Week 7 covers through the end of the planning horizon.

The least unit cost run size and total cost are shown in the bottom half of Exhibit 7.16.

CHOOSING THE BEST LOT SIZE

Using the lot-for-lot method, the total cost for the eight weeks is $376; the EOQ total cost is $171.05; the least total cost method is $140.50; and the least unit cost is $153.50. The lowest cost was obtained using the least total cost method of $140.50. If there were more than eight weeks, the lowest cost could differ.

The advantage of the least unit cost method is that it is a more complete analysis and would take into account ordering or setup costs that might change as the order size increases. If the ordering or setup costs remain constant, the lowest total cost method is more attractive because it is simpler and easier to compute; yet it would be just as accurate under that restriction.

Least Unit Cost Run Size for an MRP Schedule

exhibit 7.16

WEEKS	QUANTITY ORDERED	CARRYING COST	ORDER COST	TOTAL COST	UNIT COST	
1	50	$ 0.00	$ 47.00	$ 47.00	$0.9400	
1–2	110	3.00	47.00	50.00	0.4545	
1–3	180	10.00	47.00	57.00	0.3167	
1–4	240	19.00	47.00	66.00	0.2750	
1–5	335	38.00	47.00	85.00	0.2537	
1–6	410	56.75	47.00	103.75	0.2530	← 1st order
1–7	470	74.75	47.00	121.75	0.2590	Least unit cost
1–8	525	94.00	47.00	141.00	0.2686	
?	60	0.00	47.00	47.00	0.7833	2nd order
7–8	115	2.75	47.00	49.75	0.4326	← Least unit cost

WEEK	NET REQUIREMENTS	PRODUCTION QUANTITY	ENDING INVENTORY	HOLDING COST	SETUP COST	TOTAL COST
1	50	410	360	$18.00	$ 47.00	$ 65.00
2	60	0	300	15.00	0.00	80.00
3	70	0	230	11.50	0.00	91.50
4	60	0	170	8.50	0.00	100.00
5	95	0	75	3.75	0.00	103.75
6	75	0	0	0	0	103.75
7	60	115	55	2.75	47.00	153.50
8	55	0	0	0	0	$ 153.50

SUMMARY

Since the 1970s, MRP has grown from its original purpose of determining simple time schedules for production and material procurement to its present use as an integral part of enterprise resource planning that ties together all the major functions of a firm. MRP has proved to be a flexible platform that has been adapted to many different situations, including repetitive manufacturing using just-in-time systems.

In this chapter the basic concepts needed to understand MRP have been covered. The MRP engine takes information from a master schedule that is a detailed plan for future production. Depending on the needs of the firm, the master schedule can be stated in terms of individual products, generic products, or modules and subassemblies. Master scheduling is part of the sales and operations planning process that is critical to implementing the firm's operations strategy successfully.

The bill of materials depicts exactly how a firm makes the items in the master schedule. The "structure" of the bill of materials (sometimes referred to as the "product structure") captures how raw materials and purchased parts come together to form subassemblies and how those subassembles are brought together to make the items in the master schedule.

The MRP "explosion" process is the heart of the system. Using the master schedule and bill of materials, together with the current inventory status (amount on-hand and on-order) of each part in the bill of materials, detailed schedules are calculated that show the exact timing of needed parts in the future. In a typical company, this process can require a significant computation effort involving literally thousands of detailed schedules.

In this chapter, the important topic of how to consider inventory-related costs was addressed. A number of common MRP lot-sizing rules were described that consider the fixed cost and variable cost trade-off that can be significant in minimizing inventory costs.

KEY TERMS

Material requirements planning (MRP) The logic for determining the number of parts, components, and materials needed to produce a product. MRP also provides the schedule specifying when each of these materials, parts, and components should be ordered or produced.

Master production schedule (MPS) A time-phased plan specifying how many and when the firm plans to build each end item.

Available to promise A feature of MRP systems that identifies the difference between the number of units currently included in the master schedule and the actual (firm) customer orders.

Bill of materials (BOM) A computer file that contains the complete product description, listing the materials, parts, and components and the sequence in which the product is created.

Net change system An MRP system that calculates the impact of a change in the MRP data (the inventory status, BOM, or master schedule) immediately. This is a common feature in current systems.

SOLVED PROBLEMS

Excel: Solved Problem

SOLVED PROBLEM 1

Product X is made of two units of Y and three of Z. Y is made of one unit of A and two units of B. Z is made of two units of A and four units of C.

Lead time for X is one week; Y, two weeks; Z, three weeks; A, two weeks; B, one week; and C, three weeks.

a. Draw the bill of materials (product structure tree).

b. If 100 units of X are needed in week 10, develop a planning schedule showing when each item should be ordered and in what quantity.

Solution

a.

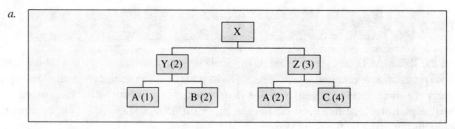

b.

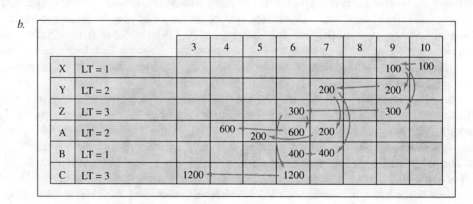

SOLVED PROBLEM 2

Product M is made of two units of N and three of P. N is made of two units of R and four units of S. R is made of one unit of S and three units of T. P is made of two units of T and four units of U.

a. Show the bill of materials (product structure tree).

b. If 100 M are required, how many units of each component are needed?

c. Show both a single-level parts list and an indented parts list.

Solution

a.

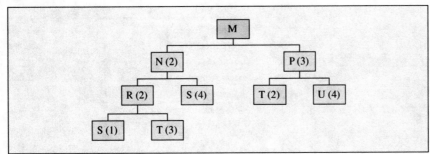

b.

M = 100	S = 800 + 400 = 1,200
N = 200	T = 600 + 1,200 = 1,800
P = 300	U = 1,200
R = 400	

c.

SINGLE-LEVEL PARTS LIST	INDENTED PARTS LIST
M	M
N (2)	N(2)
P (3)	R(2)
N	S (1)
R (2)	T (3)
S (4)	S (4)
R	P (3)
S (1)	T (2)
T (3)	U (4)
P	
T (2)	
U (4)	

REVIEW AND DISCUSSION QUESTIONS

1 Discuss the meaning of MRP terms such as *planned order release* and *scheduled order receipt.*

2 Many practitioners currently update MRP weekly or biweekly. Would it be more valuable if it were updated daily? Discuss.

3 What is the role of safety stock in an MRP system?

4 Contrast the significance of the term *lead time* in the traditional EOQ context and in an MRP system.

5 Discuss the importance of the master production schedule in an MRP system.

6 "MRP just prepares shopping lists. It does not do the shopping or cook the dinner." Comment.

7 What are the sources of demand in an MRP system? Are these dependent or independent, and how are they used as inputs to the system?

8 State the types of data that would be carried in the bill of materials file and the inventory record file.

PROBLEMS

1 Semans is a manufacturer that produces bracket assemblies. Demand for bracket assemblies (X) is 130 units. The following is the BOM in indented form:

ITEM	DESCRIPTION	USAGE
X	Bracket assembly	1
A	Wall board	4
B	Hanger subassembly	2
D	Hanger casting	3
E	Ceramic knob	1
C	Rivet head screw	3
F	Metal tong	4
G	Plastic cap	2

Below is a table indicating current inventory levels:

Item	X	A	B	C	D	E	F	G
Inventory	25	16	60	20	180	160	1000	100

   a. Using Excel, create the MRP using the product tree structure.
   b. What are the net requirements of each item in the MPS?

2 In the following MRP planning schedule for Item J, indicate the correct net requirements, planned order receipts, and planned order releases to meet the gross requirements. Lead time is one week.

		WEEK NUMBER				
ITEM J	0	1	2	3	4	5
Gross requirements			75		50	70
On-hand	40					
Net requirements						
Planned order receipt						
Planned order release						

3 Repeat Solved Problem 1 using current on-hand inventories of 20 X, 40 Y, 30 Z, 50 A, 100 B, and 900 C.

4 Assume that Product Z is made of two units of A and four units of B. A is made of three units of C and four D. D is made of two units of E.

   Lead times for purchase or fabrication of each unit to final assembly are: Z takes two weeks; A, B, C, and D take one week each; and E takes three weeks.

   Fifty units are required in Period 10. (Assume that there is currently no inventory on hand of any of these items.)

   a. Show the bill of materials (product structure tree).
   b. Develop an MRP planning schedule showing gross and net requirements and order release and order receipt dates.

5 *Note:* For Problems 5 through 10, to simplify data handling to include the receipt of orders that have actually been placed in previous periods, the following six-level scheme can be used. (A number of different techniques are used in practice, but the important issue is to keep track of what is on hand, what is expected to arrive, what is needed, and what size orders should be placed.) One way to calculate the numbers is as follows:

WEEK

Gross requirements
Scheduled receipts
Projected available balance
Net requirements
Planned order receipt
Planned order release

One unit of A is made of three units of B, one unit of C, and two units of D. B is composed of two units of E and one unit of D. C is made of one unit of B and two units of E. E is made of one unit of F.

Items B, C, E, and F have one-week lead times; A and D have lead times of two weeks.

Assume that lot-for-lot (L4L) lot sizing is used for Items A, B, and F; lots of size 50, 50, and 200 are used for Items C, D, and E, respectively. Items C, E, and F have on-hand (beginning) inventories of 10, 50, and 150, respectively; all other items have zero beginning inventory. We are scheduled to receive 10 units of A in Week 2, 50 units of E in Week 1, and also 50 units of F in Week 1. There are no other scheduled receipts. If 30 units of A are required in Week 8, use the low-level-coded bill of materials (product structure tree) to find the necessary planned order releases for all components.

6 One unit of A is made of two units of B, three units of C, and two units of D. B is composed of one unit of E and two units of F. C is made of two units of F and one unit of D. E is made of two units of D. Items A, C, D, and F have one-week lead times; B and E have lead times of two weeks. Lot-for-lot (L4L) lot sizing is used for Items A, B, C, and D; lots of size 50 and 180 are used for Items E and F, respectively. Item C has an on-hand (beginning) inventory of 15; D has an on-hand inventory of 50; all other items have zero beginning inventory. We are scheduled to receive 20 units of Item E in Week 2; there are no other scheduled receipts.

Construct simple and low-level-coded bills of materials (product structure tree) and indented and summarized parts lists.

If 20 units of A are required in Week 8, use the low-level-coded bill of materials to find the necessary planned order releases for all components. (See the note in Problem 5.)

7 One unit of A is made of one unit of B and one unit of C. B is made of four units of C and one unit each of E and F. C is made of two units of D and one unit of E. E is made of three units of F. Item C has a lead time of one week; Items A, B, E, and F have two-week lead times; and Item D has a lead time of three weeks. Lot-for-lot lot sizing is used for Items A, D, and E; lots of size 50, 100, and 50 are used for Items B, C, and F, respectively. Items A, C, D, and E have on-hand (beginning) inventories of 20, 50, 100, and 10, respectively; all other items have zero beginning inventory. We are scheduled to receive 10 units of A in Week 1, 100 units of C in Week 1, and 100 units of D in Week 3; there are no other scheduled receipts. If 50 units of A are required in Week 10, use the low-level-coded bill of materials (product structure tree) to find the necessary planned order releases for all components. (See the note in Problem 5.)

8 One unit of A is made of two units of B and one unit of C. B is made of three units of D and one unit of F. C is composed of three units of B, one unit of D, and four units of E. D is made of one unit of E. Item C has a lead time of one week; Items A, B, E, and F have two-week lead times; and Item D has a lead time of three weeks. Lot-for-lot lot sizing is used for Items C, E, and F; lots of size 20, 40, and 160 are used for Items A, B, and D, respectively. Items A, B, D, and E have on-hand (beginning) inventories of 5, 10, 100, and 100, respectively; all other items have zero beginning inventories. We are scheduled to receive 10 units of A in Week 3, 20 units of B in Week 7, 40 units of F in Week 5, and 60 units of E in Week 2; there are no other scheduled receipts. If 20 units of A are required in Week 10, use the low-level-coded bill of materials (product structure tree) to find the necessary planned order releases for all components. (See the note in Problem 5.)

9 One unit of A is composed of two units of B and three units of C. Each B is composed of one unit of F. C is made of one unit of D, one unit of E, and two units of F. Items A, B, C, and D have 20, 50, 60, and 25 units of on-hand inventory. Items A, B, and C use lot-for-lot (L4L) as their lot-sizing technique, while D, E, and F require multiples of 50, 100, and 100, respectively, to be purchased. B has scheduled receipts of 30 units in Period 1. No other scheduled receipts exist. Lead times are one period for Items A, B, and D, and two

periods for Items C, E, and F. Gross requirements for A are 20 units in Period 1, 20 units in Period 2, 60 units in Period 6, and 50 units in Period 8. Find the planned order releases for all items.

10　Each unit of A is composed of one unit of B, two units of C, and one unit of D. C is composed of two units of D and three units of E. Items A, C, D, and E have on-hand inventories of 20, 10, 20, and 10 units, respectively. Item B has a scheduled receipt of 10 units in Period 1, and C has a scheduled receipt of 50 units in Period 1. Lot-for-lot (L4L) is used for Items A and B. Item C requires a minimum lot size of 50 units. D and E are required to be purchased in multiples of 100 and 50, respectively. Lead times are one period for Items A, B, and C, and two periods for Items D and E. The gross requirements for A are 30 in Period 2, 30 in Period 5, and 40 in Period 8. Find the planned order releases for all items.

11　The MRP gross requirements for Item A are shown here for the next 10 weeks. Lead time for A is three weeks and setup cost is $10. There is a carrying cost of $0.01 per unit per week. Beginning inventory is 90 units.

	WEEK									
	1	2	3	4	5	6	7	8	9	10
Gross requirements	30	50	10	20	70	80	20	60	200	50

Use the least total cost and the least unit cost lot-sizing method to determine when and for what quantity the first order should be released.

12　Product A is an end item and is made from two units of B and four of C. B is made of three units of D and two of E. C is made of two units of F and two of E.

A has a lead time of one week. B, C, and E have lead times of two weeks, and D and F have lead times of three weeks.

a. Show the bill of materials (product structure tree).

b. If 100 units of A are required in Week 10, develop the MRP planning schedule, specifying when items are to be ordered and received. There are currently no units of inventory on hand.

13　Product A consists of two units of Subassembly B, three units of C, and one unit of D. B is composed of four units of E and three units of F. C is made of two units of H and three units of D. H is made of five units of E and two units of G.

a. Construct a simple bill of materials (product structure tree).

b. Construct a product structure tree using low-level coding.

c. Construct an indented parts list.

d. To produce 100 units of A, determine the numbers of units of B, C, D, E, F, G, and H required.

14　The MRP gross requirements for Item X are shown here for the next 10 weeks. Lead time for A is two weeks, and setup cost is $9. There is a carrying cost of $0.02 per unit per week. Beginning inventory is 70 units.

	WEEK									
	1	2	3	4	5	6	7	8	9	10
Gross requirements	20	10	15	45	10	30	100	20	40	150

Use the least total cost and the least unit cost lot-sizing method to determine when and for what quantity the first order should be released.

15　Audio Products, Inc., produces two AM/FM/CD players for cars. The radio/CD units are identical, but the mounting hardware and finish trim differ. The standard model fits intermediate and full-size cars, and the sports model fits small sports cars.

Audio Products handles the production in the following way. The chassis (radio/CD unit) is assembled in Mexico and has a manufacturing lead time of two weeks. The mounting hardware is purchased from a sheet steel company and has a three-week lead time. The finish trim is purchased from a Taiwan electronics company with offices in Los Angeles as prepackaged units consisting of knobs and various trim pieces. Trim packages have a two-week lead time. Final assembly time may be disregarded because adding the trim package and mounting are performed by the customer.

Audio Products supplies wholesalers and retailers, who place specific orders for both models up to eight weeks in advance. These orders, together with enough additional units to satisfy the small number of individual sales, are summarized in the following demand schedule:

	WEEK							
MODEL	1	2	3	4	5	6	7	8
Standard model				300				400
Sports model					200			100

There are currently 50 radio/CD units on hand but no trim packages or mounting hardware.

Prepare a material requirements plan to meet the demand schedule exactly. Specify the gross and net requirements, on-hand amounts, and the planned order release and receipt periods for the radio/CD chassis, the standard trim and sports car model trim, and the standard mounting hardware and the sports car mounting hardware.

CASE: BRUNSWICK MOTORS, INC.—AN INTRODUCTORY CASE FOR MRP

Recently, Phil Harris, the production control manager at Brunswick, read an article on time-phased requirements planning. He was curious about how this technique might work in scheduling Brunswick's engine assembly operations and decided to prepare an example to illustrate the use of time-phased requirements planning.

Phil's first step was to prepare a master schedule for one of the engine types produced by Brunswick: the Model 1000 engine. This schedule indicates the number of units of the Model 1000 engine to be assembled each week during the last 12 weeks and is shown below. Next, Phil decided to simplify his requirements planning example by considering only two of the many components that are needed to complete the assembly of the Model 1000 engine. These two components, the gear box and the input shaft, are shown in the product structure diagram shown on the next page. Phil noted that the gear box is assembled by the Subassembly Department and subsequently is sent to the main engine assembly line. The input shaft is one of several component parts manufactured by Brunswick that are needed to produce a gear box subassembly. Thus, levels 0, 1, and 2 are included in the product structure diagram to indicate the three manufacturing stages that are involved in producing an engine: the Engine Assembly Department, the Subassembly Department, and the Machine Shop.

The manufacturing lead times required to produce the gear box and input shaft components are also indicated in the product structure diagram. Note that two weeks are required to produce a batch of gear boxes and that all the gear boxes must be delivered to the assembly line parts stockroom before Monday morning of the week in which they are to be used. Likewise, it takes three weeks to produce a lot of input shafts, and all the shafts that are needed for the production of gear boxes in a given week must be delivered to the Subassembly Department stockroom before Monday morning of that week.

In preparing the MRP example Phil planned to use the worksheets shown on the next page and make the following assumptions:

1. Seventeen gear boxes are on hand at the beginning of week 1, and five gear boxes are currently on order to be delivered at the start of week 2.
2. Forty input shafts are on hand at the start of week 1, and 22 are scheduled for delivery at the beginning of week 2.

ASSIGNMENT

1. Initially, assume that Phil wants to minimize his inventory requirements. Assume that each order will be only for what is required for a single period. Using the following forms, calculate the net requirements and planned order releases for the gear boxes and input shafts. Assume that lot sizing is done using lot-for-lot.
2. Phil would like to consider the costs that his accountants are currently using for inventory carrying and setup for the gear boxes and input shafts. These costs are as follows:

PART	COST
Gear Box	Setup = $90/order
	Inventory carrying cost = $2/unit/week
Input Shaft	Setup = $45/order
	Inventory carrying cost = $1/unit/week

Given the cost structure, evaluate the cost of the schedule from (1). Assume inventory is valued at the end of each week.

3. Calculate a schedule using least-total-cost lot sizing. What are the savings with this new schedule?

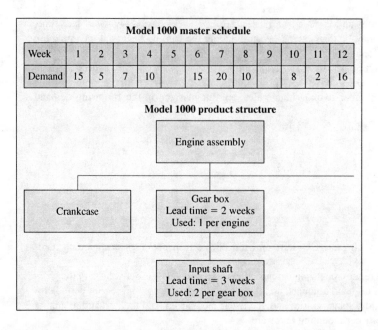

Model 1000 master schedule

Week	1	2	3	4	5	6	7	8	9	10	11	12
Demand	15	5	7	10		15	20	10		8	2	16

Model 1000 product structure

Engine assembly

Crankcase

Gear box
Lead time = 2 weeks
Used: 1 per engine

Input shaft
Lead time = 3 weeks
Used: 2 per gear box

Engine assembly master schedule

Week	1	2	3	4	5	6	7	8	9	10	11	12
Quantity												

Gear box requirements

Week	1	2	3	4	5	6	7	8	9	10	11	12
Gross requirements												
Scheduled receipts												
Projected available balance												
Net requirements												
Planned order release												

Input shaft requirements

Week	1	2	3	4	5	6	7	8	9	10	11	12
Gross requirements												
Scheduled receipts												
Projected available balance												
Net requirements												
Planned order release												

SUPER QUIZ

1 Logic used to calculate the needed parts, components, and other materials needed to produce an end item.

2 This drives the MRP calculations and is a detailed plan for how we expect to meet demand.

3 Period of time during which a customer has a specified level of opportunity to make changes.

4 This identifies the specific materials used to make each item and the correct quantities of each.

5 If an item is used in two places in a bill of material, say, level 3 and level 4, what low-level code would be assigned to the item?

6 One unit of Part C is used in item A and in item B. Currently, we have 10 A's, 20 B's, and 100 C's in inventory. We want to ship 60 A's and 70 B's. How many additional C's do we need to purchase?

7 These are orders that have already been released and are to arrive in the future.

8 This is the total amount required for a particular item.

9 This is the amount needed after considering what we currently have in inventory and what we expect to arrive in the future.

10 The planned order receipt and planned order release are offset by this amount of time.

11 These are the part quantities issued in the planned order release section of an MRP report.

12 Ordering exactly what is needed each period without regard to economic considerations.

13 None of the techniques for determining order quantity consider this important noneconomic factor that could make the order quantity infeasible.

1. Material requirements planning (MRP) 2. Master schedule 3. Time fence 4. Bill of materials 5. Level 4 6. Zero 7. Scheduled receipts 8. Gross requirements 9. Net requirements 10. Lead time 11. Lot sizes 12. Lot-for-lot ordering 13. Capacity

SELECTED BIBLIOGRAPHY

Orlicky, J. *Materials Requirements Planning.* 2nd ed. New York: McGraw-Hill, 1994. (This is the classic book on MRP)

Sheikh, K. *Manufacturing Resource Planning (MRP II) with Introduction to ERP, SCM, and CRM.* New York: McGraw-Hill, 2002.

Vollmann, T. E.; W. L. Berry; D. C. Whybark; and F. R. Jacobs. *Manufacturing Planning and Control Systems for Supply Chain Management.* 5th ed. New York: McGraw-Hill, 2004.

LEAN AND SUSTAINABLE SUPPLY CHAINS

chapter 8

GREEN IS THE NEW BLACK[1]

SURVEY SUGGESTS THAT ENVIRO-CONSCIOUS MANUFACTURERS ARE THE BEST RISK FOR INVESTORS

Many manufacturers still have a long way to go to address the risks and opportunities posed by the push toward more environment-friendly production processes, according to a new study conducted by RiskMetrics Group, a provider of risk management services. Those risks include higher energy costs due to tighter

After reading this chapter you will:

1. Describe how Green and Lean can complement each other.

2. Explain how a production pull system works.

3. Understand Toyota Production System concepts.

4. Summarize important attributes of a lean supply chain.

5. Analyze a supply chain process using value stream mapping.

6. Know the principles of supply chain design.

greenhouse gas (GHG) emissions standards, and the opportunities include growing global demand for more energy-efficient products.

The report ranks large manufacturers and other companies on their effectiveness in such areas as reducing GHG emissions, introducing energy-efficient projects, expanding renewable energy purchases, and integrating climate factors into product designs. However, perhaps reflecting

Top Ten Green Manufacturers

1. IBM Corp.
2. Dell Inc.
3. Intel
4. Johnson & Johnson
5. Nike
6. Applied Materials
7. Coca-Cola
8. Sun Microsystems
9. Hewlett-Packard
10. Molson Coors

SOURCE: RISKMETRICS GROUP

Supply Chain

the skepticism many people still have as to exactly what role, if any, manufacturing plays in global warming, many companies are largely ignoring climate change, particularly at the board and CEO level.

According to the report, which was sponsored by the Ceres Investor coalition, only 17 percent of the respondent companies say their boards receive climate-specific updates from management; 11 percent of the CEOs have taken leadership roles on climate change initiatives. The survey indicates that none of the companies have linked executive compensation directly to climate-related performance.

The survey indicates that green strategies that save energy and fight global warming have broad consumer appeal and political support. Companies that seize the initiative can gain market share, build investor confidence, and insulate themselves against future energy shocks and climate change regulations. It's simply smart business to employ these governance practices today.

The highest ranking green manufacturers in the study tend to be high-tech, with IBM leading the way, followed by Dell, Intel, Johnson & Johnson and Nike (see chart, "Top Ten Green Manufacturers"). High-tech companies were noteworthy for their product and service innovation, when it comes to making their operations, data centers, and product lines more energy efficient. IBM's energy conservation programs, for instance, helped save the company nearly $20 million last year.

Among other suggestions, the report recommends that companies raise supply chain awareness by including supply chain greenhouse gas emissions—those emissions that result from raw material extraction, production, transport, and packaging—in emissions inventories, as well as setting emission standards for suppliers.

LEAN PRODUCTION

Lean production

Supply Chain

Global

Customer value

The most significant operations and supply management approach of the past 50 years is lean production. In the context of supply chains, lean production refers to a focus on eliminating as much waste as possible. Moves that are not needed, unnecessary processing steps, and excess inventory in the supply chain are targets for improvement during the *learning* process. Some consultants in industry have coined the phrase *value chain* to refer to a process that identifies each step in the supply chain that delivers products and services to customers, emphasizes those that create value, and removes those that do not create value. Lean production may be one of the best tools for implementing green strategies in manufacturing and service processes.

The basis of lean thinking came from the just-in-time (JIT) production concepts pioneered in Japan at Toyota. Even though JIT gained worldwide prominence in the 1970s, some of its philosophy can be traced to the early 1900s in the United States. Henry Ford used JIT concepts as he streamlined his moving assembly lines to make automobiles. For example, to eliminate waste, he used the bottom of the packing crates for car seats as the floor board of the car. Although elements of JIT were being used by Japanese industry as early as the 1930s, it was not fully refined until the 1970s when Tai-ichi Ohno of Toyota Motors used JIT to take Toyota's cars to the forefront of delivery time and quality.

Customer value, in the context of lean production, is defined as something for which the customer is willing to pay. Value-adding activities transform materials and information into something the customer wants. Non-value-adding activities consume resources and do

not directly contribute to the end result desired by the customer. Waste, therefore, is defined   Waste
as anything that does not add value from the customer's perspective. Examples of process
wastes are defective products, overproduction, inventories, excess motion, processing steps,
transportation, and waiting.

Lean concepts also apply to service industries. Consider the nonmanufacturing example of a
flight to the Bahamas.[2] The value-adding part of that process is the flight itself. The non-value-
added parts of that process are driving to the airport, parking, walking to the terminal, checking-in,
waiting in line at check-in, walking to the security check, and so on. Many times the non-value-
added time far exceeds the value-added time in this type of process. Where should improvement
efforts be focused—on the non-value-added steps or on making the plane fly faster?

Understanding the difference between value and waste and value-added and non-value-
added processes is critical to understanding lean production. Sometimes it is not easy to
discern the difference when looking at the entire supply chain. The best way is to look at the
individual components and apply lean thinking to each one. Then determine how to link the
processes to reduce waste.

This chapter starts by reviewing the evolution of lean concepts from Japan and Toyota. We
then expand this view to encompass a complete supply chain. The remainder of the chapter is
devoted to value stream mapping, a tool that can be used to drive out waste and improve the
efficiency of the supply chain.

LEAN LOGIC

Lean production is an integrated set of activities designed to achieve production using
minimal inventories of raw materials, work-in-process, and finished goods. Parts arrive at
the next workstation "just-in-time" and are completed and move through the process quickly.
Lean is also based on the logic that nothing will be produced until it is needed. Exhibit 8.1
illustrates the process. Production need is created by actual demand for the product. When an
item is sold, in theory, the market pulls a replacement from the last position in the system—
final assembly in this case. This triggers an order to the factory production line, where a
worker then pulls another unit from an upstream station in the flow to replace the unit taken.
This upstream station then pulls from the next station further upstream and so on back to
the release of raw materials. To enable this pull process to work smoothly, lean production
demands high levels of quality at each stage of the process, strong vendor relations, and a
fairly predictable demand for the end product.

Lean Production Pull System   exhibit 8.1

Each stage of the system is tightly linked. Material is pulled through the system only when there is demand.

Sub = Subassembly
Fab = Fabrication

THE TOYOTA PRODUCTION SYSTEM

In this section we examine the philosophy and elements of lean production developed in Japan and embodied in the Toyota Production System—the benchmark for lean manufacturing. The Toyota Production System was developed to improve quality and productivity and is predicated upon two philosophies that are central to the Japanese culture: elimination of waste and respect for people.[3]

Global

ELIMINATION OF WASTE

Waste, as defined by Toyota's past president, Fujio Cho, is "anything other than the minimum amount of equipment, materials, parts, and workers (working time) which are absolutely essential to production." An expanded lean definition advanced by Fujio Cho identifies seven prominent types of waste to be eliminated from the supply chain: (1) waste from overproduction, (2) waste of waiting time, (3) transportation waste, (4) inventory waste, (5) processing waste, (6) waste of motion, and (7) waste from product defects.[4]

Global

RESPECT FOR PEOPLE

Respect for people is a key to the Toyota Production System. Toyota has traditionally strived to ensure lifetime employment for permanent positions and to maintain level payrolls even when business conditions deteriorate. Permanent workers (about one-third of the total workforce of Japan) have job security and tend to be more flexible, remain with a company, and do all they can to help a firm achieve its goals. (Global recessions have caused many Japanese companies to move away from this ideal.)

Company unions at Toyota as well as elsewhere in Japan exist to foster a cooperative relationship with management. All employees receive two bonuses a year in good times. Employees know that if the company performs well, they will get a bonus. This encourages workers to improve productivity. Management views workers as assets, not as human machines. Automation and robotics are used extensively to perform dull or routine jobs so employees are free to focus on important improvement tasks.

Toyota relies heavily on subcontractor networks. Indeed, more than 90 percent of all Japanese companies are part of the supplier network of small firms. Some suppliers are

TOYOTA'S DESIGN TEAM AT THEIR CALTY DESIGN RESEARCH FACILITIES IN CALIFORNIA. FROM CONCEPT TO COMPETITION VEHICLES, EACH TEAM MEMBER IS CONSIDERED AS IMPORTANT AS THE VEHICLES THEY DESIGN. CALTY PROVIDES DESIGN SOLUTIONS FOR TOYOTA, LEXUS AND SCION PRODUCT DEVELOPMENT.

specialists in a narrow field, usually serving multiple customers. Firms have long-term partnerships with their suppliers and customers. Suppliers consider themselves part of a customer's family.

A study by Christer Karlsson of the Stockholm School of Economics points out that the lean ideas found here are not universally used in all manufacturing companies in Japan. Rather, they are applied situationally and where appropriate. However, the fundamental ideas of elimination of waste and respect for workers are still foundations of the exceptional productivity of most Japanese manufacturing companies.[5]

LEAN SUPPLY CHAINS

The focus of the Toyota Production System is on elimination of waste and respect for people. As the concepts have evolved and become applied to the supply chain, the goal of maximizing customer value has been added. Customer value when considered in the context of the entire supply chain should center on the perspective of the end customer with the goal being to maximize what the customer is willing to pay for a firm's goods or services. The value stream consists of the value-adding and non-value-adding activities required to design, order, and provide a product or service from concept to launch, order to delivery, and raw materials to customers. Exhibit 8.2 is a map that depicts the flow of an item through a supply chain. This all-inclusive view of the system is a significant expansion of the scope of application of the lean concepts pioneered by Toyota. When applied to supply chains, waste reduction relates to the optimization of the value-adding activities and the elimination of non-value-adding activities that are part of the value stream.

Supply Chain

Value stream

Waste reduction

In the following we discuss the different components of a supply chain and what would be expected using a lean focus:

Lean Suppliers Lean suppliers are able to respond to changes. Their prices are generally lower due to the efficiencies of lean processes, and their quality has improved to the point that incoming inspection at the next link is not needed. Lean suppliers deliver on time and their culture is one of continuous improvement. To develop lean suppliers, organizations should include them in their value stream planning. This will help them fix problems and share savings.

Lean Procurement A key to lean procurement is automation. The term *e-procurement* relates to automatic transaction, sourcing, bidding, and auctions using Web-based applications, and the use of software that removes human interaction and integrates with the financial reporting of the firm. The key to lean procurement is visibility. Suppliers must be able to "see" into the customers' operations and customers must be able

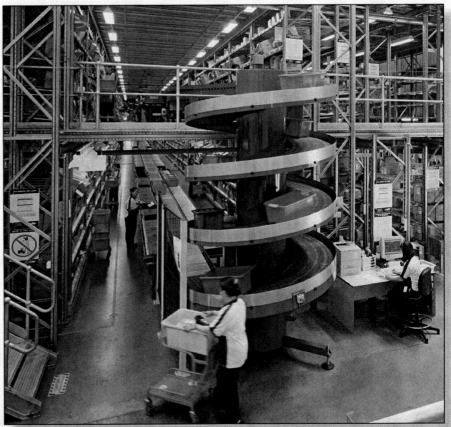

POST LOGISTICS IN AUSTRALIA DISTRIBUTES THE SPEEDO SWIMWEAR BRAND. THREE LEVELS OF STORAGE ARE CONNECTED BY A SPIRAL CONVEYOR LINKED TO A "SMART" HORIZONTAL CONVEYOR SYSTEM THAT INTERCONNECTS PICKING ZONES ON EACH OF THE THREE LEVELS AND CARRIES THROUGH TO A SIX-LANE PACKING AND DISTRIBUTION AREA.

exhibit 8.2   ACME Fulfillment Stream Current State: SKU 918

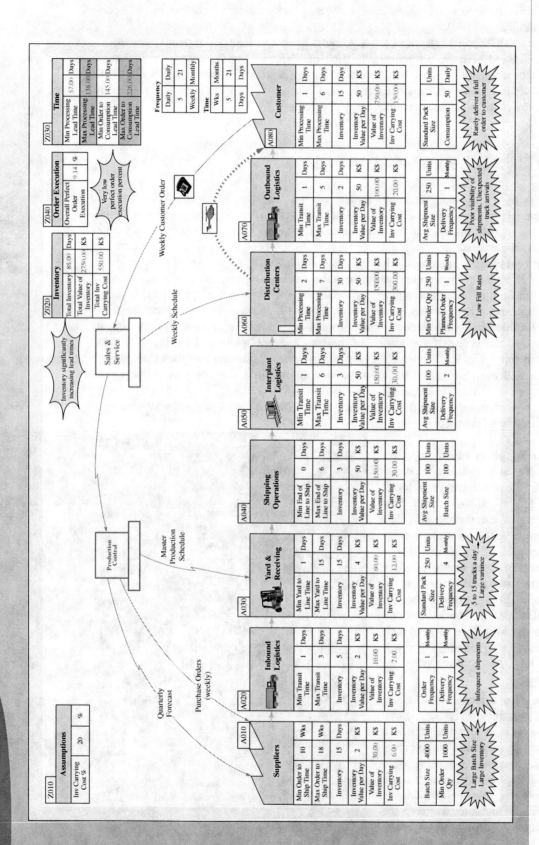

to "see" into their suppliers' operations. The overlap of these processes needs to be optimized to maximize value from the end customer perspective.

Lean Manufacturing   Lean manufacturing systems produce what customers want, in the quantity they want, when they want it, and with minimum resources. Applying lean concepts in manufacturing typically presents the greatest opportunities for cost reduction and quality improvement.

VOICE-DIRECTED ORDER FULFILLMENT ALLOWS WORKERS HANDS-FREE OPERATION FOR FASTER, SAFER, AND MORE ACCURATE INVENTORY PICKING. IT ALSO SUPPORTS THE USE OF MULTIPLE LANGUAGES.

Lean Warehousing   This relates to eliminating non-value-added steps and waste in product storage processes. Typical functions include the following: receiving of material; put-away/storing; replenishment of inventory; picking inventory; packing for shipment; and shipping. Waste can be found in many warehousing processes, including shipping defects, which create returns; overproduction or overshipment of products; excess inventory, which requires extra space and reduces warehouse efficiency; excess motion and handling; waiting for parts; and inadequate information systems.

Lean Logistics   Lean concepts can be applied to the functions associated with the movement of material through the system. Some of the key areas include optimized mode selection and pooling orders; combined multistop truckloads; optimized routing; cross docking; import/export transportation processes; and backhaul minimization. Just as with the other areas, these logistics functions need to be optimized by eliminating non-value-adding activities while improving the value-adding activities.

Lean Customers   Lean customers have a great understanding of their business needs and specify meaningful requirements. They value speed and flexibility and expect high levels of delivery performance. Lean customers are interested in establishing effective partnerships with their suppliers. Lean customers expect value from the products they purchase and provide value to their customers.

The benefits of a lean supply chain primarily are in the improved responsiveness to the customer. As business conditions change, the supply chain adapts to dynamic needs. The ideal is a culture of rapid change with a bias for change when it is needed. The reduced inventory inherent in a lean supply chain reduces obsolescence and reduces flow time through the value-added processes. The reduced cost along with improved customer service affords the firms using a lean supply chain a significant competitive advantage in the global marketplace.

VALUE STREAM MAPPING

Value stream mapping (VSM) is a special type of flowcharting tool that is valuable for the development of lean processes. The technique is used to visualize product flows through various processing steps. The tool also illustrates information flows that result from the process as well as information used to control flow through the process. The aim of this section is to provide a brief introduction to VSM and to illustrate its use with an example.

Value stream mapping

To create a lean process, one needs to have a full understanding of the business, including production processes, material flows, and information flows. In this section we discuss this in the context of a production process where a product is being made. VSM is not limited to this context and can be readily applied to service, logistics, distribution, or virtually any type of process.

exhibit 8.3   Manufacturing Process Map

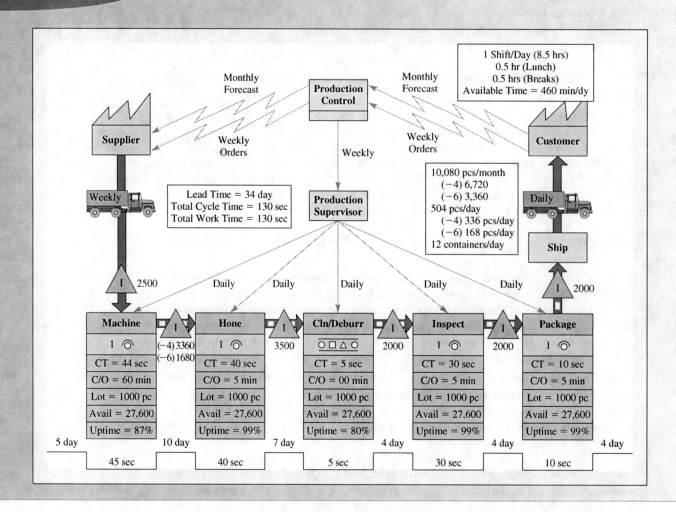

In the context of a production process such as a manufacturing plant, the technique is used to identify all of the value-adding as well as non-value-adding processes that materials are subjected to within a plant, from raw material coming into the plant through delivery to the customer. Exhibit 8.3 is a sample map that depicts a production process. With this map, identification of wasteful processes and flows can be made so that they can be modified or eliminated, and the manufacturing system can be made more productive.

Details explaining the symbols will be discussed later in the section but here it is useful to discuss what the information in the map depicted in Exhibit 8.3 actually means.[6] Starting from the left, we see that material is supplied on a weekly basis and deposited in a raw material inventory indicated by the triangle. The average level for this inventory is 2,500 units. This material is run through a five-step process consisting of machining, honing, cleaning, inspection, and packaging. The machining, honing, inspection, and packaging process all use a single operator. Under each of these process symbols is the activity cycle time (CT), changeover time (C/O time to switch from one type of item to another), lot size, available number of seconds per day, and percent uptime. The cleaning/duburring activity is a multistep process where items are handled on a first-come-first-served basis. Between each process are inventory buffers with the average inventory in these buffers depicted in the exhibit.

Information flows are shown on the map. In Exhibit 8.3 we see that production control issues monthly demand forecasts, weekly orders to the supplier, and a weekly production

Value Stream Mapping Symbols

exhibit 8.4

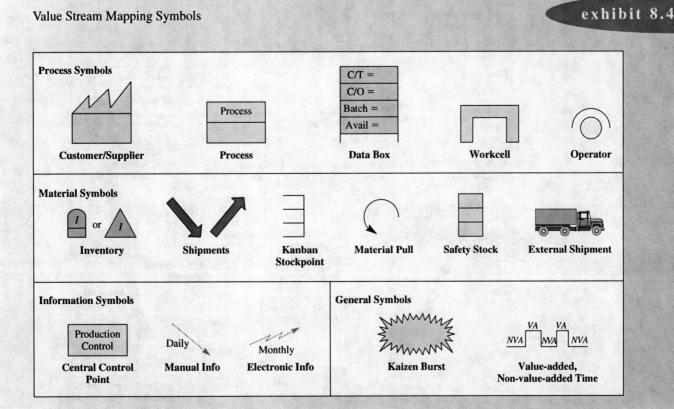

schedule that is managed by the supervisor on a daily basis. Monthly forecasts are provided by customers, and they place their orders on a weekly basis. The time line at the bottom shows the processing time for each production activity (in seconds) together with the average inventory wait time. Adding these times together gives an estimate of the lead time through the entire system.

VSM symbols are generally standardized but there are many variations. Several common symbols are depicted in Exhibit 8.4. These are categorized as process, material, information, and general symbols.

Value stream mapping is a two-part process—first depicting the "current state" of the process, and second a possible "future state." Exhibit 8.5 depicts another map of the same process with suggested improvements. The map has been annotated using Kaizen bursts that suggest the areas for improvement. Kaizen is the Japanese philosophy that focuses on continuous improvement. In this exhibit we see a totally redesigned process where the individual production operations have been combined into a workcell operated by three employees. In addition, rather than "pushing" material through the system based on weekly schedules generated by production control, the entire process is converted to a pull system that is operated directly in response to customer demand. Note that the lead time in the new system is only 5 days, compared to the 34-day lead time with the old system.

Kaizen

VSM is a great visual way to analyze an existing system and to find areas where waste can be eliminated. Value stream maps are simple to draw and it is possible to construct the maps totally using paper and pencil. These maps can, however, be more easily constructed using standard office software or graphics packages. Additionally, dedicated VSM software is available from Strategos (**www.strategosinc.com**) and System2win (**www.Systems2win.com**).

exhibit 8.5   Analysis Showing Potential Areas for Improving a Process

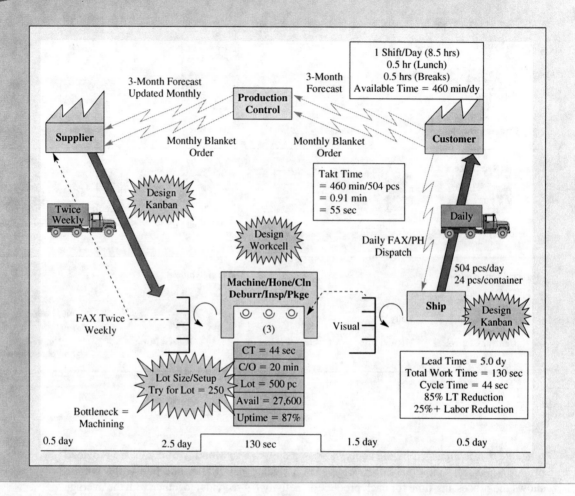

LEAN SUPPLY CHAIN DESIGN PRINCIPLES

Supply Chain

Value stream mapping is a great way to analyze existing processes. Looking for ways to improve supply chain processes should be based on ideas that have been proven over time. In the following we review a set of key principles which can guide the design of lean supply chains. We divide our design principles into three major categories. The first two sets of principles relate to internal production processes. These are the processes that actually create the goods and services within a firm. The third category applies lean concepts to the entire supply chain. These principles include:

1. Lean Layouts
   a. Group technology
   b. Quality at the source
   c. JIT production
2. Lean Production Schedules
   a. Uniform plant loading
   b. Kanban production control system
   c. Determination of number of Kanbans needed
   d. Minimized setup times
3. Lean supply chains
   a. Specialized plants
   b. Work with suppliers
   c. Building a lean supply chain

LEAN LAYOUTS

Lean requires the plant layout to be designed to ensure balanced work flow with a minimum of work-in-process inventory. Each workstation is part of a production line, whether or not a physical line actually exists. Capacity is balanced using the same logic for an assembly line, and operations are linked through a pull system. In addition, the system designer must visualize how all aspects of the internal and external logistics system tie to the layout.

Preventive maintenance is emphasized to ensure that flows are not interrupted by downtime or malfunctioning equipment. Preventive maintenance involves periodic inspection and repair designed to keep a machine reliable. Operators perform much of the maintenance because they are most familiar with their machines and because machines are easier to repair, as lean operations favor several simple machines rather than one large complex one.

Preventive maintenance

Group Technology   Group technology (GT) is a philosophy in which similar parts are grouped into families, and the processes required to make the parts are arranged in a manufacturing cell. Instead of transferring jobs from one specialized department to another, GT considers all operations required to make a part and groups those machines together. Exhibit 8.6 illustrates the difference between the clusters of different machines grouped into cells versus departmental layouts. The group technology cells eliminate movement and queue (waiting) time between operations, reduce inventory, and reduce the number of employees required. Workers, however, must be flexible to run several machines and processes. Due to their advanced skill level, these workers have increased job security.

Group technology

Quality at the Source   Quality at the source means do it right the first time and, when something goes wrong, stop the process or assembly line immediately. Factory workers become their own inspectors, personally responsible for the quality of their output. Workers concentrate on one part of the job at a time so quality problems are uncovered. If the pace is too fast, if the worker finds a quality problem, or if a safety issue is discovered, the worker is obligated to push a button to stop the line and turn on a visual signal. People from other areas respond to the alarm and the problem. Workers are empowered to do their own maintenance and housekeeping until the problem is fixed.

Quality at the source

JIT Production   JIT (just-in-time) means producing what is needed when needed and no more. Anything over the minimum amount necessary is viewed as waste, because effort

Group Technology versus Departmental Specialty

exhibit 8.6

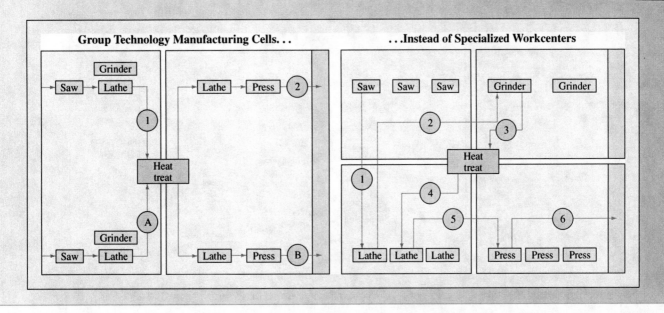

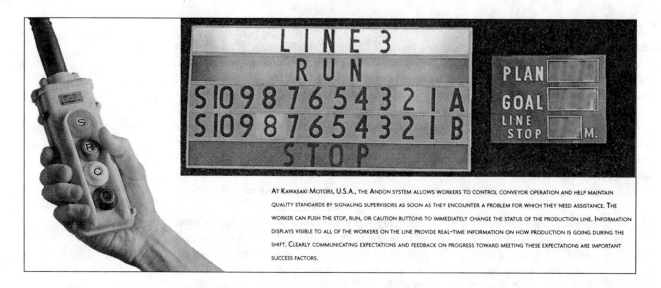

AT KAWASAKI MOTORS, U.S.A., THE ANDON SYSTEM ALLOWS WORKERS TO CONTROL CONVEYOR OPERATION AND HELP MAINTAIN QUALITY STANDARDS BY SIGNALING SUPERVISORS AS SOON AS THEY ENCOUNTER A PROBLEM FOR WHICH THEY NEED ASSISTANCE. THE WORKER CAN PUSH THE STOP, RUN, OR CAUTION BUTTONS TO IMMEDIATELY CHANGE THE STATUS OF THE PRODUCTION LINE. INFORMATION DISPLAYS VISIBLE TO ALL OF THE WORKERS ON THE LINE PROVIDE REAL-TIME INFORMATION ON HOW PRODUCTION IS GOING DURING THE SHIFT. CLEARLY COMMUNICATING EXPECTATIONS AND FEEDBACK ON PROGRESS TOWARD MEETING THESE EXPECTATIONS ARE IMPORTANT SUCCESS FACTORS.

and material expended for something not needed now cannot be utilized now. This is in contrast to relying on extra material just in case something goes wrong.

JIT is typically applied to repetitive manufacturing, which is when the same or similar items are made one after another. JIT does not require large volumes and can be applied to any repetitive segments of a business regardless of where they appear. Under JIT the ideal lot size or production batch is one. Although workstations may be geographically dispersed, it is important to minimize transit time and keep transfer quantities small—typically one-tenth of a day's production. Vendors even ship several times a day to their customers to keep lot sizes small and inventory low. The goal is to drive all inventory queues to zero, thus minimizing inventory investment and shortening lead times.

When inventory levels are low, quality problems become very visible. Exhibit 8.7 illustrates this idea. If the water in a pond represents inventory, the rocks represent problems that could occur in a firm. A high level of water hides the problems (rocks). Management assumes everything is fine, but as the water level drops in an economic downturn, problems are presented. If you deliberately force the water level down (particularly in good economic times), you can expose and correct problems before they cause worse problems. JIT manufacturing exposes problems otherwise hidden by excess inventories and staff.

exhibit 8.7   Inventory Hides Problems

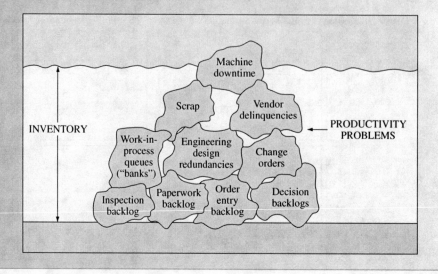

LEAN PRODUCTION SCHEDULES

As noted earlier, lean production requires a stable schedule over a lengthy time horizon. This is accomplished by level scheduling, freeze windows, and underutilization of capacity. A level schedule is one that requires material to be pulled into final assembly in a pattern uniform enough to allow the various elements of production to respond to pull signals. It does not necessarily mean that the usage of every part on an assembly line is identified hour by hour for days on end; it does mean that a given production system equipped with flexible setups and a fixed amount of material in the pipelines can respond.[7]

Level schedule

The term freeze window refers to that period of time during which the schedule is fixed and no further changes are possible. An added benefit of the stable schedule is seen in how parts and components are accounted for in a pull system. Here, the concept of backflush is used where the parts that go into each unit of the product are periodically removed from inventory and accounted for based on the number of units produced. This eliminates much of the shop-floor data collection activity, which is required if each part must be tracked and accounted for during production.

Freeze window

Backflush

Underutilization and overutilization of capacity are controversial features of lean production. Conventional approaches use safety stocks and early deliveries as a hedge against production problems like poor quality, machine failures, and unanticipated bottlenecks in traditional manufacturing. Under lean production, excess labor, machines, and overtime provide the hedge. The excess capacity in labor and equipment that results is much cheaper than carrying excess inventory. When demand is greater than expected, overtime must be used. Often part-time labor is used when additional capacity is needed. During idle periods, personnel can be put to work on other activities such as special projects, work group activities, and workstation housekeeping.

Uniform Plant Loading Smoothing the production flow to dampen the reaction waves that normally occur in response to schedule variations is called uniform plant loading. When a change is made in a final assembly, the changes are magnified throughout the line and the supply chain. The only way to eliminate the problem is to make adjustments as small as possible by setting a firm monthly production plan for which the output rate is frozen.

Uniform plant loading

Toyota found it could do this by building the same mix of products every day in small quantities. Thus, a total mix is always available to respond to variations in demand. A Toyota example is shown in Exhibit 8.8. Monthly car style quantities are reduced to daily quantities (assuming a 20-day month) in order to compute a model *cycle time* (defined here as the time between two identical units being completed on the line). The cycle time figure is used to adjust resources to produce the precise quantity needed. The speed of equipment or of the production line is adjusted so only the needed quantity is produced each day. JIT strives to produce on schedule, on cost, and on quality.

Kanban Production Control Systems A kanban control system uses a signaling device to regulate JIT flows. Kanban means "sign" or "instruction card" in Japanese. In a paperless control system, containers can be used instead of cards. The cards or containers

Kanban

Toyota Example of Mixed-Model Production Cycle in a Japanese Assembly Plant

exhibit 8.8

MODEL	MONTHLY QUANTITY	DAILY QUANTITY	MODEL CYCLE TIME (MINUTES)
Sedan	5,000	250	2
Hardtop	2,500	125	4
Wagon	2,500	125	4

SEQUENCE: SEDAN, HARDTOP, SEDAN, WAGON, SEDAN, HARDTOP, SEDAN, WAGON, AND SO ON (ONE MINUTE APART)

exhibit 8.9   Flow of Two Kanbans

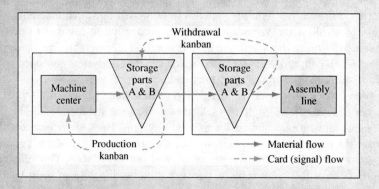

Kanban pull system

make up the kanban pull system. The authority to produce or supply additional parts comes from downstream operations. Consider Exhibit 8.9, where we show an assembly line that is supplied with parts by a machine center. The machine center makes two parts, A and B. These two parts are stored in containers that are located next to the assembly line and next to the machine center. Each container next to the assembly line has a withdrawal kanban, and each container next to the machine center has a production kanban. This is often referred to as a two-card kanban system.

When the assembly line takes the first part A from a full container, a worker takes the withdrawal kanban from the container, and takes the card to the machine center storage area. In the machine center area, the worker finds a container of part A, removes the production kanban, and replaces it with the withdrawal kanban. Placement of this card on the container authorizes the movement of the container to the assembly line. The freed production kanban is placed on a rack by the machine center, which authorizes the production of another lot of material. A similar process is followed for part B. The cards on the rack become the dispatch list for the machine center. Cards are not the only way to signal the need for production of a part; other visual methods are possible, as shown in Exhibit 8.10.

exhibit 8.10   Diagram of Outbound Stockpoint with Warning Signal Marker

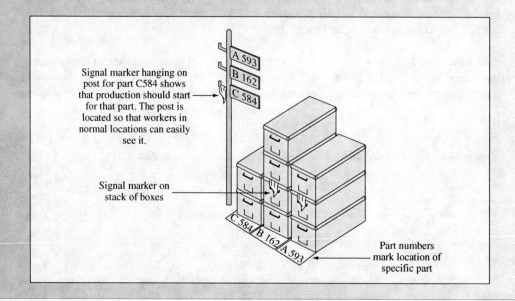

The following are some other possible approaches:

Kanban squares. Some companies use marked spaces on the floor or on a table to identify where material should be stored. When the square is empty, the supplying operations are authorized to produce; when the square is full, no parts are needed.

Container system. Sometimes the container itself can be used as a signal device. In this case, an empty container on the factory floor visually signals the need to fill it. The amount of inventory is adjusted by simply adding or removing containers.

Colored golf balls. At a Kawasaki engine plant, when a part used in a subassembly is down to its queue limit, the assembler rolls a colored golf ball down a pipe to the replenishment machine center. This tells the operator which part to make next. Many variations have been developed on this approach.

The kanban pull approach can be used not only within a manufacturing facility but also between manufacturing facilities (pulling engines and transmissions into an automobile assembly operation, for example) and between manufacturers and external suppliers.

Supply Chain

Determining the Number of Kanbans Needed Setting up a kanban control system requires determination of the number of kanban cards (or containers) needed. In a two-card system, we are finding the number of sets of withdrawal and production cards. The kanban cards represent the number of containers of material that flow back and forth between the supplier and the user areas. Each container represents the minimum production lot size to be supplied. The number of containers, therefore, directly controls the amount of work-in-process inventory in the system.

Accurately estimating the lead time needed to produce a container of parts is the key to determining the number of containers. This lead time is a function of the processing time for the container, any waiting time during the production process, and the time required to transport the material to the user. Enough kanbans are needed to cover the expected demand during this lead time plus some additional amount for safety stock. The number of kanban card sets is

$$k = \frac{\text{Expected demand during lead time} + \text{Safety stock}}{\text{Size of the container}}$$

$$= \frac{DL(1 + S)}{C} \qquad [8.1]$$

where

k = Number of kanban card sets

D = Average number of units demanded per period (lead time and demand must be expressed in the same time units)

L = Lead time to replenish an order (expressed in the same units as demand)

S = Safety stock expressed as a percentage of demand during the lead time (This can be based on a service level and variance.)

C = Container size

Observe that a kanban system does not produce zero inventory; rather, it controls the amount of material that can be in process at a time—the number of containers of each item. The kanban system can be easily adjusted to fit the current way the system is operating, because card sets can be easily added or removed from the system. If the workers find that they are not able to consistently replenish the item on time, an additional container of material, with the accompanying kanban cards, can be added. If it is found that excess containers of material accumulate, card sets can be easily removed, thus reducing the amount of inventory.

EXAMPLE 8.1: Determining the Number of Kanban Card Sets

Arvin Automotive, a company that makes muffler assemblies for the Big Three, is committed to the use of kanban to pull material through its manufacturing cells. Arvin has designed each cell to fabricate a specific family of muffler products. Fabricating a muffler assembly involves cutting and bending pieces

Step by Step

of pipe that are welded to a muffler and a catalytic converter. The mufflers and catalytic converters are pulled into the cell based on current demand. The catalytic converters are made in a specialized cell.

Catalytic converters are made in batches of 10 units and are moved in special hand carts to the fabrication cells. The catalytic converter cell is designed so that different types of catalytic converters can be made with virtually no setup loss. The cell can respond to an order for a batch of catalytic converters in approximately four hours. Because the catalytic converter cell is right next to the muffler assembly fabrication cell, transportation time is virtually zero.

The muffler assembly fabrication cell averages approximately eight assemblies per hour. Each assembly uses the same catalytic converter. Due to some variability in the process, management has decided to have safety stock equivalent to 10 percent of the needed inventory.

How many kanban sets are needed to manage the replenishment of the catalytic converters?

SOLUTION

In this case, the lead time for replenishment of the converters (L) is four hours. The demand (D) for the catalytic converters is eight per hour. Safety stock (S) is 10 percent of the expected demand, and the container size (C) is 10 units.

$$k = \frac{8 \times 4(1 + .1)}{10} = \frac{35.2}{10} = 3.52$$

In this case, we would need four kanban card sets, and we would have four containers of converters in the system. In all cases, when we calculate k, we will round the number up because we always need to work with full containers of parts. ●

Minimized Setup Times   The reductions in setup and changeover times are necessary to achieve a smooth flow. Exhibit 8.11 shows the relationship between lot size and setup costs. Under a traditional approach, setup cost is treated as a constant, and the optimal order quantity is shown as six. Under the kanban approach, setup cost is significantly reduced and

exhibit 8.11   Relationship between Lot Size and Setup Cost

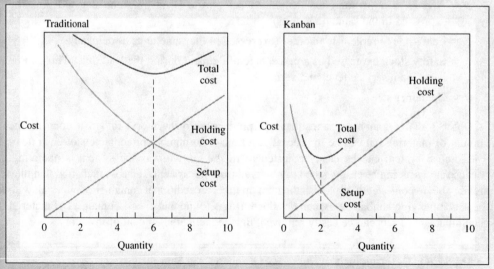

Definitions: *Holding* cost includes the costs of storing inventory and the cost of money tied up in inventory. Setup cost includes the wage costs attributable to workers making the setup, and various administrative and supplies costs.

the corresponding optimal order quantity is reduced. In the exhibit, the order quantity has been reduced from six to two under lean methods by employing setup-time–saving procedures. This organization will ultimately strive for a lot size of one.

In a widely cited example from the late 1970s, Toyota teams of press operators producing car hoods and fenders were able to change an 800-ton press in 10 minutes, compared with the average of six hours for U.S. workers and four hours for German workers. (Now, however, such speed is common in most U.S. auto plants.) To achieve such setup time reduction, setups are divided into internal and external activities. Internal setups must be done while a machine is stopped. External setups can be done while the machine is running. Other time-saving devices such as duplicate tool holders also are used to speed setups.

Global

LEAN SUPPLY CHAINS

Building a lean supply chain involves taking a systems approach to integrating the partners. Supply must be coordinated with the need of the production facilities and production must be tied directly to the demand of the customers for products. The importance of speed and steady, consistent flow that is responsive to actual customer demand cannot be overemphasized. Concepts that relate to lean network design are discussed next.

Supply Chain

Specialized Plants   Small specialized plants rather than large vertically integrated manufacturing facilities are important. Large operations and their inherent bureaucracies are difficult to manage and not in line with the lean philosophy. Plants designed for one purpose can be constructed and operated more economically. These plants need to be linked so they can be synchronized to one another and to the actual need of the market. Speed and quick response to changes are keys to the success of a lean supply chain.

Work with Suppliers   Just as customers and employees are key components of lean systems, suppliers are also important to the process. If a firm shares its projected usage requirements with its vendors, they have a long-run picture of the demands that will be placed on their production and distribution systems. Some vendors are linked online with a customer to share production scheduling and input needs data. This permits them to develop level production systems. Confidence in the supplier or vendor's delivery commitment allows reductions of buffer inventories. Maintaining stock at a lean level requires frequent deliveries during the day. Some suppliers even deliver directly to a location on the production line and not at a receiving dock. When vendors adopt quality practices, incoming receiving inspections of their products can be bypassed.

Building a Lean Supply Chain   A supply chain is the sum total of organizations involved—from raw materials firms through tiers of suppliers to original equipment manufacturers, onward to the ultimate distribution and delivery of the finished product to the customer. Womack and Jones, in their seminal work *Lean Thinking,* provide the following guidelines for implementing a lean supply chain:[8]

- Value must be defined jointly for each product family along with a target cost based on the customer's perception of value.
- All firms along the value stream must make an adequate return on their investments related to the value stream.
- The firms must work together to identify and eliminate *muda* (waste) to the point where the overall target cost and return-on-investment targets of each firm are met.
- When cost targets are met, the firms along the stream will immediately conduct new analyses to identify remaining *muda* and set new targets.
- Every participating firm has the right to examine every activity in every firm relevant to the value stream as part of the joint search for waste.

To summarize: To be lean, everyone's got to be on the same page!

LEAN SERVICES

Service

Global

Many lean techniques have been successfully applied by service firms. Just as in manufacturing, the suitability of each technique and the corresponding work steps depend on the characteristics of the firm's markets, production and equipment technology, skill sets, and corporate culture. Service firms are not different in this respect. Here are 10 of the more successful techniques applied to service companies:

1. **Organize Problem-Solving Groups** Honeywell is extending its use of quality teams from manufacturing into its service operations. Other corporations as diverse as First Bank/Dallas, Standard Meat Company, and Miller Brewing Company are using similar approaches to improve service. British Airways used quality teams as a fundamental part of its strategy to implement new service practices.

2. **Upgrade Housekeeping** Good housekeeping means more than winning the clean broom award. It means that only the necessary items are kept in a work area, that there is a place for everything, and that everything is clean and in a constant state of readiness. The employees clean their own areas.

   Service organizations such as McDonald's, Disneyland, and Speedi-Lube have recognized the critical nature of housekeeping. Their dedication to housekeeping has meant that service processes work better, the attitude of continuous improvement is easier to develop, and customers perceive that they are receiving better service.

3. **Upgrade Quality** The only cost-effective way to improve quality is to develop reliable process capabilities. Process quality is quality at the source—it guarantees first-time production of consistent and uniform products and services.

   McDonald's is famous for building quality into its service delivery process. It literally "industrialized" the service delivery system so that part-time, casual workers could provide the same eating experience anywhere in the world. Quality doesn't mean producing the best; it means consistently producing products and services that give the customers their money's worth.

4. **Clarify Process Flows** Clarification of flows, based on JIT themes, can dramatically improve the process performance. Here are three examples.

   First, Federal Express Corporation changed air flight patterns from origin-to-destination to origin-to-hub, where the freight is transferred to an outbound plane heading for the destination. This revolutionized the air transport industry. Second, the order-entry department of a manufacturing firm converted from functional subdepartments to customer-centered work groups and reduced the order processing lead time from eight to two days. Finally, Supermaids sends in a team of house cleaners, each with a specific responsibility, to clean a part of each house quickly with parallel processes. Changes in process flows can literally revolutionize service industries.

5. **Revise Equipment and Process Technologies** Revising technologies involves evaluation of the equipment and processes for their ability to meet the process requirements, to process consistently within tolerance, and to fit the scale and capacity of the work group.

   Speedi-Lube converted the standard service station concept to a specialized lubrication and inspection center by changing the service bays from drive-in to drive-through and by eliminating the hoists and instead building pits under the cars where employees have full access to the lubrication areas on the vehicle.

   A hospital reduced operating room setup time so that it had the flexibility to perform a wider range of operations without reducing the operating room availability.

6. **Level the Facility Load** Service firms synchronize production with demand. They have developed unique approaches to leveling demand so they can avoid making customers wait for service. McDonald's offers a special breakfast menu in the morning. Retail stores use take-a-number systems. The post office charges more for next-day delivery. These are all examples of the service approach for creating uniform facility loads.

7. **Eliminate Unnecessary Activities**   A step that does not add value is a candidate for elimination. A step that does add value may be a candidate for reengineering to improve the process consistency or to reduce the time to perform the tasks.

   A hospital discovered that significant time was spent during an operation waiting for an instrument that was not available when the operation began. It developed a checklist of instruments required for each category of operation. Speedi-Lube eliminated steps, but also added steps that did not improve the lubrication process but did make customers feel more assured about the work being performed.

8. **Reorganize Physical Configuration**   Work area configurations frequently require reorganization during a lean implementation. Often manufacturers accomplish this by setting up manufacturing cells to produce items in small lots, synchronous to demand. These cells amount to microfactories inside the plant.

   Most service firms are far behind manufacturers in this area. However, a few interesting examples do come out of the service sector. Some hospitals—instead of routing patients all over the building for tests, exams, X-rays, and injections—are reorganizing their services into work groups based on the type of problem. Teams that treat only trauma are common, but other work groups have been formed to treat less immediate conditions like hernias. These amount to microclinics within the hospital facility.

9. **Introduce Demand-Pull Scheduling**   Due to the nature of service production and consumption, demand-pull (customer-driven) scheduling is necessary for operating a service business. Moreover, many service firms are separating their operations into "back room" and "customer contact" facilities. This approach creates new problems in coordinating schedules between the facilities. The original Wendy's restaurants were set up so cooks could see cars enter the parking lot. They put a preestablished number of hamburger patties on the grill for each car. This pull system was designed to have a fresh patty on the grill before the customer even placed an order.

10. **Develop Supplier Networks**   The term *supplier networks* in the lean context refers to the cooperative association of suppliers and customers working over the long term for mutual benefit. Service firms have not emphasized supplier networks for materials because the service costs are often predominantly labor. Notable exceptions include service organizations like McDonald's, one of the biggest food products purchasers in the world, which has been developing lean practices. Manpower and other employment agencies have established lean-type relationships with a temporary employment service and a trade school to develop a reliable source of trained assemblers.

SUMMARY

Lean production has proven its value to thousands of companies throughout the world. The idea behind *lean* is achieving high volume with minimal inventory. Toyota pioneered the ideas associated with *lean production* with the Toyota Production System. Lean concepts are best applied in environments where the same products are produced over and over at relatively high volume. Value stream mapping is a useful tool for visualizing supply chains and for applying lean concepts.

KEY TERMS

Lean production Integrated activities designed to achieve high-volume, high-quality production using minimal inventories of raw materials, work-in-process, and finished goods.

Customer value In the context of lean, something for which the customer is willing to pay.

Waste Something that does not add value from the customer's perspective.

Value stream These are the value-adding and non-value-adding activities required to design, order, and provide a product from concept to launch, order to delivery, and raw materials to customers.

Waste reduction The optimization of value-adding activities and elimination of non-value-adding activities that are part of the value stream.

Value stream mapping A graphical way to analyze where value is or is not being added as material flows through a process.

Kaizen Japanese philosophy that focuses on continuous improvement.

Preventive maintenance Periodic inspection and repair designed to keep equipment reliable.

Group technology A philosophy in which similar parts are grouped into families, and the processes required to make the parts are arranged in a specialized work cell.

Quality at the source Philosophy of making factory workers personally responsible for the quality of their output. Workers are expected to make the part correctly the first time and to stop the process immediately if there is a problem.

Level schedule A schedule that pulls material into final assembly at a constant rate.

Freeze window The period of time during which the schedule is fixed and no further changes are possible.

Backflush Calculating how many of each part were used in production and using these calculations to adjust actual on-hand inventory balances. This eliminates the need to actually track each part used in production.

Uniform plant loading Smoothing the production flow to dampen schedule variation.

Kanban and the kanban pull system An inventory or production control system that uses a signaling device to regulate flows.

FORMULA REVIEW

Determining the number of kanbans

$$k = \frac{DL(1 + S)}{C} \qquad [8.1]$$

SOLVED PROBLEMS

SOLVED PROBLEM 1

Value Stream Mapping Example: Bolt Manufacturing[9]

A simple example will illustrate the use of value stream mapping. Exhibit 8.12 depicts a bolt manufacturing operation that ships 7,500 bolts per week. The current state map provides cycle time and setup time information for each of the 15 processes used, and it provides inventory levels at each location. The map also depicts information flow between the steel supplier, the bolt customer, and management via production scheduling. The total value-added time, denoted as processing time, is obtained by summing all of the individual value-added contributions at each processing step on the time line. For the example, it equals 28.88 seconds. At each inventory location, lead time is calculated by dividing inventory level by daily production demand, which is 1,500 bolts. Summing all of the lead time produces an overall production lead time of 66.1 days, which is the entire time it takes an individual bolt to make its way through the plant.

There are several possibilities to optimize the current production scenario. Exhibit 8.13 provides a few of these, shown as Kaizen bursts, including eliminating several processing steps, modifying some of the existing processes, and reducing travel distances between processes. Exhibit 8.14, the future state map, illustrates the incorporation of these modifications. As shown, the changes reduce production lead time to 50.89 days, which is a 23 percent reduction. The production scenario could be enhanced even more if pull systems were incorporated at various locations.

SOLVED PROBLEM 2

A local hospital wants to set up a kanban system to manage its supply of blood with the regional blood bank. The regional blood bank delivers blood to the hospital each day with a one-day order lead time (an order placed by 6 P.M. today will be delivered tomorrow afternoon). Internally, the hospital purchasing group places orders for blood each day at 5 P.M. Blood is measured by the pint and is shipped in containers that contain six pints. For a particular blood type, the hospital uses an average of 12 pints per day. Due to the critical nature of a blood shortage, the hospital wants to carry a safety stock of two days' expected supply. How many kanban card sets should the hospital prepare?

exhibit 8.12   Current State Map for Bolt Manufacturing Example

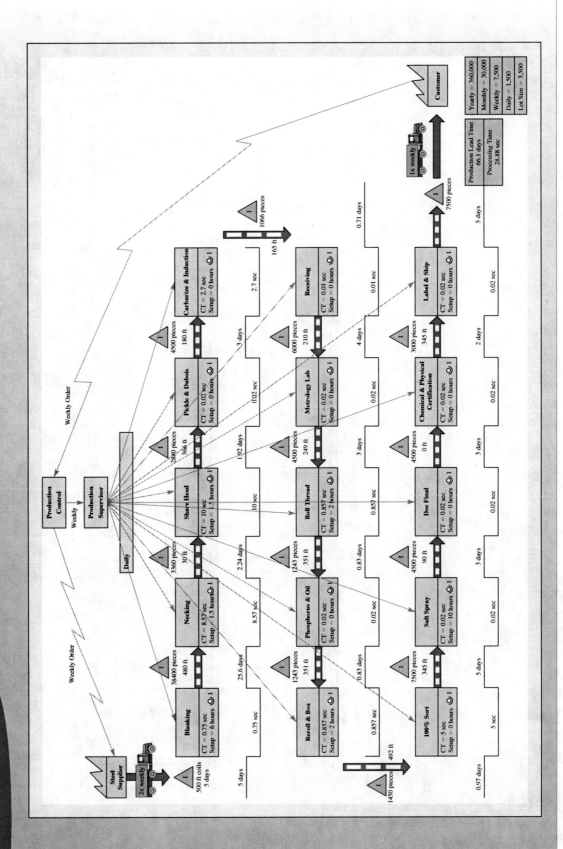

exhibit 8.13 Potential Process Changes for Bolt Manufacturing Example

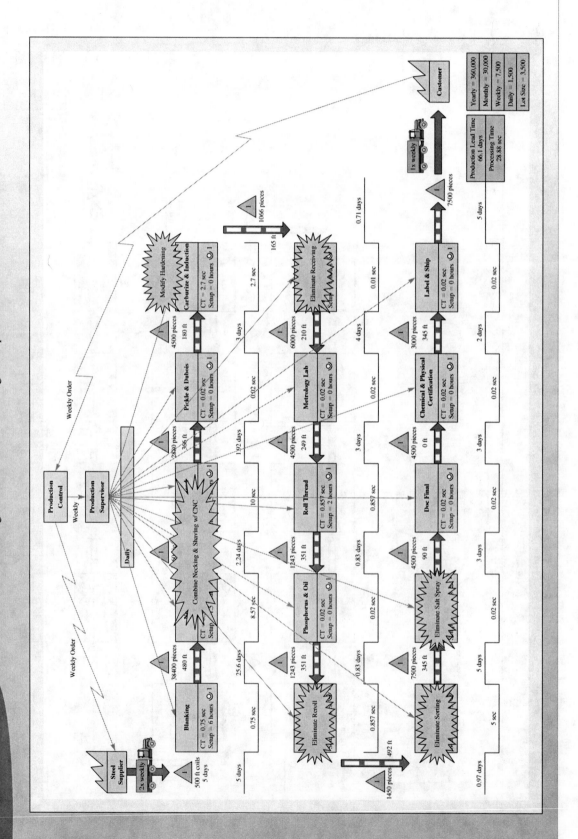

exhibit 8.14   Future State Map for Bolt Manufacturing Example

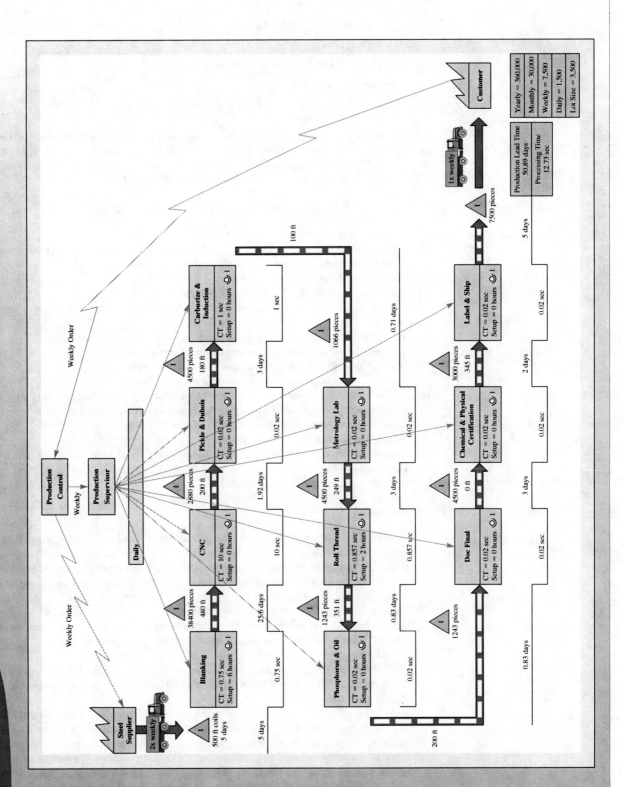

Solution

This problem is typical of how a real application might look. Using the data given, the variables for this problem are as follows:

D = 12 pints per day (average demand)

L = 1 day (lead time)

S = 200 percent (safety stock, as a fraction this is 2.0)

C = 6 pints (container size)

$$k = \frac{DL(1 + S)}{C} = \frac{12(1 + 2)}{6} = 6$$

This indicates that we need to prepare six kanban card sets. Each time a new container of blood (containing six pints) is opened, the card will be sent to purchasing and another six pints of blood will be ordered. When the blood is received, the card will be attached to the new container and moved to the blood storage area.

REVIEW AND DISCUSSION QUESTIONS

1   Is it possible to achieve zero inventories? Why or why not?
2   Stopping waste is a vital part of lean. Using value stream mapping, identify some sources of waste in your home or dorm and discuss how they may be eliminated.
3   Why must lean have a stable schedule?
4   Will lean work in service environments? Why or why not?
5   Discuss ways to use lean to improve one of the following: a pizza restaurant, a hospital, or an auto dealership.
6   What objections might a marketing manager have to uniform plant loading?
7   What are the implications for cost accounting of lean production?
8   What are the roles of suppliers and customers in a lean system?
9   Explain how cards are used in a kanban system.
10 In which ways, if any, are the following systems analogous to kanban: returning empty bottles to the supermarket and picking up filled ones; running a hot dog stand at lunchtime; withdrawing money from a checking account; raking leaves into bags?
11 Why is lean hard to implement in practice?
12 Explain the relationship between quality and productivity under the lean philosophy.
13 How would you show a pull system in VSM symbols between the blanking and CNC stages of the bolt manufacturing solved problem?

PROBLEMS

1   A supplier of instrument gauge clusters uses a kanban system to control material flow. The gauge cluster housings are transported five at a time. A fabrication center produces approximately 10 gauges per hour. It takes approximately two hours for the housing to be replenished. Due to variations in processing times, management has decided to keep 20 percent of the needed inventory as safety stock. How many kanban card sets are needed?
2   Transmissions are delivered to the fabrication line four at a time. It takes one hour for transmissions to be delivered. Approximately four vehicles are produced each hour, and management has decided that 50 percent of expected demand should be maintained as safety stock. How many kanban card sets are needed?
3   A bottling plant fills 2,400 bottles every two hours. The lead time is 40 minutes and a container accommodates 120 bottles. The safety stock is 10 percent of expected demand. How many kanban cards are needed?
4   Refer to Example 8.1 as the basis for this problem. Arvin Meritor hires a team of consultants. The consultants suggest a partial robotic automation as well as an increase in safety stock to 0.125. Arvin Automotive implements these suggestions. The result is an increase in efficiency in both the fabrication of muffler assembly and the making of catalytic converters. The muffler assembly fabrication cell now averages 16 assemblies per hour and the lead time has been decreased to two hours' response time for a batch of 10 catalytic converters. How many kanban cards are now needed?
5   Arvin Meritor is so pleased with the outcome from previous suggestions that the consultants are invited back for more work. The consultants now suggest a more complete robotic automation of the making of muffler assemblies and also a reduction in container size to eight per container. Arvin Meritor implements these suggestions and the result is that the muffler assembly

fabrication cell now averages approximately 32 assemblies per hour, and the catalytic converter assembly cell can now respond to an order for a batch of catalytic converters in one hour. The safety stock remains at 0.125. How many kanban cards are needed?

6   A manufacturer of high-end leather bracelets uses a kanban system to control material flow. The bracelets are transported in sets of 12. A cutting operation, on average, produces approximately 200 bracelets per hour. It takes one hour for the sets of collars to be replenished. Due to variations in processing times due to the size and length of the bracelets, it has been decided to keep 25 percent of the needed inventory as safety stock. How many kanban card sets are needed?

7   Suppose a switch assembly is assembled in batches of 4 units from an "upstream" assembly area and delivered in a special container to a "downstream" control-panel assembly operation. The control-panel assembly area requires 5 switch assemblies per hour. The switch assembly area can produce a container of switch assemblies in 2 hours and safety stock has been set at 10 percent of needed inventory.

CASE: QUALITY PARTS COMPANY

Quality Parts Company supplies gizmos for a computer manufacturer located a few miles away. The company produces two different models of gizmos in production runs ranging from 100 to 300 units.

The production flow of models X and Y is shown in Exhibit 8.15. Model Z requires milling as its first step, but otherwise follows the same flow pattern as X and Y. Skids can hold up to 20 gizmos at a time. Approximate times per unit by operation number and equipment setup times are shown in Exhibit 8.16.

Demand for gizmos from the computer company ranges between 125 and 175 per month, equally divided among X, Y, and Z. Subassembly builds up inventory early in the month to make certain that a buffer stock is always available. Raw materials and purchased parts for subassemblies each constitute 40 percent of the manufacturing cost of a gizmo. Both categories of parts are multiple-sourced from about 80 vendors and are delivered at random times. (Gizmos have 40 different part numbers.)

Scrap rates are about 10 percent at each operation, inventory turns twice yearly, employees are paid on a day rate, employee turnover is 25 percent per year, and net profit from operations is steady at 5 percent per year. Maintenance is performed as needed.

The manager of Quality Parts Company has been contemplating installing an automated ordering system to help control inventories and to "keep the skids filled." (She feels that two days of work in front of a workstation motivates the worker to produce at top speed.) She is also planning to add three inspectors to clean up the quality problem. Further, she is thinking about setting up a rework line to speed repairs. Although she is pleased with the high utilization of most of her equipment and labor, she is concerned about the idle time of the milling machine. Finally, she has asked the industrial engineering department to look into high-rise shelving to store parts coming off machine 4.

QUESTIONS

1   Which of the changes being considered by the manager of Quality Parts Company are counter to the lean philosophy?

2   Make recommendations for lean improvements in such areas as scheduling, layout, kanban, task groupings, and inventory. Use quantitative data as much as possible; state necessary assumptions.

3   Sketch the operation of a pull system for running Quality Parts Company's current system.

4   Outline a plan for introducing lean at Quality Parts Company.

CASE: VALUE STREAM MAPPING

Value stream mapping involves first developing a baseline map of the current situation of a company's external and/or internal operations and then, applying lean concepts, developing a future state map that shows improved operations. Exhibit 8.17, for example, shows the current state with a production lead time of 4.5 days. This system is a batch/push system (indicated by striped arrows) resulting in long delays and inventory buildups. Exhibit 8.18 shows the future state map with production lead time of 0.25 day. This was accomplished by moving to a continuous-flow pull system and attacking the seven wastes. Value stream mapping uses a number of special icons and display format of boxes and flows. For a more complete discussion of the methodology, see Jared Lovelle.[10]

QUESTIONS

1   Eliminating the queue of work dramatically quickens the time it takes a part to flow through the system. What are the disadvantages of removing those queues?

2   How do you think the machine operators would react to the change?

3   What would you do to ensure that the operators were kept busy?

exhibit 8.15 Gizmo Production Flow

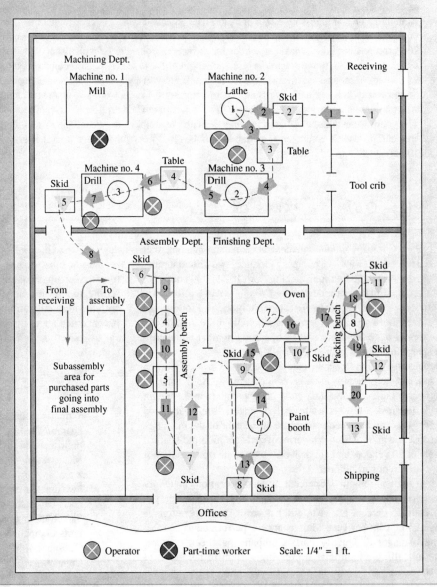

exhibit 8.16 Operations and Setup Time

OPERATION NUMBER AND NAME	OPERATION TIME (MINUTES)	SETUP TIME (MINUTES)
Milling for Model Z	20	60
1 Lathe	50	30
2 Mod. 14 drill	15	5
3 Mod. 14 drill	40	5
4 Assembly step 1	50	
Assembly step 2	45	
Assembly step 3	50	
5 Inspection	30	
6 Paint	30	20
7 Oven	50	
8 Packing	5	

Map of the Current State

exhibit 8.17

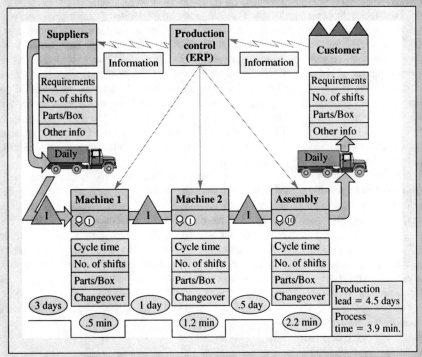

SOURCE: JARED LOVELLE, "MAPPING THE VALUE STREAM," *IIE SOLUTIONS* 33, NO. 2 (FEBRUARY 2001), P. 32.

Map of the Future State

exhibit 8.18

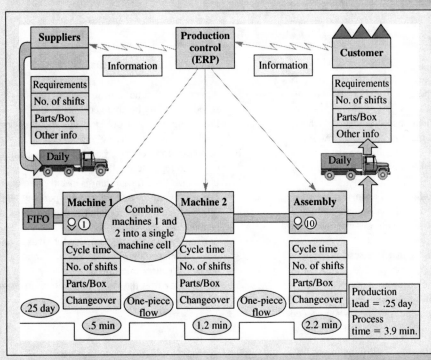

SOURCE: JARED LOVELLE, "MAPPING THE VALUE STREAM," *IIE SOLUTIONS* 33, NO. 2 (FEBRUARY 2001), P. 30.

CASE: PRO FISHING BOATS—A VALUE STREAM MAPPING EXERCISE

A fishing boat manufacturer, Pro Fishing Boats, is having many problems with critical globally sourced parts. Pro Fishing has two manufacturing facilities in the United States. The firm's reliance on efficient global supply chain operations is increasing as the manufacturer is sourcing more and more parts overseas, including critical components. Recent problems with a number of these critical parts have caused line shutdowns. In response, Pro Fishing has *mandated* a six-week inventory on all globally sourced parts. Management has asked you to evaluate whether this is the right decision.

First, you must understand Pro Fishing's supply chain. Currently, there is very little visibility (knowledge of the current status) of inventory in the supply chain and communication with the supply base is minimal. In fact, the boat manufacturer does not have *any* visibility past the Tier I suppliers. Adding to the complexity of this problem, each part of the supply chain is handled by different departments within the company.

In order to understand the supply chain, Pro Fishing has asked you to map their supply chain. To do so, the company identified a critical component to follow in the supply chain. After having the opportunity to interview supply chain participants, including suppliers, you have collected the following information.

The component is manufactured overseas in China by the Tier I supplier, Manufacturing Inc. The Manufacturing Inc. production schedule is based on orders sent via fax from the Pro Fishing warehouse. The supplier operates on a 90-60-30 day forecast along with a weekly order. Upon completion of the component, Manufacturing Inc. sends the component via truck to the Shanghai Port where it is loaded onto a ship heading to the United States. Loading at the port takes 1 week and truck transport takes 3 days. Manufacturing Inc. holds a 9-week finished goods buffer inventory. Manufacturing time for each component is only about 3 days. The ship bound to the United States takes about 14 days to travel overseas. Upon arrival in the United States the component is unloaded at the Los Angeles port. This takes about 5 days and customs inspects in Los Angeles. The goods travel by train to Chicago, which takes about 7 days. Goods are held in Chicago for about half a week. From there, the component is trucked to a Pro Fishing warehouse where the 6-week inventory buffer has been mandated. Shipment to the Pro Fishing warehouse takes 2 days. From the warehouse, the components are trucked to plants in the United States triggered by electronic orders from each of the Pro Fishing plants.

In talking to Manufacturing Inc., Pro Fishing has learned that its component is made up of two main raw materials: one from China and the other from the United States. To avoid the risk of running out of these raw materials, Manufacturing Inc. maintains a 4-week buffer on the China-based raw materials and a 12-week buffer in the U.S. based raw material. These Tier II supplier orders are by formal purchase order only. It is interesting to note that Manufacturing Inc. uses these suppliers to fulfill Pro Fishing's strict supplier qualification requirements.

QUESTIONS

1. Create a value stream map (VSM) of this supply chain. What other information is needed?
2. Where is there risk for supply chain disruptions or stoppages to the flow of materials?
3. Where do opportunities reside in improving supply chain operations and how has VSM helped to reveal these?

SUPER QUIZ

1. Anything that does not add value from the customer's perspective.
2. An integrated set of activities designed to achieve production using minimal inventories of raw materials, work-in-process, and finished goods.
3. The Toyota Production System is founded in these two philosophies.
4. The set of value-adding and non-value-adding activities required to design, order, and provide a product from concept to launch, order to delivery, and raw materials to customers.
5. The Japanese philosophy that focuses on continuous improvement.
6. A philosophy in which similar parts are brought together in families for production purposes.
7. Means only producing what is needed when needed and no more.
8. A period of time during which the production schedule cannot be changed.
9. Producing a mix of products that matches demand as closely as possible.
10. A production control system that uses a signaling device to regulate the flow of material.
11. If the lead time for an item is exactly five days, the demand is a constant four units per day, and the shipment container contains two units, how many kanban card sets would be needed?
12. A firm wants to justify smaller lot sizes economically. Management knows that it cannot change the cost to carry one unit in inventory since this is largely based on the value of the item. To justify a smaller lot size what must they do?

1. Waste 2. Lean production 3. Elimination of waste and respect for people 4. Value stream 5. Kaizen
6. Group technology 7. JIT (just-in-time) production 8. Freeze window 9. Uniform plant loading
10. Kanban 11. 10 card sets 12. Reduce setup cost

SELECTED BIBLIOGRAPHY

Allen, M. "Picture-Perfect Manufacturing [Using Value Stream Mapping]." *Modern Machine Shop Magazine Online,* August 2004.

George, M. L. *Lean Six Sigma.* New York: McGraw-Hill, 2002.

Gross, J. M., and K. R. McInnis. *Kanban Made Simple: Demystifying and Applying Toyota's Legendary Manufacturing Process.* New York: AMACOM, 2003.

Monden, Y. *Toyota Production System: An Integrated Approach to Just-in-Time.* Atlanta, GA: Institute of Industrial Engineers, 1998.

Phelps, T.; M. Smith; and T. Hoenes. "Building a Lean Supply Chain." *Manufacturing Engineering* 132, no. 5 (May 2004), pp. 107–13.

Womack, J. P., and D. T. Jones. *Lean Thinking: Banish Waste and Create Wealth in Your Corporation.* New York: Simon & Schuster, 1996.

Womack, J. P.; D. T. Jones; and D. Roos. *The Machine That Changed the World.* New York: R. A. Rawston Associates, 1990.

FOOTNOTES

1 Adapted from D. Blanchard, *Green Is the New Black,* March 1, 2009, IndustryWeek.com.

2 Adapted from B. Tompkins, *Lean Thinking for the Supply Chain,* from www.tompkinsinc.com.

3 K. A. Wantuck, *The Japanese Approach to Productivity* (Southfield, MI: Bendix Corporation, 1983).

4 K. Suzaki, *The New Manufacturing Challenge: Techniques for Continuous Improvement* (New York: Free Press, 1987), pp. 7–25.

5 C. Karlsson, *Japanese Production Management in Sunrise or Sunset* (Stockholm, Sweden: Stockholm School of Economics, EFI/The Economic Research Institute. 1999).

6 This was adapted from material from Strategos Consultants. See www.strategosinc.com.

7 R. H. Hall, *Zero Inventories* (Homewood, IL: Dow Jones-Irwin, 1983), p. 64.

8 J. P. Womack and D. T. Jones, *Lean Thinking* (New York: Simon & Schuster, 1996), p. 277.

9 K. A. Rosentrater and R. Balamuralikrishna, *Value Stream Mapping—A Tool for Engineering and Technology Education and Practice.* ASEE Illinois-Indiana Sectional Conference, Fort Wayne, IN. American Society for Engineering Education. Presented April 1, 2006.

10 J. Lovelle, "Mapping the Value Stream," *IIE Solutions* 33, no. 2 (February 2001), pp. 26–33.

SUPPLEMENTARY NOTES

Additional information on Chapters 2, 3, 4, 5, 6 and 7 is included in the following notes.

CHAPTER 2: PROCESS ANALYSIS

A *process* is any part of an organization that takes *inputs* and *transforms* them into *outputs* that, it is hoped, are of *greater value*_than the original inputs. *Transactions* go through a process; transactions can be **people**, material, etc. Operations require *resources*; these resources can include **people**, machines, etc.

DIAGRAMS

The textbook uses the terminology *Process Flowchart*; we may use the term *Process Flow Diagram* and use the following symbols (other terms: process flow, value stream mapping). In our class we may use many of the symbols (below left) regularly. First we will start with another diagram called a draw a *precedence diagram* (below right).

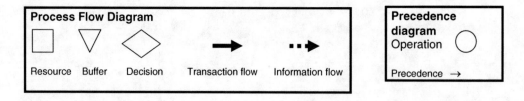

PROCESS TYPES

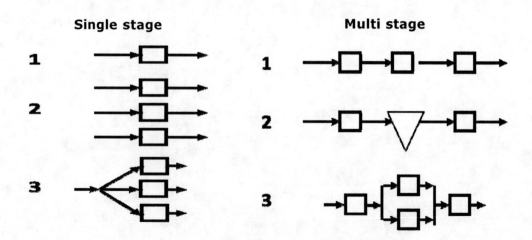

In the single stage process 2 and 3 on the left (above), there are multiple stations. Each station at a stage carries out similar operations. When there is only one station at each stage, we may use the word station and stage somewhat interchangeably. Process 3 on right (above) is called hybrid process.

Another way to classify processes is by how end product is utilized. ***Make to stock*** process is activated to meet expected or forecasted demand. ***Make to order*** process is activated only in response to an actual order. A ***hybrid*** process has a mixture of the other to processes.

PROCESS DESIGN:

1. We first determine what operations involved and how long it takes to perform each operation.
2. We need to know precedence relationship between operations (what goes before what).
3. The first two steps will help us draw a precedence diagram.

We will use intuitive method for the time being to develop process designs.

EXAMPLE 1

Suppose we have to stuff thousands of envelopes on a daily basis. Since this is a repetitive work, we would like to design an efficient process. Therefore we first determine tasks involved, time for each task and precedence relationship (which task must be done before which task). Suppose there are five tasks (times shown in parenthesis seconds).

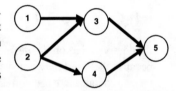

1. **Get material (30)**
2. **Get envelope (2)**
3. **Insert and seal (8)**
4. **Put label (5)**
5. **Drop in proper box (3)**

Precedence relationships are shown in the diagram to the right. This diagram shows the following. Tasks 1 and 2 have no precedence (can be done in any order). You can insert and seal (task 3) only after doing tasks 1 and 2. We will now develop some processes.

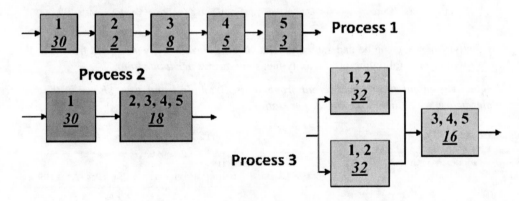

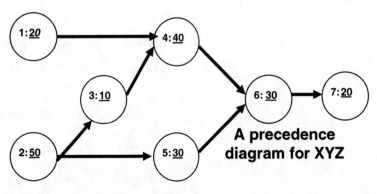

EXAMPLE 2

Figure to the right shows a precedence diagram for a process to make a product XYZ. There are 7 tasks [shown by (circular) nodes]. The first number in the node indicates the task number and the second number indicates the processing time in seconds. Arrows show precedence. For example, task 4 can be performed only after completing tasks 1 and 3. When you start performing these tasks on a new product, you can either complete task 1 first or task 2. In fact you could perform tasks 2, 3 and 5 before you undertake task 1. If you add up all processing times, you will find that it takes a total of 200 seconds to complete the product. ***There are no standard conventions for precedence diagrams.***

Here we see four possible layouts:

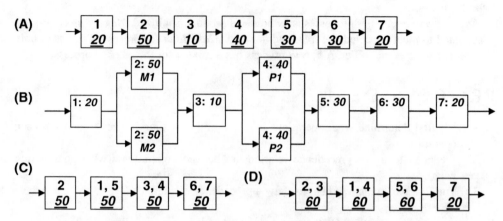

Various process flows diagrams for the product XYZ

PRODUCTIVITY

Productivity is simply defined as the ratio of output to input. It is not a simple measure because the input may consist of many resources and it is not easy to convert all into a single measurement. Here are some of the productivity measures used in practice.

TOTAL	(Output/Input) or (Goods and services produced/All resources used)
PARTIAL	(Output/Labor) or (Output/Capitol) or (Output/Materials) or (Output/Energy)
MULTIFACTOR	[Output/(Labor + Capitol + Energy)] or [Output/(Labor + Capitol + Material)]

Productivity measure can be understood in relative terms: ***productivity increased from X to Y***
We will use the following productivity measure: ***output per labor hour.***

Productivity calculations for different processes in Example 1 and 2 are shown in the two tables below, we assume one worker per station.

EXAMPLE 1: PRODUCTIVITY

PROCESS	LABOR	CAPACITY [UNITS/HR]	PRODUCTIVITY: UNITS PER LABOR HOUR.
1	5	120	24
2	2	120	60
3	3	225	75

EXAMPLE 2: PRODUCTIVITY

PROCESS	LABOR	CAPACITY [UNITS/HR]	PRODUCTIVITY: UNITS PER LABOR HOUR.
A	7	72	72/7 = 10.3
B	9	120	120 /9 = 13.3
C	4	72	72/4 = 18
D	4	60	60/4 = 15

PROCESS PARAMETERS

Consider three examples of a simple process with a single task.

A1.   Components are processed on an automated machine.
A2.   People walk to a window, buy a ticket (operation/transformation) and leave with a ticket.
A3.   People arrive at scheduled times and receive some service.

In example A1, the processing times are known (and fixed). We can schedule these operations at appropriate times; thus the transaction arrival time to the system is also known.

When arrival times and processing times are fixed (for all practical purposes), we have a *deterministic process*.

In example A2, arrivals may be random and processing times may vary. If arrivals and processing times behave according to some probability distributions, we have probabilistic or *stochastic processes*.

In A3, arrivals are deterministic while processing times may be stochastic.

We will mainly deal with deterministic processes although we will provide some discussion on stochastic processes towards the end of this note.

We can analyze a process through different *parameters*[1]. The parameters can be of two types: Design parameters and Run Time Parameters. These are summarized in the table below.

DESIGN PARAMETERS	RUN TIME PARAMETERS	OTHER TERMINOLOGY
	Input Rate: *Transaction arrival rate*	
Capacity: *Maximum rate of transaction processing*	**Output Rate:** *Current rate of transaction processing*	Output rate: throughput rate **(TPR)**, flow rate, production rate
Productivity = Capacity/labor	Productivity = Output rate/labor	
(Design) Cycle Time = 1/ (capacity)	**(Actual) Cycle Time: CT** = 1/(output rate)	
Minimum Throughput Time (Min TPT)	**Average TPT:** *Average time spent by a transaction to go through a stable process.*	TPT: flow time, manufacturing lead time
	Average WIP: *Average number of transactions in the process.*	

Instead of *operations*, we may use words such as *tasks or activities*. In any process, we say that transactions pass (flow) through the process. Typical *transactions* in business processes include *materials, work orders, customers, patients, products, projects, cash, claims forms*, etc. We may use these terms or *jobs* instead of transactions. A process may consist of operations in *series, parallel* or a *hybrid combination*. A process may have multiple input points involving *assembly* operations; there may be multiple output points. For each operation, we use *resources* such as *people machines*, etc. Notice that a person (customer) can be a transaction while another person (operator) can be a resource. To simplify our discussion, we will use manufacturing examples most of the time and will use *job* and *machine* (instead of transaction and resource).

At the run time, we can look at the concept of a *schedule*. Assume that we determine the schedule. Consider the following two schedules. In the first schedule, transactions are released every 10 minutes. In the second schedule, two transactions are released simultaneously every 20 minutes. Although both schedules represent the input rate of 6 transactions per **hour**, the values of run time parameters such as WIP will be different.

The *capacity* (design parameter) assumes that we can generate the best possible schedule. At the run time, the following two points may be noted.

1. If the input rate is greater than the capacity, the process will not become stable.
2. For a stable process, output rate = input rate.

Another important concept is *dimensional analysis*. We will use a square bracket [ ] to denote dimension of any term: *Time* **[T]**, *Number of units or quantity* **[Q]** and *Cost* **[$]**.

Capacity, output rate, input rate: [Q/T]. Cycle time: [T/Q], WIP [Q] Throughput Time-TPT: [T].

We will also use *Gantt Charts* to depict information pictorially. The horizontal axis of a Gantt chart generally represents time scale. In a machine based Gantt chart, different machines (resources) are plotted along the vertical axis and machine utilization is shown. In a job based Gantt chart, jobs (transactions) are plotted on the vertical axis to show the progress of each job. We will generally use machine-based charts.

---

[1] Some parameters also used for the part of a process (called stage or station).

EXAMPLE 3

A service involves one machine (M1) performing a single task and it takes exactly 4 minutes per task. Component (we will use the word "job") "X" is processed at M1 and comes out as product Y.

We will first calculate design parameters. Then we will analyze three run time situations.

(a) A new job is scheduled every 4 minutes.

(b) A new job is scheduled every 10 minutes.

(c) A new job is scheduled every 3 minutes.

Since it takes 4 minutes to process a job, we first calculate design parameters.

Capacity = 60 [min./hour]/4 [min./job] = **15 [jobs/hour]**

Cycle time = 4 [min./ job]

Minimum TPT = 4 [min.]

Part (a):   Since each job enters the system every four minutes, the input rate is calculated as follows.

$$M1 \quad \boxed{\text{Job 1} \quad \text{Job 2} \quad \text{Job 3} \quad \text{Job}}$$

$$\quad\quad\quad 4 \quad\quad\quad 8 \quad\quad\quad 12$$

Input rate = 1 **[unit]**/4 **[min]** = (1/4) **[unit/min]**, or

Input rate = (1/4) **[unit/min]** × (60) **[min/hour]** = 15 **[units/hour]**

Job 1 will go immediately to M1. After 4 minutes, job 1 will be released from M1, Job 2 will enter the system at the same time and will go to M1. Also, the output rate will be same as the input rate, i.e.

Output rate = 15 **[units/hour]**

We will draw a Gantt chart for the situation. The Gantt chart is shown to the right.

Part (b):   Since each job enters the system every ten minutes, the input rate will be 6 **[units/hour]**. The output rate will be 6 **[units/hour]**. Notice in the Gantt chart that between time units 4 to 10, the machine is ***idle***.

$$M1 \quad \boxed{\text{Job1} \quad\quad\quad\quad\quad\quad \text{Job 2}}$$

$$\quad\quad\quad 4 \quad\quad\quad\quad\quad 10$$

Part (c):   Since each job enters the system every three minutes, the input rate will be 20 **[units/hour]**. But the capacity is only 15 **[units/hour]**. So, the output rate will be only 15 **[*units/hour*]**. Here is what will happen as time progresses.

TIME	ARRIVING TRANSACTION #	PRIOR ARRIVALS	DEPARTURES	TPT FOR ARRIVING TRANSACTION
0	1	0	0	$(0 - 0) \times 4 + 4 = 4$ min
60	21	20	15	$(20 - 15) \times 4 + 4 = 24$ min
120	41	40	30	$(40 - 30) \times 4 + 4 = 44$ min

Each successive arriving transaction stays 1 minute longer and the ***system never becomes stable***. This is true for any process when ***input rate is greater than the system capacity***.

Comments on Example 3   In the above example, since there was only one machine in the process, we do not need to make distinction between stage values and process values of different parameters. We considered three different schedules (for the input to the system), there can be many more.

For our example, the capacity is 15 **[units/hour].** The actual cycle time for parts (**a**) and (**c**) is 4 **[min./unit]** and for part (**b**) it is 10 **[min./unit].** The minimum TPT is 4 **[min.].** The average TPT for parts (a) and (b) is 4 **[min.].**

Some important observations:
- For sequential stages, the capacity is determined by the slowest stage called the bottleneck.
- When machines are in parallel (performing the same operation), capacities add.

EXAMPLE 4

A single stage process has 3 machines (M1, M2, M3) operating in parallel. A product can be processed on any one of the three machines with per unit processing times of 10 seconds on M1, 16 seconds f on M2 and 20 seconds on M3.

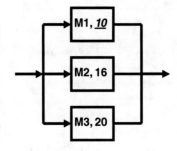

Part (a):   What is the process cycle time?

Part (b):   If you need to produce a minimum of 1200 units per hour, what should be the cycle time a new machine used in parallel?

SOLUTION

Part (a):   When machines are in parallel, the capacity is equal to sum of capacities of individual machines.

$$\text{Capacity of M1} = 1/10 \ \textbf{[units/second]}$$
$$= 1/10 \ \textbf{[units/second]} \times 3600 \ \textbf{[sec/ hour]}$$
$$= 360 \ \textbf{[units/hour]},$$
$$\text{Capacity of M2} = 225 \ \textbf{[units/hour]},$$
$$\text{Capacity of M3} = 180 \ \textbf{[units/hour]}.$$

System capacity = 765 **[units/hour].**
Process cycle time = 3600/765 = 4.706 sec./unit

Part (b):   Since we need the capacity of 1200, we need an extra machine with capacity of $(1200 - 765) = 435$ **[units/hour].** Per unit processing time on M4 will be $3600/435 = 8.275$ **seconds.** ●

RELATIONSHIP BETWEEN CERTAIN PROCESS PARAMETERS

In the analysis of a model called "Single server queuing model" involving arrivals based on Poisson probability distributions and exponential service times, it has been shown that when the process becomes stable, there is a relationship between process parameters. In particular, the relationship can be expressed by $L = \lambda \times W$, where L is the average number of customers in the system, λ is the arrival rate and W is the average time in the system. Prof. J. D. C. Little of MIT developed the proof for this formula. This formula can be applied to a wide variety of processes in steady state and can be written as WIP = Flow time × Flow rate.

$$[Q] = [T] \times [Q/T]$$

We will use this ***Little's formula*** to analyze many different situations in the next few sections.

WIP represents the total of average number of transactions occupying each resource in a process. We can write Little's formula as

$$\text{WIP} = \text{TPT} \times \text{TPR} = \text{TPT/CT}$$

PROCESS PARAMETER CALCULATIONS

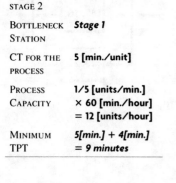

CT FOR STAGE 1	5 [min./unit]
CT FOR STAGE 2	*2 is 4 [min./unit]*
BOTTLENECK STATION	*Stage 1*
CT FOR THE PROCESS	5 [min./unit]
PROCESS CAPACITY	1/5 [units/min.] × 60 [min./hour] = 12 [units/hour]
MINIMUM TPT	*5[min.] + 4[min.] = 9 minutes*

EXAMPLE 5

A process involves two sequential tasks performed at two stages as shown.

Part (a): Design parameters are shown to the right.

Part (b): Consider the following schedule. Starting at time 0, one new job enters the process at stage 1 **every 5 minutes**.

  i. Calculate the actual cycle time and the flow rate (i.e. output rate).
 ii. Calculate average TPT
iii. Calculate WIP contribution of each resource and the total.
 iv. Verify Little's formula.

To begin with, we will plot the Gantt chart for this schedule.

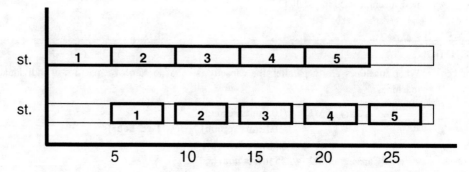

  i. From the Gantt chart, a job will come out the process at time 9, 14, 19, 24, i.e., every 10 minutes. The **actual CT = 5[min./unit]** and the **flow rate = 1/5 [units/min]**.
 ii. The first job enters the process at 0 and comes out at 9, the second job enters the process at 5 and comes out (after 9 minutes) at 14. In fact every job will stay in the process for 9 minutes. Therefore **average TPT = 9 [min.]**
iii. Notice from the Gantt chart that station 1 is always occupied by a job. So the contribution of station 1 to the WIP is 1.00 [**units**]. The process is considered to be stable after the cycle repeats itself. On station 2, if you ignore the first 5 minutes of idle time, you will notice that a job occupies the resource for 4 minutes and the resource (i.e. station 2) is idle for 1 minute (and the cycle repeats). Therefore the WIP contribution of station 2 is 0.80 [**units**] and the total WIP is 1.80 [**units**].
 iv. You can now easily verify Little's formula: WIP = TPT × Flow rate = TPT/CT

EXAMPLE 6

Consider example 5 again. Suppose we add another identical machine in parallel at stage 1. The two machines, M1 and M2 require 5 minutes to complete the first task. At stage 2, M3 requires 4 minutes. Thus a product will be processed on M1 and M3 or M2 and M3. A buffer (not shown) may be needed between two stations.

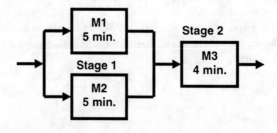

(a) Table below shows design parameters.

CT FOR STAGE 1	**2.5 [min./unit]** **
CT FOR STAGE 2	**4 [min./unit]**
BOTTLENECK	**Station 2**
PROCESS CT	**4 [min./unit]**
PROCESS CAPACITY	**1/4 [units/min.] = 15 [*units/hour*]**
MINIMUM TPT	**5 + 4 = 9 [min.]** ▲▲

**: *Capacity of M1 or M2 is 12 [units/hour]; the total stage capacity will be 24 [units/hour]. This means that CT for station 1 will be 1/24 [hours/unit] or 2.5 [min./unit].*

▲▲: *Since both machines at stage 1 take 5 minutes, we could send the job to any of these two machines (followed by M3) for minimum TPT calculations.*

<u>*Schedule 1:*</u> Jobs are released simultaneously to M1 and M2 every 8 minutes starting at time 0. Verify Little's formula. Note that since two jobs will finish simultaneously at M1 and M2 and only one can be scheduled on M3, we need a buffer and we need to consider this in WIP calculations.

Odd numbered jobs (processed on M1) stay in the system for 9 minutes. Even numbered jobs stay in the buffer for additional 5 minutes. *Average TPT* = (9 + 13)/2 = 11 **[min.]**

Actual CT = 4 **[min./unit]** since the situation is similar to schedule 1. From ***Little's formula, WIP = TPT/CT*** = 11 **[min.]**/4 **[min./unit]** = 2.75 **[units]**.

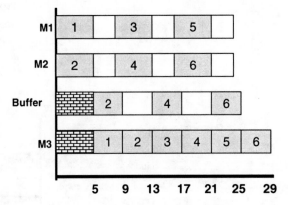

WIP CONTRIBUTIONS**	
M1	5/(5 + 3) = 0.625 [units]
M2	5/(5 + 3) = 0.625 [units]
BUFFER	4/(4 + 4) = 0.500 [units]
M3	1.000 [units]
TOTAL	2.750 [units]

** *Shaded area before the first job on each resource is ignored.*

<u>*Schedule 2:*</u> Jobs are sent to M1 every 8 minutes starting at time 0 and to M2 every 8 minutes starting at time 8. *Verify Little's formula.*

Notice that this schedule does not require buffer. Each job stays in the system for 9 minutes, hence *average TPT* = 9 **[min.]**

From the Gantt chart, each job following the first one comes out after the next one with 8-minute interval, hence *actual CT* = 4 **[min./unit]**. From Little's formula, ***WIP = TPT/CT*** = 9 **[min.]**/4 **[min./unit]** = 2.25 **[units]**.

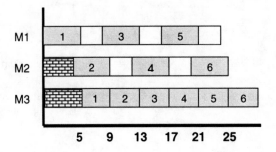

WIP CONTRIBUTIONS	
M1	5/(5 + 3) = 0.625 [units]
M2	5/(5 + 3) = 0.625 [units]
M3	1.000 [units]
TOTAL	2.250 [units]

Comments on Example 6 In both schedules the input and output rates were the same as the system capacity. However, schedule 2 appears to be better than schedule 1 since it has lower TPT and WIP.

If we do not have sufficient orders and reduce the input rate below capacity, there will be no bottleneck station and WIP contribution of each resource will be less than 1.

Example 7

Consider a process similar to example **6**. At stage 1, we have two ***non-identical*** machines (M1 and M2) in parallel. M1 requires 10 minutes while M2 requires 6 minutes. At stage 2, there is only one machine M3. The processing time is 4 minutes.

(a): Table to the right shows design parameters.

CT FOR STAGE 1	**3.75 [min./unit] **
CT FOR STAGE 2	**4 [min./unit]**
BOTTLENECK	**Station 2**
CT FOR THE PROCESS	**4 [min./unit]**
PROCESS CAPACITY	**1/4 [units/min.] = 15 [*units/hour*]**
MINIMUM TPT	**6 + 4 = 10 [min.]**

*** Capacity of M1 is 6 [**units/hour**] and M2 is 10 [**units/hour**]. The total system capacity will be 16 [units/hour]. This means that CT for station 1 will be 1/16 [hours/unit] or 3.75 [min./unit].*

WIP CONTRIBUTIONS	
M1	10/(10 + 2) = 5/6 [units]
M2	1 [units]
BUFFER	2/(2 + 10) = 1/6 [units]
M3	1 [units]
TOTAL	3 [units]

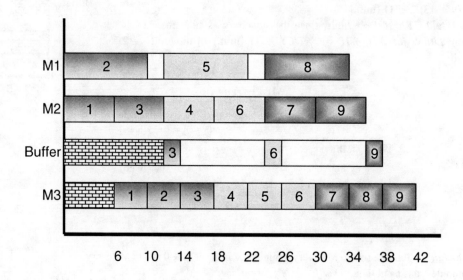

(b): Gantt chart for a schedule is shown below. Verify Little's formula.

Note that after every three jobs, the cycle will repeat and the process becomes stable.

Every job after job 1 comes out of the process every 4 minutes. Hence,

$$flow\ rate = 15\ [\text{units/hr}].$$

Every job marked 1 stays in the system for 10 minutes, job 2 stays for 14 minutes and job 3 stays for 12 minutes. Hence average ***flow time*** = (10 + 14 + 12)/3 = 12 minutes = 1/5 [**hours**].

$$WIP = \text{flow time} \times \text{flow rate}$$
$$3[\textbf{units}] = 1/5\ [\textbf{hours}] \times 15\ [\textbf{units/hr}]$$

LITTLE'S FORMULA: APPLICATION TO NON-DETERMINISTIC PROCESSES

In general, **if a process is stable, we can apply Little's formula** for transactions passing through the system. In the following examples, we assume stable processes.

Example 8

A large fast food restaurant processes on average 200 customers in a busy two-hour period. On average, there are 45 customers inside (waiting to place the order or for the order to arrive, eating, going back to counter to order more, etc.) How much time (on average) does a customer spend in the facility?

We need to find *flow time*, given Flow rate = 100 [customers/hour], WIP = 45 [customers] *Flow time* = WIP/Flow rate = 45 [customers]/100 [customers/hr] = 0.45 hours = 0.45 [hours] $\times$ 60 [min/hr] = *27* [**minutes**].

Example 9

An insurance company office processes 6,000 claims per year. The average processing time is 2 weeks. Assume 50 weeks per year. On average, how many applications are in the process?

We need to find **WIP**, given flow rate and flow time. Flow rate = 6000 [**units/year**]/50 [**weeks/year**] = 120 [**units/ week**]. Flow time = 2 [**weeks**] **WIP** = 120 [**units/week**] $\times$ 2 [**weeks**] = **240** [**units**] of claims.

Example 10

A company sells $100M worth of equipment per year. The average amount in Accounts Receivable is 15M$. On average, how many days does it take for a customer to make the payment (assume 360 days per year)?

We need to find *flow time*, given Flow rate = 100M [**$/year**]. WIP = 15M [**$**] *Flow time* = WIP/Flow rate = 15M [**$**]/100M [**$/year**] = 0.15 [**years**] = 0.15 [**years**] $\times$ 360 [**days/year**] = 54 [**days**].

Example 11

A bank finds that the average number of people waiting in queue during lunch hour is 15. On average, during this period 2.5 people per minute leave the bank after receiving service. How long do people wait on average in the queue?

We need to find *flow time*, given Flow rate 2.5 [**people/ min**]. WIP = 15 [**people**] *Flow time* = 15 [**people**]/2.5 [**people/ min**] = 6 *minutes*

Example 12

At a local bank, Jerry has a checking account with an average balance of $3,000. The money is turned over 6 times a year. On average, how many dollars flow through the account per year?

Find *flow rate* given, WIP = 3000 [**$**]. Flow time = 1/6 [**year**] *Flow rate* = 3000 [**$**]/(1/6) [**year**] = 18,000 [**$**]/[**year**].

PROCESS PARAMETER CALCULATIONS: ASSEMBLY OPERATIONS

Example 13

Product AA is processed at stage 1 (2 machines in parallel). Product BB is processed at stage 2 then at stage 3. One unit of AA and one unit of BB is picked from the buffer and assembled at stage 4. The assembled product is then processed at stage 5 (three machines in parallel).

In this example, we are not in a position to determine the WIP in a true sense because two transactions (AA and BB) are merging to form a new product. We can however find station capacities and other parameters associated with the process.

CT values for stage 2, 3 and 4 are 3 **min./unit**], 5 [**min./unit**] and 4 [**min./unit**] respectively.

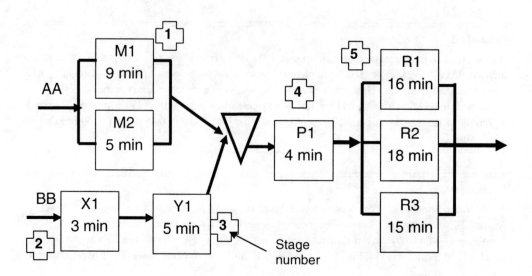

A process flow diagram for an assembly operation

Stage 1: In 45 minutes we can process 5 jobs on M1 and 9 jobs on M2, or a total of 14. Therefore ***CT*** for station 1 = 45/14 [**min./unit**] = 3.21 [**min./unit**],

Stage 5: In 720 minutes we can process 45 jobs on R1 and 40 jobs on R2 and 48 jobs on R3 or a total of 133. Therefore ***CT*** for station 5 = 720/133 [**min./unit**] = 5.41 [**min./unit**].

Bottleneck is station 5. The process capacity will be [60/5.41] ≈ 11.1 [**units/hour**].

Minimum TPT: One unit of AA will reach the buffer in 5 minutes (through M2) and one unit of BB will reach the buffer in 8 minutes. Thus we need at least 8 minutes before we can start the assembly at station 4. At station 5, the smallest time is 15 min. Therefore ***minimum TPT*** = 8 + 4 + 15 = 27 [**minutes**].

OTHER PROCESS CHARACTERISTICS

Suppose we want to process three jobs X, Y and Z on two machines "A" and "B". X must be processed first on "A" (10 minutes), then on "B" (5 minutes). Y requires only processing on "B" (16 minutes). Z is to be processed on "A" (12 minutes), then on "B" (4 minutes). Let's assume that transportation times (from one machine to the other) are negligible. Figure below shows two Gantt charts for two different processes.

Figure on left shows a schedule for the process with ***buffer space available*** between machines to store partially completed jobs. We schedule X followed by **Z** on machine A. The processing order is Y, X, Z on machine B. Notice that when X is finished on A, it is kept in the buffer until Y is completed on B. The gap between X and Z on machine B indicates ***idle time***.

Figure on right shows the same schedule for the process with ***no buffer space available***. The shaded area between X and Z on machine A indicates that when job X is completed on A, it ***blocks*** the machine until the job can be loaded on B. **For the figure on the left**, the

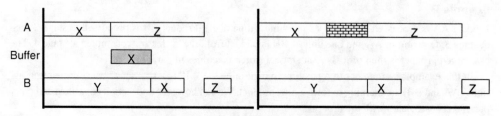

Gantt charts for processes with buffer (left) / without buffer (right)

Utilization refers to the **productive use of the resource.** Thus when a machine is idle or blocked or under repair or being set up of the next job, it is not being utilized productively.

WIP contribution refers to average number of jobs (transactions) on a resource.

following can be observed. ***Machine A has 100% utilization and WIP contribution is 1.*** Machine B has less than 100% utilization and WIP contribution is less than 1.

For the figure on the right: ***Machine A has less than 100% utilization while WIP contribution is 1.*** Machine B has less than 100% utilization and WIP contribution is less than 1. The reason for the difference in utilization and contribution on machine A is due to the fact that blocking is non-productive and does not add to the utilization. Since WIP contribution is based on a job occupying a machine, blocking will increase WIP contribution.

Some insights

1. Capacity of a process is the maximum output rate. If input rate becomes higher than the capacity, the process will not become stable.
2. If we need to increase the capacity of any process, we need to add resources at the bottleneck stage.
3. For two schedules it is possible to have same cycle time but different WIP and TPT.
4. In a number of cases, a batch of jobs is released and the whole batch moves from station to station. Obviously TPT values will be higher since the whole batch must be completed. Batching of products means more WIP and need for buffer space.
5. Analysis for nondeterministic cases can be complex. Since processing times are variable, bottleneck operations can shift frequently.
6. If an important job is to be completed as fast as possible, we may have to free up the fastest resource at every stage. The time required to complete this is given by the minimum TPT.

CHAPTER 3: PROCESS SELECTION

ASSEMBLY LINE BALANCING

<u>Given</u>: A set of "n" tasks with: Task processing times T_1, T_2, ...,T_n, precedence relationships, target cycle time and other restrictions (called constraints), if any.

<u>To determine</u>: *Minimum number of stations* (and a "good" balance) for a specified target cycle time.

<u>Assumptions:</u> Cycle time $\geq$ max $\{T_1, T_2, ...,T_n\}$. A task cannot be split.

Target cycle time is based on production requirement per shift (or per day) and tells at what interval a product is to be completed.

Station time is equal to the sum of task times included in that station. Obviously, no station time can exceed target cycle time.

Effective cycle time is the *maximum station time*; it may be less than or equal to target cycle time.

A lower bound on number of stations needed is calculated as follows. Divide the total task time by the target cycle time. *Round up* this ratio, if it does not have an integer value. No matter what method you use, you will need at least these many stations.

Line efficiency = 100 $\times$ (total task time)/(# of stations $\times$ effective cycle time).

Minimum Cycle time is equal to the largest task time. If you visualize an assembly line where there is only one task per station, the effective cycle time of this line is equal to the minimum cycle time just defined.

Maximum Cycle time is equal to the sum of all task times. If you visualize an assembly line where there is only per station doing all tasks, the effective cycle time of this line is equal to the maximum cycle time just defined.

How To Balance A Line?

Draw a task diagram based on product data (tasks, times, precedence relationships). Calculate target cycle time based on production requirements. (Calculate the lower bound on the number of stations needed.) Calculate number of stations by the method described below. Calculate, *effective cycle time*, line efficiency and draw a layout.

A task is *eligible* to be included in a station, if all preceding tasks have been included in the current or prior stations.

Step 0: Set k = 1. Arrange all tasks according to a selected *priority rule*.

Step 1: Create a new station numbered k with station time = 0

Step 2: List all eligible tasks. If there are no eligible tasks, stop (final cycle time = largest station time, number of work stations = current value of k).

Step 3: Select the first eligible task according to a specified priority rule. *If (task time + current station time) $\leq$ target cycle time and if there are no other restrictions*, go to step 5.

Step 4: Ignore this eligible task. If there are more eligible tasks, return to step 3 otherwise increase k by 1 and return to step 1.

Step 5: Remove the task from the eligible list; add it to the current station. Increment current station time by the task time, find new eligible tasks and return to step 2.

For step 0, we may use one of the following three priority rules (with tie-breaking):

SPT rule: Select the task with the *smallest processing time.*

LPT rule: Select the task with the *largest processing time.*

RPW rule: Determine Rank Positional Weights (RPW) for all tasks. *The rank positional weight of any task is equal to the task time plus the sum of task times of all succeeding tasks.* Select the task with the *largest RPW.*

Tie breaking: While applying a priority rule, two or more tasks may be tied with same priority value. To break the tie, we will select the *task with the smaller task number* (we may change this rule later).

Example 1

Target cycle time = 60 sec.
Total time for 7 tasks = 200
Lower bound on number of stations = 200/60 3.33 ≈ 4 (round up).

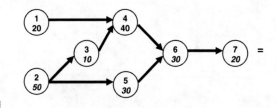

(a) Line balancing with SPT method:

SPT ORDER	3	1	7	5	6	4	2

STATION	SELECTED TASK	STATION CUM. TIME	ELIGIBLE TASKS
I	1	20	1,2/2
II	2, 3	50, 60	2/3,5/5,4
III	5	30	5,4/4
IV	4	40	4/6
V	6, 7	30, 50	6/7

Effective cycle time = 60 sec/unit

Efficiency = 100 × [200 /(5 × 60)] = 66.7%

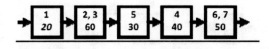

(b) Line balancing with LPT method:

LPT ORDER	2	4	5	6	1	7	3

STATION	SELECTED TASK	STATION CUM. TIME	ELIGIBLE TASKS
I	2, 3	50, 60	2,1/5,1,3/5,1
II	5, 1	30, 50	5,1/1/4
III	4	40	4/6
IV	6, 7	30, 50	6/7

Effective cycle time = 60 sec/unit

Efficiency = 100 × [200 /(4 × 60)] = 83.3%

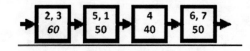

Example 2

For the task diagram shown here, production requirement is 1800 units per day (in 7.5 hours). We will solve this by the *SPT*.

Target Cycle time
= 7.5 [**Hrs/day**] × 3600 [**sec/hr**]/1800 [**units/day**]
= 15 [**sec/unit**]
Total task time = 74 [sec.]
Lower bound on number of stations = 74 /15 = 4.93 ≈ 5.

SPT ORDER	4	2	5	6	7	10	1	8	11	9	12	3

STATION	SELECTED TASK	STATION CUM. TIME	ELIGIBLE TASKS
I	2, 6	5, 10	2,1,3 /6,1,3 /1,3
II	1, 4, 5	6, 10, 15	1, 3 /4,5,3/5,9,3
III	10, 9	5, 13	10, 9, 3/9, 3/3
IV	3, 7	10, 15	3/7, 8/8
V	8, 11	6, 12	8/11/12
VI	12	9	9

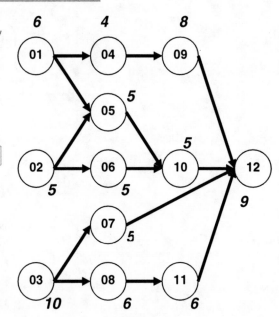

Example 1: Part C

Target cycle time = 60 sec
Line balancing with RPW method:

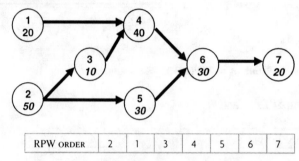

RPW ORDER	2	1	3	4	5	6	7

Effective cycle time = 60 sec/unit

Efficiency = 100 × [200 /(4 × 60)] = 83.3%

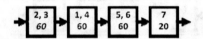

STATION	SELECTED TASK	STATION CUM. TIME	ELIGIBLE TASKS
I	2, 3	50, 60	2,1/1,3,5/1,5
II	1, 4	20, 60	1,5/4,5/5
III	5, 6	30, 60	5/6/7
IV	7	20	7

Example 2

RPW method.

Target Cycle time = 15 [sec/unit]
We have calculated weights for each task and shown these in the diagram as the underlined.

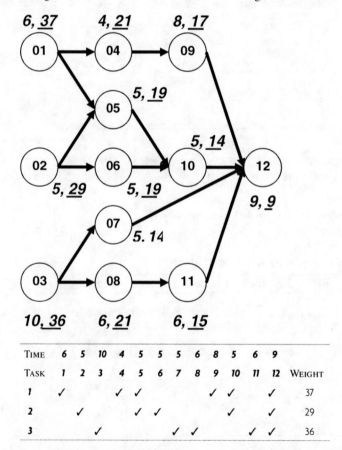

TIME	6	5	10	4	5	5	5	6	8	5	6	9	
TASK	1	2	3	4	5	6	7	8	9	10	11	12	WEIGHT
1	✓			✓	✓				✓	✓		✓	37
2		✓			✓	✓				✓		✓	29
3			✓				✓	✓			✓	✓	36

Tasks in decreasing order of RPW

01	03	02	04	08	05	06	09	11	07	10	12

STATION	SELECTED TASK	STATION CUM. TIME	ELIGIBLE TASKS
I	1, 2, 4	6, 11, 15	1,3,2 3,2,4 3,4,5,6 3,5,6,9
II	3, 5	10, 15	3,5,6,9 8,5,6,9,7 8,6,9,7
III	8, 6	6, 11	8,6,9,7 6,9,11,7 9,11,7,10
IV	9, 11	8, 14	9,11,7,10 11,7,10 7,10
V	7, 10	5, 10	7,10 10 12
VI	12	9	12

Effective Cycle time = 15 sec/unit.

Efficiency = $100 \times (74)/(6 \times 15) = 82.2\%$

Layout:

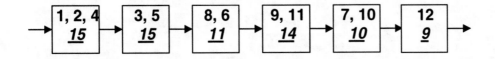

PROCESS SELECTION EXAMPLE (TIME IN MINUTES):

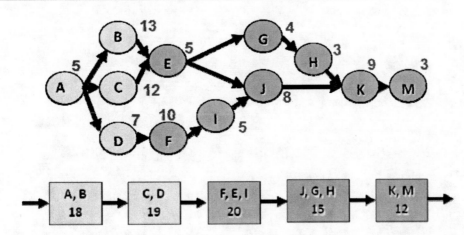

MACHINE	OPERATIONS
X	A, B, C, D
Y	E, F, I
Z	G, H, J, K, M

A - Line layout: Suppose we use a target CT = 20 min/unit. One possible layout is shown below.

Effective CT = 20 min/unit. We will produce $(7 \times 60/20) = 21$ units per day (7 hour working)

If we need to produce 100 units per day, we will need 100/≈ 5 lines in parallel (with capacity = $21 \times 5 = 105$ units per day.

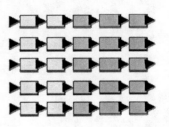

B - Cell layout: Each worker builds the entire product. We need to provide 3 machines (X, Y and Z) to each worker.

Total time needed = 5 + 13 + .. +9 + 3 = 84 min/unit

Worker capacity = 420[min/day]/84[min/unit] = 5 [units/day]

# of worker s = 100 [units/day]/5 [units/day * worker] = 20 workers.

Capacity = 100 units/day.

Costing for the cell layout:
Costing for the cell layout - Total workers: 20
Daily salary = 20[workers]*16[$/hr * worker]*8[hrs/day] = 2560 [$ /day]

Overheads = 2560 [$/ day] * 0.6 = 1536[$/ day]
Production cost = (2560 + 1536) [$/ day]/100 [units/day] = $40.96/ unit
Unit Product cost = Material cost + Production cost = $125.52 + $40.96 = $166.48.

C – Batch process: We will now calculate number of workers needed for each department. All workers work for 7 hours (420 min) and we need to produce 100 units in one day.

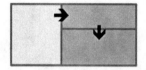

	X	Y	Z
TIME/UNIT	37 min	5 + 10 + 5 = 20 min.	27 min
TIME FOR 100 UNITS	3700 min	100 * 20 = 2000 min.	2700 min
WORKERS NEEDED	9	2000/420 ≈ 5	7
DEPT. CAPACITY	102	5 * 420/20 = 105	108

Total workers = 21. Capacity = 102

CHAPTER 4: AGGREGATE PLANNING

The main objective of "aggregate planning" is to develop a feasible production plan on an aggregate level based on demand, capacities, costs and other factors.

EXAMPLE 1

There are four products AA, BB, CC and DD. Product "AA" is the standard product. The third column shows demand for the next month.

PRODUCT	PRODUCTION TIME [HRS. / UNIT]	DEMAND [UNITS]	PRODUCTION TIME [HRS]	DEMAND IN STANDARD UNITS
AA	2.0	2000	2.0 × 2000 = 4000	4000/2.0 = 2000
BB	3.0	1000	3.0 × 1000 = 3000	3000/2.0 = 1500
CC	1.5	2400	1.5 × 2400 = 3600	3600/2.0 = 1800
DD	1.0	1200	1.0 × 1200 = 1200	1200/2.0 = 600
			Aggregate demand	5900

(a) Calculate aggregate demand (requirement) for the month.

(b) If the plant capacity for the next month is 5000 standard units, what suggestions can you make to meet demands calculated in part (a)?

SOLUTION

Part (a): See entries in the table in the last two columns.

Part (b): Since the plant capacity is 5000 and we need 5900 units, we could take several actions.

A4. Increase the capacity in month X through over time or temporary hiring or subcontracting.

A5. Produce extra 900 units in earlier months.

A6. Produce extra 900 in later months (assuming customers will accept orders late – this is called *backordering*).

A7. Decide not to meet this additional demand.

A8. A combination of the above four choices. ●

Example 2

Demand for three products (standard product: Deluxe) for January is as shown in the table below. Calculate the aggregate demand for the month. Note that instead of *"per unit production time"* (as in the previous example), here we have *"production rate"*.

PRODUCT	PRODUCTION RATE [UNITS/DAY]	DEMAND [UNITS]	PRODUCTION TIME [DAYS]	DEMAND IN STANDARD UNITS
Economy	200	3000	3000 / 200 = 15.0	15.0 × 160 = 2400
Deluxe	160	880	880 / 160 = 5.5	5.5 × 160 = 880
Imperial	60	120	120 / 60 = 2.0	2.0 × 160 = 320
			Aggregate Demand	3600

Aggregate Plan To prepare the aggregate plan over the *planning horizon*, we need to calculate aggregate demand for all periods. Then we apply a *planning strategy* and obtain an *aggregate production plan*. We are going to study simplified versions of two strategies used in aggregate planning: *Chase strategy* and *Level strategy*. We will use the term *Chase plan* to indicate production plan obtained using Chase strategy and *Level plan* for the plan obtained using level strategy.

The main idea behind the ***chase strategy*** is to ***produce quantity equal to aggregate demand for each period in order to keep inventory level zero***. The main idea behind the *level strategy* is to ***produce quantity equal to the average demand over the planning horizon***.

Using aggregate demands, we produce a ***basic plan*** (either using chase or level strategy). Then we consider ***policies (constraints),*** if any. To satisfy these policies, we make one or more adjustments to produce the ***final plan***. **Sometime we may have *soft constraints*. We try to meet these constraints as much as possible.**

Adjustments: The basic plan must be adjusted if there is a ***capacity restriction*** or a company policy such as "***no shortages permitted***" (in order to provide maximum service to the customer). Sometimes, we will permit shortages to be made up in the future period; this is called ***backordering***. The plan is also adjusted for any initial inventory on hand at the beginning of the planning horizon or if we need to keep certain inventory on hand at the end of the horizon.

The final plan can be ***expanded*** to indicate how a production quantity is broken down into regular production quantity, overtime production quantity, sub-contracted quantity, etc.
In more ***complex models*** (***not considered in our course***), capacity adjustments are also done with hiring or firing of workforce. Some models try to minimize costs when multiple choices are available.

EXAMPLE 3

For the aggregate demand shown, obtain **a chase plan** and **a level plan**, taking into account the ***capacity constraints*** and the fact that ***no shortages are permitted***. Whenever an adjustment is made to the chase plan, produce closest to the desired month.

PERIOD	1	2	3	4
TOTAL CAPACITY	8000	8000	8000	8000
AGGREGATE DEMAND	5000	6000	8500	4500

SOLUTION

Adjustment in Chase Strategy   In the *basic plan*, we are over capacity in period 3 (see the underlined entry in the table). So we shift 500 units from period 3 to period 2. The resulting plan meets all demands.

Adjustment in Level Strategy   Total demand is 24,000. Average demand will be 6000. In the *basic plan*, we have a shortage of 1500 period 3. So we produce 500 units extra in each of the first three periods. Since there is only one more period (period 4) in the planning horizon, we will reduce production in period 4 by 1500. The resulting plan meets all demands.

		CHASE					LEVEL		
PERIOD	1	2	3	4	1	2	3	4
DEMAND	5000	6000	8500	4500	5000	6000	8500	4500
BASIC PLAN	5000	6000	*8500*	4500	6000	6000	6000	6000
INVENTORY	0	0	0	0	1000	1000	*−1500*	0
ADJUSTED PLAN	5000	6500	8000	4500	6500	6500	6500	4500
INVENTORY	0	500	0	0	1500	2000	0	0

Note: It is possible to get more than one acceptable plan for the level strategy ⬤

Example 4

Aggregate demand for 6 months is shown in the table below.

	JAN	FEB	MARCH	APRIL	MAY	JUNE
DEMAND	2000	4500	4800	4300	2900	2700

CHASE		JAN	FEB	MAR	APRIL	MAY	JUNE
DEMAND		2000	4500	4800	4300	2900	2700
BASIC PLAN		1200	4500	4800	4300	2900	2700
INVENTORY	800	0	0	0	0	0	0
ADJUSTED PLAN I		3400	4000	4000	4000	2900	2700
INVENTORY	800	2200	1700	900	600	600	600
FINAL PLAN		3400	4000	4000	4000	2300	2700
INVENTORY	800	2200	1700	900	600	0	0

On December 31, you have 800 units on hand. On April 30, you must leave at least 600 units in inventory. Capacity in each month is **4000**. **No shortages** are permitted. Determine the aggregate plan using **(a) Chase strategy. (b) Level strategy.**

SOLUTION

Part (a): Chase Strategy

The basic plan: This plan produces 500 units more than capacity in February, 800 more in March and 300 more in April (see the underlined entries). Furthermore, this plan does not leave 600 units in inventory at the end of April. We should therefore produce $(500+800+300) + 600 = 2200$ additional units in January.

LEVEL		JAN	FEB	MAR	APRIL	MAY	JUNE
DEMAND		2000	4500	4800	4300	2900	2700
BASIC PLAN		3400	3400	3400	3400	3400	3400
INVENTORY	800	2200	1100	-300	-1200	-700	0
ADJUSTED PLAN		3850	3850	3850	3850	3400	3400
INVENTORY		2650	2000	1050	600	1100	1800
FINAL PLAN		3850	3850	3850	3850	2500	2500
INVENTORY		2650	2000	1050	600	200	0

Adjusted plan I: *When capacity in a month is insufficient we should shift production to the month as close to desired month as possible.*

Final Plan: We should produce 600 units less in May to get June inventory down to zero.

Part (b) Level Strategy   Since there are 800 units on hand on December 31, the total (adjusted) demand over the planning horizon will be $2000 + 4500 + 4800 + 4300 + 2900 + 2700 - 800 = 20,400$. Hence the average demand will be $(20,400/6) = 3400$.

The basic plan: This plan produces negative inventories in March, April and May (see the underlined entries). Furthermore, we need 600 units at the end of April. Let's look at the inventory of -1200 at the end of April. To make this number 600, we need to produce 1800 additional units between January and April or $(1800/4) = 450$ units more per month.

Adjusted plan I: Since this adjustment will leave 1800 units in inventory at the end of June, we should produce 1800 units less in May and June or 900 fewer units per month.

Final Plan: This plan meets all demands. ●

Example 5 **This example involves a soft constraint.**

Solve the aggregate planning problem with *chase strategy. Use the following constraints.*

1. **Maximum end inventory is limited to 500 units for any period.**
2. **Avoid shortages but if you cannot avoid, keep backordering as small as possible.**

We will use the following procedure: Start with the basic plan. Then adjust for capacity violation assuming no shortages are permitted. Then adjust for excess inventory (now you can permit shortages).

Basic plan: Capacity exceeded by 600 in P4
Adjustment 1: From P4, move 300 units to P3 and 300 to P2. Now inventory in P3 exceeds 500.
Adjustment 2: Move 100 units from P2 to P5. Plan is now acceptable.

CHASE	0	1	2	3	4	5
CAPACITY		**5000**	**5000**	**5000**	**5000**	**5000**
DEMAND		**4250**	**4000**	**4700**	**5600**	**4600**
BASIC PLAN		4250	4000	4700	5600	4600
INVENTORY	**0**	0	0	0	0	0
ADJUST. 1		4250	4300	5000	5000	4600
INVENTORY	**0**	0	300	600	0	0
ADJUST. 2		4250	4200	5000	5000	4700
INVENTORY	**0**	0	200	500	−100	0

Example 6

For the information shown in the table to the right, obtain plans using chase strategy as well as level strategy. No shortages are permitted. Note that due to plant shutdown in month 5, no regular or overtime production is possible.

After obtaining the final plan (for chase and level strategies), split the production quantities into regular, overtime and sub-contracted numbers choosing lower cost method of production first. Then calculate the production costs for each month in the tables provided. Regular production cost is $1000 per unit. Overtime production cost is $1150 per unit. Sub-contracting cost is $1250 per unit. Inventory holding cost is $60 per unit per period on leftover units at the end any month.

MONTH	1	2	3	4	5	6
DEMAND	5000	6000	8000	9000	9000	11000
PRODUCTION CAPACITIES						
REGULAR	6000	6000	6000	6000	0	6000
OVERTIME	1200	1200	1200	1200	0	1200
SUBCONTRACT	4000	4000	4000	4000	6000	4000
TOTAL	11200	11200	11200	11200	6000	11200

Chase Strategy: The basic plan produces 3000 units over capacity in period 5. Of these, 2200 are moved to period 4 and the remaining 800 to period 3. This gives the final plan. Monthly production is then broken into regular, overtime and subcontracting and costs are calculated. The total cost over the planning horizon is 52,618,000 dollars.

CHASE	1	2	3	4	5	6	TOTAL
TOTAL CAPACITY	11200	11200	11200	11200	6000	11200	
DEMAND	5000	6000	8000	9000	9000	11000	**48000**
BASIC PLAN	**5000**	**6000**	**8000**	**9000**	**9000**	**11000**	

Continued

CHASE	1	2	3	4	5	6	TOTAL
INVENTORY	0	0	0	0	0	0	
FINAL PLAN	**5000**	**6000**	**8800**	**11200**	**6000**	**11000**	
INVENTORY	0	0	800	3000	0	0	
FINAL PLAN DIVISION							
REGULAR	5000	6000	6000	6000	0	6000	
OVERTIME	0	0	1200	1200	0	1200	
SUBCONTRACT	0	0	1600	4000	6000	3800	
COSTS IN THOUSAND DOLLARS							
REGULAR	5000	6000	6000	6000	0	6000	
OVERTIME	0	0	1380	1380	0	1380	
SUBCONTRACT	0	0	2000	5000	7500	4750	
HOLDING COST	0	0	48	180	0	0	
TOTAL COST	**5000**	**6000**	**9428**	**12560**	**7500**	**12130**	**52618**

Level Strategy: Notice that the basic plan produces 2000 units over capacity in period 5. Since there is sufficient inventory at the end of period 5, we can distribute excess production units over the remaining 5 periods equally (400 in each period). This gives the final plan. Monthly production is then broken into regular, overtime and subcontracting. Then the costs are calculated. The total cost over the planning horizon is 53,316,000 dollars.

LEVEL	1	2	3	4	5	6	TOTAL
TOTAL CAPACITY	11200	11200	11200	11200	6000	11200	
DEMAND	5000	6000	8000	9000	9000	11000	**48000**
BASIC PLAN	**8000**	**8000**	**8000**	**8000**	**8000**	**8000**	
INVENTORY	3000	5000	5000	4000	3000	0	
FINAL PLAN	**8400**	**8400**	**8400**	**8400**	**6000**	**8400**	
INVENTORY	3400	5800	6200	5600	2600	0	
FINAL PLAN DIVISION							
REGULAR	6000	6000	6000	6000	0	6000	
OVERTIME	1200	1200	1200	1200	0	1200	
SUBCONTRACT	1200	1200	1200	1200	6000	1200	
COSTS IN THOUSAND DOLLARS							
REGULAR	6000	6000	6000	6000	0	6000	
OVERTIME	1380	1380	1380	1380	0	1380	
SUBCONTRACT	1500	1500	1500	1500	7500	1500	
HOLDING COST	204	348	372	336	156	0	
TOTAL COST	**9084**	**9228**	**9252**	**9216**	**7656**	**8880**	**53316**

EFFECT OF SETUP TIME ON CAPACITY

When multiple products are produced in the same facility, certain time is lost due to time required to set up machines. This results in loss of capacity. This will be illustrated through an example.

Example

Suppose we have two products X and Y requiring the same machine. One unit of X can be produced in 4 minutes, Y needs 3 minutes. The machine is available for 7 hour per day, 20 days per month. If we produce only X, we can produce $(20 \times 60 \times 7)/4 = 2100$ units. If X is the standard product, the machine capacity per month is 2100 units.

Suppose X and Y are used to assemble a product and the assembly requires 1 unit of X and 2 units of Y, or for every 4 minutes devoted to X, we must devote 6 minutes to Y or we can say that 40% time for X and 60% time for Y.

Part I: *Our aim is to maximize monthly production*: Obviously, we should start with one product (say X) at the beginning of the month and switch to the other product at appropriate time. From this point onwards, we should produce the other product for the rest of the month. This way we will lose only 1 hour in set up time during the month. Our output (in terms of standard units) will be 2085 units in one month.

MONTHLY ↓	MAXIMIZE MONTHLY PRODUCTION	PRODUCE BOTH PRODUCTS EVERY DAY
PRODUCTION TIME	139 hours = 8340 minutes	6 hours/day = 120 hours/month = 7200 minutes
TIME FOR XX	8340 × 0.4 = 3336 minutes	7200 × 0.4 = 2880 minutes
TIME FOR YY	8340 × 0.6 = 5004 minutes	7200 × 0.6 = 4320 minutes
PRODUCTION: XX	3336/4 = 834 units	2880/4 = 720 units
PRODUCTION: YY	5004/3 = 1668 units, or 1668 × 0.75 = 1251 units of XX	4320/3 = 1440 units, or 1440 × 0.75 = 1080 units of XX
PRODUCTION IN STANDARD UNITS	834 + 1251 = 2085 units.	720 + 1080 = 1800 units.
Comments	2085 is close to 2100	Significant loss in capacity.

Part II: *We must produce both products every day*: The best alternative for this situation is as follows. We should start with X at the beginning of day 1 and switch to the other product at appropriate time during the day. From this point onwards, we should produce the Y for the rest of the day. On day 2, we should start with Y (keeping the same set up from the previous day). We will lose only 1 hour in set up time every day (or a total of 20 hours in a month). Our output (in terms of standard units) will be 1800 units in one month.

 Since the actual production process may be more complex (multiple machines, multiple products, down times for scheduled maintenance), one can approximate this by assuming smaller capacity in aggregate planning. If we were to do aggregate planning for the process discussed in the example 1, we may want to assume monthly capacity to be less than 2100. We could assume 10 to 15% lower capacity for planning purposes.

CHAPTER 5: INVENTORY MANAGEMENT

Inventory: Stock or store of goods. Examples:
Manufacturing: raw material, purchased parts, partially finished and finished goods. Machine spares, tools, other supplies.
Department Stores: Clothing, furniture, carpeting, white goods, shoes, gift items, toys, cards, etc.
Hospitals: drugs, surgical supplies, life-monitoring equipment, sheets, etc.
Supermarkets: fresh and canned food, frozen food, dairy products, produce, magazines, etc.
Objective: Provide right material at the right time with right quality and price.
Inventory Control: factors – Customer service, ordering/carrying costs.

MATERIAL MANAGEMENT: TYPICAL ACTIVITIES

MATERIAL PLANNING & CONTROL	PURCHASING	STORES MGMT
Inventory Control	Source Selection	Systems & Procedures
Material Planning	Purchase Systems	Incoming Material
ABC Analysis	Price Forecasting	Material Handling
Budgeting	Seasonal Buying	Transportation
Material Research	Capital Equipment	Scrap Management
Codification	International Buying	Stock Checking
Standardization	Legal Aspects	Obsolete Items Mgmt.

We will consider inventory control of a single product through several models. In an inventory model, we specify an *objective*. We also need to know *demand type* (deterministic/stochastic). We make certain *assumptions* and there may be certain *constraints*. We then come up with *ordering policy – when to order, how much to order.*

Suppose the physical stock is 25 and demand is 30. We will deliver 25 and there will be a shortage of 5 (making OH = 0 and IL = -5). Suppose the customer does not want 5 units in future or the customer wants all 30 units and will cancel the order. This is called *lost sales case.* We will not consider lost sales in our class. We will always assume that when shortages occur, the shortages are taken care of first when fresh shipment arrives.

TERM		EXPLANATION	
Lead Time	**LT**	Time between placing and receiving order	
On Hand Inventory	**OH**	Physical stock	**OH $\geq$ 0**
Inventory Level	**IL**	Units available to meet future demand.	**IL = OH − Q on backorder**
Inventory Position	**IP**	Inventory level + Order in transit	**IP = IL + Q in transit, IP $\geq$ IL**

I INVENTORY MODELS: DETERMINISTIC DEMAND

Notation/assumptions for Models 1, 2 and 3:
D: annual demand [Q/T]. Demand occurs at uniform rate.
S: ordering/setup cost [$].
H: holding (carrying) cost in $ per unit per year based on average inventory.
LT: lead time (can be negligible).
C: unit purchase price. *No shortages are permitted.*

No.	MODEL	OBJECTIVE
1	EOQ	Min. Inv. cost
2	EPQ	Min. Inv. cost
3	EOQ with discounts	Min. Total cost
4	Lot Sizing	??

1 EOQ MODEL:

Objective: Minimize *annual inventory cost (AIC)*. The textbook uses the term *total cost*.

Example 1.1

D = 12,000 units/year, S = \$140, C = \$15 /unit and annual holding cost: 24% of C. H = \$3.6 per unit per year

LOT SIZE Q	NUMBER OF ORDERS/YEAR	ORDERING COST [\$/YEAR]	AVG. INVENTORY [UNITS]	HOLDING COST [\$/YEAR]	AIC [\$/YEAR]
400	30.0	4200	200	720	4920
800	15.0	2100	400	1440	3540
1200	10.0	1400	600	2160	3560
1600	7.5	1050	800	2880	3930

SOLUTION

Annual costs shown in the table. The best lot size among the above four is 800 with annual inventory cost of \$3540.

Derivation of the optimal lot size: We define $AIC(Q)$ = ordering cost/year + hoding cost/year for a lot size Q.

$$AIC(Q) = S \times (D/Q) + H \times (Q/2) \text{ .... Equation 1}$$

Solving this equation, we can show that the ordering and holding costs are equal for the optimal order quantity $Q = Q_0$. Equating $S * (D/Q_0) = H * (Q_0/2)$, we get

$$Q_0 = \sqrt{\frac{2.D.S}{H}} \text{ .... Equation 2}$$

It is a *common practice to round off* Q_0 *within* ± *5%* to a convenient round number as the annual inventory cost does not increase appreciably in this range. We will use Q^* final lot size we select (may be equal to Q_0 or within ± 5%). ●

Example 1.2

For data in example 1.1, calculate optimal lot size and corresponding *AIC*.

LOT SIZE	NUMBER OF ORDERS /YEAR	ORDERING COST [\$/YEAR]	INVENTORY [UNITS]	HOLDING COST [\$/YEAR]	AIC [\$/YEAR]
Q_0: 966.1	12.421	1738.94	483.05	1738.98	3477.96
Q^*:1000	12	1680	500	1800	3480

SOLUTION

From equation 2, we get $Q_0 = \sqrt{[(2 \times 12000 \times 140)/(3.6)]} = 966.1$. We will round off to $Q^* = 1000$. We will calculate costs for both 966.1 and 1000 to show that the cost difference is very small.

Ordering policy [x, Q] means when inventory position = x, order Q units. For the example above, the ordering policy is [0, 1000].

Graphs of lot size (Q) vs. various costs are shown in the figure to the left ●

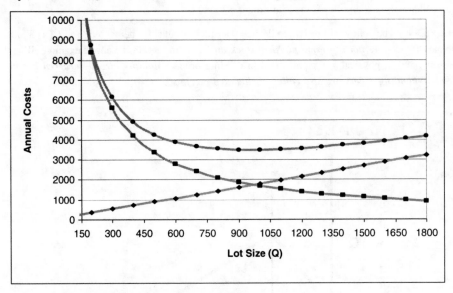

VARIATIONS OF THE BASIC EOQ MODEL:

Example 1.3

Consider examples 1.1 and 1.2 again.

1. What should be the ordering policy if minimal order quantity in a lot must be 1500?

SOLUTION   From the graph in figure above, higher the lot size over 966, the cost is going to go up. So the ordering policy should be [0, 1500].

2. What should be the ordering policy if minimal order quantity in a lot must be 750?

SOLUTION   Obviously we can use [0, 1000] as it meets the requirement of buying at least 750.

3. Suppose the product is packed in boxes containing 150 items each and a lot size must contain full boxes. What should be the ordering policy?

SOLUTION   Now the lot size should be a multiple of 150 (750, 900, 1050, 1200, etc,). Since Q_0 = 966.1, one can show that the lowest cost occurs either with 900 or 1050. You can verify that $AIC(900)$ = 3486.67 and $AIC(1050)$ = 3490. So the ordering policy should be [0, 900].

In the EOQ model, it was assumed that the lead-time is negligible. If *LT* is not negligible, what happens to the ordering policy? First, *the lot size is not affected*. This means that we still calculate the lot size (how much to order) in the same way described thus far. However the first part of the ordering policy (when to order), i.e. *the inventory position is no longer zero*. We should order when the IP becomes equal to the *demand during the lead-time*. **IP = D × LT**.

Example 1.4

Consider example 1.2 where the ordering policy was [0, 1000]

1. What will be the policy if the lead-time is 1/2 month?

SOLUTION   D × *LT* = {12000 [**units/year**]/12 [**months/year**]} × 1/2 [**month**] = 500 [**units**]

The policy will be: [when IP = 500, order 1000].

2.   What will be the policy if the lead-time is $1^1/2$ months?

SOLUTION   The policy will be [when IP = 1500, order 1000] since demand during *LT* is 1500.

3.   What will be the policy if the lead-time is 3 months?

SOLUTION   The policy will be [when IP = 3000, order 1000] since demand during *LT* is 3000.

Note that *IP does not represent physical stock on hand*. In fact, in the above example, IP = 1500 represents 500 in physical stock plus 1000 in pending orders (*quantity already ordered but not yet received). Pending orders are also called "Scheduled receipts".*

2 EPQ MODEL:

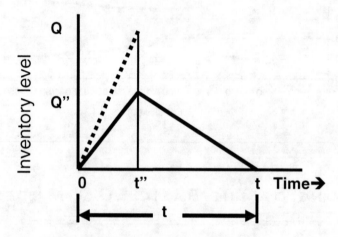

Inventory vs. time for the EPQ model

Objective: Minimize *annual inventory cost (AIC)*.
Annual Demand = D
Daily demand (called *usage rate*) = u
Daily production rate = p.
If we assume 360 days per year, u = D/360.
Run time is the interval of time for which the machine is run. This is equal to Q/p.
Cycle time is time between beginning of runs. This is equal to Q/u
Maximum inventory Q" = Q $\times$ (p −u)/p; average inventory is half of that amount.
Annualy, there will be *D/Q number of runs*.

The *AIC* will be given by
AIC(Q) = Setup cost /year + holding cost year = S $\times$ (D/Q) + H $\times$ (Q/2) $\times$ (p−u)/p.

Q_0 will be given by the formula to the right.

$$Q_0 = \sqrt{\frac{2.D.S}{H}} \sqrt{\frac{p}{(p-u)}}$$

Example 2.1

Demand (D) is 18000 units/year. Assume 360 days /year. We can produce this product at the rate of p = 90 units/day. The production set up cost (S) is $175 and inventory holding cost (H) is $4.2 per unit per year.

(a) Find the optimal lot size.

(b) Calculate run time, cycle time and AIC for the lot size in part (a).

(c) What if the machine cannot be run for more than 15 days at a time?

SOLUTION

Usage rate u = 18000/360 = 50 units/day.

(a) Substituting values in the above formula, we get Q_0 = 1837 and Q* = 1800.

(b) Now, t" = Q/p = 1800 [units]/90 [units/day] = 20 days.

Also, t = Q/u = 1800 [units]/50 [units/day] = 36 days.

Maximum inventory = Q × (p−u)/p = 1800 × 40/90 = 800.

AIC(1800) = S × (D/Q) + H × (Q/2) × (p−u)/p = $1750 + $1680 = $3430.

(c) Now run time = 15 days. Hence Q* = 1350, cycle time = 27 days and AIC(1350) = $3593.33. ●

3 EOQ MODEL WITH QUANTITY DISCOUNTS:

Objective: Minimize ***annual total cost***.

When you buy material in large quantities, you may get some discount on the purchase price and your annual cost could be lower. In the EOQ model discussed earlier, we did not consider the purchase cost in the total cost because it was independent of the order lot size. ***Now we will consider total annual cost in our decision. This cost is the sum of the annual purchase cost and annual inventory cost.***

We will consider only the model involving "***all units discount***". In the "all units" discount, the lower price applies to all units as soon as you buy large quantity.

To solve this problem, we start with the lowest unit price and calculate Q_0. If this is feasible, we calculate total annual cost and stop. If Q_0 is not feasible, we find feasible Q* and calculate total annual cost. Repeat this for next higher unit price. If we have done calculations for more than 1 unit price, we select the lot size with lowest total annual cost. This will be illustrated through examples.

Example 3.1

D = 10,000 units/year, S = $5.5, H: 20% per year of purchase price

LOT SIZE	1 to 399	400 to 699	700 and up
PRICE PER UNIT	$2.20	$2.00	$1.80
H ($/UNIT PER YEAR)	0.44	0.40	0.36
Q0 = √{2 × D × S/H}		524.40	552.80
SOLUTION			
·LOT SIZE Q*		500.00	**700.00**
PURCHASE $		20,000.00	18,000.00
ORDERING $		110.00	78.57
HOLDING $		100.00	126.00
TOTAL $		20210.00	**18204.47**

Part (a):   Calculate optimal policy and corresponding total annual cost.

We start with unit price = $1.80. Q_0 = 552.8. Since this is not feasible, we select Q* = 700 and TC(700)=$18204.47.

Now we try unit price = $2.00. Q_0 = 524.4, This is *feasible* and we will round this off to 500 and TC(500) = 20210.0

Since feasible Q_0 was found, we select the lot size with lower annual total cost.

Policy [0, 700], TC(700) = $18204.47

Part (b):   What if there is lead time = 2 weeks? Assume 50 weeks per year.

Demand during LT = 2 × (10000/50) = 400 units. Optimal policy [400, 700]

Example 3.2

A product satisfying EOQ assumptions has demand D = 6000 units/year. Other parameters are: ordering cost S = $200, holding cost: 20% of per unit purchase price per year. Information about quantity discount is given in the table below. Find the optimal lot size and total annual cost.

PRICE/UNIT	$2.50	$2.45	$2.40
ORDER QUANTITY	1 To 1000	1001 To 5999	6000 and up
HOLDING COST	$0.50	2.45 × 0.2 = $0.49	$0.48
Q_0		2213.23	2236.07
LOT SIZE Q*		**2250**	6000
ANNUAL COSTS			
PURCHASE		6000 × 2.45 = 14700.00	6000 × 2.40 = 14400.00
ORDERING		(6000/2250) × 200 = 533.33	(6000/6000) × 200 = 200.00
HOLDING		(2250/2) × 0.49 = 551.25	(6000/2) × 0.48 = 1440.00
TOTAL		**15784.58**	16040.00

SOLUTION

Start calculations from the lowest unit cost.

$$Q_0 = \sqrt{[(2 \cdot D \cdot S)/H]} = \sqrt{[(2 \cdot 6000 \cdot 200)/(0.48)]} = 2236 \text{ units.}$$

We must use 6000 as the lot size. Annual cost calculations are shown in the table. Since Q_0 (= 2236) is not in the feasible range (6000 and up), we continue our calculations for thext higher unit price.

$$Q_0 = \sqrt{[(2 \cdot D \cdot S)/H]} = \sqrt{[(2 \cdot 6000 \cdot 200)/(0.49)]} = 2213.33 \text{ units.}$$

We will use 2250 as the lot size. Annual cost calculations are shown in the table. Since Q_0 (= 2213) is in the feasible range (1001 and 5999), we can select our policy. ●

Optimal ordering policy: (0,2250). Annual cost $15784.58

4 LOT SIZING INVENTORY MODELS (DETERMINISTIC DEMAND)

In many situations we work with discrete periods and demand fluctuates from period to period as shown in the table to the right. Here we use lot sizing models. Although no shortages are permitted, some *safety stock (SS)* may be specified. This means that the inventory should not fall below the safety stock in any period. Many models do not use costs while some the others use ordering cost, holding cost, etc. We will consider situations involving no costs; then we do not have any specific objective function. *Lot sizing models can be used for purchase or production.*

We will consider three rules and calculate lot sizes using these three rules. The following is true for every rule. Suppose we consider period k. We assume that the *lot (Q_k) is received* at the *beginning of the period, demand (D_k)* occurs *during the period* and we consider *inventory (I_k)* at the *end of the period*. The following should be kept in mind.

$$I_k \geq SS \text{ and } I_k = I_{k-1} + Q_k - D_k,$$

Let's use D_k^* to denote *net demand* for period k. Then, $D_k^* = D_k + SS - I_{k-1}$

PERIOD	1	2	3	4	5	6	7	8	9	10
DEMAND	20	40	30	0	80	20	0	0	75	70

Model A: Lot for lot (L4L) *Policy: Order D_k^* units if $0 < D_k^*$.*

Model B: Fixed order Quantity (FOQ) Order a fixed quantity Q_F (based on some judgment, intuition, experience, etc) or a multiple of this fixed quantity, to cover the *net demand* for the period.

Policy: Order Q_F units if $0 < D_k^* \le Q_F$.
Order $2Q_F$ units if $Q_F < D_k^* \le 2Q_F$ and so on.

Model C: Period order quantity (POQ) If the net demand is positive, add up demand for a specified number of periods (say X) and order that quantity. *Policy: If $0 < D_k^*$, order D_k^* plus demand for next X-1 periods.*

Exception: Towards the end of the planning horizon, there may be fewer than X-1 periods left. *Then the tentative lot size is $< D_k^*$ plus demand for the remaining periods.*

Example

Calculate order quantities in the example below using *L4L, FOQ 50 and POQ 3. Initial inventory is 30 units and safety stock is 10.*

SOLUTION

FOQ 50 means we order 50 (or a multiple of 50). POQ 3 means we order for 3 periods. The second column shows initial inventory of 30.

PERIOD K		0	1	2	3	4	5	6	7	8	9	10
L4L	D_k		35	40	30	0	80	20	0	0	75	70
	ORDER		15	40	30	–	80	20	0	0	75	70
	I_k	30	10	10	10	10	10	10	10	10	10	10
FOQ 50	D_k		35	40	30	0	80	20	0	0	75	70
	ORDER		50	50	–	–	100	–			100	50
	I_k	30	45	55	25	25	45	25	25	25	50	30
POQ 3	D_k		35	40	30	0	80	20	0	0	75	70
	ORDER		85	–	–	–	100	–	–	–	145	–
	I_k	30	80	40	10	10	30	10	10	10	80	10

II INVENTORY MODELS: PROBABILISTIC DEMAND

Models considered so far (EOQ, EPQ, etc) had deterministic demand. In all of these models, no shortages were permitted. This resulted in 100% service level. Now we will consider probabilistic demand models. We will have occasional shortages and service level may be less than 100%. *The objective for Q and P system models is to determine an ordering policy to meet the desired service level. In the newsvendor model, we want to minimize expected cost (i.e. average cost).*

NO.	MODEL TYPE
5	When to reorder: re-order point model (Q system)
6	How much to order: Fixed order interval model (P system)
7	Single period model (Newsvendor)

5   MODEL BASED ON CONTINUOUS REVIEW (Q SYSTEM):

Here we are looking at the demand for a single product. We assume that the demand distribution is known and will continue to be the same for some time. We will also assume that lead time is fixed and we permit backordering when shortages occur.

In the ***continuous review system (also called Q system),*** inventory is monitored continuously. When ***inventory position*** falls below a ***predetermined level*** (called ***re-order point: ROP***), an order is placed. We are going to assume that the order quantity (lot size Q) is fixed. The ordering policy can be written as: Order Q units when $IP \leq ROP$. In many cases continuous review may simply mean ***checking IP at the beginning of each day.***

Inventory Level (IL) means units available to meet future demand. A negative value indicates backorder. ***Inventory Position (IP)*** is equal to IL plus quantity ordered but not received. For the manual systems, we will use the following formulas (assume $Y \geq X$).

Closing IL (day Y) = Opening IL (day X) + Receipts from X to Y − Withdrawals from X to Y.

Closing IP (day Y) = Opening IP (day X) + Orders from X to Y − Withdrawals from X to Y.

Example 5.1

Suppose the reorder point ***ROP*** = 320 and the order quantity Q = 450. The lead-time (***LT***) is 4 days (if you order at the beginning of the day x, you receive the lot at the beginning of day x + 4). ***Opening stock is 190.*** An order is expected to arrive on day 2. Withdrawals during next 8 days are shown in the table (in the shaded area). We will fill out the remaining entries.

Day	Opening IL	Opening IP	Receipt	Order	Withdrawal During day	Closing IL	Closing IP
1	190	640	0	-	80	110	560
2	110	560	450	-	110	450	450
3	450	450	0	-	130	320	320
4	320	320	0	450	90	230	680
5	230	680	0	-	110	120	570
6	120	570	0	-	50	70	520
7	70	520	0	-	80	−10	440
8	−10	440	450	-	70	370	370
Total			900	450	720		

Note the following.

- Orders were placed only on days when $IP \leq 320$.
- $IL = -10$ at the end of day 7 indicates shortage; it was made up on day 8.

We will apply IL formula for X = 2 and Y = 6. IL: 70 = 110 + 450 − 490.
We will apply IP formula for X = 1 and Y = 8. IP: 370 = 640 + 450 − 720

Normally distributed demand   Let the demand per unit time be normally distributed with mean = μ and standard deviation = σ. Let the lead-time be ***LT***. We will also assume that demand in each unit time period is independent of demand in other periods. Then, we can show that the demand during lead-time ***LT*** is also normally distributed with parameters as shown.

Given: Demand per unit time	**Demand during lead time LT**
N[mean = μ, standard deviation = σ]	N[mean μ_L = LT × μ, standard deviation σ_L = $(\sqrt{LT})* \sigma$]

Calculation value of reorder point (s) for a specified service level λ (say 95%)

Note that average demand during lead time is $LT \times \mu$. If we set $ROP \nabla LT \times \mu$, we will run out of stock 50% of the time, i.e. service level will be only 50%

We need to set the reorder point at $(LT \times \mu + Z_{SL} \times \sigma \times \sqrt{LT})$. The first term in the formula $(L \times \mu)$ is the *average demand during lead time*. The second term is called the *safety stock*.

Example 5.2

Demand per week: $N(\mu = 500, \sigma = 20)$. Lead-time = 4 weeks. Service level = 98%.

Part (a): *What should be reorder point (ROP)? Round up to the nearest multiple of 10.*
For $SL = 98\%$, $Z_{SL} = Z_{0.98} = 2.06$, $LT = 4$, $ROP = \mu_{LT} + Z_{0.98} \times \sigma_{LT}$
Demand during lead-time: $N[\mu_{LT} = 4 \times 500 = 2000, \sigma_{LT} = (\sqrt{4}) \times 20 = 40]$
$ROP = 2000 + 2.06 \times 40 = 2082.4 \approx \textbf{2090}$.

Part (b): *Calculate safety stock.*
SS = 2090 – 2000 5 90

Part (C): Calculate ROP and SS for $LT = 2$. Use same SL and rounding up.
$N[\mu_{LT} = 2 \times 500 = 1000, \sigma_{LT} = (\sqrt{2}) \times 20 = 28.284]$
$ROP = 1000 + 2.06 \times 28.284 = 1058.27 \approx \textbf{1060}$.
SS = 1060 – 1000 = **60**

Example 5.3

Demand per week: $N(\mu = 200, \sigma = 25)$. Lead-time = 5 weeks. Service level = 95%.

(a) What should be the value of reorder point ROP?
For 95% service level, from Normal tables: $Z_{0.95} = 1.65$ Lead-time is 5 weeks. Demand during lead-time: $N(\mu_L = 5 \times 200, \sigma_{LT} = \sqrt{5} \times 25) = N(\mu_L = 1000, \sigma_{LT} = 55.90)$
Reorder point, $ROP = 1000 + 1.65 \times 55.90 = 1092.235 \approx 1100$
Why did we round up? It increases the service level slightly.

(b) What is the safety stock?
Safety Stock = 1100 – 1000 = 100

Suppose Ordering cost: $60, Purchase price $12.50/unit, holding cost fraction f = 0.25 per year. Assume 1 year = 50 weeks.

(c) Assume that the EOQ model can approximate annual demand. What will be the lot size?
$Q^* = [2 (200 \times 50) (60)/(0.25 \times 12.5)]^{1/2} = 619. Q^* \approx 600.$

(d) What is the average time between orders for the lot size calculated in part (c)?
Average time between orders = 600/200 = 3 weeks

6 FIXED ORDER INTERVAL MODEL (P SYSTEM):

This is also known as *periodic review system*. In the *periodic review system (also called P system)*, inventory is reviewed and ordered at fixed intervals. On the review day, the order quantity is selected such that it *raises the inventory position to a predetermined level* (called *order-up-to level: "OUL"*). Use *LT* to denote lead time and *OI* to denote order interval. The ordering policy can be written as: Order (*OUL – IP*) units on each review date. We will start with an example where records are kept manually.

Example 6.1

Suppose the *OUL* = 600 and the review period *OI* = 4 days. Reviews will be carried out on **Day 1, 5, 9, etc**. The lead-time (*LT*) is 2 days. Inventory level on day 1 is 210. Assume that there are no orders are expected to arrive on day 1 and day 2. Withdrawals during next 9 days are shown in the table below (in the shaded area). Notice that some cells in the "order" column are shaded as *no orders will be placed on these days*. We will fill out the remaining entries. Notice that the order quantity varies. You can verify that the formulas shown below are applicable here.

Closing IL (day Y) = Opening IL (day X) + Receipts from X to Y – Withdrawals from X to Y.

Closing IP (day Y) = Opening IP (day X) + Orders from X to Y – Withdrawals from X to Y.

Day	Opening *IL*	Opening *IP*	Receipt	Order	Withdrawal during day	Closing *IL*	Closing *IP*
1	210	210	0	390	120	90	480
2	90	480	0		80	10	400
3	10	400	390		130	270	270
4	270	270	0		80	190	190
5	190	190	0	410	90	100	510
6	100	510	0		110	−10	400
7	−10	400	410		135	265	265
8	265	265	0		80	185	185
9	185	185	0	415	120	65	480
Total			800	1215	945		

Normally distributed demand Let the demand per unit time be normal with mean = μ and standard deviation = σ. Let the order interval be *OI*, let the lead-time be *LT*. We will also assume that demand in each unit time period is independent of demand in other periods. Here the decision we take to order affects not only the lead time, but we have to worry about demand during the order interval. If we define

Protection period = order interval + lead time = *OI* + *LT*,

OUL = Demand during protection period + SS = $(OI + LT) \times \mu + Z_{SL} \times \sigma \times \sqrt{(OI + LT)}$.

Example 6.2

demand per week ~ N(μ = 90, σ = 15), 50 weeks per year, *LT* = 3 weeks.

Part (a): Determine a suitable review period using EOQ approximation (S = $80, Purchase price $12.00 per unit, holding cost is 27% of per unit purchase price per year)

Qo = [2 x (90 x 50) x 80/(0.27 x 12)]$^{1/2}$ = 471. Q* ≈ 450

OI = 450 [units]/90 [units/week] = 5 [weeks]

Part (b): Use information in part (a) and find S for *SL* = 80%.

$Z_{0.8}$ = 0.85 (from standard normal tables)

$OUL = (OI+LT) \times \mu + Z_{SL} \{\sqrt{(OI+LT)}\} \times \sigma$

= (5+3) × 90 + 0.85 × ($\sqrt{8}$) × 15 = 720 + 36.1 = 756.1 ≈ 760

Part (c): Find *OUL* for *SL* = 98%

From the standard normal tables, $Z_{0.98}$ = 2.06

OUL = (5+3) × 90 + 2.06 × ($\sqrt{8}$) × 15 = 720 + 87.4 = 807.4 ≈ 810

Example 6.3

Demand per day ~ N[2000 gal, 500 gal]. Delivery lead-time is 1 day.

Part (a): Suppose we use continuous review system and do not want stock-outs (shortages) to occur in more than 1 out of 10 cycles. What should be reorder point s?

Shortages in 1 out of 10 cycles means service level SL = 9/10 = 0.9

$Z_{0.9} = 1.29$ and $ROP = LT \times \mu + Z_{SL} \sigma_L = (1) \times 2000 + 1.29 \times \{\sqrt{(1)}\} \times 500 = 2,645$ **gallons**

Suppose we switch to P system and order sufficient quantity to fill 10,750-gallon tank.

(i) What is order up to level S? *OUL = 10,750 gal.*

(ii) If we order every 4 days ($OI = 4$), what is the service level *SL* equal to?

$OI + LT = 5$ $OUL = (OI+LT) \times \mu + Z_{SL} \{\sqrt{(OI+LT)}\} \times \sigma$

$10,750 = (5) \times 2000 + Z_{SL} \{\sqrt{(5)}\} \times 500 = 10,000 + Z_{SL} \times 1118.$ $Z_{SL} = 0.6708. SL = 74.86\%$

(iii) What will be the service level if we review every 3 days?

$OI + LT = 4$ $10,750 = (4) \times 2000 + Z_{SL} \{\sqrt{(4)}\} \times 500.$ $Z_{SL} = 2.75, SL = 99.7\%$

---

7   NEWSVENDOR MODEL:

R: Revenue: Selling price. C: Cost: Purchase price. V: Salvage value.

$$SL = C_s/(C_s + C_e) = (R - C)/(R - V)$$

Demand based on continuous distribution   Suppose demand X has a probability distribution Pr(X) and the cumulative distribution F(X). To find the optimal order quantity Q_O, we need to solve for $F(Q_0) = SL$. *We will consider the following distributions.*

	UNIFORM	NORMAL	DISCRETE
DEMAND DISTRIBUTION	X~U[A, B]	X~N[μ, σ]	X: X1, X2,... Prob(X): 0.05, 0.1, ...
AVERAGE DEMAND	(A + B)/2	μ	0.05(X1) + 0.1(X2) + ..

Uniform Distribution   For the **uniform distribution**, we need the range of X. We write this as **X ~ U[A, B]**. We can get the optimal order quantity Q_0 using $Q_0 = A + SL \times (B - A)$.

If the order quantity is Q ($A \leq Q \leq B$), we have the following formulas

Avg. number of units sold = Q − (Q−A)²/[2 × (B−A)]
Avg. number of units unsold = Q – number sold
Avg. (expected) profit: P(Q) = [(R − C) × Q] – [(R – V) × (Q – A)²/{2 × (B – A}]

Example 7.1

Demand distribution: uniform X – U[800, 1200].

Revenue = $10/unit, Cost = $5.5 per unit and salvage = $5.00 per unit. How much should we order to maximize expected profit? Assume that newsvendor model assumptions are satisfied. *What should be the order quantity? What would be expected profit for this lot size?*

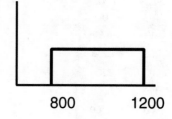

SOLUTION

Step 1: $SL = F(Q_0) = (R - C)/(R - V) = (10.00 - 5.5)/(10.00 - 5.00) = 0.90.$

Step 2: $Q_0 = A + SL^* (B - A) = 800 + 0.9^*(1200 - 800) = 1160.$

Step 3: Expected profit = $(10 - 5.5)^*1160 - [(10-5) ^* (1160-800)^2]/\{2 ^* (1200 - 800)\} = \$4410$

Expected profit for different values of Q is shown in the table below.

Q	800	900	1000	1100	1130	**1160**	1200
P(Q)	3600	3987.5	4250	4387.5	4404.375	**4410**	4400

Normal distribution   For the **normal distribution**, we generally write the function as **X ~ N[μ_x, σ_x]**. For the normal distribution, we are going to calculate only the optimal order quantity. Calculations for expected profit are somewhat involved and we won't consider them here.

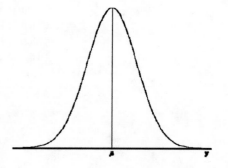

Example 7.2

Demand distribution normal. Demand $X \sim N[1000, 100]$.
Use data from the previous problem [R = $10/unit, C = $5.5 per unit and V = $5.00 per unit] and find optimal lot size.

SOLUTION

Step 1: $SL = F(Q_0) = (R - C)/(R - V) = (10.00 - 5.5)/(10.00 - 5.00) = 0.90$.
Step 2: From the **standard normal table**, we have to find the Z value corresponding to cumulative probability of 0.90. This value is $Z = 1.29$. Therefore $Q_0 = \mu + Z\sigma = 1000 + 1.29(100) = 1129$

Demand based on discrete distribution: Suppose demand X has a probability distribution $Pr(X)$ and the cumulative distribution $F(X)$. Suppose X varies from X_{min} to X_{max}. If we buy $(Q =) X_{max}$ units, we will satisfy all demand (regardless of the actual value of demand) and we will provide 100% service level. However, we may have to sell some units at loss when actual demand is less than X_{max}. What is the best service level to maximize expected profit? To find the optimal value Q_0, select the *smallest value* of $X = Q_0$ such that $F(Q_0) \geq SL$.

Example 7.3

Product – Jackets. Revenue = $100/unit, C = $30/unit and salvage value = $20/unit. Demand distribution is in the table.

DEMAND X	100	200	300	400	500	600
PROBABILITY PR(X)	0.100	0.150	0.275	0.225	0.185	0.065
CUM. PROBABILITY F(X)	0.100	0.250	0.525	0.750	0.935	1.000

Part (a): What is the average demand?

Part (b): If we stock 400 units, what will be the average sale?

Part (c): If we stock 400 units, what will be the average profit?
Part (d): What will be the optimal lot size and the corresponding profit?

SOLUTION

Part (a): Average demand $= \Sigma Pr(X) \times X = 0.1(100) + 0.15(200) + 0.275(300) + 0.225(400) + 0.185(500) + 0.065(600) = 344$

Part (b): Average sale (for Q = 400) $= \Sigma Pr(X) \times min(X, Q) = 0.1(100) + 0.15(200) + 0.275(300) + 0.225(400) + 0.185(400) + 0.065(400) = 312.5$

Part (c): Average sale (for Q = 400) is 312.5. So average leftover $= 400 - 312.5 = 87.5$
Average profit $= 312.5 \times (100 - 30) - 87.5 \times (30 - 20) = \$21,000$
You can verify average profit shown in the table to the right for different values of Q.

Q	AVERAGE PROFIT
100	7000
200	13200
300	18200
400	21000
500	22000
600	21520

Part (d): **Now we apply the three step procedure.**

Step 1: $SL = F(Q_0) = (R - C)/(R - V) = (100 - 30)/(100 - 20) = 70/80 = 7/8 = 0.875$
Step 2: From the cumulative probabilities, $F(400) = 0.75$ and $F(500) = 0.935$. Therefore $Q_0 = 500$.
Step 3: Expected profit is calculated using the procedure similar to parts b and c.
The corresponding profit will be $22,000. Note that the optimal service level is 0.875. However, due to discrete numbers, we are actually providing a service level of 0.935 (93.5%). ●

CHAPTER 6: QUALITY MANAGEMENT

1. CONTROL CHARTS

Control charts are used to determine if a process that is currently running, is in (statistical) control or not. Various types of charts are used: X, X bar, R, C, p, etc. We will study only X bar and R charts here. For every chart, there are two stages involved: The first is to start with trial control limits and establish stable limits. The second stage is to use the stable limits to monitor the process and control it by eliminating problems detected when the process starts going out of control.

1.1 $\overline{X}$ CONTROL CHARTS:

Suppose we are manufacturing a product and we want to control the process on a critical dimension. Each product dimension we measure will be denoted by X with a proper set of subscripts. Assume that X is normally distributed and the current process value is μ_x. Usually, there is a *natural variation* (also called *common variation, random variation*) in the process resulting in some value for process standard deviation (σ_x). The values of mean and standard deviation are not known and must be estimated.

Establishing trial control limits:
From the process, we collect "*m*" random samples, each of size of size "*n*" at random intervals.

SAMPLE NO	OBSERVATION NUMBER					SAMPLE STATISTICS
	I	2	....	$n-I$	n	
I	$X_{1,1}$	$X_{1,2}$		$X_{1,n-1}$	$X_{1,n}$	$\overline{X}_1 = (X_{1,1} + X_{1,2} + .. X_{1,n})/n$
2	$X_{2,1}$	$X_{2,2}$		$X_{2,n-1}$	$X_{2,n}$	
....	....	....		....	....	
m	$X_{m,1}$	$X_{m,2}$		$X_{m,n-1}$	$X_{m,n}$	$\overline{X}_m - (X_{m,1} + X_{m,2} + .. X_{m,n})/n$

For these m samples, we calculate sample statistics shown in the last column. Since X is normally distributed, we know that the distribution of $\overline{X}$ is also normally distributed. We can write this as $\overline{X} \sim N[\mu_{\overline{x}}, \sigma_{\overline{x}}]$. Now the center line of this distribution is at the mean and traditionally the upper and the lower control limits are taken at a distance of three standard deviations from the mean. Therefore CL = $\mu_{\overline{x}}$, LCL = $\mu_{\overline{x}} + 3\sigma_{\overline{x}}$ and LCL = $\mu_{\overline{x}} - 3\sigma_{\overline{x}}$.
Knowing the relationship between the distribution of $\overline{X}$ and X, we can write
CL = μ_x, LCL = $\mu_x + 3 (\sigma_x)/\sqrt{n}$ and LCL = $\mu_x . (\sigma_x)/\sqrt{n}$
Since the values of the mean and the standard deviation are not known, these must be estimated from the samples collected. Let $R_1, R_2, ..., R_m$ be the range values of m samples.
Define $\overline{\overline{X}}$ as the grand mean, i.e. mean of m sample means: $\overline{\overline{X}} = (\overline{X}_1 + \overline{X}_2 + ... + \overline{X}_1)/m$
Let $\overline{R} = (R_1 + R_2 + ... + R_m)/m$
The estimated values of CL, UCL and LCL are given by formulas in the box; **values of A₂ for different sample sizes (n) are given on the cover page.**

$$CL = \overline{\overline{X}}, UCL = \overline{\overline{X}} + A_2 \times \overline{R}, LCL = \overline{\overline{X}} - A_2 \times \overline{R}$$

Example 1

Twenty samples of *size five* each were taken for a product for the purpose of establishing control charts. Note that the actual observations in sample 1 were 2.030, 2.030, 2.034, 2.033 and 2.032 but we are recording only the last two digits. The largest and the smallest values in each column are shown in bold; these are used in the calculation of range (if there are multiple values, only one in shown in bold).

SAMPLE NO.		1	2	3	4	5	6	7	8	9	10	11	12	13	14	15	16	17	18	19	20
	1	**30**	**55**	**19**	36	36	34	32	42	**29**	29	36	20	33	27	27	36	27	**29**	**30**	30
	2	30	51	25	36	35	**38**	31	**40**	24	**28**	35	**22**	37	24	29	**23**	27	32	34	**31**
OBSERVATION	3	**34**	47	21	37	**36**	36	**39**	42	26	**34**	**39**	21	**26**	**22**	**26**	45	**26**	34	34	**29**
NUMBER	4	33	**33**	44	35	**31**	29	37	**46**	25	33	32	**20**	29	25	28	35	**29**	**35**	35	29
	5	32	48	28	**38**	36	36	**24**	44	29	32	**26**	21	**38**	**31**	**31**	31	27	34	**36**	29
	MEAN	31.8	46.8	27.4	36.4	34.8	34.6	32.6	42.8	26.6	31.2	33.6	20.8	32.6	25.8	28.2	34	27.2	32.8	33.8	29.6
	R	4	22	25	3	5	9	15	6	5	6	13	2	12	9	5	22	3	6	6	2

Trial control limits: From data above, $\bar{\bar{X}}$ = (31.8 +... + 29.6)/20 = **32.17** and $\bar{R}$ = (4 + ... +2)/20 = **9.00**.

From the table just before this example, **CL = 32.17** and for sample size n = 5, A_2 = 0.577.

Hence **UCL = 32.17 + (0.577) × (9.00) = 37.36, LCL = 32.17 − (0.577) × (9.00) = 26.98.**

Using these values for the trial control limits, we draw the control chart as shown below.

Points 2, 8, 9, 12 and 14 are outside the limits. After investigations, we are able to find assignable causes and eliminate these points. We remove these points and calculate new control limits.

Revision 1: New value: $\bar{\bar{X}}$ = **32.04**, $\bar{R}$ = **9.07, UCL = 32.04 + (0.577) × (9.07) = 37.27, LCL = 32.04 − (0.577) × (9.07) = 26.81**

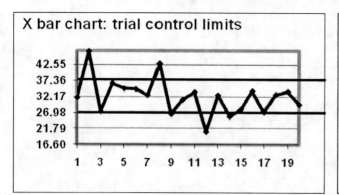

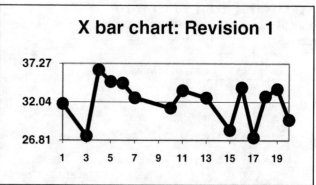

All points are within limits now. We use these limits for future control.

- If many observations fall outside the limits, we may want to collect additional data before obtaining the revised limits.
- Once points are found to be in control, we go to the second stage, i.e. maintaining control.

1.2 R CHARTS:

Consider sample numbers 1 and 7 from the previous example. Sample 1: 30, 30, 34, 33, 32 with average = 31.8 Sample 7: 32, 31, 39, 37, 24 with average = 32.6. Since the averages are close to the center lines, both points were acceptable for the X-bar chart. However the range of sample 1 is only 4 while the range of sample 7 is 15. A higher value of range indicates higher variability. Since higher variability is not considered to be good, X-bar chart alone may not be a good measure for checking whether the process is in control or not. We need to check the variability too and this is done through R chart.

The procedure for the R chart is similar to the X-bar control chart. Control limits are given by formulas below. Notice that these limits are not at equal distance from the centerline (CL).

The estimated values of CL, UCL and LCL are given by formulas in the box; **values of D_3 and D_4 for different sample sizes (n) are given on the cover page.**

$$CL = \bar{R}, \; UCL = D_4 * \bar{R}, \; LCL = D3 * \bar{R},$$

Example 2

We will use data in example 1 again for the R chart, we will plot the trial control limits

Trial control limits: $\bar{R}$ = **9.00**, D_4 = 2.114, D_3 = 0, UCL = **19.03**, LCL = **0**. Points 2, 3 and 16 are out of control. We find assignable causes for these points and eliminate them.

Revision 1: $\bar{R}$ = **6.53, D_4 = 2.114, D_3 = 0, UCL = 13.80, LCL = 0.** Point 7 is out of control now.

Revision 2: $\bar{R}$ = **6.00, D_4 = 2.114, D_3 = 0, UCL = 12.68, LCL = 0.** Point 11 is out of control.

Revision 3: $\bar{R}$ = **5.53, D_4 = 2.114, D_3 = 0, UCL = 11.7, LCL = 0.** Now we find point 13 to be out of control.

Revision 4: $\bar{R}$ = **5.07, D_4 = 2.114, D_3 = 0, UCL = 10.72, LCL = 0.** Now all points are in control.

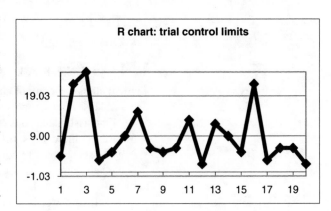

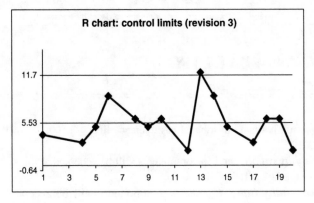

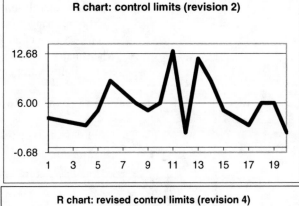

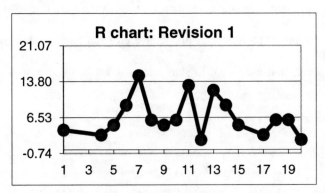

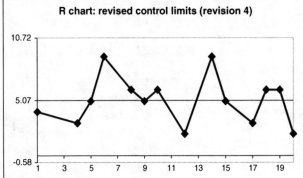

1.3 SIMULTANEOUS USE OF $\bar{X}$ AND R CHARTS:

Since X bar chart looks at changes in process average and R chart looks at changes in variability, many times both charts are used simultaneously.

In example 1, we eliminated points 2, 8, 9, 12 and 14 from the trial limits of the X bar charts before calculating the revised limits. For the R chart, we eliminated points 2, 3 and 16. If we were using both charts simultaneously we would have eliminated points 2, 3, 8, 9, 12, 14 and 16 from both charts. Verify the following.

					$\overline{X}$ CHART				R CHART		
	$\overline{X}$	$\overline{R}$	UCL	LCL	OUT OF CONTROL	UCL	LCL	OUT OF CONTROL	POINTS ELIMINATED
TRIAL LIMITS	32.17	9.00	37.36	26.98	2, 8, 9, 12, 14	19.03	0	2, 3, 16	2,3,8,9,12,14,16
REVISION 1	32.25	6.85	36.20	28.30	4, 15, 17	14.47	0	7	4,7,15,17
REVISION 2	32.76	7.00	36.79	28.72	–	14.8	0	–	none

1.4 GENERAL COMMENTS:

Typical steps for control charts
- Take several samples and establish trial control limits.
- Find assignable causes for points outside control limits; and establish new limits.
- Repeat these steps, till stable limits are established (you may need additional samples).
- Use stable units to control the process as follows.

Take new samples as per some established procedure and plot points to see if the process remains within control.

- – Take corrective action (such as tool change, adjusting pressure, etc,) when process goes out of control but do not recalculate control limits.
- – If the process is in control, do not make adjustments (even if values are fluctuating within control limits).
- – Normal changes (sharpening of tools, change of operator, etc) may happen while the process is in control.
- When major changes occur, you may have to start again by establishing new trial control limits.

Determination of "out of control"

A point falls outside control limits.	Seven consecutive points above/below CL.
Cycle pattern repeating	All points appear close to CL (hugging).
Sudden shift in process average	A run of 2 or 3 points outside 2-sigma, 4 or 5 outside 1-sigma
Trends	Instability (You need some judgment to determine instability).

2. PROCESS CAPABILITY

Example 1

A stable process with critical dimension normally distributed has tolerance limits: 2.500 ± 0.0035". Estimated standard deviation is 0.001".

Part 1: Calculate the ***process capability ratio*** C_p and % components will be accepted at this C_p. Suppose the current process average is 2.501".

Part 3: Calculate the ***process capability index*** C_{pk} and % components will be accepted at this C_{pk}.

Solution

Part 1: $Cp = (UTL - LTL)/(6\sigma) = (2.5035 - 2.4965)/(6 \times 0.001) = (0.007)/(0.006) = \boldsymbol{1.167}$
Prob. of accepting = Pr (LTL $\leq$ × $\leq$ UTL) with $\mu = 2.500$
= Pr(2.4965 $\leq$ × $\leq$ 2.5035) = Pr[(2.4965 − 2.5000)/0.001 $\leq$ Z $\leq$ (2.5035 − 2.5000)/0.001]
= Pr(−3.5 $\leq$ Z $\leq$ 3.5) = 0.9996   **So 99.96% components will be accepted.**
Part 3: $C_{pk} = min[(UTL - \mu)/(3\sigma), (\mu - LTL)/(3\sigma)]$
$(UTL - \mu)/(3\sigma) = (2.5035 - 2.501)/(3 \times 0.001) = 0.833$
$(\mu - LTL)/(3\sigma) = (2.501 - 2.4965)/(3 \times 0.001) = 1.500$ $\boldsymbol{C_{pk} = \min \{0.883, 1.500\} = 0.883.}$

Prob. of accepting = Pr (LTL $\leq$ X $\leq$ UTL) with μ = 2.501
= Pr(2.4965 $\leq$ X $\leq$ 2.5035) = Pr[(2.4965 − 2.501)/0.001 $\leq$ Z $\leq$ (2.5035 − 2.501)/0.001]
= Pr(− 4.5 $\leq$ Z $\leq$ 2.5) = 0.9938   **So 99.38% components will be accepted.** ●

Example 2

A stable process with critical dimension normally distributed has tolerance limits: 4.000 ± 0.003".
Estimated standard deviation is 0.002".
Part 1: Calculate the ***process capability ratio C_p*** and % components will be accepted at this ***Cp***.
Suppose the current process average is 4.001".
Part 3: Calculate the ***process capability index C_{pk}*** and % components will be accepted at this ***C_{pk}***.

SOLUTION

Part 1: C_p = (UTL − LTL)/(6σ) = (4.003 − 3.997)/(6 * 0.002) = (0.006)/(0.012) = ***0.5***
Prob. of accepting = Pr (LTL $\leq$ X $\leq$ UTL) with μ = 4.000
= Pr(3.997 $\leq$ X $\leq$ 4.003) = Pr[(3.997 − 4.000)/0.002 $\leq$ Z $\leq$ (4.003 − 4.000)/0.002]
= Pr(−1.5 $\leq$ Z $\leq$ 1.5) = 0.8664   **So 86.64% components will be accepted.**
Part 3: C_{pk} = min[(UTL − μ)/(3σ), (μ − LTL)/(3σ)]
(UTL − μ)/(3σ) = (4.003 − 4.001)/(3 * 0.002) = 0.333
(μ − LTL)/(3σ) = (4.001 − 3.997)/(3 * 0.002) = 0.667   ***C_{pk}* = min {0.333, 0.667) = 0.333.**
Prob. of accepting = Pr (LTL $\leq$ X $\leq$ UTL) with μ = 4.001
= Pr(3.997 $\leq$ X $\leq$ 4.003) = Pr[(3.997 − 4.001)/0.002 $\leq$ Z $\leq$ (4.003 − 4.001)/0.002]
= Pr(−2 $\leq$ Z $\leq$ 1) = 0.8185   **So 81.85% components will be accepted.** ●

3. ACCEPTANCE SAMPLING

Suppose we are ordering parts from a supplier and we have received a shipment of 1000 units. We want to ensure that these parts meet the quality specifications. We may take the following types of actions.

1. Accept the material without inspection (may be count the number or perform only visual inspection to check for scratches, dents or other types of damage). This action is taken on many occasions. For example, if we buy 50 lb. bags of chemicals, we may use them without testing. On many other occasions, customer carry out rigorous inspection of supplier's processes and issue a certificate that quality of incoming material will be accepted without inspection.
2. Check 100% of the item. If the material received is very critical, one may have to carry out 100% inspection. Many times such task is automated.
3. Select a few items and test them to decide on the overall quality of the lot. This may be the most common method used. However, how many items to select, method of selection, etc. cannot be arbitrary. For example, suppose 1000 items are sent by a truck. Should you select item from the top layer (because it is easy to pick from there)? How many should you test so that you can say with reasonable confidence that the overall lot is acceptable? *Acceptance sampling methodology* provides us some answers to these questions.

Acceptance sampling uses statistics to arrive at the size of the sample for inspection so that one can get optimal results (minimizing the risk of accepting bad products − consumer's risk or rejecting good products − producer's risk). This technique uses an approach between no inspection and 100% inspection.

Some points to note:
- Plans may be based on ***attributes*** (go, no-go) or ***variables*** (measuring dimensions).
- Many different plans exist: ***Single/double sampling plan***, ***Sequential sampling plan***, etc.
- Many of standards have been developed: Mil-Std (Military standard), ISO, etc.

H.F. Dodge and H. G. Romig, who worked for the Bell Labs, were pioneers in the development of acceptance sampling plans. The earliest plan was proposed in 1930s. We will briefly describe two plans.

Single sampling plan:

When a lot of size N is received, "n" items are randomly selected and inspected. If "c" or fewer items are rejected, the entire lot is accepted. With more than "c" rejections, the entire lot is rejected.

Double sampling plan:

When a lot of size N is received, "n_1" items are randomly selected and inspected. If "c_1" or fewer items are rejected, the entire lot is accepted. If greater than "c_2" items are rejected, the entire lot is rejected. If the number rejected is between "c_1" and "c_2", a second random sample of size "n_2" is selected and inspected. If the total number of rejected items in both samples is "c_2" or less, the entire lot is accepted. With more than "c_2" rejections, the entire lot is rejected.

4. QUALITY GURUS

W. EDWARD DEMING (1900-1993)[2]

1. Create constancy of purpose for improvement of product and service.
2. Adopt the new philosophy.
3. Cease dependence on mass inspection.
4. End the practice of awarding on the basis of price tag alone.
5. Improve constantly and forever the system of production and service.
6. Institute training.
7. Adopt and institute leadership.
8. Drive out fear.
9. Break down barriers between staff areas.
10. Eliminate slogans, exhortations, and targets.
11. Eliminate numerical quotas for the work force. Eliminate numerical goals for the people in management.
12. Remove barriers that rob the people of pride of workmanship.
13. Encourage education and self-improvement for everyone.
14. Take action to accomplish the transformation.

JOSEPH JURAN (1904 – 2008)

1. Build awareness of the need and opportunity for improvement.
2. Set improvement goals.
3. Organize to teach the goals (establish a Q. council, identify problems, select projects, appoint teams, designate facilitators).
4. Provide training.
5. Carry out projects to solve problems.
6. Report progress.
7. Give recognition.
8. Communicate results.
9. Keep score.
10. Maintain momentum by making annual improvement part of the regular systems and processes of the company.

CHAPTER 7: MRP

Each *end item* is built using *items* (components, sub-assemblies).
Demand for end items is based on customer orders, forecasts, etc. and is considered to be *independent*.
The *demand for items* is *dependent* on end item demand.
MRP starts with *Master Production Schedule (MPS)* for end items. *MPS* is prepared with *inputs from the aggregate plan,* confirmed orders from the customers (*firm orders*) and *latest forecasts.*
MRP uses *parent-child relationship* and *time buckets.*
MRP looks at the product structure diagram and determines requirements for each item systematically by considering information such as lead time, lot sizing method, multiplicity, etc.

PRODUCT STRUCTURE DIAGRAM

A *product structure diagram* is shown to the right. A product structure diagram includes multiple levels. An *end item* (a finished product) appears at the *highest level* (called level zero), *items* appear at *lower levels*. Of any two items connected to each other, the one appearing at a higher level is called the *parent* and the other one appearing at the lower level is called a *child* below). Items used in several places are assigned to the same level across all products.

DETERMINING PRODUCT STRUCTURE

Step 1: Assign level $K = 0$ to all items. All items are active.
Step 2: Scan the "children" of all active items. If no children appear, then stop. Otherwise assign (next lower) level $K + 1$ to each child. For every item remaining at level k after scanning is complete, put a check mark in front of the level and make this item inactive.
Step 3: Increase K by 1 and go back to step 2.
The following three examples show how the levels are determined from information in the first two columns of each table. Product structure diagram is drawn only for example 1.

Example 1

ITEM	CHILD	LEVEL	FINAL
A	–	0 1 ✓	1
B	E	0 1 2 ✓	2
C	–	0 1 2 ✓	2
D	–	0 1 2 ✓	2
E	–	0 1 2 3 ✓	3
G	B, C, D	0 1 ✓	1
X	A, G, D	0 ✓	0

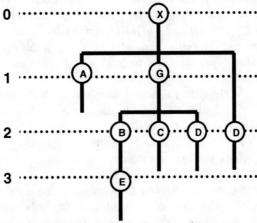

Example 2

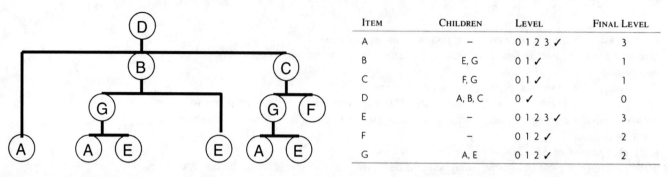

ITEM	CHILDREN	LEVEL	FINAL LEVEL
A	–	0 1 2 3 ✓	3
B	E, G	0 1 ✓	1
C	F, G	0 1 ✓	1
D	A, B, C	0 ✓	0
E	–	0 1 2 3 ✓	3
F	–	0 1 2 ✓	2
G	A, E	0 1 2 ✓	2

Example 3

ITEM	CHILDREN	LEVEL				FINAL
A	L, H1, H2	0	1	2	✓	**2**
B	–	0	1	✓		**1**
CA	A, SW	0	1	✓		**1**
H1	–	0	1	2	3	**3**
H2	–	0	1	2	3	**3**
L	–	0	1	2	3	**3**
Q	–	0	1	✓		**1**
R	–	0	1	✓		**1**
SC	B, CA, R, V	0	✓	2		**0**
ST	A, Q	0	✓	2		**0**
SW		0	1	2	✓	**2**
V	–	0	1	✓		**1**

For the table shown to the right, you can draw the product structure diagram.

MRP Calculations

To perform MRP calculations one needs the following three sets of information: Bill of materials (BOM), Item master and Master production schedule (MPS). The information may be stored in different formats in different companies.

Bill of material stores information on *items, children and multiplicity*.

Item master stores information about *lead time (L), lot sizing* method used, *safety stock (SS),* current *on hand (OH)* quantity and orders that are expected to arrive (called *scheduled receipt: SR*) either through purchasing or through production in progress.

Master production schedule (MPS) specifies demand for end items during the planning horizon.

GR - Gross Requirement (this is actually the demand for reach item)

SR - Scheduled Receipt (quantity that has been already ordered in prior periods and will be received in a future period)

OH - On Hand quantity (we will also calculate *"projected"* on hand quantities for subsequent periods and write these values in this row). Our textbook calls this as *"Projected Available Balance"*.

PR - Planned Receipt (how much we need to receive in a period - we will calculate this value). Our textbook calls this as *"Planned Order Receipt"*.

POR - Planned Order Release (when do we need to release an order so that we get *PR* quantity at the right time). If the lead time is greater than zero, we need to release the order in advance.

Example 4

Information is provided below for MRP calculations (planning horizon of 9 weeks).

BILL OF MATERIALS	
ITEM	CHILD, MULTIPLICITY
A	C4, D
B	C3, E2
D	C, E3
C	–
E	–

ITEM MASTER					
ITEM	L	LOT SIZING	SS	OH	SR
A	2	L4L	0	0	1-80
B	1	L4L	20	70	1-60
D	2	POQ 3	0	0	–
C	3	FOQ 300	100	360	1-300, 2-300, 3-300
E	1	L4L	50	950	

Using the procedure from the previous section, we can determine item levels. "A" and "B" are end items. "A" has two children "C" and "D". Number 4 after "C" gives the *multiplicity:* for each "A" you need 4 units of "C". When multiplicity is 1 (for "D"), the number is usually not written.

MASTER PRODUCTION SCHEDULE

	1	2	3	4	5	6	7	8	9
A	0	30	50	0	90	100	60	0	50
B	100	80	60	0	20	50	70	80	100

From the item master, item "C" has a lead of 3 periods, lot sizing method is FOQ 300, safety stock is 100 and on hand quantity is 360. Three hundred units are expected to arrive for each of the next 3 periods as shown in the scheduled receipt column.

MRP programs take this information and do the calculations for material planning by *exploding* (converting parent requirement to the child) and *time phasing* (using lead times). The final plan gives period by period *planned order release* for all items. The following terminology is used.

LEVEL	ITEM	PARENT
0	A	†-
0	B	†-
1	D	† A
2	C	† 4A, 3B, D
2	E	† 2B, 3D

SOLUTION

We have to first determine the all the parents (shown in the table to the right).
Complete MRP calculations are shown in the table below. ●

		0	1	2	3	4	5	6	7	8	9
A L = 2 L4L SS = 0 †	GR		0	30	50	0	90	100	60	0	50
	SR		80	0	0	0	0	0	0	0	0
	OH	0	80	50	0	0	0	0	0	0	0
	PR		0	0	0	0	90	100	60	0	50
	POR		0	0	90	100	60	0	50	0	0
B L = 1 L4L SS = 20 †	GR		100	80	60	0	20	50	70	80	100
	SR		60	0	0	0	0	0	0	0	0
	OH	70	30	20	20	20	20	20	20	20	20
	PR		0	70	60	0	20	50	70	80	100
	POR		70	60	0	20	50	70	80	100	0
D L = 2 POQ 3 SS = 0 †A	GR		0	0	90	100	60	0	50	0	0
	SR		0	0	0	0	0	0	0	0	0
	OH	0	0	0	160	60	0	0	0	0	0
	PR		0	0	250	0	0	0	50	0	0
	POR		250	0	0	0	50	0	0	0	0

C	GR		460	180	360	460	440	210	440	300	0
L = 3	SR		300	300	300	0	0	0	0	0	0
FOQ 300	OH	360	200	320	260	100	260	350	210	210	210
SS = 100	PR		0	0	0	300	600	300	300	300	–
† 4A, 3B, D	POR		300	600	300	300	300	0	0	0	0
E	GR		890	120	0	40	250	140	160	200	0
L = 1	SR		0	0	0	0	0	0	0	0	0
L4L	OH	950	60	50	50	50	50	50	50	50	0
SS = 50	PR		0	110	0	40	250	140	160	200	0
†2B, 3D	POR		110	0	40	250	140	160	200	0	0

Example 5

Use information in the first two tables here and perform MRP calculations

LEVEL	ITEM	PARENT
0	X	–
0	Y	–
1	G	† 2Y
1	P	†2X, Y
2	J	†X, G
3	F	†G, J

ITEM	CHILD, MULTIPLICITY	LEAD-TIME L	LOT SIZING	SS	OH	SR
X	P2, J	2	L4L	–	–	1-60 2-25
Y	P1, G2	1	L4L	–	–	1-30
G	J, F	2	FOQ 250	–	150	–
P	–	1	POQ 3	50	250	–
J	F	3	FOQ 600	–	420	2-600, 3-600
F	–	2	L4L	20	520	1-250

MPS	1	2	3	4	5	6	7	8	9	10
X	60	25	40	50	80	20	90	60	50	100
Y	30	60	0	80	200	120	30	0	80	70

SOLUTION

We can calculate item levels in the table to the right. Table below shows complete MRP calculations. ●

		0	1	2	3	4	5	6	7	8	9	10
ITEM X	GR		60	25	40	50	80	20	90	60	50	100
L=2	SR		60	25	0	0	0	0	0	0	0	0
L4L	OH	0	0	0	0	0	0	0	0	0	0	0
SS = 0	PR		0	0	40	50	80	20	90	60	50	100
†	POR		40	50	80	20	90	60	50	100	0	0
ITEM Y	GR		30	60	0	80	200	120	30	0	80	70
L=1	SR		30	0	0	0	0	0	0	0	0	0
L4L	OH	0	0	0	0	0	0	0	0	0	0	0
SS = 0	PR		0	60	0	80	200	120	30	0	80	70
†	POR		60	0	80	200	120	30	0	80	70	0

ITEM G	GR		120	0	160	400	240	60	0	160	140	0
L=2	SR		0	0	0	0	0	0	0	0	0	0
FOQ 250	OH	150	30	30	120	220	230	170	170	10	120	120
SS = 0	PR		0	0	250	500	250	0	0	0	250	0
† 2Y	POR		250	500	250	0	0	0	250	0	0	0
ITEM P	GR		140	100	240	240	300	150	100	280	70	0
L=1	SR		0	0	0	0	0	0	0	0	0	0
POQ 3	OH	250	110	530	290	50	300	150	50	120	50	50
SS = 50	PR		0	520	0	0	550	0	0	350	0	0
†2X, Y	POR		520	0	0	550	0	0	350	0	0	0
ITEM J	GR		290	550	330	20	90	60	300	100		
L=3	SR		0	600	600	0	0	0	0	0	0	0
FOQ 600	OH	420	130	180	450	430	340	280	580	480	480	480
SS = 0	PR		0	0	0	0	0	0	600	0	0	0
† X, G	POR		0	0	0	600	0	0	0	0	0	0
ITEM F	GR		250	500	250	600	0	0	250	0	0	0
L=2	SR		250	0	0	0	0	0	0	0	0	0
L4L	OH	520	520	20	20	20	20	20	20	20	20	20
SS = 20	PR		0	0	250	600	0	0	250	0	0	0
† G, J	POR		250	600	0	0	250	0	0	0	0	0

MISCELLANEOUS TOPICS

A: REVIEW OF PROBABILITY AND STATISTICS

Consider an experiment of tossing a coin four times. Let X represent the total number of heads appearing in these tosses. Obviously X can take values 0, 1, 2, 3 and 4. Assuming a "fair" coin, we can observe that X follows a probability distribution called "**binomial distribution**". X is called a **random variable**.

In the following we will discuss different distribution in which X is either **_discrete_** or **_continuous_**. A general comparison of these two types of distribution is presented in Table 1.

Continuous Probability distributions:
Here is a list of few known distributions: Uniform, normal, exponential, beta and Weibull. We will discuss only the uniform and the normal distribution.

Example 1

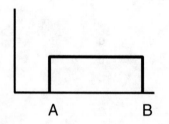

Uniform distribution $X \sim U[A, B]$
In the notation above, X is the random variable, U stands for the uniform distribution. A and B indicate the limits for X.
$f(X) = 1/(B - A)$ and $Pr(X \leq C) = (C - A)/(B - A)$
Suppose $A = 100$, $B = 500$. If $Pr(X \leq C) = 0.65$, what is C equal to?
$C = 0.65(B - A) + A = 0.65(400) + 100 = 360$

Example 2

Normal distribution $X \sim N[\mu_x, \sigma_x]$
X varies from $-\infty$ to $+\infty$. The distribution is symmetrical with mean equal to μ_x and standard deviation equal to σ_x. A special case of the normal distribution is called **standard normal distribution** when the mean $= 0$ and the standard deviation $= 1$. We denote this variable by Z. $Z \sim N[0, 1]$.

Discrete Probability distributions:
Here is a list of few known distributions: Uniform, binomial, hyper-geometric and Poisson. We will use another distribution called "empirical distribution". This distribution is built from data collected. We will briefly discuss some of these distributions through examples.

Example 3

If we toss a coin 5 times and indicate number of heads appearing by X, the resulting **binomial** distribution will be as shown in the table. The **expected value of X** gives us the average number of heads (since X denotes heads). This is written as
$E[X] = \sum X * Pr(X) = 0*(1/32) + 1*(5/32) + 2*(10/32) + 3*(10/32) + 4*(5/32) + 5*(1/32) = \mathbf{2.5}$

X	0	1	2	3	4	5
PR(X)	1/32	5/32	10/32	10/32	5/32	1/32

X	0	1	2	3	4	5
PR(X)	1/32	5/32	10/32	10/32	5/32	1/32
Y	−10	−8	−4	+5	+6	+10

Now we define another variable for the same experiment. Suppose we bet some money on the number of heads appearing. Let Y denote "profit" made when "X" number of heads appear. The expected profit can be denoted by E[Y] and

E[Y] = (−10)*(1/32) + (−8) * (5/32) + (−4) * (10/32) + 5 * (10/32) + 4 * (5/32) + 10 * (1/32) = −1/8 = −0.125

This means that we will lose on an average 12.5 cents when the experiment is repeated many times.

Example 4

Based on past experience, we find that the daily demand for a product is 10 to 50 with the probability as shown. The distribution involved here is an *empirical distribution*.

X	10	20	30	40	50
$P_R(X)$	0.05	0.14	0.20	0.45	0.16
$X.P_R(X)$	0.5	2.8	6.0	18.0	8.0

The expected (average) demand will be:

E[X] = 10 * (0.05) + 20 * (0.14) + 30 * (0.20) + 40 * (0.45) + 50* (0.16) = **35.3**

Suppose you hold 36 items in the stock. What would be the expected number sold?

X	10	20	30	40	50
$P_R(X)$	0.05	0.14	0.20	0.45	0.16
Y	10	20	30	36	36
$Y.P_R(Y)$	0.5	2.8	6.0	16.2	5.76

We will define a new variable Y denoting number of units sold. When the demand (X) is 10, we will sell only 10 units out of 36. So Y = 10. In fact, when demand X is less than or equal to 36, Y will be equal to X. When demand exceeds the stock, we can sell only the units in stock (= 36). Hence, when X > 36, Y = 36. Probability of Y is the same as the probability of X for each column. The average number of units sold will be: 10 * (0.05) + 20 * (0.14) + 30 * (0.20) + 36 * (0.45) + 36* (0.16) = **31.26**

Sampling distributions:

Suppose a *random variable X* has *some probability distribution* with mean μ_x and standard deviation σ_x. Suppose we take a *random sample of size n*. Let X_1, X_2, ..., X_n denote n observations randomly taken and let the sample average be given by

$$\overline{X} = (X_1 + X_2 + ... + X_n)/n.$$

POPULATION PARAMETERS	SAMPLE STATISTICS
μ_x, σ_x	$\overline{X}$, R, s

The *difference* between the *largest value* and the *smallest value* in a sample is called *sample range* and is denoted by *R*. Values associated with a sample are called "*sample statistics*". Another sample statistic is the *sample standard deviation s*. Values associated with a distribution (population) are called *parameters*.

The value $\overline{X}$(i.e. the sample mean) is also a random variable. Relationships of parameters of the distributions shown in the table below.

	PARAMETERS		
	MEAN	STD. DEVIATION	RELATIONSHIPS
INDIVIDUAL OBSERVATIONS X **	μ_x	σx	$\mu_{\overline{x}} = \mu_x$ $(\sigma_{\overline{x}}) = \sigma_x/(\sqrt{n})$
AVERAGES (OF RANDOM SAMPLES OF SIZE N) } X	$\mu_{\overline{x}}$	$\sigma_{\overline{x}}$	

** Note: Many times when we deal with distribution of X, we may drop the subscript x .

When X is large, the distribution of X-bar becomes normal (for all practical purposes) even if the original distribution of X was not normal. This is called the *"Central Limit Theorem"*. On the other hand the *distribution of R is not normal* (even when X is normal).

B: NUMBER ROUNDING

On many occasions we do the rounding of numbers: round down, round off and round up. This concept is explained in the Table 2.

The subject of rounding (how much) is based on judgment. If we talk of rainfall, one would probably use one or two decimal places 2.1" or 2.13". Sometimes we may even use integer numbers when we are giving approximate numbers: Annual rainfall is 35". When we discuss average annual household income, we may round off to nearest 1000 dollars. For national budgets we may use millions or even billions. Here are some guidelines for our course.

TABLE 2: ROUNDING RULES

	45.79 to integer	45
	45.79 to one decimal	45.7
ROUNDDOWN(TRUNCATE) TO LOWER VALUE	45.79 to multiple of 10	40
	31.23 to one decimal	31.2
	31.23 to multiple of 10	30
	40 to multiple of 10	40
	45.79 to integer	46
	45.79 to one decimal	45.8
	45.79 to multiple of 10	50
ROUND-OFF TO NEAREST VALUE UP OR DOWN	31.23 to integer	31
	31.23 to one decimal	31.2
	31.23 to multiple of 10	30
	31.23 to two decimal	31.23
	45.79 to integer	46
ROUND UP TO HIGHER VALUE	45.79 to one decimal	45.8
	45.79 to multiple of 10	50
	31.23 to integer	32

Assembly line balancing:

When we calculate a lower bound on number of stations needed, we ***round up*** to an integer value. When we calculate the number of operators needed to meet certain production target, we ***round up*** to an integer value. When we calculate stage capacity as 7.47 units per hour we will not round it off to 7 because the production does not stop after 1 hour. If the number were 7.47132, would probably use 7.47 or 7.5 as five-digit accuracy is not expected. If the capacity per shift is 241.31, we could say 241, as the operator will generally stop after producing 241.

EOQ model: The *optimal lot size Q^** is calculated with the square root formula. This number can be *rounded off within $\pm$ 5%* to a nice round number since the cost goes up very slightly in this range. Occasionally, *we even go as high as $\pm$ 10%*. For example, suppose monthly demand is 500 units and we obtain $Q^* = 460$. We may round this to 500 (8.7% up) since the lot size now becomes equal to the monthly demand.

INDEX

Note: Page numbers followed by *n* refer to footnotes.